Scott Foresman-Addison Wesley
enVisionMATH®
Common Core

Authors

Randall I. Charles
Professor Emeritus
Department of Mathematics
San Jose State University
San Jose, California

Janet H. Caldwell
Professor of Mathematics
Rowan University
Glassboro, New Jersey

Mary Cavanagh
Executive Director of Center for Practice,
Research, and Innovation in Mathematics
Education (PRIME)
Arizona State University
Mesa, Arizona

Juanita Copley
Professor Emerita, College of Education
University of Houston
Houston, Texas

Warren Crown
Professor Emeritus of Mathematics Education
Graduate School of Education
Rutgers University
New Brunswick, New Jersey

Francis (Skip) Fennell
L. Stanley Bowlsbey Professor of Education and
Graduate and Professional Studies
McDaniel College
Westminster, Maryland

Stuart J. Murphy
Visual Learning Specialist
Boston, Massachusetts

Kay B. Sammons
Coordinator of Elementary Mathematics
Howard County Public Schools
Ellicott City, Maryland

Jane F. Schielack
Professor of Mathematics
Associate Dean for Assessment and
Pre K-12 Education, College of Science
Texas A&M University
College Station, Texas

William Tate
Edward Mallinckrodt Distinguished University
Professor in Arts & Sciences
Washington University
St. Louis, Missouri

Mathematicians

David M. Bressoud
DeWitt Wallace Professor of Mathematics
Macalester College
St. Paul, Minnesota

Roger Howe
Professor of Mathematics
Yale University
New Haven, Connecticut

Gary Lippman
Professor of Mathematics and Computer Science
California State University East Bay
Hayward, California

PEARSON

Glenview, Illinois • Boston, Massachusetts • Chandler, Arizona • Upper Saddle River, New Jersey

Consulting Author

Grant Wiggins
Researcher and Educational Consultant
Hopewell, New Jersey

ELL Consultant

Jim Cummins
Professor
The University of Toronto
Toronto, Canada

Common Core State Standards Reviewers

Elizabeth Baker
Mathematics Coordinator
Gilbert Public Schools
Gilbert, Arizona

Amy Barber
K-12 Math Coach
Peninsula School District ESC
Gig Harbor, Washington

Laura Cua
Teacher
Columbus City Schools
Columbus, Ohio

Wafa Deeb-Westervelt
Assistant Superintendent for
Curriculum, Instruction, and
Professional Development
Freeport Public Schools
Freeport, New York

Lynn Gullette
Title 1 Math Intervention
Mobile County Public Schools
Gilliard Elementary
Mobile, Alabama

Beverly K. Kimes
Director of Mathematics
Birmingham City Schools
Birmingham, Alabama

Kelly O'Rourke
Elementary School Assistant Principal
Clark County School District
Las Vegas, Nevada

Piper L. Riddle
Evidence-Based Learning Specialist
Canyons School District
Sandy, Utah

Debra L. Vitale
Math Coach
Bristol Public Schools
Bristol, Connecticut

Diane T. Wehby
Math Support Teacher
Birmingham City Schools
Birmingham, Alabama

Scott Foresman·Addison Wesley

enVisionMATH®
Common Core

ISBN-13: 978-0-328-67263-9
ISBN-10: 0-328-67263-7

9 10 V063 15 14 13

Common Core

Standards for Mathematical Content

Domain: Number and Operations in Base Ten
Topics: 1, 2, 3, 4, 5, 6, and 7

Domain: Operations and Algebraic Thinking
Topic: 8

Domain: Number and Operations—Fractions
Topics: 9, 10, and 11

Domain: Measurement and Data
Topics: 12, 13, and 14

Domain: Geometry
Topics: 15 and 16

Standards for Mathematical Practice

- ☑ Make sense of problems and persevere in solving them.
- ☑ Reason abstractly and quantitatively.
- ☑ Construct viable arguments and critique the reasoning of others.
- ☑ Model with mathematics.
- ☑ Use appropriate tools strategically.
- ☑ Attend to precision.
- ☑ Look for and make use of structure.
- ☑ Look for and express regularity in repeated reasoning.

Common Core

Standards for Mathematical Practices

☑ Make sense of problems and persevere in solving them.

☑ Reason abstractly and quantitatively.

☑ Construct viable arguments and critique the reasoning of others.

☑ Model with mathematics.

☑ Use appropriate tools strategically.

☑ Attend to precision.

☑ Look for and make use of structure.

☑ Look for and express regularity in repeated reasoning.

Grade 5 Domain Colors

● **Domain: Number and Operations in Base Ten**
Topics: 1, 2, 3, 4, 5, 6, and 7

● **Domain: Operations and Algebraic Thinking**
Topic: 8

● **Domain: Number and Operations—Fractions**
Topics: 9, 10, and 11

● **Domain: Measurement and Data**
Topics: 12, 13, and 14

● **Domain: Geometry**
Topics: 15 and 16

Topic 1

Place Value

Standards for Mathematical Content

Domain
Number and Operations in Base Ten

Cluster
• Understand the place value system.

Standards
5.NBT.1, 5.NBT.3, 5.NBT.3.a, 5.NBT.3.b

v

Topic 6 — Multiplying Decimals

Standards for Mathematical Content

Domain

Number and Operations in Base Ten

Clusters

• Understand the place value system.

• Perform operations with multi-digit whole numbers and with decimals to hundredths.

Standards

5.NBT.1, 5.NBT.2, 5.NBT.7

Topic 7 — Dividing Decimals

Standards for Mathematical Content

Domain

Number and Operations in Base Ten

Clusters

• Understand the place value system.

• Perform operations with multi-digit whole numbers and with decimals to hundredths.

Standards

5.NBT.1, 5.NBT.2, 5.NBT.7

Standards for Mathematical Content

Domain
Measurement and Data

Cluster
• Geometric measurement: understand concepts of volume and relate volume to multiplication and to addition.

Standards
5.MD.3, 5.MD.3.a, 5.MD.3.b, 5.MD.4, 5.MD.5, 5.MD.5.a, 5.MD.5.b, 5.MD.5.c

Standards for Mathematical Content

Domain
Measurement and Data

Cluster
• Convert like measurement units within a given measurement system.

Standard
5.MD.1

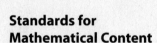

Problem-Solving Handbook

Scott Foresman·Addison Wesley

en**Vision**MATH®
Common Core

Problem-Solving Handbook

Use this Problem-Solving Handbook throughout the year to help you solve problems.

Pictures help me understand!

Explaining helps me understand!

Everybody can be a good problem solver!

There's almost always more than one way to solve a problem!

Don't give up!

Problem-Solving Process

Read and Understand

© Answer these questions to make sense of problems.

❓ **What am I trying to find?**
  - Tell what the question is asking.

❓ **What do I know?**
  - Tell the problem in my own words.
  - Identify key facts and details.

Plan and Solve

© Choose an appropriate tool.

❓ **What strategy or strategies should I try?**

❓ **Can I show the problem?**
  - Try drawing a picture.
  - Try making a list, table, or graph.
  - Try acting it out or using objects.

❓ **How will I solve the problem?**

❓ **What is the answer?**
  - Tell the answer in a complete sentence.

Strategies
- Show What You Know
- Draw a Picture
- Make an Organized List
- Make a Table
- Make a Graph
- Act It Out/ Use Objects
- Look for a Pattern
- Try, Check, Revise
- Write an Equation
- Use Reasoning
- Work Backward
- Solve a Simpler Problem

Look Back and Check

© Give precise answers.

❓ **Did I check my work?**
  - Compare my work to the information in the problem.
  - Be sure all calculations are correct.

❓ **Is my answer reasonable?**
  - Estimate to see if my answer makes sense.
  - Make sure the question was answered.

Using Bar Diagrams

© Bar diagrams are tools that will help you understand and solve word problems. Bar diagrams show how the quantities in a problem are related.

Problem 1

A recipe calls for $3\frac{2}{4}$ cups of orange juice and $1\frac{1}{4}$ cups of lemon juice. How much juice is needed for the recipe?

Bar Diagram

TOTAL: Total amount of juice needed for the recipe →

?

| $3\frac{2}{4}$ | $1\frac{1}{4}$ |

↑ PART: Amount of orange juice needed ↑ PART: Amount of lemon juice needed

$$3\frac{2}{4} + 1\frac{1}{4} = \blacksquare$$

Think I can add to find the total.

Problem 2

Ethan is building a model plane. He has a strip of wood that is $6\frac{7}{8}$ inches long. He cuts a piece that is $1\frac{3}{8}$ inches long. How long is the remaining piece?

Bar Diagram

$6\frac{7}{8}$

TOTAL: The original length of the strip of wood →

| $1\frac{3}{8}$ | ? |

↑ PART: The length of the part cut off ↑ PART: The length of the remaining strip

$$6\frac{7}{8} - 1\frac{3}{8} = \blacksquare$$

Think I can subtract to find the missing part.

Pictures help me understand!

Don't trust key words!

Problem 3

Ziva gave her friends 5 pieces of cake. Each piece of the cake was $\frac{1}{8}$ of the whole cake. How much of the cake did Ziva give to her friends?

Bar Diagram

TOTAL: Total amount of cake given to her friends → ?

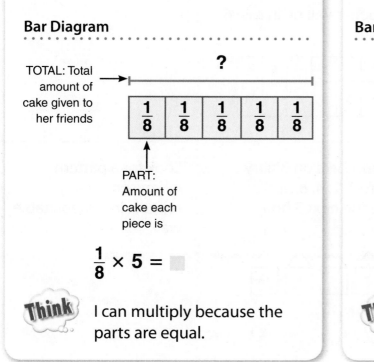

| $\frac{1}{8}$ | $\frac{1}{8}$ | $\frac{1}{8}$ | $\frac{1}{8}$ | $\frac{1}{8}$ |

PART: Amount of cake each piece is

$$\frac{1}{8} \times 5 = \blacksquare$$

Think I can multiply because the parts are equal.

Problem 4

Lin, Alexis, and Andy are planning to share a used bike that costs $37.50. They are splitting the cost equally. How much should each person pay?

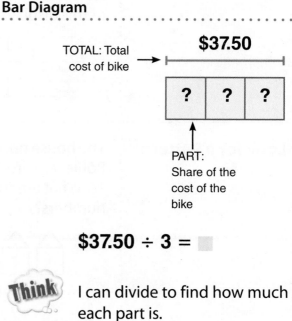

$37.50

Bar Diagram

TOTAL: Total cost of bike → **$37.50**

| ? | ? | ? |

PART: Share of the cost of the bike

$$\$37.50 \div 3 = \blacksquare$$

Think I can divide to find how much each part is.

Problem-Solving Strategies

Ⓒ Strategies are tools for understanding and solving problems.

Strategy	Example	When I Use It
Draw a Picture	How many diagonals can be drawn from one vertex of a hexagon?	Try drawing a picture when it helps you visualize the problem or when relationships such as joining or separating are involved.
Make a Table	Kevin is building a store display with boxes of raisins. How many boxes will be in row 6 of this display?	Try making a table when: • there are two or more quantities, • amounts change using a pattern.
Look for a Pattern	The house numbers on Binary Boulevard are 1, 2, 4, 8, and 16. What are the next 3 house numbers?	Look for a pattern when something repeats in a predictable way.

Row	1	2	3	4	5	6
Number of boxes of raisins	1	3	5	7	9	11

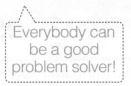

MATHEMATICAL PRACTICES

Strategy	Example	When I Use It
Make an Organized List	How many different sandwiches can you make choosing one from each: rye bread or wheat bread and chicken, tuna salad, or ham?	Make an organized list when asked to find combinations of two or more items.
	Rye Chicken Wheat Chicken Rye Tuna salad Wheat Tuna Salad Rye Ham Wheat Ham	
Try, Check, Revise	Jamal spent $10, not including tax, on school supplies. He bought 3 items. What did he buy? $3.50 + $1.15 + $7.50 = $12.15 $3.50 + $1.15 + $1.45 = $6.10 $3.50 + $1.15 + $5.35 = $10	Use Try, Check, Revise when quantities are being combined to find a total, but you don't know which quantities. **School Supplies Sale!** Pack of pads .... $3.50 Ruler .... $1.15 Pack of markers .... $7.50 Sticky notes .... $1.45 Calculator.............................. $5.35
Write an Equation	Della wants to copy her playlist onto CDs. She gets 20 songs onto one CD. How many CDs does she need for 260 songs? Find $260 \div 20 = n$	Write an equation when the story describes a situation that uses an operation or operations.

Even More Strategies

© These are more tools for understanding and solving problems.

Strategy	Example	When I Use It
Act It Out	Which figure has more lines of symmetry, a square or a rectangle that is not a square?	Think about acting out a problem when the numbers are small and there is action in the problem you can do.
Use Reasoning	The starting line for one relay-race is a rope that is 54 inches long. The starting line for another race is a rope that is 2 yards long. Are the ropes the same length? If not, which is longer? 1 yard = 36 inches 2 yards = 72 inches	Use reasoning when you can use known information to reason out unknown information.
Work Backward	The school play is scheduled to begin at 8 PM. Performers need to arrive $1\frac{1}{2}$ hours before the start of the play to get in costume and make-up. A snack is served $\frac{1}{2}$ hour before the costume time. What time is the snack served? $\frac{1}{2}$ hour $1\frac{1}{2}$ hours 6:00 6:30 8:00 Snack served. Play begins.	Try working backward when: • you know the end result of a series of steps, • you want to know what happened at the beginning.

MATHEMATICAL PRACTICES

Strategy	Example	When I Use It
Solve a Simpler Problem	At the first meeting of soup kitchen volunteers, each of the 15 people present gave cards with his or her phone number to every other person there. How many cards were given out? I can think about the cards for fewer people. If there are . . . 2 people each gives 1 card = 2 3 people each gives 2 cards = 6 4 people each gives 3 cards = 12	Try solving a simpler problem when you can create a simpler case that is easier to solve.
Make a Graph	Emma surveyed her 5th-grade class and the 6th-grade class about the number of pets there were at home. Do more 5th or 6th graders have either no pets or 1 pet at home? **Pets at Home** *(bar graph: Number of Students vs. Pets)* No pets: 5th grade 10, 6th grade 8 1 pet: 5th grade 8, 6th grade 11 2 pets: 5th grade 9, 6th grade 6 3 or more pets: 5th grade 5, 6th grade 7	Make a graph when: • data for a survey are given, • the question can be answered by reading the graph.

Writing to Explain

© Good written explanations communicate your reasoning to others. Here is a good math explanation.

Writing to Explain Use blocks to model 13 × 24.
Draw a picture and explain what you did with the blocks.

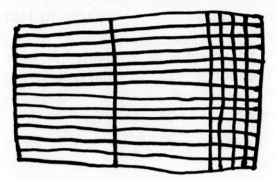

First we made a row of 24 using 2 tens and 4 ones.
Then we made more rows until we had 13 rows. Then
we said 13 rows of 2 tens is 13 × 2 tens = 26 tens or
260. Then we said 13 rows of 4 once is 13 × 4 = 52.
Then we added the parts.
260 + 52 = 312 So, 13 × 24 = 312.

Tips for Writing Good Math Explanations ...

A good explanation should be:
- correct
- simple
- complete
- easy to understand

Math explanations can use:
- words
- pictures
- numbers
- symbols

Problem-Solving Recording Sheet

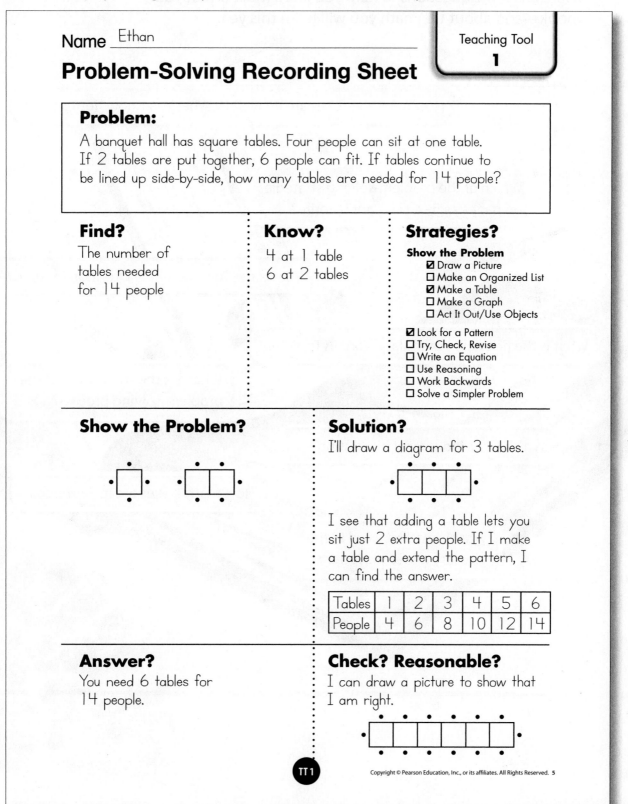

MATHEMATICAL PRACTICES

ⓒ This helps you organize your work and make sense of problems.

Name _Ethan_

Teaching Tool **1**

Problem-Solving Recording Sheet

Problem:
A banquet hall has square tables. Four people can sit at one table. If 2 tables are put together, 6 people can fit. If tables continue to be lined up side-by-side, how many tables are needed for 14 people?

Find?
The number of tables needed for 14 people

Know?
4 at 1 table
6 at 2 tables

Strategies?
Show the Problem
☑ Draw a Picture
☐ Make an Organized List
☑ Make a Table
☐ Make a Graph
☐ Act It Out/Use Objects

☑ Look for a Pattern
☐ Try, Check, Revise
☐ Write an Equation
☐ Use Reasoning
☐ Work Backwards
☐ Solve a Simpler Problem

Show the Problem?

Solution?
I'll draw a diagram for 3 tables.

I see that adding a table lets you sit just 2 extra people. If I make a table and extend the pattern, I can find the answer.

Tables	1	2	3	4	5	6
People	4	6	8	10	12	14

Answer?
You need 6 tables for 14 people.

Check? Reasonable?
I can draw a picture to show that I am right.

TT 1

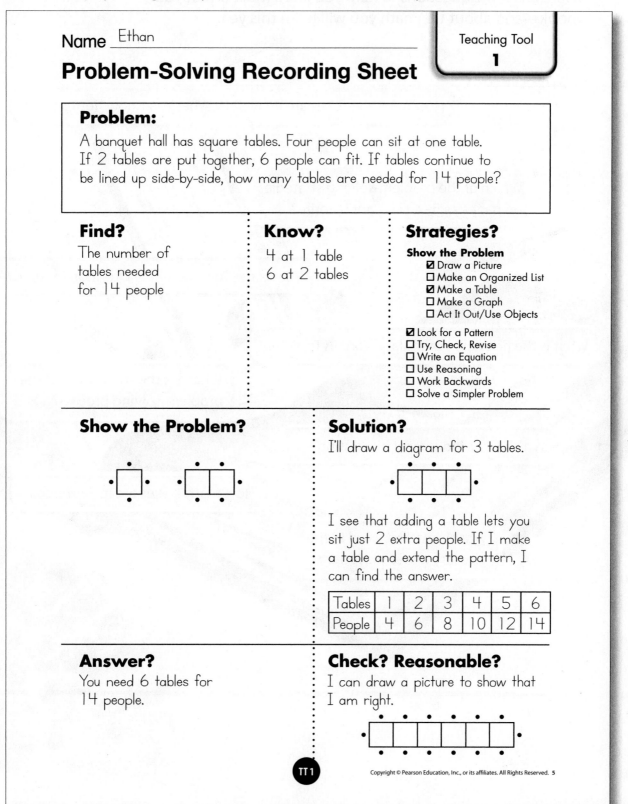

Getting to Know Your Math Book

Before you start working on lessons, look through your textbook. Here are some questions to help you learn more about your book—and about the math you will learn this year.

How many exercises are in "Review What You Know" for Topic 1?

Which of the problem-solving strategies on pages xviii–xxiii is your favorite?

What is the Topic Essential Question in Topic 6?

What is the first new vocabulary word in Topic 16?

What are the three parts of the problem-solving process?

Which topic looks most interesting?

How many pages are in your book?

What is the first word in the glossary under the letter H?

DOMAIN Number and Operations in Base Ten

Topic

1

Place Value

▼ The longest stick insect in the world lives in Borneo. How long is the Borneo stick insect? You will find out in Lesson 1-4.

Review What You Know!

Vocabulary

Choose the best term from the box.

- digits
- place value
- period
- whole numbers

1. __?__ are the symbols used to show numbers.

2. A group of 3 digits in a number is a __?__.

3. __?__ is the position of a digit in a number that is used to determine the value of the digit.

Adding Whole Numbers

Find each sum.

4. 800 + 90 + 2

5. 3,000 + 400 + 50

6. 10,000 + 2,000 + 60 + 1

7. 37 + 85

8. 124 + 376

Comparing

Compare. Use <, >, or = for each ◯.

9. 869 ◯ 912

10. 9,033 ◯ 9,133

11. 1,338 ◯ 1,388

12. 7,325 ◯ 7,321

Place Value

© 13. **Writing to Explain** In the number 767, does the first 7 have the same value as the final 7? Why or why not?

Topic Essential Question
• How are whole numbers and decimals written, compared, and ordered?

 Topic 1   3

Interactive Learning

Pose the problem. Start each lesson by working together to solve problems. It will help you make sense of math.

Applying Math Practices

- What am I asked to find?
- What else can I try?
- How are quantities related?
- How can I explain my work?
- How can I use math to model the problem?
- Can I use tools to help?
- Is my work precise?
- Why does this work?
- How can I generalize?

Lesson 1-1

© **Reason** The chart at the right shows place values through billions. Use it to help you solve this problem.

How many millions does it take to make one billion? Tell how you decided.

Place-Value Chart 1

Lesson 1-2

© **Use Structure** Use what you know about fractions to solve this problem.

Betty made 3 out of 10 shots or $\frac{3}{10}$ of her shots while playing basketball. Give three fractions that are equivalent to $\frac{3}{10}$ using denominators of 20, 50, and 100. Explain how you decided.

Lesson 1-3

© **Use Structure** The cube at the right is made up of 1,000 smaller cubes. Each is $\frac{1}{1,000}$ of the whole.

Jennie is training for a race. On Tuesday she finished her sprint 0.305 seconds faster than she did on Monday. Use the cube at the right and what you know about decimal place value to explain in writing the meaning of 0.305.

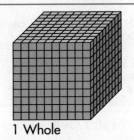

1 Whole

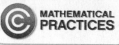

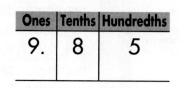

Lesson 1-4

© **Use Structure** Solve.

A runner won the men's 100-meters race in the 2004 Olympics with a time of 9.85 seconds. How can you use place-value to explain this time?

Ones	Tenths	Hundredths
9.	8	5

Lesson 1-5

© **Reason** Solve any way you choose.

The lengths of three kinds of ants are shown in the chart. Which ant was the longest? Which was the shortest? Tell how you decided.

Ant Label	Length (cm)
A	0.521
B	0.498
C	0.550

Lesson 1-6

© **Use Structure** Solve using the diagram shown.

An interior designer has received a shipment of flooring tiles. Each tile is identified by a code made up of a number and a letter. The designer has recorded the tile codes on the floor layout chart shown, but he is missing some tiles. What are the letter and number codes of the tiles he still needs? Tell how you decided.

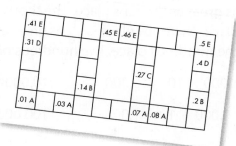

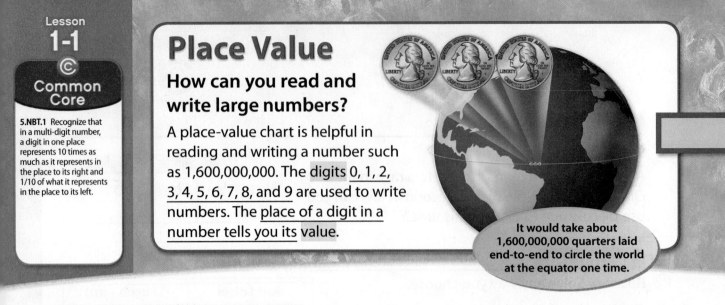

© Common Core

5.NBT.1 Recognize that in a multi-digit number, a digit in one place represents 10 times as much as it represents in the place to its right and 1/10 of what it represents in the place to its left.

Place Value

How can you read and write large numbers?

A place-value chart is helpful in reading and writing a number such as 1,600,000,000. The digits 0, 1, 2, 3, 4, 5, 6, 7, 8, and 9 are used to write numbers. The place of a digit in a number tells you its value.

It would take about 1,600,000,000 quarters laid end-to-end to circle the world at the equator one time.

Another Example   What patterns do you notice about place value?

$10 \times 1 = 10$ $10 \times 10 = 100$ $10 \times 100 = 1,000$

$10 \div 10 = 1$ $100 \div 10 = 10$ $1,000 \div 10 = 100$

The tens place is 10 times as great as the ones place. The hundreds place is 10 times as great as the tens place. The thousands place is 10 times as great as the hundreds place. The ones place is $\frac{1}{10}$ as great as the tens place. The tens place is $\frac{1}{10}$ as great as the hundreds place. The hundreds place is $\frac{1}{10}$ as great as the thousands place.

$1,000 \times 10 = 10,000$ $10,000 \times 10 = 100,000$

$10,000 \div 10 = 1,000$ $100,000 \div 10 = 10,000$

Explain It

1. Describe the relationship between the thousands place and the ten thousands place.

2. Describe the relationship between the ten thousands place and the hundred thousands place.

Guided Practice*

MATHEMATICAL PRACTICES

Do you know HOW?

In **1** through **2**, write each number in standard form.

1. forty billion, forty-eight million

2. $90,000,000,000 + 5,000,000 + 300$

Do you UNDERSTAND?

3. Ehrin has $200. Kerry has 10 times as much money as Ehrin. How much money does Kerry have?

© 4. **Look for Patterns** Luis has ten times as much money as Kerry. How much money does he have?

DIGITAL   Animated Glossary
www.pearsonsuccessnet.com

*For another example, see Set A on page 22.

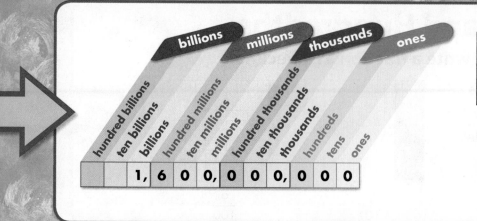

1 is in the billions place. Its value is 1,000,000,000

Standard form:
1,600,000,000

Expanded form:
1,000,000,000 + 600,000,000

Word form:
one billion, six hundred million

Independent Practice

Write each number in word form.

5. 7,123

6. 18,345

7. 10,010,468

8. 300,014,000,056

Write each number in standard form.

9. 8,000,000 + 300 + 9

10. 60,000,000 + 10,000 + 20 + 3

Write each number in expanded form.

11. 670,200,640

12. 1,000,102,200

13. 85,000,011,000

Problem Solving

MATHEMATICAL PRACTICES

© **14. Be Precise** The Milky Way Galaxy has at least two hundred billion stars. Write this number in standard form.

15. Neptune is 4,498,252,900 km from the Sun. Write this number in expanded form.

© **16. Reason** In a recent U.S. Census, the population of Illinois was 12,419,293. What is this population after

  a an increase of 100,000.

  b an increase of 1,000,000.

  c a decrease of 10,000.

17. There can be up to 22,000,000 individuals in a colony of driver ants. Write this number in word form and expanded form.

© **18. Critique Reasoning** For the standard form of two billion, three hundred fifty thousand, four, Danielle wrote 2,350,400,000. What error did she make? What is the correct standard form of the number?

© Common Core

5.NBT.3.a Read and write decimals to thousandths using base-ten numerals, number names, ... Also 5.NBT.1

Tenths and Hundredths

How can you write a fraction as a decimal?

A fraction such as $\frac{3}{10}$ or $\frac{9}{100}$ can be shown by a model.

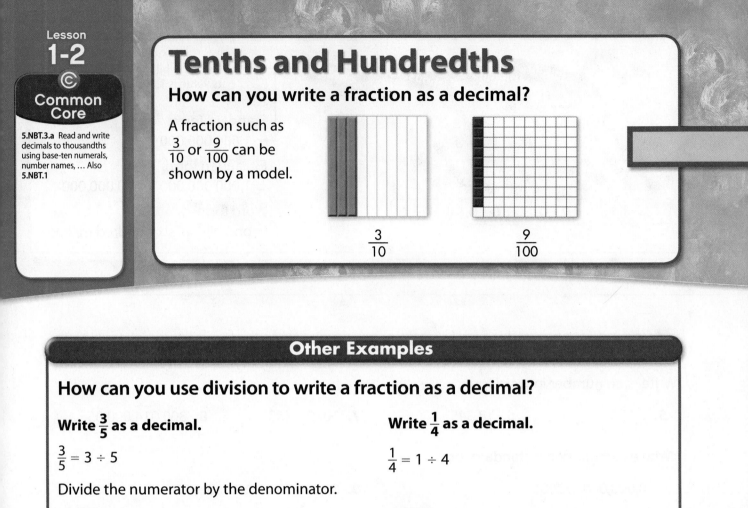

$\frac{3}{10}$ $\frac{9}{100}$

Other Examples

How can you use division to write a fraction as a decimal?

Write $\frac{3}{5}$ as a decimal.

$\frac{3}{5} = 3 \div 5$

Divide the numerator by the denominator.

$$\begin{array}{r} 0.6 \\ 5\overline{)3.0} \\ -\ 3\,0 \\ \hline 0 \end{array}$$ Insert a decimal point after 3 and annex zeros as needed.

So, $\frac{3}{5} = 0.6$.

Write $\frac{1}{4}$ as a decimal.

$\frac{1}{4} = 1 \div 4$

$$\begin{array}{r} 0.25 \\ 4\overline{)1.00} \\ -\ \ 8\downarrow \\ \hline 20 \\ -\ 20 \\ \hline 0 \end{array}$$ Insert a decimal point after 1 and annex zeros as needed.

So, $\frac{1}{4} = 0.25$.

Explain It

1. How can you write $\frac{9}{100}$ as a division problem?

2. In the second example, how many zeros did you need to annex after 1 when you divided 1 by 4?

Guided Practice*

© MATHEMATICAL PRACTICES

Do you know HOW?

Write each decimal as a fraction and each fraction as a decimal.

1. 0.1   2. 0.02

3. $\frac{9}{10}$ 4. $\frac{7}{100}$

5. Use division to change $\frac{11}{20}$ to a decimal.

Do you UNDERSTAND?

© 6. **Look for Patterns** How are the two 4s in the decimal 0.44 related?

© 7. **Communicate** How is $\frac{3}{10}$ equal to 0.3?

*For another example, see Set B on page 22.

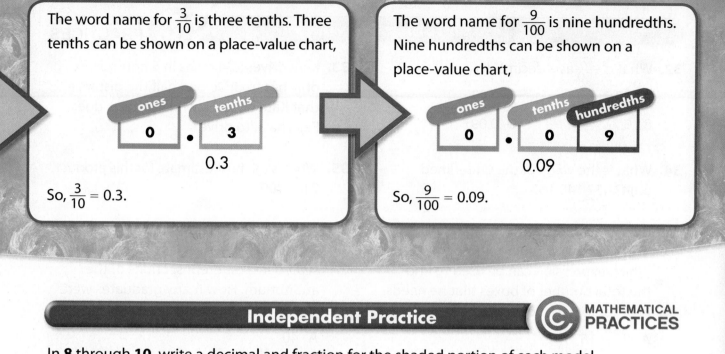

The word name for $\frac{3}{10}$ is three tenths. Three tenths can be shown on a place-value chart,

ones	tenths
0	3

0.3

So, $\frac{3}{10} = 0.3$.

The word name for $\frac{9}{100}$ is nine hundredths. Nine hundredths can be shown on a place-value chart,

ones	tenths	hundredths
0	0	9

0.09

So, $\frac{9}{100} = 0.09$.

Independent Practice

MATHEMATICAL PRACTICES

In **8** through **10**, write a decimal and fraction for the shaded portion of each model. Then write the word name for each number.

8.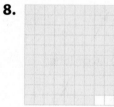

9.

10.

Ⓒ **11. Look for Patterns** How does the decimal 0.9 relate to 0.09 at the top of the page?

In **12** through **19**, write each decimal as either a fraction or a mixed number.

12. 3.2

13. 0.7

14. 0.23

15. 9.75

16. 7.7

17. 0.4

18. 0.81

19. 2.43

In **20** through **27**, write each fraction or mixed number as a decimal.

20. $2\frac{1}{100}$

21. $9\frac{3}{10}$

22. $\frac{9}{10}$

23. $1\frac{18}{100}$

24. $6\frac{31}{100}$

25. $4\frac{1}{10}$

26. $\frac{4}{10}$

27. $6\frac{6}{100}$

Use division to change each fraction to a decimal.

28. $\frac{2}{5}$

29. $\frac{3}{25}$

30. $\frac{7}{50}$

31. $\frac{9}{20}$

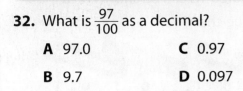
32. What is $\frac{97}{100}$ as a decimal?

A 97.0   **C** 0.97

B 9.7   **D** 0.097

33. Kate drives 234 miles in 5 hours. Felix only has to drive one half the distance that Kate does. How many miles does Felix have to drive?

34. What is the value of the underlined digit? 457,140,167

35. What is the best estimate for this product? 81×409

© **36.** **Persevere** Jorge is packing books into boxes. Each box can hold 16 books. Which expression can be used to find the total number of boxes that he needs in order to pack 96 books?

A $96 \div 16$

B $96 - 16$

C $96 + 16$

D 96×16

37. At a high-school graduation, there were 200 students in the class. They were seated in 5 different sections of the auditorium. How many graduates were seated in each section?

A 40

B 195

C 400

D 1,000

38. *Titanus giganteus* is one of the largest known beetles on Earth.

   a How long is *Titanus giganteus* as a mixed number?

   b How long is *Titanus giganteus* as an improper fraction?

17.6 cm long

39. The Great Owlet Moth of Brazil has a wingspan of 12.13 inches. Write this number as a mixed number.

© **40.** **Think About the Structure** A design is divided into 5 equal parts and $\frac{2}{5}$ are shaded. How would you change $\frac{2}{5}$ to a decimal?

A Divide 2 by 5.

B Divide 5 by 2.

C Multiply 2 by 5.

D Add 2 and 5.

12.13 inches

Changing from Fraction to Decimal Form

Write $\frac{17}{50}$ and $\frac{33}{50}$ in decimal form.

Step 1 To write $\frac{17}{50}$ in decimal form, divide 17 by 50.

Press: 17 ÷ 50 **ENTER =**

Display: .34

So, $\frac{17}{50} = 0.34$.

Step 2 To write $\frac{33}{50}$ in decimal form, divide 33 by 50.

Press: 33 ÷ 50 **ENTER =**

Display: .66

So, $\frac{33}{50} = 0.66$.

When the denominator of a fraction is 50, one way to find the decimal form is to put 2 times the numerator in the tenths and hundredths places. Look at the example above. $2 \times 33 = 66$. Place 66 in the tenths and hundredths places, and the answer is 0.66.

Practice

Write each fraction in decimal form.

1. $\frac{3}{10}$ 2. $\frac{7}{10}$ 3. $\frac{1}{10}$

4. $\frac{2}{5}$ 5. $\frac{4}{5}$ 6. $\frac{3}{5}$

7. $\frac{7}{25}$ 8. $\frac{9}{25}$ 9. $\frac{21}{25}$

10. $\frac{9}{20}$ 11. $\frac{11}{20}$ 12. $\frac{19}{20}$

13. $\frac{6}{10}$ 14. $\frac{8}{10}$ 15. $\frac{2}{10}$

16. $\frac{1}{5}$ 17. $\frac{5}{5}$ 18. $\frac{0}{5}$

19. $\frac{13}{20}$ 20. $\frac{15}{20}$ 21. $\frac{18}{20}$

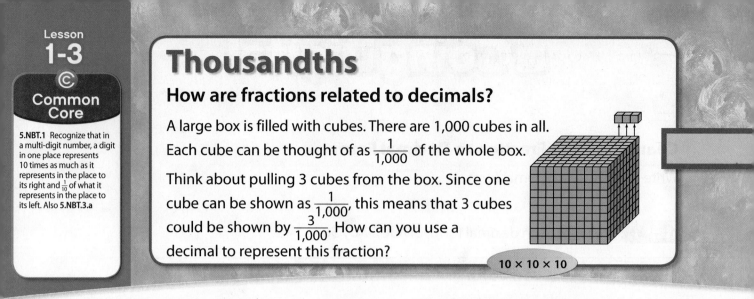

Lesson 1-3

Common Core

5.NBT.1 Recognize that in a multi-digit number, a digit in one place represents 10 times as much as it represents in the place to its right and $\frac{1}{10}$ of what it represents in the place to its left. Also **5.NBT.3.a**

Thousandths

How are fractions related to decimals?

A large box is filled with cubes. There are 1,000 cubes in all. Each cube can be thought of as $\frac{1}{1,000}$ of the whole box.

Think about pulling 3 cubes from the box. Since one cube can be shown as $\frac{1}{1,000}$, this means that 3 cubes could be shown by $\frac{3}{1,000}$. How can you use a decimal to represent this fraction?

10 × 10 × 10

Guided Practice*

MATHEMATICAL PRACTICES

Do you know HOW?

In **1** through **4**, write each decimal as a fraction or mixed number.

1. 0.003　　　　**2.** 0.050

3. 7.001　　　　**4.** 0.393

In **5** through **8**, write each fraction as a decimal.

5. $\frac{389}{1,000}$　　　　**6.** $3\frac{673}{1,000}$

7. $\frac{211}{1,000}$　　　　**8.** $\frac{90}{1,000}$

Do you UNDERSTAND?

9. Reason How is $\frac{3}{10}$ different from $\frac{3}{1000}$ in place value?

10. Be Precise How would you write the fraction of cubes that are left when 3 cubes are pulled from the box in the model above?

Independent Practice

In **11** through **18**, write each decimal as a fraction or mixed number.

11. 0.007　　　**12.** 0.008　　　**13.** 0.065　　　**14.** 0.900

15. 0.832　　　**16.** 0.023　　　**17.** 3.078　　　**18.** 5.001

In **19** through **26**, write each fraction or mixed number as a decimal.

19. $\frac{434}{1,000}$　　　**20.** $3\frac{499}{1,000}$　　　**21.** $\frac{873}{1,000}$　　　**22.** $\frac{309}{1,000}$

23. $1\frac{17}{1,000}$　　　**24.** $\frac{9}{1,000}$　　　**25.** $\frac{990}{1,000}$　　　**26.** $5\frac{707}{1,000}$

The word name for $\frac{3}{1,000}$ is three thousandths. A decimal place-value chart can help you determine the decimal.

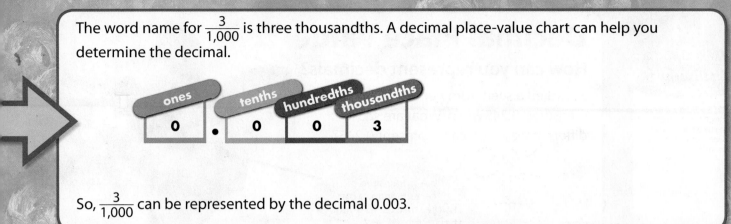

So, $\frac{3}{1,000}$ can be represented by the decimal 0.003.

Problem Solving

MATHEMATICAL PRACTICES

27. Persevere Which illustrates the Associative Property of Multiplication?

A $5 \times 7 = 7 \times 5$

B $0 \times 8 = 0$

C $6 \times 1 = 6$

D $1 \times (2 \times 3) = (1 \times 2) \times 3$

28. The largest egg on record was laid by an ostrich. The weight was 5.476 pounds. Which digit is in the tenths place?

A 4   **C** 6

B 5   **D** 7

29. Look for Patterns Write the fractions $\frac{9}{10}$, $\frac{9}{100}$, and $\frac{9}{1,000}$ as decimals.

30. Critique Reasoning Frank reasoned that $\frac{97}{1,000}$ can be written as 0.97. Is this correct? If not, justify your reasoning.

31. Communicate How many cubes are in the box? What fraction of the entire box do the 7 cubes represent? Explain your answer.

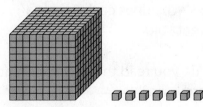

$10 \times 10 \times 10$

32. Model What part of the entire square is shaded?

A 0.007   **C** 0.7

B 0.07   **D** 7.0

33. A bagel costs $1.25 and a glass of juice costs $2.75. Write 1.25 and 2.75 in word form.

34. Paul has a toy train that is 3.37 inches long. Write 3.37 as a mixed number.

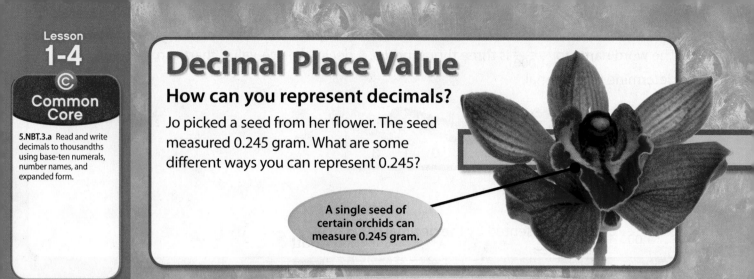

Lesson 1-4

Common Core

5.NBT.3.a Read and write decimals to thousandths using base-ten numerals, number names, and expanded form.

Decimal Place Value

How can you represent decimals?

Jo picked a seed from her flower. The seed measured 0.245 gram. What are some different ways you can represent 0.245?

> A single seed of certain orchids can measure 0.245 gram.

Another Example **What are equivalent decimals?**

Equivalent decimals <u>name the same amount.</u>

Name two other decimals equivalent to 1.4.

One and four tenths is the same as one and forty hundredths.
So, 1.4 = 1.40.

One and four tenths is the same as one and four hundred thousandths.
So, 1.4 = 1.400.

So, 1.4 = 1.40 = 1.400.

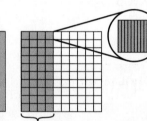

1 whole

4 columns = 4 tenths
40 small squares = 40 hundredths
= 400 thousandths

Guided Practice* **MATHEMATICAL PRACTICES**

Do you know HOW?

Write the word form for each number and give the value of the underlined digit.

1. 4.7<u>3</u>7 **2.** 9.80<u>6</u>

Write each number in standard form.

3. 6 + 0.6 + 0.03 + 0.007

4. four and sixty-eight hundredths

Write two decimals that are equivalent to the given decimal.

5. 3.700 **6.** 5.60

Do you UNDERSTAND?

7. Reason The number 3.453 has two 3s. Why does each 3 have a different value?

8. How do you read the decimal point in word form?

9. Generalize José finished a race in 2.6 hours and Pavel finished the same race in 2.60 hours. Which runner finished the race first?

---

14 *For another example, see Set D on page 23.*

Animated Glossary, eTools
www.pearsonsuccessnet.com

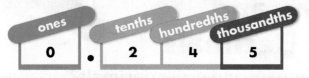

ones	tenths	hundredths	thousandths
0 .	2	4	5

Standard Form: 0.245

└─ The 5 is in the thousandths place. Its value is 0.005.

Expanded Form: 0.2 + 0.04 + 0.005

Word Form: two hundred forty-five thousandths

Independent Practice

Write the word form for each number and give the value of the underlined digit.

10. 2.<u>3</u>00   **11.** 9.<u>2</u>07   **12.** 1.9<u>8</u>2   **13.** 6.17<u>8</u>

Write each number in standard form.

14. two and six thousandths   **15.** five and one hundred four thousandths

16. 3 + 0.3 + 0.009   **17.** 7 + 0.6 + 0.05 + 0.007

Write two decimals that are equivalent to the given decimal.

18. 2.200   **19.** 8.1   **20.** 9.50   **21.** 4.200

Problem Solving

MATHEMATICAL PRACTICES

© **22. Be Precise** Kay is buying juice at the market. She has $9 and each bottle of juice costs $2. Does she have enough money to buy 5 bottles of juice? Explain.

© **23. Model** Which point on the number line below best represents 0.368?

```
            W  X      Y   Z
  ◄─┼─┼─┼─┼─┼─●─┼─●─┼─┼─┼─●─┼─●─┼─►
 0.350                      0.370
```

A W   **B** X   **C** Y   **D** Z

24. The Borneo stick insect has a total length, including legs, of 21.5 inches. Write 21.5 in word form.

25. Worker leafcutter ants can measure 0.5 inches. Name two decimals that are equivalent to 0.5.

© **26. Generalize** Why are 7.630 and 7.63 equivalent?

Common
Core

5.NBT.3.b Compare two decimals to thousandths based on meanings of the digits in each place, using >, =, and < symbols to record the results of comparisons.

Comparing and Ordering Decimals

How can you compare and order decimals?

Scientists collected and measured the lengths of different cockroach species. Which cockroach had the greater length, the American or the Oriental cockroach? Use these three steps to find out.

Oriental
3.432 centimeters

American
3.576 centimeters

Australian
3.582 centimeters

Another Example **How can you order decimals?**

Order the cockroaches from least to greatest length. Use the three steps below to help you.

Step 1

Write the numbers, lining up the decimal points. Start at the left. Compare digits of the same place-value.

3.576
3.432
3.582

3.432 is the least.

Step 2

Write the remaining numbers, lining up the decimal points. Start at the left. Compare.

3.576
3.582

3.582 is the greater.

Step 3

Write the numbers from least to greatest.

3.432, 3.576, 3.582

In order of their lengths from least to greatest, the cockroaches are the Oriental, the American, and the Australian.

Guided Practice*

 MATHEMATICAL PRACTICES

Do you know HOW?

Compare the two numbers. Write >, <, or = for each $\bigcirc$.

1. 3.692 $\bigcirc$ 3.697 **2.** 7.216 $\bigcirc$ 7.203

Order these numbers from least to greatest.

3. 5.540, 5.631, 5.625, 5.739

4. 0.675, 1.529, 1.35, 0.693

Do you UNDERSTAND?

5. Write a number that is greater than 4.508 but less than 4.512.

6. **Reason** Scientists measured a Madeira cockroach and found it to be 3.438 cm long. If they were ordering the lengths of the cockroaches from least to greatest, between which two cockroaches would the Madeira cockroach belong?

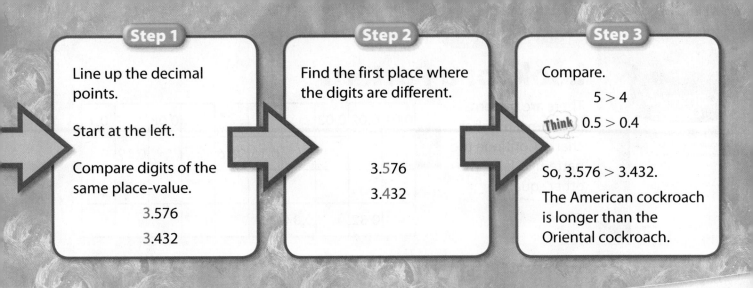

Step 1

Line up the decimal points.

Start at the left.

Compare digits of the same place-value.

3.576
3.432

Step 2

Find the first place where the digits are different.

3.576
3.432

Step 3

Compare.

5 > 4

Think 0.5 > 0.4

So, 3.576 > 3.432.

The American cockroach is longer than the Oriental cockroach.

Independent Practice

Copy and complete. Write >, <, or = for each ◯.

7. 0.890 ◯ 0.89   **8.** 5.733 ◯ 5.693   **9.** 9.707 ◯ 9.717

10. 4.953 ◯ 4.951   **11.** 1.403 ◯ 1.4   **12.** 3.074 ◯ 3.740

Order from least to greatest.

13. 2.912, 2.909, 2.830, 2.841   **14.** 8.541, 8.314, 8.598, 8.8

Order from greatest to least.

15. 5.132, 5.123, 5.312, 5.231   **16.** 62.905, 62.833, 62.950, 62.383

Problem Solving

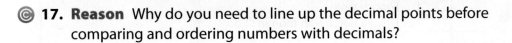

MATHEMATICAL
PRACTICES

ⓒ **17. Reason** Why do you need to line up the decimal points before comparing and ordering numbers with decimals?

ⓒ **18. Persevere** Judith wants to buy her mother flowers. Judith earns $4 a week doing chores. If each flower costs $2, how many flowers can Judith buy her mother if she saves for three weeks?

ⓒ **19. Reasonableness** There are five types of grains of sand: coarse, very coarse, medium, fine, and very fine. A grain of fine sand can have a diameter of 0.125 millimeters.

Which number is less than 0.125?

A 0.5   **C** 0.13

B 0.2   **D** 0.12

Lesson
1-6

©
Common Core

5.NBT.3 Read, write, and compare decimals to thousandths.

Look for a Pattern

There are patterns in decimal number charts. Continue the pattern to label the other squares.

0.01	0.02	0.03					0.08		0.1
				0.15	0.16			0.19	
								0.29	
	0.32		0.34			0.37			

Another Example

In this decimal number chart, what are the patterns in the diagonals?

Using the same system as above, you could fill in the diagonals of a decimal number chart.

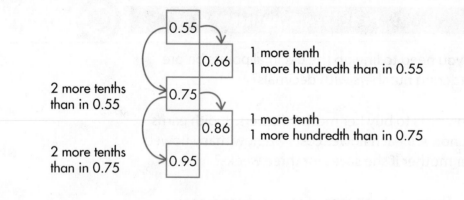

0.55

0.66 — 1 more tenth
1 more hundredth than in 0.55

2 more tenths than in 0.55

0.75

0.86 — 1 more tenth
1 more hundredth than in 0.75

2 more tenths than in 0.75

0.95

Explain It

1. If the grid in Another Example above were extended by 2 cells in the same design, what decimals would be used to complete the grid?

What are the missing decimals?

0.01

As you work with vertical columns, you will see the tenths increase by 1 and the hundredths stay the same as you move down.

0.01
0.11
0.21
0.31

What are the missing decimals?

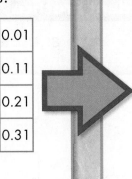

			0.29	

Moving from left to right, tenths are the same in each row except for the last number; the hundredths increase by 1.

0.26	0.27	0.28	0.29	0.30

Guided Practice*

 MATHEMATICAL PRACTICES

Do you know HOW?

In **1** and **2**, determine the patterns, and then complete the decimal grids.

1.

0.42

2.

0.16

Do you UNDERSTAND?

© **3. Use Structure** In a completed decimal chart, look at the first row, which begins with 0.01, 0.02 . . . . If Rene were to create a thousandths chart, what two numbers would immediately follow 0.001?

© **4. Look for Patterns** Write a real-world problem that you could solve by looking for a pattern.

Independent Practice

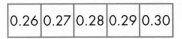 **MATHEMATICAL PRACTICES**

© **Reasonableness** In **5** and **6**, determine the patterns, and then complete the decimal grids.

5.

		0.14

6.

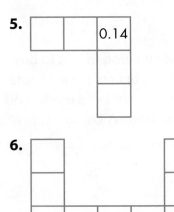

0.87

Applying Math Practices

- What am I asked to find?
- What else can I try?
- How are quantities related?
- How can I explain my work?
- How can I use math to model the problem?
- Can I use tools to help?
- Is my work precise?
- Why does this work?
- How can I generalize?

---

*For another example, see Set F on page 23.

© **7. Look for Patterns** Describe the patterns you should use to complete the following grid, then complete it.

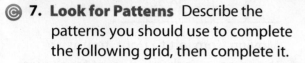

© **8. Use Structure** Determine the patterns, and then complete the grid.

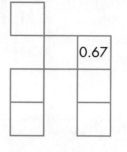

© **9. Look for Patterns** Determine the patterns, and then complete the grid.

© **10. Reason** What is the missing number in the grid?

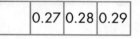

© **11. Use Structure** Drake drew a grid of five cells in a row. The number 0.75 was in the middle cell. What did Drake's grid look like?

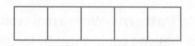

© **12. Look for Patterns** Determine a pattern, and then complete the grid.

13. Juan and his family went to a movie. They bought 2 adult tickets at $8 each and 3 student tickets at $5 each. They paid with two $20 bills. How much change did they get?

14. The greatest distance of Mercury from Earth is 136,000,000 miles. Write this number in expanded form.

© **Think About the Structure**

15. You buy three items that cost $0.37, $0.35, and $0.19, and give the clerk $1.00. Which expression shows how to find the amount of change you would get from $1.00?

   A $0.37 + $0.35 + $0.19 + $1.00

   B $1.00 − $0.37

   C $1.00 − ($0.37 + $0.35 + $0.19)

   D $1.00 + $0.37 + $0.35 − $0.19

16. If 100 people are waiting in line to buy tickets and only 53 tickets are available, which expression would you use to find how many people won't be able to buy tickets?

   A 100 + 53

   B 100 − 53

   C 100 × 53

   D 53 + 53

Decimal Place Value

To subtract 0.008 from 3.695, you can subtract 0.01, and then add 0.002.
Do this subtraction on the calculator.
Next, tell how to change 3.695 to 3.685, and then 3.685 to 3.687 on a calculator.

Step 1   Turn the calculator on, enter 3.695.
Subtract 0.01 and add 0.002.

Press: 3.695 $-$ 0.01 $+$ 0.002   **ENTER =**

Display: *3.687*

Step 2   When 3.695 changes to 3.685, the digit in the hundredths place decreases from 9 to 8, so subtract one hundredth, or 0.01.

Press: 3.695 $-$ 0.01   **ENTER =**

Display: *3.685*

Step 3   When 3.685 changes to 3.687, the digit in the thousandths place increases from 5 to 7, so add two thousandths, or 0.002.

Press: $+$ 0.002   **ENTER =**

Display: *3.687*

Press (Clear) before starting a new problem.

Practice

Make each change on a calculator and tell how you made it.

1. 2.659 to 2.658   **2.** 8.356 to 8.456   **3.** 7.348 to 7.328

4. 5.148 to 5.178   **5.** 4.251 to 4.253   **6.** 9.462 to 9.062

7. 3.272 to 3.27   **8.** 1.605 to 1.635   **9.** 6.537 to 6.534

10. 0.659 to 0.658   **11.** 7.492 to 7.495   **12.** 5.219 to 5.209

13. 8.674 to 8.676   **14.** 3.21 to 3.23   **15.** 7.41 to 7.45

16. 3.673 to 3.671   **17.** 5.483 to 5.479   **18.** 3.618 to 3.612

Set A, pages 6–7

Write the word form and tell the value of the underlined digit for 930,365.

Nine hundred thirty thousand, three hundred sixty-five.

Since the 0 is in the thousands place, its value is 0 thousands or 0.

Remember that, starting from the right, each group of three digits forms a period. Periods are separated by commas.

Write the word form and tell the value of the underlined digit.

1. 9,000,009

2. 300,000,000,000

3. 25,678

4. 17,874,000,000

5. 4,000,345,000

6. 105,389

Set B, pages 8–10

Write $\frac{60}{100}$ as a decimal.

You can write fractions as decimals using a place-value chart. You read $\frac{60}{100}$ as 60 hundredths.

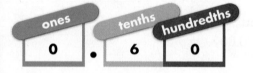

You can see that $\frac{60}{100}$ = 0.60.

Remember that to write a decimal, you need to pay particular attention to the denominator of the fraction.

For **1** through **4**, write each fraction or mixed number as a decimal.

1. $1\frac{2}{10}$ **2.** $\frac{9}{100}$

3. $\frac{7}{10}$ **4.** $2\frac{35}{100}$

Set C, pages 12–13

Write $\frac{7}{1,000}$ as a decimal.

You can write fractions as decimals using a place value chart. You read $\frac{7}{1,000}$ as seven thousandths.

You can see that $\frac{7}{1,000}$ = 0.007.

Remember that to write a decimal with thousandths place, you need to use three decimal places after the decimal.

Write each decimal as a fraction.

1. 0.192   **2.** 0.042

Write each fraction as a decimal.

3. $\frac{189}{1,000}$ **4.** $\frac{3}{1,000}$

Write the word form and tell the value of the underlined digit for the number 8.0<u>2</u>6.

Write the numbers on a place value chart.

ones		tenths	hundredths	thousandths
8	.	0	2	6

Eight and twenty-six thousandths

The 2 is in the hundredths place.
Its value is 0.02.

Remember to write the word *and* for the decimal point.

Write the word form and tell the value of each underlined digit.

1. 8.<u>5</u>9
2. 2.25<u>1</u>
3. 7.00<u>3</u>
4. 3.20<u>4</u>
5. 6.8<u>3</u>7
6. 0.6<u>3</u>6

Compare. Write <, >, or =.

8.45 ◯ 8.47.

Line up the numbers above each other by the decimals.

8.4<u>5</u>

8.4<u>7</u>

5 hundredths < 7 hundredths

So, 8.45 < 8.47.

Remember that equivalent decimals, such as 0.45 and 0.450, can help you compare numbers.

Compare. Write >, <, or =.

1. 0.584 ◯ 0.58
2. 9.327 ◯ 9.236
3. 5.2 ◯ 5.20
4. 5.643 ◯ 5.675
5. 0.07 ◯ 0.08

The table below shows the number of new members each month for a club. If the pattern continues, how many new members will there be in June?

Jan.	Feb.	Mar.	Apr.	May	June
15	30	60	120	▪	▪

Pattern: The number doubles each month.

May: $120 \times 2 = 240$ June: $240 \times 2 = 480$

In June, there will be 480 new members.

Remember to look for a pattern.

1. On the board, Andrea's teacher wrote the pattern below. Find the next three numbers in the pattern.

   2, 4, 8, 14, 22, ▪, ▪, ▪

2. Sean bought a rare stamp for $15. He was told that it would increase in value by $11 each year. What will the stamp's value be after 4 years?

Multiple Choice

© ASSESSMENT

1. About 885,000,000 people speak Mandarin Chinese. How is 885,000,000 written in words? (1-1)

   A eight hundred million, eighty-five thousand

   B eight hundred eighty-five million

   C eight billion, eighty-five million

   D eight hundred eighty-five billion

2. A National Park in Alaska has eighty thousand, nine-hundred twenty-three and eighty-six hundredths acres of nonfederal land. Which shows this number in standard form? (1-4)

   A 80,923.68

   B 80,923.86

   C 80,923.086

   D 80,923.806

3. The circumference of a bowling ball is less than 27.002 inches. Which of the following numbers is less than 27.002? (1-5)

   A 27.02

   B 27.2

   C 27.004

   D 27.001

4. In the year 2000, the population of New York City was about 14,700,000. Which of the following is another way to write this number? (1-1)

   A 10,000,000 + 4,000,000 + 70,000

   B 10,000,000 + 4,000 + 700

   C 10,000,000 + 4,000,000 + 700

   D 10,000,000 + 4,000,000 + 700,000

5. A certain machine part must be between 2.73 and 3.55 inches. Which number is greater than 2.73 and less than 3.55? (1-5)

   A 3.73

   B 3.6

   C 2.55

   D 2.75

6. What part of the figure is shaded? (1-2)

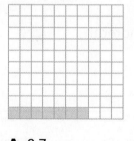

   A 0.7

   B 0.70

   C 0.07

   D 0.007

7. Lead melts at 327.46 degrees Celsius. What is 327.46 written in expanded form? (1-4)

8. Use place value to solve. Kendra has $70. Alonzo has $\frac{1}{10}$ as much money as Kendra. Mariko has 10 times as much money as Kendra. How much money does Alonzo have? How much money does Mariko have? (1-1)

9. About $\frac{2}{5}$ of U.S. households own at least one dog. What is $\frac{2}{5}$ written as a decimal? (1-2)

10. Determine the pattern, then fill in the decimal grid. (1-6)

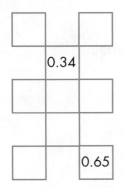

11. Determine the pattern, then fill in the grid. (1-6)

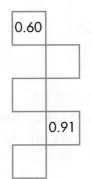

12. In basketball, Dimitri is averaging 12.375 rebounds per game in a tournament. What is 12.375 in expanded form? In word form? (1-3)

13. Use place value to solve. Pablo has a piece of wire that is 0.08 meters long. Beth has a piece of wire that is ten times as long as Pablo's wire. Li's wire is $\frac{1}{10}$ as long as Pablo's. How long is Beth's wire? How long is Li's wire? (1-1)

14. Determine the pattern, then fill in the decimal grid. (1-6)

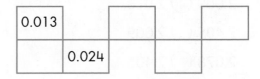

15. Thomas says that $\frac{35}{1000}$ can be written as 0.35. Is this correct? If not, justify your reasoning and give the correct decimal equivalent. (1-3)

16. What fraction is shown by the shaded part of the model? (1-2)

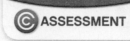
Dwayne has $5.00. Kendra has $\frac{1}{10}$ as much money as Dwayne. Juan has $\frac{1}{10}$ as much money as Kendra. Tom has 10 times as much money as Dwayne, and Ruth has 10 times as much money as Tom.

1. Create a chart to show how much money each person has. List them in order from greatest amount to least amount.

Use the following information for items 2 and 3.

Mr. Bhatia has a cantaloupe that weighs 2.009 kilograms. Mrs. Roberts has a cantaloupe that weighs 2.078 kilograms, and Mr. Carroll's cantaloupe weighs 2.405 kilograms.

2. Compare each pair of decimals using >, =, or <.

2.009 $\bigcirc$ 2.078

2.405 $\bigcirc$ 2.009

2.078 $\bigcirc$ 2.405

3. Write the expanded form and word form for each decimal.

4. Determine the pattern, then fill in the decimal grid.

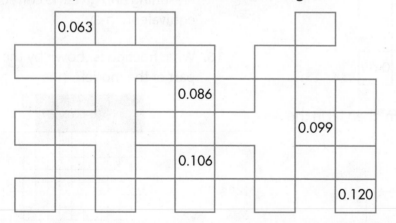

5. Kayla is asked to write an 8-digit number with 3 in the hundred thousands place and 7 in the hundreds place. She writes 13,246,708. Is she correct? If not, explain and write a number that would satisfy the requirements.

Adding and Subtracting Decimals

▼ The bones in a human's leg are not the same length. Do you know the difference in the length of the bones? You will find out in Lesson 2-7.

Review What You Know!

Vocabulary

Choose the best term from the box.

- Associative Property of Addition
- Commutative Property of Addition
- difference
- sum

1. Using the __?__ you can add two numbers in any order.

2. The __?__ is the answer to a subtraction problem.

3. When you can change the grouping of numbers when adding you are using the __?__.

4. The answer in an addition problem is called the __?__.

Rounding

Round each number to the nearest hundred.

5. 748   6. 293   7. 139

Round each number to the nearest thousand.

8. 3,857   9. 2,587   10. 2,345

Round each number to the underlined digit.

11. 84.59   12. 2.948   13. 3.0125

Estimating

© **Writing to Explain** Write an answer for the question.

14. Explain how to use rounding when estimating.

Topic Essential Questions

- How can sums and differences of decimals be estimated?
- What are the standard procedures for adding and subtracting whole numbers and decimals?

Interactive Learning

Pose the problem. Start each lesson by working together to solve problems. It will help you make sense of math.

Applying Math Practices

- What am I asked to find?
- What else can I try?
- How are quantities related?
- How can I explain my work?
- How can I use math to model the problem?
- Can I use tools to help?
- Is my work precise?
- Why does this work?
- How can I generalize?

Lesson 2-1

© **Reason** Solve using mental math – no paper and pencil.

Suppose you want to buy software for your computer. One piece of software costs $20.75. Another costs $10.59 and a third costs $18.25. (a) Use mental math to find the total cost. Explain how you found the answer. (b) How much more is the first piece of software than the second?

Lesson 2-2

© **Reason** Use the numbers at the right to answer the question.

Which of the numbers at the right are closer to 1,200 and which are closer to 1,300? Tell how you decided.

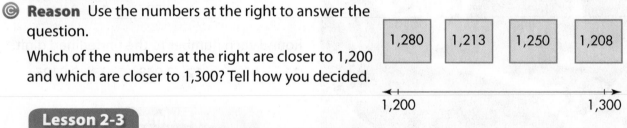

| 1,280 | 1,213 | 1,250 | 1,208 |

1,200   1,300

Lesson 2-3

© **Reasonableness** Solve. All you need are estimates.

An amusement park has two roller coasters and a train ride. About how many feet long are the roller coaster rides combined? About how many feet longer is one than the other? Tell how you found each estimate.

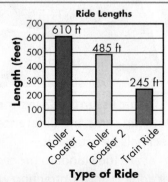

Ride Lengths

Length (feet) / Type of Ride
- Roller Coaster 1: 610 ft
- Roller Coaster 2: 485 ft
- Train Ride: 245 ft

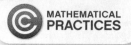

Lesson 2-4

© **Use Tools** Use the grid paper to represent decimals and solve this problem.

Gloria rode her bicycle 0.75 mile in the morning and 1.10 miles in the afternoon. How many miles did Gloria ride in all? Tell how you found the answer.

One ☐ = 0.01 mile.

Lesson 2-5

© **Model** Solve. Use the Problem Solving Recording Sheet.

Myra scored 10 points. Kari scored 14 more points than Myra. How many points did Kari score? Draw a picture to help you solve this problem.

Lesson 2-6

© **Generalize** Solve any way you choose. Use what you know about adding whole numbers.

Mr. Davidson has two sacks of potatoes shown at the right. How many pounds of potatoes does Mr. Davidson have in all?

14.27 pounds   **11.39 pounds**

Lesson 2-7

© **Generalize** Solve any way you choose. Use what you know about subtracting whole numbers.

Ms. Garcia has a length of wire that is 32.7 m long. She has another length of wire that is 15.33 m long. How much longer is the one wire than the other?

Lesson 2-8

© **Model** Solve. Use skills you have learned previously.

Sheena bought 3 student tickets to a softball game for $1.75 each. How much did she spend? Now write another problem whose solution uses the answer to the first problem. Tell what operation or operations you used and why.

© Common Core

5.NBT.7 Add, subtract... decimals to hundredths, using...strategies based on... properties of operations, and/or the relationship between addition and subtraction...

Mental Math

How can you use mental math to add and subtract?

Properties of addition can help you find the total cost of these three items.

Commutative Property
You can add two decimals in any order.

$11.45 + $3.39 = $3.39 + $11.45

Associative Property
You can change the grouping of addends.

($11.45 + $3.39) + $9.55 = $11.45 + ($3.39 + $9.55)

$9.55

$11.45 $3.39

Another Example How can you use compensation to add or subtract?

With compensation, adjust one or both numbers to make the computation easier; then compensate to get the final answer.

Use compensation to subtract.

Find 4.25 − 3.08 mentally.

Think 4.25 − 3.10 = 1.15

0.02 too much was subtracted   Compensate, add back 0.02

4.25 − 3.08 = 1.17

Use compensation to add.

Find $3.47 + $4.35 mentally

Think $3.50 + $4.35 = $7.85

Add 0.03   Compensate, take away 0.03

$3.47 + $4.35 = $7.82

Explain It

1. In the first example above, why is the answer 0.02 greater than 1.15? In the second example above, why is the answer 0.03 less than $7.85?

2. The equation 0 + 0.5 = 0.5 is an example of the Identity Property of Addition. What is the sum when you add zero to any number?

What You Think

The Commutative and Associative Properties make it easy to add $11.45 + $3.39 + $9.55.

$11.45 and $9.55 are compatible numbers. These are numbers that are easy to compute mentally.

11 + 9 = 20	0.45 + 0.55 = 1.00
20 + 1 = 21	21 + 3.39 = 24.39

The three items cost a total of $24.39.

Why It Works

Commutative Property: change the order

($11.45 + $3.39) + $9.55 = ($3.39 + $11.45) + $9.95

Associative Property: change the grouping

($3.39 + $11.45) + $9.95 = $3.39 + ($11.45 + $9.95)

Guided Practice*

Do you know HOW?

In **1** through **6**, use mental math to add or subtract.

1. 2.1 + 0.9 + 1.2   **2.** 3.5 + 4.6 + 0.4

3. 1.9 + 3.4   **4.** 3.8 + 1.5

5. 4.7 − 1.9   **6.** 8.6 − 4.9

Do you UNDERSTAND?

© **7. Communicate** If 9.8 − 5.29 is changed to 9.8 − 5.3 = 4.5, what must be done to 4.5 to get the exact answer for 9.8 − 5.29? Explain.

8. Jim earns $22.50, $14.75, and $8.50 on three different days. How much did he earn in all? Use mental math to find the sum.

Independent Practice

In **9** through **26**, use mental math to add or subtract.

Tip *When you add 3 or more numbers, look for compatible numbers.*

9. 66 + 1.8 + 2.2   **10.** 9.7 + 3 + 6.3   **11.** 22 + 4.6 + 4.4

12. 23.7 + 1.95 + 2.3   **13.** 3.99 + 3.11 + 6.3   **14.** 5.75 + 4.66 + 4.25

15. 96.6 + 1.48 + 3.4   **16.** 2.99 + 14 + 6.31   **17.** 3.06 + 11.99

18. 14.53 − 9.8   **19.** 4.9 + 8.07 + 9.1   **20.** 6.8 − 2.9

21. 10.03 + 5.8 + 8.2   **22.** 7.65 + 13 + 6.35   **23.** 25.25 + 4.6 + 4.75

24. 66.5 − 24.98   **25.** 8.75 − 2.26   **26.** 99 − 8.95

*For another example, see Set A on page 54.

© 27. Look for Patterns Use the Equal Additions Property shown at the right to find each difference mentally. Explain how you found each difference.

a 6.7 − 2.9   **b** $4.56 − $1.98

Tip *Equal Additions Property:*

Subtract $3.69 − $1.99 mentally.

$3.69 − $1.99.   *If the same number is added to each, the difference is the same.*
+0.01   +0.01
↓   ↓
$3.70 − $2.00 = $1.70

© 28. Be Precise Use mental math to find how many points the football team had scored after the first three quarters.

Quarter	Points
1	14
2	9
3	6
4	10

Data

© 29. Persevere On three different days at her job, Sue earned $27.50, $33.75, and $49.25. She needs to earn $100 to buy a desk for her computer. The cost of the desk includes tax. If she buys the desk, how much money will she have left over?

30. A CD shelf can hold 50 CDs. Jill has 27 CDs. She plans to buy 5 new ones. Each CD costs $9. After she buys the new ones, how many more CDs will the shelf hold?

31. Three different gymnasts had scores of 8.903, 8.827, and 8.844. Which of the scores is the greatest?

© 32. Reason Which shows the Associative Property of Addition?

A 1.3 + 10 = 10 + 1.3

B 15.5 + 0 = 15.5

C (3 + 10) + 7 = 3 + (10 + 7)

D (3 + 10) + 7 = (10 + 3) + 7

33. André buys 12 apples at $1 each. He uses a coupon for $1.50 off the total purchase. How much did André spend on apples?

A $10.50

B $11.00

C $11.50

D $12.00

34. Which number, when rounded to the nearest ten thousand, is 70,000?

A 6,499

B 7,499

C 64,985

D 74,999

Mixed Problem Solving

© **1. Model** How many more species of fish are there than mammals?

Fish	19,000

Mammals	4,000	?

2. What is the total number of species of fish, birds, and mammals?

Some Facts About Animal Species	
Animal	**Species**
Arthropods	1,100,000
Fish	19,000
Birds	9,000
Mammals	4,000
Reptiles	6,000
Amphibians	4,000

3. Is the number of arthropod species greater or less than a million? By how much?

© **4. Persevere** What is the total number of species of birds, mammals, reptiles, and amphibians? Is the total greater or less than the number of species of fish? By how much?

5. What is the total number of reptile and amphibian species? Is the total greater or less than the number of species of birds? By how much?

6. Arthropods have the most species. Find the total number of species of fish, birds, mammals, reptiles, and amphibians. How many more arthropod species are there than that total?

- -

7. A zoo has 1,123 mammals, 745 birds, 1,078 fish, and 134 amphibians. They want to increase the number of amphibians to 200. How many more amphibians do they need?

9. A single drip of water doesn't seem like much, but many drips of water from one faucet can quickly add up to several gallons per day. If the number of drips from a faucet is 30 per minute, how many drips is this for 10 minutes? Use repeated addition.

8. The diagram below shows about how much of the Earth's surface is covered by water. About how much of the Earth's surface is not covered by water?

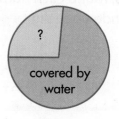

Lesson
2-2

©
Common
Core

5.NBT.4 Use place value
understanding to round
decimals to any place.

Rounding Whole Numbers and Decimals

How can you round whole numbers?

Rounding replaces one number with another number that tells about how many or how much. Round 634 to the nearest hundred.

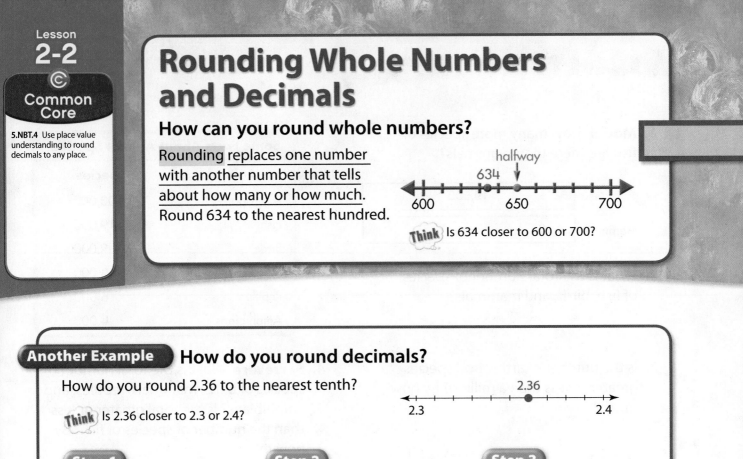

halfway

634

Think Is 634 closer to 600 or 700?

Another Example **How do you round decimals?**

How do you round 2.36 to the nearest tenth?

Think Is 2.36 closer to 2.3 or 2.4?

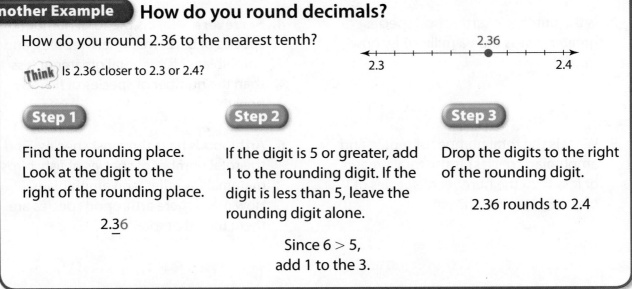

2.36

Step 1

Find the rounding place. Look at the digit to the right of the rounding place.

2.36

Step 2

If the digit is 5 or greater, add 1 to the rounding digit. If the digit is less than 5, leave the rounding digit alone.

Since 6 > 5, add 1 to the 3.

Step 3

Drop the digits to the right of the rounding digit.

2.36 rounds to 2.4

Guided Practice*

MATHEMATICAL PRACTICES

Do you know HOW?

In **1** through **6**, round each number to the place of the underlined digit.

1. 1<u>6</u>

2. 56.<u>1</u>

3. 1.3<u>2</u>

4. 4<u>2</u>7,841

5. <u>1</u>,652

6. <u>5</u>82,062

Do you UNDERSTAND?

© **7. Reason** To round 7,458 to the nearest hundred, which digit do you look at? What is 7,458 rounded to the nearest hundred?

8. A runner is running on a track with markers every 10 meters. If the runner has run 368 meters, is she closer to the 360-meter marker or the 370-meter marker?

Animated Glossary
www.pearsonsuccessnet.com

For another example, see Set B on page 54.

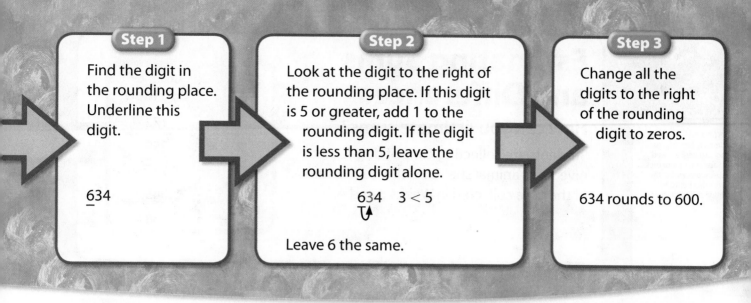

Step 1

Find the digit in the rounding place. Underline this digit.

<u>6</u>34

Step 2

Look at the digit to the right of the rounding place. If this digit is 5 or greater, add 1 to the rounding digit. If the digit is less than 5, leave the rounding digit alone.

6<u>3</u>4   3 < 5

Leave 6 the same.

Step 3

Change all the digits to the right of the rounding digit to zeros.

634 rounds to 600.

Independent Practice

In **9** through **16**, round each whole number to the place of the underlined digit.

9. 6<u>7</u>7   **10.** 4,5<u>2</u>6   **11.** 12,0<u>6</u>4   **12.** <u>5</u>73

13. 34,<u>7</u>39   **14.** <u>5</u>9,304   **15.** 930,<u>9</u>98   **16.** 748,<u>3</u>97

In **17** through **24**, round each number to the place of the underlined digit.

17. 7<u>5</u>.8   **18.** 0.7<u>5</u>8   **19.** 643.8<u>2</u>   **20.** 0.4<u>7</u>2

21. 84.<u>7</u>32   **22.** 738.2<u>9</u>   **23.** 5.0<u>2</u>8   **24.** 23.0<u>0</u>9

Problem Solving

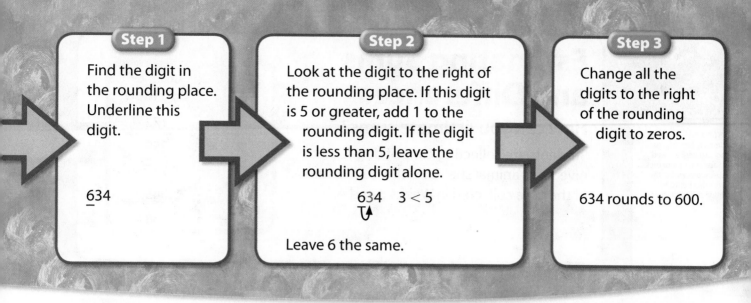 **MATHEMATICAL PRACTICES**

25. The world's largest aloha shirt measures 4.26 meters around the chest. Round 4.26 to the nearest ones place and to the nearest tenths place.

26. In the first 3 quarters of a basketball game, a team scored 17, 25, and 13 points. Their final score was 75. How many points did the team score in the fourth quarter?

27. An African Watusi steer's horn measures 95.25 cm around. What is 95.25 when rounded to the nearest tenth? Nearest whole number? Nearest ten?

© **28. Be Precise** In a recent year, the population of Illinois was 12,653,544. What is that population when rounded to the nearest million?

   A 10,000,000   **B** 12,000,000   **C** 12,600,000   **D** 13,000,000

29. The world land speed record set on October 15, 1997, was 763.03 miles per hour. What is this speed rounded to the nearest one?

Lesson
2-3

Common
Core

5.NBT.7 Add, subtract...
decimals to hundredths,
using...strategies based
on place value, properties
of operations, and/or the
relationship between
addition and subtraction...

Estimating Sums and Differences

How can you estimate sums?

Students are collecting cans of dog food to give to an animal shelter. Estimate the sum of the cans collected in Weeks 3 and 4.

Week	Cans of dog food
1	172
2	298
3	237
4	345
5	338

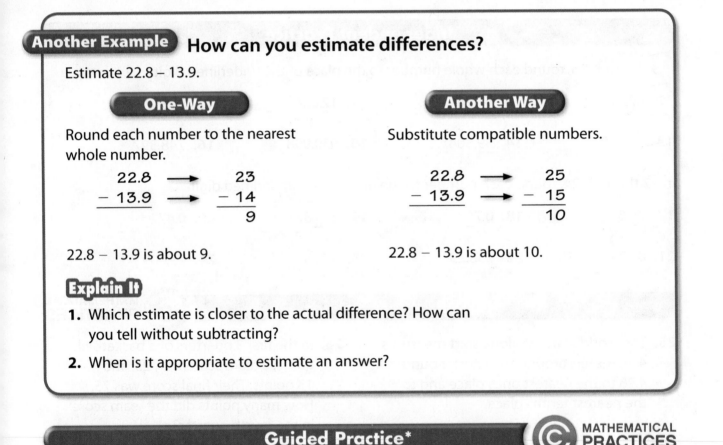

Another Example **How can you estimate differences?**

Estimate 22.8 – 13.9.

One-Way

Round each number to the nearest whole number.

$$\begin{array}{r} 22.8 \longrightarrow 23 \\ -\ 13.9 \longrightarrow -14 \\ \hline 9 \end{array}$$

22.8 – 13.9 is about 9.

Another Way

Substitute compatible numbers.

$$\begin{array}{r} 22.8 \longrightarrow 25 \\ -\ 13.9 \longrightarrow -15 \\ \hline 10 \end{array}$$

22.8 – 13.9 is about 10.

Explain It

1. Which estimate is closer to the actual difference? How can you tell without subtracting?

2. When is it appropriate to estimate an answer?

Guided Practice*

MATHEMATICAL
PRACTICES

Do you know HOW?

In **1** through **6**, estimate the sums and differences.

1. 49 + 22

2. 86 – 18

3. 179 + 277

4. 232 – 97

5. 23.8 – 4.7

6. 87.2 + 3.9

Do you UNDERSTAND?

7. **Communicate** Give an example of when estimating is useful.

8. In the example at the top, the students collected more cans of dog food in week 4 than in week 3. Estimate about how many more cans.

*For another example, see Set C on page 55.

One Way

Round each addend to the nearest hundred.

$$237 \longrightarrow 200$$
$$+\ 345 \longrightarrow +\ 300$$
$$\overline{500}$$

237 + 345 is about 500. The students collected about 500 cans of dog food in Weeks 3 and 4.

Another Way

Substitute compatible numbers. Compatible numbers are easy to add.

$$237 \longrightarrow 250$$
$$+\ 345 \longrightarrow +\ 350$$
$$\overline{600}$$

237 + 345 is about 600. The students collected about 600 cans of dog food in Weeks 3 and 4.

Independent Practice

Estimate each sum or difference.

9.
$$\begin{array}{r} 79 \\ +\ 32 \\ \hline \end{array}$$

10.
$$\begin{array}{r} 788 \\ -\ 572 \\ \hline \end{array}$$

11.
$$\begin{array}{r} 103 \\ +\ 798 \\ \hline \end{array}$$

12.
$$\begin{array}{r} 2{,}488 \\ -\ 1{,}320 \\ \hline \end{array}$$

13.
$$\begin{array}{r} 64 \\ +\ 48 \\ \hline \end{array}$$

14.
$$\begin{array}{r} 837 \\ +\ 488 \\ \hline \end{array}$$

15.
$$\begin{array}{r} 51 \\ -\ 18 \\ \hline \end{array}$$

16.
$$\begin{array}{r} 7{,}889 \\ +\ 6{,}455 \\ \hline \end{array}$$

17.
$$\begin{array}{r} 184 \\ -\ 58 \\ \hline \end{array}$$

18.
$$\begin{array}{r} 847 \\ -\ 379 \\ \hline \end{array}$$

19.
$$\begin{array}{r} 3{,}856 \\ -\ 2{,}357 \\ \hline \end{array}$$

20.
$$\begin{array}{r} 7{,}647 \\ -\ 369 \\ \hline \end{array}$$

21. 3,205 − 2,812   **22.** 93 − 46   **23.** 1,052 + 963   **24.** 149 − 51

Estimate each sum or difference.

25.
$$\begin{array}{r} 2.9 \\ +\ 3.9 \\ \hline \end{array}$$

26.
$$\begin{array}{r} 7.28 \\ -\ 1.32 \\ \hline \end{array}$$

27.
$$\begin{array}{r} \$11.33 \\ +\ 32.43 \\ \hline \end{array}$$

28.
$$\begin{array}{r} \$12.99 \\ -\ 3.95 \\ \hline \end{array}$$

29.
$$\begin{array}{r} 8.1 \\ 3.7 \\ +\ 7.9 \\ \hline \end{array}$$

30.
$$\begin{array}{r} 3.8 \\ 4.1 \\ +\ 3.3 \\ \hline \end{array}$$

31.
$$\begin{array}{r} 67.9 \\ +\ 81.34 \\ \hline \end{array}$$

32.
$$\begin{array}{r} 78.11 \\ +\ 46.03 \\ \hline \end{array}$$

33. 77.11 − 8.18   **34.** 35.4 − 7.8   **35.** 89.66 − 27.9   **36.** 99.9 − 27.9

37. 22.8 + 49.2 + 1.7   **38.** 67.5 − 13.7   **39.** $9.10 + $48.50 + $5.99

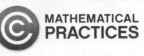
40. Critique Reasoning/Arguments The cost of one CD is $16.98 and the cost of another CD is $9.29. Brittany estimated the cost of these two CDs to be about $27. Did she overestimate or underestimate? Explain.

41. Martha cycled 14 miles each day on Saturday and Monday and 13 miles each day on Tuesday and Thursday. How many miles did she cycle in all?

42. Persevere One fifth-grade class has 11 boys and 11 girls. A second fifth-grade class has 10 boys and 12 girls. There are 6 math teachers. To find the total number of fifth-grade students, what information is not needed?

    A The number of girls in the first class.

    B The number of boys in the first class.

    C The number of math teachers.

    D The number of boys in the second class.

43. On vacation, Steven spent $13 each day on Monday and Tuesday. He spent $9 each day on Wednesday and Thursday. If Steven brought $56 to spend, how much did he have left to spend?

44. Estimate 74.05 + 9.72 + 45.49 by rounding to the nearest whole number. What numbers did you add?

    A 75, 10, and 46   **C** 74, 10, and 45

    B 74.1, 9.7, and 45.5   **D** 75, 10, and 50

45. Golden Gate Park is located in San Francisco, California. The park covers 1,017 acres and has been compared to the size and shape of Central Park in New York City. Central Park covers 843 acres. About how many more acres does Golden Gate Park cover than Central Park?

Central Park

Golden Gate Park

Algebra Connections

Number Patterns

The following numbers form a pattern.

3, 7, 11, 15, 19, …

In this case the pattern is a simple one. The pattern is add 4.

Some patterns are more complicated. Look at the following pattern.

20, 24, 30, 34, 40, 44, 50, …

In this case, the pattern is add 4, add 6.

Example:

What are the next two numbers in the pattern?

24, 29, 28, 33, 32, 37, 36, …

Think The first number is increased by 5. The next number is decreased by 1. I see that the pattern continues.

24, 29, 28, 33, 32, 37, 36, …
+5 −1 +5 −1 +5 −1

To find the next two numbers, add 5, and then subtract 1. The next two numbers are 41 and 40.

Look for a pattern. Find the next two numbers.

1. 9, 18, 27, 36, 45, …

2. 90, 80, 70, 60, 50, …

3. 2, 102, 202, 302, …

4. 26, 46, 66, 86, …

5. 20, 31, 42, 53, 64, …

6. 100, 92, 84, 76, 68, …

7. 1, 3, 9, 27, …

8. 800, 400, 200, 100, …

9. 20, 21, 19, 20, 18, 19, 17, …

10. 10, 11, 21, 22, 32, 33, …

11. 25, 32, 28, 35, 31, 38, …

12. 5, 15, 10, 20, 15, 25, 20, …

13. The following numbers are called Fibonacci numbers.

1, 1, 2, 3, 5, 8, 13, 21, 34, 55, …

Explain how you could find the next two numbers.

14. Use Structure Make up a number pattern that involves two operations.

Common
Core

5.NBT.7 Add, subtract...
decimals to hundredths,
using concrete models or
drawings...

Modeling Addition and Subtraction of Decimals

Hands-On
grid paper

How do you add decimals using grids?

Use the table at the right to find the total monthly cost of using the dishwasher and the DVD player.

Data

Device	Cost/month
DVD player	$0.40
Microwave oven	$3.57
Ceiling light	$0.89
Dishwasher	$0.85

Another Example How do you subtract decimals with grids?

Find the difference between the cost per month to run the microwave oven and the ceiling light.

Use hundredths grids to subtract 3.57 − 0.89.

Step 1 Shade three grids and 57 squares to show 3.57.

Step 2 Cross out 8 columns and 9 squares of the shaded grid to show 0.89 being subtracted from 3.57.

Count the squares that are shaded but not crossed out to find the difference.
3.57 − 0.89 = 2.68

Explain It

© 1. **Reasonableness** How could you use the grids to check your answer above?

2. How would the grid above be different if the cost per month to run the microwave were $2.57?

Use hundredths grids to add $0.85 + $0.40.

It costs $0.85 to use the dishwasher per month.

Shade 85 squares to show $0.85.

It costs $0.40 to use the DVD player per month.

Use a different color and shade 40 more squares to show $0.40. Count all of the shaded squares to find the sum.

$0.85 + $0.40 = $1.25

The monthly cost of using the dishwasher and DVD player is $1.25.

Guided Practice*

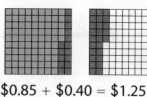

MATHEMATICAL
PRACTICES

Do you know HOW?

In **1** through **6**, use hundredths grids to add or subtract.

1. 1.22 + 0.34   **2.** 0.63 + 0.41

3. 2.73 − 0.94   **4.** $1.38 − $0.73

5. 0.47 − 0.21   **6.** 2.02 + 0.8

Do you UNDERSTAND?

7. If you were to shade 40 squares first, and then shade 85 more, would the answer be the same as shading 85 squares and then 40 more?

© 8. Model Show the difference between the monthly cost of using the DVD player and the dishwasher.

Independent Practice

In **9** through **18**, add or subtract. Use hundredths grids to help.

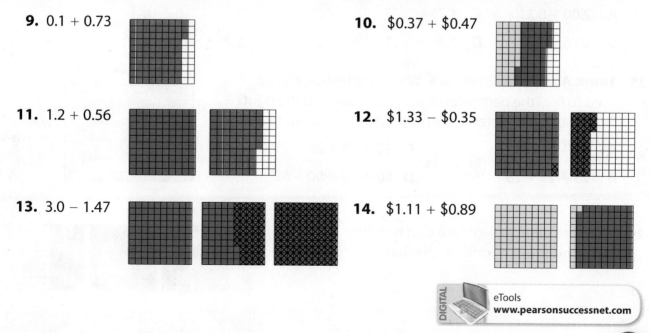

9. 0.1 + 0.73

10. $0.37 + $0.47

11. 1.2 + 0.56

12. $1.33 − $0.35

13. 3.0 − 1.47

14. $1.11 + $0.89

eTools
www.pearsonsuccessnet.com

15. 2.23 − 1.8

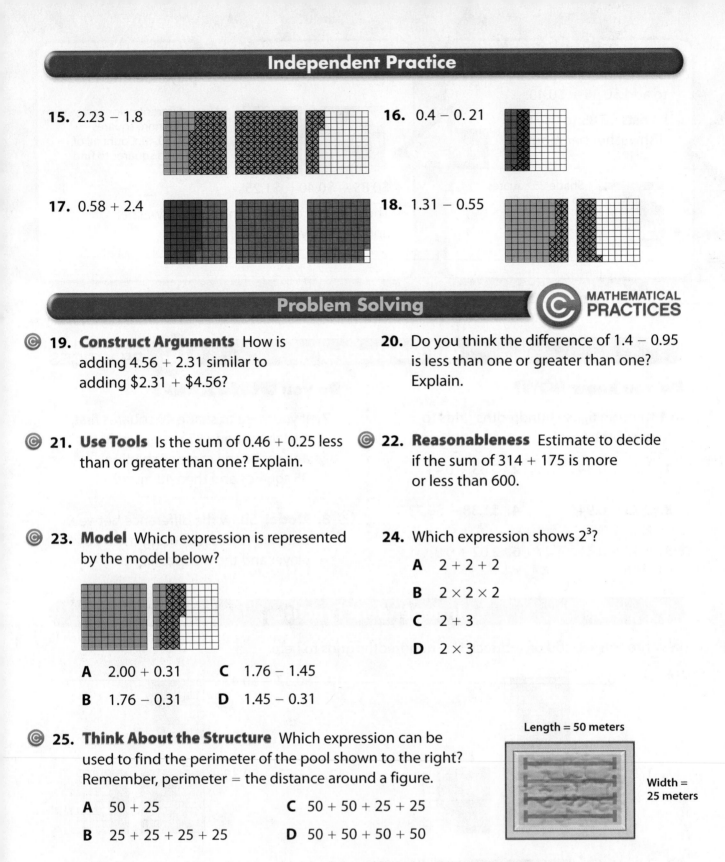

16. 0.4 − 0. 21

17. 0.58 + 2.4

18. 1.31 − 0.55

Problem Solving

19. Construct Arguments How is adding 4.56 + 2.31 similar to adding $2.31 + $4.56?

20. Do you think the difference of 1.4 − 0.95 is less than one or greater than one? Explain.

21. Use Tools Is the sum of 0.46 + 0.25 less than or greater than one? Explain.

22. Reasonableness Estimate to decide if the sum of 314 + 175 is more or less than 600.

23. Model Which expression is represented by the model below?

A 2.00 + 0.31   **C** 1.76 − 1.45

B 1.76 − 0.31   **D** 1.45 − 0.31

24. Which expression shows 2^3?

A 2 + 2 + 2

B 2 × 2 × 2

C 2 + 3

D 2 × 3

25. Think About the Structure Which expression can be used to find the perimeter of the pool shown to the right? Remember, perimeter = the distance around a figure.

A 50 + 25   **C** 50 + 50 + 25 + 25

B 25 + 25 + 25 + 25   **D** 50 + 50 + 50 + 50

Length = 50 meters

Width = 25 meters

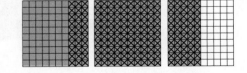

26. Write the number sentence that is shown by the hundredths grids to the right.

Going Digital

Reasonableness of Differences

Estimate 4.72 − 2.85. Use a calculator to subtract. Then explain whether or not the sum you found is reasonable.

Step 1 Estimate 4.72 − 2.85.

5 − 3 = 2

Step 2 Use a calculator to subtract.

Press: 4.72 [−] 2.85 [ENTER =]

Display: 1.87

Step 3 Explain whether or not the difference is reasonable.

Since 1.87 is close to the estimate of 2, the difference is reasonable.

Press (Clear) before starting a new problem.

Estimate 7.51 − 6.49 and use a calculator to subtract. Explain the difference between the estimation and the calculator result.

The estimated difference is 2, and the calculator result is 1.02. The two answers have a difference of about 1, because the first number rounded up and the second number rounded down.

Practice

Estimate each difference. Find the difference on a calculator. Then explain whether or not the difference is reasonable.

1. 28.34 − 7.85

2. 6.86 − 2.18

3. 5.2 − 0.74

4. 1.73 − 0.8

5. 14.97 − 12.39

6. 9.05 − 5.92

7. 2.4 − 0.56

8. 65.47 − 38.19

9. 16.15 − 3.9

10. 3.7 − 1.2

11. 2.82 − 1.21

12. 5.76 − 3.21

13. 8.47 − 7.08

14. 6.59 − 6.03

15. 8.88 − 3.84

Lesson
2-5

ⓒ
Common
Core

5.NBT.7. Add, subtract...
decimals to hundredths,
using concrete models or
drawings...

Problem Solving

Draw a Picture and Write an Equation

Three friends have music collections. How many more CDs does Susan have than Larry?

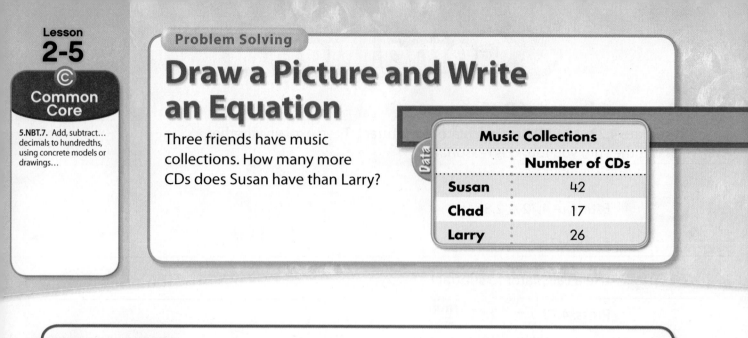

Music Collections	
	Number of CDs
Susan	42
Chad	17
Larry	26

Another Example

Rori had some balloons and then gave 35 of them away. She now has 21 left. How many balloons did Rori have to begin with?

x	
35	21

One Way

Think The total is unknown.

35 were given away and 21 are left.

Write an Equation

$x - 35 = 21$

$21 + 35 = 56$, so 56 is the total.

$x = 56$

Another Way

Think 35 were given away. Rori has 21 left.

The total is unknown.

Write an Equation

$35 + 21 = x$

$35 + 21 = 56$, so 56 is the total.

$x = 56$

Rori had 56 balloons to begin with.

Explain It

1. Why do both ways use addition to solve for x?

2. How can you check if 56 is a reasonable answer?

Read and Understand

What do I know?

Susan has 42 CDs
and Larry has 26 CDs.

What am I asked to find?

The difference between
the number of CDs from
these two collections.

Plan and Solve

Draw a Picture

Susan	42 CDs	
Larry	n	26

Write an Equation

Let n = the number of
additional CDs Susan has.

$42 - 26 = n$

$$\begin{array}{r} \overset{3}{\cancel{4}}\overset{1}{2} \\ -\ 2\ 6 \\ \hline 1\ 6 \end{array}$$

Susan has 16 more CDs in her collection than Larry.

Guided Practice*

MATHEMATICAL PRACTICES

Do you know HOW?

Draw a picture and write an equation. Solve.

1. Alec prints digital photos at a camera store. The first order was for 24 prints. The second order was for 85 prints, and the third for 60 prints. How many fewer prints were in the first order than the third order?

Do you UNDERSTAND?

2. What phrase from the above example gives you a clue that you will use subtraction in your drawing to solve the problem?

© 3. **Be Precise** Write a real-world problem that uses subtraction and can be solved by drawing a picture and writing an equation.

Independent Practice

MATHEMATICAL PRACTICES

In **4**, copy and complete the picture. Then write an equation and solve.

4. Rose needs 22 tacos for a party. She has made 12 tacos so far. How many more tacos does Rose need to make?

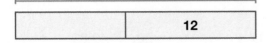

	12

In **5**, draw a picture, write an equation in two different ways, then solve.

© 5. **Model** Aryanna is planning to spend a certain number of days on a trip to Florida. If she plans to spend 5 of the days in Orlando, she'll have 16 more days for the rest of her vacation. How many days does Aryanna plan to spend in Florida?

Applying Math Practices

- What am I asked to find?
- What else can I try?
- How are quantities related?
- How can I explain my work?
- How can I use math to model the problem?
- Can I use tools to help?
- Is my work precise?
- Why does this work?
- How can I generalize?

For another example, see Set E on page 56.

© Common Core

5.NBT.7 Add...decimals to hundredths, using... strategies based on... properties of operations...; relate the strategy to a written method and explain the reasoning used.

Adding Decimals

How can you add decimals?

What was the combined time for the first two legs of the relay race?

Choose an Operation Add to join groups.

Find 21.49 + 21.59.

Estimate: 21 + 22 = 43

Swimmers	Times in Seconds
Caleb	21.49
Bradley	21.59
Vick	20.35
Matthew	19.03

Guided Practice*

MATHEMATICAL PRACTICES

Do you know HOW?

In **1** through **6**, find each sum.

1. 0.82 + 4.21

2. 9.1 + 7.21

3. 9.7 + 0.24

4. 3.28 + 6.09

5. 0.26 + 8.3

6. 4.98 + 3.02

Do you UNDERSTAND?

© **7. Reasonableness** How do you know the total time for the first two legs of the race is reasonable?

© **8. Communicate** How is finding $4.25 + $3.50 like finding 4.25 + 3.5? How is it different?

Independent Practice

In **9** through **26**, find each sum.

9.
```
   1.03
+ 0.36
```

10.
```
   6.9
+ 2.8
```

11.
```
  45.09
+ 2.005
```

12.
```
   2.02
+ 0.78
```

13.
```
  13.094
+ 4.903
```

14.
```
  356.2
+ 12.45
```

15.
```
  4.298
+ 0.65
```

16.
```
  9.001
+ 1.999
```

17.
```
   $8.23
+ $64.10
```

18.
```
   $44.00
+ $91.46
```

19.
```
  17.49
+  9
```

20.
```
  42.89
+  8.2
```

21. $271.90 + $34.22

22. 658.2 + 0

23. 0.922 + 6.4

24. 8.02 + 9.07

25. 13.9 + 0.16

26. 0.868 + 15.973

For another example, see Set F on page 56.

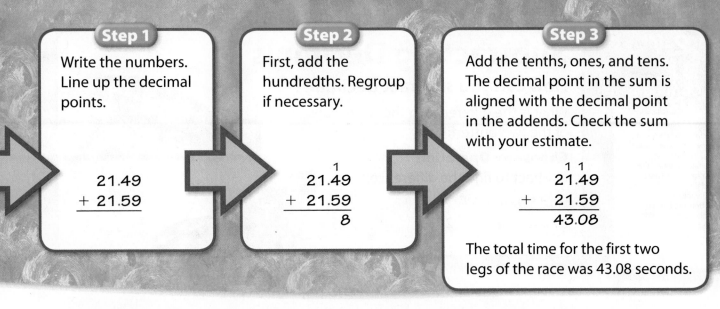

Step 1

Write the numbers. Line up the decimal points.

21.49
+ 21.59

Step 2

First, add the hundredths. Regroup if necessary.

$\overset{1}{2}$1.49
+ 21.59
8

Step 3

Add the tenths, ones, and tens. The decimal point in the sum is aligned with the decimal point in the addends. Check the sum with your estimate.

$\overset{1\ 1}{2}$1.49
+ 21.59
43.08

The total time for the first two legs of the race was 43.08 seconds.

Problem Solving

 MATHEMATICAL PRACTICES

27. Reason A balloon mural of the Chicago skyline measures 17.6 m on two sides and 26.21 m on the other two sides. What is the perimeter of the mural?

A 38.81 m **B** 48.21 m **C** 55.74 m **D** 87.62 m

28. Critique Reasoning Juan adds 3.8 + 4.6 and gets a sum of 84. Is his answer correct? Tell how you know.

29. Think About the Structure Jamie earned $27 taking care of a neighbor's dog for one week. She spent $19.95 on a new DVD. Later, she earned $15 for raking leaves. Which expression shows how to find the money Jamie has left?

A $27 + $19.95 + $15
B $19.95 − $15 + $27
C $27 − $19.95 + $15
D $27 − $19.95 − $15

30. At a flower shop, Teri sees that roses are $3 each, carnations are $4 for 3 flowers, and tulips are $4 for 4 flowers. She buys 3 roses and 3 carnations. She has $20. How much change does Teri get back?

31. Persevere Which two cities had the greatest combined rainfall for the period given?

A Caribou and Boise
B Springfield and Macon
C Macon and Boise
D Caribou and Springfield

Location	Rainfall amount in a typical year (in inches)
Macon, GA	45
Boise, ID	12.19
Caribou, ME	37.44
Springfield, MO	44.97

32. What is the typical yearly rainfall for all four cities?

33. Which location had less than 45 inches of rain but more than 40 inches of rain?

Lesson
2-7

Common
Core

5.NBT.7 …subtract…
decimals to hundredths,
using…strategies based
on…properties of
operations, and/or the
relationship between
addition and subtraction;
relate the strategy to a
written method and
explain the reasoning
used.

Subtracting Decimals

How can you subtract decimals?

What is the difference in the wingspans
of the two butterflies?

Choose an Operation

Subtract to find the difference.

Find $5.92 - 4.37$.

Estimate: $6 - 4 = 2$

4.37 cm

5.92 cm

Other Examples

Using 0 as a placeholder

Find $49.59 - 7.9$.

$$
\begin{array}{r}
\overset{8}{\cancel{9}}\ \overset{15}{\cancel{5}} \\
4\ 9.\ 5\ 9 \\
-\ \ 7.\ 9\ 0 \\
\hline
4\ 1.\ 6\ 9
\end{array}
$$

Annex a
0 as a
placeholder
to show
hundredths.

Using 0 as a placeholder

Find $24.6 - 8.27$.

$$
\begin{array}{r}
1\ 14\ 5\ 10 \\
\cancel{2}\ \cancel{4}.\ \cancel{6}\ \cancel{0} \\
-\ \ 8.\ 2\ 7 \\
\hline
1\ 6.\ 3\ 3
\end{array}
$$

←Annex a
0 as a
placeholder
to show
hundredths.

Subtracting money

Find $\$26.32 - \$5.75$.

$$
\begin{array}{r}
12 \\
5\ \overset{2}{\cancel{3}}\ \overset{12}{\cancel{2}} \\
\$2\ 6.\ 3\ 2 \\
-\ \ \ 5.\ 7\ 5 \\
\hline
\$2\ 0.\ 5\ 7
\end{array}
$$

Guided Practice*

MATHEMATICAL
PRACTICES

Do you know HOW?

In **1** through **8**, find each difference.

1.
$$
\begin{array}{r}
16.82 \\
-\ \ 5.21 \\
\hline
\end{array}
$$

2.
$$
\begin{array}{r}
7.21 \\
-\ \ 6.1 \\
\hline
\end{array}
$$

3.
$$
\begin{array}{r}
23.06 \\
-\ \ 8.24 \\
\hline
\end{array}
$$

4.
$$
\begin{array}{r}
\$4.08 \\
-\ \ 2.12 \\
\hline
\end{array}
$$

5. $56.8 - 2.765$

6. $\$43.80 - \$16.00$

7. $22.4 - 10.7$

8. $\$36.40 - \$21.16$

Do you UNDERSTAND?

9. Reason Explain why 1.55 cm is a
reasonable answer for the difference in
the wingspans of the two butterflies.

10. In the other examples above, is the
value of 7.9 changed when you annex
a zero after 7.9? Why or why not?

11. Construct Arguments How is finding
$9.12 - 4.8$ similar to finding
$\$9.12 - \$4.80$? How is it different?

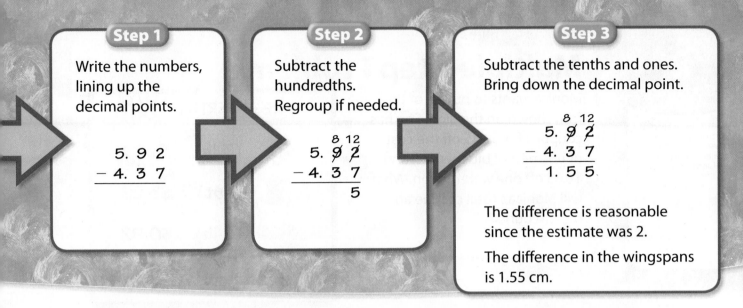

Step 1

Write the numbers, lining up the decimal points.

```
  5. 9 2
− 4. 3 7
```

Step 2

Subtract the hundredths. Regroup if needed.

```
      8 12
  5. 9 2
− 4. 3 7
        5
```

Step 3

Subtract the tenths and ones. Bring down the decimal point.

```
      8 12
  5. 9 2
− 4. 3 7
  1. 5 5
```

The difference is reasonable since the estimate was 2.

The difference in the wingspans is 1.55 cm.

Independent Practice

In **12** through **23**, find each difference.

12.
```
  7.8
− 4.9
```

13.
```
  $20.60
− $14.35
```

14.
```
  43.905
−  7.526
```

15.
```
  65.29
− 28.038
```

16. 15.03 − 4.121

17. 13.9 − 3.8

18. 65.18 − 12.005

19. $52.02 − $0.83

20. 7.094 − 3.657

21. 34.49 − 12.619

22. 85.22 − 43.548

23. $10.05 − $4.50

Problem Solving

Ⓒ **MATHEMATICAL PRACTICES**

Ⓒ **24. Use Structure** Why is it necessary to line up decimal points when subtracting decimals?

Ⓒ **25. Be Precise** Sue subtracted 2.9 from 20.9 and got 1.8. Explain why this is not reasonable.

26. The pyramid of Khafre measured 143.5 meters high. The pyramid of Menkaure measured 65.5 meters high. What is the difference in the heights of these two pyramids?

A 68.8 meters

B 69.3 meters

C 78 meters

D 212.3 meters

27. An average person's upper leg bone measures 19.88 in. and the lower leg bone measures 16.94 in. How much longer is the upper leg bone than the lower leg bone?

upper leg bone	19.88 in.

lower leg bone	?	16.94 in.

Khafre
143.5 meters

Menkaure
65.5 meters

Lesson
2-8

Common Core

5.NBT.7 Add, subtract… decimals to hundredths…; relate the strategy to a written method and explain the reasoning used.

Problem Solving

Multiple-Step Problems

Monica wants to buy all of the fruit shown on this sign. She has coupons for $0.45 off the cost of one pint of blueberries, and $0.35 off one watermelon. What will Monica's total cost be after the discounts?

FRESH FRUIT TODAY		
	(3 lb)	$1.29
	(1 pt)	$3.29
	(2 lb)	$0.92
	(each)	$5.65

Another Example

A children's news and talk show is broadcast for 2 hours each weekday. On Saturday and Sunday, the show is an hour longer than during the week. How many hours is this show broadcast each week?

What is one hidden question?

How many hours of the show are broadcast during weekdays?

? total hours

2	2	2	2	2

↑ hours per weekday

$5 \times 2 = 10$

The show is on for 10 hours during weekdays.

What is another hidden question?

How many hours of the show are broadcast during the weekend?

? total hours

3	3

↑ hours per weekend day

$2 \times 3 = 6$

The show is on for 6 hours during the weekend.

Add the number of weekday and weekend hours.

10 weekday hours + 6 weekend hours = 16 hours
The show is on for 16 hours each week.

Check for reasonableness: I can estimate 2 hrs × 7 days = 14 hrs. This is close to 16 hours.

Explain It

© **1. Persevere** Why do you find and answer the hidden questions before solving the problem?

What do I know?

Monica wants to buy the fruit with prices shown on a store sign. She has coupons for $0.45 and $0.35 off the price of one pint of blueberries and one watermelon.

What am I asked to find?

The cost of all the fruit after the discount

Find and answer the hidden question or questions.

1. How much does the fruit cost?

? total cost

$1.29	$3.29	$0.92	$5.65

$1.29 + $3.29 + $0.92 + $5.65 = $11.15

2. How much are the coupons worth?

? total saved

$0.45	$0.35

$$\begin{array}{r} \$0.45 \\ + \$0.35 \\ \hline \$0.80 \end{array}$$

Subtract the total saved from the cost of the fruit.
$11.15 − $0.80 = $10.35

Monica will pay $10.35 for the fruit after the discount.

Guided Practice*

MATHEMATICAL PRACTICES

Do you know HOW?

Solve.

1. Nate has a $5 bill and a $10 bill. He spends $2.50 for a smoothie and $2 for a muffin. How much money does he have left?

Do you UNDERSTAND?

2. What are the hidden questions and answers for Problem 1?

3. Be Precise Write a real-world multiple-step problem that can be solved using addition and subtraction.

Independent Practice

MATHEMATICAL PRACTICES

In **4** through **6**, write and answer the hidden question or questions. Then solve.

4. Elias saved $30 in July, $21 in August, and $50 in September. He spent $18 on movies and $26 on gas. How much money does Elias have left?

5. Persevere Paige takes riding lessons 5 days per week for 2 hours each day. Maggie takes guitar lessons twice a week for $2\frac{1}{2}$ hours each day, and piano lessons three days per week for 1 hour each day. Which girl spends more hours on lessons? How many more hours?

6. Lonny planted 15 roses, 12 geraniums, and 6 daisies. His dog digs up 4 roses and 2 daisies. How many flowers are left planted?

> **Applying Math Practices**
> - What am I asked to find?
> - What else can I try?
> - How are quantities related?
> - How can I explain my work?
> - How can I use math to model the problem?
> - Can I use tools to help?
> - Is my work precise?
> - Why does this work?
> - How can I generalize?

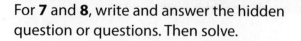
For **7** and **8**, write and answer the hidden question or questions. Then solve.

Driving Log		
	Business	**Personal Use**
Monday	48 mi	11 mi
Tuesday	59 mi	8 mi
Wednesday	78 mi	28 mi

7. At the right is a driving log that Mr. Smith kept for the last three days of his trip. How many more miles did he drive for business than for personal use?

ⓒ **8. Reason** The table at the right shows the amount of salad a deli had on Monday morning. During the morning, the deli sold 5 lb of macaroni salad, 16 lb of pasta salad, and 14 lb of potato salad. How many total pounds of salad did the deli have left Monday afternoon?

Salad Inventory	
Macaroni Salad	11 lb
Pasta Salad	22 lb
Potato Salad	15 lb

9. At the craft festival, Tuan spent $12 for food, $19.50 for a small painting, and $6 for a straw hat. Tuan had $4 left. How much did Tuan spend on the small painting and the hat together? Draw a picture and write an equation to solve.

ⓒ **10. Look for Patterns** Look for a pattern, and then describe it. What are the next three missing numbers?

0.39, 0.45, 0.51, ▮, ▮, ▮

ⓒ **11. Reasonableness** Pull-over shirts cost $24.95 each. Describe how to estimate the cost of 4 shirts. What is the estimate?

ⓒ **Think About the Structure**

12. A men's store has 63 blue oxford shirts and 44 tan oxford shirts. The same store has 39 red rugby shirts. Which hidden question needs to be answered to find the difference between the number of oxford shirts and rugby shirts?

A How many oxford shirts does the store have?

B How many blue and red shirts does the store have?

C How many total shirts does the store have?

D Why does the store sell oxford shirts?

13. Rita budgeted $250 to refurnish her home. She spent $156 on two rugs and $205 on a new lamp. Rita wants to know how much more money she'll need. Which expression can be evaluated to answer this hidden question: How much has Rita spent on the rugs and the lamp?

A $156 + $205

B $250 − $156

C $156 + $250

D $250 + $205

Going Digital

Adding Decimals

Use tools

Place-Value Blocks

Use the Place-Value Blocks eTool to add 1.46 + 0.285.

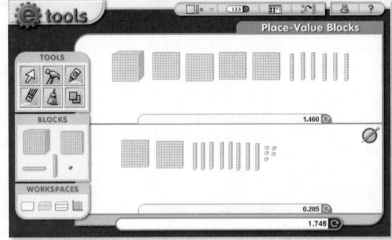

Step 1 Go to the Place-Value Blocks eTool. Use the pull-down menu at the top of the page to select Large as the unit block. Select the two-part workspace icon. Click on the large cube, which represents one whole, and then click in the top part of the workspace. In the same way as above, show 4 flat place-value blocks and 6 long place-value blocks. The odometer should read 1.460.

Step 2 Show 0.285 in the bottom part of the workspace, using the small cube for thousandths. The odometer for the bottom workspace should read 0.285.

Step 3 Use the arrow tool to select the 5 thousandths in the bottom part of the workspace and move them to the top. Move the 8 hundredths so they are next to the 6 hundredths in the top. Click on the glue icon, and then click on a long block. This will change 10 hundredths to 1 tenth. Move the remaining 2 tenths to the top space and look at the blocks to find the sum. 1.46 + 0.285 = 1.745.

Practice

Use the Place-Value Blocks eTool to find each sum.

1. 1.728 + 0.154   **2.** 0.375 + 0.29   **3.** 0.569 + 0.253   **4.** 0.86 + 0.649

5. 1.649 + 0.123   **6.** 1.223 + 0.789   **7.** 0.123 + 1.223   **8.** 0.789 + 1.649

9. 1.518 + 0.456   **10.** 1.527 + 0.912   **11.** 0.456 + 1.527   **12.** 0.912 + 1.518

13. 1.312 + 0.708   **14.** 1.630 + 0.815   **15.** 1.847 + 0.217   **16.** 1.309 + 0.219

Set A, pages 30–32

Add 5.3 + 1.1 + 1.7 using mental math.

Use compatible numbers.

Tip *Compatible numbers are easy to add.*

5.3 and 1.7 are compatible numbers.

The Commutative Property of Addition allows us to add in any order.

$$5.3 + 1.1 + 1.7 = 5.3 + 1.7 + 1.1$$
$$= 7.0 + 1.1$$
$$= 8.1$$

So, 5.3 + 1.1 + 1.7 = 8.1

Remember that you can use compatible numbers or compensation to find sums and differences.

Use mental math to add or subtract.

1. 67 + 28

2. 130 + 470

3. 35 + 14 + 6

4. 8.6 + 23.4 + 1.4

5. 27 − 9.9

6. 127 + 9.9

7. 24.1 + 1.2 + 8.8

8. 86 − 4.9

Set B, pages 34–35

Round 12.0$\underline{8}$7 to the place of the underlined digit.

12.0$\underline{8}$7   Look at the digit following the underlined digit. Look at 7.

Round to the next greater digit of hundredths because 7 > 5.

12.087 is about 12.09.

Round $\underline{9}$.073 to the place of the underlined digit.

$\underline{9}$.073   Look at the digit following the underlined digit. Look at 0.

Since 0 < 5 the digit in the ones place remains the same.

9.073 is about 9.

Remember that rounding a number means replacing it with another number that tells about how much or how many.

Round each number to the place of the underlined digit.

1. 10.2$\underline{4}$5   **2.** $\underline{7}$3.4

3. 9.1$\underline{4}$5   **4.** 3.9$\underline{9}$9

5. 67,9$\underline{0}$1   **6.** 13.0$\underline{2}$3

7. $\underline{9}$9,102   **8.** 45.3$\underline{9}$8

9. 0.1$\underline{5}$3   **10.** 0.6$\underline{2}$5

11. 8.$\underline{9}$78   **12.** 5.7$\underline{3}$9

13. 9,$\underline{9}$99   **14.** 79.5

15. 3.$\underline{0}$91   **16.** 2.4$\underline{3}$2

Estimate 19.9 + 17.03.

$$
\begin{array}{r}
19.9 \longrightarrow 20 \\
+ 17.03 \longrightarrow + 17 \\
\hline
37
\end{array}
$$

Tip *Round to the nearest whole number.*

19.9 + 17.03 is about 37.

Estimate 22.4 − 16.2.

$$
\begin{array}{r}
22.4 \longrightarrow 20 \\
- 16.2 \longrightarrow - 15 \\
\hline
5
\end{array}
$$

Tip *Use compatible numbers.*

22.4 − 16.2 is about 5.

Remember using compatible numbers to estimate is easier than rounding.

Estimate each sum or difference.

1. 76 + 23

2. 15.01 − 4.4

3. 80.01 + 2.89

4. 25,003 − 12,900

5. 9.5 + 9 + 8.6

6. 3.4 + 3.7 + 2.9

Use hundredths grids to subtract 1.86 − 0.95.

Shade one whole grid and 86 squares to show 1.86.

To subtract 0.95, cross out 95 shaded squares on the grids.

Count the squares that are shaded but not crossed out.

1.86 − 0.95 = 0.91

Remember when adding decimals, shade the first number in one color and then continue on shading the second number with another color.

1. 0.02 + 0.89   **2.** 0.67 − 0.31

3. 0.34 + 0.34   **4.** 0.81 − 0.78

Set E, pages 44–45

Draw a picture and write an equation. Solve.

Over the summer, Martin exercises 190 minutes more each week than during the school year. If Martin exercises 910 minutes per week in the summer, how many minutes per week does he exercise during the school year?

```
        910 minutes
|------------------------|
|              |         |
|      m       | 190 min.|
|              |         |
```

Let m = minutes per week of exercise during the school year

$910 - 190 = m$
$m = 720$

```
  811
  9 1 0
-   1 9 0
---------
    7 2 0
```

Martin exercises 720 minutes per week during the school year.

Remember that drawing a picture can help you before writing an equation to solve a problem.

Draw a picture and write an equation. Solve.

1. Jay's parents celebrated their 25th wedding anniversary in 2005. In what year were they married?

2. One football stadium, built in 1982, has 64,035 seats. Another stadium, built in 1987, has 74,916 seats. How many more seats does the newer stadium have?

3. In Helen's class, there are 13 girls and 17 boys. Megan's class has the same number of students, but there are 20 girls in her class. How many boys are in Megan's class?

Set F, pages 46–47

Find 9.32 + 2.95.

Estimate: 9 + 3 = 12

Step 1 Write the numbers. Line up the decimal points.

```
  9. 3 2
+ 2. 9 5
--------
```

Step 2 Add as you would whole numbers. Bring the decimal point down into the answer.

```
    1
  9. 3 2
+ 2. 9 5
--------
1 2. 2 7
```

The sum 12.27 is reasonable because it is close to the estimate, 12.

Remember to line up the decimal points before you add.

Find each sum.

1. 3.77 + 4.66

2. 12.68 + 31.91

3. 6.14 + 1.32

4. 67.8 + 14.75

5. 7.03 + 48.7

6. 10.93 + 0.96

7. 1.47 + 1.80

8. 125.9 + 6.77

Find 7.83 − 3.147.

Estimate: 8 − 3 = 5.

Step 1 Write the numbers. Line up the decimal points. Annex zeros to show place value and act as placeholders.

$$
\begin{array}{r}
7.\ 8\ 3\ 0 \\
-\ 3.\ 1\ 4\ 7 \\
\hline
\end{array}
$$

Step 2 Subtract as you would whole numbers. Bring the decimal point down into the answer.

$$
\begin{array}{r}
^{7\ \ 12\ 10} \\
7.\ \cancel{8}\ \cancel{3}\ \cancel{0} \\
-\ 3.\ 1\ 4\ 7 \\
\hline
4.\ 6\ 8\ 3 \\
\end{array}
$$

Step 3 Check your answer by adding. The answer checks.

$$
\begin{array}{r}
^{1\ \ 1} \\
4.\ 6\ 8\ 3 \\
+\ 3.\ 1\ 4\ 7 \\
\hline
7.\ 8\ 3\ 0 \\
\end{array}
$$

The difference 4.683 is reasonable because it is close to the estimate, 5.

Remember that you can check your answer by adding.

Find each difference.

1. 9.21 − 1.72

2. 15.51 − 11.302

3. 5.7 − 0.623

4. 16.209 − 14.5

5. 17.099 − 9.7

6. 81.12 − 37.202

7. 61.1 − 0.008

8. 19.006 − 7.5

Gene wants to buy a catcher's mitt for $52.00 and baseball shoes for $95.75. He has a coupon for $8.50 off the price of the catcher's mitt. How much money will Gene owe for his total purchase?

What is the hidden question or questions?

How much will Gene have to pay for the catcher's mitt after he uses the coupon?

$52.00		
$8.50	? cost after coupon	

$52.00 − $8.50 = $43.50

Solve the problem.

Add the discounted price of the mitt to the price of the shoes to find the total amount Gene owes.
$43.50 + $95.75 = $139.25

Gene will pay $139.25 for his purchase.

Remember to look for the hidden question or questions first to solve the problem.

Write and answer the hidden question or questions. Then solve.

1. Pedro earned money doing different jobs for neighbors. He kept a table of what he earned. If Pedro bought a magazine subscription for $16.95 from his earnings, how much money did he have left?

Job	Earnings
Mowing lawn	$13.50
Raking leaves	$11.00
Walking dogs	$14.75

Multiple Choice

1. A dollhouse has 15.15 square feet downstairs and 6.25 square feet upstairs. Which of the following is the best estimate of the total square footage in the dollhouse? (2-3)

   A 21

   B 22

   C 23

   D 25

2. What is 2.934 rounded to the nearest hundredth? (2-2)

   A 2.90

   B 2.93

   C 2.94

   D 3.00

3. Eduardo is training for a marathon. He ran his first mile in 12.56 minutes and his second mile in 12.98 minutes. What is his combined time for the first two miles? (2-6)

   A 24.43 minutes

   B 24.54 minutes

   C 25.44 minutes

   D 25.54 minutes

4. Beth worked 33.25 hours last week and 23.75 hours this week. How many total hours did she work? Use mental math to solve. (2-1)

   A 46

   B 47

   C 56

   D 57

5. The Thomas Jefferson Memorial is on 18.36 acres of land and the Franklin Delano Roosevelt Memorial is on 7.5 acres of land. How many more acres of land is the Jefferson Memorial on than the Roosevelt Memorial? (2-7)

   A 9.86

   B 10.86

   C 11.31

   D 17.61

6. Which picture represents the problem? Parson's Sporting Goods ordered 56 T-shirts in sizes small, medium, and large. If 23 T-shirts are medium and 12 T-shirts are large, how many are small? (2-5)

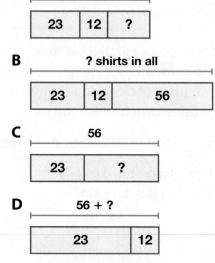

7. Which two trails combined are less than 4 miles? (2-3)

Trails	Miles
Red	2.75
Blue	3.5
Yellow	2.95
Green	1.2

8. Azim kicked a soccer ball 13.48 meters. What is 13.48 rounded to the nearest tenth? (2-2)

9. Ann has one cat that is 13.6 cm tall. She has another cat that is 6.1 cm tall. How much taller is one cat than the other? Use mental math to solve. (2-1)

10. Parker has a rabbit that is 21.9 cm long. Keenan's rabbit is 23.4 cm long. How much longer is Keenan's rabbit than Parker's? (2-7)

11. Monica bought a skirt for $14.50 and a hat for $12.25. What is a way to find how much change she would get from $40? (2-8)

12. Adam has $87.25. His friend Kyle owes him $7.69. How much money will Adam have when Kyle repays him? (2-6)

13. Estimate 84.1 + 3.65 + 41.06 by rounding to the nearest whole number. What numbers did you add? (2-3)

14. Use mental math to solve. Kerry has $16.90 in one pocket and $5.10 in another pocket. How much money does she have in all? (2-1)

15. Estimate to determine if the difference of 3.4 − 1.95 is less than or greater than one. (2-4)

16. Jared rode in a bike race and covered 7 miles on the first day. The race is 25 miles. Draw a picture and write an equation to determine how much farther he has to ride. (2-5)

17. Kerry bought a loaf of bread for $3.49, a jar of preserves for $2.29, and a jar of peanut butter for $3.89. Round to the nearest dollar to determine about how much Kerry spent. Write an equation to show your work. (2-3)

Use the table for **1** through **3**.

Craft Supplies	
Colored beads	$1.89 per bag
Yarn	$2.15 per roll
Glitter	$4.49 each
Felt	$1.12 per yard
Markers	$2.59 each
Pipe cleaners	$3.38 per bag
Set of paints	$4.89 per box
Paint brush	$1.59 each

1. The art club bought 3 bags of pipe cleaners. Round the cost of each bag of pipe cleaners to the nearest ten cents to estimate how much the club spent on pipe cleaners.

2. If the art club bought one of each item on the list, about how much did the club spend?

3. Carol bought 2 containers of glitter. Henry bought 2 markers. About how much more did Carol spend?

Use the table to solve problems **4** and **5**.

OLYMPIC GOLD MEDAL WINNERS-JAVELIN THROW			
YEAR	WINNER	NATION	MEASUREMENT
1912	Erik Lemming	Sweden	54.82 meters
1972	Klaus Wolfemann	West Germany	90.48 meters
1992	Jan Zelezny	Czechoslovakia	89.66 meters
2004	Andreas Thorkildsen	Norway	86.50 meters

4. What is the difference between the greatest measurement on the table and the least measurement on the table?

5. Find the difference between the most recent measurement and the earliest measurement.

Topic
3

Multiplying Whole Numbers

▼ This hummingbird is eating nectar from a flower. How can you make food for a hummingbird? You will find out in Lesson 3-6.

Review What You Know!

Vocabulary

Choose the best term from the box.

- equation
- factors
- product
- round

1. A(n) __?__ is another word for a number sentence.

2. One way to estimate a number is to __?__ the number.

3. A(n) __?__ is the answer to a multiplication problem.

4. In the equation $9 \times 5 = 45$, 9 and 5 are both __?__.

Multiplication Facts

Find each product.

5. 3×9 6. 5×6 7. 4×8

8. 6×9 9. 7×4 10. 9×8

Rounding

Round each number to the nearest hundred.

11. 864   12. 651   13. 348

14. 985   15. 451   16. 749

Multiplying Three Factors

© **Writing to Explain** Write an answer to the question.

17. Gina wants to multiply $9 \times 2 \times 5$. How can Gina group the factors to make it easier to multiply?

Topic Essential Question
- What are the standard procedures for estimating and multiplying whole numbers?

Interactive Learning

Pose the problem. Start each lesson by working together to solve problems. It will help you make sense of math.

Lesson 3-1

© **Generalize** Solve. Look for what's the same in each.

One classroom has 3 rows of 6 desks. Another has 6 rows of 3 desks. Do both classrooms have the same number of desks? How do you know?

Lesson 3-2

© **Reason** Solve using mental math.

Suppose 3 people can sit at a table. How many people can sit at 2 of these tables? How many people can sit at 20 of these tables? Tell how you found the answers.

Lesson 3-3

© **Reasonableness** Solve. All you need is an estimate.

A school club wants to buy shirts for each of its 38 members. Each shirt costs $23. About how much money will the shirts cost? Tell how you found your estimate.

Lesson 3-4

© **Generalize** Solve. Look for multiple ways.

Suppose 4 is multiplied by itself 5 times. How could you record this calculation? Is there more than one way? Explain.

Lesson 3-5

Ⓒ **Generalize** Use the rectangle shown on the recording sheet to solve this problem.

How can you use numerical expressions and only the numbers shown on the rectangle to find the area of the unshaded rectangle on the left? Be sure to use all three numbers. Tell how you decided.

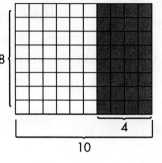

1. _____ = _____

Lesson 3-6

Ⓒ **Model** Use what you know about the meaning of multiplication to solve this problem any way you choose.

A school cafeteria orders 3 cases of milk. Each case contains 28 cartons of milk. How many cartons of milk are ordered?

Lesson 3-7

Ⓒ **Generalize** Solve any way you choose. Use what you know about multiplying with one-digit numbers.

A carpenter sells 38 chairs in one day. Each chair costs $23. How much money does the carpenter make? Show how you found the answer.

Lesson 3-8

Ⓒ **Generalize** Solve any way you choose.

A local charity collected 163 cans of food every day for 14 days. How many cans of food did the charity collect in all? Use what you know about multiplying smaller numbers to try to find the answer. Tell how you found the answer.

Lesson 3-9

Ⓒ **Model** Solve. Use the bar diagram to help.

Kevin took 248 photos on a field trip. Marco took 2 times as many. How many photos did Marco take?

248	Kevin's

		Marco's

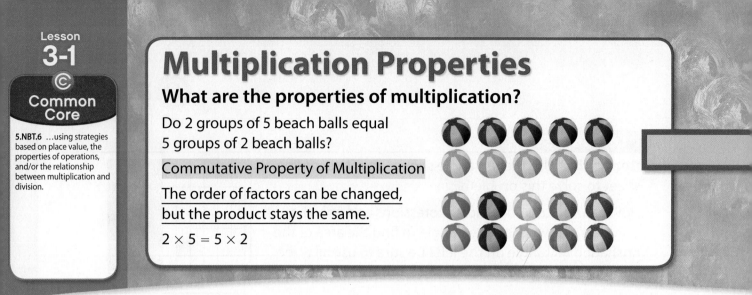

Multiplication Properties

What are the properties of multiplication?

Do 2 groups of 5 beach balls equal 5 groups of 2 beach balls?

Commutative Property of Multiplication

The order of factors can be changed, but the product stays the same.

$2 \times 5 = 5 \times 2$

5.NBT.6 …using strategies based on place value, the properties of operations, and/or the relationship between multiplication and division.

Guided Practice*

Do you know HOW?

In **1** through **5**, write the multiplication property used in each equation.

1. $65 \times 1 = 65$
2. $45 \times 6 = 6 \times 45$
3. $33 \times 0 = 0$
4. $11 \times 9 = 9 \times 11$
5. $(6 \times 20) \times 5 = 6 \times (20 \times 5)$

Do you UNDERSTAND?

6. Using equations, give an example for each property of multiplication.

7. In the following equations, what number should replace each ▧? Which property of multiplication is used?

   a $40 \times 8 = ▧ \times 40$

   b $1,037 \times ▧ = 1,037$

Independent Practice

Ⓒ **Use Structure** In **8** through **19**, write the multiplication property used in each equation.

8. $537 \times 1 = 537$
9. $24 \times 32 = 32 \times 24$
10. $400 \times 0 = 0$
11. $73 \times 14 = 14 \times 73$
12. $5 \times (40 \times 9) = (5 \times 40) \times 9$
13. $1 \times 111 = 111$
14. $0 \times 1,247 = 0$
15. $8 \times (4 \times 3) = (8 \times 4) \times 3$
16. $(9 \times 3) \times 5 = 9 \times (3 \times 5)$
17. $1 \times 90 = 90 \times 1$
18. $76 \times 1 = 76$
19. $0 \times 563 = 0$

MATHEMATICAL PRACTICES

Animated Glossary
www.pearsonsuccessnet.com

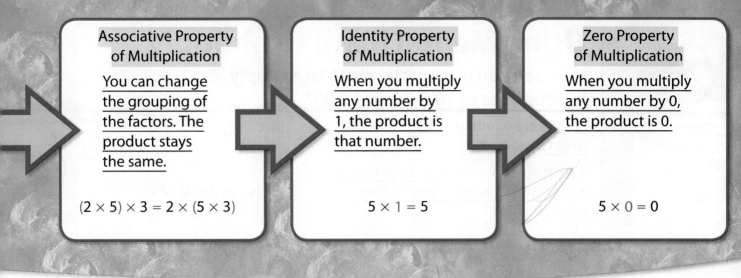

Associative Property of Multiplication	Identity Property of Multiplication	Zero Property of Multiplication
You can change the grouping of the factors. The product stays the same.	When you multiply any number by 1, the product is that number.	When you multiply any number by 0, the product is 0.
$(2 \times 5) \times 3 = 2 \times (5 \times 3)$	$5 \times 1 = 5$	$5 \times 0 = 0$

© **Reason** In **20** through **25**, use the multiplication properties to determine the number that belongs in each box.

20. $1,037 \times \boxed{} = 1,037$

21. $5 \times (20 \times 9) = (5 \times 20) \times \boxed{}$

22. $(635 \times 47) \times \boxed{} = 0$

23. $8 \times (\boxed{} \times 4) = (8 \times 5) \times 4$

24. $75 \times \boxed{} = 42 \times 75$

25. $(9 \times 6) \times 4 = 9 \times (\boxed{} \times 4)$

Problem Solving

© MATHEMATICAL PRACTICES

© **26. Communicate** Haley said that she would always know her 0 and 1 multiplication facts. Explain why Haley would say this.

© **27. Generalize** How can one of the multiplication properties help you evaluate $(77 \times 25) \times 4$?

28. Last month 48,097 people visited the zoo. The number 48,097 is how many more than 25,000?

   A 2,079   **C** 23,097

   B 12,097   **D** 320,079

© **29. Think About the Structure** Naomi ordered 2 bottles of water for $1.00 each and 1 turkey sandwich for $3.00. Which expression would you use to find how much Naomi paid?

   A $(2 \times \$1) \times \$3$

   B $2 \times (1 \times \$3)$

30. Compare. Write >, <, or = for each ◯.

   a 34,304 ◯ 43,403

   b 5.70 ◯ 5.7

   c 21,978 ◯ 21,789

   C $(2 - \$1) + \$2$

   D $(2 \times \$1) + (1 \times \$3)$

31. Three hundred fifty 10-year-olds registered for a city-wide bowling tournament. If 205 participants are boys, how many are girls?

32. Think of two numbers that will round to 14,000.

Lesson
3-2

Common
Core

5.NBT.2 Explain patterns in
the number of zeros of the
product when multiplying a
number by powers of 10...

Using Mental Math to Multiply

How can you use mental math to multiply by multiples of 10, 100, or 1,000?

Factors are numbers that are multiplied to get a product.

A multiple of a number is a product of a given whole number and another whole number.

factors   product

$3 \times 10 = 30$

30 is a multiple of 10.
30 is a multiple of 3.

Another Example How can multiplication properties help you use mental math?

Use the properties of multiplication and mental math to find $25 \times 17 \times 4$.

What You Think

25 and 4 are compatible numbers. They are easy to multiply in my head.

$25 \times 4 = 100$ and $100 \times 17 = 1,700$.

So, $25 \times 17 \times 4 = 1,700$

What You Write

Step 1 Using the Commutative Property, $25 \times (17 \times 4) = 25 \times (4 \times 17)$.

Step 2 Using the Associative Property, $25 \times (4 \times 17) = (25 \times 4) \times 17$

Guided Practice*

MATHEMATICAL
PRACTICES

Do you know HOW?

© **Look for Patterns** In **1** through **8**, use patterns and properties to compute mentally.

1. $3 \times 7 = $ ▨
   $30 \times 7 = $ ▨
   $300 \times 7 = $ ▨

2. $4 \times 8 = $ ▨
   $40 \times 8 = $ ▨
   $400 \times 8 = $ ▨

3. $20 \times 50 \times 7$

4. $50 \times 32 \times 2$

5. 600×90

6. $4 \times 33 \times 25$

7. 80×500

8. $10 \times 783 \times 10$

Do you UNDERSTAND?

© **9. Reason** Why are there two zeros in the product of 5×40?

10. When you find $50 \times 32 \times 2$, which two numbers are easy to multiply? Which multiplication property allows you to think of $50 \times 32 \times 2$ as $50 \times 2 \times 32$?

Animated Glossary
www.pearsonsuccessnet.com

*For another example, see Set B on page 84.

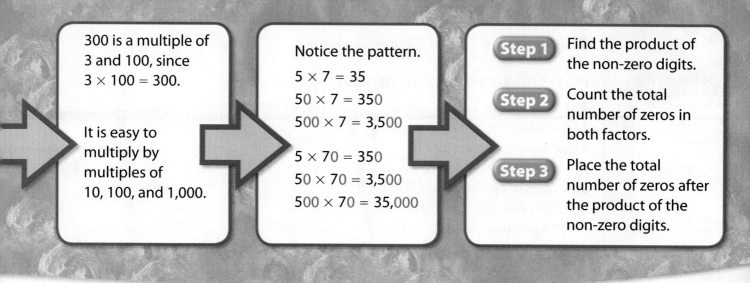

300 is a multiple of 3 and 100, since $3 \times 100 = 300$.

It is easy to multiply by multiples of 10, 100, and 1,000.

Notice the pattern.

$5 \times 7 = 35$
$50 \times 7 = 350$
$500 \times 7 = 3,500$

$5 \times 70 = 350$
$50 \times 70 = 3,500$
$500 \times 70 = 35,000$

Step 1 Find the product of the non-zero digits.

Step 2 Count the total number of zeros in both factors.

Step 3 Place the total number of zeros after the product of the non-zero digits.

Independent Practice

In **11** through **22**, use patterns and properties to compute mentally.

11. 120×30

12. $600 \times 40 \times 0$

13. $110 \times 2,000$

14. $800 \times 40 \times 3$

15. $3,000 \times 700$

16. $60 \times 90 \times 1$

17. 500×500

18. $1,000 \times 100$

19. 50×60

20. 70×80

21. 400×800

22. $1 \times 6 \times 250$

Problem Solving

MATHEMATICAL PRACTICES

23. A box of printer paper has 10 packages, with 500 sheets in each package. If a principal orders 10 boxes, how many sheets of paper does he order?

Ⓒ **24. Model** A post is put every 6 feet along a rectangular fence that is 42 ft long and 36 ft wide. How many posts are needed?

Ⓒ **25. Generalize** Write a rule that tells how to use mental math to find the product of $30,000 \times 50,000$.

26. $a \times b = 3,500$. If a and b are two-digit multiples of 10, what numbers could a and b represent?

Ⓒ **27. Use Structure** Which is a possible solution for

▨ × ▨ × ▨ = 1,500?

A $50 \times 30 \times 0$

C $5 \times 30 \times 10$

B $3 \times 5 \times 10$

D $10 \times 5 \times 10$

28. Name the solid figure shown below.

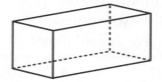

29. It takes Isaac 10 minutes to ride his bike down the hill to school and 20 minutes to ride up the hill from school. He attends school Monday through Friday. How many minutes does he spend biking to and from school in two weeks?

Lesson
3-3
ⓒ
**Common
Core**

5.NBT.5 Fluently multiply multi-digit whole numbers using the standard algorithm.

Estimating Products
How can you estimate products?

A store needs to take in at least $15,000 in sales per month to make a profit. If the store is open every day in March and takes in an average of $525 per day, will the store make a profit in March?

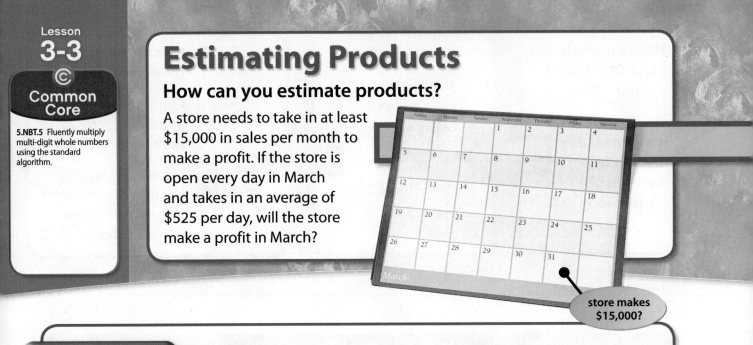

store makes $15,000?

Another Example **How can you use compatible numbers to estimate products?**

Estimate 24×39.

You can also use compatible numbers to estimate products.

It is easy to find 25×40, since 25 and 40 are compatible numbers. Remember that $25 \times 4 = 100$. So, $25 \times 40 = 1,000$, and 1,000 is a good estimate for 24×39.

Both numbers used to estimate were greater than the actual numbers. So, 1,000 is an overestimate.

Guided Practice*

ⓒ **MATHEMATICAL PRACTICES**

Do you know HOW?

In **1** and **2**, estimate by using rounding. Tell if your estimate is an overestimate or underestimate.

1. 58×6 **2.** 733×21

In **3** and **4**, estimate by using compatible numbers. Tell if your estimate is an overestimate or underestimate.

3. $43 \times 27 \times 4$ **4.** 38×69

Do you UNDERSTAND?

ⓒ **5. Construct Arguments** Susan used rounding to estimate 243×4 and found 200×4. Jeremy used compatible numbers and found 250×4. The actual product is 972. Whose method gives an estimate closer to the actual product?

ⓒ **6. Reason** In the example above, why is it better to adjust $525 to 500 rather than leave the number at 525?

DIGITAL

Animated Glossary
www.pearsonsuccessnet.com

For another example, see Set C on page 84.

You can use rounding to estimate.

$525 rounds to $500.

31 rounds to 30.

Find 30 × 500.

Think I know that 3 × 5 = 15.

30 × 500 = 15,000

Both numbers used to estimate were less than the actual numbers, so 15,000 is an underestimate. The store will actually take in more than $15,000.

So, the store will make a profit in March.

Independent Practice

In **7** through **18**, estimate each product.

7. 75 × 28

8. 3 × 118

9. 39 × 58

10. 97 × 15

11. 513 × 19

12. 64 × 55

13. 286 × 9

14. 11 × 83

15. 10 × 66

16. 26 × 29 × 41

17. 18 × 586

18. 26 × 3 × 101

Problem Solving

MATHEMATICAL PRACTICES

© **19. Reason** Estimate 53 × 375. Is the estimated product closer to 15,000 or 20,000?

© **20. Persevere** Kilauea Volcano has been active since 1983. Lava is discharged from the volcano at about 7 cubic meters per second. About how many cubic meters of lava is discharged in one minute?

© **21. Look for Patterns** Samuel needs to estimate the product of 95 × 23 × 4. Explain two different methods Samuel could use to estimate.

22. Give two factors whose estimated product is about 800.

© **23. Reasonableness** Jacque uses 11 sheets of notebook paper each day at school. If he has a package of 150 sheets, will that be enough paper for him to use for 3 weeks at school? Use an estimate to find out.

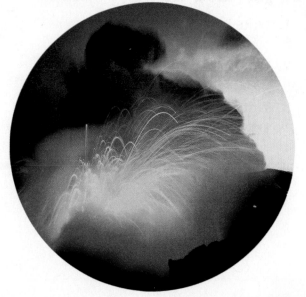

Lesson
3-4

Common
Core

5.NBT.2 Explain patterns in the number of zeros of the product when multiplying a number by powers of 10, and explain patterns in the placement of the decimal point when a decimal is multiplied or divided by a power of 10. Use whole-number exponents to denote powers of 10.

Exponents

How can you use exponents to write large numbers?

A box of cubes has 5 layers. Each layer has 5 rows, with 5 cubes in each row.

There are $5 \times 5 \times 5$ cubes in the box.

You can use exponential notation to represent repeated multiplication of the *same* number such as $5 \times 5 \times 5$.

Other Examples

Exponential notation
Write $4 \times 4 \times 4$ in exponential notation.

$4 \times 4 \times 4 = 4^3$

Expanded form
Write 10^4 in expanded form.

$10^4 = 10 \times 10 \times 10 \times 10$

Standard form
Write 2^5 in standard form.

$2^5 = 2 \times 2 \times 2 \times 2 \times 2$
$= 32$

An exponent is also called a power. You can read 4^6 as "4 to the sixth power". The second and third powers have special names. Read 3^2 as "3 to the second power," or 3 squared. Read 6^3 as "6 to the third power," or 6 cubed.

Guided Practice*

Do you know HOW?

1. Write 3^5 in expanded form.

2. Write 2^4 in standard form.

3. Write $7 \times 7 \times 7 \times 7 \times 7$ using exponential notation.

4. Write 5^4 in expanded form and standard form.

Do you UNDERSTAND?

5. In 3^5, what is the base? The exponent?

6. In the example at the top, how is 125 written in expanded form?

7. What is the standard form of 3 squared? For 6 cubed?

Animated Glossary
www.pearsonsuccessnet.com

*For another example, see Set D on page 84.

The base is the number to be multiplied.

The exponent is the number that tells how many times the base is used as a factor.

factors   exponent

$5 \times 5 \times 5 = 5^3$

base

Numbers involving exponents can be written in three different forms.

Exponential notation	5^3
Expanded form	$5 \times 5 \times 5$
Standard form	125

Independent Practice

MATHEMATICAL PRACTICES

Look for Patterns In **8** through **14**, write in exponential notation.

8. $10 \times 10 \times 10 \times 10 \times 10$ **9.** $9 \times 9 \times 9$ **10.** 81×81 **11.** $5 \times 5 \times 5 \times 5$

12. $7 \times 7 \times 7$ **13.** $13 \times 13 \times 13 \times 13 \times 13 \times 13$ **14.** $6 \times 6 \times 6 \times 6$

In **15** through **22**, write in expanded form.

15. 10^9 **16.** 35 squared   **17.** 4^3 **18.** 7^6

19. 55^4 **20.** 11^6 **21.** 8 cubed   **22.** 1^9

In **23** through **30**, write in standard form.

23. 5^4 **24.** 10^3 **25.** $4 \times 4 \times 4$ **26.** 12 squared

27. 1^{10} **28.** 2^6 **29.** 3 cubed   **30.** $10 \times 10 \times 10 \times 10 \times 10$

Problem Solving

MATHEMATICAL PRACTICES

31. Communicate Why is the standard form of 8^2 NOT equal to 16?

32. Reason Find the number that equals 81 when it is squared.

33. Darnell earned $10 each week for 10 weeks walking a neighbor's dog.

  a How much did he earn?

  b Write the amount Darnell earned using exponential notation.

34. Be Precise Which of the following, when written in standard form, is equal to the standard form of 2^6?

  A 6^2 **C** 8^2

  B 3^4 **D** 4^4

Lesson 3-5

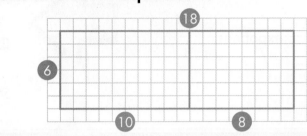

Distributive Property

How can you use the Distributive Property to write expressions and solve equations?

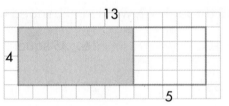

Common Core

5.NBT.5 Fluently multiply multi-digit whole numbers using the standard algorithm. Also 5.OA.1

What expressions can you write to represent the number of square units inside the rectangle?

18

6

10   8

Guided Practice*

MATHEMATICAL PRACTICES

Do you know HOW?

1. Use the Distributive Property to complete the equation.

$12 \times 308 = 12 \times (\boxed{} + 8)$

$= (12 \times \boxed{}) + (\boxed{} \times 8)$

$= \boxed{} + \boxed{}$

$= \boxed{}$

2. Show how you can use the Distributive Property to find the product of 4×105.

3. Show how you can use the Distributive Property to find the product of 20×32.

Do you UNDERSTAND?

4. Do these expressions name the same number of square units in the shaded area?

$4 \times (13 - 5)$ and $(4 \times 13) - (4 \times 5)$

13

4

5

© 5. Generalize Write the Distributive Property to state that multiplication distributes over subtraction.

© 6. Construct Arguments Is $20 - (4 \times 2) = (20 - 4) \times (20 - 2)$? Explain your answer.

Independent Practice

Use the Distributive Property to complete each equation.

7. $509 \times 11 = (500 + 9) \times 11$

$= (500 \times \boxed{}) + (9 \times \boxed{})$

$= \boxed{} + 99$

$= \boxed{}$

8. $12 \times 47 = 12 \times (50 - \boxed{})$

$= (12 \times \boxed{}) - (12 \times 3)$

$= 600 - \boxed{}$

$= \boxed{}$

Animated Glossary
www.pearsonsuccessnet.com

DIGITAL

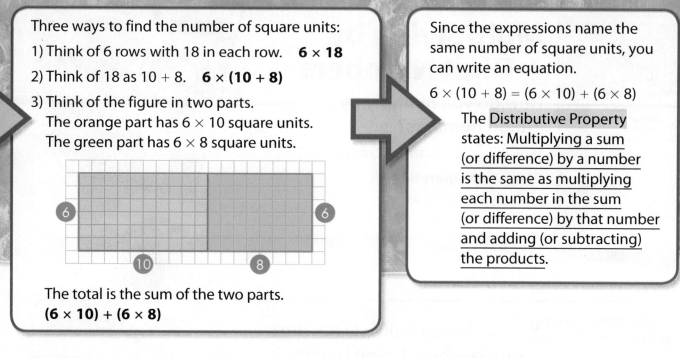

Three ways to find the number of square units:

1) Think of 6 rows with 18 in each row. **6 × 18**

2) Think of 18 as 10 + 8. **6 × (10 + 8)**

3) Think of the figure in two parts.
The orange part has 6 × 10 square units.
The green part has 6 × 8 square units.

The total is the sum of the two parts.
(6 × 10) + (6 × 8)

Since the expressions name the same number of square units, you can write an equation.

6 × (10 + 8) = (6 × 10) + (6 × 8)

The Distributive Property states: Multiplying a sum (or difference) by a number is the same as multiplying each number in the sum (or difference) by that number and adding (or subtracting) the products.

For **9** through **16**, rewrite each expression using the Distributive Property. Then find each product.

9. 7 × 86

10. 7 × 420

11. 220 × 8

12. 45 × 60

13. 80 × 64

14. 16 × 102

15. 101 × 23

16. 390 × 40

Problem Solving

© MATHEMATICAL PRACTICES

© **Look for Patterns** For **17** through **19**, use the table at the right and the following information.

Wendy brought the lemonade and iced tea for the school picnic. Since more people like lemonade than iced tea, she brought 2 gallons of lemonade for every 10 people. She also brought 5 gallons of iced tea for people who don't like lemonade.

Number of People	Gallons of Lemonade	Total Gallons
10	2	
20		
30		
40		

17. Write an algebraic expression to show the total number of gallons Wendy would need to bring. Let n represent the number of groups of ten people.

18. How many gallons does Wendy need for 10 people?

19. Complete the rest of the table.

20. Use the Distributive Property to find another expression for $3(2x + 7)$.

　A $6x + 7$

　B $3(14x)$

　C $(9x) × 3$

　D $6x + 21$

© **21. Reasonableness** The highest point in Colorado is Mount Elbert, at 14,433 feet. About how many miles is that?

Tip *1 mile = 5,280 feet*

ⓒ
Common Core

5.NBT.5 Fluently multiply multi-digit whole numbers using the standard algorithm.

Multiplying by 1-Digit Numbers

How do you multiply by 1-digit numbers?

How many beads are in 7 containers?

Choose an Operation
Multiply to join equal groups.

36 Beads

Another Example How do you multiply a 1-digit number by a 3-digit number?

A theater has 5 sections with 347 seats in each section. What is the total number of seats in the theater?

A 1,505 seats   **C** 1,705 seats

B 1,535 seats   **D** 1,735 seats

? seats in theater

| 347 | 347 | 347 | 347 | 347 |

↑
└ seats in each section

Choose an Operation Multiply to join equal groups.

Step 1

Multiply the ones, and regroup if necessary.

$$\begin{array}{r} \overset{3}{34}7 \\ \times \quad 5 \\ \hline 5 \end{array}$$

5 × 7 ones = 35 ones
Regroup 35 ones as 3 tens 5 ones.

Step 2

Multiply the tens. Add any extra tens. Regroup if necessary.

$$\begin{array}{r} \overset{2\,3}{34}7 \\ \times \quad 5 \\ \hline 35 \end{array}$$

5 × 4 tens = 20 tens
20 tens + 3 tens = 23 tens
Regroup as 2 hundreds 3 tens.

Step 3

Multiply the hundreds. Add any extra hundreds. Regroup if necessary.

$$\begin{array}{r} \overset{2\,3}{34}7 \\ \times \quad 5 \\ \hline 1,735 \end{array}$$

5 × 3 hundreds = 15 hundreds
15 hundreds + 2 hundreds = 17 hundreds
Regroup as 1 thousand 7 hundreds.

The theater has 1,735 seats, so the correct choice is **D**.

Explain It

1. In Step 1, how do you know that 35 ones is 3 tens and 5 ones?

2. In Step 3, why are 2 hundreds added to the 15 hundreds?

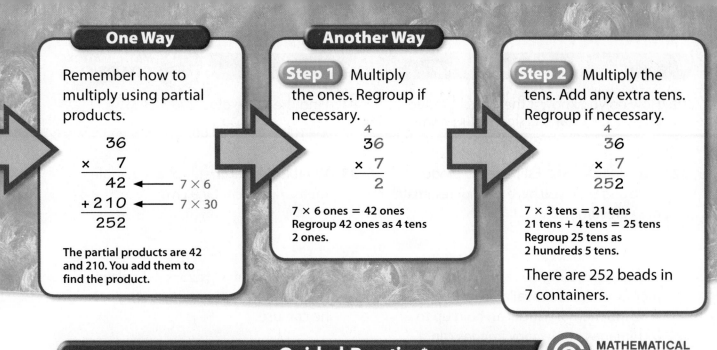

One Way

Remember how to multiply using partial products.

$$\begin{array}{r} 36 \\ \times 7 \\ \hline 42 \\ +210 \\ \hline 252 \end{array}$$

42 ← 7 × 6
+210 ← 7 × 30

The partial products are 42 and 210. You add them to find the product.

Another Way

Step 1 Multiply the ones. Regroup if necessary.

$$\begin{array}{r} \overset{4}{3}6 \\ \times 7 \\ \hline 2 \end{array}$$

7 × 6 ones = 42 ones
Regroup 42 ones as 4 tens
2 ones.

Step 2 Multiply the tens. Add any extra tens. Regroup if necessary.

$$\begin{array}{r} \overset{4}{3}6 \\ \times 7 \\ \hline 252 \end{array}$$

7 × 3 tens = 21 tens
21 tens + 4 tens = 25 tens
Regroup 25 tens as
2 hundreds 5 tens.

There are 252 beads in 7 containers.

Guided Practice*

MATHEMATICAL PRACTICES

Do you know HOW?

In **1** and **2**, find each product. Estimate to check that your answer is reasonable.

1.
$$\begin{array}{r} 63 \\ \times 8 \\ \hline \end{array}$$

2.
$$\begin{array}{r} 274 \\ \times 3 \\ \hline \end{array}$$

Do you UNDERSTAND?

3. Use Structure In Step 2 of Another Example, why is it necessary to regroup the 23 tens?

4. In the example above, how many beads would be in 9 containers?

Independent Practice

MATHEMATICAL PRACTICES

Look for Patterns In **5** through **29**, find each product. Estimate to check that your answer is reasonable.

5.
$$\begin{array}{r} 111 \\ \times 7 \\ \hline \end{array}$$

6.
$$\begin{array}{r} 873 \\ \times 6 \\ \hline \end{array}$$

7.
$$\begin{array}{r} 795 \\ \times 5 \\ \hline \end{array}$$

8.
$$\begin{array}{r} 227 \\ \times 3 \\ \hline \end{array}$$

9.
$$\begin{array}{r} 459 \\ \times 4 \\ \hline \end{array}$$

10.
$$\begin{array}{r} 25 \\ \times 9 \\ \hline \end{array}$$

11.
$$\begin{array}{r} 633 \\ \times 9 \\ \hline \end{array}$$

12.
$$\begin{array}{r} 41 \\ \times 8 \\ \hline \end{array}$$

13.
$$\begin{array}{r} 552 \\ \times 6 \\ \hline \end{array}$$

14.
$$\begin{array}{r} 69 \\ \times 7 \\ \hline \end{array}$$

15. 62×7

16. 124×2

17. 921×8

18. 55×4

19. 438×3

20. 29×6

21. 73×9

22. 264×4

23. 18×5

24. 38×8

25. 705×9

26. 351×2

27. 826×3

28. 79×8

29. 26×6

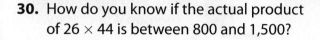
30. How do you know if the actual product of 26 × 44 is between 800 and 1,500?

31. Find the value of *x*.

$$x + 100 = 100{,}000{,}000$$

32. Reasonableness Estimate the product of 76 and 8. Do you have an underestimate or overestimate?

33. What is the perimeter of a rectangle measuring 5 cm by 9 cm?

34. A memory stick can be used to store images from a digital camera. The first memory stick was available in 1998. A 32 MB memory stick can hold up to 491 images. How many images can 7 memory sticks hold?

35. Use Structure Paul needs to estimate the product of 87 × 23 × 4. Explain two different estimation strategies he can use.

36. Use partial products to find 89 × 6.

37. When multiplying 37 × 4, how would you regroup the 14 tens?

38. Estimation A popular restaurant has 48 tables. On each table are 3 different types of salsa. In one day, all of the tables are used for 9 different sets of customers. Which expression can be used to estimate how many containers of salsa are needed for all the tables in one day?

  A 50 × 9   **C** 50 × 3 × 10

  B 16 × 3 × 9   **D** 40 × 5 × 5

39. A group of 24 students and 2 teachers went to a school fair. Each student and teacher spent $8 on tickets and $3 on snacks. What information is NOT needed to find out how much the 24 students and 2 teachers spent on tickets?

  A The number of teachers

  B The amount spent on snacks

  C The amount spent on tickets

  D The number of students

40. Be Precise A man set a world record by holding nine eggs in one hand. Each egg weighed about 57 grams. What was the total weight of all of the eggs?

  A 513 grams

  B 456 grams

  C 540 grams

  D 570 grams

41. Model One type of food that hummingbirds like to eat is a simple syrup made from sugar and water. To make simple syrup you need 1 part sugar and 4 parts water. If you have 12 cups of sugar, how many cups of water do you need?

? cups of water

| 4 | 4 | 4 | 4 | 4 | 4 | 4 | 4 | 4 | 4 | 4 | 4 |

↑ parts water for 1 part sugar

Algebra Connections

Simplifying Numerical Expressions

In order to simplify numerical expressions, you must follow the order of operations.

- Complete the operations inside the parentheses.

- Multiply and/or divide in order from left to right.

- Add and/or subtract in order from left to right.

Example:

Simplify $50 - (9 \times 3)$.

Start with the operation inside the parentheses. What is 9×3?

$9 \times 3 = 27$

Then subtract.

$50 - 27 = 23$

So, $50 - (9 \times 3) = 23$.

Simplify. Follow the order of operations.

1. $4 + 2 \times 9$

2. $16 + 8 \div 2$

3. $25 + (3 \times 6) - 5$

4. $8 \times 6 + 9$

5. $10 + 27 \div 3$

6. $(6 + 3) \times 5$

7. $(5 \times 2) + (10 \div 2)$

8. $5 \times 7 \times (6 - 3)$

9. $(12 - 3) \times (3 + 4)$

10. $35 + 5 \div 5 - 2$

11. $20 \times 2 + 3 \times (8 + 2)$

12. $(10 + 7) \times 3 - 4 \times (2 + 5)$

13. $3 \times 3 \div 3 + 6 - 3$

14. $(5 + 63) - 4 \times (12 \div 4)$

Insert parentheses to make each statement true.

15. $11 - 6 - 1 = 6$

16. $10 + 2 \times 4 + 1 = 60$

17. $30 - 4 \times 2 + 5 = 2$

18. $64 \div 2 \times 4 \div 2 = 4$

© **19. Be Precise** Write a real-world problem that you could solve by simplifying the expression $50 - (2 \times 9)$.

Lesson
3-7

©
Common Core

5NBT.5 Fluently multiply multi-digit whole numbers using the standard algorithm.

Multiplying 2-Digit by 2-Digit Numbers

How do you multiply by 2-digit numbers?

Sammy's Car Wash had 38 full-service car washes in one day. How much money did Sammy's Car Wash make in one day from full-service car washes?

Choose an Operation
Multiply to join equal groups.

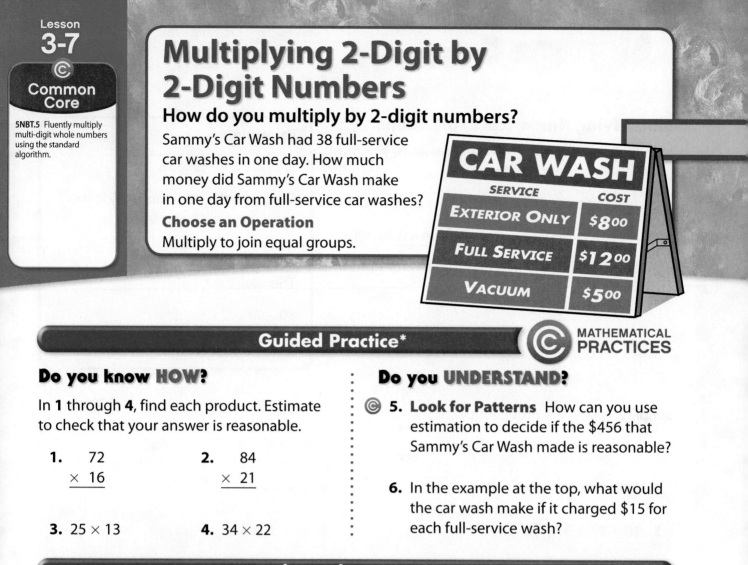

CAR WASH

SERVICE	COST
EXTERIOR ONLY	$8.00
FULL SERVICE	$12.00
VACUUM	$5.00

Guided Practice*

© MATHEMATICAL PRACTICES

Do you know HOW?

In **1** through **4**, find each product. Estimate to check that your answer is reasonable.

1.	72	**2.**	84
	× 16		× 21

3. 25 × 13

4. 34 × 22

Do you UNDERSTAND?

© **5. Look for Patterns** How can you use estimation to decide if the $456 that Sammy's Car Wash made is reasonable?

6. In the example at the top, what would the car wash make if it charged $15 for each full-service wash?

Independent Practice

Leveled Practice In **7** through **23**, find each product. Estimate to check that your answer is reasonable.

7.
```
    44
×   23
  ▢▢2
  8 0
▢▢▢1
```

8.
```
    89
×   11
  8▢▢
 ▢▢0
 9▢▢
```

9.
```
    67
×   57
  ▢69
 ▢350
 3▢1
```

10.
```
    98
×   45
  ▢9▢
 3 20
 4▢0
```

11.
```
    17
×   12
  3▢
 1▢0
 ▢▢4
```

12.
```
    35
×   71
   ▢5
  2 5
  2▢8
```

13.
```
    26
×   18
```

14.
```
    35
×   29
```

15.
```
    72
×   51
```

16.
```
    19
×   15
```

17.
```
    83
×   47
```

18.
```
    45
×   16
```

19. 52 × 36

20. 77 × 18

21. 24 × 21

22. 64 × 32

23. 96 × 33

DIGITAL   Animated Glossary
www.pearsonsuccessnet.com

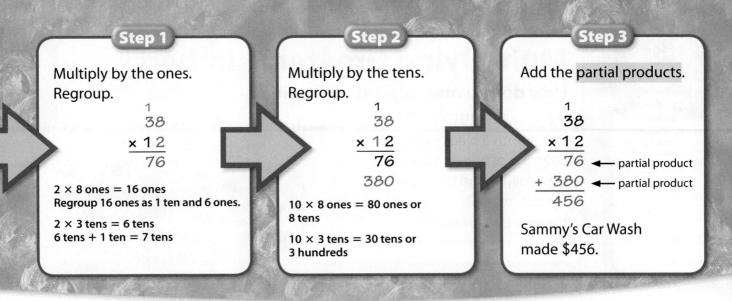

Step 1

Multiply by the ones.
Regroup.

$$\begin{array}{r} 1 \\ 38 \\ \times\ 12 \\ \hline 76 \end{array}$$

2 × 8 ones = 16 ones
Regroup 16 ones as 1 ten and 6 ones.

2 × 3 tens = 6 tens
6 tens + 1 ten = 7 tens

Step 2

Multiply by the tens.
Regroup.

$$\begin{array}{r} 1 \\ 38 \\ \times\ 12 \\ \hline 76 \\ 380 \end{array}$$

10 × 8 ones = 80 ones or
8 tens

10 × 3 tens = 30 tens or
3 hundreds

Step 3

Add the partial products.

$$\begin{array}{r} 1 \\ 38 \\ \times\ 12 \\ \hline 76 \\ +\ 380 \\ \hline 456 \end{array}$$

76 ← partial product
380 ← partial product

Sammy's Car Wash
made $456.

Problem Solving

MATHEMATICAL PRACTICES

24. The 2001 record for balancing drinking glasses was 75 glasses. If the capacity of each glass was 20 fluid ounces, how many total fluid ounces could all of the glasses contain?

25. The principal of a school is buying 3 computers at $900 each. She can pay $98 per month instead of paying for them at once. Will she have paid for the computers by the end of 12 months?

C 26. Critique Reasoning How can finding the product of 5 × 700 help you check the product of 5 × 789?

27. The label on a jigsaw puzzle states that it has more than 1,000 pieces. After Bonnie put the puzzle together, she counted 44 pieces across the top and 28 pieces down the side. Estimate to determine if the label was correct.

C 28. Persevere There are 21 classrooms at Pine School. There are between 27 and 33 students per room. Which is the best estimate of the total number of students in the school?

A 300 **B** 400 **C** 500 **D** 600

For **29** and **30**, use the table at the right.

29. The Explorer Hiking Club has 64 members. How much will it cost for all members to buy new Terrain backpacks?

30. The club also needs to buy 16 dome tents and 16 propane stoves. Will they spend more or less on these items than on the backpacks? How much more or less?

Camping Gear Prices	
Gear	**Price**
Dome Tent	$99
Propane Stove	$28
Terrain Backpack	$87

Lesson 3-8

Common Core

5.NBT.5 Fluently multiply multi-digit whole numbers using the standard algorithm.

Multiplying Greater Numbers

How do you multiply 3-digit numbers by 2-digit numbers?

Last month a bakery sold 389 trays of bagels. How many bagels did the store sell last month?

Choose an Operation
Multiply to join equal groups.

12 bagels per tray

Guided Practice*

MATHEMATICAL PRACTICES

Do you know HOW?

In **1** through **4**, find each product. Estimate to check that your answer is reasonable.

1. 236
     × 46

2. 425
     × 61

3. 827 × 23

4. 745 × 13

Do you UNDERSTAND?

5. In Step 2 of the example at the top, do you multiply 1×9 or 10×9?

6. Reasonableness Is 300×10 a good estimate for the number of bagels sold at the bakery?

Independent Practice

In **7** through **31**, find each product. Estimate to check that your answer is reasonable.

7. 451
     × 10

8. 892
     × 18

9. 655
     × 98

10. 132
      × 47

11. 381
      × 27

12. 901
      × 62

13. 185
      × 55

14. 227
      × 87

15. 946
      × 33

16. 735
      × 41

17. 25×100

18. 529×47

19. 19×763

20. 498×42

21. 106×72

22. 289×26

23. 390×59

24. 35×515

25. 81×11

26. 785×58

27. 25×314

28. 602×14

29. 40×719

30. 500×62

31. 199×99

For another example, see Set F on page 85.

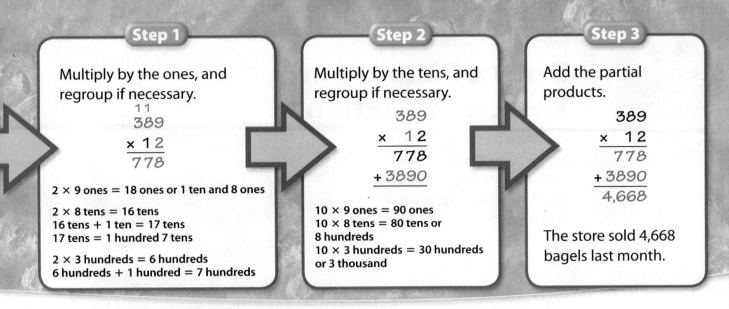

Step 1

Multiply by the ones, and regroup if necessary.

$$\begin{array}{r} {\scriptstyle 1\,1} \\ 389 \\ \times\ 12 \\ \hline 778 \end{array}$$

2 × 9 ones = 18 ones or 1 ten and 8 ones

2 × 8 tens = 16 tens
16 tens + 1 ten = 17 tens
17 tens = 1 hundred 7 tens

2 × 3 hundreds = 6 hundreds
6 hundreds + 1 hundred = 7 hundreds

Step 2

Multiply by the tens, and regroup if necessary.

$$\begin{array}{r} 389 \\ \times\ 12 \\ \hline 778 \\ +\ 3890 \end{array}$$

10 × 9 ones = 90 ones
10 × 8 tens = 80 tens or 8 hundreds
10 × 3 hundreds = 30 hundreds or 3 thousand

Step 3

Add the partial products.

$$\begin{array}{r} 389 \\ \times\ 12 \\ \hline 778 \\ +\ 3890 \\ \hline 4,668 \end{array}$$

The store sold 4,668 bagels last month.

Problem Solving

Ⓒ MATHEMATICAL PRACTICES

Ⓒ Use Tools For **32** through **34**, use the data chart.

32. How many times does a dog's heart beat in 15 minutes?

33. In 20 minutes, how many more times does a gerbil's heart beat than a rabbit's?

Data	Animal	Heart Rate (beats per minute)
	Dog	100
	Gerbil	360
	Rabbit	212

Ⓒ 34. Think About the Structure Which expression shows how to find the total number of heartbeats in 1 hour for a dog and a rabbit?

A $(100 \times 1) + (212 \times 1)$

B $60 \times 100 \times 212$

C $(60 \times 100) + (60 \times 212)$

D $(212 \times 100) + 60$

35. The length of the Nile River in Africa is about 14 times the length of Lake Michigan. About how many miles long is the Nile River?

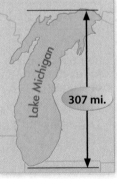

Lake Michigan

307 mi.

36. The fifth-grade class at Monticello Middle School sold more bags of popcorn than any other class. They ordered 17 cases of popcorn. Each case had 242 bags. How many bags of popcorn did the class sell?

37. A nursery sells plants in flats. There are 6 plants in each tray. Each flat has 6 trays. The nursery sold 18 flats on Saturday and 21 flats on Sunday. How many plants did the nursery sell in all?

Ⓒ 38. Reasonableness Is 3,198 a reasonable product for 727×44? Why or why not?

39. A theater in Darling Harbour, Australia, can seat 540 people at one time. How many tickets can be sold if the theater sells out every seat for one 30-day month?

Common
Core

5.NBT.5 Fluently multiply
multi-digit whole numbers
using the standard
algorithm. Also **5.OA.2**

Problem Solving

Draw a Picture and Write an Equation

In 1990, a painting was bought
for $575. In 2006 the same
painting sold for 5 times as
much. What was the price of
the painting in 2006?

Another Example

Each artist at a large art show is assigned to a team of 5 judges.
There are 9 teams of judges at the show. If each team reviews
the work of 27 artists, how many artists attend the show?

Think There are 9 teams of judges. Each team reviews 27 artists.
The total number of artists at the show is unknown.

Draw a Picture

a number of artists

27	27	27	27	27	27	27	27	27

↑
number of artists
for each team
of judges

Write an Equation

Let *a* = the number
of artists at the show.

$9 \times 27 = a$
$a = 243$

$$\begin{array}{r} \overset{6}{2\,7} \\ \times\ \ \ 9 \\ \hline 2\,4\,3 \end{array}$$

There are 243 artists at the show.

Explain It

1. Which of the 2 diagrams shown in the 2 examples models
   "times as many"?

2. What does the variable *a* represent in the example?

3. How can you check if 243 is a reasonable product?

4. Jupiter is roughly 5 times the distance Earth is from the Sun.
   Earth is about 93,000,000 miles from the sun. About how far
   is Jupiter from the Sun?

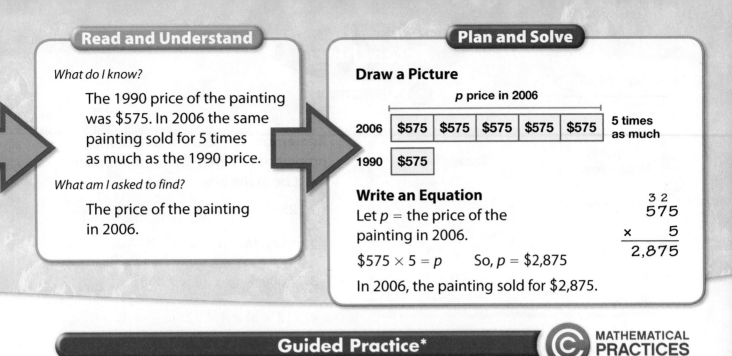

What do I know?

The 1990 price of the painting was $575. In 2006 the same painting sold for 5 times as much as the 1990 price.

What am I asked to find?

The price of the painting in 2006.

Draw a Picture

p price in 2006

2006	$575	$575	$575	$575	$575	5 times as much

1990	$575

Write an Equation

Let p = the price of the painting in 2006.

$575 \times 5 = p$ So, $p = \$2,875$

$$\begin{array}{r} \overset{3\ 2}{575} \\ \times \quad 5 \\ \hline 2{,}875 \end{array}$$

In 2006, the painting sold for $2,875.

Guided Practice*

MATHEMATICAL PRACTICES

Do you know HOW?

Copy and complete the picture and write an equation. Solve.

1. Sharon's Stationery Store has 219 boxes of cards. May's Market has 3 times as many boxes of cards. How many boxes of cards does May's Market have?

   b boxes of cards

Do you UNDERSTAND?

2. What phrase from the top example gives you a clue that you will use multiplication in your drawing to solve the problem?

3. **Construct Arguments** Write a real-world problem that uses multiplication and can be solved by drawing a picture and writing an equation.

Independent Practice

MATHEMATICAL PRACTICES

For **4** and **5**, draw a picture and write an equation. Solve.

4. **Use Tools** Brad lives 10 times as far away from Dallas as Jennie. If Jennie lives 44 miles from Dallas, how many miles from Dallas does Brad live?

5. **Reasonableness** Gamal helped his dad clean the garage and attic over the weekend. They took eight 15-minute breaks. How many minutes did they spend on breaks?

Applying Math Practices

- What am I asked to find?
- What else can I try?
- How are quantities related?
- How can I explain my work?
- How can I use math to model the problem?
- Can I use tools to help?
- Is my work precise?
- Why does this work?
- How can I generalize?

For another example, see Set G on page 85.

Reteaching

Set A, pages 64–65

Property of Multiplication	Example
Commutative	$4 \times 8 = 8 \times 4$ $32 = 32$
Associative	$(4 \times 5) \times 6 = 4 \times (5 \times 6)$ $120 = 120$
Zero	$12 \times 0 = 0$
Identity	$9 \times 1 = 9$

Remember to use the multiplication properties to determine what number must be in the box.

1. $256 \times \boxed{} = 256$

2. $157{,}678 \times 0 = \boxed{}$

3. $7{,}000 \times \boxed{} = 20 \times 7{,}000$

4. $(12 \times 3) \times 4 = 12 \times (\boxed{} \times 4)$

Set B, pages 66–67

Find $3{,}000 \times 500$.

Step 1 Find the product of the non-zero digits. $3 \times 5 = 15$

Step 2 Count the total number of zeros in both factors. 5 zeros

Step 3 Place the total number of zeros after the product of the non zero digits. 1,500,000

Remember to count the total number of zeros in both factors.

Find each product.

1. 12×30 **2.** 600×40

3. $10 \times 9{,}000$ **4.** $5{,}000 \times 80$

5. $9 \times 10 \times 800$

Set C, pages 68–69

Estimate 37×88.

Step 1 Round both factors. 37 is about 40 and 88 is about 90.

Step 2 Use mental math and multiply the rounded factors. $40 \times 90 = 3{,}600$

Remember to either round the factors or use compatible numbers.

Estimate each product.

1. 7×396 **2.** 17×63

3. 91×51 **4.** 70×523

Set D, pages 70–71

Write 7^3 in expanded form and standard form.

Tip The base is 7.
The exponent is 3.

Expanded form: $7 \times 7 \times 7$
Standard form: 343

Remember that the exponent tells how many times the base is used as a factor.

Write each in expanded form and standard form.

1. 17^2 **2.** 10^5 **3.** 2^6 **4.** 5^4

The Distributive Property states that multiplying a sum by a number is the same as multiplying each number in the sum by the number, and then adding the products.

Use the Distributive Property to find 5 × 23.

Think of 23 as 20 + 3.

$$5 \times 23 = 5 \times (20 + 3)$$
$$= (5 \times 20) + (5 \times 3)$$
$$= 100 + 15 = 115$$

Remember that you write one of the numbers as a sum, multiply each of those numbers by the other number, and then add the products.

Use the Distributive Property to find each product.

1. 7 × 45   **2.** 29 × 9

3. 72 × 6   **4.** 3 × 46

A store received a shipment of 38 TV's valued at $425 each. What is the total value of the shipment?
$p = 425 \times 38$

Step 1

Multiply the ones.

```
 2 4
 425
×  38
3400
```

Step 2

Multiply the tens.

```
    1
  425
×  38
 3400
12750
```

Step 3

Add the partial products.

```
   425
×   38
  3400
+12750
16,150
```

Remember to regroup if necessary. Estimate to check that your answer is reasonable.

Find each product.

1. 54 × 9   **2.** 92 × 6

3. 189 × 3   **4.** 708 × 5

5. 67 × 48   **6.** 81 × 19

7. 51 × 605   **8.** 32 × 871

Draw a picture and write an equation. Solve.

The length of James's pool is 16 ft. The length of the pool at Wing Park is 4 times as long. How long is the pool at Wing Park?

Let ℓ = the length of Wing Park pool.

$16 \times 4 = \ell$
$\ell = 64$ ft

The length of Wing Park pool is 64 ft.

ℓ length of Wing Park Pool
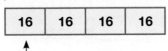

| 16 | 16 | 16 | 16 |

length of James's pool in feet

Remember that a picture can help you visualize an equation.

Solve.

1. Mia has a collection of 34 dolls. A toy store's warehouse has 15 times as many dolls. How many dolls are in the warehouse?

2. Lea has given 23 surveys at school. She needs to give twice this amount before the end of the week. How many more surveys does Lea need to give?

Multiple Choice

1. Dr. Peterson works about 11 hours each day. Which of the following can be used to find the best estimate of the number of hours he works in 48 days? (3-3)

   A 10 × 40

   B 9 × 50

   C 10 × 50

   D 15 × 45

2. A banana contains 105 calories. Last week, Brendan and Lea ate a total of 14 bananas. How many calories does this represent? (3-8)

   A 525

   B 1,450

   C 1,470

   D 4,305

3. Four bags with 7 apples in each bag is the same amount as 7 bags with 4 apples in each bag. Which property of multiplication does this represent? (3-1)

   A Associative

   B Commutative

   C Identity

   D Zero

4. Which of the following is equal to 4^5? (3-4)

   A 4 × 5

   B 5 × 5 × 5 × 5

   C 4 × 4 × 4 × 4

   D 4 × 4 × 4 × 4 × 4

5. The latest mystery novel costs $24. The table shows the sales of this novel by a bookstore. What is the total amount of sales on Saturday? (3-8)

Day	Books Sold
Thursday	98
Friday	103
Saturday	157
Sunday	116

   A $3,768

   B $3,748

   C $2,784

   D $942

6. Mr. Leim spends $24 on parking each week. He works 48 weeks a year. How much does he spend on parking in a year? (3-7)

   A $1,152

   B $1,122

   C $1,022

   D $288

7. Jasmin's parents allow her to use the family computer 90 minutes each day. How many minutes is she allowed to use the computer during a month that is 30 days in length? (3-2)

8. The average rainfall at Mt. Waialeale in Hawaii is 460 inches per year. How much rain would this location expect to receive in 5 years? (3-6)

9. Tyrone scored 24 touchdowns this year. Each touchdown scored was 6 points. How many points did Tyrone score this year? (3-6)

10. Use compatible numbers to estimate $4 \times 26 \times 7$. (3-3)

11. Kai has 35 baseball cards. Sharon has 6 times as many cards as Kai. Complete the picture, write an equation, and determine the number of baseball cards Sharon has. (3-9)

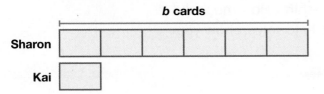

12. Myra needs to order food for the school picnic. Use the price list to determine the cost of 16 packages of hot dogs, 16 packages of buns, and 1 bottle of ketchup. (3-7)

Item	Price
Package of hot dogs	$5.00
Package of buns	$2.00
Bottle of ketchup	$1.00

13. Use the distributive property to complete each line of the equation. (3-5)

$$46 \times 12 = 46 \times (10 + \underline{\quad})$$

$$= (\underline{\quad} \times 10) + (\underline{\quad} \times 2)$$

$$= \underline{\quad} + 92$$

$$= \underline{\quad}$$

14. Four buses are available for a field trip. Each bus can hold 48 people. Write an equation to find the number of people that can ride the buses. (3-9)

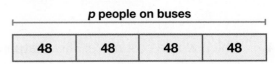

15. What number makes the number sentence true? (3-1)

$$(4 \times 8) \times 7 = 4 \times (8 \times \underline{\quad})$$

16. Sasha bikes 25 miles every day for two weeks. How many miles does she bike during this time? (3-7)

17. Write fifteen cubed in exponential notation, expanded form, and standard form. (3-4)

Coach Vandersea wants to buy items for the baseball team. The team already has hats with the team logo on them, but the coach would like them to have a T-shirt, sweatshirt, sweatpants, and a jacket with the team logo.

Use the table to solve the problems.

Jackie's Sports and Team Store	
Item	Item Price
jacket	$53
sweatshirt	$32
T-shirt	$14
sweatpants	$24

1. There are 16 players on the baseball team. How much would it cost to order each player a jacket?

2. Coach Vandersea ordered 23 sweatshirts. What was the total cost of his order?

3. The players asked their families and friends if they wanted T-shirts with the team logo. If 68 people wanted T-shirts, what would be the total cost?

4. Which would cost more: 38 sweatpants or 29 sweatshirts? How much more?

5. Molly ordered 12 T-shirts. Teena ordered 23 T-shirts. How much did they spend in all? Use the distributive property to solve. Show your work.

6. Which costs more, 14 sweatshirts or 32 T-shirts? What property can be used to find the answer?

Topic 4

Dividing by 1-Digit Divisors

▼ Scientists have been tagging turtles at Turtle Island for years in order to study their behavior. How many turtles have the scientists tagged? You will find out in Lesson 4-5.

Vocabulary

Choose the best term from the box.

- compatible numbers
- multiple
- inverse
- quotient

1. The number 800 is a(n) __?__ of 100.

2. One way to estimate is to use __?__.

3. In the equation 12 ÷ 4 = 3, the number 3 is the __?__.

4. Multiplication and division have a(n) __?__ relationship.

Place Value

Copy and complete with the word tens, hundreds, or thousands.

5. 6,200 is the same as 6 __?__ and 2 __?__.

6. 150 is the same as 15 __?__.

7. 2,300 is the same as 23 __?__.

8. 750 is the same as 75 __?__.

Rounding

Round each number to the place value of the underlined digit.

9. 4̲56   10. 3̲8   11. 1̲,600

12. 9̲20   13. 6̲1   14. 3̲,205

© **Writing to Explain** Write an answer to the question.

15. Explain how to round 768 to the hundreds place.

Topic Essential Question
- What is the standard procedure for division and why does it work?

Interactive Learning

Hands-On Minds-On

Pose the problem. Start each lesson by working together to solve problems. It will help you make sense of math.

Applying Math Practices

- What am I asked to find?
- What else can I try?
- How are quantities related?
- How can I explain my work?
- How can I use math to model the problem?
- Can I use tools to help?
- Is my work precise?
- Why does this work?
- How can I generalize?

Lesson 4-1

Generalize Solve using any method you choose. Look for basic facts to help.

Suppose 24,000 people in all attended a county fair. The fair lasted 3 days, and the same number of people went each day. How many people went to the fair each day?

• The Sun Times •

RECORD SET- 24,000 attend fair!

Lesson 4-2

Reasonableness Solve. You only need an estimate.

Suppose you have 134 stamps in your collection. You want to display them on 5 pages of an album with about the same number of stamps on each page. About how many stamps should go on each page?

Lesson 4-3

Reasonableness Solve any way you choose. Check that your answers are reasonable.

How many 6 oz glasses can you fill with 32 oz of orange juice? How many bags are needed for 32 apples if each bag holds 6 apples?

Lesson 4-4

© **Reason** Solve. Share money to find the answer.

How can 4 people share $108 equally?

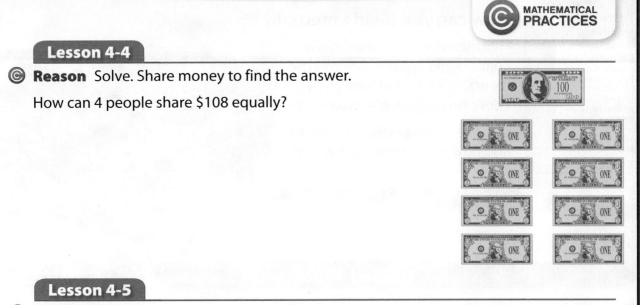

Lesson 4-5

© **Generalize** Solve any way you choose, but use numbers only.

A fifth-grade class collected $108 to share equally among 4 charities. How much will they donate to each charity?

Lesson 4-6

© **Generalize** Solve any way you choose. Be prepared to explain how you found the answer.

The cycling team raises money to buy a bike that costs $312. The team collects the same amount of money each week for 3 weeks to pay for the bike. How much money does the team collect each week?

Lesson 4-7

© **Model** Solve. Use the problem-solving recording sheet.

There are 119 campers. Eight campers are assigned to a group for hiking. How many hiking groups are needed for all the campers?

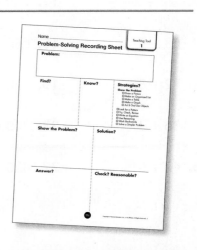

Common Core

5.NBT.6 Find whole-number quotients of whole numbers with up to four-digit dividends and two-digit divisors, using strategies based on place value, the properties of operations, and/or the relationship between multiplication and division. Illustrate and explain the calculation by using equations, rectangular arrays, and/or area models.

Dividing Multiples of 10 and 100

How can you divide mentally?

Five friends want to share these comic books equally. Can you use mental math to find how many comic books each friend will get?

Choose an Operation Divide to find how many are in each group.

1,000 comic books

Guided Practice*

MATHEMATICAL PRACTICES

Do you know HOW?

In **1** through **6**, use mental math to find each quotient.

1. 540 ÷ 9   **2.** 490 ÷ 7

3. 28,000 ÷ 4   **4.** 48,000 ÷ 6

5. 360 ÷ 6   **6.** 81,000 ÷ 9

Do you UNDERSTAND?

7. Reason How can you use the division fact 54 ÷ 9 to find 5,400 ÷ 9?

8. In the example at the top, how many comic books would each friend get if there were 300 comic books?

9. How could you use multiplication to check your answer of 200 comic books per person?

Independent Practice

In **10** through **29**, use mental math to find each quotient.

10. 22 ÷ 2   **11.** 220 ÷ 2   **12.** 2,200 ÷ 2   **13.** 22,000 ÷ 2

14. 63 ÷ 9   **15.** 630 ÷ 9   **16.** 6,300 ÷ 9   **17.** 63,000 ÷ 9

18. 72 ÷ 8   **19.** 720 ÷ 8   **20.** 7,200 ÷ 8   **21.** 72,000 ÷ 8

22. 36 ÷ 3   **23.** 360 ÷ 3   **24.** 3,600 ÷ 3   **25.** 36,000 ÷ 3

26. 42 ÷ 6   **27.** 420 ÷ 6   **28.** 4,200 ÷ 6   **29.** 42,000 ÷ 6

Animated Glossary
www.pearsonsuccessnet.com

*For another example, see Set A on page 112.

Notice the pattern.

$10 \div 5 = 2$

$100 \div 5 = 10$ tens $\div 5 = 2$ tens $= 20$

$1{,}000 \div 5 = 10$ hundreds $\div 5 = 2$ hundreds $= 200$

$10{,}000 \div 5 = 10$ thousands $\div 5 = 2$ thousands $= 2{,}000$

Use the division fact $10 \div 5 = 2$.

Count the additional zeros in the dividend (the number you are dividing). The number you are dividing by, in this case 5, is the divisor.

There are two more zeros in 1,000 than in 10. Annex the additional zeros to the quotient (the number that is the result of dividing).

So, $1{,}000 \div 5 = 200$.

Each friend will get 200 comic books.

Problem Solving

MATHEMATICAL PRACTICES

30. The Paloma family has 1,000 minutes per month on their cell phone plan. Mr. and Mrs. Paloma each use the number of minutes shown, and their children divide the remaining minutes equally. How many minutes do the children use per month?

Name	Minutes
Mr. Paloma	400 minutes
Mrs. Paloma	440 minutes
Maria	minutes
Luz	minutes

Data

31. Reason How can you find the quotient of $56{,}000 \div 7$ mentally? Find the quotient.

32. Reasonableness Estimate the product of 88×7. Do you have an underestimate or an overestimate?

33. Use Structure If $18{,}000 \div n = 300$, then what is the value of n?

34. Reason Why does $3{,}600 \div 6$ have the same quotient as $1{,}800 \div 3$?

35. Reason If a cyclist rides 200 miles in 5 days and rides the same distance each day, how many miles does the cyclist ride each day?

36. DVDs at the mall are on sale 3 for $25. If 400 DVDs are put on 5 shelves with an equal number on each shelf, how many DVDs are on each shelf?

  A 8   **C** 800

  B 80   **D** 8,000

37. Saturn's average distance from the Sun is 886,000,000 miles. Jupiter's average distance from the Sun is 484,000,000 miles. Which planet's distance from the Sun is greater?

38. Communicate For each pair, determine if the quotient is the same or different. Explain.

  a $72{,}000 \div 9$ and $40{,}000 \div 5$

  b $3{,}600 \div 12$ and $1{,}800 \div 6$

Lesson
4-2

Common
Core

5.NBT.6 Find whole-number quotients of whole numbers with up to four-digit dividends and two-digit divisors, using strategies based on place value, the properties of operations, and/or the relationship between multiplication and division. Illustrate and explain the calculation by using equations, rectangular arrays, and/or area models.

Estimating Quotients

How can you estimate quotients?

Jorge is putting shells into 6 boxes. He wants to put about the same number in each box. About how many shells could Jorge put in each box?

Choose an Operation Divide to separate an amount into equal groups.

258 total shells

Guided Practice*

MATHEMATICAL
PRACTICES

Do you know HOW?

In **1** through **8**, estimate each quotient.

1. 520 ÷ 4   **2.** 444 ÷ 8

3. 640 ÷ 6   **4.** 310 ÷ 5

5. 683 ÷ 2   **6.** 297 ÷ 3

7. 700 ÷ 9   **8.** 507 ÷ 7

Do you UNDERSTAND?

9. Construct Arguments In the rounding example above, how do you know the actual quotient should be less than 50?

10. In the example above, about how many shells could Jorge put into each box if he had 8 boxes?

Independent Practice

In **11** through **22**, use rounding to estimate each quotient.

11. 312 ÷ 5   **12.** 792 ÷ 4   **13.** 834 ÷ 2   **14.** 518 ÷ 4

15. 586 ÷ 5   **16.** 419 ÷ 7   **17.** 635 ÷ 8   **18.** 287 ÷ 2

19. 975 ÷ 5   **20.** 359 ÷ 6   **21.** 695 ÷ 7   **22.** 187 ÷ 4

In **23** through **34**, use compatible numbers to estimate each quotient.

23. 263 ÷ 3   **24.** 317 ÷ 7   **25.** 477 ÷ 6   **26.** 378 ÷ 9

27. 641 ÷ 6   **28.** 433 ÷ 4   **29.** 256 ÷ 3   **30.** 182 ÷ 7

31. 545 ÷ 8   **32.** 239 ÷ 5   **33.** 772 ÷ 7   **34.** 324 ÷ 8

For another example, see Set B on page 112.

Use rounding to estimate 258 ÷ 6.

Remember that you can round to the nearest tens or hundreds.

Round 258 to 300.

$300 \div 6 = 50$

50 shells is an overestimate, since 258 was rounded up to 300.

Use compatible numbers.

Replace 258 with 240.

240 and 6 are compatible, since $24 \div 6 = 4$. You can use mental math to find $240 \div 6 = 40$.

40 shells is an underestimate, since 258 was rounded down to 240.

Jorge should put between 40 and 50 shells in each box.

Problem Solving

MATHEMATICAL
PRACTICES

35. While shopping, Tina's mom bought 7 tacos for the family for lunch. Each taco cost $2.25, including tax. How much change did Tina's mom get from a $20 bill?

36. Writing to Explain If you want to use compatible numbers to estimate 262 ÷ 7, is it better to use 210 ÷ 7 or 280 ÷ 7? Explain.

37. Seven friends collected coats for a clothing drive. The students gathered 61 coats. Each person collected about the same number. About how many coats did each student collect?

38. Model A new auditorium has 7 sections. Each section has the same number of seats. The auditorium seats 560 people. How many seats are in each section?

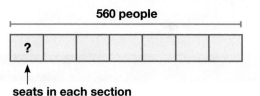

39. Toby earned $596 in 3 months for mowing lawns. If he was paid the same amount each month, about how much did he earn per month?

40. Think About the Structure A digital camera costs $499. A laser printer for the camera costs $277. If you have $100 to spend, which expression can you use to find how much more money you need to save to buy the digital camera?

A 499 − 100

C 499 + 100

B 277 + 100 + 499

D 277 − 100

41. Reasonableness Horses are measured in hands. Three hands equal 1 foot. If a horse is about 19 hands high, about how many feet tall is it?

A 5 feet

C 7 feet

B 6 feet

D 8 feet

Common Core

5.NBT.6 Find whole-number quotients of whole numbers with up to four-digit dividends and two-digit divisors, using strategies based on place value, the properties of operations, and/or the relationship between multiplication and division. Illustrate and explain the calculation by using equations, rectangular arrays, and/or area models.

Problem Solving

Reasonableness

There are 60 students attending a field trip. One chaperone is needed for every 8 students. How many chaperones are needed?

Answer: $60 \div 8 = 7 R4$

So, 7 chaperones are needed.

After you solve a problem, check to see if your answer is reasonable.

60 students

8   ? chaperones →

↑
**1 chaperone
per 8 students**

Guided Practice*

MATHEMATICAL **PRACTICES**

Do you know HOW?

Look back and check. Tell if the answer is reasonable. Explain why or why not.

1. Myrna has 26 daisies. She can plant 3 daisies in each pot. How many pots can she completely fill?

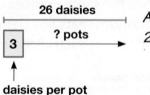

26 daisies

3   ? pots →

daisies per pot

Answer: 8 pots with 2 daisies left

Do you UNDERSTAND?

2. In the problem above, why did the remainder need to be interpreted before the final answer was given?

© 3. **Write a Problem** Write a real-world problem that you can solve by dividing. Give an answer to be checked for reasonableness.

Independent Practice

MATHEMATICAL **PRACTICES**

In **4** through **6**, look back and check. Tell if the answer is reasonable. Explain why or why not.

4. In the school cafeteria, each table holds 10 students. There are 48 students who will eat lunch. How many tables are needed to seat all of the students?

Answer: Four tables with 8 students left

Applying Math Practices

• What am I asked to find?
• What else can I try?
• How are quantities related?
• How can I explain my work?
• How can I use math to model the problem?
• Can I use tools to help?
• Is my work precise?
• Why does this work?
• How can I generalize?

Is my calculation reasonable?

Think I can check by using multiplication.

I know that $7 \times 8 = 56$. I can add the remainder to the product. $56 + 4 = 60$.

So, 7 R4 is reasonable.

Did I answer the right question?

Think The question asks for the number of chaperones needed for ALL students. Seven chaperones is not reasonable because 4 students will be without a chaperone.

Think When there is a remainder in a division problem, you must always interpret the remainder.

So, the correct answer should be that 8 chaperones are needed for the field trip.

For **5,** the table at the right shows how many students can use each supply per case.

5. Mrs. Goia has 49 students in her art classes. She is ordering art supplies.

a How many cases of pastels does she need to order?

Answer: 17 cases

b How many cases of charcoals does she need to order?

Answer: 8 cases with 1 student left

Art Supplies	
Item	**Number of Students**
Case of pastels	3
Case of paints	4
Case of charcoals	6

Data

6. Lionel is buying ice chests to hold 144 bottles of lemonade for a picnic. Each ice chest holds 20 bottles. How many ice chests should he buy?

Answer: 8 chests

ⓒ **7. Reasonableness** Bridget sold 62 tickets to a school concert at $3.95 each. About how much money did she collect for all 62 tickets?

8. How many 6-bottle packages of bottled water must Rashmi's mom buy if she plans to serve 1 bottle to each of the 28 people who will attend the school fair?

ⓒ **9. Model** Marcia has 27 red beads and 42 blue beads. How many beads does she have in all? Write an equation and solve.

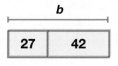

10. Pia needs 100 red beads to make a necklace. She already has 38 red beads. How many more red beads does she need? Write an equation and solve.

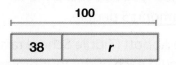

11. A wood carver has made 179 carved animals. The animals will be shipped in boxes that hold only 8 animals each. How many boxes will be completely filled? How many animals will be left over?

5.NBT.6 Find whole-number quotients of whole numbers with up to four-digit dividends and two-digit divisors, using strategies based on place value, the properties of operations, and/or the relationship between multiplication and division. Illustrate and explain the calculation by using equations, rectangular arrays, and/or area models.

Connecting Models and Symbols

Hands-On
play money

How can you model division?

Abbott Middle School raised $148 selling spaghetti at the school's fund-raiser dinner. How can the principal divide the money equally among 4 school projects?

Choose an Operation Divide since you are sharing.

10
10

Another Example How can you record division?

Suppose 4 people needed to share $148.

What You Think

The $100 bill needs to be shared. Exchange the $100 bill for ten $10 bills. There are now 14 $10 bills.

Each person gets three $10 bills. (4 × 3 = 12).

Two $10 bills are left to share. Exchange the $10 bills for 20 $1 bills.

That gives 28 $1 bills to be divided into four groups.

Each person gets seven $1 bills (4 × 7 = 28).

After each person gets seven $1 bills, there is no money left to share.

What You Write

$$\begin{array}{r} 3 \\ 4\overline{)148} \\ -12 \\ \hline 2 \end{array}$$

$$\begin{array}{r} 37 \\ 4\overline{)148} \\ -12 \\ \hline 28 \\ -28 \\ \hline 0 \end{array}$$

Each person gets $37.

Explain It

1. Explain how you can exchange bills to divide four $10 bills equally among 5 people.

2. Suppose Abbott Middle School raised $76 more. In all, how much would each of the four projects receive?

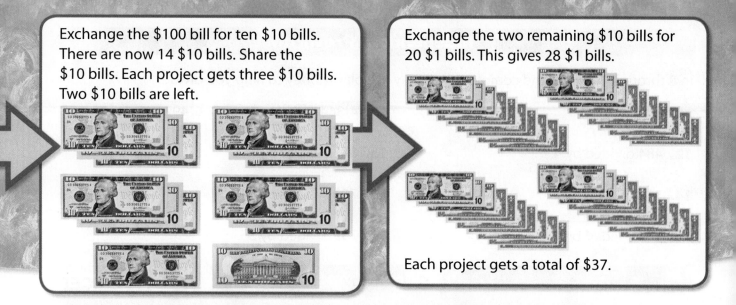

Exchange the $100 bill for ten $10 bills. There are now 14 $10 bills. Share the $10 bills. Each project gets three $10 bills. Two $10 bills are left.

Exchange the two remaining $10 bills for 20 $1 bills. This gives 28 $1 bills.

Each project gets a total of $37.

Guided Practice*

MATHEMATICAL PRACTICES

Do you know HOW?

In **1** through **4**, use models to help you divide.

1. $3\overline{)69}$

2. $7\overline{)490}$

3. $9\overline{)225}$

4. $3\overline{)186}$

Do you UNDERSTAND?

© **5. Reason** In the example above, why do you have to exchange the two remaining $10 bills?

6. If 4 people divide $244 equally, how much will each person get?

Independent Practice

Leveled Practice In **7**, use play money or draw diagrams of the bills shown at the right to symbolize division. Copy and complete the calculation as you answer the questions below.

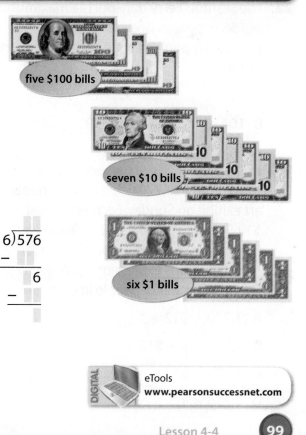

five $100 bills

seven $10 bills

six $1 bills

7. Six people need to share $576 equally.

a All $100 bills are replaced with $10 bills. How many $10 bills are there altogether?

b How many $10 bills will each person get?

c How many $10 bills are left?

d Replace the remaining $10 bills with $1 bills. How many $1 bills are left in all to divide among 6 people?

e What is the total amount each person gets?

$$6\overline{)576}$$

eTools
www.pearsonsuccessnet.com

In **8** through **17**, copy and complete. You may use play money to help you divide.

8. 5)355   **9.** 7)693   **10.** 4)364   **11.** 6)492

12. 484 divided by 4   **13.** 672 divided by 6

14. 312 divided by 2   **15.** 765 divided by 5

16. 385 divided by 7   **17.** 759 divided by 3

Problem Solving    MATHEMATICAL PRACTICES

18. Twenty bags of dog food were donated to the animal shelter. The total cost of the dog food, including $5.95 tax, was $145.95. How much did one bag of dog food cost before taxes?

19. Paulo helped his grandmother with her garden for five days after school. He worked for two hours each day. Paulo's grandmother gave him $75. How much money did Paulo earn each day?

20. Be Precise Nick and 3 friends unloaded 224 folding chairs for the community theater. Each person unloaded the same number of chairs. How many chairs did Nick unload?

21. Construct Arguments Explain how division facts and patterns can help you find 20,000 ÷ 5.

22. The Stanton Ferry transports a maximum of 756 people to Green Island in 4 trips. How many people can the ferry transport in 1 trip?

   A 151   **C** 189

   B 164   **D** 199

23. The Napoleon Bonaparte Broward Bridge is 10,646 feet long. The Sunshine Sky Bridge is 29,040 feet long. Which bridge is shorter and by how much?

24. Communicate Why is 3.892 greater than 3.289?

25. Think About the Structure The art museum sold 1,770 tickets to the modern art exhibit on Sunday. Each ticket cost $12. The ticket holders were divided into five groups to organize the viewing for that day. Which expression tells how to find the number of people in each group?

   A 1,770 ÷ $12 + 5

   B 1,770 ÷ 5 + $12

   C 1,770 ÷ $12

   D 1,770 ÷ 5

26. Kirstin is starting a swimming club. She is the only member the first month. She plans to have each member find 2 new members each month. How many members will the club have at the end of 4 months?

27. Look for Patterns Find the next three numbers in the pattern shown below.

10, 15, 12, 17, 14, . . .

Algebra Connections

Completing Number Sentences

Remember that a number sentence has two numbers or expressions that are connected by the symbols >, <, or =.

Estimation can be used to see if the left or right side is greater.

Copy and complete the comparisons using estimation. Check your answers.

Remember:
> means "is greater than."
< means "is less than."
= means "is equal to."

Example: $6 \times 80 \bigcirc 6 \times 77$

Think Is 6 groups of 80 more than 6 groups of 77?

Since 80 is more than 77, 6 groups of 80 is more than 6 groups of 77. Complete the comparison with ">."

$$6 \times 80 > 6 \times 77$$

This means 6 groups of 80 is greater than 6 groups of 77.

Copy and complete. Write <, >, or = in the circle.

1. $6 \times 50 \bigcirc 51 \times 6$ **2.** $40 \times 5 \bigcirc 45 \times 5$ **3.** $56 + 56 \bigcirc 55 \times 2$

4. $7 \times 67 \bigcirc 67 \times 7$ **5.** $320 \bigcirc 8 \times 43$ **6.** $8 \times 72 \bigcirc 560$

7. $20 \times 20 \bigcirc 17 \times 18$ **8.** $5 \times 20 \bigcirc 100$ **9.** $3 + 48 \bigcirc 3 \times 48$

10. $3 \times 19 \bigcirc 60$ **11.** $5 \times 20 \bigcirc 19 \times 4$ **12.** $6 + 18 \bigcirc 6 \times 18$

For **13** through **14**, write a number sentence to help solve each problem.

© **13. Look for Patterns** Marina bought a lavender backpack for herself and a green backpack for her brother. Charley bought an orange backpack. Who spent more money?

14. Mr. Wozniak purchased a green backpack. Ms. Chivas purchased 4 lavender backpacks. Who paid more?

15. Write a word problem using the price of the backpacks.

$9

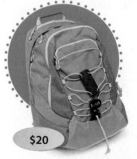
$20

$40

$50

Common Core

5.NBT.6 Find whole-number quotients of whole numbers with up to four-digit dividends and two-digit divisors, using strategies based on place value, the properties of operations, and/or the relationship between multiplication and division. Illustrate and explain the calculation by using equations, rectangular arrays, and/or area models.

Dividing by 1-Digit Divisors

Why use division?

Students are selling candles to raise money. A shipment arrived yesterday. The candles will be sold in boxes of 6 each. How many boxes can be filled? A diagram can help you decide what operation to use.

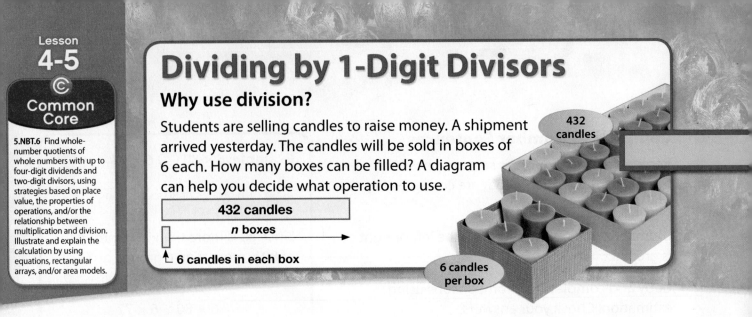

432 candles

432 candles

n boxes

6 candles in each box

6 candles per box

Another Example **How do you find a quotient with a remainder?**

2-digit quotient with remainder

Find 380 ÷ 6.

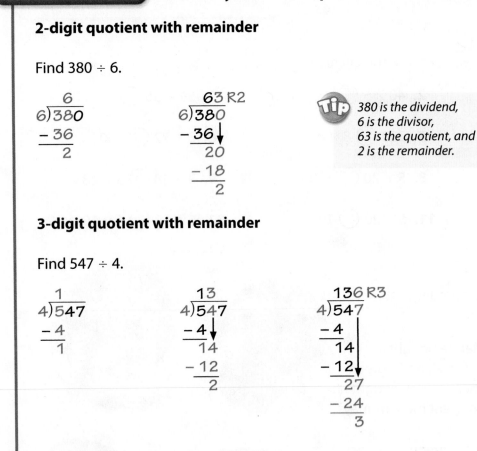

```
      6
6)380
  -36
    2
```

```
     63 R2
6)380
  -36↓
    20
   -18
     2
```

Tip 380 is the dividend, 6 is the divisor, 63 is the quotient, and 2 is the remainder.

3-digit quotient with remainder

Find 547 ÷ 4.

```
     1
4)547
  -4
   1
```

```
    13
4)547
  -4↓
   14
  -12
    2
```

```
   136 R3
4)547
  -4│
   14│
  -12↓
   27
  -24
    3
```

Explain It

1. Name the quotient, divisor, remainder, and dividend in these two examples.

2. Why did the second example have a 3-digit quotient?

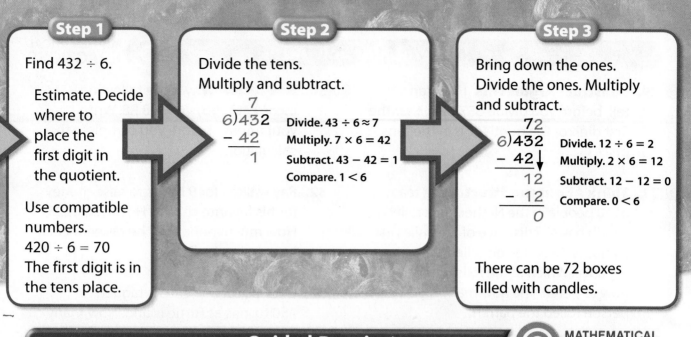

Step 1

Find 432 ÷ 6.

Estimate. Decide where to place the first digit in the quotient.

Use compatible numbers.
420 ÷ 6 = 70
The first digit is in the tens place.

Step 2

Divide the tens.
Multiply and subtract.

$$6\overline{)432} \atop -42 \atop 1 \text{ with } 7 \text{ above}$$

Divide. 43 ÷ 6 ≈ 7
Multiply. 7 × 6 = 42
Subtract. 43 − 42 = 1
Compare. 1 < 6

Step 3

Bring down the ones. Divide the ones. Multiply and subtract.

$$6\overline{)432} \atop -42 \atop 12 \atop -12 \atop 0 \text{ with } 72 \text{ above}$$

Divide. 12 ÷ 6 = 2
Multiply. 2 × 6 = 12
Subtract. 12 − 12 = 0
Compare. 0 < 6

There can be 72 boxes filled with candles.

Guided Practice*

MATHEMATICAL PRACTICES

Do you know HOW?

In **1** through **6**, find each quotient.

1. $9\overline{)270}$ **2.** $6\overline{)684}$

3. $3\overline{)65}$ **4.** $5\overline{)339}$

5. $5\overline{)564}$ **6.** $4\overline{)724}$

Do you UNDERSTAND?

7. Construct Arguments How can estimating with compatible numbers help you find the quotient?

8. In the first example, find the quotient if the total number of candles is 561.

Independent Practice

In **9** through **16**, use compatible numbers to estimate each quotient. Then decide where to place the first digit of the quotient.

9. $5\overline{)762}$ **10.** $3\overline{)289}$ **11.** $8\overline{)607}$ **12.** $3\overline{)567}$

13. $6\overline{)960}$ **14.** $7\overline{)973}$ **15.** $5\overline{)373}$ **16.** $9\overline{)462}$

In **17** through **28**, copy and complete the calculation.

17. $8\overline{)616}$ **18.** $6\overline{)486}$ **19.** $4\overline{)448}$ **20.** $9\overline{)828}$

21. $2\overline{)131}$ **22.** $9\overline{)836}$ **23.** $5\overline{)413}$ **24.** $5\overline{)469}$

25. $7\overline{)644}$ **26.** $2\overline{)995}$ **27.** $4\overline{)139}$ **28.** $5\overline{)625}$

---

29. Construct Arguments How can you tell, before you divide 387 by 4, that the first digit of the quotient is in the tens place?

30. Be Precise Why is the following incorrect? $296 \div 6 = 48$ R8. Write your answer before you complete the calculation.

31. Think About the Structure A team of 10 people in the Netherlands rolled a 140-lb barrel a distance of 164 miles in 24 hours. Each person rolled the same distance. Which of the following shows how to determine how many miles each person rolled the barrel?

A $164 \div 24$ **C** $140 \div 24$

B $164 \div 10$ **D** $140 \div 10$

32. Ray walked for 9 hours to raise money for his favorite charity. He raised $225. How much money did he raise for each hour he walked?

33. Over 9 years, scientists tagged 450 turtles at Turtle Island. How many turtles did they tag each year if each year they tagged the same number of turtles?

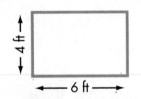

450 turtles								
?	?	?	?	?	?	?	?	?

34. The High Sierra Trail at Mt. Whitney is 49 miles long each way. Park rangers report that to walk the trail one way takes hikers 6 days. About how many miles must the hikers walk each day to finish all 49 miles in 6 days?

A 6 miles   **C** 10 miles

B 8 miles   **D** 12 miles

35. Reason What is the value of c in the equation $c \times 3 = 324$?

A 18   **C** 180

B 108   **D** 1,080

36. Reason Find the value of n.

$3 \times 7 = n \times 3$

37. Model What is the perimeter of the rectangle in inches? (Hint: 1 ft = 12 in.)

4 ft
6 ft

38. Suppose there were 8 cowboys that herded 104 cattle. If each cowboy herded the same number of cattle, how many animals was each cowboy responsible for?

39. Model Willis Tower in Chicago is 1,450 feet tall. First Interstate Plaza in Houston is 973 feet tall. How many feet taller is the Willis Tower than the First Interstate Plaza building? Finish drawing the picture. Write an equation, then solve. Let h = the difference in height.

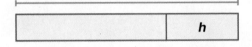

	h

Find the product. Estimate to check if the answer is reasonable.

1. 58
   × 4

2. 355
   × 7

3. 6,044
   × 6

4. 5,137
   × 3

5. 236
   × 17

6. 23
   × 25

7. 117
   × 33

8. 65
   × 29

9. 45 × 12

10. 1,001 × 25

11. 8 × 3,030

12. 6 × 3,373

Find the sum. Estimate to check if the answer is reasonable.

13. 76,095
    + 3,950

14. 9,713
    + 9,328

15. 888
    + 726

16. 7,566
    + 8,092

17. 27,444
    + 9,507

Error Search Find each answer that is not correct.
Write it correctly and explain the error.

18. 703
    × 88
    ──────
    11,248

19. 348
    × 17
    ──────
    5,916

20. 202
    × 15
    ──────
    1,010

21. 19
    × 18
    ──────
    344

22. 2,456
    × 73
    ──────
    179,288

Number Sense

© **Reasonableness** Write whether each statement is true or false.
Explain your reasoning.

23. The product of 7 and 6,943 is closer to 42,000 than 49,000.

24. The difference of 15.9 and 4.2 is closer to 11 than 12.

25. The sum of 33,345 and 60,172 is less than 93,000.

26. The product of 43 and 5,116 is greater than 200,000.

27. The sum of 3.98 + 4.62 is 0.02 less than 8.62.

28. The product of 9 and 48 is 18 less than 450.

Common
Core

5.NBT.6 Find whole-
number quotients of
whole numbers with up to
four-digit dividends and
two-digit divisors, using
strategies based on place
value, the properties of
operations, and/or the
relationship between
multiplication and division.
Illustrate and explain the
calculation by using
equations, rectangular
arrays, and/or area models.

Zeros in the Quotient

When do you write a zero in the quotient?

On vacation the McQueen family drove a total of 830 miles in four days. What is the average number of miles they drove each day?

Choose an Operation Divide to find how many miles per day.

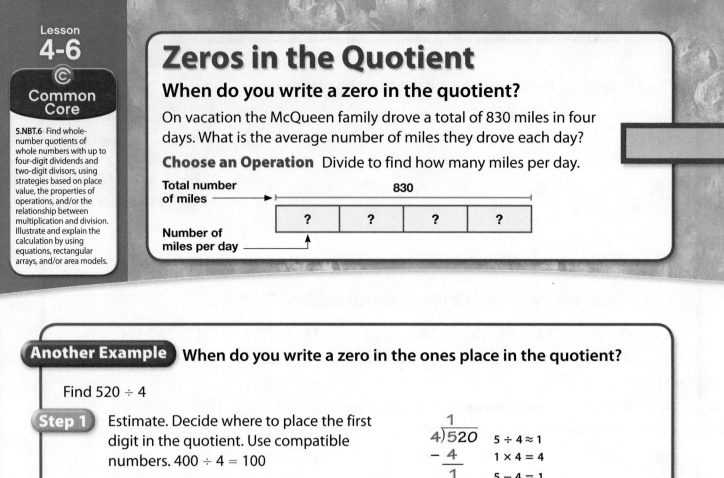

Another Example When do you write a zero in the ones place in the quotient?

Find 520 ÷ 4

Step 1 Estimate. Decide where to place the first digit in the quotient. Use compatible numbers. 400 ÷ 4 = 100

$$4\overline{)520} \quad \begin{array}{l} 5 \div 4 \approx 1 \\ 1 \times 4 = 4 \\ 5 - 4 = 1 \\ 1 < 4 \end{array}$$

The first digit in the quotient is in the hundreds place.

Divide the hundreds. Multiply, subtract, and compare.

Step 2 Bring down the tens.
Divide the tens.
Multiply, subtract, and compare.

$$\begin{array}{r} 13 \\ 4\overline{)520} \\ -4\downarrow \\ \overline{12} \\ -12 \\ \overline{0} \end{array} \quad \begin{array}{l} \\ \\ 12 \div 4 = 3 \\ 3 \times 4 = 12 \\ 12 - 12 = 0 \\ 0 < 4 \end{array}$$

Step 3 Bring down the ones.
There are 0 ones.
Write 0 in the ones place in the quotient.

$$\begin{array}{r} 130 \\ 4\overline{)520} \\ -4 \\ \overline{12} \\ -12\downarrow \\ \overline{00} \end{array}$$

There are 0 ones.
Write 0 in the
ones place in
the quotient.

Explain It

1. In the example at the top, why is the zero in the tens place of the quotient, but in the ones place in Another Example?

2. Explain how to check your answers in both examples.

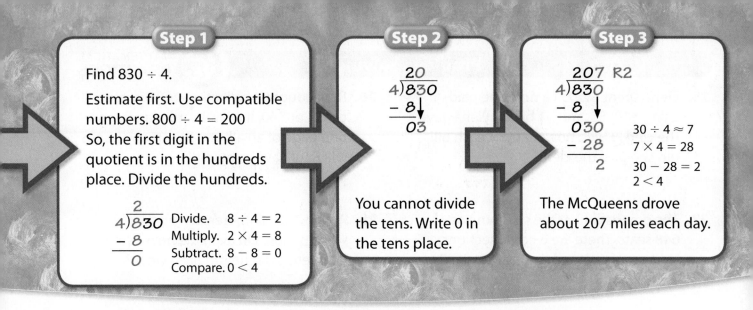

Step 1

Find 830 ÷ 4.

Estimate first. Use compatible numbers. 800 ÷ 4 = 200
So, the first digit in the quotient is in the hundreds place. Divide the hundreds.

$$\begin{array}{r} 2 \\ 4\overline{)830} \\ -8 \\ \hline 0 \end{array}$$

Divide.   8 ÷ 4 = 2
Multiply. 2 × 4 = 8
Subtract. 8 − 8 = 0
Compare. 0 < 4

Step 2

$$\begin{array}{r} 20 \\ 4\overline{)830} \\ -8\downarrow \\ \hline 03 \end{array}$$

You cannot divide the tens. Write 0 in the tens place.

Step 3

$$\begin{array}{r} 207 \;\; R2 \\ 4\overline{)830} \\ -8\downarrow \\ \hline 030 \\ -28 \\ \hline 2 \end{array}$$

30 ÷ 4 ≈ 7
7 × 4 = 28
30 − 28 = 2
2 < 4

The McQueens drove about 207 miles each day.

Guided Practice*

MATHEMATICAL PRACTICES

Do you know HOW?

In **1** through **4**, find each quotient. Check your answers.

1. $9\overline{)972}$

2. $7\overline{)714}$

3. $5\overline{)453}$

4. $2\overline{)941}$

Do you UNDERSTAND?

© 5. **Be Precise** In the example at the top, what would happen if you do not bring down the zero in the ones place?

6. Suppose the McQueens only drove 424 miles in 4 days. If they drove an equal number of miles each day, how many miles did they drive in 1 day?

Independent Practice

In **7** through **24**, find each quotient. Check your answers.

7. $2\overline{)880}$

8. $5\overline{)540}$

9. $6\overline{)840}$

10. $3\overline{)323}$

11. $7\overline{)563}$

12. $3\overline{)624}$

13. $2\overline{)801}$

14. $5\overline{)180}$

15. $8\overline{)816}$

16. $3\overline{)912}$

17. $5\overline{)547}$

18. $7\overline{)284}$

19. $9\overline{)455}$

20. $2\overline{)420}$

21. $6\overline{)648}$

22. $4\overline{)816}$

23. $3\overline{)512}$

24. $7\overline{)776}$

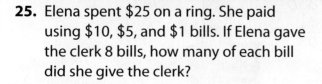

25. Elena spent $25 on a ring. She paid using $10, $5, and $1 bills. If Elena gave the clerk 8 bills, how many of each bill did she give the clerk?

26. Raul bought a collection of 856 baseball cards for $40. If only 8 cards can fit on one page of an album, how many pages will Raul have to buy?

27. The grandstand at the stadium has 648 seats. There are 6 equal sections. How many seats are in each section?

28. Ali ran 120 kilometers over a four week period. On average, how many kilometers did he run each week?

29. Persevere Harry filled one box with 9 pints of blueberries. He picked 97 pints of blueberries. If Harry filled 10 boxes, how many pints were left for the last box?

30. A school raised $306 washing cars. The money will be used to buy new recycling containers for the school. If each container costs $8, how many containers can the school buy?

31. Construct Arguments Clare's teacher has a box of 180 stickers for a group of students to share equally. Does each student get more stickers if there are 6 students or if there are 9 students?

32. Be Precise Each car of the roller coaster can hold 6 people. If 63 people are waiting in line to ride the roller coaster, how many cars will be needed?

33. Dora has 24 pairs of earrings. She keeps them in 6 boxes. Each box has the same number of earrings. Each pair of earrings costs between $10 and $20. How many pairs of earrings are in each box?

    A 4

    B 8

    C 10

    D 12

34. Think About the Structure A home and garden show ran for two days. Tickets cost $2 each. On the first day, ticket sales totaled $322. On the second day, ticket sales were $294. Which of the following shows how to determine the number of tickets sold?

    A $(322 + 294) \div 2$

    B $322 \times 294 \div 2$

    C $(322 + 294) \times 2$

    D $322 \div 2 + 294$

35. Reasonableness The world's longest cartoon strip has 242 panels. It was drawn by 35 artists in about 8 hours. About how many panels were drawn in one hour?

    A 15   **B** 20   **C** 30   **D** 45

Choose a Computation Method

In many airports, people ride minibuses between terminals. The minibuses leave only when they are full. If a minibus carried 297 passengers in a day, and it holds 11 passengers at a time, how many times did it fill up?

Step 1 Draw a picture and choose an operation.

297 passengers

11

? times

number of passengers in each bus

Divide 297 ÷ 11.

Step 2 Choose the best computation method. Decide whether to use mental math, paper and pencil, or a calculator.

Since 11 has two-digits, use a calculator.

Step 3 Solve.

Press: 297 ÷ 11 **ENTER =**   Display: 27

The minibus filled up 27 times.

Practice

For each problem, draw a picture and choose an operation. Then choose the best computation method and solve.

1. If each of the 297 passengers paid $2, how could the driver find the amount of money he collected? How much did he collect?

2. Four drivers had 293, 147, 307, and 284 passengers. How many passengers did the four drivers have in all?

3. One of the drivers had 150 passengers on Monday and 250 passengers on Tuesday. How many passengers does he need on Wednesday to have 500 passengers for the week?

4. A special pass for frequent travelers cost $50 a year. If 200 travelers bought the special pass, how much was the bus company paid?

Common
Core

5.NBT.6 Find whole number quotients of whole numbers with up to four-digit dividends and two-digit divisors, using strategies based on place value, the properties of operations, and/or the relationship between multiplication and division. Illustrate and explain the calculation by using equations, rectangular arrays, and/or area models. Also **5.OA.2**

Problem Solving

Draw a Picture and Write an Equation

There are 112 campers going boating. The size of the boat and number of people it can hold is shown at the right. How many boats will be needed to hold all the campers?

Another Example

Arturo is putting 114 portable DVD players into boxes. Each box holds 9 DVD players. How many boxes will Arturo need?

You can use repeated subtraction to find the answer. Take one group of 9 and subtract it from 114. Keep subtracting 9 until you can no longer subtract.

$114 - 9 = 105$
$105 - 9 = 96$
$96 - 9 = 87$
$87 - 9 = 78$
$78 - 9 = 69$
$69 - 9 = 60$
$60 - 9 = 51$
$51 - 9 = 42$
$42 - 9 = 33$
$33 - 9 = 24$
$24 - 9 = 15$
$15 - 9 = 6$ You cannot subtract 9 from 6, so 6 players are left over.

114 DVD players

9   *b* boxes

players per box

Tip *You can also draw a picture and write an equation to solve.*

Let *b* = the number of boxes needed.

$114 \div 9 = b$
$b = 12 \text{ R6}$

Since you can subtract 9 *twelve times* and have 6 *left over*, $114 \div 9 = 12 \text{ R6}$.

Since there are 6 players left without a box, Arturo needs 13 boxes to pack all 114 DVD players.

Explain It

1. Why does Arturo need 13 boxes and not 12?

What do I know?   There are 112 campers. Six people can fit in a boat.

What am I asked to find?   The number of boats needed to hold all the campers.

Draw a picture.

112 campers

| 6 | n boats → |

↑ campers per boat

Write an equation.

Let n = the number of boats needed.

$$112 \div 6 = n$$

$$n = 18 \text{ R4}$$

For all campers to go boating, 19 boats will be needed.

$$\begin{array}{r} 18 \text{ R4} \\ 6\overline{)112} \\ -6 \\ \hline 52 \\ -48 \\ \hline 4 \end{array}$$

Guided Practice*

MATHEMATICAL PRACTICES

Do you know **HOW?**

Solve. Copy and complete the picture. Then, write an equation.

1. If each van holds 9 people, how many vans will be needed to take 137 people to a concert?

| 9 | → |

Do you **UNDERSTAND?**

2. How do you know your answer for Exercise 1 is reasonable?

3. **Look for Patterns** Write a real-world problem that you can solve by using repeated subtraction.

Independent Practice

MATHEMATICAL PRACTICES

In **4** through **6**, draw a picture, write an equation, then solve.

4. Steven has 140 photos. A page from a photo album contains 8 photos. How many pages does Steven have?

5. **Use Tools** If you buy a digital music player for $246, including tax, and are allowed to pay for it in 6 equal payments, how much will each payment be?

6. There are 7 players on each academic team. If there are 175 total players at the tournament, how many teams are there?

Applying Math Practices

- What am I asked to find?
- What else can I try?
- How are quantities related?
- How can I explain my work?
- How can I use math to model the problem?
- Can I use tools to help?
- Is my work precise?
- Why does this work?
- How can I generalize?

*For another example, see Set C on page 112.

Set A, pages 92–93

Find 48,000 ÷ 6.

Identify a basic fact.   48 ÷ 6 = 8

Look for a pattern.   480 ÷ 6 = 80
4,800 ÷ 6 = 800
48,000 ÷ 6 = 8,000

Remember to use basic facts and patterns to divide mentally.

1. 810 ÷ 9   **2.** 360 ÷ 6

3. 2,400 ÷ 6   **4.** 4,500 ÷ 9

5. 64,000 ÷ 8   **6.** 42,000 ÷ 7

Set B, pages 94–95

Estimate 330 ÷ 8.

Think of a number close to 33 that is a multiple of 8, so a basic fact can be used. Then divide.

32 ÷ 8 = 4
320 ÷ 8 = 40

So, 330 ÷ 8 is about 40.

Remember to use rounding or compatible numbers when estimating quotients.

Estimate.

1. 410 ÷ 6   **2.** 653 ÷ 8

3. 8,243 ÷ 9   **4.** 14,368 ÷ 5

5. 26,952 ÷ 7   **6.** 22,487 ÷ 3

Set C, pages 96–97, 98–100, 110–111

A company ships 4 basketballs in a box. How many boxes will be needed to ship 30 balls?

30 balls

? boxes

4

number of balls per box

Calculate the division.

$$\begin{array}{r} 7\,R2 \\ 4)\overline{30} \\ -28 \\ \hline 2 \end{array}$$

Seven boxes will be completely filled, but another box is needed to hold the remainder of 2 balls.

It is reasonable to say that 8 boxes are needed to ship 30 balls.

Remember you need to check the reasonableness of a solution by interpreting a remainder of a division problem.

Solve.

1. Sarah's DVD collection is stored in a cabinet that holds 6 DVDs on each shelf. How many shelves will she need to hold her collection of 89 DVDs?

2. There are 135 fifth-grade students in a certain school. Each table in the lunchroom seats six students. How many tables are needed to seat all fifth graders?

3. A large group of people is going to the baseball game. If 97 people are going, and each bus holds 32 people, how many buses will need to be ordered?

Find 549 ÷ 6.

Estimate first. 540 ÷ 6 = 90.

```
      91 R3
  6)549
   − 54
      09
    −  6
       3
```

Check:

```
      91
   ×   6
     546
   +   3
     549
```

The quotient 91 R3 is close to the estimate, 90.

Remember that you can check your answer by multiplying the quotient and the divisor, and then add the remainder.

Divide.

1. 74 ÷ 5
2. 89 ÷ 9
3. 232 ÷ 4
4. 488 ÷ 8
5. 682 ÷ 7
6. 735 ÷ 6
7. 856 ÷ 4
8. 492 ÷ 6

Find 839 ÷ 4.

Estimate first. 800 ÷ 4 = 200.

```
     209 R3
  4)839
   − 8
     03
    − 3
      39
    − 36
       3
```

Check:
```
      209
    ×   4
      836
    +   3
      839
```

The quotient 209 R3 is close to the estimate, 200. The answer is reasonable.

Remember that you sometimes need to write a zero in the quotient when you divide.

Divide. Estimate to check that your answer is reasonable.

1. 720 ÷ 6
2. 661 ÷ 3
3. 424 ÷ 4
4. 914 ÷ 3
5. 6)185
6. 9)1,872
7. 7)2,940
8. 5)1,532

Multiple Choice

ASSESSMENT

1. If the money shown is to be divided among 4 people, what should be the first step? (4-4)

A Exchange the $100 bill for eight $10 bills and twenty $1 bills.

B Exchange the four $10 bills for forty $1 bills.

C Exchange the $100 dollar bill for a hundred $1 bills.

D Exchange the $100 dollar bill for ten $10 bills.

2. If $2,400 is divided evenly by 3 charities, how many dollars does each charity get? (4-1)

A 60

B 80

C 800

D 8,000

3. If 283 is divided by 4, where should the first digit of the quotient be placed? (4-5)

A Because 4 is greater than 2, it should be in the tens place.

B Because 4 is less than 2, it should be in the tens place.

C Because 4 is greater than 2, it should be in the hundreds place.

D Because 4 is less than 2, it should be in the hundreds place.

4. Which of the following is the most reasonable estimate of 913 ÷ 4? (4-3)

A 200

B 225

C 250

D 300

5. The table shows the amount raised by teams for the children's hospital. Raquel's team raised 4 times the amount that Jeremy's team raised. How much did Jeremy's team raise? (4-6)

Data

Team Leader	Amount Raised
Raquel	$836
Jeremy	
Charles	$448

A $209

B $204

C $112

D $29

6. Which of the following shows the best way to estimate 712 ÷ 8 using compatible numbers? (4-2)

A 700 ÷ 8

B 720 ÷ 8

C 730 ÷ 8

D 800 ÷ 8

7. The student council has 186 members divided as evenly as possible into 8 committees. How many members are on each committee? (4-5)

8. A marathon race has 522 runners divided as evenly as possible into 6 groups. About how many runners are in each group? Use compatible numbers to solve. (4-3)

9. A set of 490 DVDs is being divided equally by 7 people. How many DVDs does each person get? (4-1)

10. A prize of $820 is being shared equally by 4 students. How much money does each student receive? (4-6)

11. A florist is making flower arrangements. She has 108 roses to place in 9 arrangements. What equation can be used to find r, the number of roses in each arrangement? (4-7)

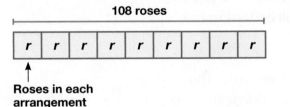

108 roses

| r | r | r | r | r | r | r | r | r |

↑
Roses in each
arrangement

12. A high school has $1,016 available for scholarships and $2,592 available for grants. If 8 students are awarded equal parts of the money for scholarships, how much does each student receive? (4-5)

13. Write an equation to show the best way to estimate 208 ÷ 7 using compatible numbers. (4-2)

14. If the money below is divided among 5 people, how much money would each person get? (4-4)

15. Margaret's Farm has 840 peaches ready to sell. If 105 peaches fit in each crate, how many crates can be filled? (4-7)

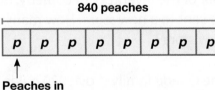

840 peaches

| p | p | p | p | p | p | p | p |

↑
Peaches in
each crate

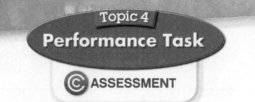
Use the data in the table for **1** through **4**.

Video Store Movies	
Category	**Number of Videos**
Comedy	512
Drama	378
Action	456
Horror	392
New Releases	425

1. How many shelves are needed for the new releases if each shelf holds 8 videos?

2. Half of the action movies are on DVD and the other half are on VHS. How many action DVDs does the video store have?

3. About 416 of the new releases can be equally divided among the other categories. How many new releases could be added to each category?

4. Half of the inventory of comedy, drama, and horror movies will be sent to a new store. How many movies will be sent to the new store?

5. The Quade family drove 920 miles in 3 days. They drove the same number of miles the first 2 days and then drove 50 miles the third day. How many miles did they drive on each of the first two days? Explain how you found your answer.

6. Four families went out for dinner. The total food bill came to $327. The families also left a $50 tip for the waiter. If each family spent the same amount, about how much did each family spend on dinner? Explain how you found your answer.

Topic 5

Dividing by 2-Digit Divisors

▼ Some comets can be seen from Earth fairly often. About how many of these comets are seen each year? You will find out in Lesson 5-2.

Review What You Know!

Vocabulary

Choose the best term from the box.

- dividend
- quotient
- divisor
- remainder

1. In the equation $180 \div 45 = 4$, the number 180 is the __?__ and the number 4 is the __?__.

2. The number used to divide another number is the __?__.

3. $15 \div 6 = 2$ with a __?__ of 3.

Place Value

Copy and complete.

4. 7,896 is the same as 7 __?__ + 8 __?__ + 9 __?__ + 6 __?__.

5. 36,000 is the same as 36 __?__.

6. 75,800 is the same as 75 __?__ + 8 __?__.

Rounding

Round each number to the place of the underlined digit.

7. 6<u>7</u>9   8. <u>3</u>,769   9. 90,<u>3</u>24

10. <u>8</u>77   11. <u>6</u>,542   12. 42,<u>3</u>76

© **Writing to Explain** Write an answer for item 13.

13. Explain one way to estimate $738 \div 84$.

Topic Essential Question
- What is the standard procedure for dividing with two-digit divisors?

Topic 5

Interactive Learning

Pose the problem. Start each lesson by working together to solve problems. It will help you make sense of math.

Applying Math Practices

- What am I asked to find?
- What else can I try?
- How are quantities related?
- How can I explain my work?
- How can I use math to model the problem?
- Can I use tools to help?
- Is my work precise?
- Why does this work?
- How can I generalize?

Lesson 5-1

© **Use Structure** Solve. Look for patterns.

A bakery sells muffins in boxes shown at the right. If 60 muffins were sold, how many boxes were used? 600 muffins? 6,000 muffins? Describe patterns you found.

Lesson 5-2

© **Reasonableness** Solve. All you need is an estimate.

Your school needs to buy posters for a fundraiser. The school has a budget of $147. Each poster costs $13. About how many posters can your school buy for the fundraiser? Tell how you found an estimate.

Lesson 5-3

© **Use Tools** Use grid paper and an array to solve this problem.

A parking lot holds 270 cars. Each row holds 15 cars. How many rows are in this parking lot?

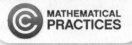

Lesson 5-4

© **Use Structure** Solve. Look for basic facts.

Suppose your soccer team has $160 to buy uniforms that cost $20 each. How many uniforms can your team buy? What if the team has $168? Show how you found each answer.

Lesson 5-5

© **Use Tools** Solve any way you choose. Estimate the quotient first.

You need 250 yards of string to fly a kite. How many balls of string like the one at the right do you need to buy? Show how you found the answer.

75 Yards

Lesson 5-6

© **Generalize** Solve. Use what you learned with one-digit quotients.

A factory is going to ship 814 stuffed animals. Each of the packing boxes will hold 18 stuffed animals. How many boxes are needed? How many boxes will be filled? Show how you found the answers.

Lesson 5-7

© **Reasonableness** Solve. All you need is an estimate.

Marcia's choir needs to raise $5,390 for its annual trip. Each of the 25 members of the choir will need to contribute equally. About how much money does each person need to raise?

Lesson 5-8

© **Model** Make up any data that may be missing. Then solve the problem.

Juno rides his bike twice as far on Sunday as he does on Saturday. How many miles does he ride on Sunday?

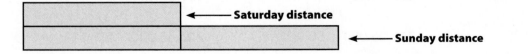

Saturday distance

Sunday distance

Common Core

5.NBT.6 Find whole-number quotients of whole numbers with up to four-digit dividends and two-digit divisors, using strategies based on place value…

Using Patterns to Divide

How can patterns help you divide large multiples of 10?

A jet carries 18,000 passengers in 90 trips. The plane is full for each trip. How many passengers does the plane hold?

Choose an Operation Divide to find how many people were on each trip.

18,000 passengers in 90 trips

Guided Practice*

MATHEMATICAL PRACTICES

Do you know HOW?

In **1** through **4**, find each quotient. Use mental math.

1. $210 \div 30 = 21$ tens $\div 3$ tens = ▢

2. $480 \div 60 = 48$ tens $\div 6$ tens = ▢

3. $8,100 \div 90 =$ ▢

4. $2,800 \div 70 =$ ▢

Do you UNDERSTAND?

© 5. **Reason** In Exercise 1, why is $210 \div 30$ the same as 21 tens $\div$ 3 tens?

6. In the example at the top, if the jet carried 10,000 people in 40 trips, how many people did it carry for each trip?

Independent Practice

In **7** through **22**, use mental math to find the missing numbers.

7. $560 \div 70 = 56$ tens $\div 7$ tens = ▢

8. $360 \div 60 = 36$ tens $\div 6$ tens = ▢

9. $6,000 \div 50 = 600$ tens $\div 5$ tens = ▢

10. $24,000 \div 60 = 2,400$ tens $\div 6$ tens = ▢

11. $2,000 \div 20 =$ ▢

12. $6,300 \div 90 =$ ▢

13. $240 \div 10 =$ ▢

14. $21,000 \div$ ▢ $= 700$

15. $8,100 \div 90 =$ ▢

16. $72,000 \div$ ▢ $= 200$

17. $30,000 \div$ ▢ $= 600$

18. $7,200 \div$ ▢ $= 80$

19. $56,000 \div$ ▢ $= 800$

20. $10,000 \div 100 =$ ▢

21. $25,000 \div 50 =$ ▢

22. $45,000 \div 90 =$ ▢

*For another example, see Set A on page 138.

Think of a basic fact to help you solve.

$18 \div 9 = 2$

Think about multiples of 10:

$180 \div 90 = 18 \text{ tens} \div 9 \text{ tens} = 2$

$1,800 \div 90 = 180 \text{ tens} \div 9 \text{ tens} = 20$

$18,000 \div 90 = 1,800 \text{ tens} \div 9 \text{ tens} = 200$

The pattern shows us that
$18,000 \div 90 = 200$.

So, the jet can hold 200 people during each trip.

You can multiply to check your answer.

$200 \times 90 = 18,000$

Problem Solving

MATHEMATICAL PRACTICES

For **23** and **24**, use the information at the right.

© 23. **Be Precise** If all the flights were full and all planes carried the same number of passengers, how many people were on each flight?

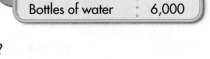

Data		
Total passengers	:	3,000
Flights per day	:	20
Bottles of water	:	6,000

24. If each flight was stocked with the same number of bottles of water, how many bottles were on each flight?

25. There are 12 school campuses in the community. Each campus has a 14-member volleyball team. How many students play volleyball?

26. Helen bowled 5 games. Her scores were 97, 108, 114, 99, and 100. What was the total of her scores?

© 27. **Thinking About the Structure** Dividing 480 by 60 is the same as

    A dividing 48 ones by 6 ones.

    B dividing 48 tens by 6 ones.

    C dividing 48 tens by 6 tens.

    D dividing 48 hundreds by 6 tens.

© 28. **Look for Patterns** Suppose there are 1,500 pencils in 20 bins. You want to put the same number of pencils in each bin. Which expression shows how to find the number of pencils in each bin?

    A $1,500 + 20$ **C** $1,500 \times 20$

    B $1,500 - 20$ **D** $1,500 \div 20$

29. One dozen eggs is 12 eggs. A farmer harvested 1,260 eggs from the hen-house. Which expression shows how to find how many dozen eggs the farmer harvested?

    A $1,260 + 12$ **C** $1,260 \div 12$

    B $1,260 - 12$ **D** $1,260 \times 12$

30. It takes 18,000 kg of sand to fill 600 school sandboxes. How much sand will a construction company need to put in each of the 600 sandboxes to get ready for the new school year?

5.NBT.6 Find whole-number quotients of whole numbers with up to four-digit dividends and two-digit divisors, using strategies based on...the properties of operations, and/or the relationship between multiplication and division ...

Estimating Quotients with 2-Digit Divisors

How can you use compatible numbers to estimate quotients?

$159 for 75 bracelets

Betty made $159 by selling 75 bracelets. Each bracelet costs the same. About how much did each bracelet cost?

Choose an Operation We know the total amount made and the number of bracelets. Divide to find the price.

Guided Practice*

MATHEMATICAL
PRACTICES

Do you know HOW?

In **1** through **6**, estimate using compatible numbers.

1. 287 ÷ 42

2. 320 ÷ 11

3. 208 ÷ 72

4. 554 ÷ 62

5. 1,220 ÷ 59

6. 3,390 ÷ 42

Do you UNDERSTAND?

© **7. Use Structure** If you use rounding to estimate in the example above, can you divide easily? Explain.

© **8. Reasonableness** Betty has 425 more bracelets to sell. She wants to store these in plastic bags that hold 20 bracelets each. She estimates she will need about 25 bags. Is she right? Why or why not?

Independent Practice

In **9** through **26**, estimate using compatible numbers.

9. 412 ÷ 84

10. 288 ÷ 37

11. 2,964 ÷ 73

12. 228 ÷ 19

13. 1,784 ÷ 64

14. 7,620 ÷ 53

15. 2,280 ÷ 12

16. 485 ÷ 92

17. 540 ÷ 61

18. 1,710 ÷ 32

19. 2,740 ÷ 67

20. 4,322 ÷ 81

21. 5,700 ÷ 58

22. 7,810 ÷ 44

23. 6,395 ÷ 84

24. 4,877 ÷ 74

25. 2,495 ÷ 48

26. 6,284 ÷ 93

For another example, see Set B on page 138.

| The question asks, "About how much?" So, an estimate is enough.

Use compatible numbers to estimate 159 ÷ 75. | Find compatible numbers for 159 and 75.

Think 16 can be divided evenly by 8.

160 and 80 are close to 159 and 75.

So, 160 and 80 are compatible numbers. | Divide.

160 ÷ 80 = 2.

So, Betty charged *about* $2 for each bracelet.

Check for reasonableness:
2 × 80 = 160 |

Problem Solving

MATHEMATICAL
PRACTICES

27. A high school volleyball team has made it to the state tournament. There are 586 students that want to go, and 32 students can fit on each bus. About how many buses are needed?

28. Each player contributed $3 for a gift for the head coach. The two assistant coaches each donated $10. If there were 22 players on the team, how much money did the team raise in all?

29. There are 135 comets that are visible from Earth every 20 years or less. What is an estimate of how many of these comets are seen each year?

30. Leon bought 8 CDs on sale for $88. The regular price for 8 CDs is $112. How much did Leon save per CD by buying them on sale?

31. Estimate the product for the following expression.

805 × 62

A 4,800

B 48,000

C 54,000

D 64,000

© 32. Use Structure Which property does the following equation illustrate?

2 + (11 + 19) = (2 + 11) + 19

A Commutative Property of Addition

B Associative Property of Addition

C Identity Property of Addition

D Commutative Property of Multiplication

33. Donald bought a clock radio. The radio weighs 18 ounces. Donald paid $12 less than the normal sales price. If the normal sales price was $38, how much did Donald spend on the radio?

© 34. Construct Arguments Autumn needs to estimate the quotient 817 ÷ 91. Explain how she can use compatible numbers to make a reasonable estimate.

Lesson
5-3

Common
Core

5.NBT.6 Find whole-number quotients of whole numbers with up to four-digit dividends and two-digit divisors, using strategies based on...the properties of operations... Illustrate and explain the calculation by using equations, rectangular arrays, and/or area models.

Connecting Models and Symbols

How can you use models and symbols to find quotients?

A theater has 375 seats arranged in rows with 15 seats in each row. How many rows are in this theater? Let R equal the number of rows.

Think: $15 \times R = 375$ or $375 \div 15 = R$

15 seats in each row.

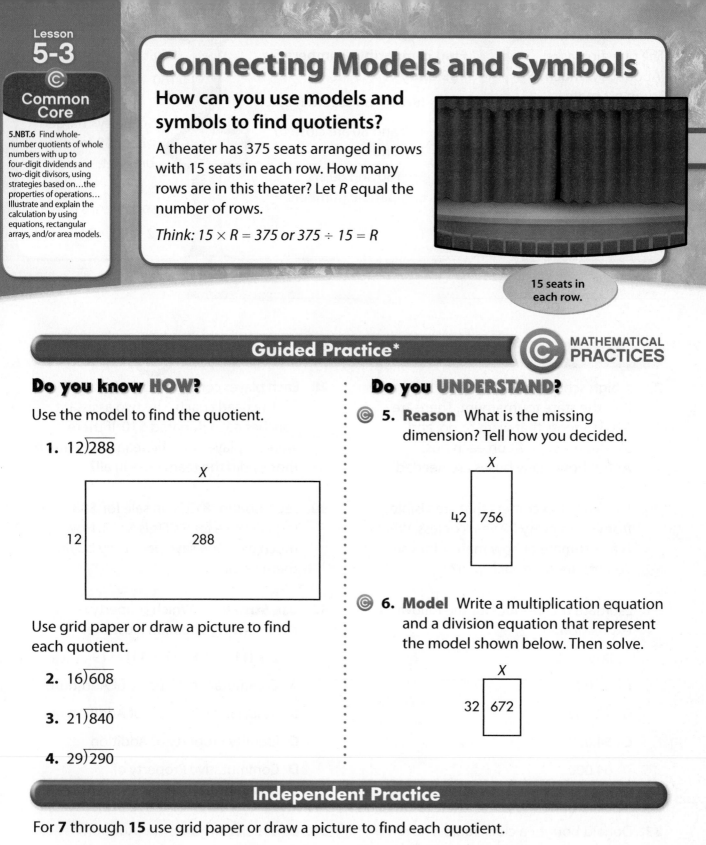

Guided Practice*

MATHEMATICAL PRACTICES

Do you know HOW?

Use the model to find the quotient.

1. $12\overline{)288}$

	X
12	288

Use grid paper or draw a picture to find each quotient.

2. $16\overline{)608}$

3. $21\overline{)840}$

4. $29\overline{)290}$

Do you UNDERSTAND?

5. Reason What is the missing dimension? Tell how you decided.

	X
42	756

6. Model Write a multiplication equation and a division equation that represent the model shown below. Then solve.

	X
32	672

Independent Practice

For **7** through **15** use grid paper or draw a picture to find each quotient.

7. $132 \div 11$

8. $690 \div 12$

9. $247 \div 19$

10. $189 \div 21$

11. $630 \div 14$

12. $304 \div 16$

13. $450 \div 11$

14. $600 \div 20$

15. $186 \div 31$

For another example, see Set C on page 138.

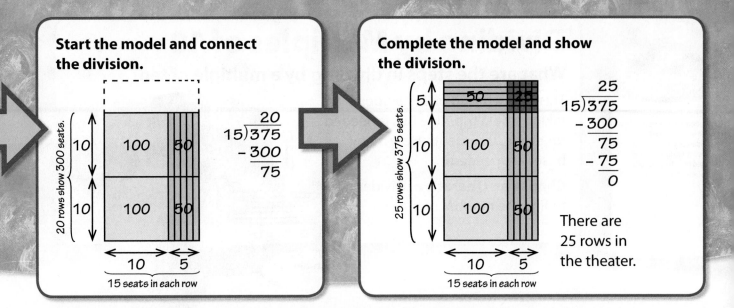

Start the model and connect the division.

20 rows show 300 seats.

10 | 100 | 50
10 | 100 | 50

10   5

15 seats in each row

$$\begin{array}{r} 20 \\ 15\overline{)375} \\ -300 \\ \hline 75 \end{array}$$

Complete the model and show the division.

25 rows show 375 seats.

5 | 50 | 25
10 | 100 | 50
10 | 100 | 50

10   5

15 seats in each row

$$\begin{array}{r} 25 \\ 15\overline{)375} \\ -300 \\ \hline 75 \\ -75 \\ \hline 0 \end{array}$$

There are 25 rows in the theater.

Problem Solving

16. A factory produces 264 chairs in a 12-hour shift. How many chairs does the factory produce per hour?

17. A hotel sets up tables for a conference for 286 people. If each table seats 11 people, how many tables will be needed?

18. Peter is driving 992 miles from Chicago to Dallas. His sister is driving 1,068 miles from Phoenix to Dallas. How much farther does she have to drive?

19. Mental Math Shannon biked in an endurance cycling race. She traveled 2,912 mi and biked about 95 miles each day. About how many days did it take her to complete the race?

20. Persevere The cost of each plane ticket for the Baltazar family's summer vacation is $329. If there are 7 family members, what is the total cost of the plane tickets?

21. Estimation A 969 acre wildlife preserve has 19 cheetahs. About how many acres does each cheetah have if each cheetah roams the same number of acres?

22. Twelve buses bring a total of 420 people to The Alhambra in Granada, Spain. Each bus carries the same number of people. How many people are on each bus?

23. Look for Patterns Carly is burning 1,200 minutes of music onto CDs for a road trip. If each CD holds 80 minutes, how many will she need to use?

80 Min.

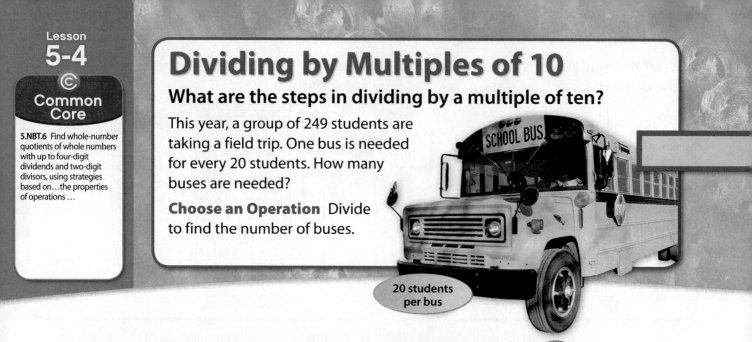

Dividing by Multiples of 10

What are the steps in dividing by a multiple of ten?

This year, a group of 249 students are taking a field trip. One bus is needed for every 20 students. How many buses are needed?

Choose an Operation Divide to find the number of buses.

20 students per bus

© Common Core

5.NBT.6 Find whole-number quotients of whole numbers with up to four-digit dividends and two-digit divisors, using strategies based on…the properties of operations …

Guided Practice*

© MATHEMATICAL PRACTICES

Do you know HOW?

In **1** through **6**, divide.

1. $30\overline{)345}$ **2.** $20\overline{)282}$

3. $50\overline{)467}$ **4.** $60\overline{)841}$

5. $40\overline{)413}$ **6.** $80\overline{)766}$

Do you UNDERSTAND?

7. In the example above, if only 137 students were going on the trip, how many buses would be needed?

© **8. Reason** In the example above, why is 12 buses a reasonable estimate?

Independent Practice

Leveled Practice Copy and complete.

9.
```
      5 R1▢
20)318
   2▢
   1▢
   1▢▢
   1▢
```

10.
```
      1▢ R 2
60)712
   6▢
   1▢▢
    6▢
    ▢2
```

11.
```
      1▢ R▢
30)328
   ▢▢
   ▢▢
    0
    2▢
```

12. $40\overline{)348}$ **13.** $70\overline{)618}$ **14.** $80\overline{)939}$

15. $697 \div 90$ **16.** $114 \div 30$ **17.** $766 \div 50$

18. $724 \div 60$ **19.** $841 \div 20$ **20.** $222 \div 30$

21. $936 \div 40$ **22.** $295 \div 20$ **23.** $479 \div 60$

For another example, see Set D on page 139.

Find 249 ÷ 20.

Estimate: 240 ÷ 20 = 12
Divide the tens.

$$20\overline{)249}$$
$$- 20$$
$$4$$

Divide   24 ÷ 20 = 1
Multiply 1 × 20 = 20
Subtract 24 − 20 = 4
Compare 4 < 20

Bring down the ones. Divide the ones.

$$20\overline{)249}$$
$$- 20$$
$$49$$
$$- 40$$
$$9$$

Divide   49 ÷ 20 = 2
Multiply 2 × 20 = 40
Subtract 49 − 40 = 9
Compare 9 < 20

Since the remainder is 9, one more bus is needed. A total of 13 buses are needed.

The answer is reasonable since 13 is close to the estimate, 12.

Problem Solving

MATHEMATICAL
PRACTICES

Use the chart to answer **24** through **26**.

24. Rita's family is moving from Grand Junction to Dallas. The van that is moving them averages 60 miles an hour. About how many hours does it take the family to reach their new home in Dallas?

Data		
Dallas, TX, to Grand Junction, CO	980 miles
Nashville, TN, to Norfolk, VA	670 miles
Charleston, SC, to Atlanta, GA	290 miles
Denver, CO, to Minneapolis, MN	920 miles
Little Rock, AR, to Chicago, IL	660 miles

25. A van driver ran into construction delays on her trip from Denver to Minneapolis. She averaged 50 miles an hour. About how long did the trip take?

26. Charlie has to pay a toll of $2 for every 30 miles on his trip from Charleston to Atlanta. How much money does Charlie pay in tolls?

27. Manchaca school district has 32,020 students, while the Saddle River school district has 56,212 students. How many more students are there in the Saddle River than in the Manchaca school district?

28. The Port Lavaca fishing pier is 3,200 feet long. If there is one person fishing every ten feet, then how many people are fishing from the pier?

ⓒ **29. Persevere** Each person on a boat ride pays $26 for a ticket. There are 63 passengers. How much money is collected from all the passengers?

   A $89

   B $504

   C $1,538

   D $1,638

ⓒ **30. Think About the Structure** What is the first step in finding 383 ÷ 30?

   A Regroup 8 tens as 80 ones

   B See how many are in the remainder

   C Regroup 3 hundreds as 30 tens

   D Multiply 3 by 38

Lesson
5-5

©
Common
Core

5.NBT.6 Find whole-number quotients of whole numbers with up to four-digit dividends and two-digit divisors, using strategies based on place value, the properties of operations …

1-Digit Quotients

What are the steps for dividing by 2-digit numbers?

A theater sold 428 tickets for a show. A section in this theater has 64 seats. How many sections must there be to seat all the ticket holders?

Choose an Operation Divide to find the total number of sections.

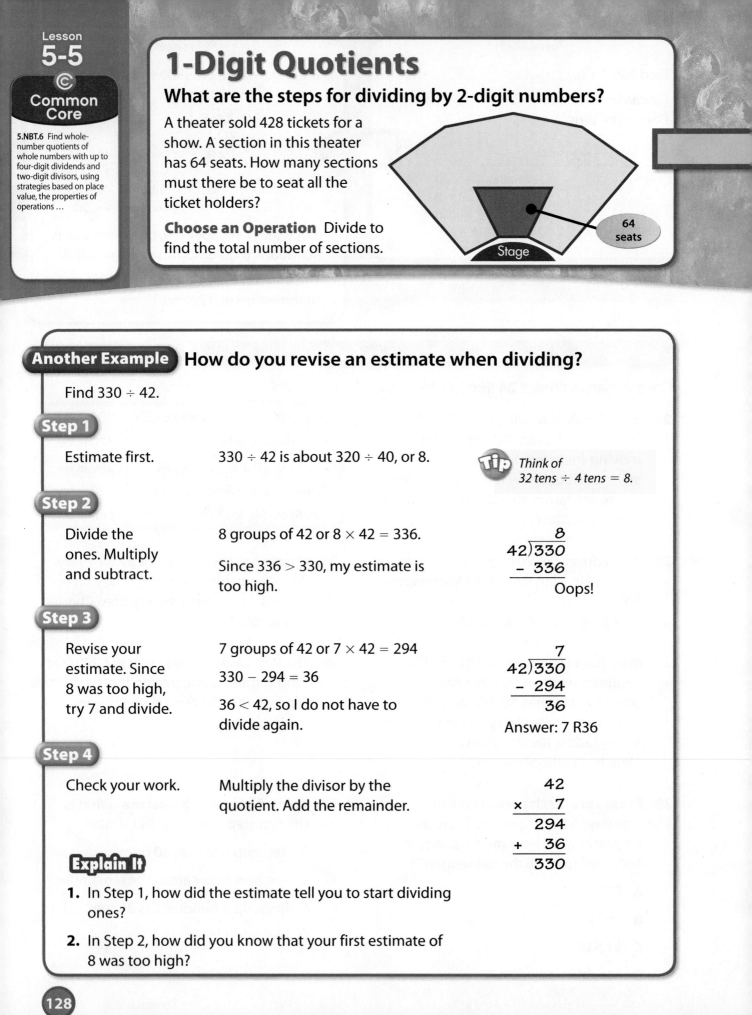

64 seats

Stage

Another Example **How do you revise an estimate when dividing?**

Find $330 \div 42$.

Step 1

Estimate first. $330 \div 42$ is about $320 \div 40$, or 8.

Tip *Think of 32 tens ÷ 4 tens = 8.*

Step 2

Divide the ones. Multiply and subtract.

8 groups of 42 or $8 \times 42 = 336$.

Since $336 > 330$, my estimate is too high.

$$\begin{array}{r} 8 \\ 42\overline{)330} \\ -\ 336 \\ \hline \text{Oops!} \end{array}$$

Step 3

Revise your estimate. Since 8 was too high, try 7 and divide.

7 groups of 42 or $7 \times 42 = 294$

$330 - 294 = 36$

$36 < 42$, so I do not have to divide again.

$$\begin{array}{r} 7 \\ 42\overline{)330} \\ -\ 294 \\ \hline 36 \end{array}$$

Answer: 7 R36

Step 4

Check your work.   Multiply the divisor by the quotient. Add the remainder.

$$\begin{array}{r} 42 \\ \times\quad 7 \\ \hline 294 \\ +\quad 36 \\ \hline 330 \end{array}$$

Explain It

1. In Step 1, how did the estimate tell you to start dividing ones?

2. In Step 2, how did you know that your first estimate of 8 was too high?

128

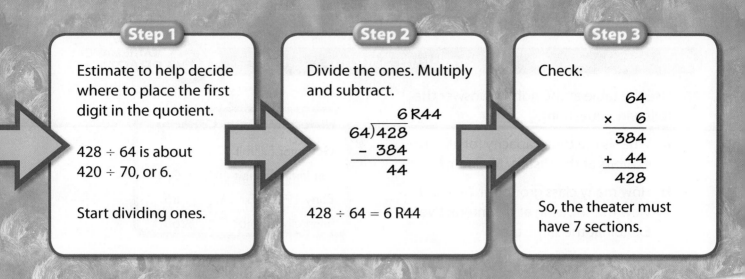

Estimate to help decide where to place the first digit in the quotient.

$428 \div 64$ is about $420 \div 70$, or 6.

Start dividing ones.

Divide the ones. Multiply and subtract.

$$\begin{array}{r} 6\ R44 \\ 64\overline{)428} \\ -\ 384 \\ \hline 44 \end{array}$$

$428 \div 64 = 6\ R44$

Check:

$$\begin{array}{r} 64 \\ \times\ \ 6 \\ \hline 384 \\ +\ \ 44 \\ \hline 428 \end{array}$$

So, the theater must have 7 sections.

Guided Practice*

MATHEMATICAL PRACTICES

Do you know HOW?

Copy and complete.

1. $12\overline{)115}$ R
  − ▦▦▦
  ▦

2. $31\overline{)243}$ R
  − ▦▦▦
  ▦▦

Do you UNDERSTAND?

ⓒ **3. Generalize** Can the remainder in either example be greater than the divisor? Why or why not?

4. In the example above, if the theater had sold 612 tickets, how many sections must it have?

Independent Practice

Leveled Practice Copy and complete.

5. R2
  $38\overline{)325}$
  − 3▦
  2▦

6. 7 R 9
  $52\overline{)403}$
  − ▦▦ 4
  9

7. R 7
  $74\overline{)693}$
  − 66▦
  ▦ 7

8. R
  $33\overline{)301}$
  − ▦▦▦
  ▦

In **9** through **24** divide.

9. $57\overline{)550}$ **10.** $29\overline{)254}$ **11.** $46\overline{)260}$ **12.** $56\overline{)528}$

13. $51\overline{)293}$ **14.** $19\overline{)119}$ **15.** $91\overline{)628}$ **16.** $40\overline{)180}$

17. $396 \div 42$ **18.** $275 \div 38$ **19.** $179 \div 22$ **20.** $345 \div 85$

21. $214 \div 28$ **22.** $748 \div 81$ **23.** $671 \div 79$ **24.** $476 \div 68$

25. Use the table at the right to answer the following questions.

a What is the total capacity for all four exhibits at the History Museum?

b How many class groups of 24 could view the showing at the Interactive Exhibit at the same time?

History Museum Capacity	
Governor Exhibit	68
Landmark Exhibit	95
Early 1900s Exhibit	85
Interactive Exhibit	260

26. Chen's band put on a concert at school. There were 720 people in the audience. Each ticket cost $8. The audience was seated in 12 sections. If each section had the same number of people, how many people were in each section?

27. Mrs. Dugan collects antiques. She bought 7 antique chairs for which she paid a total of $1050. Each chair was made with a different type of wood. If each chair cost the same amount, how much did each chair cost?

28. Mr. Nolan changes the oil in his car every 4,000 miles. He uses 3 quarts of oil each time. How many quarts of oil will he have used after 12,000 miles?

29. If you estimate 124 × 22 by rounding to the nearest ten, will you get an overestimate or an underestimate?

30. Twenty members of the photography club took 559 pictures. If they use memory cards that hold 85 pictures per card, how many cards will they use?

31. The annual music festival featured different posters for sale. The sale of jazz band posters brought in $1,240. If each poster was $20, how many were sold?

32. Construct Arguments Explain how you know the answer to the problem shown below has an error.

$$\frac{8 \text{ R}24}{16 \overline{)152}}$$
$$\frac{-128}{24}$$

33. Use Structure Rachel wanted to get 8 hours of sleep before a test. She went to bed at 9:00 P.M. and woke up at 6:00 A.M. How many more hours of sleep did Rachel get than the 8 hours she wanted?

A 3 more hours   **C** 1 more hour

B 9 more hours   **D** No more hours

34. Reason Explain why 0.2 and 0.02 are NOT equivalent.

35. Model In a large restaurant, there are 9 times as many chairs as tables. The restaurant is famous for its very spicy chili. If the restaurant has 360 chairs, how many tables are in the restaurant?

Algebra Connections

Completing Tables

Remember that multiplication and division have an inverse relationship.

Since $9 \times 7 = 63$, you also know:

$$63 \div 9 = 7$$

$$63 \div 7 = 9$$

You can use inverse relationships to help complete tables.

Example:

There are 4 quarts in a gallon. Complete the table.

gallons	1	3	8	■
quarts	4	12	■	40

You can multiply the number of gallons by 4 to find the number of quarts.

$8 \times 4 = 32$. So, 8 gallons = 32 quarts.

You can divide the number of quarts by 4 to find the number of gallons.

$40 \div 4 = 10$. So, 40 quarts = 10 gallons.

Copy and complete each table below.

1. Each box holds 5 pencils.

Pencils	15	30	35	40	45
Boxes	3	■	■	■	9

2. Each shelf has 10 books.

Shelves	2	3	4	■	■
Books	20	■	■	50	90

3. A frame holds 4 photos.

Frames	2	3	■	5	■
Photos	■	■	16	■	36

4. Each package has 8 markers.

Packages	2	4	5	■	■
Markers	■	■	■	72	80

5. Mallory swims 2 miles per day.

Days	1	3	■	10	■
Miles	■	■	16	■	60

6. Each week has 7 days.

Weeks	2	4	■	■	12
Days	■	■	35	63	■

© Common Core

5.NBT.6 Find whole-number quotients ... with ... two-digit divisors, using strategies based on ... the properties of operations...

2-Digit Quotients

How can you divide larger numbers?

So far, 467 tortillas have been made. These tortillas will be placed in packages of 15. How many complete packages will be filled?

Choose an Operation Divide to find the number of packages of tortillas.

15 tortillas per package

Guided Practice*

© **MATHEMATICAL PRACTICES**

Do you know HOW?

Copy and complete.

1. 47)985 R
   – ▯▯
   ▯▯

2. 33)678 R ▯▯
   – ▯▯
   ▯▯

For **3** and **4**, divide.

3. 16)298

4. 23)292

Do you UNDERSTAND?

© 5. **Communicate** In the problem above, why will 31 packages be filled instead of 32?

6. How many packages will 627 tortillas fill?

7. How do you decide where to place the first digit in the quotient for Exercises 1–4?

Independent Practice

Leveled Practice Copy and complete.

8. 36)584 R
   – ▯▯
   ▯▯
   – 1▯
   8

9. 45)981 R▯▯
   – ▯0
   1
   – ▯▯
   ▯▯

10. 56)674 R
   – ▯▯
   ▯▯▯
   – ▯▯▯
   ▯

In **11** through **22**, divide.

11. 76)864

12. 23)279

13. 63)710

14. 18)638

15. 48)582

16. 26)784

17. 13)989

18. 72)2,532

19. 4,328 ÷ 93

20. 678 ÷ 27

21. 980 ÷ 45

22. 717 ÷ 31

For another example, see Set E on page 139.

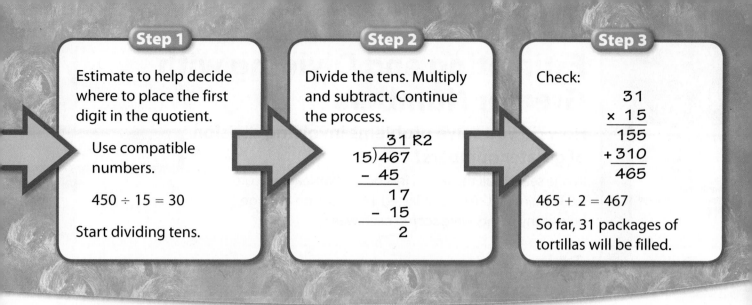

Step 1

Estimate to help decide where to place the first digit in the quotient.

Use compatible numbers.

$450 \div 15 = 30$

Start dividing tens.

Step 2

Divide the tens. Multiply and subtract. Continue the process.

$$
\begin{array}{r}
31 \text{ R2} \\
15\overline{)467} \\
-\ 45 \\
\hline
17 \\
-\ 15 \\
\hline
2
\end{array}
$$

Step 3

Check:

$$
\begin{array}{r}
31 \\
\times\ 15 \\
\hline
155 \\
+310 \\
\hline
465
\end{array}
$$

$465 + 2 = 467$

So far, 31 packages of tortillas will be filled.

Problem Solving

 MATHEMATICAL PRACTICES

©ⓒ 23. Construct Arguments If you are asked to find $621 \div 59$, how do you know the quotient will be greater than 10 before you actually divide?

24. Julita bought a sandwich for $3.50 and a glass of juice for $1.75. The tax was $0.42. She paid with a $10 bill. How much change did she get?

©ⓒ 25. Critique Reasoning An outdoor concert company is putting on 12 concerts this summer. Each concert is sold out. The company sold a total of 972 seats. How many people will attend each performance?

  A 8   **C** 80

  B 79   **D** 81

©ⓒ 26. Look for Patterns Julio spends about $\frac{1}{2}$ hour reading every night. He owns 8 science fiction books, 12 mystery books, and 7 history books. He wants to add enough books to his collection to have 40 books. How many more books does he need?

27. There are 120 minutes in 2 hours. How many minutes are there in 15 hours?

28. What compatible numbers can you use to estimate $803 \div 86$?

29. One of the Thorny Devil lizard's favorite foods is ants. It can eat up to 45 ants per minute. How long would it take it to eat 540 ants?

  A 9 minutes

  B 10 minutes

  C 12 minutes

  D 15 minutes

30. Decide if each statement is true or false. Explain.

  a $710 \div 20$ is greater than 30.

  b $821 \div 40$ is less than 20.

  c $300 \div 15$ is exactly 20.

31. Braedy had $5.00 when she left the county fair. She spent $11.00 on her ticket, and she bought lunch for $6.00. After lunch, she spent $17.00 on games and rides. How much money did Braedy bring to the county fair?

Lesson
5-7

©
Common
Core

5.NBT.6 Find whole-number quotients of whole numbers … using strategies based on place value, the properties of operations, and/or the relationship between multiplication and division …

Estimating and Dividing with Greater Numbers

How do you solve problems involving division of greater numbers?

In one season, all the teams in a basketball league scored 7,832 points. If the season lasted 14 weeks, on average, how many points were scored each week?

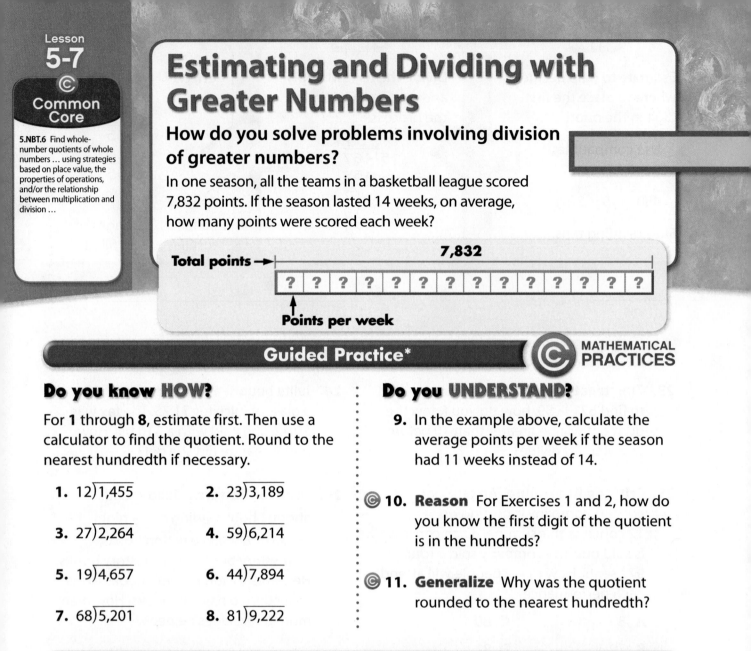

Total points → | 7,832 |
? ? ? ? ? ? ? ? ? ? ? ? ? ?
↑
Points per week

Guided Practice*

MATHEMATICAL PRACTICES

Do you know HOW?

For **1** through **8**, estimate first. Then use a calculator to find the quotient. Round to the nearest hundredth if necessary.

1. $12\overline{)1,455}$ **2.** $23\overline{)3,189}$

3. $27\overline{)2,264}$ **4.** $59\overline{)6,214}$

5. $19\overline{)4,657}$ **6.** $44\overline{)7,894}$

7. $68\overline{)5,201}$ **8.** $81\overline{)9,222}$

Do you UNDERSTAND?

9. In the example above, calculate the average points per week if the season had 11 weeks instead of 14.

© **10. Reason** For Exercises 1 and 2, how do you know the first digit of the quotient is in the hundreds?

© **11. Generalize** Why was the quotient rounded to the nearest hundredth?

Independent Practice

For **12** through **31**, estimate first. Then use a calculator to find the quotient. Round to the nearest hundredth if necessary.

12. $4,457 \div 31$ **13.** $5,232 \div 47$ **14.** $9,137 \div 84$ **15.** $3,201 \div 68$

16. $5,792 \div 51$ **17.** $7,274 \div 68$ **18.** $8,728 \div 83$ **19.** $8,415 \div 81$

20. $3,972 \div 32$ **21.** $6,281 \div 24$ **22.** $8,264 \div 35$ **23.** $5,423 \div 71$

24. $4,896 \div 71$ **25.** $2,482 \div 25$ **26.** $5,016 \div 50$ **27.** $2,915 \div 52$

28. $6,321 \div 84$ **29.** $9,852 \div 11$ **30.** $3,233 \div 77$ **31.** $8,932 \div 92$

Estimate

7,832 ÷ 14 is close to 7,500 ÷ 15, or 500.

The quotient should be close to 500.

Use a Calculator

Dividing on a calculator gives 559.428 ... , or 559 R6.

÷   =

7,832 ÷ 14 = 559.428 ... .

Round 559.428 to the nearest hundredth—559.43.

Since 559.43 is close to the estimate—500, it is reasonable.

About 559 points were scored during each week of the basketball season.

Problem Solving

MATHEMATICAL PRACTICES

32. The city of Linton is holding a chess tournament. Use the data at the right to answer the problems.

   a The total student entry fees paid were $3,105. How many students participated?

   b There are about ten times as many students as adults registered for the tournament. About how many adults are registered?

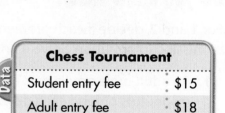

Chess Tournament	
Student entry fee	$15
Adult entry fee	$18
Reserve a chess board	$12

33. Give three factors whose product is about 10,000.

34. There are 12 inches in 1 foot. How many inches are there in 120 feet?

35. There are 1,185 possible words that can be used for the spelling bee. This number is 15 times more than will be used in the contest. How many words will be used in the contest?

   A 7.9 words   **C** 709 words

   B 79 words   **D** 790 words

36. Reasonableness The Arches National Park in Utah covers more than 73,000 acres and has 2,000 stone arches. A 40-mile road in the park takes visitors past most of the arches. If a visitor drove the entire paved road, about how many arches would he or she see per mile?

   A 20   **B** 26   **C** 50   **D** 75

37. Model Tabitha's class makes a flash card for each of the 1,185 words. The work of making the flash cards is divided equally among 5 teams. How many flash cards will each team need to make?

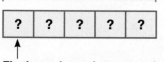

1,185 words

| ? | ? | ? | ? | ? |

Flash cards each team makes

38. Darci wants to buy a computer that costs $1,236. She works at the grocery store where she earns $11 an hour. How many hours will she have to work to earn enough money to purchase the computer?

Lesson
5-8

Common Core

5.NBT.6 Find whole-number quotients with up to four-digit dividends and two-digit divisors, using strategies based on…the properties of operations… Illustrate and explain the calculation by using equations…and/or area models.

Missing or Extra Information

A 1920 antique bicycle that had once belonged to 2 owners recently sold for $850. A 2008 lightweight mountain bike recently sold for 3 times as much. What was the cost of the 2008 bike?

$?

Guided Practice*

MATHEMATICAL PRACTICES

Do you know HOW?

For **1** and **2**, decide if each problem has extra or missing information. Solve if possible.

1. An adult male gorilla eats about 40 pounds of food each day. An adult female gorilla eats about half as much. How many pounds of food does an adult male gorilla eat in one week?

2. Lacey is buying dried fruit to feed her pet bird. How much will it cost to feed the bird for one month?

Do you UNDERSTAND?

3. Draw a diagram to show what you know and want to find in Problem 1.

4. **Be Precise** Why is it important to find the extra or missing information before solving a problem?

5. **Generalize** Write a real-world problem that does not include all of the information to solve it. Under the problem, write the missing information.

Independent Practice

MATHEMATICAL PRACTICES

For **6** and **7**, decide if each problem has extra or missing information. Solve if possible.

6. Eli has played 5 baseball games so far this season. How many runs did he score if he scored 2 runs each game for the first 4 games?

7. Sonja posted 45 band concert flyers in 2 days. Over the next 2 days, Elsie posted 60 flyers, and Frank posted 30 flyers. How many flyers did the 3 students post altogether?

Applying Math Practices

- What am I asked to find?
- What else can I try?
- How are quantities related?
- How can I explain my work?
- How can I use math to model the problem?
- Can I use tools to help?
- Is my work precise?
- Why does this work?
- How can I generalize?

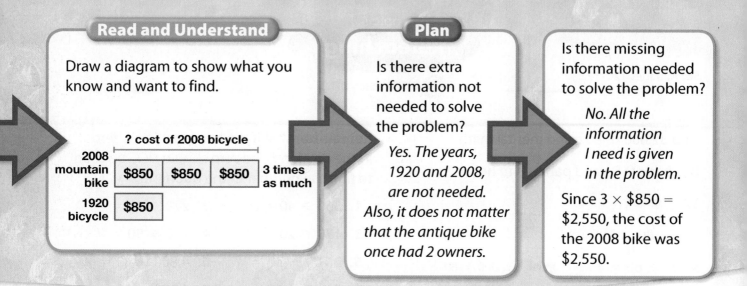

Draw a diagram to show what you know and want to find.

? cost of 2008 bicycle

| 2008 mountain bike | $850 | $850 | $850 | 3 times as much |
| 1920 bicycle | $850 | | | |

Plan

Is there extra information not needed to solve the problem?

Yes. The years, 1920 and 2008, are not needed. Also, it does not matter that the antique bike once had 2 owners.

Is there missing information needed to solve the problem?

No. All the information I need is given in the problem.

Since 3 × $850 = $2,550, the cost of the 2008 bike was $2,550.

8. Mrs. Torance has invited 16 people to a party. What information is missing if she wants to serve enough submarine sandwiches at her party?

Each sub feeds 3 children or 2 adults

9. Kara and her 4 friends went camping. Each day they hiked 2 miles before lunch and 3 miles after lunch. How many total miles did all the girls hike on their camping trip? Provide possible information needed to solve the problem, then solve it.

© 10. **Use Tools** Fox Meadow Farm boards show horses. Fifteen of their horses are in the arena. The other 21 horses are in the barn. How many horses board at the farm? Draw a picture and write an equation to solve.

11. Jun and his sister visited Texas State Aquarium in Corpus Christi. While there, they learned that 1 catfish produces 40 eggs. How many eggs will 60 catfish produce?

12. Sylvia had $20 to spend at the circus. She spent $5.00 on admission. During lunch, Sylvia bought a hot dog and drink for $6.50. How much money did Sylvia have left to spend after lunch?

13. Greg bought a sandwich and a drink at Dunstan's Deli. He paid $4.50. Which sandwich and drink did he buy?

Dunstan's Deli	
Chicken	$4.25
Roast Beef	$3.75
Tuna	$3.50
Milk	$0.60
Juice	$0.75

14. Roses are on sale at the market 2 for $1.00. Mindy has $20.00. If she buys 16 roses, how much will they cost?

© 15. **Communicate** There are 24 hours in one day. How can you use addition to find the number of hours in one week? How can you use multiplication?

© 16. **Reason** One decade equals 10 years and one century equals 100 years. Are there more years in 11 decades or 1 century?

Set A, pages 120–121

Find 32,000 ÷ 80 using mental math.

Use basic facts and patterns to help.

32 ÷ 8 = 4

320 ÷ 80 = 4

3,200 ÷ 80 = 40

32,000 ÷ 80 = 400

Think 32,000 ÷ 80
is the same as
3,200 tens ÷ 8 tens.

Remember that if the basic fact has a zero in the dividend, the zero should NOT be used to find the number in the quotient.

1. 360 ÷ 40 =   **2.** 270 ÷ 90 =

3. 180 ÷ 20 =   **4.** 750 ÷ 50 =

5. 2,100 ÷ 30 =   **6.** 4,800 ÷ 80 =

7. 5,400 ÷ 60 =   **8.** 6,300 ÷ 90 =

9. 30,000 ÷ 50 =   **10.** 21,000 ÷ 30 =

11. 72,000 ÷ 80 =   **12.** 81,000 ÷ 90 =

Set B, pages 122–123

Estimate 364 ÷ 57.

Use compatible numbers and patterns to divide.

364 ÷ 57

360 ÷ 60 = 6

So, 364 ÷ 57 is about 6.

Remember that compatible numbers are numbers that are easy to compute in your head.

1. 168 ÷ 45   **2.** 525 ÷ 96

3. 379 ÷ 63   **4.** 234 ÷ 72

5. $613 ÷ 93   **6.** $748 ÷ 92

Set C, pages 124–125

A farmer has 120 eggs. How many dozen eggs is this?

Write an equation for the problem.

120 ÷ 12 = d or 12 × d = 120

Use an array to model the equation.

Add groups of 12 until you have a sum of 120. For each group of 12 you add, add 1 to the quotient.

| 12 | 12 | 12 | 12 | 12 | 12 | 12 | 12 | 12 | 12 |

d

It takes 10 groups of 12 to make 120, so 120 ÷ 12 = 10

Remember that in a division array, the number of groups represents the quotient.

Use an array or area model to solve.

1. 63 ÷ 21 =   **2.** 112 ÷ 14 =

3. 243 ÷ 27 =   **4.** 192 ÷ 16 =

5. 143 ÷ 11 =   **6.** 62 ÷ 31 =

7. 130 ÷ 26 =   **8.** 270 ÷ 18 =

Find 461 ÷ 50.

Estimate to decide where to put the first digit in the quotient.

Use compatible numbers. 450 ÷ 50 = 9

Start dividing the ones. Multiply and subtract. Compare the remainder to the divisor.

$$
\begin{array}{r}
9\,R11 \\
50\overline{)461} \\
-450 \\
\hline
11
\end{array}
$$

To check, compare the quotient to your estimate.

Remember that if the product of your first quotient and the divisor is larger than the dividend, your estimate is too high. Try dividing again with the next lower number.

1. $20\overline{)428}$ **2.** $30\overline{)547}$

3. $40\overline{)387}$ **4.** $50\overline{)653}$

5. $60\overline{)589}$ **6.** $70\overline{)912}$

7. $80\overline{)698}$ **8.** $90\overline{)849}$

Find 789 ÷ 19.

Estimate first.

800 ÷ 20 = 40.

Divide the tens. Multiply, subtract, and compare.

Bring down the ones. Divide the ones. Multiply, subtract, and compare. Check the quotient with your estimate.

$$
\begin{array}{r}
41\,R10 \\
19\overline{)789} \\
-76 \\
\hline
29 \\
-19 \\
\hline
10
\end{array}
$$

Remember that you can check your answer by multiplying the quotient by the divisor, and then adding the remainder to that product. The sum should be your dividend.

1. $74\overline{)389}$ **2.** $28\overline{)119}$

3. $36\overline{)234}$ **4.** $38\overline{)792}$

5. $42\overline{)523}$ **6.** $47\overline{)5,190}$

7. $58\overline{)7,211}$ **8.** $12\overline{)3,549}$

Decide if the problem has missing or extra information. Solve if possible.

Kay has 3 folders. Each folder has 6 pockets for subjects. How many sheets of paper are in each folder?

What you know: 3 folders, 6 pockets per folder.

What you want to find: How many sheets of paper in each folder.

Can you solve? No, it does not mention paper being in folders or pockets.

Remember that some problems have too much information, but can be solved.

1. Mario has $40.20. He went to the store and bought apples, cereal, and bread. How much change did he get back?

2. Alanna bought 6 books. Each book costs $13 and each bookmark cost $2. How much did she spend on books?

1. The city of Seattle has 1,242 law enforcement officers in the police department. If the officers are divided into groups of 18, about how many officers will be in each group? (5-7)

   A 30

   B 60

   C 130

   D 700

2. Which of the following is the best way to estimate 487 ÷ 67 with compatible numbers? (5-2)

   A 480 divided by 70

   B 485 divided by 60

   C 490 divided by 60

   D 490 divided by 70

3. The carnival committee has purchased 985 small prizes. If the prizes are to be divided among the 20 game booths, how many prizes will each booth have and how many prizes will be left over? (5-4)

   A 44 per booth with 5 left over

   B 49 per booth with none left over

   C 49 per booth with 5 left over

   D 490 per booth with 5 left over

4. Which of the following is another way to think of 27,000 ÷ 30? (5-1)

   A 27 tens ÷ 30 tens

   B 27 tens ÷ 3 tens

   C 270 tens ÷ 3 tens

   D 2,700 tens ÷ 3 tens

5. The table shows how many employees are going to a conference. If 27 employees can sit in each row of chairs, how many rows of chairs will they need? (5-6)

Group	Number signed up to attend
Accounting	137
Marketing	146
Central Office	41

   A 12

   B 14

   C 54

   D 324

6. Shady Rivers summer camp has 188 campers this week. If there are 22 campers to each cabin, what is the least number of cabins needed? (5-5)

   A 7

   B 8

   C 9

   D 10

7. Alberto is saving for an item that costs $384. If he saves $30 each week, how long will it take him to buy the item? (5-4)

8. The lengths of two canals are given in the table. About how many times as long as the Chesapeake and Delaware Canal is the Erie Canal? Write and solve an equation to show your estimate. (5-2)

Ship Canal	Length (in miles)
Chesapeake and Delaware Canal	14
Erie Canal	363

9. Mrs. Reiss has 264 crayons for her art class of 22 students. How many crayons, c, will each student get if they are divided equally? Use the area model to help. (5-3)

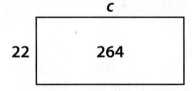

10. About 300,000 Mexican Free-tailed Bats occupy the caves at Carlsbad Caverns during the summer months. Each bat can eat about 800 insects in one hour. What other information is needed to find the number of insects a bat can eat each day? (5-8)

11. A company ordered 384 note pads. If there are 48 note pads in each box, how many boxes were ordered? (5-5)

12. Morning Star Farm purchased 2,400 apple trees. If 80 trees can be planted on each acre of land, how many acres will be needed to plant all the trees? (5-1)

13. The cost to rent a lodge for a reunion is $975. If 65 people attend, and pay the same price each, how much will each person pay? (5-6)

14. Write a multiplication equation and a division equation that represent the model shown below. (5-3)

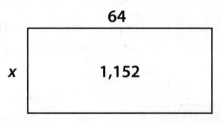

15. Charles burns 4,350 calories hiking 15 miles of the Appalachian Trail. How many calories does the he burn every mile? Estimate first and then find the exact answer. (5-7)

Use the table for **1** through **5**.

School Supplies Sold					
School Supplies	Paper	Book Bags	Notebooks	Pens	Pencils
Number Sold	616	64	432	572	784

1. Pencils are packaged 16 pencils to a box. How many boxes of pencils did the store sell?

2. The total sales of bookbags was $1,664. How much did each bookbag cost?

3. Paper is delivered in cartons of 48 packs of paper each. If the store orders 624 packs of paper, how many cartons will they receive?

4. Notebooks are packaged in sets of 15 notebooks each. How many complete sets of notebooks did the store sell?

5. The store wants to order at least as many pens as they sold. If the pens are sold in boxes of 24 pens each, how many boxes should they order? Explain how you found your answer.

6. The total sale of notebooks was $6,048. How much does each individual notebook cost?

7. School policy states that on field trips, there should be one adult chaperone for every 9 students. If 164 students are attending, how many adult chaperones are needed? Explain how you found your answer.

Topic
6

Multiplying Decimals

▼ The fastest growing flowering plant is the *Hesperoyucca Whipplei.* How many centimeters did one of these plants grow in 7 days? You will find out in Lesson 6-5.

Review What You Know!

Vocabulary

Choose the best term from the box.

- equivalent fractions
- mixed numbers
- factors
- product

1. In the equation 5 × 5 = 25, the number 25 is the __?__ and the digits 5 and 5 are __?__.

2. __?__ have a whole number and a fraction.

3. Fractions that name the same part of a whole are __?__.

Multiplying and Dividing

Find each product.

4. 58 × 10   **5.** 58 × 100   **6.** 58 × 1,000

Find each quotient.

7. 24 ÷ 8   **8.** 240 ÷ 8   **9.** 240 ÷ 80

Fractions

Write each quotient as a fraction.

10. 5 ÷ 18   **11.** 5 ÷ 6   **12.** 9 ÷ 12

Using Number Lines

© **Writing to Explain** Write an answer for the question.

340   350

13. How can you use this number line to round 347 to the nearest ten?

Topic Essential Question
- What are the standard procedures for estimating and finding products involving decimals?

Interactive Learning

Pose the problem. Start each lesson by working together to solve problems. It will help you make sense of math.

Applying Math Practices

- What am I asked to find?
- What else can I try?
- How are quantities related?
- How can I explain my work?
- How can I use math to model the problem?
- Can I use tools to help?
- Is my work precise?
- Why does this work?
- How can I generalize?

Lesson 6-1

© **Look for Patterns** Solve. Draw pictures to help you see the patterns.

David has a coin collection made up of 10 nickels, 10 dimes, and 10 quarters. How much are his coins worth? What would be the total value of each type of coin if he had 100 of each? 1,000 of each?

Lesson 6-2

© **Reasonableness** Solve. All you need is an estimate.

Mrs. Cash made the list shown at the right for grocery shopping. Will $50 cover the total cost? Tell how you decided.

Mrs. Cash's Grocery List

Item	Price	Amount needed	Estimated Cost	Actual Cost
Bread	$2.39 per loaf	4 loaves		
Chopped Meat	$3.89 per pound	3 pounds		
Eggs	$2.10 per dozen	2 dozen		
Cheese	$4.70 per package	3 packages		
Milk	$2.90 per gallon	2 gallons		
		Total cost:		

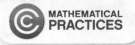
MATHEMATICAL
PRACTICES

Lesson 6-3

ⓒ **Reasoning** Use number sense and estimation to complete these problems.

Think about the size of the factors to complete these problems. Be prepared to explain your reasoning.

For each of these problems, the correct digits in the product are given, but the product may be rounded. Think about the size of each factor to decide where the decimal point should be in the product. Write the decimal point.	For each of these problems, use number sense to write a decimal that makes each statement correct. There may be more than one correct answer.
1) 7.86 x 16 = 12576	5) ___ x 0.92 is about 50
2) 0.98 x 0.95 = 93	6) 24.6 x ___ is about 12
3) 1.06 x 1.6 = 17	7) ___ x 2.5 is about 20
4) 2.43 x 7.05 = 1713	8) 0.8 x ___ is about 0.75

Lesson 6-4

ⓒ **Use Tools** Solve using grid paper and pencil.

Phara is attaching 3 planks of wood together end-to-end to begin making a fence. Each plank is 0.45 meters long. What is the total length of the wood? Use the grid paper to find the answer. Record your work with paper and pencil.

Lesson 6-5

ⓒ **Generalize** Solve. Use the data shown.

Four cars travel at different rates. If each car maintains its speed, how far will each travel in 3 minutes?

Distances Traveled

Car	1 minute	3 minutes	5 minutes
1	1.3 km		
2	0.75 km		
3	2.15 km		
4	1.8 km		

Lesson 6-6

ⓒ **Generalize** Solve any way you choose. Use the data shown.

Suppose you are going to make fruit salad. About how much will each kind of fruit cost?

Item	Price per pound	Number of pounds	Estimated Costs	Exact Costs	Practical Answers
Apples	$2.29	3.2			
Pears	$1.89	4.1			
Bananas	$0.89	4.9			
Strawberries	$2.99	2.3			

Lesson 6-7

ⓒ **Model** Solve any way you choose. Show your work.

Trey signed up for 120 hours of saxophone lessons. He meets with his music teacher for the same amount of time each Monday and Wednesday for 30 weeks. How long is each lesson?

Common
Core

5.NBT.2 Explain patterns in the number of zeros of the product...and...in the placement of the decimal point when a decimal is multiplied...by a power of 10. Use whole-number exponents to denote powers of 10. Also 5.NBT.1, 5.NBT.7

Multiplying Decimals by 10, 100, or 1,000

$0.45 per lb

What is the rule for multiplying decimals by 10, 100, or 1,000?

A baker needs to purchase 10 lb of pecans and 100 lb of flour. Recall that $10 = 10^1$ and $100 = 10^2$. How much will the baker spend for each ingredient?

Choose an Operation Multiply to join equal groups.

$2.89 per lb

Guided Practice*

MATHEMATICAL
PRACTICES

Do you know HOW?

In **1** through **6**, use mental math to find each product.

1. 0.009×10 **2.** 4.5×10

3. 3.1×10^3 **4.** 7.4×10^1

5. 0.062×100 **6.** 1.24×10^3

Do you UNDERSTAND?

7. **Look for Patterns** Find the product of 5.8×10^3.

8. How much will the baker spend if he buys 10 lb of flour? 1,000 lb of flour? Remember to use powers of 10.

Independent Practice

In **9** through **36**, use mental math to find each product.

9. 4.23×1 **10.** 4.23×10 **11.** 4.23×100 **12.** 4.23×10^3

13. 0.0867×10 **14.** 0.0867×10^2 **15.** 0.0867×1 **16.** $0.0867 \times 1,000$

17. 63.7×10^1 **18.** $56.37 \times 1,000$ **19.** 0.365×100 **20.** $5.02 \times 1,000$

21. $94.6 \times 1,000$ **22.** 0.9463×100 **23.** 0.678×10^1 **24.** 681.7×100

25. 4.3×10 **26.** 0.32×100 **27.** 5.1×100 **28.** $1.02 \times 1,000$

29. 0.004×10^3 **30.** 0.001×10 **31.** 6.02×10^2 **32.** 5.07×10

33. 0.063×100 **34.** $7.25 \times 1,000$ **35.** 19.212×100 **36.** 0.62×10

*For another example, see Set A on page 162.

Use the patterns in this table to find 0.45×10^2 and 2.89×10^1.

Multiply by		Examples
Standard Form	Exponential Form	
10	10^1	$0.45 \times 10^1 = 4.5$
100	10^2	$0.45 \times 10^2 = 45$
1,000	10^3	$0.45 \times 10^3 = 450$

So, $0.45 \times 10^2 = 45$
and $2.89 \times 10^1 = 28.9$.

The flour will cost $45.00, and the pecans will cost $28.90.

If 100 lb or 1,000 lb of pecans needed to be purchased, the pattern can be continued to find the cost.

$2.89 \times 10^2 = 289$

$2.89 \times 10^3 = 2,890$

So, 100 lb of pecans would cost $289. 1,000 lb of pecans would cost $2,890.

Problem Solving

© **MATHEMATICAL PRACTICES**

© **Look for Patterns** The table at the right shows the coins saved by Tina and her sister for one year.

37. Find the total value of each type of coin the girls have saved.

38. Find the total value for the coins saved by the sisters.

© **39. Persevere** The principal of Mountain Middle School has a big glass jar of marbles. The empty jar weighs 40.5 ounces, and each of the 1,000 marbles weighs 1.25 ounces. Find the total weight in ounces of the marbles.

Type of Coin	Number Saved
	1,000
	100
	1,000
	10

© **40. Construct Arguments** Marcia and David each multiplied 5.6×10 and 0.721×100. Marcia got 0.56 and 7.21 for her products. David got 56 and 72.1 for his products. Which student multiplied correctly? How do you know?

© **42. Structure** In which of the following equations does $n = 1,000$?

A $n \times 0.426 = 42.6$　　**C** $n \times 100 = 630$

B $7.078 \times n = 7,078$　　**D** $5.9 \times n = 0.59$

41. The Parents' Club is trying to decide on favors for International Night. They will need 100 items, and they have a budget of $250. They can choose from 100 baseball hats at $2.45 each, 100 sports bottles at $2.50 each, or 100 flags at $2.75 each. Which item(s) can they afford to buy?

Lesson
6-2

Common
Core

5.NBT.7 …Multiply…
decimals to hundredths…
using strategies based on
place value…the properties
of operations…

Estimating the Product of a Decimal and a Whole Number

What are some ways to estimate products with decimals?

A planner for a wedding needs to buy 16 pounds of sliced cheddar cheese. About how much will the cheese cost?

Estimate 2.15×16.

$2.15 per pound

Another Example **How can you estimate products of decimals that are less than 1?**

You already know how to estimate products of whole numbers using rounding and compatible numbers. You can use the same methods to estimate products with decimals.

Manuel found the total distance he walks to and from school is equal to 0.75 mile. If Manuel walks to and from school 184 days in one year, about how many total miles will he walk?

Using rounding

184×0.75

$200 \times 0.8 = 160.0$

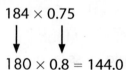 *Be sure to place the decimal point correctly.*

Using compatible numbers

184×0.75

$180 \times 0.8 = 144.0$

Compatible numbers are close to the actual numbers and are easy to multiply.

Since the compatible numbers are closer to the actual numbers than the rounded numbers, that estimate is closer to the actual product.

Manuel will walk about 144 miles to and from school in one year.

Guided Practice*

MATHEMATICAL PRACTICES

Do you know HOW?

In **1** through **6**, estimate each product using rounding or compatible numbers.

1. 0.87×412 **2.** 104×0.33

3. 9.02×80 **4.** 0.54×24

5. 33.05×200 **6.** 0.79×51

Do you UNDERSTAND?

© **7. Reasonableness** How can estimating be helpful before finding an actual product?

8. About how much money would have to be spent on 18 pounds of cheese if the price is $3.95 per pound?

For another example, see Set A on page 162.

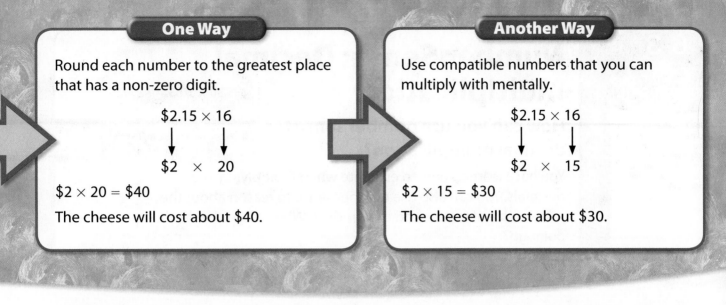

One Way
Round each number to the greatest place that has a non-zero digit.

$$\$2.15 \times 16$$

$$\$2 \quad \times \quad 20$$

$\$2 \times 20 = \$40$

The cheese will cost about $40.

Another Way
Use compatible numbers that you can multiply with mentally.

$$\$2.15 \times 16$$

$$\$2 \quad \times \quad 15$$

$\$2 \times 15 = \$30$

The cheese will cost about $30.

Independent Practice

Estimate each product.

9. 0.12×5

10. 45.3×4

11. 99.2×82

12. 37×0.93

13. 0.667×4

14. 0.6×184

15. 25×0.37

16. 0.904×75

Problem Solving

MATHEMATICAL
PRACTICES

For **17** and **18**, use the chart.

17. About how much money does Stan need to buy 5 T-shirts and 10 buttons?

18. Pat has $55. Does she have enough money to buy 4 T-shirts?

Souvenir	Cost
Button	$1.95
T-Shirt	$12.50

19. Think About the Structure You want to estimate 0.67×85. Which way will give you an estimate that is closest to the actual product?

A Round 0.67 to 1.0 and 85 to 90, multiply.

B Round 0.67 to 0.7 and 85 to 90, multiply.

C Round 0.67 to 70 and 85 to 80, multiply.

D Round 0.67 to 1.0 and 85 to 80, multiply.

20. Dentalia shells were used by some Native American tribes to make jewelry. Each dentalia shell is 1.25 inches long. If a necklace had been made with 18 dentalia shells, about how long was this necklace? Explain your estimate.

21. Reasonableness Will the actual product of 7.69×5 be greater than or less than its estimate of 8×5? Why?

22. If $n \times 4.16$ is about 200, what is a reasonable estimate for n?

Lesson
6-3

Common
Core

5.NBT.7 ... Multiply ...
decimals to hundredths,
using ... strategies based
on place value ... relate
the strategy to a written
method and explain the
reasoning used.

Number Sense: Decimal Multiplication

How can you use number sense for decimal multiplication?

You have learned how to estimate when multiplying with decimals. You can also use number sense to reason about the relative size of factors and the product. Where does the decimal point go?

$45.30 \times 0.55 = 2492

↑

What happened to the decimal point?

Guided Practice*

Do you know HOW?

Use number sense to decide where the decimal point belongs in the product. Tell the place.

1. $5 \times 3.4 = 17$

2. $3.1 \times 6.2 = 1922$

3. $0.6 \times 0.4 = 24$

Do you UNDERSTAND?

The decimal point in each of the products below MAY be in the wrong place. Use number sense to decide. If it is incorrect, give the correct product.

4. $7.8 \times 0.3 = 23.4$

5. $12 \times 4.8 = 57.6$

6. $0.6 \times 0.7 = 0.042$

Independent Practice

MATHEMATICAL PRACTICES

Ⓒ **Reason** For **7** through **11** the product is shown without the decimal point. Use number sense to place the decimal point appropriately.

7. $5.01 \times 3 = 1503$

8. $6.22 \times 3 = 1866$

9. $0.9 \times 0.9 = 81$

10. $1.8 \times 1.9 = 342$

11. $6 \times 5.01 = 3006$

For **12** through **16** tell whether or not the decimal point has been placed correctly in the product. If not, rewrite the product with the decimal point correctly placed.

12. $5.23 \times 6.4 = 3.3472$

13. $0.05 \times 12.4 = 6.2$

14. $6.99 \times 21.6 = 1,509.84$

15. $1.1 \times 13.8 = 1.518$

16. $8.06 \times 3 = 241.8$

Think about the relative size of the factors.

Multiplying a number by a decimal less than 1 gives a product less than the other factor.

Since 0.55 is less than 1, the product is less than $45.30.

Since 0.55 is about half, the decimal point should be between the 4 and 9.

$45.30 × 0.55 = $24.92

Use number sense to think about factors.

What <u>decimal</u> can be written to give the reasonable answer shown?

_____ × 5.1 is about 30.

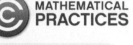 Think 6 times 5 equals 30, so the other factor has to be close to 6.

6.1 × 5.1 is about 30.

Problem Solving

MATHEMATICAL
PRACTICES

17. Charles is at the grocery store. His wife wants him to buy 2 loaves of bread. How much will this cost him?

18. Janet has $20.00 in her pocket. Will she be able to buy 11 bars of soap? If so, how much will the 11 bars cost?

At the Grocery Store	
Item	**Price**
Bar of soap	$1.60
Bag of chips	$2.75
Loaf of bread	$3.48
Pound cake	$8.95

Ⓒ 19. Structure Given a product of 7.5, find two factors that would complete the equation. One factor must be a decimal to the tenths place.

Ⓒ 20. Reason Why is 2 not a good estimate for 13.68 × 0.04?

21. What would be a more reasonable estimate for the expression in Exercise 20? Explain the method you used.

Ⓒ 22. Communicate Quincey says that 3 is a good estimate for 3.4 × 0.09, is he correct? Why?

23. A pig farmer needs 65 ft² to house a sow. Is the pen pictured below large enough?

24. Jordan's calculator will perform computations but it will not show the decimal point. He enters 3.04 × 6.04 and gets an answer of 183616. Where should he put the decimal point?

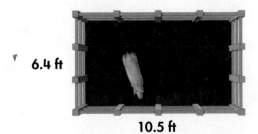

6.4 ft

10.5 ft

Lesson
6-4

©
Common
Core

5.NBT.7 …Multiply…
decimals to hundredths,
using concrete models
or drawings…properties
of operations…; relate
the strategy to a written
method and explain the
reasoning used.

Models for Multiplying Decimals

Hands-On
grid paper

How can you multiply whole numbers and decimals?

Bari displayed four paintings side-by-side in one row.
Each painting has the same width. What is the total
width of the 4 paintings?

Choose an Operation Multiply to find the total
width of the four paintings.

Each is 0.36
meters wide.

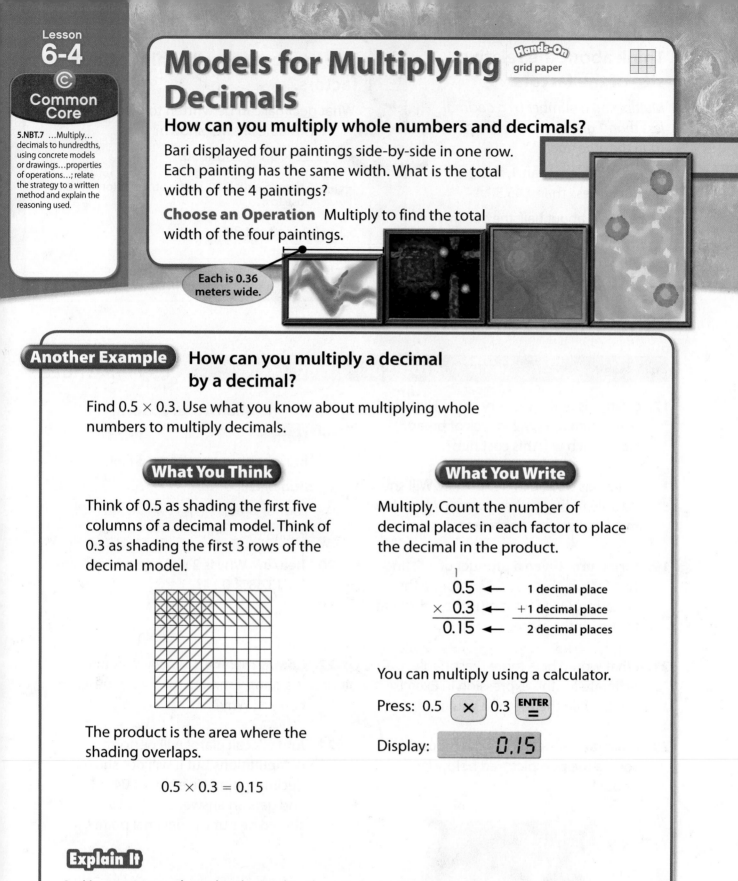

Another Example How can you multiply a decimal
by a decimal?

Find 0.5 × 0.3. Use what you know about multiplying whole
numbers to multiply decimals.

What You Think

Think of 0.5 as shading the first five
columns of a decimal model. Think of
0.3 as shading the first 3 rows of the
decimal model.

The product is the area where the
shading overlaps.

$$0.5 \times 0.3 = 0.15$$

What You Write

Multiply. Count the number of
decimal places in each factor to place
the decimal in the product.

$$
\begin{array}{r}
1 \\
0.5 \quad \leftarrow \quad \text{1 decimal place} \\
\times \ 0.3 \quad \leftarrow \quad +\text{1 decimal place} \\
\hline
0.15 \quad \leftarrow \quad \text{2 decimal places}
\end{array}
$$

You can multiply using a calculator.

Press: 0.5 × 0.3 ENTER
=

Display: *0.15*

Explain It

1. How can you place the decimal in the product when you
   multiply with decimals?

Find 0.36 × 4. Multiplying 0.36 × 4 is like adding 0.36 four times on a decimal model.

The product is the total area shaded.

0.36 × 4 = 1.44

Multiply. Add the number of decimal places to place the decimals.

$$
\begin{array}{r}
1\ 2 \\
0.36 \\
\times\ \ \ \ 4 \\
\hline
1.44
\end{array}
$$

← 2 decimal places
← + 0 decimal places
← 2 decimal places

The total width is 1.44 meters. You can also multiply using a calculator.

Press: 0.36 [×] 4 [ENTER =]

Display: 1.44

Other Examples

Use area models to multiply a decimal by a decimal.

Find 0.9 × 0.7

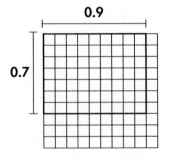

0.9

0.7

Use each factor as a side of a rectangle on a hundredths grid.

Shade the area of the rectangle bound by side lengths 0.9 and 0.7. Count the number of hundredths cells in the shaded area to find the product.

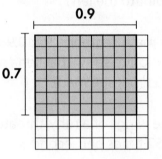

0.9

0.7

The shaded area contains 63 hundredths cells, so **0.7 × 0.9 = 0.63**.

Guided Practice*

MATHEMATICAL PRACTICES

Do you know HOW?

In **1** through **4**, place the decimal point in the product. You may use grids to help.

1. 2 × 0.32 = 64

2. 3 × 0.92 = 276

3. 4.2 × 5.4 = 2268

4. 5.7 × 0.03 = 171

In **5** and **6**, find the product.

5. 0.8 × 4

6. 0.7 × 21

Do you UNDERSTAND?

7. Explain when you need to add zeros to the left of a product.

© **8. Use Tools** In the example at the top, which method is easier to use to find the product, paper and pencil or a calculator?

DIGITAL

eTools
www.pearsonsuccessnet.com

Independent Practice

Leveled Practice In **9** through **14**, place the decimal point in each product.

9. $0.7 \times 12 = 84$

10. $4 \times 0.27 = 108$

11. $6 \times 0.13 = 078$

12. $3 \times 0.13 = 390$

13. $0.78 \times 5 = 390$

14. $0.23 \times 9 = 2070$

In **15** through **25,** find the product. You may use grids to help.

15. 10×0.32

16. 3×0.232

17. 0.7×0.8

18. 22.3×1.2

19. 100×0.12

20. 18×2.04

21. 33.3×0.3

22. 1.235×4.8

23. $3.2 \times 2.8 \times 6.1$

24. $1.8 \times 0.5 \times 100$

25. $74.3 \times 0.1 \times 2.1$

Problem Solving

MATHEMATICAL PRACTICES

© 26. Use Structure Why does multiplying numbers by 10 move the decimal point to the right, but multiplying by 0.10 move the decimal point to the left?

27. Jen solved this math sentence: $9 \times 0.989 = 89.01$. How can you use estimation to show that Jen's answer is wrong? What mistake do you think she made?

© 28. Persevere The wings of a ruby-throated hummingbird beat an average of 52 times per second.

    a If a ruby-throated hummingbird hovers for 35.5 seconds, on average how many times does its wings beat?

    b Estimate about how many times its wings would beat in a minute.

© 29. Reason Which expression does this decimal model show?

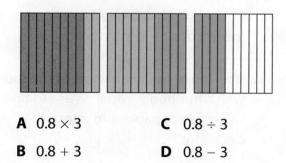

  A 0.8×3 **C** $0.8 \div 3$

  B $0.8 + 3$ **D** $0.8 - 3$

© 30. Model Which expression does this decimal model show?

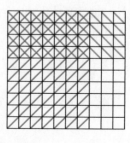

  A $0.7 \div 0.4$ **C** $0.7 - 0.4$

  B 0.7×0.4 **D** $0.7 + 0.4$

Algebra Connections

True or False?

Remember that a variable is a value that can change and is often represented by a letter. If you are given the value of the variable, you can substitute the value for the letter to evaluate an expression or equation.

> **Example:** Evaluate $x - 0.5 = 0.8$ for $x = 1.3$.
>
> Substitute 1.3 for the variable.
>
> $1.3 - 0.5 = 0.8$
>
> $\qquad 0.8 = 0.8$
>
> The equation is **true** when $x = 1.3$.

In **1** through **8**, evaluate for the variable. Write **true** or **false** for each equation.

1. $x + 7 = 8.3$; $x = 1.3$

2. $x - 2.88 = 7.11$; $x = 4$

3. $6x = 12.6$; $x = 21$

4. $0.5 + x = 1.2$; $x = 0.7$

5. $x \div 3 = 4.8$; $x = 14.4$

6. $x - 4.5 = 5.9$; $x = 9.4$

7. $7x = 21.35$; $x = 3.5$

8. $27.6 \div x = 9.2$; $x = 3$

. . . .

ⓒ **Look for Patterns** In **9** through **12**, evaluate the equations to find the answers.

9. If $b = 5.7$, which equation is true?

   A $3 + b = 6$

   B $b - 2 = 5.5$

   C $b + 4.4 = 9.1$

   D $6 - b = 0.3$

10. If $s = 8.9$, which equation is true?

   A $0.1 + s = 8.8$

   B $s - 0.01 = 8.807$

   C $s + 1.1 = 10$

   D $11.1 - s = 3.2$

11. If $g = 0.29$, which equation is true?

   A $g - 0.02 = 0.27$

   B $g - 0.22 = 0.7$

   C $g + 0.2 = 0.31$

   D $g + 2 = 0.49$

12. If $n = 1.78$, which equation is true?

   A $n - 0.3 = 2.08$

   B $2.3 + n = 4.08$

   C $n + 0.3 = 1.48$

   D $5 - n = 4.22$

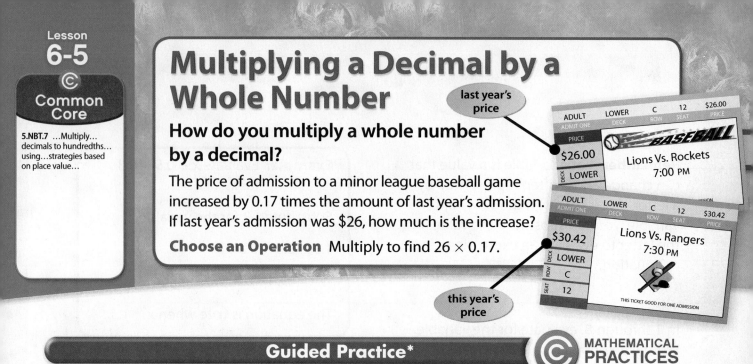

Lesson
6-5

Common Core

5.NBT.7 …Multiply…
decimals to hundredths…
using…strategies based
on place value…

Multiplying a Decimal by a Whole Number

last year's price

How do you multiply a whole number by a decimal?

The price of admission to a minor league baseball game increased by 0.17 times the amount of last year's admission. If last year's admission was $26, how much is the increase?

Choose an Operation Multiply to find 26×0.17.

ADULT   LOWER   C   12 $26.00
ADMIT ONE   DECK   ROW   SEAT   PRICE

PRICE
$26.00
DECK   LOWER

BASEBALL
Lions Vs. Rockets
7:00 PM

ADULT   LOWER   C   12 $30.42
ADMIT ONE   DECK   ROW   SEAT   PRICE

PRICE
$30.42
DECK   LOWER
ROW   C
SEAT   12

Lions Vs. Rangers
7:30 PM

THIS TICKET GOOD FOR ONE ADMISSION

this year's price

Guided Practice*

MATHEMATICAL PRACTICES

Do you know HOW?

Find each product.

1.
$$\begin{array}{r} 9.8 \\ \times\ \ 2 \\ \hline \end{array}$$

2.
$$\begin{array}{r} 0.67 \\ \times\ \ 8 \\ \hline \end{array}$$

3. 0.457×3

4. 34×5.3

5. 45×0.003

6. 34.6×21

Do you UNDERSTAND?

7. Critique Reasoning What is the difference between multiplying a whole number by a decimal and multiplying two whole numbers?

8. Use the information from the example above. How much will admission cost for 3 tickets to a minor league game this year?

Independent Practice

Find each product.

9.
$$\begin{array}{r} 34.6 \\ \times\ \ 9 \\ \hline \end{array}$$

10.
$$\begin{array}{r} 56.3 \\ \times\ \ 22 \\ \hline \end{array}$$

11.
$$\begin{array}{r} 405 \\ \times\ 0.47 \\ \hline \end{array}$$

12.
$$\begin{array}{r} 9.32 \\ \times\ \ 16 \\ \hline \end{array}$$

13.
$$\begin{array}{r} 12.9 \\ \times\ \ 8 \\ \hline \end{array}$$

14.
$$\begin{array}{r} 27.4 \\ \times\ \ 7 \\ \hline \end{array}$$

15.
$$\begin{array}{r} 336 \\ \times\ 0.4 \\ \hline \end{array}$$

16.
$$\begin{array}{r} 88 \\ \times\ 1.8 \\ \hline \end{array}$$

17. 84×0.005

18. $34,000 \times 2.65$

19. 64.2×20

20. 38.6×19

21. 40×0.22

22. 57×2.3

23. 5.8×11

24. 56×0.4

25. 0.1×22

26. 170×0.003

27. 4.02×9

28. 514×0.4

29. 0.3×99

30. 52×3.6

31. 105×0.4

32. 92×0.9

For another example, see Set B on page 162.

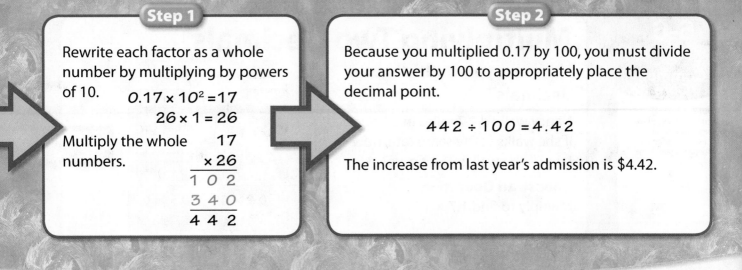

Rewrite each factor as a whole number by multiplying by powers of 10.

$$0.17 \times 10^2 = 17$$
$$26 \times 1 = 26$$

Multiply the whole numbers.

$$
\begin{array}{r}
17 \\
\times 26 \\
\hline
1\ 0\ 2 \\
3\ 4\ 0 \\
\hline
4\ 4\ 2
\end{array}
$$

Because you multiplied 0.17 by 100, you must divide your answer by 100 to appropriately place the decimal point.

$$442 \div 100 = 4.42$$

The increase from last year's admission is $4.42.

Problem Solving

MATHEMATICAL PRACTICES

For **33**, refer to the prices at the right.

33. Persevere Mia is shopping and finds a sale. She has $25 in her wallet and a coupon worth $4 off the cost of a dress.

   a How much money will the dress cost if she uses the coupon?

   b Find the total cost of 3 T-shirts.

   c How much change will Mia get back from $25 after she buys the 3 T-shirts?

$7.55

$15.50

34. To determine the tip for a restaurant server, many people multiply the amount of the check by 0.15. Find the amount of the tip on a check of $20.

35. Gary had 10 rosebushes to plant. On Friday, he planted 4 of the bushes. In simplest form, what fraction of the bushes did he plant?

36. The fastest growing flowering plant is the *Hesperoyucca Whipplei*. It was recorded that one of these plants grew at a rate of 25.4 cm per day. How many centimeters did this plant grow in 7 days?

37. Critique Reasoning/Arguments The airline that Vince is using has a baggage weight limit of 41 pounds. He has two green bags, each weighing 18.4 pounds, and one blue bag weighing 3.7 pounds. What is the combined weight of his baggage?

  A 22.1 lb   **C** 40.5 lb

  B 38.7 lb   **D** 41 lb

38. Raul, Tim, Yuko, and Joe have to line up according to height from tallest to shortest. Raul is 145.52 cm tall; Tim is 151 cm tall; Yuko is 159.5 cm tall; and Joe is 145.25 cm tall. Who is first in line?

Lesson
6-6

Common
Core

5.NBT.7 …Multiply…
decimals to hundredths,
using…drawings and
strategies based on…
properties of operations.

Multiplying Two Decimals

How can you multiply two decimals?

Nancy walked 1.7 miles in 1 hour. If she walks at the same rate, how far will she walk in 1.5 hours?

Choose an Operation
Multiply to find 1.7×1.5.

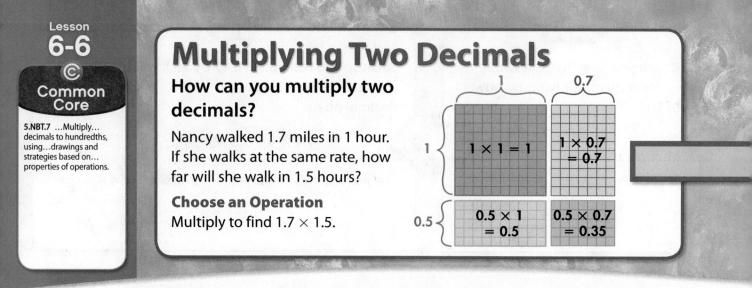

Guided Practice*

MATHEMATICAL PRACTICES

Do you know HOW?

For **1** through **6**, estimate first. Then find each product. Check that your answer is reasonable.

1. $\begin{array}{r} 9.3 \\ \times\ 4.1 \\ \hline \end{array}$

2. $\begin{array}{r} 3.02 \\ \times\ 0.6 \\ \hline \end{array}$

3. 0.7×1.9

4. 12.6×0.2

5. 8.3×10.7

6. 2.04×1.8

Do you UNDERSTAND?

7. **Communicate** How is multiplying two decimals different from multiplying one decimal by a whole number?

8. Using the example above, how many miles will Nancy walk in 2.8 hours? Show an estimate first.

Independent Practice

For **9** through **28**, estimate first. Then find each product. Check that your answer is reasonable.

9. $\begin{array}{r} 5.2 \\ \times\ 4.6 \\ \hline \end{array}$

10. $\begin{array}{r} 0.05 \\ \times\ 4.5 \\ \hline \end{array}$

11. $\begin{array}{r} 19.1 \\ \times\ 8.5 \\ \hline \end{array}$

12. $\begin{array}{r} 8.6 \\ \times\ 0.08 \\ \hline \end{array}$

13. 0.6×0.49

14. 32.3×0.7

15. 3.42×4.7

16. 8.11×0.05

17. 3.5×0.4

18. 28.6×0.17

19. 0.21×1.5

20. 1.11×6.1

21. 6.8×7.2

22. 8.3×6.4

23. 9.1×11.6

24. 0.04×15.6

25. 18.1×3.7

26. 0.06×15

27. 0.28×3.7

28. 3.14×6.2

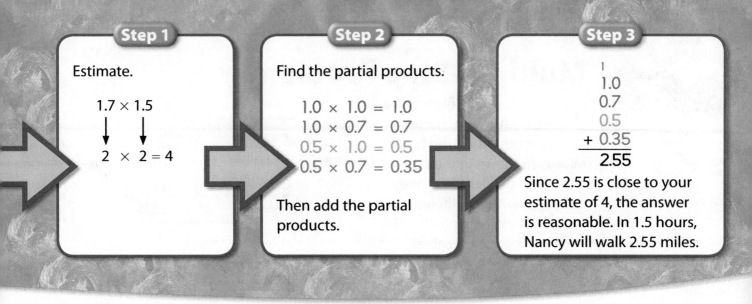

Step 1

Estimate.

1.7×1.5

$2 \times 2 = 4$

Step 2

Find the partial products.

$1.0 \times 1.0 = 1.0$
$1.0 \times 0.7 = 0.7$
$0.5 \times 1.0 = 0.5$
$0.5 \times 0.7 = 0.35$

Then add the partial products.

Step 3

$$
\begin{array}{r}
1 \\
1.0 \\
0.7 \\
0.5 \\
+ \ 0.35 \\
\hline
2.55
\end{array}
$$

Since 2.55 is close to your estimate of 4, the answer is reasonable. In 1.5 hours, Nancy will walk 2.55 miles.

Problem Solving

29. The fifth-grade planning committee needs to buy items for sandwiches for its annual lunch. Fill in the chart and determine the amount of money they'll need to buy the items for sandwiches.

Item	Amount	Price	Total
	15.5 pounds	$3.50 per pound	
	10.5 pounds	$2.90 per pound	
	12 packages	$2.50 per package	

30. Karly's bedroom measures 13.2 feet long by 10.3 feet wide. Use the formula Area = length × width to determine the number of square feet for the floor of Karly's bedroom.

31. A bag of grass seed weighs 5.8 pounds. How many pounds would 2.5 bags weigh?

  A 14.5

  B 13.8

  C 8.3

  D 3.3

© **32. Be Precise** Joy drinks 4 bottles of water per day. Each bottle contains 16.5 fluid ounces. How many fluid ounces of water does she drink per day?

  A 66 fluid ounces   **C** 660 fluid ounces

  B 68 fluid ounces   **D** 680 fluid ounces

© **33. Construct Arguments** Mary Ann ordered 3 pens and a box of paper on the Internet. Each pen cost $1.65 and the paper cost $3.95 per box. How much did she spend?

34. An astronaut's Apollo space suit weighs 29.8 pounds on the moon. It weighs approximately 6.02 times as much on Earth. About how much does an Apollo space suit weigh on Earth?

© **35. Writing to Explain** How does estimation help you place the decimal point in a product correctly?

Common
Core

5.NBT.7 Add, subtract, multiply...decimals to hundredths, using concrete models... and strategies based on place value...; relate the strategy to a written method and explain the reasoning used.

Multiple-Step Problems

For three months, a fifth-grade class held a fun fair to raise money for charities. The funds raised are shown in the table. If the class divides the money equally among 30 different organizations, how much will each organization receive?

Funds Raised	
September	$435
October	$460
November	$605

Data

Guided Practice*

MATHEMATICAL
PRACTICES

Do you know HOW?

1. Nancy wants to transfer 11 movies to her 8 gigabyte (GB) memory card. Each movie is 0.25 GB and she has already used 4.3 GB. How much free space will she have left on the card after she transfers the movies?

Ⓒ **2. Persevere** What is the hidden question and answer in Problem 1?

Do you UNDERSTAND?

Ⓒ **3. Construct Arguments** Were you able to use mental math in Problem 1?

4. Write a real-world multiple-step problem that can be solved by using multiplication.

Independent Practice

MATHEMATICAL
PRACTICES

Solve **5** through **12**.

5. A 3 lb bag of apples costs $3.75. A 2 lb bag costs $2.58. If you want to spend as little as possible to buy 6 lb of apples, how should you buy them?

6. Ariane is selling jewelry at the state fair. She sells bracelets for $8.50 each, rings for $5.75 each, and earrings for $11.20 per pair. How much will she make if she sells 9 bracelets, 14 rings, and 10 pairs of earrings?

Applying Math Practices

- What am I asked to find?
- What else can I try?
- How are the quantities related?
- How can I explain my work?
- How can I use math to model the problem?
- Can I use tools to help?
- Is my work precise?
- Why does this work?
- How can I generalize?

What do I know?

A class raised $435, $460, and $605. Thirty charities will receive the same amount of money from the total amount raised.

What am I asked to find?

The amount of money each charity will receive.

Find the hidden question or questions.

How much money was raised altogether?

? total amount raised		
$435	$460	$605

$435 + $460 + $605 = $1,500

Solve. Use mental math.

$1,500 ÷ 30 = ☐

Think 150 tens ÷ 3 tens = 50

Each charity will receive $50.

© 7. **Use Structure** Use the table at the right to compare the amount of fat contained in 2 slices of pizza, 1.5 cups of macadamia nuts, and 6 cups of popcorn. Which quantity of food contains the most fat? How much more fat does it contain than the quantity with the least fat?

Data

Fat in Food	
Food Description	Grams of Fat
1 slice pepperoni pizza	55.25
1 cup macadamia nuts	101.4
3 cups popcorn	1.3

8. Mason is growing tomatoes in his garden this year. Every 1.5 ft of stalk yields about 3.4 lbs of tomatoes. He has four plants with a combined stalk length of 10.5 feet. How many pounds of tomatoes can he expect to harvest?

9. Thomas's cat, Rainwright, eats 0.8 cans of food every day. How much will Thomas spend on food in one week if each can costs $1.75?

10. Use the table at the right to answer. How much would 5 chicken and noodle meals and 1 order of chicken and potatoes be if the tax on one meal is $0.18?

Data

Dinner Specials	
Chicken and Noodle	$7.35
Chicken and Rice	$7.15
Chicken and Potatoes	$6.25

© 11. **Look for Patterns** A glacier advances toward the sea 0.04 mile annually. In 2010 the front of the glacier is 6.9 miles from the mouth of the sea. How far will it be from the sea in 2030?

12. In 1995 the size of a typical personal computer processor was 3.8 cm × 2.9 cm. In 2009 a smartphone processor can be as small as 1.1 cm × 0.8 cm. How much larger is the 1995 processor than one found in today's phones?

Set A, pages 146–147, 148–149

Use the patterns in this table to find
$8.56 × 10 and 0.36 × 100.

Multiply by	Move the decimal point to the right
10^1	1 place
10^2	2 places
10^3	3 places

$8.56 × 10 = $85.6 = $85.60

0.36 × 100 = 36.0 = 36

Remember when you need to move the decimal point beyond the number of digits in the number you are multiplying, annex 1 or more zeros.

Use mental math to solve 1–4.
Estimate the products of 5–8.

1. 10 × 4.5

2. 100 × 4.5

3. 1,000 × 4.5

4. 10 × 0.89

5. 24 × 3.67

6. 5.86 × 52

7. 14 × 9.67

8. 8 × 56.7

Set B, pages 150–151, 152–154, 156–157

Find 52.5 × 1.9 Estimate: 50 × 2 = 100

Step 1

Multiply as you would with whole numbers.

$$\begin{array}{r} 525 \\ \times\ \ 19 \\ \hline 9975 \end{array}$$

Step 2

Since 1.9 is greater than 1, the product will be greater than 52.5. Since 1.9 is about 2, the decimal point should be between the 9 and the 7.

$$\begin{array}{r} 52.5 \\ \times\ \ 1.9 \\ \hline 99.75 \end{array}$$

So, 52.5 × 1.9 = 99.75

Remember to compare each factor to 1 in order to determine the relative size of the product. Use area models or arrays if necessary.

Find each product.

1. 5 × 98.2

2. 4 × 0.21

3. 4.4 × 6

4. 7 × 21.6

5. 12.5 × 163.2

6. 16 × 52.3

7. 0.8 × 0.11

8. 0.07 × 0.44

9. 6.4 × 3.2

10. 31.5 × 0.01

Set C, pages 158–159

Find 0.9×0.1

Estimate: $1 \times 0.1 = 0.1$

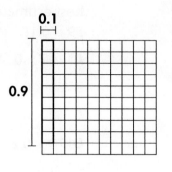

Step 1

Mark the dimensions of each factor on a hundredths square.

Step 2

Shade the area of the rectangle created by the factors and count the squares to find the product.

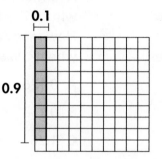

So, $0.9 \times 0.1 = 0.09$

Remember to use area models and arrays to help you find the product if needed.

Find each product.

1. 2.4×3.67
2. 5.86×5.2
3. 8.3×10.7
4. 3.42×4.7
5. 1.4×9.67
6. 11.2×9.7
7. 23.3×60.5
8. 9.03×67.98

Set D, pages 160–161

The football coach spent a total of $890.40 including $50.40 tax for 35 shirts for the team. The price of each shirt was the same. How much did one shirt cost before tax was added?

Identify the hidden question or questions.

How much did all the shirts cost without tax?

$890.40 − $50.40 = $840.00

Solve the problem.

$840 ÷ 35 = $24   Each shirt cost $24.00.

Remember that you need to identify the hidden question or questions and answer them before solving the problem.

Write and answer the hidden question or questions. Then solve.

1. At the city triathlon, athletes bike 110 miles, run a 23.5-mile marathon, and swim. If the total distance of this triathlon is 135.7 miles, how far do the athletes swim?

2. A gymnast practices 6 days per week. If the same gymnast practices a total of 120 hours in a 4-week period, how many hours per day does the gymnast practice?

1. Lucia scored an 8.65 on her first gymnastics event at a meet. If she gets the same score on each of the four events, what will be her total score? (6-5)

   A 32.48

   B 34.6

   C 34.8

   D 346

2. Mrs. Delgado needs to buy 160 begonias for her flowerbed. At the prices shown, how much would she save if she bought them by the flat instead of buying them separately? (6-7)

   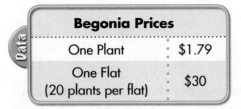

Begonia Prices	
One Plant	$1.79
One Flat (20 plants per flat)	$30

   A $160.24

   B $45.50

   C $170

   D $46.40

3. What is 0.76×10^3? (6-1)

   A 0.076

   B 7.60

   C 76.0

   D 760

4. Which of the following provides the best estimate of the product of 59×0.19? (6-2)

   A $100 \times 0.15 = 15$

   B $60 \times 0.2 = 12$

   C $60 \times 0.1 = 6$

   D $70 \times 0.2 = 14$

5. A farmer plants 0.4 of a field with wheat. The field is 3.45 acres in size. How many acres are planted with wheat? (6-6)

   A 0.126

   B 0.138

   C 1.26

   D 1.38

6. What expression does this decimal model show? (6-4)

   A 0.08×0.03

   B 0.8×0.3

   C 0.7×0.2

   D 0.4×0.6

   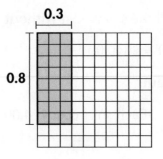

7. Estimate the product of 204 and 0.46. Explain what method of estimation you used and why it works. (6-2)

8. Sue bought 4.6 meters of fabric that cost $3.57 per meter. What was her total cost? (6-6)

9. What is 0.42×10^2? (6-1)

10. Al and Barb each go to the store to buy school supplies. Al buys 11 colored pencils for $0.69 each and Barb buys 3 packs of folders for $2.70 per pack. Who spent more at the store? Explain. (6-7)

11. Alyssa is painting her bedroom blue. Each of four walls has dimensions 12.9 ft. by 11.1 ft. How much area will she paint? (6-4)

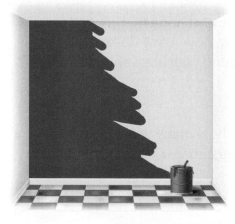

Use the table below for **12–14**.

Michelle's Fruit Stand	
Type of fruit	**Cost (per pound)**
Apples	$1.29/lb
Lemons	$2.49/lb
Oranges	$1.69/lb
Tangerines	$1.19/lb

12. Mario is buying oranges from the stand. He buys 4 pounds. Estimate how much he spends. Is your estimate an underestimate or overestimate? Explain. (6-2)

13. Antoinette buys 6 pounds of tangerines. She pays with a $10 bill. How much did she spend? How much change does she receive? (6-5)

14. Nico buys 3 pounds of lemons and 4 pounds of apples. How much does he spend in all? Write and solve an equation. (6-7)

15. Kendall worked 25.5 hours one week. If he earns $12.50 per hour, how much did he earn that week? How did you know where to put the decimal point? (6-3)

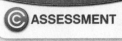
An *exchange rate* is how much of one country's currency (money) you would get for another country's currency. The table below shows the recent exchange rate between the U.S. dollar and the currency of some other countries.

U.S. $1.00 =
4.29 Venezuelan bolívares
6.88 Swedish Krona
45.02 Indian rupees
83.66 Japanese yen
80.65 Kenyan shillings
12.45 Mexican pesos

For example, if you had $2 (U.S.) dollars, you could exchange that for 24.9 Mexican pesos:

$2 \times 12.45 = 24.90$.

1. Jade has $10, Julio has $100, and Anna has $1,000. How many Japanese yen would each person get in exchange for the dollars they have?

2. Ivana has $5.50. How many Indian rupees could she exchange for this amount? Luc has 1.4 times as much money as Ivana. How many dollars does he have? How many rupees could he get? Round your answer to the nearest hundredth.

3. Use estimation to solve. Marcus has $25.10. About how many Venezuelan bolívares could he obtain? Is your estimate an overestimate or an underestimate? Explain.

4. Jorge is traveling to Kenya to photograph wildlife. How many Kenyan shillings will he receive for $500? His friends give him a $50 gift certificate right before he leaves. How many Kenyan shillings can he exchange for that amount?

5. Kofi is taking a trip to Mexico to see Mayan and Aztec pyramids. He wants to exchange $300 before arriving there. How many Mexican pesos can he receive? Write and solve an equation.

DOMAIN

Topic 7 — Dividing Decimals

▼ The longest spin of a basketball on one finger is 255 minutes. How many hours is this? You will find out in Lesson 7-4.

Review What You Know!

Vocabulary

Choose the best term from the box.

- dividend
- divisor
- decimal
- quotient

1. ___?___ is the name for the answer to a division problem.

2. A number that is being divided by another number is called the ___?___ .

3. A number that uses a decimal point and has one or more digits to the right of the decimal point is a ___?___ .

4. A number that is divided into another number is called the ___?___ .

Whole Number Operations

Calculate each value.

5. $9{,}007 - 3{,}128$

6. $7{,}964 + 3{,}872$

7. 35×17

8. 181×42

9. $768 \div 6$

10. $506 \div 22$

11. $6{,}357 \div 10$

12. $6{,}357 \div 100$

13. $10{,}500 \div 10$

14. $10{,}500 \div 100$

Decimals

© 15. **Writing to Explain** What decimal does this model represent? Explain.

Topic Essential Question

- What are the standard procedures for estimating and finding quotients involving decimals?

Interactive Learning

Pose the problem. Start each lesson by working together to solve problems. It will help you make sense of math.

Applying Math Practices

- What am I asked to find?
- What else can I try?
- How are quantities related?
- How can I explain my work?
- How can I use math to model the problem?
- Can I use tools to help?
- Is my work precise?
- Why does this work?
- How can I generalize?

Lesson 7-1

Ⓒ **Reasonableness** Suppose an object is 279.4 cm wide. If you divide the object into 10 equal parts, how wide will each part be? How wide will each part be if you divide the object into 100 equal parts? What if you divide it into 1,000 parts? What pattern do you see?

279.4 cm

Lesson 7-2

Ⓒ **Communicate** A 12.5 m piece of construction material needs to be cut into pieces 0.65 m long.

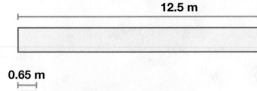

12.5 m

0.65 m

a. About how many pieces can be made?

b. If 12.5 m of material costs $235, about how much does one meter of material cost? Estimate the answers using any technique you choose. Be prepared to explain how you found your estimate.

Lesson 7-3

Ⓒ Construct Arguments Think about the relative size of the divisor, dividend, and quotient to complete Sets A and B. Be prepared to explain your reasoning. Set A: Think about the size of the dividend and the divisor to decide where the decimal point should be in the quotient. Set B: Use number sense to write a decimal that makes each statement correct.

Set A
1) 12.4 ÷ 4.1 = 3 0 2
2) 63 ÷ 0.52 = 1 2 1 1 5
3) 0.25 ÷ 0.31 = 8 1

Set B
4) ____ ÷ 0.95 is about 5
5) 14.6 ÷ ____ is about 0.5
6) ____ ÷ 2.5 is about 20

Lesson 7-4

Ⓒ Model Chris and two friends count $3.60 in loose change. How can they divide the money equally among themselves?

3)3.6

Lesson 7-5

Ⓒ Be Precise A hiking trail is 2 kilometers long. There is a distance marker at the end of every 0.5 kilometer. How many markers are on the trail? Use a decimal grid like that shown to draw and solve the problem.

Lesson 7-6

Ⓒ Use Tools Aaron buys erasers for his pencils. Each eraser costs $0.20. The total cost is $1.20. How many erasers does Aaron buy? Use the decimal models on your Teaching Tool to help you divide.

Lesson 7-7

Ⓒ Reason Samuel wants to buy thank-you cards. A box of 5 cards costs $6.40 and a box of 6 cards costs $6.90. Which package is the better buy?

THANK YOU
$6.40

THANK YOU
$6.90

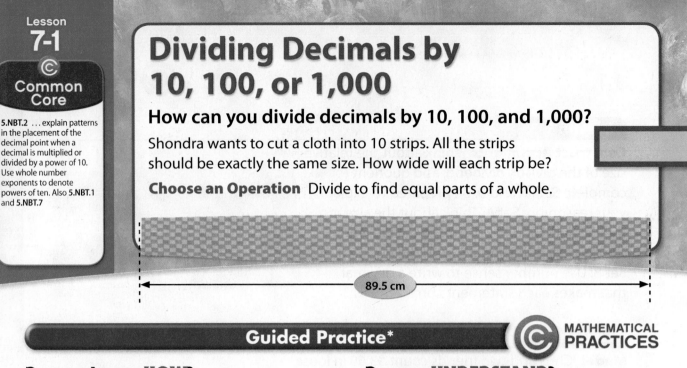

Common Core

5.NBT.2 ...explain patterns in the placement of the decimal point when a decimal is multiplied or divided by a power of 10. Use whole number exponents to denote powers of ten. Also 5.NBT.1 and 5.NBT.7

Dividing Decimals by 10, 100, or 1,000

How can you divide decimals by 10, 100, and 1,000?

Shondra wants to cut a cloth into 10 strips. All the strips should be exactly the same size. How wide will each strip be?

Choose an Operation Divide to find equal parts of a whole.

89.5 cm

Guided Practice*

MATHEMATICAL PRACTICES

Do you know HOW?

In **1** through **6**, use mental math to find each quotient.

1. $370.2 \div 10$

2. $126.4 \div 10^2$

3. $684.5 \div 1,000$

4. $72.5 \div 10^1$

5. $28.14 \div 100$

6. $42.5 \div 10^3$

Do you UNDERSTAND?

7. Construct Arguments Look at the table above. When dividing by 1,000, why was it necessary to place a zero in the tenths place?

8. Persevere If Shondra wanted to cut the cloth into 100 strips, how wide would each strip be?

Independent Practice

In **9** through **31**, find each quotient. Use mental math.

9. $23.75 \div 1$
$23.75 \div 10$
$23.75 \div 100$
$23.75 \div 1,000$

10. $509.3 \div 10^3$
$509.3 \div 10^2$
$509.3 \div 10^1$
$509.3 \div 10^0$

11. $98.2 \div 100$
$98.2 \div 1$
$98.2 \div 1,000$
$98.2 \div 10$

12. $13.65 \div 10$

13. $75.3 \div 100$

14. $890.1 \div 1,000$

15. $5.67 \div 100$

16. $8.74 \div 10^2$

17. $32.40 \div 10^3$

18. $12.33 \div 10$

19. $0.5 \div 10^1$

20. $4.5 \div 10$

21. $9.78 \div 100$

22. $7,446.5 \div 1,000$

23. $234.5 \div 10$

24. $0.27 \div 100$

25. $121.6 \div 1,000$

26. $8.373 \div 10^1$

27. $6.9 \div 10^3$

28. $8.25 \div 10^1$

29. $31.8 \div 10^2$

30. $0.36 \div 1,000$

31. $9.47 \div 100$

*For another example, see Set A on page 186.

Find 89.5 ÷ 10.

A number divided by 10 is less than the number. Moving the decimal point to the left decreases the number's value.

Place value is based on powers of 10. Dividing by 10 gives the same result as moving the decimal point one place to the left.

Notice the patterns in the table.

Divisor		
Standard Form	Exponential Form	Examples
10	10^1	$12.5 \div 10 = 1.25$
100	10^2	$12.5 \div 100 = 0.125$
1,000	10^3	$12.5 \div 1,000 = 0.0125$

So, $89.5 \div 10 = 8.95$

Each cloth strip will be 8.95 centimeters wide.

Problem Solving

MATHEMATICAL PRACTICES

© **Use Tools** For **32** through **34**, use the chart.

Pacific Middle School posted the winning times at the swim meet.

50-yard freestyle	22.17 seconds
100-yard backstroke	53.83 seconds
100-yard butterfly	58.49 seconds

32. What was the time per yard of the swimmer who swam the butterfly?

© 33. **Look for Patterns** If the 50-yard freestyle swimmer could swim the 100-yard freestyle in exactly double his 50-yard time, what would his time per yard be?

34. What was the time per yard of the swimmer who swam the backstroke?

35. Rodella has a jar full of dimes. The total amount of money in her jar is $45.60. How many dimes does she have?

© 36. **Reason** How is dividing 360 by 10^1 similar to dividing 3,600 by 10^2? Explain.

37. Helen is saving to buy a Koala Club child's membership to the San Diego Zoo as a present for her brother. The membership fee is $21.50. Helen has 10 weeks in which to save for it. How much money should she save each week?

© 38. **Generalize** In which of the following equations does $n = 100$?

A $1946.8 \div n = 1.9468$

B $61.5 \div n = 0.615$

C $11.73 \div n = 0.01173$

D $4.12 \div n = 0.412$

© 39. **Model** The dimensions of a room are shown on a blueprint with the measures of 12 inches long and 10 inches wide. The dimensions of the actual room are 12 times as big. How many feet long and wide is the actual room?

Lesson
7-2

Common Core

5.NBT.7 ...divide decimals to hundredths, using concrete models or drawings and strategies based on place value, ...; relate the strategy to a written method and explain the reasoning used.

Estimating Decimal Quotients

How can you use estimation to find quotients?

Suppose you purchase a video gaming system for $473.89 (including tax). About how much are the monthly payments if you want to pay this off in one year?

Since you need to separate the total into 12 equal groups, divide.

├----------------- $473.89 ----------------┤

Game System Version 4 $473.89

Other Examples

Compatible numbers

34.2 ÷ 6.8

34.2 ÷ 6.8 is about 35 ÷ 7 = 5

34.2 ÷ 6.8 is about 5

Estimation

Is 0.45 ÷ 23 > 1?

45 ÷ 2300 < 1

Think *Because the dividend is less than the divisor, the quotient will be less than 1.*

Guided Practice*

MATHEMATICAL PRACTICES

Do you know HOW?

Estimate each quotient. Use rounding or substitute compatible numbers.

1. 42 ÷ 2.8   **2.** 102 ÷ 9.6

3. 48.9 ÷ 4   **4.** 72.59 ÷ 7

5. Use estimation to decide if each quotient is greater than or less than 1.

   a 0.2 ÷ 4   **b** 1.35 ÷ 0.6

Do you UNDERSTAND?

6. Reason In the example at the top, which estimate is closer to the exact answer? Tell how you decided.

7. Persevere Hodi is building a birdhouse. Each of the four sides of the birdhouse needs to be 5.5 inches long. She has a scrap of wood that is 24.5 inches long. Is it long enough to get the four sides of the birdhouse? Estimate using compatible numbers.

Independent Practice

In **8–13** estimate each quotient.

8. 7 ÷ 0.85   **9.** 9.6 ÷ 0.91   **10.** 17.7 ÷ 3.2

11. 91.02 ÷ 4.9   **12.** 45.64 ÷ 6.87   **13.** 821.22 ÷ 79.4

For another example, see Set B on page 186.

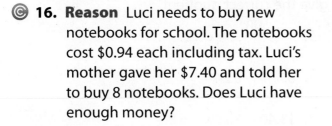

One Way

Estimate $473.89 ÷ 12. Use rounding.

To the nearest whole number, 473.89 rounds to 474.

12 rounds to 10.

$473.89 ÷ 12 is about $474 ÷ 10

$474 ÷ 10 = $47.40.

Each monthly payment will be about $47.40.

Another Way

Estimate $473.89 ÷ 12. Use compatible numbers.

Look for compatible numbers.

Think $48 ÷ 12 = 4$.

$473.89 ÷ 12 is close to $480 ÷ 12 = $40.

Each monthly payment will be about $40.

Determine whether each statement is true or false. Explain your answer.

14. The quotient of 27.2 and 5 is less than 3.

15. The quotient of 0.62 and 0.11 is less than 1.

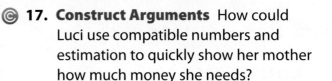

Problem Solving

MATHEMATICAL PRACTICES

16. Reason Luci needs to buy new notebooks for school. The notebooks cost $0.94 each including tax. Luci's mother gave her $7.40 and told her to buy 8 notebooks. Does Luci have enough money?

17. Construct Arguments How could Luci use compatible numbers and estimation to quickly show her mother how much money she needs?

18. Model Mauricio scored a total of 34.42 points in five gymnastic events. Which number sentence shows how you would estimate Mauricio's average score?

A $35 ÷ 5 = 7$ **B** $35 ÷ 7 = 5$

C $30 ÷ 10 = 3$ **D** $40 ÷ 10 = 4$

19. Pei Lei has a car that averages 14.5 miles per gallon while Roman's car averages 28.5 miles per gallon. Use estimation to compare how many times as many miles per gallon Roman's car gets to Pei Lei's car.

20. Be Precise Which sample from the experiment had the least mass? Which had the lowest temperature?

21. Without dividing, how do you know that the quotient of 95.5 ÷ 12 will NOT be 14?

Sample	Mass	Temperature
1	0.98 g	37.57°
2	0.58 g	57.37°
3	0.058 g	75.50°
4	0.098 g	73.57°

Lesson
7-3

Common
Core

5.NBT.7 ...Divide decimals to hundredths, using concrete drawings and strategies based on place value... Relate the strategy to a written method and explain the reasoning used.

Number Sense: Decimal Division
How can you use number sense for decimal division?

You have learned how to estimate when dividing with decimals. You can also use number sense to reason about the relative size of the dividend, divisor, and quotient. Use number sense to tell where to place the decimal point in the quotient at the right.

How many quarters are in $15.50?
$15.50 ÷ $0.25 = 6 2 0

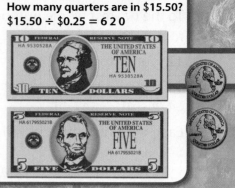

Guided Practice*

Do you know HOW?

Use number sense to decide where the decimal point belongs in the quotient.

1. $7.68 \div 1.5 = 5\ 1\ 2$

2. $256.5 \div 2.5 = 1\ 0\ 2\ 6$

3. $1127.84 \div 3.8 = 2\ 9\ 6\ 8$

4. $196.8 \div 0.1968 = 1\ 0\ 0\ 0\ 0$

Do you UNDERSTAND?

The decimal point in each of the quotients below *may* be in the wrong place. Use number sense to decide. If it is incorrect, give the correct quotient.

5. $1.44 \div 1.2 = 0.12$

6. $0.384 \div 0.24 = 1.6$

7. $\$3.40 \div \$0.05 = 6.80$

Independent Practice

 MATHEMATICAL
PRACTICES

© **Reasonableness** In **8–11**, use number sense to decide where the decimal point belongs in the quotient.

8. $14.73 \div 6.96 = 2\ 1\ 1\ 6\ 3\ 7\ 9\ 3$

9. $20.15 \div 31.2 = 6\ 4\ 5\ 8\ 3\ 3\ 3$

10. $0.985 \div 0.504 = 1\ 9\ 5\ 4\ 3\ 6\ 5$

11. $107.22 \div 0.991 = 1\ 0\ 8\ 1\ 9\ 3\ 7\ 4$

The decimal point in each of the quotients below may be in the wrong place. In **12–15**, use number sense to decide. If it is incorrect, give the correct quotient.

12. $7.02 \div 2.6 = 2.7$

13. $49.84 \div 0.56 = 8.9$

14. $337.5 \div 0.75 = 450$

15. $0.3696 \div 0.12 = 30.8$

For another example, see Set B on page 186.

Think about the relative size of the dividend and the divisor.

Dividing a decimal dividend greater than 1 by a divisor less than 1 gives a quotient greater than the dividend.

Since 0.25 is less than 1, the quotient is greater than $15.50.

Since there are 4 quarters in $1, there are about 4 × 15 = 60 quarters in $15.50.

The decimal point is between the 2 and the 0; $15.50 ÷ $0.25 = 62.0.

Use number sense to think about the dividend, divisor, and quotient.

What <u>decimal</u> can be written to give the reasonable answer shown?

_____ ÷ 2.2 is about 0.52.

Think *Because 0.52 is about 0.5 or $\frac{1}{2}$, the dividend has to be about half of 2. Possible dividends are 1.2 and 1.1.*

Problem Solving

MATHEMATICAL PRACTICES

16. Mr. Jones has a new car. The manufacturer says that the car should get about 28 miles per gallon in the city. About how many miles can Mr. Jones drive on 11.5 gallons of gas? At $2.89 gallon, how much would that cost?

17. Mason and Thomas are working on a decimal division problem. Mason states that 3.96 ÷ 0.3 = 1.32. Thomas states that the quotient is 13.2. Who is correct?

Explain your answer.

© 18. **Reasonableness** Jane needs to know how many dimes are in $45.60. After dividing on the calculator, she sees the display read 4 5 6 0. Where should Jane place the decimal in her answer?

© 19. **Reasonableness** Which shows the quotient of the following divison problem: 0.42 ÷ 1.4?

A 30   C 0.3

B 3   D 0.03

© 20. **Look for Patterns** Make up two decimals with an answer close to the given quotient.

_____ ÷ _____ = 2.3

© 21. **Communicate** A 26.2 mile marathon has water stops every 0.5 miles. Is it reasonable to say that there are about 40 water stops? Explain your answer.

22. A quarter horse can run 53.16 miles per hour. A garden snail moves at 0.02 miles per hour. How much faster is the quarter horse than the snail?

A about 2 times as fast   C about 200 times as fast

B about 20 times as fast   D about 2000 times as fast

23. How could you use estimation to check the reasonableness of the quotient for 3.99 ÷ 0.84?

Dividing by a Whole Number
How can you write a quotient for a decimal dividend?

Three friends received $2.58 for aluminum cans they recycled. They decided to share the money equally. How much will each friend get?

Choose an Operation Divide to find how much each friend will get.

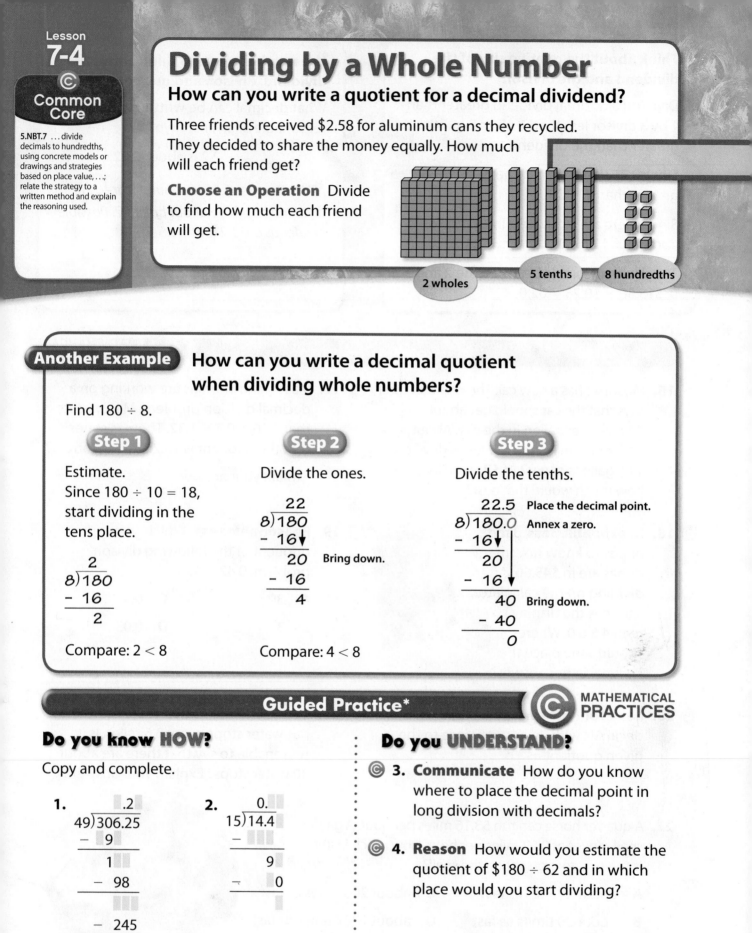

2 wholes   5 tenths   8 hundredths

Another Example How can you write a decimal quotient when dividing whole numbers?

Find 180 ÷ 8.

Step 1

Estimate.
Since 180 ÷ 10 = 18, start dividing in the tens place.

$$
\begin{array}{r}
2 \\
8\overline{)180} \\
-16 \\
\hline
2
\end{array}
$$

Compare: 2 < 8

Step 2

Divide the ones.

$$
\begin{array}{r}
22 \\
8\overline{)180} \\
-16\downarrow \\
\hline
20 \\
-16 \\
\hline
4
\end{array}
$$
Bring down.

Compare: 4 < 8

Step 3

Divide the tenths.

$$
\begin{array}{r}
22.5 \\
8\overline{)180.0} \\
-16\downarrow \\
\hline
20 \\
-16\downarrow \\
\hline
40 \\
-40 \\
\hline
0
\end{array}
$$
Place the decimal point.
Annex a zero.
Bring down.

Guided Practice*

MATHEMATICAL PRACTICES

Do you know HOW?

Copy and complete.

1.
$$
\begin{array}{r}
.2 \\
49\overline{)306.25} \\
-9 \\
\hline
1 \\
-98 \\
\hline
 \\
-245
\end{array}
$$

2.
$$
\begin{array}{r}
0. \\
15\overline{)14.4} \\
- \\
\hline
9 \\
-0
\end{array}
$$

Do you UNDERSTAND?

3. Communicate How do you know where to place the decimal point in long division with decimals?

4. Reason How would you estimate the quotient of $180 ÷ 62 and in which place would you start dividing?

eTools
www.pearsonsuccessnet.com

*For another example, see Set C on page 186.

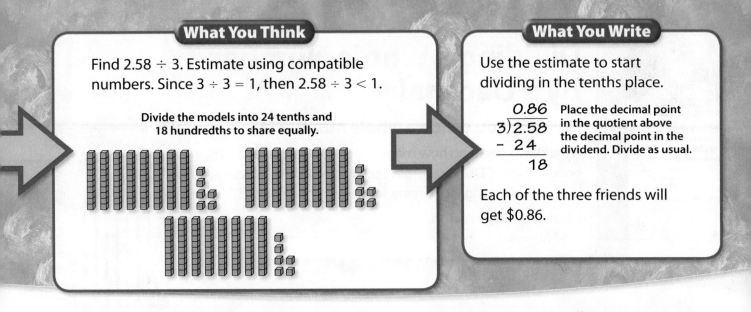

What You Think

Find 2.58 ÷ 3. Estimate using compatible numbers. Since 3 ÷ 3 = 1, then 2.58 ÷ 3 < 1.

Divide the models into 24 tenths and 18 hundredths to share equally.

What You Write

Use the estimate to start dividing in the tenths place.

$$\begin{array}{r} 0.86 \\ 3\overline{)2.58} \\ -\ 24 \\ \hline 18 \end{array}$$

Place the decimal point in the quotient above the decimal point in the dividend. Divide as usual.

Each of the three friends will get $0.86.

Independent Practice

In **5** through **20**, find each quotient.

5. $99.09 ÷ 3
6. 97.5 ÷ 6
7. 71.2 ÷ 8
8. 151.2 ÷ 6

9. 1.57 ÷ 10
10. 2.4 ÷ 8
11. $350 ÷ 40
12. 248.60 ÷ 50

13. 5 ÷ 5,000
14. 5.68 ÷ 8
15. $23.10 ÷ 11
16. 60.3 ÷ 9

17. $92.55 ÷ 5
18. 396 ÷ 88
19. 100 ÷ 1,000
20. 5.43 ÷ 15

Problem Solving

21. Admission to an amusement park cost $107.25 for three friends. If the price was the same for each friend, what was the cost of each admission?

22. Reason If Brand A dog food costs $29.95 for 30 pounds and Brand B dog food costs $50 for 45 pounds, which costs less per pound? How do you know?

23. Construct Arguments Is the work below correct? If not, explain why and give a correct response.

Find 0.9 ÷ 30.

$$\begin{array}{r} 0.30 \\ 30\overline{)0.90} \\ -\ 90 \\ \hline 0 \end{array}$$

24. Use Structure How might you best estimate the quotient of 352.25 ÷ 33?

A Round 352.25 to 352.

B Round 352.25 to 352 and 33 to 30.

C Round 352.25 to 400 and 33 to 30.

D Use compatible numbers 350 and 35.

25. Be Precise The longest spin of a basketball on one finger is 255 minutes. How many hours is this?

Lesson
7-5

Common
Core

5.NBT.7 ...divide
decimals to hundredths,
using concrete models or
drawings and strategies
based on place value,...;
relate the strategy to a
written method and explain
the reasoning used.

Dividing a Whole Number by a Decimal

How can you divide a whole number by a decimal?

A band was deciding how many songs could fit on a CD. They bought blank CDs for recording their songs. If their average song is 3.2 minutes long, how many songs can fit on each CD?

Choose an Operation
Find 80 ÷ 3.2.

Guided Practice*

MATHEMATICAL PRACTICES

Do you know HOW?

In **1** through **4**, find a power of 10 that will make the divisor a whole number and write the equivalent problem.

1. 426 ÷ 0.6   **2.** 216 ÷ 0.03

3. 2,800 ÷ 0.07   **4.** 720 ÷ 1.2

Do you UNDERSTAND?

5. Reason When changing the divisor to a whole number, why do you multiply both the divisor and the dividend by the same power of 10?

6. Generalize In the problem above, give a reason why the band might not be able to put all 25 songs on the CD?

Independent Practice

Leveled Practice In **7** through **14**, find a power of 10 that will make the divisor a whole number and write the equivalent problem.

7. 2,466 ÷ 0.9   **8.** 65 ÷ 0.05   **9.** 143 ÷ 0.22   **10.** 164 ÷ 2.05

11. 32 ÷ 8.9   **12.** 512 ÷ 2.56   **13.** 36 ÷ 0.09   **14.** 4,221 ÷ 0.7

In **15** though **26**, find each quotient. Show your work.

15. $0.03\overline{)24}$ **16.** $0.06\overline{)18}$ **17.** $0.05\overline{)12}$ **18.** $0.08\overline{)300}$

19. 114 ÷ 0.04   **20.** 51 ÷ 0.06   **21.** 126 ÷ 0.9   **22.** 11 ÷ 0.25

23. 180 ÷ 0.40   **24.** 756 ÷ 0.70   **25.** 2,550 ÷ 0.25   **26.** 110 ÷ 0.02

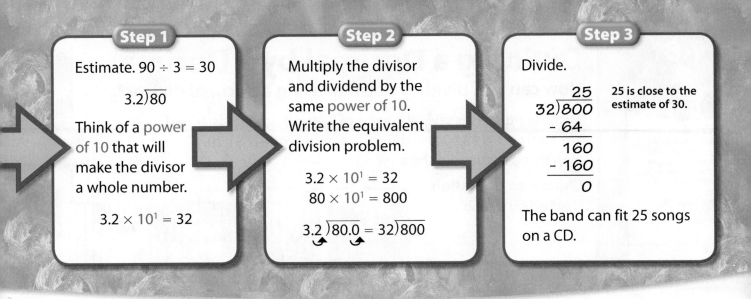

Step 1

Estimate. 90 ÷ 3 = 30

$$3.2\overline{)80}$$

Think of a power of 10 that will make the divisor a whole number.

$$3.2 \times 10^1 = 32$$

Step 2

Multiply the divisor and dividend by the same power of 10. Write the equivalent division problem.

$$3.2 \times 10^1 = 32$$
$$80 \times 10^1 = 800$$

$$3.2\overline{)80.0} = 32\overline{)800}$$

Step 3

Divide.

$$\begin{array}{r} 25 \\ 32\overline{)800} \\ -\ 64 \\ \hline 160 \\ -\ 160 \\ \hline 0 \end{array}$$

25 is close to the estimate of 30.

The band can fit 25 songs on a CD.

Problem Solving

 MATHEMATICAL PRACTICES

27. In 1927, Charles Lindbergh made the first solo, non-stop flight 3,610 miles across the Atlantic Ocean. The flight lasted about 33.5 hours. About how many miles per hour did he fly? Divide 3,610 by 33.5 and round to the nearest whole number.

Ⓒ **28. Communicate** Is the quotient for 41 ÷ 0.8 greater or less than 41? Explain.

Ⓒ **29. Persevere** In a timed typing test, Lara typed 63 words per minute. Estimate the number of words she should be able to type in half an hour.

30. The fence next to the creek near Adam's house leans a little more each year because the bank of the creek is eroding. If the fence leans about 3.7 degrees more each year, estimate how many more degrees the fence will lean after 5 years.

Use the information in the table for **31** and **32**.

Ⓒ **31. Reason** Arrange the animals at the right in order from fastest to slowest.

Ⓒ **32. Think About the Structure** At the average speed shown, the expression 2 ÷ 0.03 equals how long it would take the snail to travel 2 miles. Which expression is equivalent to 2 ÷ 0.03?

    A 2 ÷ 3   **C** 200 ÷ 3

    B 20 ÷ 3   **D** 2,000 ÷ 3

Animal	Speed (miles per hour)
Sea horse	0.01
Sloth	0.17
Snail	0.03
Tortoise	0.23

Lesson
7-6

ⓒ
Common
Core

5.NBT.7 . . .divide
decimals to hundredths,
using concrete models or
drawings and strategies
based on place value, . . .;
relate the strategy to a
written method and explain
the reasoning used.

Dividing a Decimal by a Decimal
How can you divide a decimal using a decimal divisor?

Michelle purchases several bottles of water. Before tax is added, the total cost is $3.60 and the cost of each bottle is $1.20. How many bottles did she buy?

Choose an Operation
Divide 3.60 by 1.20.

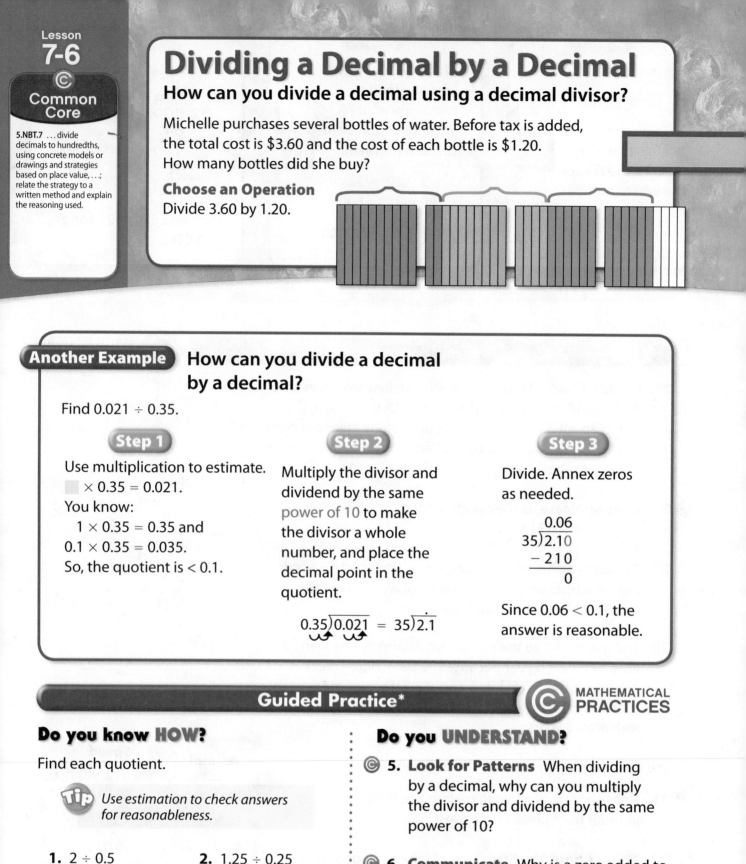

Another Example How can you divide a decimal by a decimal?

Find 0.021 ÷ 0.35.

Step 1

Use multiplication to estimate.
▨ × 0.35 = 0.021.
You know:
   1 × 0.35 = 0.35 and
0.1 × 0.35 = 0.035.
So, the quotient is < 0.1.

Step 2

Multiply the divisor and dividend by the same power of 10 to make the divisor a whole number, and place the decimal point in the quotient.

$$0.35\overline{)0.021} = 35\overline{)2.1}$$

Step 3

Divide. Annex zeros as needed.

$$\begin{array}{r} 0.06 \\ 35\overline{)2.10} \\ -210 \\ \hline 0 \end{array}$$

Since 0.06 < 0.1, the answer is reasonable.

Guided Practice*

MATHEMATICAL PRACTICES

Do you know HOW?

Find each quotient.

Tip *Use estimation to check answers for reasonableness.*

1. 2 ÷ 0.5

2. 1.25 ÷ 0.25

3. 2.1 ÷ 0.7

4. 6.6 ÷ 0.3

Do you UNDERSTAND?

ⓒ **5. Look for Patterns** When dividing by a decimal, why can you multiply the divisor and dividend by the same power of 10?

ⓒ **6. Communicate** Why is a zero added to the dividend in Step 3 of the example above?

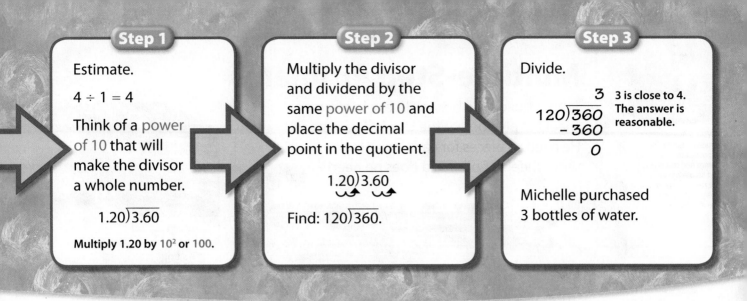

Step 1

Estimate.

$4 \div 1 = 4$

Think of a power of 10 that will make the divisor a whole number.

$1.20\overline{)3.60}$

Multiply 1.20 by 10^2 or 100.

Step 2

Multiply the divisor and dividend by the same power of 10 and place the decimal point in the quotient.

$1.20\overline{)3.60}$

Find: $120\overline{)360}$.

Step 3

Divide.

$$120\overline{)360}$$

3 is close to 4. The answer is reasonable.

Michelle purchased 3 bottles of water.

Independent Practice

Leveled Practice In **7** through **10**, estimate each quotient.

7. $3.6 \div 0.7$

8. $9.8 \div 0.2$

9. $17.8 \div 3.1$

10. $89.05 \div 4.8$

In **11** through **22**, find each quotient.

11. $62 \div 0.25$

12. $48.4 \div 0.02$

13. $0.02 \div 0.05$

14. $182.88 \div 0.08$

15. $107.25 \div 0.03$

16. $5.68 \div 8$

17. $624 \div 0.6$

18. $23.1 \div 0.7$

19. $24.2 \div 55$

20. $0.3567 \div 8.7$

21. $3.6 \div 9$

22. $4.788 \div 0.42$

Problem Solving

Ⓒ **MATHEMATICAL PRACTICES**

Ⓒ **23. Critique Reasoning/Arguments** Susan solves $1.4 \div 0.2$ using the diagram at the right. Is her reasoning correct? Explain her thinking.

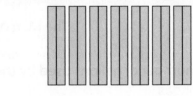

Ⓒ **24. Communicate** Tim estimates that $60 \div 5.7$ is about 10. Will the actual quotient be greater than or less than 10? Explain.

Ⓒ **25. Reason** Dex estimates that $49,892 \div 0.89$ is about 5,000. Is his estimate reasonable? Why or why not?

Ⓒ **26. Think About the Structure** What value should you multiply the divisor and dividend by to begin dividing 89 by 0.04?

A 1   **B** 10   **C** 100   **D** 1,000

Lesson
7-7

Common Core

5.NBT.7 ...divide decimals to hundredths, using concrete models or drawings and strategies based on place value, ...; relate the strategy to a written method and explain the reasoning used.

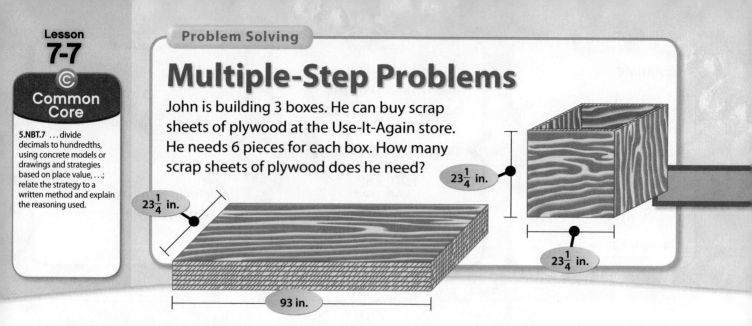

Problem Solving

Multiple-Step Problems

John is building 3 boxes. He can buy scrap sheets of plywood at the Use-It-Again store. He needs 6 pieces for each box. How many scrap sheets of plywood does he need?

$23\frac{1}{4}$ in.

$23\frac{1}{4}$ in.

$23\frac{1}{4}$ in.

93 in.

Another Example

The Marcos family went on a 2-week trip to San Diego. They drove 575 miles to get there and 627 miles to return home. In San Diego, they drove 121 miles while sightseeing. Their car can travel an average of 31.5 miles on 1 gallon of gas. If the car's gas tank can hold 14 gallons of gas, how many tanks of gas did they use on vacation?

What is one hidden question?

How many miles did the Marcos family drive during their trip?

575 miles + 627 miles + 121 miles = 1,323 miles

The Marcos family drove 1,323 miles on their trip.

What is another hidden question?

How many gallons of gas did they use on their trip?

1,323 miles ÷ 31.5 miles per gallon = 42 gallons

The Marcos family used 42 gallons of gas on their trip.

Divide the number of gallons used by the number of gallons in a full tank of gas.

42 gallons used ÷ 14 gallons in a full tank = 3 full tanks

The Marcos family used 3 tanks of gas on their trip to San Diego.

Explain It

1. Why do you need to find the hidden questions in order to solve the problem?

What do I know?

Six pieces of plywood are needed for each of 3 boxes.

Boxes are $23\frac{1}{4}$ inch cubes.

Each sheet of plywood is $23\frac{1}{4}$ inches wide and 93 inches long

What am I asked to find?

The number of sheets of plywood John needs to buy

Find the hidden question or questions.

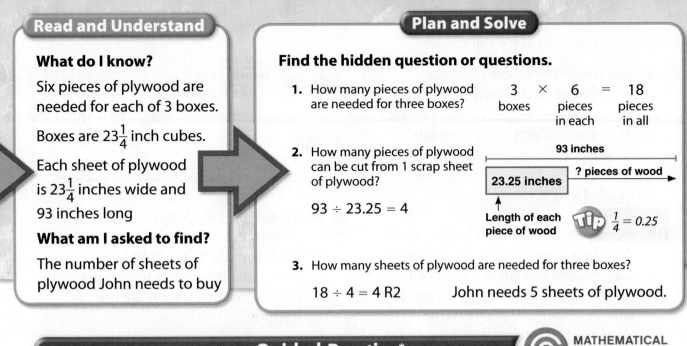

1. How many pieces of plywood are needed for three boxes?

   $3 \times 6 = 18$
   boxes / pieces in each / pieces in all

2. How many pieces of plywood can be cut from 1 scrap sheet of plywood?

   $93 \div 23.25 = 4$

   93 inches
   23.25 inches ? pieces of wood
   Length of each piece of wood
   Tip $\frac{1}{4} = 0.25$

3. How many sheets of plywood are needed for three boxes?

   $18 \div 4 = 4$ R2   John needs 5 sheets of plywood.

Guided Practice*

MATHEMATICAL PRACTICES

Do you know HOW?

Solve the problem.

1. Tom bought 8 chicken breasts and 5 steaks. Each chicken breast weighed 0.35 pound and each steak weighed 1.25 pounds. How many pounds of meat did Tom buy?

Do you UNDERSTAND?

2. **Persevere** What are the hidden questions and answers in Problem 1?

3. **Generalize** Write a real-world multiple-step problem that can be solved using multiplication and division.

Independent Practice

MATHEMATICAL PRACTICES

In **4** and **5**, write the hidden question or questions. Then solve.

4. **Reason** Alyssa has a CD that holds 700 megabytes of information. She has saved 53 pictures, each using 2.24 megabytes, to the CD. How much space is left on the CD?

5. Lori bought some plums and 4 peaches. The peaches cost $1.88 in all and the plums cost $0.33 each. She paid $3.86 in all, not including tax. How many plums did she buy?

Applying Math Practices

- What am I asked to find?
- What else can I try?
- How are quantities related?
- How can I explain my work?
- How can I use math to model the problem?
- Can I use tools to help?
- Is my work precise?
- Why does this work?
- How can I generalize?

For **6**, use the chart at the right.

6. Use Tools The school cafeteria manager needs to know how many food trays are needed during a week. All of the students eat lunch each school day, and half of all the students eat breakfast. How many trays will be needed in one week?

Grade	Number of Students	Grade	Number of Students
K	95	3	107
1	112	4	100
2	104	5	114

7. Persevere Juan used first-class mail to send two baseballs to his grandson. Each baseball weighed 5 ounces. The postage was $0.39 for the first ounce and $0.24 for each additional ounce. How much was the postage?

8. Model The Meadows Farm has 160 acres. Three times as many acres are used to plant crops as are used for pasture. Draw a picture and write an equation to find how many acres are used for pasture.

9. Be Precise A youth group charged $6 per car at their car wash to raise money. They raised $858. Of that amount, $175 was given as donations and the rest of the money came from washing cars. Stella estimated that they washed more than 100 cars. Is her estimate reasonable? Explain your reasoning.

10. Generalize A hardware store has 5 employees. Each employee works the same number of hours every week, and each one earns $10.50 per hour. Last week they worked a total of 167.5 hours. Draw a picture and write an equation to find how many hours each employee worked.

Think About the Structure

11. Persevere Matt is saving to buy a skateboard and a helmet. The skateboard costs $57 and the helmet costs $45. Matt has saved $19 so far. Which hidden question needs to be answered before you can find how much more he needs to save?

  A Is the skateboard on sale?

  B How much more does the skateboard cost than the helmet?

  C What is the price of the skateboard minus the price of the helmet?

  D What is the total price of the helmet and the skateboard?

12. Reason Two restaurant waiters share $\frac{1}{4}$ of their tips with the host. On Saturday, one waiter earned $122 in tips, and the other waiter earned $136 in tips. Which expression shows how to find the solution to the hidden question?

  A $122 + 136$

  B $136 \div \frac{1}{4}$

  C $122 \div \frac{1}{4}$

  D $136 - 122$

Find the quotient. Estimate to check if the answer is reasonable.

1. $14.5 \div 2.5$ **2.** $2.28 \div 0.6$ **3.** $69.02 \div 0.7$ **4.** $88.5 \div 0.03$

5. $0.08 \div 0.025$ **6.** $3.2 \div 0.004$ **7.** $15.5 \div 6.2$ **8.** $2.35 \div 4.7$

9. $0.81 \div 0.09$ **10.** $5.6 \div 0.08$ **11.** $13.3 \div 3.8$ **12.** $1.4 \div 0.04$

13. $66.96 \div 3.6$ **14.** $7.99 \div 0.94$ **15.** $8.88 \div 0.08$ **16.** $0.3 \div 0.03$

Use rounding to estimate the answer.

17. $598 \div 12$ **18.** $47.5 \div 23.6$ **19.** $960.7 \div 31.5$

Error Search Find each answer that is not correct.
Write it correctly and explain the error.

20. $2.748 \div 0.6 = 0.0458$ **21.** $7.86 \div 6 = 1.31$

22. $26.82 \div 3 = 0.894$ **23.** $61.25 \div 4.9 = 12.5$

Number Sense

© **Communicate** Write whether each statement is
true or false. Explain your reasoning.

24. The quotient of $4.35 \div 6$ is closer to 0.7 than 0.8.

25. The expression $8e + 6$ equals 30 when $e = 3$.

26. The quotient of $8.63 \div 5.7$ is less than 2.

27. The quotient of $3,467 \div 5$ is closer to 700 than the quotient of $5,598 \div 8$.

28. The sum of 99,999 and 3,879 is 1 more than 103,879.

29. The product of 6 and 808 is greater than the product of 8 and 606.

Set A, pages 170–171

Find 34.05 ÷ 100.

Dividing by 10, or 10^1 means moving the decimal point one place to the left.

Dividing by 100, or 10^2 means moving the decimal point two places to the left.

Dividing by 1,000, or 10^3 means moving the decimal point three places to the left.

34.05 ÷ 100 = 0.3405 = 0.3405

Remember that when dividing decimals by 10, 100, or 1,000, you may need to use one or more zeros as placeholders: 24.3 ÷ 1,000 = 0.0243.

Use mental math to find each quotient.

1. 34.6 ÷ 10
2. 64.83 ÷ 100
3. 148.3 ÷ 1,000
4. 2.99 ÷ 100
5. 7.07 ÷ 10
6. 59.13 ÷ 10^3
7. 8.94 ÷ 100
8. 6.34 ÷ 10

Set B, pages 172–173, 174–175

Estimate: 27.5 ÷ 11. Use compatible numbers.

27.5 ÷ 11
↓   ↓
30 ÷ 10 = 3

So, 27.5 ÷ 11 is about 3.

To check, use number sense to decide on the placement of the decimal point.

27.5 ÷ 11 = 2 5 0

The dividend is greater than the divisor, so the answer will be greater than 1.2 × 11 is 22, so the answer is 2.50.

Remember that compatible numbers are numbers that are easy to compute in your head.

Estimate each quotient. in **1–4.** Use number sense to correctly place the decimal point in **5–8.**

1. 26.2 ÷ 5
2. 31.9 ÷ 3
3. 49.6 ÷ 6
4. 163.5 ÷ 80
5. 4185.44 ÷ 74 = 5 6 5 6
6. 2470.4 ÷ 64 = 3 8 6
7. 1356.6 ÷ 38 = 3 5 7
8. 77.7 ÷ 21 = 3 7 0

Set C, pages 176–177

Find 3.60 ÷ 15.

$$\begin{array}{r} 0.24 \\ 15\overline{)3.60} \\ \underline{3\,0} \\ 60 \\ \underline{60} \\ 0 \end{array}$$

Place the decimal point in the quotient directly above the decimal point in the dividend. Then divide.

So, 3.60 ÷ 15 = 0.24.

Multiply to check.

0.24 × 15 = 3.60

Remember to write a zero placeholder in the quotient when you cannot divide a place in the dividend.

Find each quotient.

1. $7\overline{)12.6}$
2. $31\overline{)17.05}$
3. $8\overline{)51.2}$
4. $12\overline{)60.12}$
5. 199.68 ÷ 64
6. 152.5 ÷ 5
7. 47.61 ÷ 23
8. 51.6 ÷ 43

Find 57.9 ÷ 0.6.

Since 0.6 has one decimal place, move the decimal point one place to the right in both numbers. Then divide.

```
        96.5
0.6)57.90
     54
     ──
     39
     36
     ──
      30
      30
      ──
       0
```

Annex more zeros in the dividend if needed.

57.9 ÷ 0.6 = 96.5

Remember to place the decimal point in the quotient above the decimal point in the dividend before dividing.

1. 84 ÷ 3.2
2. 81 ÷ 3.6
3. 303 ÷ 0.03
4. 162 ÷ 0.81
5. 714 ÷ 2.1
6. 456 ÷ 0.05
7. 16.4 ÷ 0.8
8. 136.5 ÷ 4.2
9. 22.22 ÷ 2.2
10. 54.78 ÷ 6.6
11. 71.04 ÷ 7.4
12. 40.02 ÷ 8.7
13. 9.6 ÷ 0.03
14. 74.48 ÷ 9.8

Set E, pages 182–184

A football coach spent a total of $890.40, including $50.40 tax, for 35 shirts for the team. Each shirt was the same price. What was the price of one shirt?

What is the hidden question or questions?

How much did all of the shirts cost without tax?

$890.40	
$50.40	?

$890.40 − $50.40 = $840.00

What is the price of one shirt?

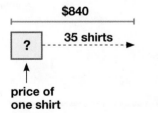

$840 ÷ 35 = $24

The price of one shirt was $24.00.

Remember to answer the hidden question or questions first to solve the problem.

Write and answer the hidden question or questions. Then solve.

1. Royce bought a book for $12.49 and 2 DVDs. Both DVDs were the same price. The tax on all the items is $1.76. He paid a total of $46.23. What was the price of each DVD?

2. Kim bought sandwiches for the football team. Each sandwich cost $3.49. She paid $142.39, including $2.79 tax. How many sandwiches did she buy?

Multiple Choice

1. Mr. Dodd filled the gas tank on his lawn mower with 3.8 gallons of gas. If he mowed his yard 10 times on the same tank of gas, how much gas did he use each time the lawn was mowed? (7-1)

   A 0.038 gallons

   B 0.38 gallons

   C 38 gallons

   D 380 gallons

2. Kimberly scored a total of 35.104 points in four events for her gymnastic competition. If she scored the same amount on each event, how many points did she score on each? (7-4)

   A 0.8776 points

   B 8.0776 points

   C 8.776 points

   D 87.76 points

3. The table shows the amount of different types of produce Mrs. Cuzalina bought, and the total price she paid for each. What is the price per pound she paid for the apples? (7-6)

Produce	Pounds	Total Price
Apples	3.4	$2.89
Bananas	2.6	$1.27
Grapes	3.7	$2.85

   A $0.09

   B $0.80

   C $0.84

   D $0.85

4. The chef at a restaurant bought 37 pounds of salad for $46.25. How much did she pay for 1 pound of salad? (7-4)

   A $0.125

   B $1.25

   C $1.30

   D $12.50

5. Consider 9.74 ÷ 0.32. Which of the following has the decimal placed in the correct location? (7-3)

   A 0.03475

   B 3.04375

   C 30.4375

   D 304.375

6. How many quarters are there in thirty dollars? (7-5)

   A 12 quarters

   B 20 quarters

   C 120 quarters

   D 200 quarters

7. Which of the following is the best estimate of 78.4 ÷ 18? (7-2)

   A 740

   B 50

   C 5

   D 4

8.

Notebook Prices	
Quantity	**Cost**
1	$1.29
2	$2.32
5	$4.80
10	$9.00

How much would 10 students save if they bought 10 notebooks as a group rather than individually? (7-7)

9. Use compatible numbers to estimate the quotient of 46.1 ÷ 2.3. (7-2)

10. Russ has a car that averages 9.8 miles per gallon while Mike's car averages 39.2 miles per gallon. How does Mike's mileage compare to Russ's? (7-6)

11. Cora is saving for a vacation. The total cost of the vacation is $1,800.36, and she has a year to save the money. How much should she save per month so she can meet her goal? (7-4)

12. Kara knows that to find the quotient of $56.9 \div 10^3$ she needs to change the divisor to standard form. Find the quotient. (7-1)

13. A developer owns 24 acres of land. He plans to use 1.2 acres for an entrance into a housing development and divide the remaining land into 0.6 acre lots. How many lots will he have? (7-7)

14. Jen says that the decimal point in the following problem belongs after the 4. Is she correct? Why? (7-3)

$$43.68 \div 5.2 = 84.0$$

15. Mrs. Frohock bought a watermelon that weighed 10.25 pounds. If she cut it into 5 pieces of equal weight, how many pounds did each piece weigh? (7-4)

16. Rudi bought 12.5 yards of fabric to make pillows. Each pillow requires 1.75 yards of fabric. Use compatible numbers to estimate the number of pillows Rudi can make. (7-2)

17. Find 0.64 ÷ 16

Is the work shown below the correct way to solve this problem? Explain why or why not. (7-3)

$$16\overline{)0.64} = 0.4$$

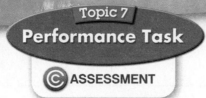
Lydia is organizing a cooking competition at her school. She ordered some basic supplies to share among the teams that are competing. The teams will be bringing other ingredients to use as well.

Use the table below to answer the questions about how Lydia will divide the supplies.

Cooking Supplies
150 meters, twine for tying
3 timers
750.75 grams, flour
36 eggs
2.75 liters, milk
5.4 liters, olive oil
24.36 grams, salt

1. One team is going to use 0.10 of the twine. How many meters of twine will they use? They are going to cut their twine into segments that are 0.5 meter long. How many segments can they make? If they cut the twine into segments that are 0.05 meter long, how many segments can they make?

2. There are 6 teams competing. If they divide the olive oil equally, how much will each team receive? Write and solve an equation to show your work.

3. Use compatible numbers to estimate. If the 6 teams divide the flour equally, about how many grams of flour will each team receive? Write an equation that shows how you estimated.

4. Only 5 teams need to use the milk that Lydia supplies. They agree to share the milk equally. How many liters of milk will each team get?

5. If 4 teams share the salt equally, how much more would each team get than if all 6 teams shared the salt equally? Show your work.

6. Lydia expects to raise $1,020.78 from the competition. If she donates the same amount to 6 different charities, how much will each charity receive?

Topic
8

Numerical Expressions, Patterns, and Relationships

▼ Passengers on a cruise ship can go ashore when the ship stops at ports of call. How can order of operations be used to find the number of passengers left on the ship when other passengers get off the ship? You will find out in Lesson 8-2.

Review What You Know!

Vocabulary

Choose the best term from the box.

- difference
- quotient
- product
- sum

1. The answer to a division problem is the __?__ .

2. The __?__ of 5 and 7 is 12.

3. To find the __?__ between 16 and 4 you subtract.

4. Multiplying is the same as finding the __?__ .

Mixed Practice

Find each answer.

5. $32 \div 4$

6. 35×100

7. $47 + 92$

8. $\frac{1}{4} + \frac{2}{4}$

9. $3.4 - 2.7$

10. $1.9 + 7$

11. $3 + \frac{1}{2}$

12. $75 \div 5$

13. $\$3.75 + \$2.49$

14. $8\frac{5}{8} - 1\frac{2}{8}$

Patterns

© **Writing to Explain** Write an answer for the question.

15. What equation comes next in the pattern below? Explain how you know.

$$7 \times 10 = 70$$
$$7 \times 100 = 700$$
$$7 \times 1,000 = 7,000$$

Topic Essential Question
- How are the values of an algebraic expression and a numerical expression found?

Topic**8**

Interactive Learning

Pose the problem. Start each lesson by working together to solve problems. It will help you make sense of math.

Persevere Use the table at the right to solve the problem.

For each of the last five years, the Hawks won 2 more games than the Metros won each year. Copy and complete the table to show how many games the Hawks won for the number of games the Metros won.

No. of Games Metros Won	No. of Games Hawks Won
1	
3	
6	
8	
10	

Be Precise Solve any way you choose.

Two students evaluated the expression 15 + 12 ÷ 3 + 5 and got two different answers. Neither made a computational mistake. How could this happen?

Use Structure Work with your partner to evaluate the following expression.

3 + (6 − 2) × 4

Show your work.

Use Structure Use order of operations to simplify the following expression.

7 + [2(8.1 + 0.9)]

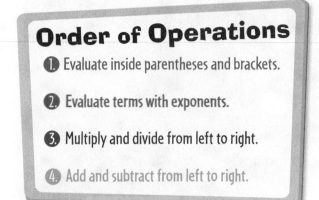

Order of Operations

1. Evaluate inside parentheses and brackets.

2. Evaluate terms with exponents.

3. Multiply and divide from left to right.

4. Add and subtract from left to right.

Lesson 8-5

© **Use Tools** Use the table to solve the problem.

Jack	17	20	25	32
Javier	13	16	21	28

Jack and Javier played a math game. Jack started by modeling a number with place-value blocks. Then Javier changed the number. The table shows the numbers that Jack modeled and also the numbers that were modeled after Javier changed them. What rule did Javier use to change the blocks? Record your work with words, symbols, or numbers.

Lesson 8-6

© **Model** Use the table to solve the problem.

Sheena	6	12	14	20
Julie	18	36	42	60

Sheena and Julie played a math game. The table shows the starting numbers Sheena modeled with place-value blocks. The table also shows the numbers of blocks modeled after Julie changed them. What rule did Julie use to change the blocks? Record your work with words, symbols, or numbers.

Lesson 8-7

© **Reason** Draw a picture to help you solve.

Maria and Elsie have new piggy banks. Maria saves two dollars each week. Elsie saves four dollars each week. If neither of them spends any of their money, how do their savings compare after a year?

Lesson 8-8

© **Look for Patterns** For the following math expressions,

$$5 + \square \text{ and } 4 \times \triangle$$

the rectangle and the triangle are each covering up one number.

Without knowing what the numbers are, what different word phrases could you use to describe each?

Lesson 8-9

© **Use Tools** A store sold 20 sweatshirts. Of these, 8 were red. Twice as many were green as yellow. How many of each color sweatshirt did the store sell? Work with your partner and use tiles to help you solve this problem. Show your work.

Show the Problem?

Lesson
8-1

Common
Core

5.OA.2 Write simple expressions that record calculations with numbers, and interpret numerical expressions without evaluating them.

Using Variables to Write Expressions

How can you write an algebraic expression?

Donnie bought CDs for $10 each. How can you represent the total cost of the CDs?

A **variable** is a quantity that can change or vary and is often represented with a letter. Variables help you translate word phrases into algebraic expressions.

$10 each

Other Examples

The table shows algebraic expressions for given situations.

Word Phrase	Operation	Algebraic Expression
three dollars more than cost c	addition	$c + 3$
twelve pencils decreased by a number n	subtraction	$12 - n$
five times a distance d	multiplication	$5 \times d$ or $5d$
a apples divided by four	division	$a \div 4$ or $\frac{a}{4}$
five less than three times an amount x	multiplication and subtraction	$3x - 5$

Guided Practice*

MATHEMATICAL PRACTICES

Do you know HOW?

Write an algebraic expression for each situation.

1. the difference of a number t and 22

2. m bicycles added to 18 bicycles

3. 11 times a number z

4. 4 less than 5 times a number g

Do you UNDERSTAND?

5. In the example at the top of the page, what does the variable n represent?

6. Reason Identify the variable and the operation in the algebraic expression $8y$.

7. Model Write an algebraic expression for this situation: n more students than the 8 students sitting in each of the 3 rows.

Animated Glossary
www.pearsonsuccessnet.com

DIGITAL

For another example, see Set A on page 214.

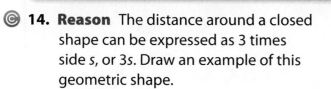

CDs cost $10 each. The operation is multiplication.

Number of CDs	Total Cost
1	$10 × 1
2	$10 × 2
3	$10 × 3
4	$10 × 4

Use the variable *n* to represent the number of CDs and write an algebraic expression.

$$\$10 \times n$$

An <mark>algebraic expression</mark> is a mathematical phrase that has at least one variable and one operation. The total cost of the CDs is represented by

$$10 \times n$$
or 10*n*.

The operation is multiplication. The variable is *n*.

Independent Practice

For **8** through **13**, write algebraic expressions.

8. A number *p* increased by 22

9. 15 divided by a number *r*

10. 12 more points than a number *p* times 8

11. 6 less than 7 times a number *b*

12. 5 more than the product of *x* and 9

13. 7 times the difference of *y* and 4

Problem Solving

MATHEMATICAL PRACTICES

14. Reason The distance around a closed shape can be expressed as 3 times side *s*, or 3*s*. Draw an example of this geometric shape.

15. Manuel sold *a* cartons of apple juice and *r* cartons of raisins. Write an algebraic expression to represent how many cartons were sold.

16. Model One float for the Tournament of Roses parade uses as many flowers as a florist usually uses in 5 years. If *x* is the number of flowers a florist uses in 1 year, write an algebraic expression for the number of flowers used to make a float.

17. Construct Arguments Devin's DVD case has 3 rows of slots, but 5 slots are broken. If *x* equals the number of slots in a row, explain how the expression 3*x* − 5 relates to Devin's DVD case.

18. Look for Patterns A group of hens laid the same number of eggs each day for a week. Kelly collected the eggs for six days. Write an expression to show the number of eggs Kelly did not collect.

19. Think About the Structure Which expression shows a quantity of rolls, *r*, added to 8 bagels?

  A 8 − *r*   **C** 8 + *r*

  B 8*r*   **D** *r* ÷ 8

Lesson
8-2

Common
Core

5.OA.1 Use parentheses, brackets, or braces in numerical expressions, and evaluate expressions with these symbols.

Order of Operations

How can you evaluate a numerical expression with more than one operation?

Two students evaluated the same expression but got different answers.

To avoid getting more than one answer, use the order of operations. Rebecca used the correct order.

Find the value of $12 \div 4 + (9 - 2) \times (3 + 5)$.

Rebecca's Way
$36 + 9 \div 3 \times 5$
$36 + 3 \times 5$
$36 + 15$
51

Juan's Way
$36 + 9 \div 3 \times 5$
$45 \div 3 \times 5$
15×5
75

Another Example ## How can you evaluate an algebraic expression with more than one operation?

You can use order of operations when evaluating algebraic expressions.

What is the value of $4v + 2w - 3$, if $v = 5$ and $w = 3$?

Step 1 Replace all of the variables with given values. Remember that $4v$ means $4 \times v$.

Step 2 Using the order of operations, multiply or divide in order from left to right.

Step 3 Add or subtract in order from left to right.

The value of the expression is 23.

$$4 \times 5 + 2 \times 3 - 3$$
$$20 + 6 - 3$$
$$26 - 3$$
$$23$$

Explain It

1. How could the value of a numerical expression such as $4 \times 5 + 2 \times 3 - 3$ be changed?

Guided Practice*

MATHEMATICAL PRACTICES

Do you know HOW?

For **1** through **4**, name the operation you should do first.

1. $6 + 27 \div 3$

2. $5 \times 2 + 12 \div 6$

3. $17 - (4 + 3)$

4. $(14 - 7) + (3 + 5)$

Do you UNDERSTAND?

5. Construct Arguments In the first example, why was Juan's answer incorrect?

6. Be Precise Insert parentheses to make the following statement true.
$3 + 5 \times 2 - 10 = 6$

Step 1	Step 2	Step 3

Step 1

In using order of operations, do the operations inside parentheses first.

$12 \div 4 + (9 - 2) \times (3 + 5)$

$12 \div 4 + \quad 7 \quad \times \quad 8$

Remember to rewrite the operations not yet performed.

Step 2

Then, multiply and divide in order from left to right.

$12 \div 4 + 7 \times 8$

$3 \quad + \quad 56$

Step 3

Finally, add and subtract in order from left to right.

$3 + 56$

59

Independent Practice

MATHEMATICAL PRACTICES

For **7** through **18**, find the value of each expression using order of operations.

7. $3 + 7 \times 6 \div 3 - 4$

8. $(29 - 18) + 14 \div 2 + 6$

9. $64 \div 8 \times 2$

10. $(19 - 5) \times 3 + 4$

11. $3(6 + 2) - 12 \times 2$

12. $36 - 5(16 - 11)$

13. $8 \times (3 + 2) - 6$

14. $3 \div (9 - 6) + 4 \times 2$

15. $(3 + 4) \times (3 + 5)$

16. $25 + 18 \div 6 - 1$

17. $4 \times (3 - 2) + 18$

18. $8 \times 6 - 4 \times 3$

For **19** through **24**, insert parentheses to make each statement true.

19. $30 - 4 \times 2 + 5 = 2$

20. $17 - 8 - 5 = 14$

21. $10 \div 2 - 3 + 1 = 3$

22. $30 - 4 \times 2 + 5 = 57$

23. $17 - 8 - 5 = 4$

24. $10 \div 2 - 3 + 1 = 1$

© **25. Be Precise** Would the value of the expression in Exercise 21 be different if no parentheses were used?

For **26** through **34**, evaluate each expression for $x = 16$ and $y = 4$.

26. $3x - 3y$

27. $x \div (2y - 4)$

28. $5y + x \div 8$

29. $4x - 2y$

30. $y \div (x \div y)$

31. $3y + 2x - 7$

32. $5x - 4y$

33. $x \div y$

34. $2x + 4y - 10$

Animated Glossary
www.pearsonsuccessnet.com

35. Draw the next figure in the following pattern.

For **36** through **38**, use the table at the right.

© **36. Use Tools** The girls' gym teacher needs to purchase 15 softballs, 5 packages of tennis balls, and 2 soccer balls. She plans to collect $1 from each of her 15 students to help pay for the balls. Write and evaluate an expression to show how much more the teacher will have to pay.

Data		
Baseballs	:	$20 per dozen
Softballs	:	$3 each
Basketballs	:	$15 each
Soccer balls	:	$17 each
Tennis balls	:	$4 per package of 3

© **37. Use Tools** The boys' gym teacher needs to buy 2 dozen baseballs, 4 basketballs, and 24 tennis balls. Write and evaluate an expression to show how much the balls will cost.

© **38. Communicate** Did you use parentheses in the expression you wrote for Exercise 36? Why or why not?

39. A small cruise ship has 220 passengers. At the Port of San Juan, 2 groups of 12 passengers go ashore to shop and 5 groups of 6 passengers go sightseeing. Evaluate $220 - (2 \times 12) - (5 \times 6)$ to find the number of passengers that are left on the ship.

40. The state of Montana is about 630 miles long and about 280 miles wide. The area of Montana could fit 3 states the size of Pennsylvania. What is the approximate area of Montana?

Tip *Area = length × width.*

© **41. Persevere** At a ski lift, 41 people are waiting to board cars that hold 6 people each. How many cars will be completely filled? How many people are left to board the last car?

A 6; 6   **C** 5; 6

B 6; 5   **D** 5; 5

© **43. Reasonableness** True or false? Explain.
$4(3 + 5) - 10 = 4 \times 3 + 5 - 10$

© **42. Use Structure** Mark bought 3 boxes of pencils that contained 20 pencils each and 4 boxes of pens that contained 10 pens each. Which expression represents the total number of pencils and pens Mark bought?

A $(3 \times 10) + (4 \times 20)$

B $(3 \times 4) + (10 \times 20)$

C $(3 \times 20) + (4 \times 10)$

D $(3 + 20) + (4 + 10)$

Mixed Problem Solving

A state song is an official symbol of the state it represents. Each of the 50 states, with the exception of New Jersey, has at least one state song. Some of the states chose songs that are famous on their own, while other states chose a song that is known only as a state song. Here are a few examples of some of the state songs:

Data

United States State Songs

State	Song Title	Year Written	Year Adopted
California	"I Love You, California"	1913	1988
Kentucky	"My Old Kentucky Home"	1853	1928
Oklahoma	"Oklahoma"	1943	1953
Maryland	"Maryland, My Maryland"	1861	1939

For **1** through **5**, use the table above.

1. How many years passed between the time Kentucky's state song was written before it was adopted?

2. **Reasonableness** About how many decades passed between the writing of "I Love You, California" and its adoption?

3. How many years earlier was "Maryland, My Maryland" written than "Oklahoma"?

4. Put the years each song was adopted in order from least to greatest.

5. **Critique Reasoning/Arguments** A lustrum is a period of 5 years. Richard said that 15 lustrums occurred between the time that California's state song was written and then adopted by the state. Is he correct? Explain.

6. **Use Tools** Solve using the strategy Draw a Picture and Write an Equation.

   Tricia ran 5 times as far as Ali. Ali ran 375 meters. How far did Tricia run?

Lesson
8-3

Common
Core

5.OA.1 Use parentheses,
brackets, or braces in
numerical expressions, and
evaluate expressions with
these symbols.

Simplifying Expressions

What order should you use when you simplify an expression?

Jack evaluated $(7 \times 2) - 3 + 2^2 \times 1$.

To avoid getting more than one answer, he used the order of operations given at the right.

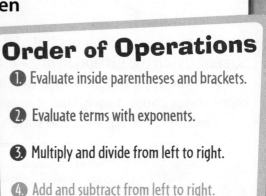

Order of Operations

1. Evaluate inside parentheses and brackets.

2. Evaluate terms with exponents.

3. Multiply and divide from left to right.

4. Add and subtract from left to right.

Other Examples

Simplify expressions with a variable

First, substitute the value for the variable.
Then follow the order of operations to simplify.

Find the value of the expression:
$(19 + a) + 16 \div 4$ for $a = 12$.

$(19 + 12) + 16 \div 4$

$31 + 16 \div 4$

$31 + 4 = 35$

Find the value of the expression:
$(16 - b) + 2 \times 3$ for $b = 9$.

$(16 - 9) + 2 \times 3$

$7 + 2 \times 3$

$7 + 6 = 13$

Guided Practice*

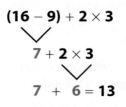

MATHEMATICAL
PRACTICES

Do you know HOW?

Use the order of operations to simplify the following expressions.

1. $8 + 14 \div 2 - (3 - 1)$

2. $7 \times (6 - 1) + 10^2$

3. $17 + 4 \times 3$

4. $(8 + 1) + 3^2 \times 7$

5. $(4 \times 3) \div 2 + 1 + 2 \times 6$

Do you UNDERSTAND?

6. In the example at the top, what operation do you do first?

7. **Communicate** Explain the steps involved in simplifying the expression $(4 + 2) - 1 \times 3$.

8. **Reason** Which is greater, $1 \times 5 + 4$ or $1 + 5 \times 4$?

9. **Be Precise** Would the value of $(15 - 3) \div 3 + 1$ change if the parentheses were removed?

*For another example, see Set B on page 214.

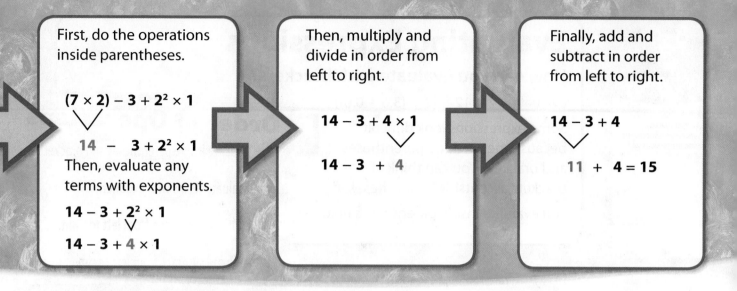

First, do the operations inside parentheses.

$(7 \times 2) - 3 + 2^2 \times 1$

$14 - 3 + 2^2 \times 1$

Then, evaluate any terms with exponents.

$14 - 3 + 2^2 \times 1$

$14 - 3 + 4 \times 1$

Then, multiply and divide in order from left to right.

$14 - 3 + 4 \times 1$

$14 - 3 + 4$

Finally, add and subtract in order from left to right.

$14 - 3 + 4$

$11 + 4 = 15$

Independent Practice

In **10** through **15**, use the order of operations to simplify the expression.

10. $6 - 3 \times 2 + 4$

11. $(4 \times 8) \div 2 + 8$

12. $(18 + 7) \times (11 - 7)$

13. $2 + 3 \times 4 + 5 \times 6$

14. $4^2 \times 3 - (17 + 20)$

15. $90 - 5 \times 5 \times 2$

In **16** through **21**, find the value of each expression for $b = 3$.

16. $39 \times 8 - (b + 4)$

17. $22 \div (2 \times 7 - b) + 1$

18. $2 \times b - 3 + b \times 4$

19. $39 \div b + 7$

20. $4 + 5 \times 6 \div b$

21. $(5^2 \times 10) \times (2 \times b - 1)$

Problem Solving

 **MATHEMATICAL PRACTICES**

22. To solve the equation $n + 20 = 25$, Darlene tested values for n until she found one that would work. She tested 5, 6, and 7. Which is correct?

ⓒ **23. Use Structure** According to the order of operations, which operation should be used first in the expression?

$6 \times 3 + 7 \div (2 - 1)$

A $\times$ **B** $+$ **C** $\div$ **D** $-$

ⓒ **24. Reason** An air tanker fights fires using lake water. The plane scoops up 2,000 pounds of water in each of its two tanks. Write an expression to find how much water the tanker carries when each tank is filled.

ⓒ **25. Construct Arguments** Use the operation signs $+$, $-$, $\times$, and $\div$ once each in the expression below to make the number sentence true.

$6 \quad (3 \quad 1) \quad 5 \quad 1 = 17$

Lesson
8-4

Ⓒ
Common
Core

5.OA.1 Use parentheses, brackets, or braces in numerical expressions, and evaluate expressions with these symbols.

Evaluating Expressions

How can you evaluate with brackets?

Evaluate $3.2 \times 12 - [2 + (3.6 \div 0.6)]$

Some expressions look difficult because they include parentheses and brackets. You can think of brackets as "outside" parentheses.

You evaluate inside parentheses first.

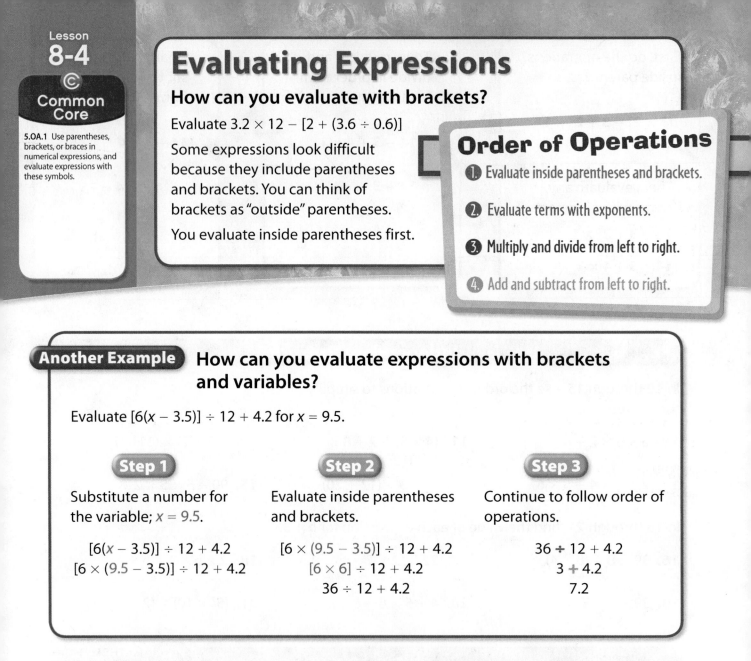

Order of Operations

❶ Evaluate inside parentheses and brackets.

❷ Evaluate terms with exponents.

❸ Multiply and divide from left to right.

❹ Add and subtract from left to right.

Another Example How can you evaluate expressions with brackets and variables?

Evaluate $[6(x - 3.5)] \div 12 + 4.2$ for $x = 9.5$.

Step 1

Substitute a number for the variable; $x = 9.5$.

$[6(x - 3.5)] \div 12 + 4.2$
$[6 \times (9.5 - 3.5)] \div 12 + 4.2$

Step 2

Evaluate inside parentheses and brackets.

$[6 \times (9.5 - 3.5)] \div 12 + 4.2$
$[6 \times 6] \div 12 + 4.2$
$36 \div 12 + 4.2$

Step 3

Continue to follow order of operations.

$36 \div 12 + 4.2$
$3 + 4.2$
7.2

Guided Practice*

Ⓒ MATHEMATICAL PRACTICES

Do you know **HOW?**

Evaluate each expression.

1. $2.3 + (4.5 - 2.1)$

2. $(9.8 + x) \times 2.8; x = 6.2$

3. $[(5.5 + 2.3) - 2.1] + 2.3$

4. $[(7.9 + 13.5) - (y + 10.4)]; y = 9.8$

Do you **UNDERSTAND?**

5. How are brackets like parentheses?

Ⓒ **6. Construct Arguments** In the example at the top, would it be easier to evaluate the expression using mental math, paper and pencil, or a calculator?

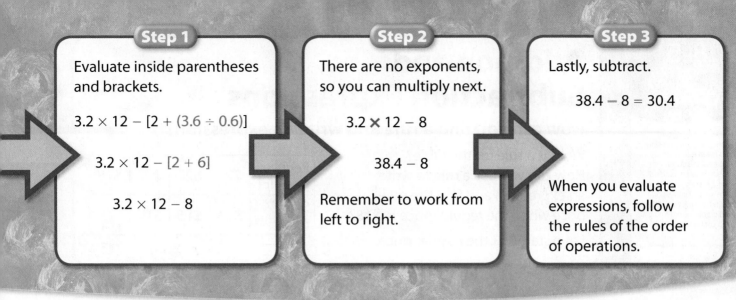

Step 1

Evaluate inside parentheses and brackets.

$3.2 \times 12 - [2 + (3.6 \div 0.6)]$

$3.2 \times 12 - [2 + 6]$

$3.2 \times 12 - 8$

Step 2

There are no exponents, so you can multiply next.

$3.2 \times 12 - 8$

$38.4 - 8$

Remember to work from left to right.

Step 3

Lastly, subtract.

$38.4 - 8 = 30.4$

When you evaluate expressions, follow the rules of the order of operations.

Independent Practice

Evaluate each expression.

7. $3.1 + (9.6 - 2.3)$

8. $(9.9 + x) \div 0.25; x = 3.6$

9. $112.5 - (3.3 \div 0.6) \times 2$

10. $[(2 + 9.8) - 2.5] + 7.7$

11. $[2.1 \times (125 \div 5)] - 2.5$

12. $[(16 \times 3.5) \div 0.25] + 1 - 10^2$

13. $14.6 + [(42 - 21.4) \times 3.5]$

14. $18.9 - [(33.3 \div 11.1) \times 6]$

15. $3 \times [(18 \times 5.5) \div y]; y = 0.3$

Problem Solving

MATHEMATICAL PRACTICES

16. Construct Arguments How do you know which part of the expression to solve first? Explain.

$(26 + 2.5) - [(8.3 \times 3) + (1 - 0.25)]$

17. Generalize Explain how you could use estimation to get an approximate answer for the expression below.

$(11.6 + 7.3) - (6.2 \times 2.1)$

18. Reasonableness Theresa bought three containers of tennis balls at $2.98 each. She had a coupon for $1 off. Her mom paid for half of the remaining cost. Evaluate the expression $[(3 \times 2.98) - 1] \div 2$.

19. Soledad solves the problem below and thinks that the answer is 92.3. Jill solves the same problem, but thinks that the answer is 67.5. Who is correct?

$[(65 + 28.2) - (7.8 + 5.5)] - 12.4$

20. Think About the Structure Using order of operations, which is the last operation you should perform to evaluate this expression?

$(1 \times 2.5) + (52 \div 13) + (5 - 6.7) - (98 + 8)$

A Addition

C Multiplication

B Subtraction

D Division

21. How long of a piece of tape would be needed to go around the perimeter of the triangle below?

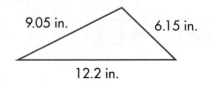

9.05 in.   6.15 in.

12.2 in.

Common Core

5.OA.3 Generate two numerical patterns using two given rules. Identify apparent relationships between corresponding terms. Form ordered pairs consisting of corresponding terms from the two patterns, and graph the ordered pairs on a coordinate plane.

Addition and Subtraction Expressions

How can you find a rule and write an expression?

What is a rule for the table?
How can you use a rule to write an expression and find the sale price when the regular price is $18?

Let *p* stand for the regular price.

Regular price *(p)*	$21	$20	$19	$18
Sale price	$16	$15	$14	

Guided Practice*

MATHEMATICAL PRACTICES

Do you know HOW?

For **1** and **2**, use the table below.

Total number of test questions *(q)*	20	30	40	50
Number of multiple-choice questions	10	20	30	

1. What is a rule for the table in words? in symbols?

2. How many multiple-choice questions would be on a 50-question test?

Do you UNDERSTAND?

© 3. **Use Tools** How could you use place-value blocks to find a rule in the table to the left?

© 4. **Model** Tony earns $7 and saves $2. When he earns $10, he saves $5. When he earns $49, he saves $44. Write an expression for the amount he saves.

Tip *Make a table to help you find a rule.*

5. In the example at the top, what is the sale price when the regular price is $30?

Independent Practice

For **6** through **11**, find a rule.

6.

n	3	4	5
n + ▨	7	8	9

7.

b	31	42	55
b − ▨	23	34	47

8.

q	0	2	8
q + ▨	15	17	23

9.

p	3	4	5
p + ▨	68	69	70

10.

x	18	21	26
x − ▨	5	8	13

11.

r	112	96	62
r − ▨	73	57	23

For another example, see Set C on page 215.

Subtract to find the sale price.	Use the expression $p - 5$ to find the missing value when $p = 18$.

Subtract to find the sale price.

For a regular price of $21:

$21 - 5 = 16$

For a regular price of $20:

$20 - 5 = 15$

For a regular price of $19:

$19 - 5 = 14$

A rule is subtract 5.
So, the expression is $p - 5$.

Use the expression $p - 5$ to find the missing value when $p = 18$.

$p - 5 = 18 - 5$

Regular price (p)	$21	$20	$19	$18
Sale price	$16	$15	$14	$18 − 5

When the regular price is $18, the sale price is $13.

For **12** through **15**, copy and complete each table, and find a rule.

12.

n	15	18	20	27
$n +$ ▨	58	61	63	▨

13.

u	212	199	190	188
$u -$ ▨	177	164	155	▨

14.

c	31	54	60	64
$c -$ ▨	5	28	34	▨

15.

a	589	485	400	362
$a -$ ▨	575	471	386	▨

Problem Solving

MATHEMATICAL PRACTICES

For **16** and **17**, use the table at the right.

16. Use Tools The United States Congress includes 2 senators from each state plus members of the House of Representatives. If r represents the number of representatives from each state, which rule represents the total number of members each state has in Congress?

A $r \times 2$

B $r \div 2$

C $r - 2$

D $r + 2$

Number of Members in the United States Congress		
State	House	Senate
Florida	25	2
Missouri	9	2
Hawaii	2	2
New York	29	2

Data

17. How many members in Congress does each state in the table have?

18. What is the value of n if $1,000 \times n = 0$?

19. Persevere Chang has driven 1,372 miles. If the total mileage for his trip is 2,800 miles, how many miles does Chang have left to drive? Explain.

20. Donna makes $10.50 each hour she works at her job. How much money does she make for 10 hours of work?

Lesson
8-6

©
Common
Core

5.OA.3 Generate two numerical patterns using two given rules. Identify apparent relationships between corresponding terms. Form ordered pairs consisting of corresponding terms from the two patterns, and graph the ordered pairs on a coordinate plane.

Multiplication and Division Expressions

How can you find a rule and write an expression?

What is a rule for the table?
How can Josie use a rule to write an expression and find the number of cards in 4 boxes?
Let *b* equal the number of boxes.

Number of boxes (b)	1	2	3	4
Number of note cards	15	30	45	

Guided Practice*

© MATHEMATICAL PRACTICES

Do you know HOW?

For **1** and **2**, use the table below.

Number of tickets (t)	2	4	6	8
Total price	$60	$120	$180	

1. What is a rule for the table in words? in symbols?

2. How much would 8 tickets cost?

Do you UNDERSTAND?

© 3. **Communicate** How could you use place-value blocks to describe a rule in the table to the left?

© 4. **Reason** How could you find the price of 1 ticket using the information from Problems 1 and 2?

5. In the example at the top, how many note cards are in 13 boxes?

Independent Practice

For **6** through **8**, find a rule.

6.
n	3	8	10
n × ▢	18	48	60

7.
p	2	4	8
p ÷ ▢	1	2	4

8.
t	2	3	4
▢ × t	16	24	32

For **9** through **12**, copy and complete each table, and find a rule.

9.
e	4	8	12	16
e ÷ ▢	1	2	3	▢

10.
j	4	9	10	16
▢ × j	28	63	70	▢

11.
w	5	7	8	10
▢ × w	45	63	72	▢

12.
s	20	35	40	45
s ÷ ▢	4	7	8	▢

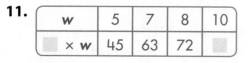

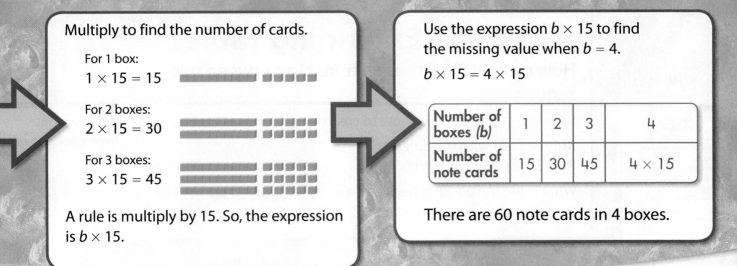

Multiply to find the number of cards.

For 1 box:
$1 \times 15 = 15$

For 2 boxes:
$2 \times 15 = 30$

For 3 boxes:
$3 \times 15 = 45$

A rule is multiply by 15. So, the expression is $b \times 15$.

Use the expression $b \times 15$ to find the missing value when $b = 4$.

$b \times 15 = 4 \times 15$

Number of boxes (b)	1	2	3	4
Number of note cards	15	30	45	4×15

There are 60 note cards in 4 boxes.

Problem Solving

For **13** and **14**, use the table at the right.

The Baker family is deciding which type of television to purchase for the family room.

ⓒ **13. Reason** How much more does a 50-inch Plasma cost than a 34-inch Flat Screen?

Type of Television	Cost
50-inch Plasma	$2,800
34-inch Flat Screen	$900
26-inch LCD	$500

Data

14. How much less does a 26-inch LCD cost than a 50-inch Plasma?

ⓒ **15. Reason** There are 60 minutes in one hour and 7 days in one week. About how many minutes are in one week?

   A About 1,500 minutes

   B About 6,000 minutes

   C About 10,000 minutes

   D About 42,000 minutes

16. Cami bought two books for $12 each and two journals for $4 each. How much change would she get if she paid with two $20 bills?

   A $2

   B $8

   C $32

   D $40

For **17**, use the table at the right.

ⓒ **17. Model** Kudzu is the world's fastest growing weed. Copy and complete the table to the right to find a rule for the growth rate of kudzu. What is a rule for the table?

Day (d)	1	2	3	4	5	6
Inches	12	24	▪	▪	▪	72

Lesson
8-7

Common
Core

5.OA.3 Generate two
numerical patterns using
two given rules. Identify
apparent relationships
between corresponding
terms. Form ordered pairs
consisting of corresponding
terms from the two patterns,
and graph the ordered pairs
on a coordinate plane.

Patterns – Extending Tables

How can you find the relationship between two sequences?

Sometimes a rule tells us how to create a sequence of numbers.

Rule A: Start with 0. Add 2.

Rule B: Start with 0. Add 6.

What is the relationship between the corresponding terms in these sequences?

Other Example

Rule C: Start with 1. Add 2.
Rule D: Start with 5. Add 2.

	First Term	Second Term	Third Term	Fourth Term
Rule C	1	3	5	7
Rule D	5	7	9	11

Rule D: Each term in Rule D is 4 more than the corresponding term in Rule C.

Guided Practice*

MATHEMATICAL
PRACTICES

Do you know HOW?

Rule E: Start with 0. Add 2.
Rule F: Start with 0. Add 8.

	First Term	Second Term	Third Term	Fourth Term
Rule E				
Rule F				

1. Complete the table to show the corresponding terms.

2. What is the relationship between the corresponding terms?

Do you UNDERSTAND?

3. **Construct Arguments** How can you tell that the relationship between the corresponding terms involves multiplication?

4. **Reason** The eleventh term using Rule E is 20. What is the eleventh term using Rule F?

5. The eighth term using Rule F is 56. What is the eighth term using Rule E?

Animated Glossary
www.pearsonsuccessnet.com

*For another example, see Set C on page 215.

Use each rule to make a table showing the corresponding terms in each sequence. The starting value for each rule is the first term.

	First Term	Second Term	Third Term	Fourth Term	Fifth Term
Rule A	0	2	4	6	8
Rule B	0	6	12	18	24

Look for a way in which the numbers in each column are related.

Each term from Rule B is three times as great as the corresponding term in Rule A.

Second Term	$2 \times 3 = 6$
Third Term	$4 \times 3 = 12$
Fourth Term	$6 \times 3 = 18$
Fifth Term	$8 \times 3 = 24$

Rule B adds 6 each time, and Rule A adds 2. So Rule B grows 3 times as fast as Rule A.

Independent Practice

In **6–9**, make a table and find the relationship between the corresponding terms.

6. Rule A: Start with 100. Subtract 3.
Rule B: Start with 150. Subtract 3.

7. Rule C: Start with 64. Divide by 2.
Rule D: Start with 128. Divide by 2.

8. Rule E: Start with 5. Add 10.
Rule F: Start with 25. Add 10.

9. Rule G: Start with 0. Add 2.
Rule H: Start with 10. Add 2.

Problem Solving

MATHEMATICAL PRACTICES

© **10. Use Tools** Anil is growing tomatoes and lettuce. He collected the information in the table. Find the number of each type of plant in Rows 4 and 5. What is the relationship between the number of lettuce plants and the number of tomato plants in each row?

	Row 1	Row 2	Row 3	Row 4	Row 5
Tomato Plants	2	4	6	▨	▨
Lettuce Plants	4	8	12	▨	▨

11. Rule M: Start with 0. Add 4. Rule N: Start with 6. Add 4. What is the relationship between the corresponding terms? If the tenth term in Rule M is 36, what is the tenth term in Rule N?

© **12. Persevere** Mr. Walker has a new motorcycle that gets 40 miles per gallon. About how many miles can Mr. Walker drive on 8.9 gallons of gas?

© **13. Reasonableness** Which shows the quotient of $0.84 \div 0.14$?

A 60

B 6

C 0.6

D 0.06

© **14. Look for Patterns** Write two decimals whose quotient is about 4.1.

Lesson
8-8

Common Core

5.OA.2 Write simple expressions that record calculations with numbers, and interpret numerical expressions without evaluating them.

Variables and Expressions

How can you translate words into expressions?

What expression shows the weight of the mixed nuts after the weight of the jar is subtracted?

A variable is a letter or symbol that represents an unknown amount that can vary, or change.

4 oz

Guided Practice*

MATHEMATICAL PRACTICES

Do you know HOW?

In **1** through **4**, use a variable to write an algebraic expression that represents the word phrase.

1. twice the number of people

2. $7 less than the current price

3. 8 more gumballs than Javier has

4. a number of students divided into 2 teams

Do you UNDERSTAND?

© 5. **Model** What would the expression for the weight of the mixed nuts be if the weight of the jar was 8 oz?

© 6. **Communicate** Why is a variable used in the example at the top?

© 7. **Look for Patterns** Write two word phrases that could be translated as $25 \times p$.

Independent Practice

For **8** through **11**, translate each algebraic expression into words.

8. $n + 9$ 9. $x \div 12$ 10. $y - 4$ 11. $8m$

For **12** through **20**, write each word phrase as an algebraic expression.

12. subtract a number from 10   13. the product of 9 and a number   14. add 6 to a number

15. 6 divided by a number   16. a number decreased by 12   17. 9 plus a number

18. a number added to 19   19. the quotient of a number and 8   20. 4 less a number

Animated Glossary
www.pearsonsuccessnet.com

An algebraic expression is a mathematical phrase involving variables, numbers, and operations.

Operation	Word Phrase	Algebraic Expression
Addition	a number *plus* 4 a number *added* to 4	$w + 4$
Subtraction	a number *minus* 4 a number *less* 4	$w - 4$
Multiplication	4 *times* a number	$4 \times w$ or $4w$
Division	a number *divided* by 4	$w \div 4$ or $\dfrac{w}{4}$

Since the weight of the mixed nuts varies, let w represent the total weight of the jar and the mixed nuts.

So, $w - 4$ is the weight of the mixed nuts after the weight of the jar is subtracted.

Problem Solving

MATHEMATICAL
PRACTICES

21. Persevere You and three of your friends are going to share a package of granola bars equally. Write an algebraic expression to show this situation.

22. In January, Winifred had $1,369.57 in her savings account. In December, she had $2,513.34 in her account. How much more money did she have in December than in January?

23. Jeff added $\frac{4}{5}$ cup of water to $\frac{2}{3}$ cup of lemonade concentrate. Is there more water or concentrate?

24. Reason How are the expressions $7 - g$ and $g - 7$ different?

25. Think About the Structure Nao has 6 fewer CDs than Emily. If c represents the number of CDs Emily has, which expression tells how many CDs Nao has?

  A $c + 6$ **C** $6 - c$

  B $c - 6$ **D** $6 + c$

26. Model A person has to be at least 48 inches tall to ride a roller coaster. Jill, who is 12 years old, is taller than 48 inches. Which expression shows Jill's height?

  A $(12 + t) - 48$ **C** $(48 - 12) + t$

  B $48t$ **D** $48 + t$

27. This drawing of the sculpture of a ball of jeans shows a stand beneath it. If the stand and sculpture measure 18 feet, which equation shows how to find the height of the sculpture?

  A $18 + x = 2$ **C** $x - 18 = 2$

  B $x + 2 = 18$ **D** $2 - 18 = x$

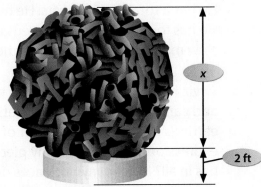

28. Juan is planning to buy a new computer monitor. He has already saved $250. Let n equal the amount Juan still needs to save. Write an algebraic expression that represents the cost of the monitor.

© **Common Core**

5.OA.2 Write simple expressions that record calculations with numbers, and interpret numerical expressions without evaluating them.

Act It Out and Use Reasoning

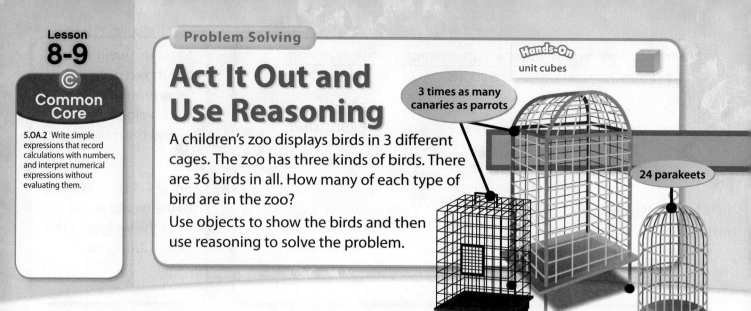

Hands-On
unit cubes

3 times as many canaries as parrots

24 parakeets

A children's zoo displays birds in 3 different cages. The zoo has three kinds of birds. There are 36 birds in all. How many of each type of bird are in the zoo?

Use objects to show the birds and then use reasoning to solve the problem.

Guided Practice*

© **MATHEMATICAL PRACTICES**

Do you know HOW?

Solve. You can use cubes to act out the problem.

1. The Rodriquez family is donating 25 baseball caps to a charity auction. There are 11 blue caps. There are 2 more white caps than green caps. How many of each color caps are they donating?

Do you UNDERSTAND?

© 2. **Use Tools** If you use 25 cubes to represent all the caps and 11 are used to show the blue caps, which expression shows how many cubes are left for the white and the green caps?
25 + 11 or 25 − 11
Solve the correct expression.

© 3. **Reason** Write a real-world problem that can be solved by acting it out and using reasoning.

Independent Practice

© **MATHEMATICAL PRACTICES**

Solve. Use cubes to act out the problems.

4. Mr. Niles has a box of accessories for clarinets. He has a total of 42 objects. He has 12 mouthpieces. He has four times as many reeds as neck straps. How many of each object does he have?

5. Sylvia has a jewelry collection of bracelets, necklaces, and earrings. She has 16 bracelets. The number of earrings is 2 times the number of necklaces. Which expression shows how many pieces of jewelry she has in all? How many necklaces does she have if she has 43 pieces of jewelry in all?

$16 + 2n + n$

$16 + 2n + 1$

Applying Math Practices

- What am I asked to find?
- What else can I try?
- How are quantities related?
- How can I explain my work?
- How can I use math to model the problem?
- Can I use tools to help?
- Is my work precise?
- Why does this work?
- How can I generalize?

For another example, see Set E on page 215.

Use objects and show what you know. Let 36 cubes represent all the birds. Use reasoning to make conclusions.

24 parakeets

12 canaries and parrots

There are 24 parakeets and 36 birds in all. That leaves a total of 12 canaries and parrots.

Use 12 cubes. There are 3 times as many canaries as parrots.

There are 24 parakeets, 9 canaries, and 3 parrots.
$24 + 9 + 3 = 36$, so the answer is correct.

For **6** through **8**, use and complete the table at the right.

6. Use Tools There are 8 students who play the tuba. There are $\frac{1}{2}$ as many students playing the clarinet as the flute. Which expression shows how to find the number of students that play each instrument? How many students play the clarinet?

$8 + 2f + f$

$8 + \frac{f}{2} + f$

Instrument	Number of Students
Group 1	44
Tuba	8
Clarinet	
Flute	
Group 2	41
Saxophone	8
Trumpet	
Trombone	

7. There are 41 students in Group 2. Twice as many students play the trumpet as play the trombone, but 8 students play the saxophone. How many students in Group 2 play each instrument?

8. Later, 7 students joined Group 2 and 1 student left to join Group 1. Some students decided to play a different instrument. Now 20 students play trombone and 7 more students play trumpet as play saxophone. How many students play each instrument?

9. Look for Patterns Jane worked 1.5 hours on Monday, 3 hours on Tuesday, and 4.5 hours on Wednesday. If the pattern continues, how many hours will she work on Friday?

10. Model The Garden Theater presented a play. A total of 179 people attended in 3 days. The first day, 58 people attended. On the second day, 47 people attended. How many attended on the third day?

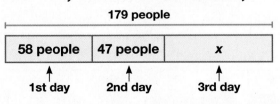

11. Model Reggie earned $360 in the summer. If he earned $40 per week, how many weeks did he work?

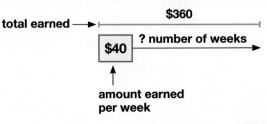

Set A, pages 194–195

Variables represent values that can change.

The expression $24 + n$ means "the sum of 24 and a number." The unknown number is a variable that is expressed by a letter, n.

Operation Terms

Addition	→	Sum
Subtraction	→	Difference
Multiplication	→	Product
Division	→	Quotient

Remember that you can use any letter as a variable that stands for an unknown value.

Write the phrases as algebraic expressions.

1. 22 less forks than a number, f

2. 48 times a number of game markers, g

3. a number of eggs, e, divided by 12

4. 3 times the number of milk cartons, m, used by the 5th grade class

Set B, pages 196–198, 200–201, 202–203

Use the order of operations to evaluate expressions with brackets.

Order of Operations

1. Compute inside parentheses and brackets.

2. Evaluate terms with exponents.

3. Multiply and divide from left to right.

4. Add and subtract from left to right.

Step 1	**Step 2**	**Step 3**
Perform the operations inside the parentheses.	Multiply and divide in order from left to right.	Add and subtract in order from left to right.
$(8 + 2) \times (3 + 7) + 50 = 10 \times 10 + 50$	$10 \times 10 + 50 = 100 + 50$	$100 + 50 = 150$

Remember that you can think of brackets as outside parentheses and evaluate the inside parentheses first.

Evaluate each expression.

1. $(7.8 + 4.7) \div 0.25$

2. $4 + 8 \times 6 \div 2 + 3$

3. $[(8 \times 2.5) \div 0.5] + 120$

4. $31.2(40 + 60) \div 0.6$

5. $(8.7 - 3.2) \div 0.5$

6. $92.3 - (3.2 \div 0.4) \times 2^3$

7. $(18 - 3) \div 5 + 4$

8. $8 \times 5 + 7 \times 3 - (10 - 5)$

Use the values given for variables to evaluate each expression.

9. $4.2 + 5 \times x \div 0.10; x = 4$

10. $2^2 \times (4.2 - y); y = 1.2$

11. $12 + (4^2 \div z); z = 0.04$

Look at the table below. Start with the number in the first column. What rule tells you how to find the number in the second column?

Regular price (p)	Sale price
$43	$41
$45	$43
$46	$44
$47	

$43 - 2 = 41$

$45 - 2 = 43$

$46 - 2 = 44$

The rule is subtract 2, or $p - 2$.

Use this rule to find the missing number in the table.

$47 - 2 = 45$

The sale price is $45.

Remember to ask "What is a rule?"

Copy and complete each table and find a rule.

1.

n	n − ▇
18	3
20	5
25	10
37	▇

2.

x	x + ▇
34	100
0	66
8	74
13	▇

3.

n	2	6	8	9
▇ × n	6	18	24	▇

4.

s	45	40	35	15
s ÷ ▇	9	8	▇	3

Translate a word phrase into an algebraic expression.

Five more cards than Steve owns

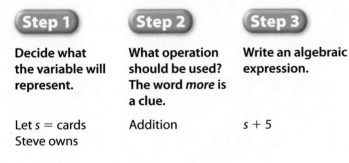

Step 1

Decide what the variable will represent.

Let s = cards Steve owns

Step 2

What operation should be used? The word *more* is a clue.

Addition

Step 3

Write an algebraic expression.

$s + 5$

Remember to look for words that give you clues as to what operation to use.

Write an algebraic expression for each.

1. A puzzle costs p less than a magazine. The magazine costs $1.99. How much is the puzzle?

2. The evergreen is twice as tall as a hosta. The hosta is h inches tall. How tall is the evergreen?

A pet shop has a total of 19 dogs, cats, and ferrets. There are 4 ferrets, and twice as many cats as dogs. How many of each kind of pet are in the shop?

Use 19 cubes and let 4 of them represent the ferrets. That leaves 15 cubes to represent the cats and dogs. There must be 10 cats and 5 dogs.

Remember that objects can help you reason through a problem.

1. Kerry has 12 paperweights in her collection. She has twice as many glass paperweights as metal, and 3 are wood. How many of each type of paperweight does she have?

1. Which expression can be used to represent the phrase "three times the amount of money"? (8-1)

   A $3 + m$

   B $3 - m$

   C $3 \times m$

   D $3 \div m$

2. If Lisa travels an average of 65 miles per hour for 8 hours, she will travel 8×65 miles. Which of the following is equal to 8×65? (8-2)

   A $(8 + 60) \times (8 + 5)$

   B $(8 + 60) - (8 + 5)$

   C $(8 \times 60) + (8 \times 5)$

   D $(8 \times 60) - (8 \times 5)$

3. Ryan had 18 more shots on goal during the soccer season than Peyton, who had 36. Evaluate the expression $x + 18$ for $x = 36$. (8-4)

   A 2

   B 18

   C 52

   D 54

4. Jerry has a coupon for $3 off the price of an item. If p represents the original price of a shirt, which expression tells Jerry's cost, before tax, when he uses the coupon? (8-8)

   A $p \div 3$

   B $3 - p$

   C $p - 3$

   D $p + 3$

5. The expression $f - 3$ represents the number of years Mark has taken piano lessons when Fatima has taken lessons for f years. How many years of lessons will Mark have when Fatima has 9 years? (8-5)

   A 27

   B 12

   C 6

   D 3

6. What is the first step in evaluating the expression shown below? (8-2)

   $8 - 7 + 12 \div (3 + 1)$

   A Add 3 and 1.

   B Divide 12 by 3.

   C Add 7 and 12.

   D Subtract 7 from 8.

7. What value of n makes the equation true? (8-2)

   $15 \times 110 = (15 \times 100) + (15 \times n)$

   A 10

   B 15

   C 90

   D 110

8. The cost for n students to attend a workshop is $7n + 12$ dollars. What is the cost for 6 students to attend? (8-6)

   A $25

   B $54

   C $126

   D $156

9. Tennessee, New Mexico, and Michigan have a total of 27 representatives in the U.S. House of Representatives. Michigan has 15 representatives and Tennessee has 3 times as many as New Mexico. How many representatives does the state of Tennessee have? (8-6)

10. Write the expression represented by n students divided into groups of 6. (8-1)

11. What is the value of the expression $6 + (13 - 1) \div 4 + 2$? (8-3)

12. Alex starts with $5 and saves $10 each week. Nora starts with $14 and saves $10 each week. Copy and complete the chart to show how much money each has saved at the end of each week. What is the relationship between how much money each has at the end of each week? (8-7)

	Alex's Savings	Nora's Savings
Start	$5	$14
1st week		
2nd week		
3rd week		
4th week		
5th week		

13. Jannah purchased flowers to plant in her garden. She planted 2 flowers in each of her 5 garden beds. If t represents the total number of flowers, write an expression that shows how many flowers she planted. (8-1)

14. Joshua is watching a parade. He makes the table below to record his observations. (8-7)

	Row 1	Row 2	Row 3	Row 4	Row 5
Drummers	3	6	9	12	15
Trumpeters	6	12	18	24	30

What is the relationship between the number of drummers and the number of trumpeters in each row?

15. What is the value of $7 + 3m - 2$ when $m = 4$? (8-4)

16. The table shows the cost to board Lucy's dog at a kennel. Write the expression that shows the cost to board the dog for d days? (8-9)

Number of Days	Total Cost
3	$36
4	$48
5	$60

Use the following expression to answer **17** and **18**.

$$6 \times (24 \div 4) \times y$$

17. Which operation do you perform first in simplifying this expression? (8-2)

18. Write the simplified form of the expression. (8-3)

1. Use the table to the right.

If one serving has *C* calories, write an expression to show the number of calories in 3 servings. Explain how to use your expression to find the number of calories in 3 servings of lettuce.

2. Plan a dinner party. Choose one food from each food group to serve. List your choices. Then, using the number of servings given per person, complete the columns for fat and calories.

Food Item	Fat Grams	Calories
Meat group		
Turkey, 1 ounce	2	51
Ham, 3.5 ounces	5	159
Hamburger, 3 ounces	20	286
Dairy group		
Milk, 1 cup whole	8	150
American cheese 1 oz.	9	110
Yogurt, 1 cup plain	4	144
Vegetable group		
Green beans, 1 cup	0.2	36
Lettuce, 1 cup	0.2	10
Peas, 1 cup	0.4	134
Fruit group		
Banana, 1	0.6	105
Apple, 1	0.5	81
Bread and pasta group		
Wheat bread, 1 slice	1	70
Macaroni, 1 cup	0	159

Food item	Number of Servings for Each Person	Grams of Fat for that Portion	Calories for that Portion
Meat	2		
Dairy	2		
Vegetable	3		
Fruit	1.5		
Bread or pasta	2.5		
Total			

3. To complete the table, which computations did you do with mental math? Why?

4. Explain how you could reduce the total amount of fat and calories for each person by changing one item.

Topic
9

Adding and Subtracting Fractions

▼ Coral reef formations near coastal regions can be very large. About what fraction of the ocean floor is covered by coral reefs? You will find out in Lesson 9-6.

Review What You Know!

Vocabulary

Choose the best term from the box.

- difference
- quotient
- product
- thousandths

1. In $55 \div 5 = 11$, the 11 is the _?_.

2. In 0.456, the 6 is in the _?_ place.

3. To find the _?_ between 16 and 4 you subtract.

4. Multiplying is the same as finding the _?_.

Division

Find each answer.

5. $32 \div 4$ 6. $97 \div 8$

7. $69 \div 16$ 8. $95 \div 10$

9. $163 \div 31$ 10. $725 \div 25$

Multiplication

Find each answer.

11. 40×8 12. 30×500

13. 31×46 14. 92×18

15. 319×4 16. $2 \times 25 \times 30$

Properties of Multiplication

©**Writing to Explain** Write an answer for each question.

17. Explain how you can use the Associative Property to evaluate $(7 \times 50) \times 4$.

18. Can you use the Associative Property to evaluate $3 \times (4 + 5)$?

Topic Essential Questions

- What does it mean to add and subtract fractions with unlike denominators?
- What is a standard procedure for adding and subtracting fractions with unlike denominators?

Interactive Learning

Pose the problem. Start each lesson by working together to solve problems. It will help you make sense of math.

Lesson 9-1

Ⓒ **Reason** Solve. Use fraction strips to help.

How many fractions can you find that show the same amount as $\frac{4}{6}$? Write each fraction and use drawings or words to explain your work.

| $\frac{1}{6}$ | $\frac{1}{6}$ | $\frac{1}{6}$ | $\frac{1}{6}$ | | |

Lesson 9-2

Ⓒ **Use Tools** Use the recording sheet to complete this task.

Use the area models to write the fraction of squares that are shaded and the fraction of squares that are unshaded. Are there other ways you can express the same fraction using a different numerator and a different denominator? Explain.

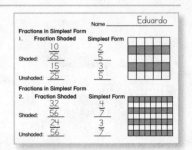

Lesson 9-3

Ⓒ **Communicate** Write a good explanation.

Draw two rectangles on a sheet of paper. Shade $\frac{1}{4}$ of one rectangle and then shade $\frac{1}{3}$ of the other rectangle. Write and explain how you decided how much of each rectangle to shade.

Lesson 9-4

Ⓒ **Use Tools** Solve using any tool you choose.

Jack needs about $1\frac{1}{2}$ yards of string. He can choose only two pieces from the following: $\frac{2}{5}$ yard, $\frac{1}{6}$ yard, and $\frac{7}{8}$ yard. Without finding the exact amount, which two pieces should he choose to get closest to $1\frac{1}{2}$ yards of string? Justify your solution using words, drawings, and numbers.

Lesson 9-5

Ⓒ **Model** Solve any way you choose. Tell how you found the answer.

Pads of paper come in packages of 10, and pencils come in packages of 12. Without opening the packages, what is the minimum number of pads and pencils that Sarah needs to buy to have an equal number of each? Explain.

Lesson 9-6

ⓒ **Model** Solve any way you choose. Tell how you found the answer.

Sue wants $\frac{1}{2}$ of a pan of cornbread. Dejah wants $\frac{1}{3}$ of the same pan of cornbread. How should you cut the cornbread so that Sue and Dejah each get the size piece they want?

Lesson 9-7

ⓒ **Use Tools** Solve any way you choose. Tell how you found the answer.

Over the weekend, Eleni ate $\frac{1}{4}$ box of cereal, and Freddie ate $\frac{3}{8}$ of the same box. What portion of the box of cereal did they eat in all? You may use a number line or fraction strips to help.

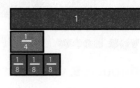

Lesson 9-8

ⓒ **Use Tools** Solve any way you choose. Tell how you found the answer.

Rose bought $\frac{4}{6}$ yard of copper pipe. She used $\frac{1}{2}$ yard to repair the shower. How much pipe does she have left? You may use a number line or fraction strips to help.

Lesson 9-9

ⓒ **Model** Solve any way you choose. Tell how you found the answer.

Tyler ate $\frac{1}{2}$ of the pizza, and Dejah ate $\frac{1}{3}$ of the same pizza. How much of the pizza was eaten, and how much is left over?

Lesson 9-10

ⓒ **Model** Solve any way you choose. Tell how you found the answer.

Michelle rode her bike $\frac{3}{4}$ mile on Thursday, $\frac{6}{8}$ mile on Friday, and $\frac{1}{2}$ mile on Saturday. How far did she ride her bike in all? Choose an operation, and write an equation to solve the problem. Use the bar diagram to help.

	x	
$\frac{3}{4}$	$\frac{6}{8}$	$\frac{1}{2}$

Equivalent Fractions

Hands-On
fraction strips

$\frac{1}{8}$

How can you find equivalent fractions?

Fractions that have different numerators and denominators but name the same amount are called equivalent fractions.

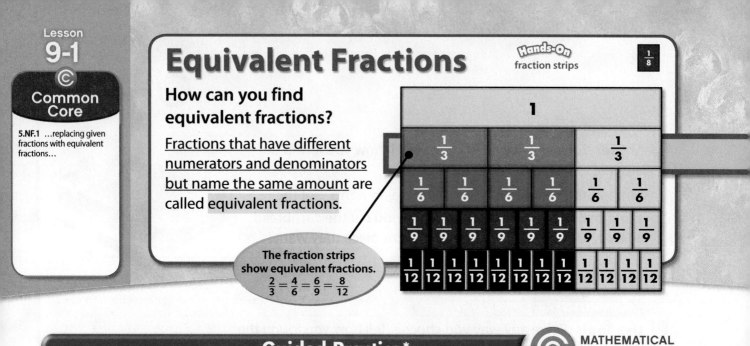

The fraction strips show equivalent fractions.
$\frac{2}{3} = \frac{4}{6} = \frac{6}{9} = \frac{8}{12}$

Guided Practice*

MATHEMATICAL PRACTICES

Do you know HOW?

In **1** through **5**, write two fractions that are equivalent to the one fraction given. You may use fraction strips to help.

1. $\frac{2}{4}$ $\frac{2 \times 2}{4 \times 2} = \blacksquare$ $\frac{2 \div 2}{4 \div 2} = \blacksquare$

2. $\frac{24}{48}$

3. $\frac{10}{35}$

4. $\frac{6}{10}$

5. $\frac{4}{9}$

Do you UNDERSTAND?

6. **Look for Patterns** Why is multiplying or dividing the numerator and denominator by the same nonzero number the same as multiplying or dividing the fraction by 1?

7. Why wouldn't you use division to find an equivalent fraction for $\frac{7}{15}$?

Independent Practice

Leveled Practice In **8** through **21**, write two fractions that are equivalent to each fraction given. You may use fraction strips to help.

8. $\frac{3}{12}$ $\frac{3 \times 2}{12 \times 2} = \blacksquare$ $\frac{3 \div 3}{12 \div 3} = \blacksquare$

9. $\frac{6}{12}$ $\frac{6 \div 3}{12 \div 3} = \blacksquare$ $\frac{6 \div 6}{12 \div 6} = \blacksquare$

10. $\frac{6}{9}$

11. $\frac{35}{56}$

12. $\frac{32}{40}$

13. $\frac{5}{7}$

14. $\frac{3}{15}$

15. $\frac{7}{21}$

16. $\frac{9}{10}$

17. $\frac{25}{30}$

18. $\frac{14}{35}$

19. $\frac{121}{132}$

20. $\frac{28}{36}$

21. $\frac{1}{1000}$

DIGITAL Animated Glossary, eTools
www.pearsonsuccessnet.com

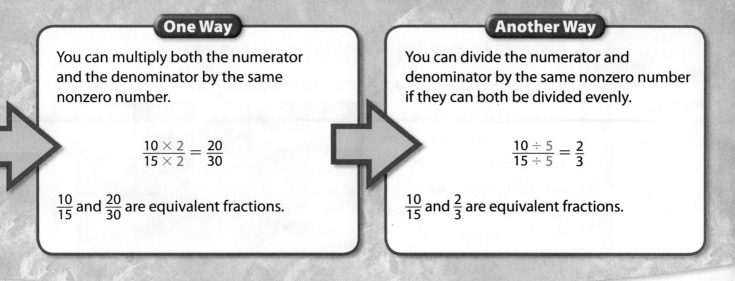

One Way

You can multiply both the numerator and the denominator by the same nonzero number.

$$\frac{10 \times 2}{15 \times 2} = \frac{20}{30}$$

$\frac{10}{15}$ and $\frac{20}{30}$ are equivalent fractions.

Another Way

You can divide the numerator and denominator by the same nonzero number if they can both be divided evenly.

$$\frac{10 \div 5}{15 \div 5} = \frac{2}{3}$$

$\frac{10}{15}$ and $\frac{2}{3}$ are equivalent fractions.

Problem Solving

MATHEMATICAL PRACTICES

22. **Construct Arguments** How can you use equivalent fractions to know that $\frac{43}{200}$ is between $\frac{1}{5}$ and $\frac{1}{4}$?

23. Kai says that $\frac{3}{7} = \frac{9}{14}$. Is Kai correct? Explain.

24. **Critique Reasoning** Jenna claims that no matter how many equivalent fractions are found for any fraction, she can always find one more. Is she right? Explain.

25. **Reason** Find the value of x that makes the fractions equivalent.

a $\frac{10}{14} = \frac{x}{42}$ b $\frac{x}{200} = \frac{3}{4}$

26. There are 206 bones in the body. The fraction $\frac{54}{206}$ represents the number of bones in both hands compared to the total number of bones in the body. Write an equivalent fraction.

There are 27 bones in each human hand.

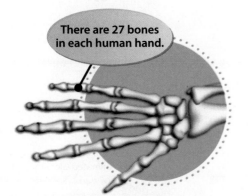

27. **Use Structure** Which of the following fractions is NOT equivalent to the others?

A $\frac{1}{3}$ B $\frac{4}{12}$ C $\frac{5}{21}$ D $\frac{3}{9}$

28. **Use Tools** How does this diagram help show that $\frac{2}{7} = \frac{8}{28}$?

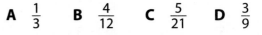

29. Draw a grid like the one in Exercise 28 to show that $\frac{5}{6} = \frac{15}{18}$.

Common
Core

5.NF.1 …replacing given
fractions with equivalent
fractions… Also 5.NF.2

Fractions in Simplest Form

How can you write a fraction in simplest form?

A stained glass window has 20 panes. Out of 20 sections, 12 are yellow. So $\frac{12}{20}$ of the panes are yellow. Notice how the picture also shows that $\frac{3}{5}$ are yellow.

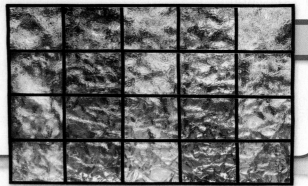

Guided Practice*

MATHEMATICAL
PRACTICES

Do you know HOW?

In **1** through **6**, write each fraction in simplest form.

1. $\frac{16}{32}$
2. $\frac{10}{14}$
3. $\frac{33}{77}$
4. $\frac{16}{20}$
5. $\frac{30}{40}$
6. $\frac{10}{15}$

Do you UNDERSTAND?

7. In the stained glass window pattern above, what fraction in simplest form names the green tiles?

8. **Writing to Explain** Can a fraction with an even numerator and an even denominator be in simplest form? Why or why not?

Independent Practice

For **9** through **32**, write each fraction in simplest form.

9. $\frac{300}{400}$
10. $\frac{55}{60}$
11. $\frac{3}{6}$
12. $\frac{75}{100}$

13. $\frac{14}{21}$
14. $\frac{4}{12}$
15. $\frac{42}{48}$
16. $\frac{63}{70}$

17. $\frac{18}{21}$
18. $\frac{22}{44}$
19. $\frac{6}{42}$
20. $\frac{15}{25}$

21. $\frac{9}{81}$
22. $\frac{12}{100}$
23. $\frac{7}{21}$
24. $\frac{16}{30}$

25. $\frac{99}{121}$
26. $\frac{122}{144}$
27. $\frac{28}{42}$
28. $\frac{32}{80}$

29. $\frac{40}{80}$
30. $\frac{11}{22}$
31. $\frac{60}{80}$
32. $\frac{8}{100}$

Animated Glossary
www.pearsonsuccessnet.com

For another example, see Set A on page 244.

A fraction is in simplest form when its numerator and denominator have no common factor other than 1.

To write $\frac{12}{20}$ in simplest form, find a common factor of the numerator and the denominator. Since 12 and 20 are even numbers, they have 2 as a factor.

Divide both 12 and 20 by 2.

$$\frac{12 \div 2}{20 \div 2} = \frac{6}{10}$$

Both 6 and 10 are even. Divide both by 2.

$$\frac{6 \div 2}{10 \div 2} = \frac{3}{5}$$

Since 3 and 5 have no common factor other than 1, you know that $\frac{3}{5}$ is in simplest form.

Problem Solving

MATHEMATICAL PRACTICES

33. Construct Arguments Can you assume that any fraction is in simplest form if either the numerator or denominator is a prime number?

34. Mrs. Lok is planning a 600-mile trip. Her car has an 18-gallon gas tank and gets 29 miles per gallon. Will 1 tank full of gas be enough for the trip?

35. Be Precise Explain how you know that $\frac{55}{80}$ is not in simplest form.

36. If 5 packages of hot dogs cost $10.25, what is the cost of 1 package?

37. Look for Patterns Write a fraction in simplest form that shows the shaded part of the figure.

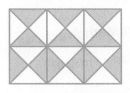

38. A store manager wants to give away the last 84 samples of hand cream. She counts 26 customers in the store. She will give each customer the same number of free samples. How many free samples will each customer get?

39. Persevere Mayflies can live at the bottom of lakes for 2 to 3 years before they become winged adults. Mayflies are between $\frac{4}{10}$ inches and 1.6 inches long. If this mayfly is $\frac{4}{10}$ of an inch long, how can you write $\frac{4}{10}$ in simplest form?

A $\frac{1}{6}$

B $\frac{1}{4}$

C $\frac{2}{5}$

D $\frac{8}{20}$

40. Reason Use divisibility rules to find a number that satisfies the given conditions.

a a number greater than 75 that is divisible by 2 and 5.

b a three-digit number divisible by 3, 5 and 6.

Lesson
9-3

Common
Core

5.NF.2 ...Use benchmark
fractions and number
sense of fractions to
estimate mentally and
assess the reasonableness
of answers.

Problem Solving

Writing to Explain

How do you write a math explanation?

The circle graph shows the continents where the 20 most populated countries of the world are located. Estimate the fractional part for each continent. Explain how you decided.

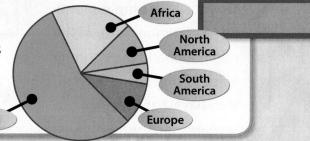

Locations of the 20 Most Populated Countries in the World

Africa
North America
South America
Europe
Asia

Guided Practice*

MATHEMATICAL PRACTICES

Do you know HOW?

1. Estimate the fractional part of the square that is shaded. Explain how you decided.

Do you UNDERSTAND?

2. Draw a picture to show $\frac{2}{3}$ as a benchmark fraction.

3. **Be Precise** Write a real-world problem that involves a benchmark fraction. Your problem should ask for an explanation as part of the solution.

Independent Practice

MATHEMATICAL PRACTICES

For **4** and **5**, use the picture below.

4. Estimate the part of the table that is covered with plates. Explain how you decided.

5. Estimate the part of the table that is covered with glasses. Explain how you decided.

6. Draw a kitchen table. Using plates, show the benchmark fraction, $\frac{3}{4}$. Explain how you decided the number of plates to draw.

Applying Math Practices

- What am I asked to find?
- What else can I try?
- How are quantities related?
- How can I explain my work?
- How can I use math to model the problem?
- Can I use tools to help?
- Is my work precise?
- Why does this work?
- How can I generalize?

Animated Glossary
www.pearsonsuccessnet.com

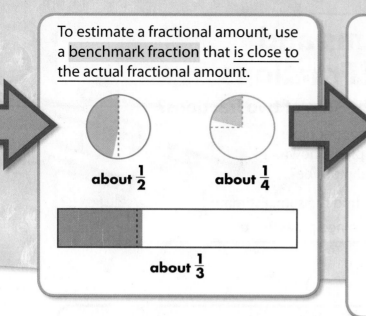

To estimate a fractional amount, use a benchmark fraction that is close to the actual fractional amount.

about $\frac{1}{2}$ about $\frac{1}{4}$

about $\frac{1}{3}$

Writing a Math Explanation

Use *words*, *pictures*, *numbers*, or *symbols* to write a good math explanation.

Asia: *If you draw a line from the top of the graph to the bottom, you can see this continent is a little more than $\frac{1}{2}$.*

Africa: *This part is a little less than $\frac{1}{4}$.*

Europe and North America: *About 10 of each of these can fill the circle, so this is about $\frac{1}{10}$.*

South America: *This part is less than the part for Europe, so I'll say about $\frac{1}{20}$.*

---

7. Estimate the fractional part of the square that is shaded. Explain how you decided.

8. Estimate the part of the square that is *NOT* shaded. Explain how you decided.

9. Communicate Draw a rectangle and shade about $\frac{1}{3}$ of it. Explain how you decided how much to shade.

10. Draw two circles that are different sizes. Shade about $\frac{1}{8}$ of each. Are the shaded parts the same amount? Explain.

11. The Mayfield Little League baseball infield is being covered with a tarp because of rain. Is more or less than $\frac{3}{4}$ of the infield grass covered with the tarp?

12. Reason Cereal can be a good source of protein. How many quarter cups of cereal are there in $6\frac{1}{4}$ cups?

13. A refreshment stand at the fair was open for 3 hours. Four people each took turns working at the stand for the same amount of time. How many minutes did each person work?

For **14**, decide if there is extra or missing information. Solve if possible.

14. Persevere Gene's new car gets 35 miles per gallon. Matt's car gets 32 miles per gallon. How many more gallons of gas will Matt's car use than Gene's car to go to the beach?

Common Core

5.NF.2 ...Use benchmark fractions and number sense of fractions to estimate mentally and assess the reasonableness of answers. Also 5.NF.1

Estimating Sums and Differences of Fractions

How can you estimate the sum of two fractions?

Mr. Frish is welding together 2 copper pipes to repair a leak. He will use the pipes shown. About how long will the welded pipes be?

$\frac{5}{12}$ foot long

$\frac{1}{6}$ foot long

Choose an Operation Add to find the sum. Estimate $\frac{1}{6} + \frac{5}{12}$ to find about how long the combined pipes will be.

Another Example How can you estimate the difference of two fractions?

Estimate $\frac{15}{16} - \frac{1}{8}$.

Step 1

Replace each fraction with the nearest half or whole. A number line can make it easy to decide if each fraction is closest to 0, $\frac{1}{2}$, or 1.

$$\frac{1}{8} \qquad\qquad \frac{15}{16}$$

0        $\frac{1}{2}$ 1

$\frac{15}{16}$ is between $\frac{1}{2}$ and 1, but is closer to 1.

$\frac{1}{8}$ is between 0 and $\frac{1}{2}$, but is closer to 0.

Step 2

Subtract to find the estimate.

A good estimate of $\frac{15}{16} - \frac{1}{8}$ is $1 - 0$, or 1.

Tip You can use the symbol $\approx$ to show an estimate. The symbol $\approx$ means "approximately equal to."

So, $\frac{15}{16} - \frac{1}{8} \approx 1$.

Guided Practice*

MATHEMATICAL PRACTICES

Do you know HOW?

For **1** through **3**, use a number line to tell if each fraction is closest to 0, $\frac{1}{2}$, or 1.

1. $\frac{9}{10}$ **2.** $\frac{2}{5}$ **3.** $\frac{1}{8}$

For **4** through **7**, estimate each sum or difference by replacing each fraction with 0, $\frac{1}{2}$, or 1.

4. $\frac{9}{10} + \frac{5}{6}$ **5.** $\frac{11}{12} - \frac{5}{6}$

6. $\frac{2}{3} - \frac{1}{8}$ **7.** $\frac{5}{9} + \frac{5}{6}$

Do you UNDERSTAND?

8. Look for Patterns In the problem above, would you get the same estimate if Mr. Frish's pipes measured $\frac{2}{6}$ foot and $\frac{7}{12}$ foot?

9. Critique Reasoning Nalini says that if the denominator is more than twice the numerator, the fraction can always be replaced with 0. Is she correct? Give an example in your explanation.

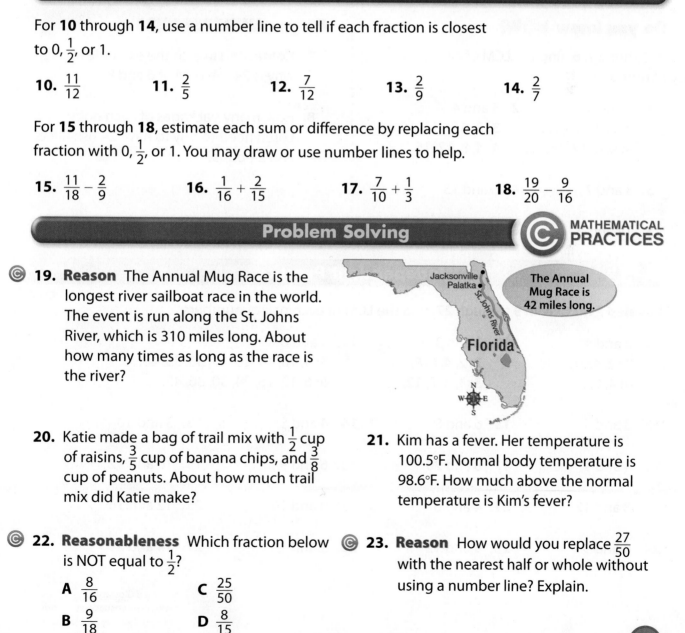

Replace each fraction with the nearest half or whole. A number line can make it easy to decide if each fraction is closest to 0, $\frac{1}{2}$, or 1.

$\frac{1}{6}$ is between 0 and $\frac{1}{2}$, but is closer to 0. Replace $\frac{1}{6}$ with 0.

$\frac{5}{12}$ is also between 0 and $\frac{1}{2}$, but is closer to $\frac{1}{2}$. Replace $\frac{5}{12}$ with $\frac{1}{2}$.

Add to find the estimate.

A good estimate of $\frac{1}{6} + \frac{5}{12}$ is $0 + \frac{1}{2}$, or $\frac{1}{2}$.

So the welded pipes will be about $\frac{1}{2}$ foot long.

Since both addends are less than $\frac{1}{2}$, it is reasonable that the sum is less than 1.

Independent Practice

For **10** through **14**, use a number line to tell if each fraction is closest to 0, $\frac{1}{2}$, or 1.

10. $\frac{11}{12}$ **11.** $\frac{2}{5}$ **12.** $\frac{7}{12}$ **13.** $\frac{2}{9}$ **14.** $\frac{2}{7}$

For **15** through **18**, estimate each sum or difference by replacing each fraction with 0, $\frac{1}{2}$, or 1. You may draw or use number lines to help.

15. $\frac{11}{18} - \frac{2}{9}$ **16.** $\frac{1}{16} + \frac{2}{15}$ **17.** $\frac{7}{10} + \frac{1}{3}$ **18.** $\frac{19}{20} - \frac{9}{16}$

Problem Solving

MATHEMATICAL PRACTICES

© **19. Reason** The Annual Mug Race is the longest river sailboat race in the world. The event is run along the St. Johns River, which is 310 miles long. About how many times as long as the race is the river?

Jacksonville
Palatka
St. Johns River

Florida

The Annual Mug Race is 42 miles long.

20. Katie made a bag of trail mix with $\frac{1}{2}$ cup of raisins, $\frac{3}{5}$ cup of banana chips, and $\frac{3}{8}$ cup of peanuts. About how much trail mix did Katie make?

21. Kim has a fever. Her temperature is 100.5°F. Normal body temperature is 98.6°F. How much above the normal temperature is Kim's fever?

© **22. Reasonableness** Which fraction below is NOT equal to $\frac{1}{2}$?

A $\frac{8}{16}$ C $\frac{25}{50}$

B $\frac{9}{18}$ D $\frac{8}{15}$

© **23. Reason** How would you replace $\frac{27}{50}$ with the nearest half or whole without using a number line? Explain.

Common Multiples and Least Common Multiple

How do you find the least common multiple?

Loren is buying fish fillets and buns for the soccer team dinner. What is the smallest number of fish fillets and buns she can buy to have the same number of each?

Guided Practice*

© MATHEMATICAL PRACTICES

Do you know HOW?

In **1** through **6**, find the LCM of each pair of numbers.

1. 2 and 4
  2: 2, 4, 6, 8, . . .
  4: 4, 8, 12, 16, . . .

2. 3 and 4
  3: 3, 6, 9, 12, 15, . . .
  4: 4, 8, 12, 16, . . .

3. 3 and 7

4. 8 and 15

5. 12 and 9

6. 6 and 18

Do you UNDERSTAND?

© **7. Communicate** In the example above, why is 24 the LCM of 6 and 8?

8. How many packages of each does Loren need to buy to have 24 fish fillets and 24 buns?

Independent Practice

Leveled Practice In **9** through **27**, find the LCM of each pair of numbers.

9. 2 and 4
  2: 2, 4, . . .
  4: 4, 8, . . .

10. 2 and 3
  2: 2, 4, 6, 8, . . .
  3: 3, 6, 9, 12, . . .

11. 5 and 6
  5: 5, 10, 15, 20, 25, 30, 35, 40, . . .
  6: 6, 12, 18, 24, 30, 36, 42, . . .

12. 3 and 5

13. 6 and 8

14. 4 and 5

15. 3 and 10

16. 4 and 9

17. 8 and 20

18. 6 and 9

19. 10 and 12

20. 8 and 12

21. 4 and 6

22. 8 and 16

23. 12 and 16

24. 8 and 9

25. 4 and 12

26. 5 and 10

27. 14 and 21

DIGITAL
Animated Glossary
www.pearsonsuccessnet.com

Find the common multiples of 6 and 8.

Remember that a multiple of a number is a product of a given whole number and another whole number.

A common multiple is a number that is a multiple of two or more numbers.

List the multiples of 6 and 8.

6: 6, 12, 18, 24, 30, 36, 42, 48, 54, …

8: 8, 16, 24, 32, 40, 48, 56, …

Two common multiples of 6 and 8 are 24 and 48.

Find the least common multiple of 6 and 8.

A least common multiple (LCM) is the least number that is a multiple of both numbers.

Both 24 and 48 are common multiples of 6 and 8. So, the LCM of 6 and 8 is 24.

Loren will need to buy 24 fish fillets and 24 buns.

Problem Solving

MATHEMATICAL
PRACTICES

28. Pecans are sold in $\frac{7}{8}$ pound bags, almonds are sold in $\frac{1}{4}$ pound bags, and peanuts are sold in $\frac{3}{8}$ pound bags. If you wanted to buy about 1 pound of nuts, which 2 kinds of nuts would you buy? Use benchmark fractions to help you decide.

29. Look for Patterns Can you always find the LCM for two numbers by multiplying them together? Why or why not?

30. Use Tools The heights of 3 house plants are $\frac{1}{8}$ ft, $\frac{3}{8}$ ft, and $\frac{7}{8}$ ft tall. Using benchmark fractions, which of these is closest to $\frac{1}{2}$ ft tall? Use a number line to help.

31. A cell phone call costs $0.07 per minute for the first 25 minutes and $0.10 per minute for each additional minute. How much would a 47-minute call cost?

32. a Peter is distributing pamphlets about dog care and samples of dog biscuits. The dog biscuits come in packages of 12 and the pamphlets are in packages of 20. What is the smallest number of samples and pamphlets he needs to distribute without having any left over?

  b How many packages of dog biscuits and pamphlets will Peter need?

33. Reason Katie bought dinner at 5 different restaurants. Each dinner cost between $12 and $24. What is a reasonable total cost for all 5 dinners?

  A Less than $60

  B More than $150

  C Between $24 and $60

  D Between $60 and $120

34. Construct Arguments Julie drank $\frac{2}{3}$ cup of cranberry juice. Her brother said she drank $\frac{4}{6}$ cup of juice. Is her brother correct? Explain your answer.

35. A factory whistle blows every half an hour. The clock tower chimes every quarter hour. If they both sounded at 1:00 P.M., at what time will they both sound at the same time again?

Lesson
9-6

Common
Core

5.NF.1 ...replacing given
fractions with equivalent
fractions in such a way as to
produce... fractions with like
denominators. Also 5.NF.2

Finding Common Denominators

How can you find a common denominator for fractions with unlike denominators?

Tyrone divided a rectangle into thirds. Sally divided a rectangle of the same size into fourths. How could you divide a rectangle of the same size so that you see both thirds and fourths?

Thirds   **Fourths**

Another Example **How can you use multiples to find a common denominator?**

Find a common denominator for $\frac{7}{12}$ and $\frac{5}{6}$. Then rename each fraction.

One Way

Multiply the denominators: $12 \times 6 = 72$. Rename each fraction to have a common denominator of 72.

$\frac{7}{12} = \frac{7 \times 6}{12 \times 6} = \frac{42}{72}$ $\frac{5}{6} = \frac{5 \times 12}{6 \times 12} = \frac{60}{72}$

So, $\frac{42}{72}$ and $\frac{60}{72}$.

Another Way

Check to see if one denominator is a multiple of the other: 12 is a multiple of 6.

$\frac{5}{6} = \frac{5 \times 2}{6 \times 2} = \frac{10}{12}$

So, $\frac{7}{12}$ and $\frac{10}{12}$.

Guided Practice*

MATHEMATICAL PRACTICES

Do you know HOW?

In **1** through **4**, find a common denominator for each pair of fractions.

1. $\frac{2}{3}$ and $\frac{3}{4}$ **2.** $\frac{1}{6}$ and $\frac{1}{3}$

3. $\frac{3}{8}$ and $\frac{2}{3}$ **4.** $\frac{3}{7}$ and $\frac{1}{2}$

In **5** and **6**, find a common denominator for each pair of fractions. Then rename each fraction.

5. $\frac{1}{5}$ and $\frac{3}{10}$ **6.** $\frac{1}{2}$ and $\frac{2}{5}$

Do you UNDERSTAND?

7. How many twelfths are in each $\frac{1}{3}$ section of Tyrone's rectangle, and how many twelfths are in each $\frac{1}{4}$ section of Sally's rectangle?

8. Construct Arguments Is the product of two denominators always a common denominator? Give an example in your explanation.

Animated Glossary
www.pearsonsuccessnet.com

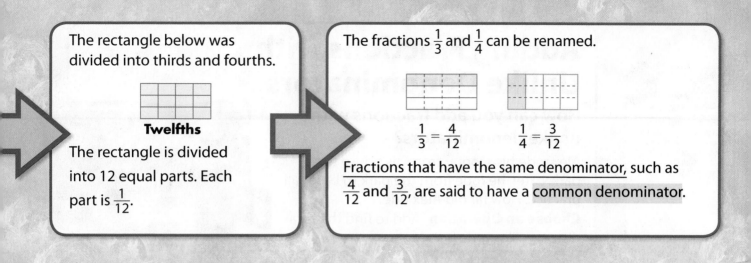

The rectangle below was divided into thirds and fourths.

Twelfths

The rectangle is divided into 12 equal parts. Each part is $\frac{1}{12}$.

The fractions $\frac{1}{3}$ and $\frac{1}{4}$ can be renamed.

$\frac{1}{3} = \frac{4}{12}$ $\frac{1}{4} = \frac{3}{12}$

Fractions that have the same denominator, such as $\frac{4}{12}$ and $\frac{3}{12}$, are said to have a **common denominator**.

Independent Practice

For **9** through **12**, find a common denominator for each pair of fractions.

9. $\frac{4}{5}$ and $\frac{3}{8}$

10. $\frac{1}{2}$ and $\frac{2}{3}$

11. $\frac{4}{5}$ and $\frac{3}{20}$

12. $\frac{3}{5}$ and $\frac{1}{2}$

For **13** through **16**, find a common denominator for each pair of fractions. Then rename each fraction.

13. $\frac{2}{5}$ and $\frac{1}{6}$

14. $\frac{1}{3}$ and $\frac{4}{5}$

15. $\frac{5}{8}$ and $\frac{3}{4}$

16. $\frac{3}{10}$ and $\frac{3}{8}$

Problem Solving

MATHEMATICAL PRACTICES

17. **Science** Coral reefs cover less than $\frac{1}{500}$ of the ocean floor, but they contain more than $\frac{1}{4}$ of all marine life. Which is a common denominator for $\frac{1}{500}$ and $\frac{1}{4}$?

A 2   **B** 100   **C** 125   **D** 500

18. Generalize Marlee is taking a class to improve her reading. She began reading a book on Monday and completed 3 pages. On Tuesday she read 6 pages, on Wednesday 12 pages. If this pattern continues, how many pages will Marlee read on Friday?

For **19** and **20**, use the table at the right.

19. Reason Mr. Paulsen rides a motorcycle. It will take $2\frac{1}{2}$ gallons of gasoline to fill his tank. He has $10 to spend on gasoline. Does he have enough money to fill his tank? Explain.

20. What is the price of premium gasoline rounded to the nearest dollar? Rounded to the nearest dime? Rounded to the nearest penny?

Gasoline Prices	
Grade	**Price (per gallon)**
Regular	$4.199
Premium	$4.409
Diesel	$5.019

Data

Common Core

5.NF.1 Add ... fractions with unlike denominators ... in such a way as to produce an equivalent sum ... of fractions with like denominators. Also 5.NF.2

Adding Fractions with Unlike Denominators

How can you add fractions with unlike denominators?

Alex rode his scooter from his house to the park. Later, he rode from the park to baseball practice. How far did Alex ride?

Choose an Operation Add to find the total distance Alex rode his scooter.

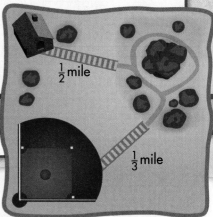

$\frac{1}{2}$ mile

$\frac{1}{3}$ mile

Guided Practice*

MATHEMATICAL PRACTICES

Do you know HOW?

In **1** through **4**, find each sum. Simplify, if necessary.

1. $\frac{1}{2} = \frac{9}{18}$
    $+ \frac{2}{9} = \frac{4}{18}$

2. $\frac{2}{6} = \frac{8}{24}$
    $+ \frac{3}{8} = \frac{9}{24}$

3. $\frac{1}{4} + \frac{7}{10}$

4. $\frac{5}{12} + \frac{1}{8}$

Do you UNDERSTAND?

5. **Look for Patterns** In the example above, would you get the same sum if you used 12 as the common denominator?

6. In the example above, if the park were $\frac{2}{5}$ mile from baseball practice, how far would Alex ride his scooter?

Independent Practice

Leveled Practice In **7** through **22**, find each sum. Simplify, if necessary.

7. $\frac{1}{9} = \frac{\blacksquare}{18}$
    $+ \frac{5}{6} = \frac{\blacksquare}{18}$

8. $\frac{1}{12} = \frac{\blacksquare}{12}$
    $+ \frac{2}{3} = \frac{\blacksquare}{12}$

9. $\frac{1}{3} = \frac{\blacksquare}{15}$
    $+ \frac{1}{5} = \frac{\blacksquare}{15}$

10. $\frac{1}{8} = \frac{\blacksquare}{56}$
    $+ \frac{3}{7} = \frac{\blacksquare}{56}$

11. $\frac{2}{9} + \frac{2}{3}$

12. $\frac{5}{8} + \frac{1}{6}$

13. $\frac{3}{20} + \frac{2}{5}$

14. $\frac{1}{6} + \frac{3}{10}$

15. $\frac{7}{8} + \frac{1}{12}$

16. $\frac{11}{16} + \frac{1}{4}$

17. $\frac{5}{16} + \frac{3}{8}$

18. $\frac{7}{12} + \frac{3}{16}$

19. $\frac{1}{2} + \frac{1}{8} + \frac{1}{8}$

20. $\frac{1}{9} + \frac{1}{6} + \frac{4}{9}$

21. $\frac{1}{4} + \frac{1}{3} + \frac{1}{4}$

22. $\frac{1}{5} + \frac{1}{4} + \frac{2}{5}$

Animated Glossary
www.pearsonsuccessnet.com

234   *For another example, see Set F on page 245.

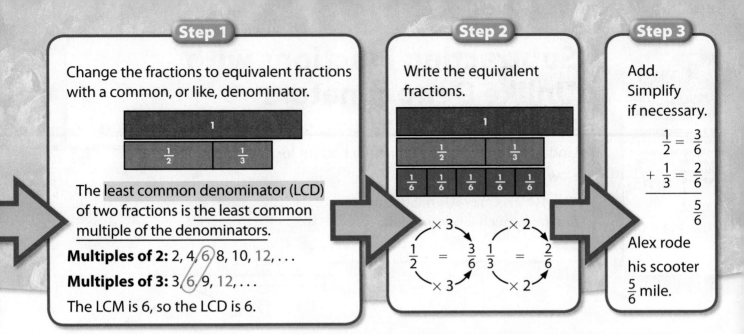

Step 1

Change the fractions to equivalent fractions with a common, or like, denominator.

The **least common denominator (LCD)** of two fractions is the least common multiple of the denominators.

Multiples of 2: 2, 4, 6, 8, 10, 12, . . .

Multiples of 3: 3, 6, 9, 12, . . .

The LCM is 6, so the LCD is 6.

Step 2

Write the equivalent fractions.

$$\frac{1}{2} = \frac{3}{6} \qquad \frac{1}{3} = \frac{2}{6}$$

Step 3

Add. Simplify if necessary.

$$\frac{1}{2} = \frac{3}{6}$$
$$+ \frac{1}{3} = \frac{2}{6}$$
$$\overline{\frac{5}{6}}$$

Alex rode his scooter $\frac{5}{6}$ mile.

Problem Solving

23. Cindy added $\frac{5}{8}$ cup of water to $\frac{1}{4}$ cup of juice concentrate. How much juice did Cindy make?

24. Abdul bought a loaf of bread for $1.59 and a package of cheese for $2.69. How much did Abdul spend?

25. Mr. Perez is building a fence. He wants to bolt together 2 boards. One is $\frac{3}{4}$ inch thick and the other is $\frac{1}{8}$ inch thick. What will be the total thickness of the 2 boards?

26. 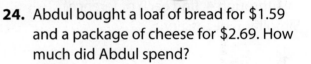 **Science** About $\frac{1}{10}$ of the bones in your body are in your skull. Your hands have about $\frac{1}{4}$ of the bones in your body. What fraction of the bones in your body are in your hands and skull?

© 27. Reason If two sides of an isosceles triangle each measure $\frac{1}{4}$ inch, and the third side measures $\frac{3}{8}$ inch, what is the perimeter of the triangle?

28. A girls' club sold hats to raise money. They ordered 500 hats that cost $5.15 each. They sold the hats for $18.50 each. All the hats were sold. Which expression shows how to find the amount of money the club made after expenses?

A $500 \times (18.50 + 5.15)$

B $(500 \times 18.50) + (500 \times 5.15)$

C $(500 \times 5.15) - (500 \times 18.50)$

D $500 \times (18.50 - 5.15)$

29. **Science** In all, 36 chemical elements were named after people or places. Of these, 2 were named for women scientists, and 25 were named for places. What fraction of these 36 elements were named for women and places? Write your answer in simplest form.

Lesson
9-8

Common Core

5.NF.1 ...subtract fractions with unlike denominators ... in such a way as to produce an equivalent ... difference of fractions with like denominators. Also 5.NF.2

Subtracting Fractions with Unlike Denominators

How can you subtract fractions with unlike denominators?

Linda used $\frac{1}{4}$ yard of the fabric she bought for a sewing project. How much fabric did she have left?

Choose an Operation Subtract to find how much fabric was left.

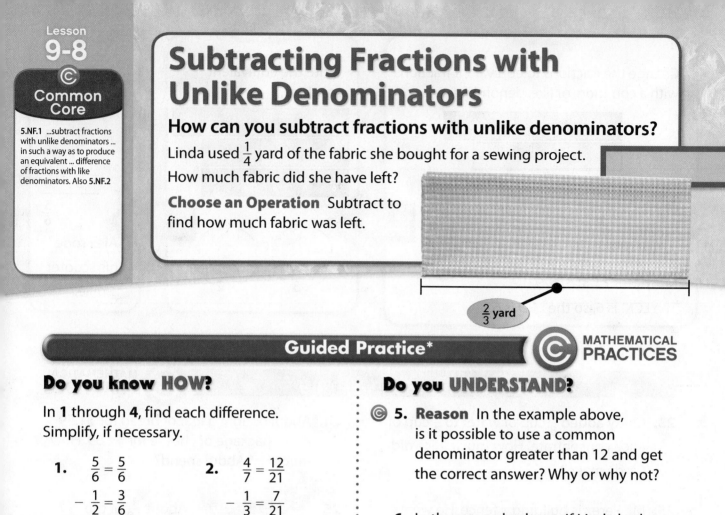

$\frac{2}{3}$ yard

Guided Practice*

MATHEMATICAL PRACTICES

Do you know HOW?

In **1** through **4**, find each difference. Simplify, if necessary.

1. $\frac{5}{6} = \frac{5}{6}$
    $-\frac{1}{2} = \frac{3}{6}$

2. $\frac{4}{7} = \frac{12}{21}$
    $-\frac{1}{3} = \frac{7}{21}$

3. $\frac{1}{2} - \frac{3}{10}$

4. $\frac{7}{8} - \frac{1}{3}$

Do you UNDERSTAND?

5. **Reason** In the example above, is it possible to use a common denominator greater than 12 and get the correct answer? Why or why not?

6. In the example above, if Linda had started with one yard of fabric and used $\frac{5}{8}$ of a yard, how much fabric would be left?

Independent Practice

Leveled Practice In **7** through **24**, find each difference. Simplify, if necessary.

7. $\frac{1}{3} = \frac{\blacksquare}{6}$
    $-\frac{1}{6} = \frac{\blacksquare}{6}$

8. $\frac{2}{3} = \frac{\blacksquare}{12}$
    $-\frac{5}{12} = \frac{\blacksquare}{12}$

9. $\frac{3}{5} = \frac{\blacksquare}{15}$
    $-\frac{1}{3} = \frac{\blacksquare}{15}$

10. $\frac{2}{9} = \frac{\blacksquare}{72}$
    $-\frac{1}{8} = \frac{\blacksquare}{72}$

11. $\frac{1}{4} = \frac{\blacksquare}{8}$
    $-\frac{1}{8} = \frac{\blacksquare}{8}$

12. $\frac{2}{3} = \frac{\blacksquare}{6}$
    $-\frac{1}{2} = \frac{\blacksquare}{6}$

13. $\frac{3}{4} = \frac{\blacksquare}{8}$
    $-\frac{3}{8} = \frac{\blacksquare}{8}$

14. $\frac{5}{6} = \frac{\blacksquare}{6}$
    $-\frac{1}{3} = \frac{\blacksquare}{6}$

15. $\frac{5}{8} - \frac{1}{4}$

16. $\frac{9}{16} - \frac{3}{8}$

17. $\frac{1}{5} - \frac{1}{7}$

18. $\frac{7}{10} - \frac{2}{4}$

19. $\frac{5}{6} - \frac{3}{4}$

20. $\frac{2}{3} - \frac{5}{9}$

21. $\frac{4}{5} - \frac{1}{4}$

22. $\frac{5}{8} - \frac{7}{12}$

23. $\frac{6}{7} - \frac{1}{2}$

24. $\frac{5}{12} - \frac{4}{16}$

*For another example, see Set F on page 245.

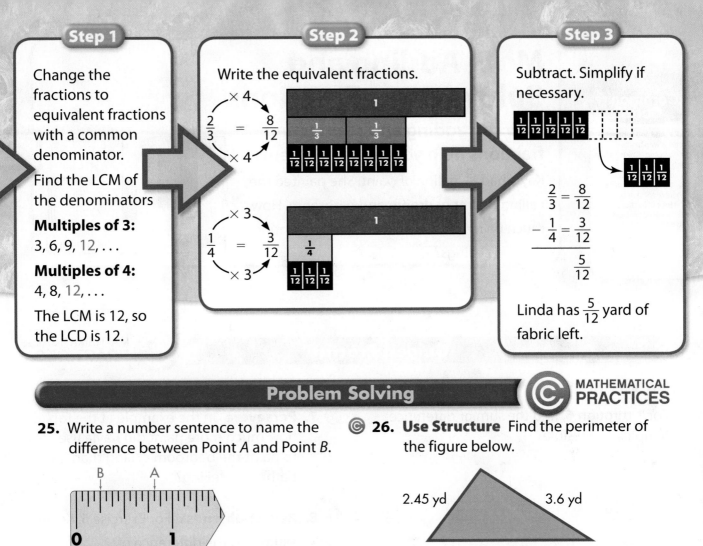

Step 1

Change the fractions to equivalent fractions with a common denominator.

Find the LCM of the denominators

Multiples of 3:

3, 6, 9, 12, . . .

Multiples of 4:

4, 8, 12, . . .

The LCM is 12, so the LCD is 12.

Step 2

Write the equivalent fractions.

$$\frac{2}{3} \stackrel{\times 4}{=} \frac{8}{12}$$

$$\frac{1}{4} \stackrel{\times 3}{=} \frac{3}{12}$$

Step 3

Subtract. Simplify if necessary.

$$\frac{2}{3} = \frac{8}{12}$$
$$-\frac{1}{4} = \frac{3}{12}$$
$$\frac{5}{12}$$

Linda has $\frac{5}{12}$ yard of fabric left.

Problem Solving

MATHEMATICAL **PRACTICES**

25. Write a number sentence to name the difference between Point *A* and Point *B*.

B   A

0   1

INCHES

© **26. Use Structure** Find the perimeter of the figure below.

2.45 yd   3.6 yd

4.5 yd

© **27. Reasonableness** Roy earned $72.50, $59, and $41.75 in tips when waiting tables last weekend. About how much did Roy earn in tips?

28. Mariko's social studies class lasts $\frac{5}{6}$ of an hour. Only $\frac{3}{12}$ of an hour has gone by. What fraction of an hour remains of Mariko's social studies class?

© **29. Construct Arguments** Why do fractions need to have a common denominator before you add or subtract them?

© **30. Generalize** What is the greatest common multiple of 3 and 4?

The hiking trail around Mirror Lake in Yosemite National Park is 5 miles long. Use the table for **31** and **32**.

31. What fraction more of the trail did Jon hike than Andrea?

32. What fraction more of the trail did Callie hike than Jon?

Hiker	Fraction of Trail Hiked
Andrea	$\frac{2}{5}$
Jon	$\frac{1}{2}$
Callie	$\frac{4}{5}$

5.NF.1 Add and subtract fractions with unlike denominators... by replacing given fractions with equivalent fractions in such a way as to produce an equivalent sum or difference of fractions with like denominators. Also 5.NF.2

More Adding and Subtracting Fractions

How can adding and subtracting fractions help you solve problems?

Kayla had $\frac{9}{10}$ gallon of paint. She painted the ceilings in her bedroom and bathroom. How much paint does she have left after painting the two ceilings?

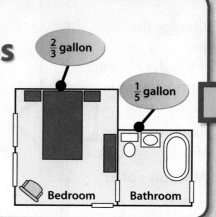

$\frac{2}{3}$ gallon

$\frac{1}{5}$ gallon

Bedroom   Bathroom

Guided Practice*

MATHEMATICAL PRACTICES

Do you know HOW?

For **1** through **6**, find the sum or difference. Simplify, if possible.

1. $\frac{1}{15}$
    $+\ \frac{1}{6}$

2. $\frac{7}{16}$
    $-\ \frac{1}{4}$

3. $\frac{25}{50} - \frac{2}{4}$

4. $\frac{2}{5} + \left(\frac{7}{10} - \frac{4}{10}\right)$

5. $\frac{7}{8} - \frac{3}{6}$

6. $\frac{7}{8} + \left(\frac{4}{8} - \frac{2}{4}\right)$

Do you UNDERSTAND?

7. Persevere In the example at the top, how much more paint did Kayla use to paint the bedroom ceiling than the bathroom ceiling?

8. Reasonableness For Exercise 5, Kevin estimated the difference of $\frac{7}{8} - \frac{3}{6}$ to be 0. Is his estimate reasonable? Explain.

Independent Practice

For **9** through **24**, find the sum or difference. Simplify, if possible.

9. $\frac{4}{50}$
    $+\ \frac{3}{5}$

10. $\frac{2}{3}$
    $-\ \frac{7}{12}$

11. $\frac{9}{10}$
    $+\ \frac{2}{100}$

12. $\frac{4}{9}$
    $+\ \frac{1}{4}$

13. $\frac{13}{15} - \frac{1}{3}$

14. $\frac{7}{16} + \frac{3}{8}$

15. $\frac{5}{7} - \frac{1}{2}$

16. $\frac{5}{6} - \frac{5}{18}$

17. $\frac{1}{12} + \frac{7}{8}$

18. $\frac{2}{75} + \frac{13}{15}$

19. $\frac{8}{25} - \frac{9}{75}$

20. $\frac{3}{50} + \frac{7}{10}$

21. $\left(\frac{7}{8} + \frac{1}{12}\right) - \frac{1}{2}$

22. $\left(\frac{11}{18} - \frac{4}{9}\right) + \frac{1}{6}$

23. $\left(\frac{9}{16} + \frac{1}{4}\right) - \frac{5}{8}$

24. $\frac{2}{3} + \left(\frac{5}{12} - \frac{1}{6}\right)$

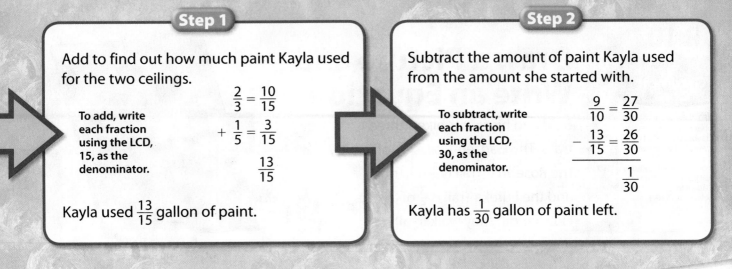

Step 1

Add to find out how much paint Kayla used for the two ceilings.

To add, write each fraction using the LCD, 15, as the denominator.

$$\frac{2}{3} = \frac{10}{15}$$
$$+ \frac{1}{5} = \frac{3}{15}$$
$$\frac{13}{15}$$

Kayla used $\frac{13}{15}$ gallon of paint.

Step 2

Subtract the amount of paint Kayla used from the amount she started with.

To subtract, write each fraction using the LCD, 30, as the denominator.

$$\frac{9}{10} = \frac{27}{30}$$
$$- \frac{13}{15} = \frac{26}{30}$$
$$\frac{1}{30}$$

Kayla has $\frac{1}{30}$ gallon of paint left.

Problem Solving

 MATHEMATICAL **PRACTICES**

25. Stefan's sculpture is $\frac{7}{12}$ foot tall. He attaches it to a base that is $\frac{1}{3}$ foot tall. How tall, in feet, is the sculpture with the base?

26. Tara made a snack mix with $\frac{3}{4}$ cup of rice crackers and $\frac{2}{3}$ cup of pretzels. She then ate $\frac{5}{8}$ cup of the mix for lunch. How much of the snack mix is left?

Ⓒ **27. Reason** Charlie's goal is to use less than 50 gallons of water per day. His water bill for the month showed that he used 1,524 gallons of water in 30 days. Did Charlie meet his goal this month? Explain how you decided.

Ⓒ **28. Construct Arguments** Jereen spent $\frac{1}{4}$ hour on homework after school, another $\frac{1}{2}$ hour after she got home, and a final $\frac{1}{3}$ hour after dinner. Did she spend more or less than 1 hour on homework in all? Explain.

29. Herb's Bakery had an electric bill for April of $112.59. The gas bill for the same month was $215.35. What was the bakery's total energy bill for the month?

Ⓒ **30. Be Precise** A cat's heart beats about 130 beats per minute. A kitten's heartbeat can be as fast as 240 beats per minute. How many times does a kitten's heart beat in one half-hour?

31. Kayla has decided to paint the ceiling in the living room. She has $\frac{1}{30}$ gallon of paint left. The living room ceiling will take $\frac{5}{6}$ gallon. After buying another gallon and painting the ceiling, how much paint will she have left?

32. What fraction of the kitten's heart rate is the cat's heart rate? Write the fraction in simplest form.

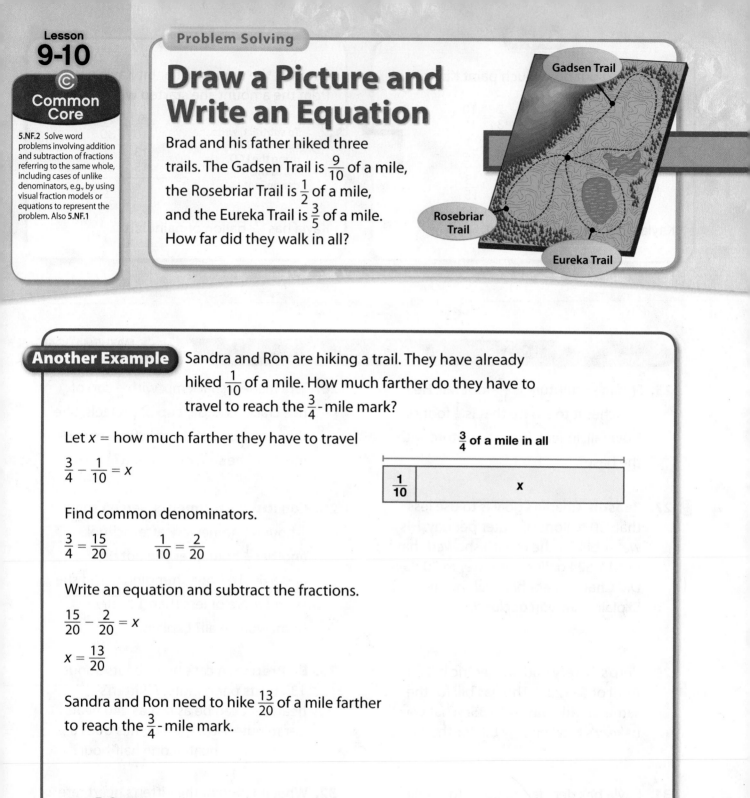

Problem Solving

Draw a Picture and Write an Equation

© Common Core

5.NF.2 Solve word problems involving addition and subtraction of fractions referring to the same whole, including cases of unlike denominators, e.g., by using visual fraction models or equations to represent the problem. Also 5.NF.1

Brad and his father hiked three trails. The Gadsen Trail is $\frac{9}{10}$ of a mile, the Rosebriar Trail is $\frac{1}{2}$ of a mile, and the Eureka Trail is $\frac{3}{5}$ of a mile. How far did they walk in all?

Gadsen Trail

Rosebriar Trail

Eureka Trail

Another Example Sandra and Ron are hiking a trail. They have already hiked $\frac{1}{10}$ of a mile. How much farther do they have to travel to reach the $\frac{3}{4}$-mile mark?

Let x = how much farther they have to travel

$\frac{3}{4} - \frac{1}{10} = x$

$\frac{3}{4}$ of a mile in all

| $\frac{1}{10}$ | x |

Find common denominators.

$\frac{3}{4} = \frac{15}{20}$ $\frac{1}{10} = \frac{2}{20}$

Write an equation and subtract the fractions.

$\frac{15}{20} - \frac{2}{20} = x$

$x = \frac{13}{20}$

Sandra and Ron need to hike $\frac{13}{20}$ of a mile farther to reach the $\frac{3}{4}$-mile mark.

Explain It

© 1. **Model** How could you find how much farther Sandra and Ron will have to hike to reach one mile?

© 2. **Reason** If Sandra and Ron turn around and hike back $\frac{1}{10}$ of a mile, how can you find the difference between the length they traveled and $\frac{3}{4}$ of a mile?

What do I know? Brad and his father hiked 3 trails.

Gadsen Trail = $\frac{9}{10}$ mi

Rosebriar Trail = $\frac{1}{2}$ mi

Eureka Trail = $\frac{3}{5}$ mi

What am I asked to find? How far did Brad and his father walk in all?

Let x = total miles hiked

$\frac{9}{10} = \frac{9}{10}$

$\frac{1}{2} = \frac{5}{10}$

$\frac{3}{5} = \frac{6}{10}$

	x miles in all	
$\frac{9}{10}$	$\frac{5}{10}$	$\frac{6}{10}$

Write an equation and add the fractions.

$x = \frac{9}{10} + \frac{5}{10} + \frac{6}{10} = \frac{20}{10}$ or 2 miles

Brad and his father walked 2 miles in all.

Guided Practice*

MATHEMATICAL PRACTICES

Do you know HOW?

Draw a picture and write an equation to solve.

1. Hannah ran $\frac{1}{3}$ of a mile. David ran $\frac{1}{6}$ of a mile. How much farther did Hannah run than David?

Do you UNDERSTAND?

2. **Look for Patterns** If you were asked to find how far Brad and his father walked on the Rosebriar and Eureka Trails alone, would the common denominator be different?

3. **Be Precise** Write a problem that you can solve by drawing a picture and writing an equation.

Independent Practice

MATHEMATICAL PRACTICES

Draw a picture and write an equation to solve.

4. Steve connected a wire extension that is $\frac{3}{8}$ foot long to another wire that is $\frac{1}{2}$ foot long. How long is the wire with the extension?

x foot	
$\frac{3}{8}$	$\frac{1}{2}$

5. The smallest female spider measures about $\frac{1}{2}$ millimeter (mm) in length. The smallest male spider measures about $\frac{2}{5}$ mm in length. How much longer is the female spider than the male spider?

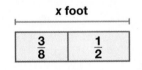

$\frac{1}{2}$ mm long	
$\frac{2}{5}$	x

Applying Math Practices

- What am I asked to find?
- What else can I try?
- How are quantities related?
- How can I explain my work?
- How can I use math to model the problem?
- Can I use tools to help?
- Is my work precise?
- Why does this work?
- How can I generalize?

6. A recipe calls for 3 times as many carrots as peas. If Carmen used 2 cups of peas, how many cups of carrots will she use?

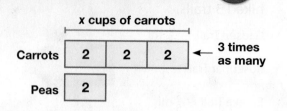

x cups of carrots

Carrots | 2 | 2 | 2 | ← 3 times as many

Peas | 2

7. Model Felix bought $\frac{5}{6}$ pound of peanuts. He ate $\frac{3}{4}$ pound of the peanuts with his friends. How much did Felix have left?

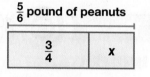

$\frac{5}{6}$ pound of peanuts

$\frac{3}{4}$ | x

8. Be Precise Jack's dog has a rectangular pen. The length is two feet longer than the width. The width is 6 feet. What is the perimeter of the pen?

9. Critique Reasoning Terrence has 8 comic books and 4 detective books. His sister says $\frac{2}{3}$ of his books are comic books. Terrence says that $\frac{8}{12}$ of his books are comic books. Who is correct? Explain your answer.

10. Persevere If the perimeter of the parallelogram below is 56 inches, and you know one side is 8 inches, will you be able to find the length of the other 3 sides? Why or why not?

8 inches

11. Model A banana bread recipe calls for $\frac{3}{4}$ cup of mashed bananas and $\frac{1}{8}$ cup of walnuts. Draw a picture and write an equation to find the total amount of bananas and walnuts added to the recipe.

Think About the Structure

12. Four relay team members run an equal part of an 8-mile race. Which equation shows how far each member runs?

A $4 + 2 = 6$ **C** $2 + 2 + 2 = 6$

B $8 \div 4 = 2$ **D** $8 + 4 = 12$

13. At an automobile dealership, there are 3 green cars, 4 blue cars, and 4 silver cars. Which equation tells how many cars are not silver?

A $4 - 3 = 1$ **C** $3 + 4 + 4 = 11$

B $11 - 4 = 7$ **D** $7 \times 4 = 28$

Algebra Connections

Equations with Fractions

Remember that you can evaluate an algebraic expression by substituting a value of the variable and simplifying.

Evaluate each equation for $v = \frac{1}{4}$ to determine whether it is true.

1. $\frac{2}{3} + v = \frac{3}{7}$

2. $v + \frac{1}{2} = \frac{3}{4}$

3. $v - \frac{1}{5} = \frac{1}{20}$

4. $\frac{1}{4} + v = \frac{3}{16}$

5. $\frac{4}{5} - v = \frac{2}{3}$

6. $\frac{3}{4} - v = \frac{1}{2}$

7. $\frac{3}{10} + v = \frac{11}{20}$

8. $v + \frac{1}{6} = \frac{5}{12}$

9. $\frac{1}{3} + v = \frac{1}{2}$

10. $v - \frac{1}{4} = 0$

11. $v - \frac{1}{8} = \frac{1}{8}$

12. $v + \frac{2}{5} = \frac{7}{8}$

Example: If $m = \frac{2}{5}$, which of the three equations listed below are true?

$\frac{1}{2} + m = 1; m + \frac{3}{5} = 1; \frac{4}{9} - m = \frac{1}{2}$

Think How can I check to see if each equation is true?

Substitute $\frac{2}{5}$ for m in each equation.

$\frac{1}{2} + \frac{2}{5} = \frac{5}{10} + \frac{4}{10} = \frac{9}{10} \neq 1$

$\frac{2}{5} + \frac{3}{5} = 1$

$\frac{4}{9} - \frac{2}{5} = \frac{20}{45} - \frac{18}{45} = \frac{2}{45} \neq \frac{1}{2}$

The only true equation is $m + \frac{3}{5} = 1$.

© **13. Model** It rained $\frac{2}{3}$ inch on Saturday. Find the total amount of rain, t, for the weekend if it rained $\frac{1}{4}$ inch on Sunday. Write and solve an equation to find the answer.

14. Jill walked $\frac{1}{3}$ mile less than Romero walked. If w equals how far Romero walked, which expression describes how far Jill walked?

A $\frac{1}{3} - w$ **C** $w - \frac{1}{3}$

B $\frac{1}{3} + w$ **D** $w + \frac{1}{3}$

© **15. Be Precise** Write a real-world problem using the equation $n = \frac{3}{8} - \frac{1}{6}$.

Set A, pages 222–223, 224–225

Write $\frac{21}{36}$ in simplest form.

To express a fraction in simplest form, divide the numerator and denominator by common factors until the only common factor is 1.

$$\frac{21 \div 3}{36 \div 3} = \frac{7}{12}$$

Write each fraction in simplest form.

1. $\frac{45}{60}$ 2. $\frac{32}{96}$

3. $\frac{24}{30}$ 4. $\frac{42}{49}$

Set B, pages 226–227

When you are asked to explain how you found your answer, follow these steps:

 Step 1

Break the process into steps.

 Step 2

Use pictures and words to explain.

 Step 3

Tell about things to watch out for and be careful about.

 Step 4

Write your steps in order using words like *find* and *put*.

Remember to show your work clearly so that others can understand it.

1. Sara's paper airplane flew $8\frac{1}{2}$ yards. Jason's flew $8\frac{2}{3}$ yards. Michael's flew $8\frac{1}{4}$ yards and Denise's flew $8\frac{1}{6}$ yards. Whose airplane flew the farthest? Explain how you found your answer.

Set C, pages 228–229

Estimate $\frac{7}{12} - \frac{1}{8}$.

Estimate the difference by replacing each fraction with 0, $\frac{1}{2}$ or 1.

Step 1 $\frac{7}{12}$ is close to $\frac{6}{12}$. Round $\frac{7}{12}$ to $\frac{1}{2}$.

Step 2 $\frac{1}{8}$ is close to 0. Round $\frac{1}{8}$ to 0.

Step 3 $\frac{1}{2} - 0 = \frac{1}{2}$

$\frac{7}{12} - \frac{1}{8}$ is about $\frac{1}{2}$.

Remember that you can use a number line to replace fractions with the nearest half or whole.

```
 ◄──┼──┼──┼──┼──┼──┼──┼──┼──►
    0              1/2            1
```

Estimate each sum or difference.

1. $\frac{2}{3} + \frac{5}{6}$ 2. $\frac{7}{8} - \frac{5}{12}$

3. $\frac{1}{8} + \frac{1}{16}$ 4. $\frac{5}{8} - \frac{1}{6}$

Set D, pages 230–231

Find the least common multiple (LCM) of 9 and 12. List the multiples of each number.

Multiples of 9: 9, 18, 27, 36, 45, …

Multiples of 12: 12, 24, 36, 48, …

Identify the least number that is a multiple of both 9 and 12. The LCM of 9 and 12 is 36.

Remember that the LCM of two numbers is the least number that is a multiple of both of the numbers.

1. 3 and 5   2. 4 and 6

3. 5 and 9   4. 6 and 10

5. 8 and 12   6. 8 and 3

Find a common denominator for $\frac{4}{9}$ and $\frac{1}{3}$.
Then rename the fractions to have that common denominator.

 Step 1 Multiply the denominators:

$9 \times 3 = 27$, so 27 is a common denominator.

Step 2 Rename the fractions:

$\frac{4}{9} \times \frac{3}{3} = \frac{12}{27}$ $\qquad$ $\frac{1}{3} \times \frac{9}{9} = \frac{9}{27}$

So, $\frac{12}{27}$ and $\frac{9}{27}$.

Remember you can check to see if one denominator is a multiple of the other. Since 9 is a multiple of 3, another common denominator of $\frac{4}{9}$ and $\frac{1}{3}$ is 9.

1. $\frac{3}{5}$ and $\frac{7}{10}$

2. $\frac{5}{6}$ and $\frac{7}{18}$

3. $\frac{3}{7}$ and $\frac{1}{4}$

4. $\frac{4}{9}$ and $\frac{3}{5}$

Find $\frac{5}{6} - \frac{3}{4}$.

Step 1 Find the least common multiple (LCM) of 6 and 4.
The LCM is 12, so the least common denominator (LCD) is 12.

Step 2 Use the LCD to write equivalent fractions.

$\frac{5}{6} = \frac{5 \times 2}{6 \times 2} = \frac{10}{12}$ $\qquad$ $\frac{3}{4} = \frac{3 \times 3}{4 \times 3} = \frac{9}{12}$

Step 3 Subtract the equivalent fractions. Simplify, if possible.

$\frac{10}{12} - \frac{9}{12} = \frac{1}{12}$

Remember to multiply the numerator and denominator by the same number when writing equivalent fractions.

1. $\frac{2}{5} + \frac{3}{10}$ $\qquad$ 2. $\frac{1}{9} + \frac{5}{6}$

3. $\frac{3}{4} - \frac{5}{12}$ $\qquad$ 4. $\frac{7}{8} - \frac{2}{3}$

5. $\frac{5}{16} - \frac{1}{8}$ $\qquad$ 6. $\frac{7}{10} - \frac{1}{6}$

7. $\frac{9}{25} + \frac{1}{3}$ $\qquad$ 8. $\frac{1}{4} + \frac{3}{8}$

9. $\frac{4}{5} - \frac{1}{3}$ $\qquad$ 10. $\frac{5}{8} - \frac{1}{2}$

11. $\frac{1}{6} + \frac{1}{2} + \frac{1}{6}$ $\qquad$ 12. $\frac{7}{100} + \frac{4}{50} + \frac{3}{25}$

Tina and Andy are building a model airplane. Tina built $\frac{1}{3}$ of the model, and Andy built $\frac{1}{5}$. How much more has Tina built than Andy?

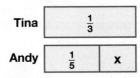

Find a common denominator and subtract.

$\frac{1}{3} = \frac{5}{15}$ $\qquad$ $\frac{1}{5} = \frac{3}{15}$ $\qquad$ So, $x = \frac{5}{15} - \frac{3}{15} = \frac{2}{15}$

Tina built $\frac{2}{15}$ more of the model than Andy.

Remember to use a picture to help you write an equation.

1. Bonnie ran $\frac{1}{4}$ of a mile. Olga ran $\frac{1}{8}$ of a mile. How far did they run in all?

2. Linda's plant was $\frac{9}{12}$ foot tall. Macy's plant was $\frac{2}{3}$ foot tall. How much taller is Linda's plant than Macy's?

Multiple Choice

 **ASSESSMENT**

1. The table shows water fowl that Hong counted at the lake. What fraction of the water fowl listed are Mallards? (9-2)

	Water Fowl Type	Number
	Canadian geese	5
	Crane	3
	Mallards	12

   A $\frac{3}{5}$

   B $\frac{8}{12}$

   C $\frac{3}{2}$

   D $\frac{5}{3}$

2. Replace each addend with 0, $\frac{1}{2}$, or 1. What is the estimate of the sum of $\frac{5}{8} + \frac{8}{9}$? (9-4)

   A $\frac{1}{2} + 1 = 1\frac{1}{2}$

   B $0 + 1 = 1$

   C $\frac{1}{2} + \frac{1}{2} = 1$

   D $1 + 1 = 2$

3. Which of the following pairs of numbers has a least common multiple of 24? (9-5)

   A 4 and 6

   B 3 and 8

   C 2 and 12

   D 3 and 6

4. What number makes the equation true? (9-1)

   $\frac{7}{12} = \frac{\blacksquare}{24}$

   A 2

   B 12

   C 14

   D 19

5. Benjamin and his sister shared a large sandwich. Benjamin ate $\frac{3}{5}$ of the sandwich and his sister ate $\frac{1}{7}$ of the sandwich. What is the best estimate of how much more Benjamin ate than his sister? (9-4)

   A $\frac{1}{2} - 0 = \frac{1}{2}$

   B $\frac{1}{2} - \frac{1}{2} = 0$

   C $1 - \frac{1}{2} = \frac{1}{2}$

   D $1 - 0 = 1$

6. Which renames $\frac{5}{12}$ and $\frac{3}{8}$ using a common denominator? (9-6)

   A $\frac{5}{12}$ and $\frac{3}{12}$

   B $\frac{10}{16}$ and $\frac{6}{16}$

   C $\frac{10}{24}$ and $\frac{12}{24}$

   D $\frac{10}{24}$ and $\frac{9}{24}$

7. Teri and her friends bought a party-size sandwich that was $\frac{7}{9}$ yard long. They ate $\frac{2}{3}$ of a yard. What part of a yard was left? (9-8)

Use the table for **8** and **9**.

Item	Number in Package
Paper	50
Pencils	12
Erasers	10

8. The table lists sizes of packages of school supplies. What is the smallest number of pencils and erasers that Mrs. Deng can buy so that she will have the same number of each? (9-5)

9. Mr. Vail purchased 1 package of each kind of school supply. What fraction of the items he purchased are pencils? Write your answer in simplest form. (9-2)

10. Sandra drove for $\frac{1}{3}$ hour to get to the store. Then she drove $\frac{1}{5}$ hour to get to the library. What fraction of an hour did Sandra drive in all? (9-7)

11. A store has the floor plan shown. Estimate the part of the store used for sporting goods. Explain how you decided. (9-3)

Women's	
Boys'	Girls'
Sporting Goods	
Bath	Men's

12. A green snake is $\frac{8}{9}$ yard long. A garter snake is $\frac{13}{18}$ yard long. How much longer is the green snake than the garter? (9-9)

13. Of the balls shown, $\frac{1}{3}$ are basketballs and $\frac{1}{15}$ are soccer balls. What fraction of the balls are either basketballs or soccer balls? (9-7)

14. What fraction of the balls above are baseballs? Write the fraction in simplest form. (9-2)

15. Rhys is kayaking down a $\frac{4}{5}$-mile stream. He has already traveled $\frac{1}{4}$ of a mile. How much farther does he need to travel? Draw a picture and write an equation to solve. (9-10)

16. Pablo and Jamie bought two pizzas that were the same size. Jamie ate $\frac{1}{4}$ of her pizza. Pablo ate $\frac{1}{3}$ of his pizza. How much more pizza did Pablo eat than Jamie? How much of a pizza did they eat in all? (9-9)

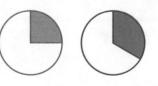

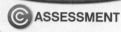
1. Pat made muffins to bring to a party. She gave $\frac{1}{6}$ of the muffins to her younger brothers. Her dad ate $\frac{1}{8}$ of the muffins. What fraction of the muffins was left to take to the party?

2. Pat also made a container of punch to bring to the party. She gave $\frac{1}{12}$ of the punch to her mother to try and $\frac{1}{8}$ of the punch to each of her two sisters. What fraction of the punch was left to take to the party?

3. To get to the party, Pat walked $\frac{1}{6}$ of an hour to the bus stop. After waiting $\frac{1}{12}$ of an hour, the bus arrived. Pat spent $\frac{2}{3}$ of an hour on the bus. What fraction of an hour did Pat spend getting to the party? Explain how you found your answer.

4. At the party, Pat estimated that about $\frac{1}{2}$ of the guests were dressed up. If $\frac{3}{16}$ of the guests were dressed up, is Pat's estimate reasonable? Explain how you decided.

5. At the party, $\frac{6}{16}$ of the guests were playing games and $\frac{3}{8}$ of the guests were singing. Pat said that the same number of guests were playing games as were singing. Is she right? Explain.

6. On her way to the party, Pat saw a group of children playing at a school. $\frac{4}{9}$ of the children were playing soccer while $\frac{5}{12}$ were playing on the playground. Pat said there are more children playing soccer than are playing on the playground. Is she correct?

Topic **10** **Adding and Subtracting Mixed Numbers**

▼ This Parson's chameleon can extend its tongue up to $1\frac{1}{2}$ times the length of its body. What is the total length of the chameleon when its tongue is fully extended? You will find out in Lesson 10-4.

Review What You Know!

Vocabulary

Choose the best term from the box.

- least common multiple (LCM)
- common multiple
- least common denominator (LCD)
- prime factorization

1. Writing a number as the product of prime numbers is called __?__ .

2. A __?__ is a number that is a multiple of two or more numbers.

3. The number 12 is the __?__ of 3, 4, and 6.

Comparing Fractions

Compare. Write >, <, or = for each $\bigcirc$.

4. $\frac{5}{25} \bigcirc \frac{2}{5}$ 5. $\frac{12}{27} \bigcirc \frac{6}{9}$

6. $\frac{11}{16} \bigcirc \frac{2}{8}$ 7. $\frac{2}{7} \bigcirc \frac{1}{5}$

Fractions in Simplest Form

Write each fraction in simplest form.

8. $\frac{6}{18}$ 9. $\frac{12}{22}$ 10. $\frac{15}{25}$

11. $\frac{8}{26}$ 12. $\frac{14}{35}$ 13. $\frac{4}{18}$

© **Writing to Explain** Write an answer for each question.

14. How do you know when a fraction is in simplest form?

15. How can you write a fraction in simplest form?

Topic Essential Questions
- What does it mean to add and subtract mixed numbers?
- What is a standard procedure for adding and subtracting mixed numbers?

Interactive Learning

Pose the problem. Start each lesson by working together to solve problems. It will help you make sense of math.

Applying Math Practices

- What am I asked to find?
- What else can I try?
- How are quantities related?
- How can I explain my work?
- How can I use math to model the problem?
- Can I use tools to help?
- Is my work precise?
- Why does this work?
- How can I generalize?

Lesson 10-1

© **Use Tools** Copy the number line. Then write the numbers most likely represented by points A and B. Can you name each in more than one way? Explain.

$$\underset{0 \qquad\qquad\quad 1 \qquad\qquad\quad 2}{\longleftrightarrow}$$

A   B

Lesson 10-2

© **Reasonableness** Solve mentally. You only need an estimate.

Alex has 5 cups of strawberries. He wants $1\frac{6}{8}$ cups of strawberries for a fruit salad and $3\frac{1}{2}$ cups of strawberries for jam. Does Alex have enough strawberries to make both recipes? Tell how you decided.

Lesson 10-3

© **Use Tools** Solve any way you choose. You may use fraction strips to help.

Tory is cutting bread loaves into fourths. She needs to wrap up $3\frac{3}{4}$ loaves to take to a potluck supper and $1\frac{2}{4}$ loaves for a bake sale. How many loaves does Tory need to wrap in all for the potluck supper and the bake sale?

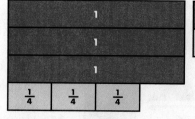

Lesson 10-4

© **Generalize** Solve in any way you choose. Record your work.

Joaquin used $1\frac{1}{2}$ cups of whole-wheat flour and $1\frac{2}{3}$ cups of buckwheat flour in a recipe. How much flour did he use in all?

$1\frac{1}{2}$ cups

Lesson 10-5

© **Generalize** Solve in any way you choose. Record your work.

Evan is walking $2\frac{1}{8}$ miles to his aunt's house. He has already walked $\frac{3}{4}$ mile. How much farther does he have to go?

Total distance = $2\frac{1}{8}$ miles

Evan's House | First Stop | Aunt's House

Start

Lesson 10-6

© **Reasonableness** Solve in any way you choose. Record your work.

Tim has 15 feet of wrapping paper. He uses $4\frac{1}{3}$ feet for his daughter's present and $5\frac{3}{8}$ feet for his niece's present. How much wrapping paper does Tim have left? Explain how you know your answer is reasonable.

Lesson 10-7

© **Model** Solve. Use the bar diagram to help choose the needed operation.

Juan biked $1\frac{1}{10}$ miles to his friend Mike's house and then to school. He biked $2\frac{7}{10}$ miles in all. What is the distance from Mike's house to school? Tell why you choose the operation you used.

$2\frac{7}{10}$

| $1\frac{1}{10}$ | x |

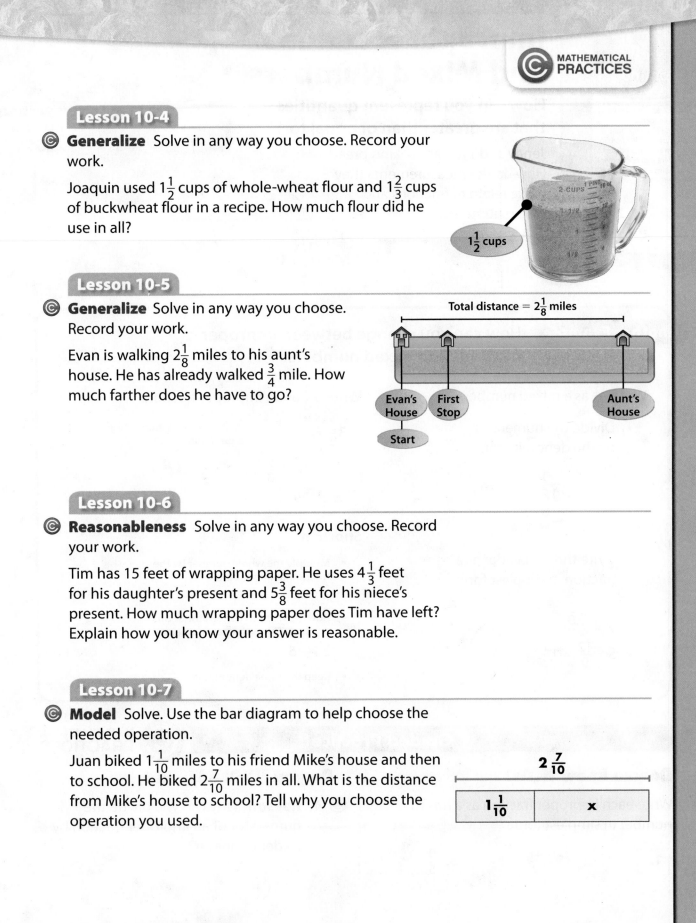

Common
Core

5.NF.1 Add and subtract...
mixed numbers by
replacing given fractions
with equivalent fractions in
such a way as to produce an
equivalent sum or difference
of fractions with like
denominators. Also 5.NF.2

Improper Fractions and Mixed Numbers

How can you represent quantities that are greater than or equal to 1?

Jenny and Tyler are baking bread. How do the measurements they make relate to fractions and mixed numbers?

$4\frac{1}{2}$ cups of flour

$\frac{1}{2}$ cup of sugar

$\frac{4}{3}$ cup of milk

Another Example How can you change between improper fractions and mixed numbers?

Write $\frac{12}{9}$ as a mixed number.

- Divide the numerator by the denominator.

$$9\overline{)12} \quad \begin{array}{r} 1\ R3 \\ \hline 12 \\ -\ 9 \\ \hline 3 \end{array}$$

- Write the remainder as a fraction in simplest form.

$$\frac{3}{9} = \frac{1}{3}$$

- So, $\frac{12}{9} = 1\frac{1}{3}$.

Write $3\frac{5}{8}$ as an improper fraction.

$$3\frac{5}{8} = 3 + \frac{5}{8} \qquad \text{Write 3 as a fraction using a denominator of 8.}$$

$$= \frac{24}{8} + \frac{5}{8}$$

$$= \frac{29}{8}$$

Shortcut

- Multiply the whole number by the fraction denominator.

$$3 \times 8 = 24$$

- Add the fraction numerator to this product. This is the new numerator.

$$24 + 5 = 29$$

- Keep the same denominator. $\frac{29}{8}$

Guided Practice*

MATHEMATICAL PRACTICES

Do you know HOW?

Write each improper fraction as a mixed number in simplest form.

1. $\frac{7}{3}$ 2. $\frac{41}{9}$ 3. $\frac{9}{5}$

Do you UNDERSTAND?

4. **Reason** Why can you divide the numerator of an improper fraction by its denominator?

Animated Glossary
www.pearsonsuccessnet.com

*For another example, see Set A on page 268.

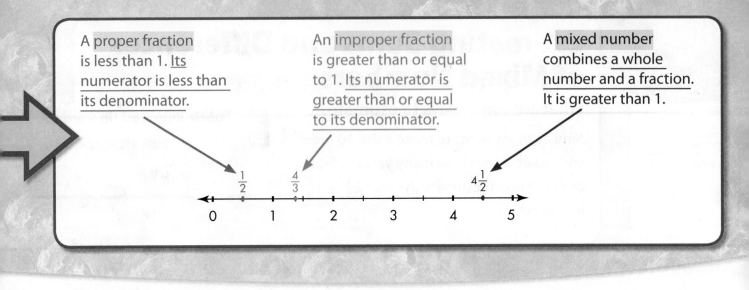

A proper fraction is less than 1. Its numerator is less than its denominator.

An improper fraction is greater than or equal to 1. Its numerator is greater than or equal to its denominator.

A mixed number combines a whole number and a fraction. It is greater than 1.

Independent Practice

Write each improper fraction as a whole number or mixed number in simplest form.

5. $\frac{38}{7}$ **6.** $\frac{14}{8}$ **7.** $\frac{8}{3}$ **8.** $\frac{42}{6}$ **9.** $\frac{17}{5}$ **10.** $\frac{21}{9}$

Write each mixed number as an improper fraction.

11. $1\frac{1}{8}$ **12.** $4\frac{2}{3}$ **13.** $3\frac{1}{11}$ **14.** $5\frac{3}{5}$ **15.** $2\frac{7}{12}$ **16.** $8\frac{1}{4}$

For **17** through **21**, which letter on the number line corresponds to each number?

17. $1\frac{3}{8}$ **18.** $\frac{4}{2}$ **19.** $3\frac{3}{4}$ **20.** $\frac{1}{2}$ **21.** $\frac{9}{4}$

Problem Solving

MATHEMATICAL PRACTICES

© **22. Be Precise** A capybara is the world's largest rodent. It can grow to be $1\frac{3}{10}$ m long. Which improper fraction represents the length of the capybara?

A $\frac{36}{13}$ m

B $\frac{13}{10}$ m

C $\frac{29}{10}$ m

D $\frac{11}{10}$ m

© **23. Critique Reasoning** Diego said that $\frac{9}{4}$ and $1\frac{1}{4}$ are equivalent. Is he right? Explain.

24. A quadrilateral has 3 angles that measure 47°, 110°, and 85°. What is the measurement of the fourth angle?

© **25. Reason** Should $\frac{15}{15}$ be expressed as a mixed number or a whole number? How do you know?

© Common Core

5.NF.2 …Use benchmark fractions and number sense of fractions to estimate mentally and assess the reasonableness of answers. Also 5.NF.1

Estimating Sums and Differences of Mixed Numbers

What are some ways to estimate?

Jamila's mom wants to make a size 10 dress and jacket. About how many yards of fabric does she need? Estimate the sum $2\frac{1}{4} + 1\frac{7}{8}$ to find out.

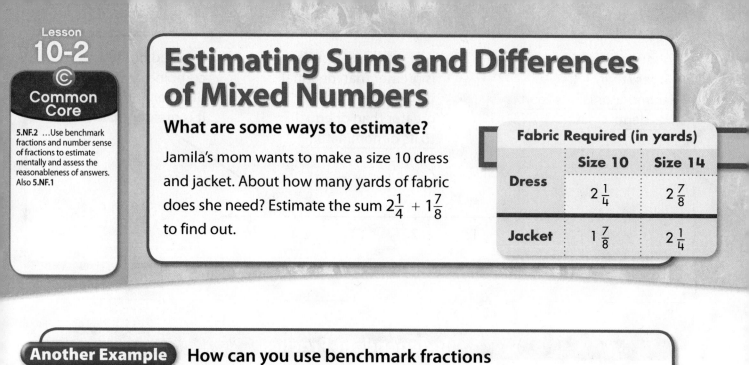

Fabric Required (in yards)		
	Size 10	Size 14
Dress	$2\frac{1}{4}$	$2\frac{7}{8}$
Jacket	$1\frac{7}{8}$	$2\frac{1}{4}$

Another Example How can you use benchmark fractions such as $\frac{1}{4}, \frac{1}{3}, \frac{1}{2}, \frac{2}{3}$, and $\frac{3}{4}$ to estimate?

Estimate $\frac{5}{8} - \frac{3}{16}$.

$\frac{5}{8}$ is close to $\frac{6}{8}$, and $\frac{6}{8} = \frac{3}{4}$.

$\frac{3}{16}$ is close to $\frac{4}{16}$, and $\frac{4}{16} = \frac{1}{4}$.

So, $\frac{5}{8} - \frac{3}{16}$ is close to $\frac{3}{4} - \frac{1}{4}$.

$\frac{3}{4} - \frac{1}{4} = \frac{2}{4}$ or $\frac{1}{2}$

So, $\frac{5}{8} - \frac{3}{16} \approx \frac{1}{2}$.

Guided Practice*

MATHEMATICAL PRACTICES

Do you know HOW?

Round to the nearest whole number.

1. $\frac{3}{4}$ **2.** $1\frac{5}{7}$ **3.** $2\frac{3}{10}$

Estimate each sum or difference using benchmark fractions.

4. $2\frac{5}{9} - 1\frac{1}{3}$ **5.** $2\frac{4}{10} + 3\frac{5}{8}$

Do you UNDERSTAND?

© **6. Use Structure** To estimate with mixed numbers, when should you round up to the nearest whole number?

7. Suppose Jamila's mom wants to make a size 14 dress and jacket. About how many yards of fabric does she need?

Independent Practice

Leveled Practice Use the number line to round the mixed numbers to the nearest whole number.

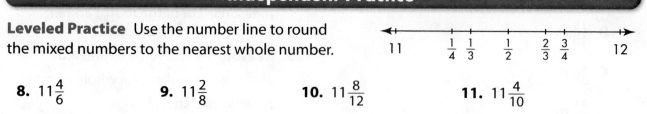

8. $11\frac{4}{6}$ **9.** $11\frac{2}{8}$ **10.** $11\frac{8}{12}$ **11.** $11\frac{4}{10}$

*For another example, see Set B on page 268.

Estimate each sum or difference.

12. $2\frac{1}{8} - \frac{5}{7}$ **13.** $12\frac{1}{3} + 2\frac{1}{4}$ **14.** $2\frac{2}{3} + \frac{7}{8}$ **15.** $1\frac{10}{15} - \frac{8}{9}$

16. $10\frac{5}{6} - 2\frac{3}{8}$ **17.** $12\frac{8}{25} + 13\frac{5}{9}$ **18.** $48\frac{1}{10} - 2\frac{7}{9}$ **19.** $33\frac{14}{15} + 23\frac{9}{25}$

Problem Solving

MATHEMATICAL PRACTICES

20. Use the recipes to answer the questions.

  a Estimate how many cups of Fruit Trail Mix this recipe can make.

  b Estimate how many cups of Traditional Trail Mix this recipe can make.

  c Estimate how much trail mix you would have if you made both recipes.

Fruit Trail Mix

- $\frac{1}{2}$ cup raisins
- $\frac{3}{8}$ cup sunflower seeds
- 1 cup unsalted peanuts
- $\frac{1}{4}$ cup coconut

Traditional Trail Mix

- $1\frac{1}{3}$ cup raisins
- 1 cup sunflower seeds
- $1\frac{3}{4}$ cup unsalted peanuts
- 1 cup cashews

© **21. Reasonableness** In the equation $5\frac{2}{9} + x = 9\frac{7}{8}$, estimate the value of x.

© **22. Look for Patterns** Scott uses a pattern to collect beetles. The table shows how many of each species he has. Use the pattern to find the missing numbers. Explain Scott's pattern.

Number of Beetles by Species							
Species	A	B	C	D	E	F	G
Number	1	3	6	10	15	▨	▨

© **23. Use Tools** Round $2\frac{3}{8}$ using benchmark fractions. Use a number line to help you solve.

  A $2\frac{1}{2}$ **C** $3\frac{1}{4}$

  B $2\frac{3}{4}$ **D** $3\frac{1}{2}$

Lesson
10-3

Common
Core

5.NF.2 Solve word problems involving addition and subtraction of fractions referring to the same whole... by using visual fraction models or equations to represent the problem. Also 5.NF.1

Modeling Addition and Subtraction of Mixed Numbers

Hands-On fraction strips

$\frac{1}{8}$

How can you model addition of mixed numbers?

Bill has 2 boards he will use to make picture frames. What is the total length of the boards Bill has to make picture frames?

Choose an Operation Add to find the total length.

$1\frac{11}{12}$ feet $2\frac{5}{12}$ feet

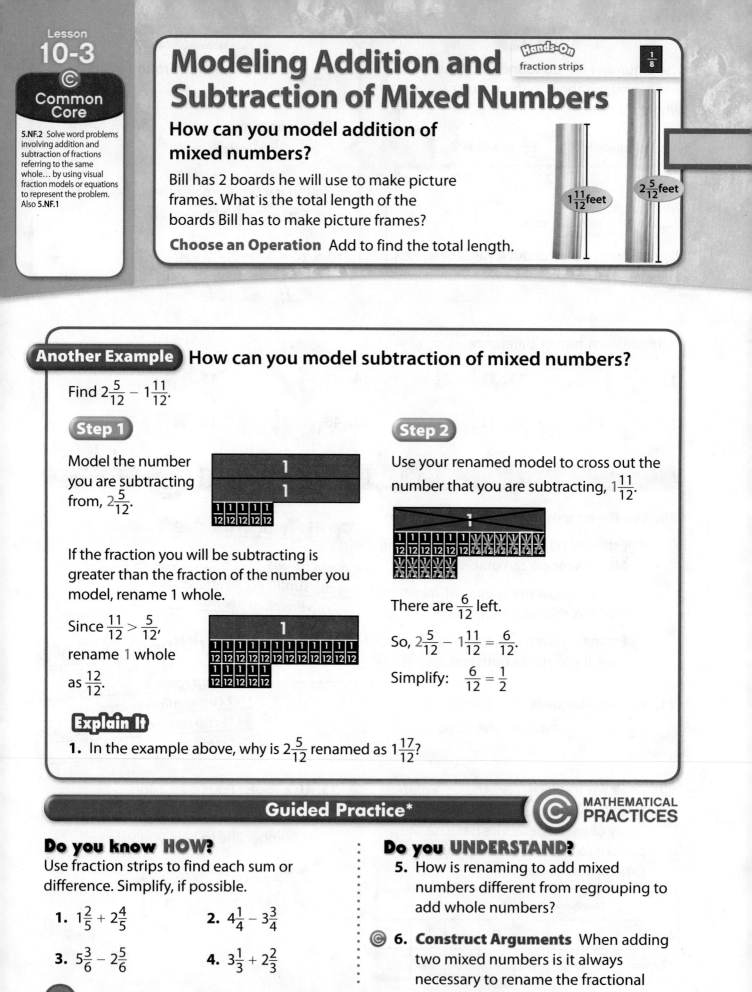

Another Example How can you model subtraction of mixed numbers?

Find $2\frac{5}{12} - 1\frac{11}{12}$.

Step 1

Model the number you are subtracting from, $2\frac{5}{12}$.

If the fraction you will be subtracting is greater than the fraction of the number you model, rename 1 whole.

Since $\frac{11}{12} > \frac{5}{12}$, rename 1 whole as $\frac{12}{12}$.

Step 2

Use your renamed model to cross out the number that you are subtracting, $1\frac{11}{12}$.

There are $\frac{6}{12}$ left.

So, $2\frac{5}{12} - 1\frac{11}{12} = \frac{6}{12}$.

Simplify: $\frac{6}{12} = \frac{1}{2}$

Explain It

1. In the example above, why is $2\frac{5}{12}$ renamed as $1\frac{17}{12}$?

Guided Practice*

MATHEMATICAL PRACTICES

Do you know HOW?

Use fraction strips to find each sum or difference. Simplify, if possible.

1. $1\frac{2}{5} + 2\frac{4}{5}$

2. $4\frac{1}{4} - 3\frac{3}{4}$

3. $5\frac{3}{6} - 2\frac{5}{6}$

4. $3\frac{1}{3} + 2\frac{2}{3}$

Do you UNDERSTAND?

5. How is renaming to add mixed numbers different from regrouping to add whole numbers?

© 6. **Construct Arguments** When adding two mixed numbers is it always necessary to rename the fractional sum? Explain.

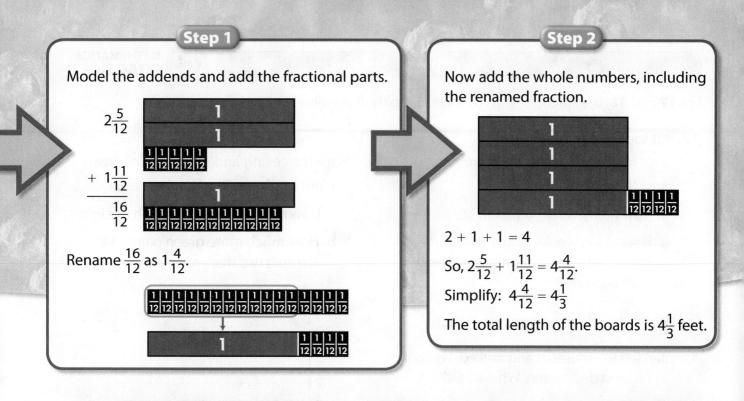

Step 1

Model the addends and add the fractional parts.

$2\frac{5}{12}$

$+ \ 1\frac{11}{12}$

$\frac{16}{12}$

Rename $\frac{16}{12}$ as $1\frac{4}{12}$.

Step 2

Now add the whole numbers, including the renamed fraction.

$2 + 1 + 1 = 4$

So, $2\frac{5}{12} + 1\frac{11}{12} = 4\frac{4}{12}$.

Simplify: $4\frac{4}{12} = 4\frac{1}{3}$

The total length of the boards is $4\frac{1}{3}$ feet.

Independent Practice

In **7** and **8**, use each model to find the sum or difference. Simplify if possible.

© **7. Model** Charles used $1\frac{2}{3}$ cups of walnuts and $2\frac{2}{3}$ cups of cranberries to make breakfast bread. How many cups of walnuts and cranberries did he use in all?

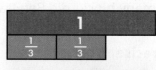

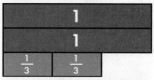

8. Terrell ran to his friend's apartment in $2\frac{5}{6}$ minutes. It took Terrell $4\frac{1}{6}$ minutes to go back home. How much more time did Terrell take to get home?

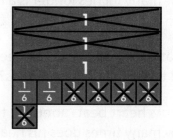

In **9** through **16**, use fraction strips to find each sum or difference. Simplify if possible.

9. $2\frac{3}{5} + 1\frac{3}{5}$ **10.** $4\frac{5}{12} + 1\frac{7}{12}$ **11.** $4\frac{9}{10} + 3\frac{7}{10}$ **12.** $5\frac{3}{4} + 2\frac{3}{4}$

13. $9\frac{1}{6} - 4\frac{5}{6}$ **14.** $12\frac{3}{8} - 9\frac{5}{8}$ **15.** $8\frac{1}{3} - 7\frac{2}{3}$ **16.** $13\frac{7}{9} - 10\frac{8}{9}$

For **17** and **18**, use fraction strips to solve. Simplify, if possible.

17. Kit said, "On summer vacation, I spent $2\frac{4}{7}$ weeks with my grandma and $1\frac{6}{7}$ weeks with my aunt."

   a How many weeks is that in all?

   b How many weeks longer did Kit spend with her grandmother than with her aunt?

18. Hannah used $1\frac{2}{3}$ gallons of white paint for the ceiling and $3\frac{2}{3}$ gallons of green paint for the walls of her kitchen.

   a How much paint did Hannah use in all?

   b How much more green paint did Hannah use than white paint?

For **19** and **20**, use the map at the right.

19. Ben left the museum and walked 4 blocks to his next destination. What was it?

© **20. Think About the Structure** Ben walked from the restaurant to the bus stop. Then he took the bus to the stadium. If he took the shortest route, how many blocks did Ben travel?

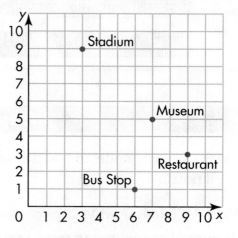

© **21. Be Precise** What is the value of the underlined digit in 6.2<u>7</u>5?

   A 7 ones   **B** 7 tenths   **C** 7 hundredths   **D** 7 thousandths

For **22** and **23**, use the table at the right.

22. How many inches longer is a Hercules beetle than a ladybug?

23. What is the difference between the largest and the smallest stag beetles?

24. Raoul's heart beats about 72 times each minute. How many times does his heart beat in 15 minutes?

Beetles by Length	
Beetle	**Length in inches**
Hercules beetle	$6\frac{3}{4}$
Ladybug	$\frac{1}{4}$
Stag beetle	$1\frac{1}{8}$ to $2\frac{4}{8}$

25. Nicole, Tasha, Maria, and Joan ran a relay race. Nicole ran the first leg of the race in $1\frac{13}{15}$ minutes. Tasha ran the second leg in $2\frac{1}{15}$ minutes. Maria ran the third leg in $1\frac{7}{15}$ minutes. Joan ran the last leg in $2\frac{2}{15}$ minutes to finish the race.

  © **a Reason** How can you find how much faster Maria ran than Joan?

   b The team wanted to run the race in less than six minutes. Did they meet their goal? Explain.

The human body is very complex. Two systems of the human body are the muscular and circulatory systems.

1. An average ten-year-old weighs about $86\frac{1}{2}$ pounds and has muscles that weigh about $34\frac{1}{5}$ pounds. Find the difference between these two weights.

2. Use the information given in Exercise 1. About how much do the muscles of two average ten-year-olds weigh? Write your answer as a mixed number.

3. Your body temperature can change from hour to hour. Tony's temperature was 98.6°F at 2 P.M. His temperature increased 0.6°F during the first hour, 0.2°F the second hour, and 0.1°F during the third hour. It decreased 0.8°F during the fourth hour. What was Tony's temperature at 6 P.M.?

4. The circulatory system includes the heart, the blood, and the blood vessels. A person is born with about 0.25 liter of blood. An adult has about 5 liters of blood. What is the difference between the amount of blood an adult has and the amount of blood a newborn baby has?

In **5** and **6**, use the following information.

The left ventricle of an average person can pump about 315 liters of blood in 1 hour.

© 5. **Reason** Estimate to find about how many liters of blood the left ventricle can pump in 1 minute. Hint: There are 60 minutes in an hour.

© 6. **Reason** The left ventricle pumps blood away from the heart into your body's largest artery, the aorta. About how much blood is pumped into the aorta in 10 minutes?

A 5 liters   C 50 liters

B 10 liters   D 500 liters

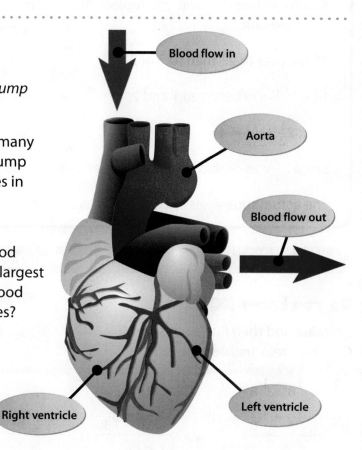

Common
Core

5.NF.1 Add…fractions
with unlike denominators
(including mixed numbers)
by replacing given fractions
with equivalent fractions in
such a way as to produce
an equivalent sum… Also
5.NF.2

Adding Mixed Numbers

How can you add mixed numbers?

Rhoda mixes sand with $2\frac{2}{3}$ cups of potting mixture
to prepare soil for her cactus plants. After
mixing them together, how many cups
of soil does Rhoda have?

Choose an Operation Add to
find the total amount of soil.

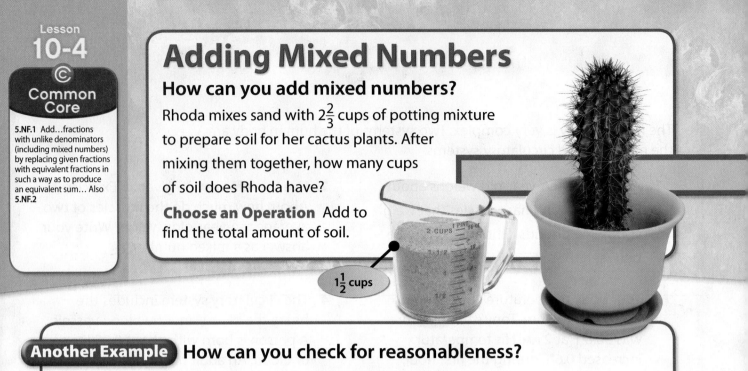

$1\frac{1}{2}$ cups

Another Example **How can you check for reasonableness?**

You just found that the sum of $2\frac{2}{3}$ and $1\frac{1}{2}$ is $4\frac{1}{6}$. You can use estimation
to check that a sum is reasonable.

Estimate $2\frac{2}{3} + 1\frac{1}{2}$.

A number line can help you replace mixed numbers with the nearest one-half
or whole unit.

$2\frac{2}{3}$ is closer to $2\frac{1}{2}$ than to 2 or 3.

$1\frac{1}{2}$ is halfway between 1 and 2.

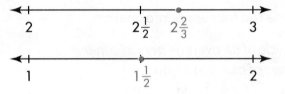

Add: $2\frac{1}{2} + 1\frac{1}{2} = 4$

Since $2\frac{2}{3}$ was replaced with $2\frac{1}{2}$, the answer will be greater than the estimate.

The actual sum, $4\frac{1}{6}$, is reasonable because it is close to the estimate, 4.

Guided Practice*

**MATHEMATICAL
PRACTICES**

Do you know HOW?

Estimate and then find each sum.
Check for reasonableness.

1. $1\frac{7}{8} = 1\frac{\square}{8}$
    $+ 1\frac{1}{4} = 1\frac{\square}{8}$
    _____

2. $2\frac{2}{5} = 2\frac{\square}{30}$
    $+ 5\frac{5}{6} = 5\frac{\square}{30}$
    _____

3. $4\frac{1}{9} + 1\frac{1}{3}$

4. $6\frac{5}{12} + 4\frac{5}{8}$

Do you UNDERSTAND?

© 5. **Reason** How is adding mixed
numbers like adding fractions and
whole numbers?

© 6. **Construct Arguments** Kyle used 9
as an estimate for $3\frac{1}{6} + 5\frac{7}{8}$. He added
and got $9\frac{1}{24}$ for the actual sum. Is his
answer reasonable?

For another example, see Set D on page 269.

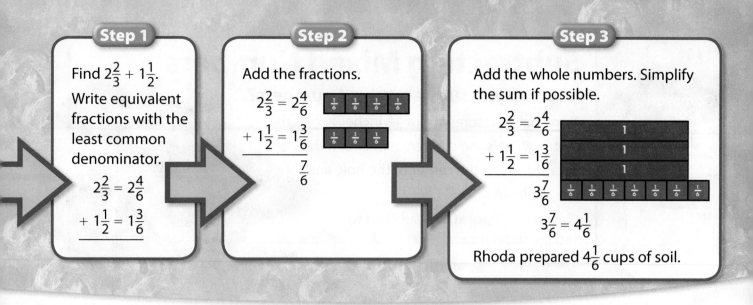

Step 1

Find $2\frac{2}{3} + 1\frac{1}{2}$.
Write equivalent fractions with the least common denominator.

$$2\frac{2}{3} = 2\frac{4}{6}$$
$$+ 1\frac{1}{2} = 1\frac{3}{6}$$

Step 2

Add the fractions.

$$2\frac{2}{3} = 2\frac{4}{6}$$
$$+ 1\frac{1}{2} = 1\frac{3}{6}$$
$$\frac{7}{6}$$

Step 3

Add the whole numbers. Simplify the sum if possible.

$$2\frac{2}{3} = 2\frac{4}{6}$$
$$+ 1\frac{1}{2} = 1\frac{3}{6}$$
$$3\frac{7}{6}$$

$$3\frac{7}{6} = 4\frac{1}{6}$$

Rhoda prepared $4\frac{1}{6}$ cups of soil.

Independent Practice

Leveled Practice For **7** through **18**, estimate and then find each sum. Check for reasonableness.

7.
$$3\frac{1}{6} = 3\frac{\square}{6}$$
$$+ 5\frac{2}{3} = 5\frac{\square}{6}$$

8.
$$11\frac{1}{2} = 11\frac{\square}{10}$$
$$+ 10\frac{3}{5} = 10\frac{\square}{10}$$

9.
$$9\frac{3}{16}$$
$$+ 7\frac{5}{8}$$

10.
$$5\frac{6}{7}$$
$$+ 8\frac{1}{7}$$

11. $4\frac{1}{10} + 6\frac{1}{2}$

12. $9\frac{7}{12} + 4\frac{3}{4}$

13. $5 + 3\frac{1}{8}$

14. $8\frac{3}{4} + 7\frac{3}{4}$

15. $2\frac{3}{4} + 7\frac{3}{5}$

16. $3\frac{8}{9} + 8\frac{1}{2}$

17. $1\frac{7}{12} + 2\frac{3}{8}$

18. $3\frac{11}{12} + 9\frac{1}{16}$

Problem Solving

© **MATHEMATICAL PRACTICES**

© **19. Persevere** Arnie skated $1\frac{3}{4}$ miles from home to the lake, then went $1\frac{1}{3}$ miles around the lake, and then back home. How many miles did he skate?

A $2\frac{1}{12}$ miles

B $3\frac{1}{12}$ miles

C $4\frac{5}{6}$ miles

D $4\frac{5}{12}$ miles

20. a Use the map below to find the distance from the start of the trail to the end.

b Louise walked from the start of the trail to the bird lookout and back. Did she walk more or less than if she had walked from the start of the trail to the end?

21. The length of a male Parson's chameleon can be up to $23\frac{1}{2}$ inches. It can extend its tongue up to $35\frac{1}{4}$ inches to catch its food. What is the total length of a male Parson's chameleon when its tongue is fully extended?

Common
Core

5.NF.1 …Subtract fractions with unlike denominators (including mixed numbers) by replacing given fractions with equivalent fractions in such a way as to produce a… difference of fractions with like denominators. Also **5.NF.2**

Subtracting Mixed Numbers

How can you subtract mixed numbers?

A golf ball measures about $1\frac{2}{3}$ inches across the center. What is the difference between the distance across the center of the hole and the golf ball?

Choose an Operation Subtract to find the difference.

$4\frac{1}{4}$ inches

Another Example **How can you check for reasonableness?**

You just found that the difference of $4\frac{1}{4}$ and $1\frac{2}{3}$ is $2\frac{7}{12}$. You can use estimation to check that a difference is reasonable.

Estimate $4\frac{1}{4} - 1\frac{2}{3}$.

$4\frac{1}{4}$ is close to 4.
Replace $4\frac{1}{4}$ with 4.

$1\frac{2}{3}$ is closer to 2 than to 1.

Subtract: $4 - 2 = 2$.

The actual difference, $2\frac{7}{12}$, is reasonable because it is close to the estimate, 2.

Guided Practice*

MATHEMATICAL
PRACTICES

Do you know HOW?

Estimate and then find each difference. Check for reasonableness.

1. $7\frac{2}{3} = 7\frac{\square}{6} = 6\frac{\square}{6}$
   $- 3\frac{5}{6} = 3\frac{\square}{6} = 3\frac{\square}{6}$

2. $5 = \quad \frac{\square}{4}$
   $- 2\frac{3}{4} = \quad 2\frac{3}{4}$

3. $6\frac{3}{10} - 1\frac{4}{5}$

4. $9\frac{1}{3} - 4\frac{3}{4}$

Do you UNDERSTAND?

5. In Exercise 2, why do you need to rename the 5?

© 6. **Reason** Could two golf balls fall into the hole at the same time? Explain your reasoning.

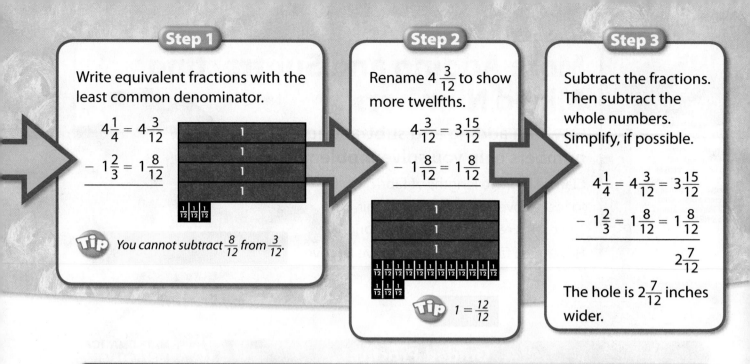

Step 1

Write equivalent fractions with the least common denominator.

$4\frac{1}{4} = 4\frac{3}{12}$

$- 1\frac{2}{3} = 1\frac{8}{12}$

Tip You cannot subtract $\frac{8}{12}$ from $\frac{3}{12}$.

Step 2

Rename $4\frac{3}{12}$ to show more twelfths.

$4\frac{3}{12} = 3\frac{15}{12}$

$- 1\frac{8}{12} = 1\frac{8}{12}$

Tip $1 = \frac{12}{12}$

Step 3

Subtract the fractions. Then subtract the whole numbers. Simplify, if possible.

$4\frac{1}{4} = 4\frac{3}{12} = 3\frac{15}{12}$

$- 1\frac{2}{3} = 1\frac{8}{12} = 1\frac{8}{12}$

$\overline{ 2\frac{7}{12}}$

The hole is $2\frac{7}{12}$ inches wider.

Independent Practice

Leveled Practice For **7** through **18**, estimate and then find each difference. Check for reasonableness.

7. $8\frac{1}{4} = 8\frac{\square}{8} = 7\frac{\square}{8}$
$\quad - 2\frac{7}{8} = 2\frac{\square}{8} = 2\frac{\square}{8}$

8. $3\frac{1}{2} = 3\frac{\square}{6}$
$\quad - 1\frac{1}{3} = 1\frac{\square}{6}$

9. $4\frac{1}{8}$
$\quad - 1\frac{1}{2}$

10. 6
$\quad - 2\frac{4}{5}$

11. $6\frac{1}{3} - 5\frac{2}{3}$

12. $9\frac{1}{2} - 6\frac{3}{4}$

13. $8\frac{3}{16} - 3\frac{5}{8}$

14. $7\frac{1}{2} - \frac{7}{10}$

15. $15\frac{1}{6} - 4\frac{3}{8}$

16. $13\frac{1}{12} - 8\frac{1}{4}$

17. $6\frac{1}{3} - 2\frac{3}{5}$

18. $10\frac{5}{12} - 4\frac{7}{8}$

Problem Solving

MATHEMATICAL
PRACTICES

19. The average weight of a basketball is $21\frac{1}{10}$ ounces. The average weight of a baseball is $5\frac{1}{4}$ ounces. How many more ounces does the basketball weigh?

20. As of 2008, the world's shortest horse is Thumbelina. She is $17\frac{1}{4}$ inches tall. The second shortest horse, Black Beauty, is $18\frac{1}{2}$ inches tall. How much shorter is Thumbelina than Black Beauty?

21. The smallest mammals on Earth are the bumblebee bat and the Etruscan pygmy shrew. A length of a bumblebee bat is $1\frac{9}{50}$ inches. A length of an Etruscan pygmy shrew is $1\frac{21}{50}$ inches. How much smaller is the bat than the shrew?

ⓒ **22. Construct Arguments** How are the parallelogram and the rectangle alike? How are they different?

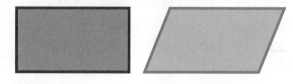

Lesson
10-6

Common
Core

5.NF.1 Add and subtract...
mixed numbers by replacing
given fractions with
equivalent fractions in
such a way as to produce
an equivalent sum or
difference of fractions
with like denominators.
Also 5.NF.2

More Adding and Subtracting Mixed Numbers

How can adding and subtracting mixed numbers help you solve problems?

Clarisse has two lengths of fabric to make covers for a sofa and chair. The covers require $9\frac{2}{3}$ yards of fabric. How much fabric will Clarisse have left over?

$7\frac{5}{6}$ yards

$5\frac{3}{4}$ yards

Guided Practice*

MATHEMATICAL PRACTICES

Do you know HOW?

1. $5\frac{1}{9}$
$-\ 2\frac{2}{3}$

2. $2\frac{1}{4}$
$+\ 8\frac{2}{3}$

3. $6\frac{7}{25}$
$-\ 3\frac{9}{50}$

For **4** through **7**, simplify each expression.

4. $\left(12\frac{1}{6} - 6\frac{5}{12}\right) + 1\frac{1}{4}$

5. $\left(7\frac{2}{3} + 3\frac{4}{5}\right) - 1\frac{4}{15}$

6. $6\frac{1}{4} + \left(2\frac{1}{3} - 1\frac{5}{8}\right)$

7. $8\frac{2}{5} - \left(3\frac{2}{3} + 2\frac{3}{5}\right)$

Do you UNDERSTAND?

8. Think About the Structure In the example above, why do you add before you subtract to solve the problem?

9. Construct Arguments In the example above, does Clarisse have enough fabric left over to make two cushions that each use $2\frac{1}{3}$ yards of fabric? Explain.

Independent Practice

10. $9\frac{1}{3}$
$-\ 4\frac{1}{6}$

11. $12\frac{1}{4}$
$-\ 9\frac{3}{5}$

12. $6\frac{3}{5}$
$+\ 1\frac{3}{25}$

13. $3\frac{4}{9}$
$+\ 2\frac{2}{3}$

14. $5\frac{31}{75}$
$-\ 3\frac{2}{25}$

15. $7\frac{1}{5}$
$+\ 4\frac{5}{6}$

16. $15\frac{4}{7}$
$-\ 6\frac{3}{4}$

17. $8\frac{1}{4}$
$-\ 5\frac{5}{12}$

18. $11\frac{7}{8}$
$+\ 3\frac{9}{24}$

19. $9\frac{3}{10}$
$+\ 5\frac{1}{2}$

In **20** through **25**, simplify each expression.

20. $\left(2\frac{5}{8} + 2\frac{1}{2}\right) - 4\frac{2}{3}$

21. $\left(5\frac{3}{4} + 1\frac{5}{6}\right) - 6\frac{7}{12}$

22. $4\frac{3}{5} + \left(8\frac{1}{5} - 7\frac{3}{10}\right)$

23. $\left(13 - 10\frac{1}{3}\right) + 2\frac{2}{3}$

24. $9\frac{9}{1,000} - 5\frac{9}{100}$

25. $2\frac{13}{20} + 11\frac{13}{25}$

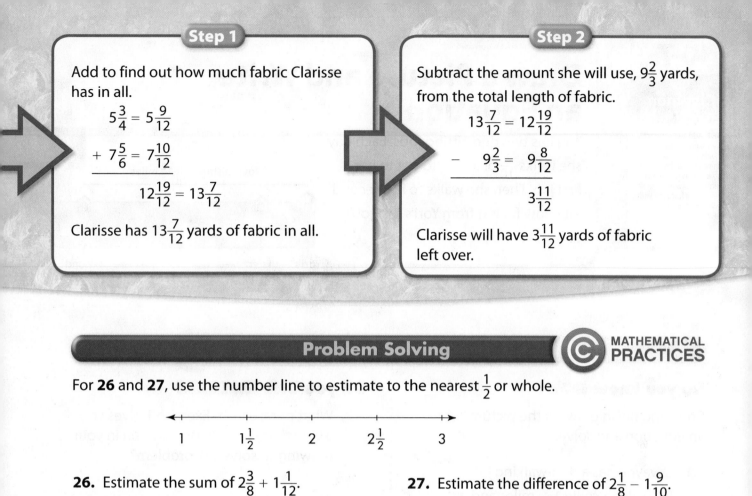

Step 1

Add to find out how much fabric Clarisse has in all.

$$5\frac{3}{4} = 5\frac{9}{12}$$
$$+ 7\frac{5}{6} = 7\frac{10}{12}$$
$$\overline{12\frac{19}{12} = 13\frac{7}{12}}$$

Clarisse has $13\frac{7}{12}$ yards of fabric in all.

Step 2

Subtract the amount she will use, $9\frac{2}{3}$ yards, from the total length of fabric.

$$13\frac{7}{12} = 12\frac{19}{12}$$
$$- \quad 9\frac{2}{3} = 9\frac{8}{12}$$
$$\overline{3\frac{11}{12}}$$

Clarisse will have $3\frac{11}{12}$ yards of fabric left over.

Problem Solving

MATHEMATICAL
PRACTICES

For **26** and **27**, use the number line to estimate to the nearest $\frac{1}{2}$ or whole.

$$1 \qquad 1\frac{1}{2} \qquad 2 \qquad 2\frac{1}{2} \qquad 3$$

26. Estimate the sum of $2\frac{3}{8} + 1\frac{1}{12}$.

27. Estimate the difference of $2\frac{1}{8} - 1\frac{9}{10}$.

28. Which is 6.245 rounded to the nearest hundredth?

   A 6.0   **C** 6.24

   B 6.2   **D** 6.25

© **29. Be Precise** Which number is NOT a common factor of 24 and 36?

   A 4   **C** 9

   B 6   **D** 12

For **30** through **32**, use the table. Simplify answers, if possible.

Frog Species	Body Length (cm)	Maximum Jump (cm)
Bullfrog	$20\frac{3}{10}$	$213\frac{1}{2}$
Leopard frog	$12\frac{1}{2}$	$162\frac{1}{2}$
South African sharp-nosed frog	$7\frac{3}{5}$	$334\frac{2}{5}$

30. How much longer is the maximum jump of a South African sharp-nosed frog than the maximum jump of a leopard frog?

31. Rounded to the nearest whole number, how many centimeters long is a bullfrog?

© **32. Reasonableness** Which frog can leap about 10 times its body length? Explain how you found your answer.

Lesson
10-7

Common
Core

5.NF.1 Add and subtract...
mixed numbers by
replacing given fractions
with equivalent fractions in
such a way as to produce
an equivalent sum or
difference of fractions with
like denominators. Also
5.NF.2

Problem Solving

Draw a Picture and Write an Equation

Yori has two dog-sitting jobs. Each day she walks $\frac{3}{10}$ of a mile to get to her first job. Then she walks to her second job. How far is it from Yori's first job to her second job?

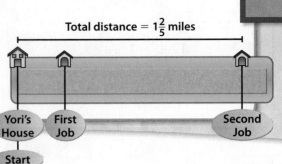

Total distance = $1\frac{2}{5}$ miles

Yori's House — Start
First Job
Second Job

Guided Practice*

MATHEMATICAL PRACTICES

Do you know HOW?

Copy and finish drawing the picture. Write an equation and solve.

1. Dwayne has a dog-walking job. He walks a collie $1\frac{9}{10}$ miles and a schnauzer $2\frac{3}{4}$ miles. What is the total distance he walks for his job?

   d total distance

Do you UNDERSTAND?

2. What phrase from Exercise 1 gives you a clue that you will use addition in your drawing to solve the problem?

3. **Model** Write a real-world problem that uses addition or subtraction of fractions with like denominators and that can be solved by drawing a picture and writing an equation.

Independent Practice

MATHEMATICAL PRACTICES

In **4** through **6**, draw a picture and write an equation. Then solve.

4. If Jessie hikes all 3 trails, how far will she hike?

5. Kent only wants to hike Wing Trail. How much farther will Jessie hike than Kent?

Trails and Distances

Wing Trail $2\frac{3}{4}$ mi

Sunset Trail $1\frac{7}{8}$ mi

Ridge Trail $1\frac{1}{3}$ mi

Applying Math Practices

- What am I asked to find?
- What else can I try?
- How are quantities related?
- How can I explain my work?
- How can I use math to model the problem?
- Can I use tools to help?
- Is my work precise?
- Why does this work?
- How can I generalize?

What do I know?

Yori walks $\frac{3}{10}$ of a mile to her first job. At her second job she will have walked a total of $1\frac{2}{5}$ miles.

What am I asked to find?

The distance from the first to the second job

Draw a Picture

$1\frac{2}{5}$ miles

$\frac{3}{10}$	d miles

Write an Equation

Let d = the distance from first to second job

$$\frac{3}{10} + d = 1\frac{2}{5} \quad \text{or} \quad 1\frac{2}{5} - \frac{3}{10} = d$$

$$1\frac{2}{5} - \frac{3}{10} = 1\frac{4}{10} - \frac{3}{10} = 1\frac{1}{10}$$

$$d = 1\frac{1}{10} \text{ miles}$$

It is $1\frac{1}{10}$ miles from Yori's first job to her second job.

6. Renee mixed red, white, and yellow paint. She used $1\frac{2}{3}$ gallons of red paint, $5\frac{5}{6}$ gallons of white paint, and $2\frac{1}{2}$ gallons of yellow. How many gallons of paint did Renee mix in all?

7. Katya needs $2\frac{5}{6}$ yards of satin fabric. She has $\frac{3}{4}$ of a yard now. How much more fabric does Katya need to buy?

© **8. Look for Patterns** Give an example of when the sum of two fractions equals 1 whole.

9. Parker's dad drove $2\frac{1}{3}$ miles from the start of a construction zone. He stopped to read this road sign. How far will Parker's dad have driven when he reaches the end of the construction zone?

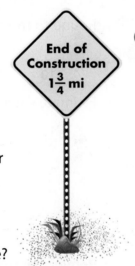

End of Construction $1\frac{3}{4}$ mi

© **10. Critique Reasoning** Gene says that the two circles below show the same amount. Do you agree? Write a good math explanation to support your decision.

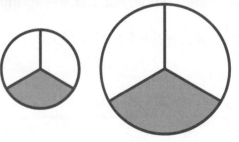

© **11. Communicate** In many cases, a baby's weight at birth is equal to one half his or her weight at age one. Explain how to estimate the weight of a baby at birth if this baby weighs 18 pounds at age one.

12. Last year, Mr. Kline's fifth-grade class planted a longleaf pine sapling that was $1\frac{5}{12}$ feet tall. Now the sapling is $3\frac{1}{4}$ feet tall. How many feet did the sapling grow from last year?

A $1\frac{1}{2}$ feet   **B** $1\frac{5}{6}$ feet   **C** $2\frac{1}{2}$ feet   **D** $3\frac{3}{12}$ feet

Set A, pages 252–253

Write $\frac{19}{3}$ as a mixed number.

- Divide the numerator by the denominator.

$$3\overline{)19} \quad 6\,R1$$

- Write the remainder as a fraction in simplest form.

$$\frac{19}{3} = 6\frac{1}{3}$$

Write $9\frac{5}{8}$ as an improper fraction.

$$9\frac{5}{8} = 9 + \frac{5}{8} \text{ and } 9 + \frac{5}{8} = \frac{72}{8} + \frac{5}{8}$$

So, $9\frac{5}{8} = \frac{77}{8}$.

Remember to always write the answer in simplest form.

Write each improper fraction as a mixed number or whole number.

1. $\frac{16}{6}$ **2.** $\frac{24}{9}$ **3.** $\frac{9}{2}$

Write each as an improper fraction.

4. $4\frac{5}{9}$ **5.** $2\frac{7}{11}$ **6.** $8\frac{5}{7}$

7. $5\frac{1}{3}$ **8.** $10\frac{4}{5}$ **9.** $8\frac{8}{11}$

Set B, pages 254–255

Estimate $5\frac{1}{3} + 9\frac{9}{11}$.

Compare fractions to $\frac{1}{2}$ to round to the nearest whole number.

Round fractions that are less than $\frac{1}{2}$ down to the nearest whole number. $5\frac{1}{3}$ rounds to 5.

Round fractions greater than or equal to $\frac{1}{2}$ up to the nearest whole number. $9\frac{9}{11}$ rounds to 10.

So, $5\frac{1}{3} + 9\frac{9}{11} \approx 5 + 10 = 15$.

Remember that you can also use benchmark fractions such as $\frac{1}{4}, \frac{1}{3}, \frac{1}{2}, \frac{2}{3},$ and $\frac{3}{4}$ to help you estimate.

Round to the nearest whole number.

1. $2\frac{9}{10}$ **2.** $9\frac{19}{20}$ **3.** $6\frac{2}{7}$

Estimate each sum or difference.

4. $3\frac{1}{4} - 1\frac{1}{2}$ **5.** $5\frac{2}{9} + 4\frac{11}{13}$

6. $2\frac{3}{8} + 5\frac{3}{5}$ **7.** $9\frac{3}{7} - 6\frac{2}{5}$

Set C, pages 256–258, 266–267

Find $2\frac{1}{6} - 1\frac{5}{6}$.

Step 1 Model the number you are subtracting from and rename 1 whole if necessary to subtract.

Step 2 Use your renamed model to cross out the number you are subtracting.

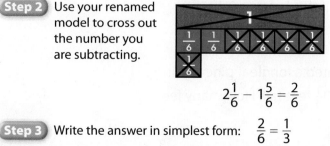

$$2\frac{1}{6} - 1\frac{5}{6} = \frac{2}{6}$$

Step 3 Write the answer in simplest form: $\frac{2}{6} = \frac{1}{3}$

Remember that when you use a model to add mixed numbers, you should rename improper fractions in the sum.

Use a model to find each sum or difference. Simplify if possible.

1. $2\frac{1}{4} + 3\frac{3}{4}$ **2.** $6\frac{2}{3} + 5\frac{2}{3}$

3. $7\frac{5}{9} + 8\frac{7}{9}$ **4.** $12\frac{1}{4} - 7\frac{2}{4}$

5. $15\frac{3}{5} - 3\frac{4}{5}$ **6.** $5\frac{5}{8} - 3\frac{1}{8}$

Find $1\frac{5}{6} + 2\frac{3}{8}$.

$1\frac{5}{6} = 1\frac{20}{24}$

$+ 2\frac{3}{8} = 2\frac{9}{24}$

$3\frac{29}{24} = 4\frac{5}{24}$

Step 1 Write equivalent fractions with the LCD.

Step 2 Add the fractions.

Step 3 Add the whole numbers. Rename improper fractions and simplify the sum, if possible.

Remember that mixed numbers are added the same way whole numbers and fractions are added.

1. $5\frac{1}{2} + 2\frac{1}{8}$　　　　**2.** $3\frac{1}{4} + 1\frac{5}{6}$

3. $5\frac{7}{10} + 4\frac{2}{5}$　　　**4.** $7\frac{3}{5} + 6\frac{2}{3}$

5. $8\frac{5}{9} + 9\frac{1}{3}$　　　　**6.** $2\frac{5}{12} + 3\frac{3}{4}$

Find $5\frac{1}{5} - 3\frac{1}{2}$.

$5\frac{1}{5} = 5\frac{2}{10} = 4\frac{12}{10}$

$- 3\frac{1}{2} = 3\frac{5}{10} = 3\frac{5}{10}$

$1\frac{7}{10}$

Step 1 Write equivalent fractions with the LCD.

Step 2 Rename $5\frac{2}{10}$ to show more tenths.

Step 3 Subtract the fractions. Subtract the whole numbers. Simplify the difference.

Remember that subtracting mixed numbers may require renaming.

1. $7\frac{5}{6} - 3\frac{2}{3}$　　　　**2.** $2\frac{3}{5} - 1\frac{1}{2}$

3. $5\frac{2}{3} - 4\frac{5}{6}$　　　　**4.** $9 - 3\frac{3}{8}$

5. $3\frac{1}{9} - 1\frac{1}{3}$　　　　**6.** $6\frac{1}{4} - 3\frac{2}{5}$

7. $9\frac{1}{4} - 2\frac{5}{8}$　　　　**8.** $4 - 1\frac{2}{5}$

Gil has two lengths of wallpaper, $2\frac{3}{4}$ yards and $1\frac{7}{8}$ yards long. He used some and now has $1\frac{5}{6}$ yards left over. How many yards of wallpaper did Gil use?

Step 1 Add to find the total amount of wallpaper Gil has.

$2\frac{3}{4} = 2\frac{18}{24}$

$+ \ 1\frac{7}{8} = 1\frac{21}{24}$

$4\frac{5}{8}$

Step 2 Subtract to find the amount of wallpaper Gil used.

$4\frac{5}{8} = 4\frac{15}{24}$

$- \ 1\frac{5}{6} = 1\frac{20}{24}$

$2\frac{19}{24}$

Gill used $2\frac{19}{24}$ yards of wallpaper.

Remember when you add or subtract mixed numbers, rename the fractional part to have a common denominator.

Simplify each expression.

1. $\left(2\frac{1}{6} + 3\frac{3}{4}\right) - 1\frac{5}{12}$

2. $\left(4\frac{4}{5} + 7\frac{1}{3}\right) - 1\frac{7}{15}$

3. $\left(8\frac{3}{8} - 4\frac{5}{6}\right) + 1\frac{11}{24}$

4. $2\frac{9}{25} + 2\frac{9}{50} + 2\frac{1}{100}$

Multiple Choice

1. Which expression is the best estimate for $1\frac{3}{4} + 2\frac{3}{8}$? (10-2)

   A $2 + 2$

   B $1 + 2$

   C $2 + 3$

   D $1 + 3$

2. Yao drank $\frac{11}{4}$ bottles of water during a soccer game. What is this number expressed as a mixed number? (10-1)

   A $3\frac{1}{4}$

   B $2\frac{3}{4}$

   C $2\frac{1}{2}$

   D $2\frac{1}{4}$

3. Which expression does the model show? (10-3)

   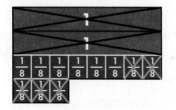

   A $3\frac{3}{8} + \frac{5}{8}$

   B $3\frac{3}{8} + 2\frac{5}{8}$

   C $3\frac{3}{8} - 2\frac{5}{8}$

   D $3\frac{3}{8} - \frac{5}{8}$

4. Marie needs $2\frac{1}{4}$ yards of fabric. She already has $1\frac{3}{8}$ yards. How many more yards of fabric does she need? (10-5)

   A $\frac{1}{8}$ yard

   B $\frac{3}{4}$ yard

   C $\frac{7}{8}$ yard

   D $1\frac{7}{8}$ yards

5. The Jacobys went on a 600-mile trip. On the first day they drove $5\frac{2}{3}$ hours and on the second day they drove $4\frac{3}{5}$ hours. How many hours did they drive during the first two days? (10-4)

   A $10\frac{4}{15}$ hours

   B 10 hours

   C $9\frac{19}{30}$ hours

   D $9\frac{4}{15}$ hours

6. Which equation does NOT match the picture? (10-7)

   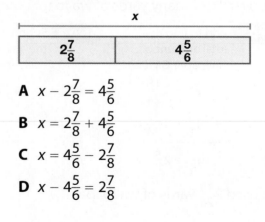

   A $x - 2\frac{7}{8} = 4\frac{5}{6}$

   B $x = 2\frac{7}{8} + 4\frac{5}{6}$

   C $x = 4\frac{5}{6} - 2\frac{7}{8}$

   D $x - 4\frac{5}{6} = 2\frac{7}{8}$

7. Rick made a paper football that was $1\frac{1}{6}$ inches long. Carly made one that was $\frac{5}{6}$ of an inch long. How much longer was Rick's paper football than Carly's? (10-5)

8. Mary weighed $7\frac{1}{2}$ pounds when she was born. What number makes the statement true? (10-1)

$$7\frac{1}{2} = \frac{\blacksquare}{2}$$

9. What expression does the model show? (10-3)

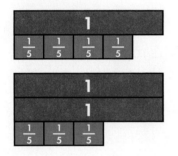

10. The square below has sides that are $1\frac{1}{4}$ inches long. What is the perimeter of the square? Write an addition equation to solve. (10-7)

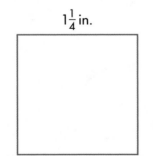

$1\frac{1}{4}$ in.

11. What is the sum of $1\frac{7}{8} + 2\frac{3}{8}$? (10-4)

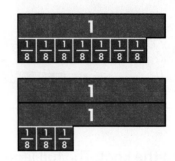

12. Dawson says that when you simplify the expression $\left(2\frac{4}{10} + 8\frac{4}{5}\right) - 3\frac{1}{5}$ you get a whole number. What whole number do you get? (10-6)

13. The equilateral triangle below has sides that are $3\frac{1}{2}$ cm long. What is the perimeter of the triangle? Write an addition equation to solve. (10-7)

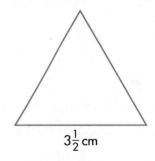

$3\frac{1}{2}$ cm

14. The main ingredients for Kayla's banana bread recipe are $2\frac{1}{3}$ cups of flour, $\frac{3}{4}$ cup of sugar, and $1\frac{1}{2}$ cups of mashed bananas. How many more cups of dry ingredients (flour and sugar) than wet ingredients (bananas) go into Kayla's banana bread? Explain. (10-6)

Liam and Pam each have a length of thick rope.

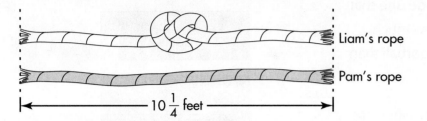

Liam's rope

Pam's rope

$10\frac{1}{4}$ feet

1. Liam untied the knot. The full length of the rope is shown below. How much rope did the knot use?

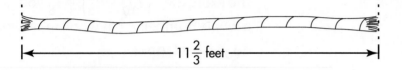

$11\frac{2}{3}$ feet

2. **Estimate** If Liam laid his untied rope end-to-end with Pam's rope, about how long would the two ropes be? Explain whether the actual length would be more or less than your estimate.

3. Liam and Pam tied their two ropes together with a square knot. The knot used $1\frac{1}{8}$ feet of rope. How long is their rope? Explain.

4. Marco has a rope that is 16 feet long. He ties his rope to Liam and Pam's with a square knot that uses $1\frac{1}{8}$ feet of rope. How long are the three ropes tied together? Write and solve an equation.

Topic
11

Multiplying and Dividing Fractions and Mixed Numbers

▼ If you rode an elevator up $\frac{3}{4}$ of the height of the Willis Tower in Chicago, about how many feet high would you be? You will find out in Lesson 11-3.

Review What You Know!

Vocabulary

Choose the best term from the box.

- estimate
- like denominators
- common factor

1. A ___?___ is a number that is a factor of two or more numbers.

2. To find an approximate answer or solution is to ___?___.

3. $\frac{4}{8}$ and $\frac{7}{8}$ have ___?___.

Estimation

Estimate each sum, difference, or product.

4. $1,478 + 2,822$ 5. $305 - 197$

6. $6,490 - 3,510$ 7. $1,213 + 4,797 + 403$

8. 38×6 9. 59×21

Fractions and Decimals

Write the shaded part as a fraction.

10. [figure]   11. [figure]

Express each decimal as a fraction or mixed number. Simplify where possible.

12. 0.80   13. 5.25   14. 15.95

Divisibility

© 15. **Writing to Explain** How can you tell if 78 is divisible by 2, 3, or 6?

Topic Essential Question
- What are standard procedures for estimating and finding products and quotients of fractions and mixed numbers?

Interactive Learning

Pose the problem. Start each lesson by working together to solve problems. It will help you make sense of math.

ⓒ **Model** Write a division expression to represent each situation. Then act out the situation with circles. What part of a waffle does each person get? (1) 3 waffles divided among 4 people; (2) 3 waffles divided among 8 people; (3) 2 waffles divided among 5 people; (4) 4 waffles divided among 5 people.

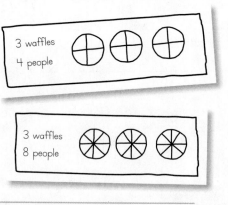

ⓒ **Reason** Emily has 6 eggs. She needs $\frac{2}{3}$ of the eggs to make an omelet. How many eggs does she need?

ⓒ **Communicate** Raul is training for a 15-mile bike race. He started riding a few miles each day. Now he is riding $\frac{3}{4}$ of the length of the race each day. About how many miles is Raul riding each day? Work with your partner to solve this problem using any way you can.

ⓒ **Reasonableness** The art teacher gave each student half a sheet of paper. Then she asked the students to color one quarter of their piece of paper. What part of the original page did the students color?

ⓒ **Use Tools** A rectangular poster is $\frac{1}{4}$ yard wide and $\frac{3}{4}$ yard tall. What is its area? Use grid paper to work the problem.

MATHEMATICAL PRACTICES

Lesson 11-6

© **Look for Patterns** Use the ingredients list to make a batch of Josie's special pancakes. How much pancake mix and milk will you need if you want to double and to triple the recipe? Decide how you would compute the amounts.

> **PANCAKE RECIPE**
> $2\frac{1}{4}$ cups pancake mix
> 1 egg
> $1\frac{2}{5}$ cups milk
> dash of vanilla

Lesson 11-7

© **Reasonableness** Which problem in each set will give the largest product and which will give the smallest **without multiplying.**

Set 1	Set 2	Set 3
a. $\frac{1}{2} \times 2$	a. $3\frac{3}{4} \times 2\frac{1}{2}$	a. $\frac{3}{4} \times \frac{6}{6}$
b. $\frac{3}{3} \times 2$	b. $\frac{3}{4} \times 2\frac{1}{2}$	b. $\frac{3}{4} \times 1\frac{5}{6}$
c. $2\frac{2}{3} \times 2$	c. $\frac{4}{4} \times 2\frac{1}{2}$	c. $\frac{3}{4} \times \frac{5}{6}$

Lesson 11-8

© **Use Tools** Jason and his sister are going to install carpet in their bedrooms. Jason's bedroom is 10 feet by 12 feet. His sister's bedroom is 9 feet by 15 feet. Which bedroom will have more carpet and how much more?

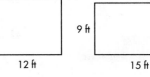

Lesson 11-9

© **Persevere** When a pizza shop makes a circular pizza, a ball of dough is stretched into a circle. Then, the sauce and toppings are added before the pizza is baked. After the pizza is cooked, it is cut into 8 equal pieces. How many pieces of pizza can you make with 3 balls of dough?

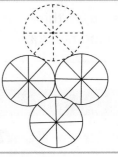

Lesson 11-10

© **Model** Yesterday Mrs. Hudson made a pan of brownies. Half of the brownies were left after lunch for the four members of the camera club to share equally. What fraction of the pan of brownies did each person get?

Lesson 11-11

© **Be Precise** A board is 2 feet long. How many $\frac{1}{4}$ foot pieces can be cut from the board?

© Common Core

5.NF.3 Interpret a fraction as division of the numerator by the denominator $(a/b = a \div b)$. Solve word problems involving division of whole numbers leading to answers in the form of fractions or mixed numbers, e.g. by using visual fraction models or equations to represent the problem.

Fractions and Division

How are fractions related to division?

Eleven members of the 6th grade Science Club stayed after school to help their teacher, Ms. Oliva, set up the laboratory. Afterwards, Ms. Oliva bought two large pizzas. If all twelve people divide the pizza equally, what fraction of a large pizza will each person get?

Two large pizzas to divide

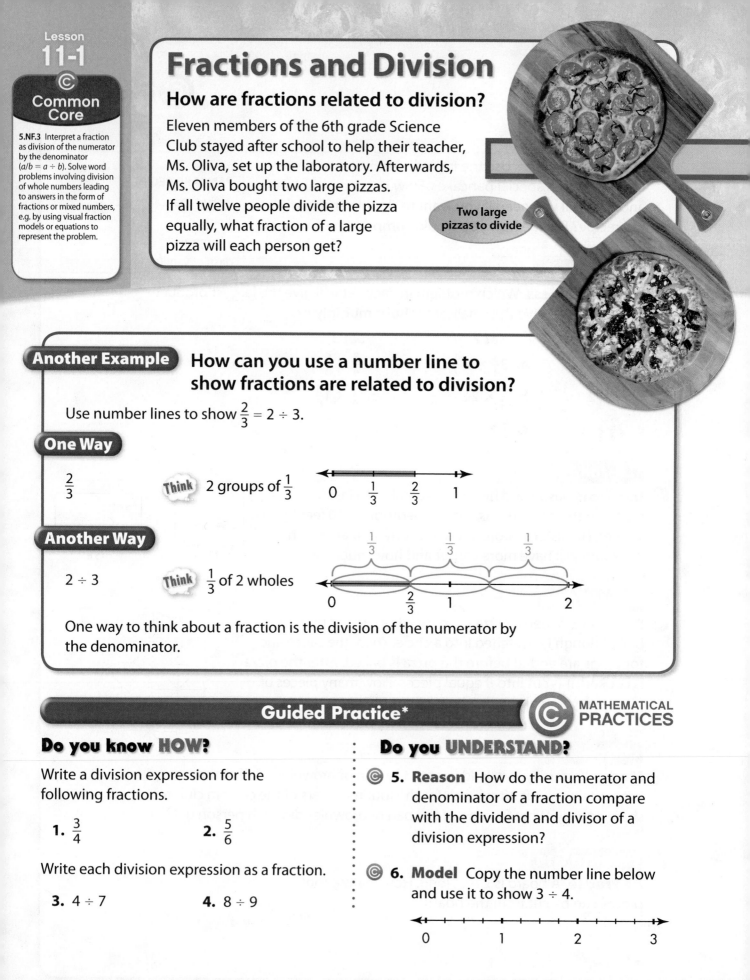

Another Example How can you use a number line to show fractions are related to division?

Use number lines to show $\frac{2}{3} = 2 \div 3$.

One Way

$\frac{2}{3}$

Think 2 groups of $\frac{1}{3}$

Another Way

$2 \div 3$

Think $\frac{1}{3}$ of 2 wholes

One way to think about a fraction is the division of the numerator by the denominator.

Guided Practice*

© MATHEMATICAL PRACTICES

Do you know HOW?

Write a division expression for the following fractions.

1. $\frac{3}{4}$

2. $\frac{5}{6}$

Write each division expression as a fraction.

3. $4 \div 7$

4. $8 \div 9$

Do you UNDERSTAND?

© **5. Reason** How do the numerator and denominator of a fraction compare with the dividend and divisor of a division expression?

© **6. Model** Copy the number line below and use it to show $3 \div 4$.

*For another example, see Set A on page 300.

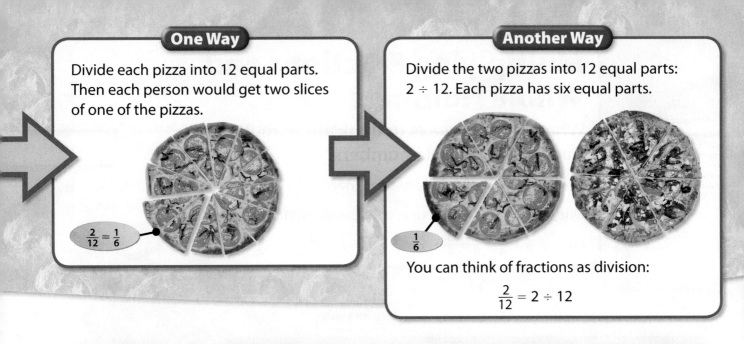

One Way

Divide each pizza into 12 equal parts. Then each person would get two slices of one of the pizzas.

$\frac{2}{12} = \frac{1}{6}$

Another Way

Divide the two pizzas into 12 equal parts: $2 \div 12$. Each pizza has six equal parts.

$\frac{1}{6}$

You can think of fractions as division:

$$\frac{2}{12} = 2 \div 12$$

Independent Practice

Write a division expression for the following fractions.

7. $\frac{7}{8}$ **8.** $\frac{1}{2}$ **9.** $\frac{3}{5}$ **10.** $\frac{6}{7}$ **11.** $\frac{15}{29}$

12. $\frac{4}{9}$ **13.** $\frac{6}{11}$ **14.** $\frac{9}{15}$ **15.** $\frac{1}{4}$ **16.** $\frac{14}{21}$

Write each division expression as a fraction.

17. $9 \div 11$ **18.** $1 \div 10$ **19.** $4 \div 9$ **20.** $7 \div 13$ **21.** $5 \div 8$

22. $3 \div 7$ **23.** $12 \div 23$ **24.** $8 \div 30$ **25.** $11 \div 17$ **26.** $25 \div 75$

Problem Solving

MATHEMATICAL PRACTICES

Ⓒ **27. Reason** Into how many sections would you divide this number line to graph $\frac{7}{10}$? Why?

0   1

The table at the right shows the weights of different materials used to build a bridge. Use the table to answer **28** and **29**.

Ⓒ **28. Model** Write a division expression that represents the weight of the steel structure compared to the total weight of the bridge's materials.

Ⓒ **29. Persevere** Which of the following fractions equals the amount of glass and granite in the bridge divided by the amount of steel, written in simplest form?

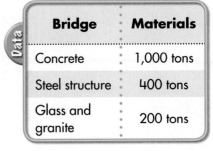

Bridge	Materials
Concrete	1,000 tons
Steel structure	400 tons
Glass and granite	200 tons

    A $\frac{1}{2}$ **B** $\frac{1}{3}$ **C** $\frac{1}{4}$ **D** $\frac{1}{8}$

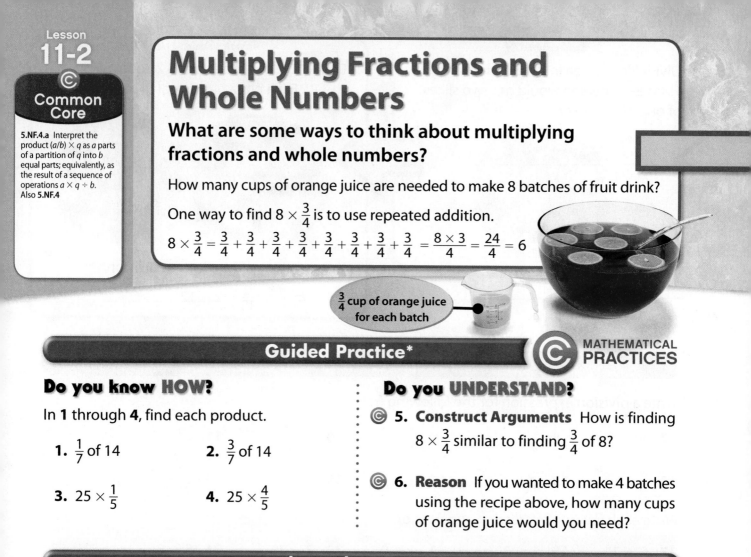

© Common Core

5.NF.4.a Interpret the product (a/b) × q as a parts of a partition of q into b equal parts; equivalently, as the result of a sequence of operations a × q ÷ b.
Also 5.NF.4

Multiplying Fractions and Whole Numbers

What are some ways to think about multiplying fractions and whole numbers?

How many cups of orange juice are needed to make 8 batches of fruit drink?

One way to find $8 \times \frac{3}{4}$ is to use repeated addition.

$$8 \times \frac{3}{4} = \frac{3}{4} + \frac{3}{4} + \frac{3}{4} + \frac{3}{4} + \frac{3}{4} + \frac{3}{4} + \frac{3}{4} + \frac{3}{4} = \frac{8 \times 3}{4} = \frac{24}{4} = 6$$

$\frac{3}{4}$ cup of orange juice for each batch

Guided Practice*

MATHEMATICAL PRACTICES

Do you know HOW?

In **1** through **4**, find each product.

1. $\frac{1}{7}$ of 14

2. $\frac{3}{7}$ of 14

3. $25 \times \frac{1}{5}$

4. $25 \times \frac{4}{5}$

Do you UNDERSTAND?

© 5. **Construct Arguments** How is finding $8 \times \frac{3}{4}$ similar to finding $\frac{3}{4}$ of 8?

© 6. **Reason** If you wanted to make 4 batches using the recipe above, how many cups of orange juice would you need?

Independent Practice

In **7** through **38**, find each product.

7. $\frac{1}{4}$ of 40

8. $\frac{1}{3}$ of 15

9. $\frac{1}{5}$ of 40

10. $\frac{1}{7}$ of 28

11. $\frac{2}{9}$ of 90

12. $\frac{2}{5}$ of 40

13. $\frac{1}{2}$ of 50

14. $\frac{5}{8}$ of 32

15. $\frac{3}{4}$ of 12

16. $\frac{6}{7}$ of 49

17. $\frac{3}{5}$ of 25

18. $\frac{2}{7}$ of 35

19. $\frac{5}{8}$ of 24

20. $\frac{3}{7}$ of 21

21. $\frac{8}{9}$ of 81

22. $\frac{7}{8}$ of 56

23. $\frac{2}{3} \times 27$

24. $\frac{3}{8} \times 16$

25. $\frac{5}{6} \times 18$

26. $50 \times \frac{7}{10}$

27. $25 \times \frac{4}{5}$

28. $12 \times \frac{2}{3}$

29. $32 \times \frac{1}{4}$

30. $18 \times \frac{2}{9}$

31. $\frac{2}{5} \times 35$

32. $\frac{8}{9} \times 18$

33. $\frac{4}{7} \times 35$

34. $\frac{5}{8} \times 16$

35. $\frac{3}{8} \times 24$

36. $\frac{7}{9} \times 36$

37. $\left(\frac{3}{4} - \frac{1}{4}\right) \times 24$

38. $\left(\frac{3}{5} - \frac{3}{10}\right) \times 30$

To find $8 \times \frac{3}{4}$, you can multiply first and then divide.

$8 \times \frac{3}{4} = \frac{24}{4} = 6$

Another way to think about multiplication of a whole number and a fraction is to find a part of a whole group.

Martin has 8 oranges to make juice. If he uses $\frac{3}{4}$ of the oranges, how many will he use? To find $\frac{3}{4}$ of 8, you can draw a picture.

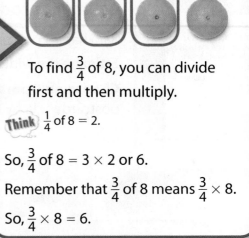

To find $\frac{3}{4}$ of 8, you can divide first and then multiply.

Think $\frac{1}{4}$ of $8 = 2$.

So, $\frac{3}{4}$ of $8 = 3 \times 2$ or 6.

Remember that $\frac{3}{4}$ of 8 means $\frac{3}{4} \times 8$.

So, $\frac{3}{4} \times 8 = 6$.

Problem Solving

MATHEMATICAL
PRACTICES

© **39. Use Structure** Explain how you would find $36 \times \frac{3}{4}$ mentally.

40. Lions spend about $\frac{5}{6}$ of their days sleeping. How many hours a day does a lion sleep?

© **41. Critique Reasoning** Jo said that when you multiply a nonzero whole number by a fraction less than 1, the product is always less than the whole number. Do you agree?

© **42. Use Tools** Who ran the most miles by the end of the week? Use the table below.

	Monday	Wednesday	Saturday
Pat	2.75 mi	3 mi	2.5 mi
Toby	2 mi	2.25 mi	3.5 mi

43. On Mars, your weight is about $\frac{1}{3}$ of your weight on Earth. If a fifth grader weighs 96 pounds on Earth, about how much would be his or her weight on Mars?

44. How much change will Stacy get if she buys two CDs and two books and gives the clerk two $20 bills?

45. A recipe calls for $\frac{1}{2}$ cup of walnuts and $\frac{3}{16}$ cup of dates. Which of the following shows the correct relationship?

A $\frac{1}{2} > \frac{3}{16}$ **C** $\frac{3}{8} < \frac{1}{4}$

B $\frac{1}{2} = \frac{3}{16}$ **D** $\frac{1}{2} < \frac{3}{16}$

46. A 1965 U.S. half dollar contains $\frac{2}{5}$ ounce of silver. How many ounces of silver do 100 of those coins contain?

Sale: CDs for $8.25 each

Sale: 2 books for $10.00

© Common Core

5.NF.5.a Comparing the size of a product to the size of one factor on the basis of the size of the other factor, without performing the indicated multiplication. Also 5.NF.5.b

Estimating Products

How can you use compatible numbers to estimate products of fractions?

Sara has 14 postcards that are each $\frac{3}{8}$ foot wide.

Estimate the width of these postcards placed side by side.

Choose an Operation Multiply to find the width of the postcards side by side.

Each postcard is $\frac{3}{8}$ foot wide.

Another Example How can you use rounding to estimate products of fractions and mixed numbers?

Estimate $3\frac{3}{4} \times 14\frac{1}{2}$. Round to the nearest whole numbers.

$$3\frac{3}{4} \times 14\frac{1}{2}$$
$$\downarrow \qquad \downarrow$$
$$4 \times 15 = 60$$

So, $3\frac{3}{4} \times 14\frac{1}{2} \approx 60$.

Estimate $\frac{5}{6} \times 3\frac{7}{8}$. Round to the nearest whole numbers.

$$\frac{5}{6} \times 3\frac{7}{8}$$
$$\downarrow \qquad \downarrow$$
$$1 \times 4 = 4$$

So, $\frac{5}{6} \times 3\frac{7}{8} \approx 4$.

Guided Practice*

© MATHEMATICAL PRACTICES

Do you know HOW?

For **1** through **4**, estimate each product.

1. $\frac{3}{4} \times 19$

2. $35 \times \frac{5}{9}$

3. $21\frac{3}{4} \times \frac{1}{5}$

4. $3 \times 6\frac{4}{5}$

Do you UNDERSTAND?

© 5. **Reason** In the example at the top, why can you have two different estimates?

© 6. **Use Tools** How can rounding to the nearest whole number help you estimate products?

Independent Practice

For **7** through **14**, estimate each product.

7. $\frac{1}{4} \times 25$

8. $70 \times \frac{5}{8}$

9. $\frac{3}{8} \times 20$

10. $5\frac{5}{6} \times 8\frac{1}{9}$

11. $11\frac{7}{8} \times 4\frac{1}{3}$

12. $\frac{11}{12} \times 4\frac{7}{8}$

13. $2\frac{3}{4} \times 30\frac{1}{16}$

14. $1\frac{4}{5} \times 75\frac{2}{9}$

*For another example, see Set D on page 300.

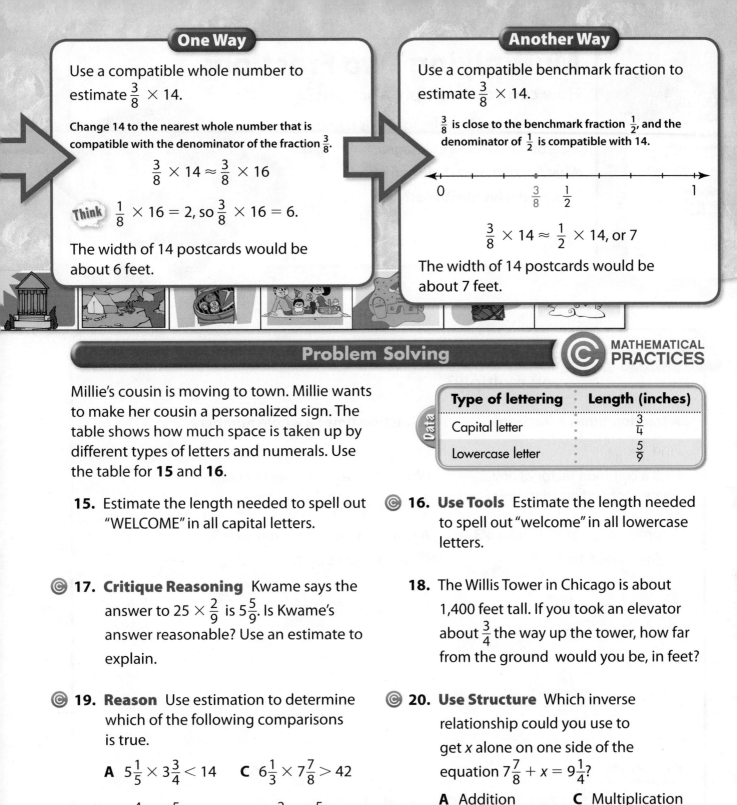

One Way

Use a compatible whole number to estimate $\frac{3}{8} \times 14$.

Change 14 to the nearest whole number that is compatible with the denominator of the fraction $\frac{3}{8}$.

$$\frac{3}{8} \times 14 \approx \frac{3}{8} \times 16$$

Think $\frac{1}{8} \times 16 = 2$, so $\frac{3}{8} \times 16 = 6$.

The width of 14 postcards would be about 6 feet.

Another Way

Use a compatible benchmark fraction to estimate $\frac{3}{8} \times 14$.

$\frac{3}{8}$ is close to the benchmark fraction $\frac{1}{2}$, and the denominator of $\frac{1}{2}$ is compatible with 14.

$$\frac{3}{8} \times 14 \approx \frac{1}{2} \times 14, \text{ or } 7$$

The width of 14 postcards would be about 7 feet.

Problem Solving

MATHEMATICAL PRACTICES

Millie's cousin is moving to town. Millie wants to make her cousin a personalized sign. The table shows how much space is taken up by different types of letters and numerals. Use the table for **15** and **16**.

Type of lettering	Length (inches)
Capital letter	$\frac{3}{4}$
Lowercase letter	$\frac{5}{9}$

15. Estimate the length needed to spell out "WELCOME" in all capital letters.

16. Use Tools Estimate the length needed to spell out "welcome" in all lowercase letters.

17. Critique Reasoning Kwame says the answer to $25 \times \frac{2}{9}$ is $5\frac{5}{9}$. Is Kwame's answer reasonable? Use an estimate to explain.

18. The Willis Tower in Chicago is about 1,400 feet tall. If you took an elevator about $\frac{3}{4}$ the way up the tower, how far from the ground would you be, in feet?

19. Reason Use estimation to determine which of the following comparisons is true.

A $5\frac{1}{5} \times 3\frac{3}{4} < 14$ **C** $6\frac{1}{3} \times 7\frac{7}{8} > 42$

B $4\frac{4}{7} \times 4\frac{5}{9} < 16$ **D** $44\frac{2}{3} \times 2\frac{5}{7} > 150$

20. Use Structure Which inverse relationship could you use to get x alone on one side of the equation $7\frac{7}{8} + x = 9\frac{1}{4}$?

A Addition   **C** Multiplication

B Subtraction   **D** Division

21. Think About the Structure Which of the following would best help you estimate $6\frac{6}{7} \times 7\frac{1}{3}$?

A Change the mixed numbers to improper fractions.

B Change the mixed numbers to decimals.

C Draw a picture to show the problem.

D Round the factors to the nearest whole numbers.

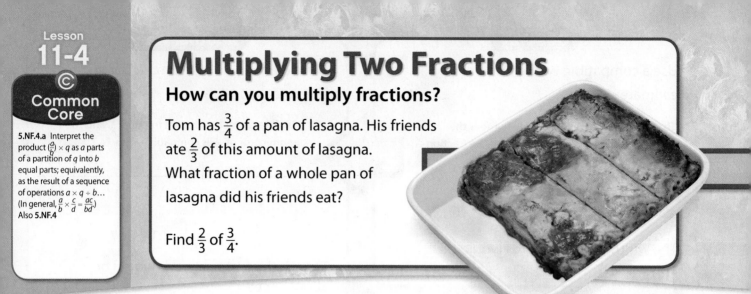

ⓒ
**Common
Core**

5.NF.4.a Interpret the product ($\frac{a}{b}$) × q as a parts of a partition of q into b equal parts; equivalently, as the result of a sequence of operations a × q ÷ b... (In general, $\frac{a}{b} \times \frac{c}{d} = \frac{ac}{bd}$.) Also **5.NF.4**

Multiplying Two Fractions

How can you multiply fractions?

Tom has $\frac{3}{4}$ of a pan of lasagna. His friends ate $\frac{2}{3}$ of this amount of lasagna. What fraction of a whole pan of lasagna did his friends eat?

Find $\frac{2}{3}$ of $\frac{3}{4}$.

Another Example **How can you simplify before you multiply?**

A fraction times a fraction

Find $\frac{3}{4} \times \frac{5}{6}$.

Find a common factor of any numerator and any denominator.

A common factor of 3 and 6 is 3.

Divide 3 and 6 by 3.

$$\frac{\overset{1}{\cancel{3}}}{4} \times \frac{5}{\underset{2}{\cancel{6}}} = \frac{1 \times 5}{4 \times 2} = \frac{5}{8}$$

So, $\frac{3}{4} \times \frac{5}{6} = \frac{5}{8}$.

A fraction times a whole number

Find $\frac{2}{3} \times 18$.

Write 18 as an improper fraction.

$$\frac{2}{3} \times 18 = \frac{2}{3} \times \frac{18}{1}$$

A common factor of 3 and 18 is 3.

Divide 3 and 18 by 3.

$$\frac{2}{3} \times 18 = \frac{2}{\underset{1}{\cancel{3}}} \times \frac{\overset{6}{\cancel{18}}}{1} = \frac{12}{1} = 12$$

Explain It

1. To find $\frac{3}{4} \times \frac{5}{6}$ in the first example above, why is the 3 crossed out with a 1 written above it, and why is the 6 crossed out with a 2 written below it?

2. To find $\frac{2}{3} \times 18$ in the second example above, how is the problem changed so that you could multiply a fraction by a fraction?

One Way

Draw a picture to represent $\frac{3}{4}$. Shade 3 of the 4 parts red. Then draw two horizontal lines to show thirds. Use yellow to shade $\frac{2}{3}$ of the whole rectangle. Where the two shadings overlap is orange.

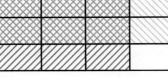

2×3 out of 3×4 parts are shaded orange.

They ate $\frac{6}{12}$ or $\frac{1}{2}$ of the pan of lasagna.

Another Way

Multiply the numerators and denominators. Simplify if possible.

$$\frac{2}{3} \times \frac{3}{4} = \frac{2 \times 3}{3 \times 4} = \frac{6}{12} = \frac{1}{2}$$

Guided Practice*

Do you know HOW?

In **1** through **4**, find each product. Simplify, if necessary.

1. $\frac{3}{4} \times \frac{7}{8}$

2. $15 \times \frac{3}{4}$

3. $\frac{3}{4} \times \frac{1}{4} \times 2$

4. $\left(\frac{2}{3} - \frac{1}{3}\right) \times \frac{5}{8}$

Do you UNDERSTAND?

5. Communicate How can you find the product of $\frac{6}{6} \times \frac{3}{8}$ mentally?

6. Use Structure In the problem above, find the fraction of a whole pan of lasagna that Tom's friends ate if he started with $\frac{7}{8}$ of a pan.

Independent Practice

In **7** through **31**, find each product. Simplify, if necessary.

7. $\frac{3}{5} \times \frac{5}{9}$

8. $13 \times \frac{1}{5}$

9. $\frac{3}{4} \times \frac{1}{3} \times 2$

10. $\frac{2}{3} \times \frac{5}{8} \times 4$

11. $\frac{1}{6} \times \frac{5}{6}$

12. $\frac{1}{3} \times \frac{1}{4} \times \frac{2}{3}$

13. $\frac{1}{7} \times \frac{2}{3} \times 6$

14. $\frac{1}{2} \times \frac{3}{8} \times \frac{3}{4}$

15. $\frac{1}{3} \times \frac{2}{5}$

16. $\frac{7}{8} \times \frac{2}{5}$

17. $\frac{2}{5} \times \frac{3}{4} \times 10$

18. $\frac{1}{8} \times \frac{1}{3} \times 24$

19. $\frac{2}{9} \times \frac{3}{10}$

20. $\frac{3}{7} \times \frac{1}{3}$

21. $\frac{1}{6} \times \frac{3}{5} \times 20$

22. $\frac{1}{2} \times \frac{2}{5} \times 5$

23. $\left(\frac{1}{4} + \frac{1}{4}\right) \times \frac{7}{8}$

24. $\left(\frac{2}{3} - \frac{1}{3}\right) \times \frac{4}{9}$

25. $\left(\frac{3}{8} + \frac{1}{8}\right) \times \frac{2}{5}$

26. $\left(\frac{2}{3} - \frac{1}{4}\right) \times \frac{5}{6}$

27. $\left(\frac{1}{8} + \frac{1}{8}\right) \times \frac{5}{9}$

28. $\left(\frac{3}{4} - \frac{1}{3}\right) \times \frac{3}{5}$

29. $\left(\frac{1}{8} + \frac{1}{4}\right) \times \frac{1}{2}$

30. $\left(\frac{4}{5} - \frac{1}{2}\right) \times \frac{3}{8}$

31. $\left(\frac{1}{2} - \frac{4}{8}\right) \times \frac{3}{7}$

*For another example, see Set C on page 300.

32. Use Tools In the voting for City Council Precinct 5, only $\frac{1}{2}$ of all eligible voters cast votes. What fraction of all eligible voters voted for Shelley? Daley? Who received the most votes?

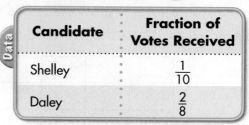

Candidate	Fraction of Votes Received
Shelley	$\frac{1}{10}$
Daley	$\frac{2}{8}$

33. Look for Patterns The stained glass shown here is a regular hexagon. How can you use multiplication to find its perimeter?

$\frac{1}{2}$ ft

$\frac{1}{2}$ ft $\frac{1}{2}$ ft

$\frac{1}{2}$ ft $\frac{1}{2}$ ft

$\frac{1}{2}$ ft

34. Communicate Will $50 be enough to buy 6 cans of paint?

$8.95

35. Reason What is the value of n in the equation $\frac{2}{3} \times n = \frac{4}{9}$?

36. Reasonableness $\frac{4}{9} \times \frac{7}{8} = \frac{7}{18}$. What is $\frac{7}{8} \times \frac{4}{9}$? How do you know without multiplying?

37. Be Precise To amend the U.S. Constitution, $\frac{3}{4}$ of the states must approve the amendment. If 35 states approve an amendment, will the constitution be amended?

38. A plumber charges $45 for the first hour and $30 for each additional hour. How much does he charge if it takes him 4 hours to make a repair?

A $165   C $120

B $135   D $75

39. Naomi has 3 pounds of apples and $2\frac{1}{2}$ pounds of grapes. If she gives $\frac{1}{3}$ of her apples to Christine, how many pounds of apples does she have left?

A $\frac{1}{6}$ pound   C 1 pound

B $\frac{1}{2}$ pound   D 2 pounds

40. Persevere A video rental store has 6,000 movies. One Friday, $\frac{3}{5}$ of the movies were rented. How many movies were rented that Friday night?

41. One lap around the Lincoln School track is $\frac{1}{4}$ mile. If Eddie runs 6 laps around the track and then runs $2\frac{1}{2}$ miles to get home, how far will he run in all?

42. Model Ben found a recipe that calls for $\frac{3}{4}$ cup of chopped apples. If he wants to make half the recipe, how many cups of chopped apples should he use?

Find each product. Simplify if possible.

1. $\frac{1}{8} \times 6$ **2.** $7 \times \frac{1}{2}$ **3.** $\frac{4}{5} \times 3$ **4.** $5 \times \frac{7}{10}$

5. $8 \times \frac{5}{6}$ **6.** $\frac{2}{3} \times 9$ **7.** $4 \times \frac{5}{12}$ **8.** $\frac{1}{6} \times 12$

Find each product. Simplify if possible.

9. $\frac{2}{3} \times \frac{1}{4}$ **10.** $\frac{3}{5} \times \frac{3}{10}$ **11.** $\frac{1}{2} \times \frac{5}{12}$ **12.** $\frac{1}{4} \times \frac{1}{8}$ **13.** $\frac{2}{3} \times \frac{4}{5}$

14. $\frac{3}{4} \times \frac{1}{3}$ **15.** $\frac{8}{9} \times \frac{1}{2}$ **16.** $\frac{1}{5} \times \frac{1}{5}$ **17.** $\frac{3}{8} \times \frac{5}{6}$ **18.** $\frac{1}{2} \times \frac{1}{2}$

Find each sum. Simplify if possible.

19. $\frac{5}{6} + \frac{1}{12}$ **20.** $\frac{1}{2} + \frac{3}{8}$ **21.** $\frac{1}{3} + \frac{5}{12}$ **22.** $\frac{2}{3} + \frac{1}{9}$ **23.** $\frac{1}{5} + \frac{3}{10}$

© **Construct Arguments** Find each product that is not correct. Write it correctly and explain the error.

24. $\frac{2}{3} \times 3 = 2$ **25.** $\frac{3}{4} \times \frac{2}{5} = \frac{3}{20}$ **26.** $\frac{2}{10} \times \frac{3}{10} = \frac{6}{10}$

Number Sense

© **Construct Arguments** Write whether each statement is true or false. Explain your reasoning.

27. The product of 7 and 4.83 is greater than 35.

28. The sum of 45,752 and 36,687 is greater than 70,000 but less than 90,000.

29. The difference of $\frac{1}{2}$ and $\frac{1}{3}$ equals their product.

30. The product of $\frac{3}{4}$ and 5 is less than 5.

31. The quotient of $534 \div 9$ is greater than 60.

32. The sum of 21.45 and 4.2 is less than 25.

Ⓒ
Common Core

5.NF.4.b Find the area of a rectangle with fractional side lengths by tiling it with unit squares of the appropriate unit fraction side lengths, and show that the area is the same as would be found by multiplying the side lengths. Multiply fractional side lengths to find areas of rectangles, and represent fraction products as rectangular areas. Also 5.NF.4

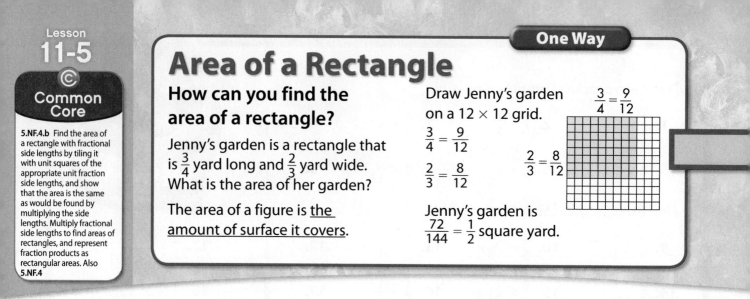

One Way

Area of a Rectangle

How can you find the area of a rectangle?

Jenny's garden is a rectangle that is $\frac{3}{4}$ yard long and $\frac{2}{3}$ yard wide. What is the area of her garden?

The area of a figure is <u>the amount of surface it covers</u>.

Draw Jenny's garden on a 12 × 12 grid.

$\frac{3}{4} = \frac{9}{12}$

$\frac{2}{3} = \frac{8}{12}$

$\frac{3}{4} = \frac{9}{12}$

$\frac{2}{3} = \frac{8}{12}$

Jenny's garden is $\frac{72}{144} = \frac{1}{2}$ square yard.

Guided Practice*

Ⓒ MATHEMATICAL PRACTICES

Do you know HOW?

1. Find the area of a rectangle with sides of lengths $\frac{2}{3}$ foot and $\frac{1}{2}$ foot.

2. Find the area of a square with sides of length $\frac{3}{4}$ inch.

Do you UNDERSTAND?

Ⓒ 3. **Generalize** If you do not remember the formula for finding the area of a rectangle, how can you find its area?

Ⓒ 4. **Use Tools** Use a 6 × 6 grid to show the product $\frac{1}{2} \times \frac{1}{3}$ as the area of a rectangle.

Independent Practice

Leveled Practice In **5–8**, copy and complete the drawing to find the area of each rectangle.

5.
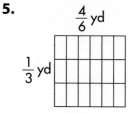
$\frac{4}{6}$ yd

$\frac{1}{3}$ yd

6.
$\frac{3}{5}$ unit

$\frac{2}{5}$ unit

1 unit

1 unit

7.
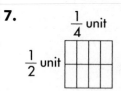
$\frac{1}{4}$ unit

$\frac{1}{2}$ unit

8.
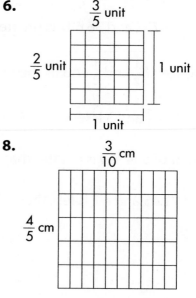
$\frac{3}{10}$ cm

$\frac{4}{5}$ cm

9. Find the area of a rectangle with side lengths $\frac{1}{8}$ foot and $\frac{1}{2}$ foot.

10. Find the area of a square with side length $\frac{3}{8}$ inch.

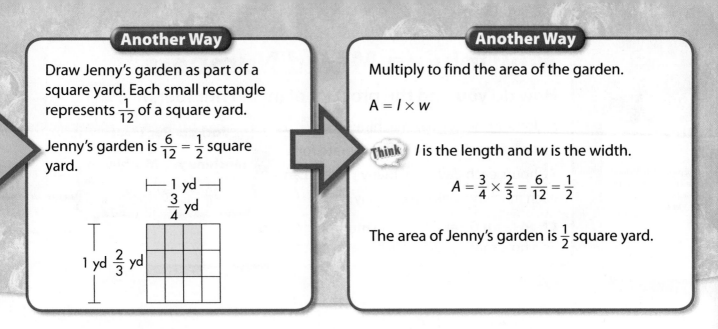

Another Way

Draw Jenny's garden as part of a square yard. Each small rectangle represents $\frac{1}{12}$ of a square yard.

Jenny's garden is $\frac{6}{12} = \frac{1}{2}$ square yard.

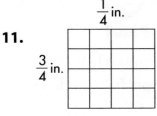

Another Way

Multiply to find the area of the garden.

$A = l \times w$

Think l is the length and w is the width.

$$A = \frac{3}{4} \times \frac{2}{3} = \frac{6}{12} = \frac{1}{2}$$

The area of Jenny's garden is $\frac{1}{2}$ square yard.

In **11–14**, find the area of each rectangle. Give your answer in simplest form.

11.

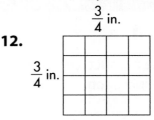

$\frac{1}{4}$ in.

$\frac{3}{4}$ in.

12.

$\frac{3}{4}$ in.

$\frac{3}{4}$ in.

13. Find the area of a square with side length $\frac{1}{6}$ foot.

14. Find the area of a rectangle with side lengths $\frac{1}{3}$ foot and 2 feet.

Problem Solving

MATHEMATICAL PRACTICES

© **15. Use Tools** Yuka is placing blue and white tile in her bathroom. She made a diagram of the layout showing the area of both colors.

Which describes the area of the blue tile?

A $\frac{2}{3} \times \frac{2}{3}$ **B** $\frac{4}{6} \times \frac{4}{6}$ **C** Both A and B **D** none of these

© **16. Construct Arguments** Daniel and Paul are working on a multiplication problem. Daniel claims that $\frac{1}{4}$ in. $\times \frac{3}{8}$ in. $= \frac{3}{32}$ sq. in. Paul claims that the correct answer is $\frac{3}{12}$ sq. in. Who is correct? Explain your answer.

© **17. Reasonableness** Emilio needs to know how much area to clear to place his son's square sandbox. Each side of the sandbox is $\frac{3}{4}$ yard. Find the area that the sandbox will cover.

© **18. Persevere** Margaret purchased a door mat measuring $\frac{1}{2}$ yard by $\frac{2}{3}$ yard for her back door step. If the step measures $\frac{1}{4}$ square yard, will the mat fit? Explain.

Common
Core

5.NF.4.a Interpret the
product $(\frac{a}{b}) \times q$ as a parts
of a partition of q into b
equal parts; equivalently, as
the result of a sequence of
operations $a \times q \div b$.
Also 5.NF.4

Multiplying Mixed Numbers

How do you find the product of mixed numbers?

A clothing factory has machines that
make jackets. The machines operate for
$7\frac{1}{2}$ hours each day. How many jackets can
each machine make in one day?

Jackets Per Hour	
Machine A	Machine B
$2\frac{3}{4}$	$3\frac{1}{3}$

Choose an Operation Use multiplication to
find how many jackets each machine can make in a day.

Guided Practice*

MATHEMATICAL
PRACTICES

Do you know HOW?

In **1** and **2**, estimate the product. Then copy
and complete the multiplication.

1. $2\frac{3}{4} \times 8 = \frac{\blacksquare}{4} \times \frac{8}{1}$

2. $4\frac{1}{2} \times 1\frac{1}{4} = \frac{\blacksquare}{2} \times \frac{\blacksquare}{4}$

Do you UNDERSTAND?

3. Communicate Explain how you
would use improper fractions to
multiply $5 \times 2\frac{1}{2}$.

4. Be Precise How many jackets a day
can Machine A make if it can make
$4\frac{1}{4}$ jackets an hour?

Independent Practice

In **5** through **10**, estimate the product. Then copy and complete the multiplication.

5. $3\frac{4}{5} \times 5 = \frac{\blacksquare}{5} \times \frac{5}{1}$

6. $1\frac{3}{5} \times 2\frac{1}{4} = \frac{\blacksquare}{5} \times \frac{\blacksquare}{4}$

7. $1\frac{1}{2} \times 3\frac{5}{6} = \frac{\blacksquare}{2} \times \frac{\blacksquare}{6}$

8. $4\frac{2}{3} \times 4 = \frac{\blacksquare}{3} \times \frac{4}{1}$

9. $3\frac{1}{7} \times 1\frac{1}{4} = \frac{\blacksquare}{7} \times \frac{\blacksquare}{4}$

10. $1\frac{1}{3} \times 2\frac{1}{6} = \frac{\blacksquare}{3} \times \frac{\blacksquare}{6}$

In **11** through **22**, estimate the product. Then find each product. Simplify if possible.

11. $2\frac{1}{6} \times 4\frac{1}{2}$

12. $\frac{3}{4} \times 8\frac{1}{2}$

13. $1\frac{1}{8} \times 3\frac{1}{3}$

14. $3\frac{1}{4} \times 6$

15. $5\frac{1}{3} \times 3$

16. $2\frac{3}{8} \times 4$

17. $\left(\frac{1}{3} + 1\frac{4}{9}\right) \times \left(2\frac{3}{4} - 1\frac{1}{2}\right)$

18. $\left(1\frac{2}{9} + 2\frac{1}{3}\right) \times \left(2\frac{3}{4} - 1\frac{1}{8}\right)$

19. $\left(1\frac{1}{8} + 1\frac{1}{2}\right) \times \left(2\frac{2}{5} - 1\frac{1}{10}\right)$

20. $\left(\frac{1}{6} + 2\frac{2}{3}\right) \times \left(1\frac{1}{4} - \frac{1}{2}\right)$

21. $\left(2\frac{4}{9} + \frac{1}{3}\right) \times \left(1\frac{1}{4} - \frac{1}{8}\right)$

22. $\left(1\frac{7}{8} + 2\frac{1}{2}\right) \times \left(1\frac{1}{5} - \frac{1}{10}\right)$

Machine A

Estimate $7\frac{1}{2} \times 2\frac{3}{4}$ is about the same as 8×3, so the answer should be about 24 jackets a day.

Change the mixed numbers to improper fractions.

$$7\frac{1}{2} \times 2\frac{3}{4} = \frac{15}{2} \times \frac{11}{4}$$
$$= \frac{165}{8}$$
$$= 20\frac{5}{8}$$

Machine A makes $20\frac{5}{8}$ jackets each day.

Machine B

Estimate $7\frac{1}{2} \times 3\frac{1}{3}$ is about the same as 8×3, so the answer should be about 24 jackets per day.

$$7\frac{1}{2} \times 3\frac{1}{3} = \frac{\overset{5}{\cancel{15}}}{2} \times \frac{\overset{5}{\cancel{10}}}{\underset{1}{\cancel{3}}}$$
$$= \frac{25}{1} = 25$$

Machine B makes 25 jackets each day.

Problem Solving

For **23** through **25**, use the diagram at the right.

Ⓒ **23. Use Tools** Bernie and Chloe hiked the Tremont Trail to the end and back. Then they hiked the Wildflower Trail to the end before stopping to eat lunch. How far did they hike before they ate lunch?

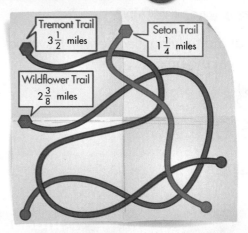

Tremont Trail $3\frac{1}{2}$ miles

Seton Trail $1\frac{1}{4}$ miles

Wildflower Trail $2\frac{3}{8}$ miles

24. In one day, Ricardo hiked $2\frac{2}{3}$ times as far as Bernie and Chloe. How far did he hike?

25. The city plans to extend the Wildflower Trail $2\frac{1}{2}$ times its current length in the next 5 years. How long will the Wildflower Trail be at the end of 5 years?

Ⓒ **26. Generalize** How can you use multiplication to find $3\frac{3}{5} + 3\frac{3}{5} + 3\frac{3}{5}$?

27. The world's smallest gecko is $\frac{3}{4}$ inch long. An adult male Western Banded Gecko is $7\frac{1}{3}$ times as long. How long is a Western Banded Gecko?

Ⓒ **28. Persevere** The Akashi-Kaikyo Bridge in Japan is about $1\frac{4}{9}$ as long as the Golden Gate Bridge in San Francisco. The Golden Gate Bridge is about 9,000 feet long. About how long is the Akashi-Kaikyo Bridge?

Ⓒ **29. Reason** Patty spent $3\frac{1}{2}$ times as much as Sandy on their shopping trip. If Sandy spent $20.50, how much did Patty spend?

A $71.75

B $92.20

C $100.25

D $143.50

Common Core

5.NF.5.b Explaining why multiplying a given number by a fraction greater than 1 results in a product greater than the given number... explaining why multiplying a given number by a fraction less than 1 results in a product smaller than the given number; and relating the principle of fraction equivalence $\frac{a}{b} = \frac{(n \times a)}{(n \times b)}$ to the effect of multiplying $\frac{a}{b}$ by 1. Also 5.NF.5, 5.NF.5.a

Multiplication as Scaling

How can multiplying by a fraction change the second factor?

Sue knitted four scarves 4 feet long for her and her friends Joe, Alan, and June. After a month, they compared the lengths of their scarves. Some scarves had stretched and some had shrunk. The results are shown in the chart.

How had the lengths of the scarves changed?

Think of multiplication as scaling or resizing.

Data		
Sue	4	
Joe	$1\frac{1}{2} \times 4$	
Alan	$\frac{3}{4} \times 4$	
June	$\frac{3}{3} \times 4$	

Guided Practice*

MATHEMATICAL PRACTICES

Do you know HOW?

Without multiplying, decide which symbol belongs in the box: $<$, $>$, or $=$.

1. $3\frac{1}{2} \times 2\frac{2}{3}$ ☐ $2\frac{2}{3}$

2. $\frac{4}{5} \times 2\frac{2}{3}$ ☐ $2\frac{2}{3}$

3. $4\frac{3}{5} \times \frac{4}{4}$ ☐ $4\frac{3}{5}$

Do you UNDERSTAND?

4. **Reason** Why does multiplying a number by $3\frac{1}{2}$ increase its value?

5. **Reason** Does the scaling factor always have to be the first factor?

Independent Practice

In **6–11**, without multiplying, decide which symbol belongs in the box: $<$, $>$, or $=$.

6. $2\frac{1}{2} \times 1\frac{2}{3}$ ☐ $1\frac{2}{3}$

7. $\frac{3}{5} \times 4\frac{4}{5}$ ☐ $4\frac{4}{5}$

8. $1\frac{2}{7} \times \frac{5}{5}$ ☐ $1\frac{2}{7}$

9. $\frac{1}{3} \times 2\frac{2}{5}$ ☐ $2\frac{2}{5}$

10. $3\frac{3}{5} \times \frac{2}{2}$ ☐ $3\frac{3}{5}$

11. $4\frac{1}{3} \times 2\frac{2}{7}$ ☐ $2\frac{2}{7}$

12. Without multiplying, order the following products from least to greatest.

$2 \times \frac{3}{5}$ $\qquad$ $2\frac{1}{4} \times \frac{3}{5}$ $\qquad$ $\frac{3}{4} \times \frac{3}{5}$ $\qquad$ $\frac{5}{5} \times \frac{3}{5}$

Animated Glossary
www.pearsonsuccessnet.com

For another example, see Set B on page 300.

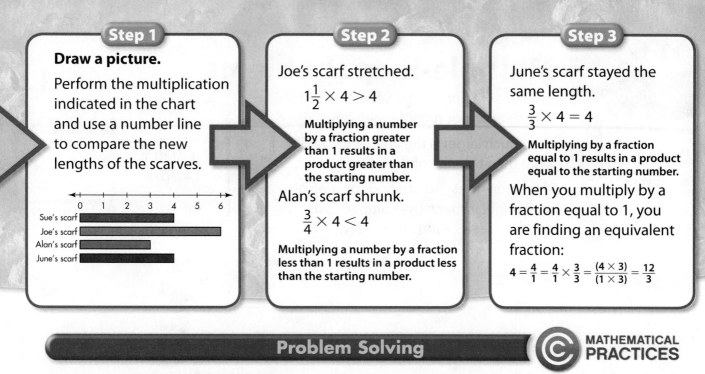

Step 1

Draw a picture.

Perform the multiplication indicated in the chart and use a number line to compare the new lengths of the scarves.

Step 2

Joe's scarf stretched.

$$1\frac{1}{2} \times 4 > 4$$

Multiplying a number by a fraction greater than 1 results in a product greater than the starting number.

Alan's scarf shrunk.

$$\frac{3}{4} \times 4 < 4$$

Multiplying a number by a fraction less than 1 results in a product less than the starting number.

Step 3

June's scarf stayed the same length.

$$\frac{3}{3} \times 4 = 4$$

Multiplying by a fraction equal to 1 results in a product equal to the starting number.

When you multiply by a fraction equal to 1, you are finding an equivalent fraction:

$$4 = \frac{4}{1} = \frac{4}{1} \times \frac{3}{3} = \frac{(4 \times 3)}{(1 \times 3)} = \frac{12}{3}$$

Problem Solving

MATHEMATICAL PRACTICES

13. At a taffy pull, George stretched the taffy to 3 feet. Jose stretched it $1\frac{1}{3}$ times as far as George. Maria stretched it $\frac{2}{3}$ as far. Sally stretched it $\frac{6}{6}$ as far. Who stretched it the farthest? the least?

© **14. Use Tools** Who ran the farthest by the end of the week? Use the table below that shows the distances in miles.

Data		Monday	Tuesday	Wednesday	Thursday	Friday
	Holly	$1\frac{1}{2}$	$\frac{1}{2}$	$2\frac{1}{4}$	$\frac{3}{4}$	$1\frac{1}{2}$
	Yu	$1\frac{3}{4}$	$1\frac{1}{2}$	$2\frac{3}{4}$	$1\frac{1}{4}$	$\frac{1}{2}$

© **15. Persevere** Joni and her friends are stretching rubber bands for an activity in science class. Joni stretched her rubber band to 24 inches. Manuel stretched it $2\frac{1}{2}$ times as far. Nicole stretched it $\frac{3}{3}$ as far. Molly stretched it $\frac{3}{5}$ as far. Put the students in order of how far they stretched their rubber bands from least to greatest.

© **16. Look for Patterns** Make up two decimals with an answer close to the given product.

___.___ × ___. ___ = 6.3

© **17. Reasonableness** Put the following products in order from greatest to least, without multiplying.

$$3 \times \frac{4}{7} \qquad \frac{1}{2} \times \frac{4}{7} \qquad 1\frac{3}{4} \times \frac{4}{7} \qquad \frac{4}{4} \times \frac{4}{7}$$

© Common Core

5.NF.6. Solve real world problems involving multiplication of fractions and mixed numbers, e.g., by using visual fraction models or equations to represent the problem.

Multiple-Step Problems

To solve some problems, you first need to answer one or more hidden questions.

How much larger is the area of the family room than the area of the kitchen?

Remember that you can find the area of a rectangular shape by multiplying its length times its width, or $A = \ell w$.

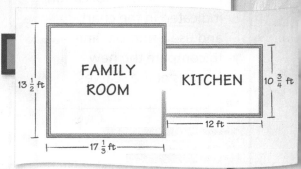

Guided Practice*

© MATHEMATICAL PRACTICES

Do you know **HOW?**

1. A Web site has a daily trivia contest. On Mondays, Wednesdays, and Fridays, you have $1\frac{1}{2}$ hours to submit an answer. On Tuesdays and Thursdays, you have $1\frac{1}{4}$ hours. How many total hours in a week do you have to submit an answer?

   a What are the hidden questions?

   b Solve the problem.

Do you **UNDERSTAND?**

© 2. **Reason** How can you find the hidden question in a problem?

© 3. **Communicate** Use a real-life situation to write a problem that contains a hidden question or hidden questions.

Independent Practice

4. Suzy runs $1\frac{1}{4}$ miles a day for a week. Gretchen walks 3 miles a day for a week. How many more miles does Gretchen cover than Suzy in a week?

   a What are the hidden questions?

   b Solve the problem.

5. John has $1\frac{1}{2}$ hours of homework from Monday through Thursday and $2\frac{3}{4}$ hours over the weekend. How much homework does John have in a week?

6. A movie costs $8.50 for adults and $5.75 for children under 13. Enrico's father took Enrico and two of his friends to the movie. If Enrico and his friends are under 13, what was the total cost for the movie?

Applying Math Practices

- What am I asked to find?
- What else can I try?
- How are quantities related?
- How can I explain my work?
- Can I use math to model the problem?
- Can I use tools to help?
- Is my work precise?
- Why does this work?
- How can I generalize?

What do I know? The family room is $17\frac{1}{3}$ ft $\times$ $13\frac{1}{2}$ ft. The kitchen is 12 ft $\times$ $10\frac{3}{4}$ ft.

What am I asked to find? How much larger is the family room than the kitchen?

Hidden Question 1: What is the area of the family room?

$A = 17\frac{1}{3} \times 13\frac{1}{2}$

$A = \overset{26}{\cancel{\frac{52}{\underset{1}{3}}}} \times \overset{9}{\cancel{\frac{27}{\underset{1}{2}}}} = 234$

Hidden Question 2: What is the area of the kitchen?

$A = 12 \times 10\frac{3}{4}$

$A = \overset{3}{\cancel{\frac{12}{1}}} \times \overset{}{\frac{43}{\cancel{4}_{1}}} = 129$

$234 - 129 = 105$

The family room is 105 square feet larger than the kitchen.

Problem Solving

MATHEMATICAL PRACTICES

In **7** and **8**, identify the hidden questions. Then solve the problem.

7. Crystal has a choice of buying either lunch at the right. Which lunch costs less? How much less?

LUNCH AT THE DELI
Drinks: $1\frac{25}{}$
Sandwich: $5\frac{50}{}$

LUNCH at MANNY'S
Drinks: $2\frac{00}{}$
Burritos: $4\frac{50}{}$

© **8. Persevere** Chris has a choice of two cell phone plans. Plan A charges a flat fee of $20 per month for 300 minutes and $0.20 for every minute over 300. Plan B charges $0.10 per minute with no fee. Which plan would be cheaper for 442 minutes?

Use the table at the right for **9** and **10**.

© **9. Be Precise** What is the difference in length between a Lion's Mane jellyfish and a Thimble jellyfish?

Jellyfish	Length
Thimble jellyfish	1 inch
Lion's Mane jellyfish	7 feet

Data

10. How many times as long as a Thimble jellyfish is a Lion's Mane jellyfish?

11. Kathy is measuring the rainfall in a rain gauge for her science project. The first week, she measured $2\frac{1}{4}$ inches of rain. The second week, she measured twice as much rain, and the third week, she measured half as much rain as the first week. It did not rain at all in the fourth week. How much rainfall did Kathy measure for the entire month? Explain.

© **12. Persevere** The Spanish Club is selling folders to advertise their club. Rob, the president of the club, had 50 folders printed. Janice, the vice president of the club, had a different design printed on four and a half times as many folders. How many folders does the Spanish Club have?

A 50

B 200

C 250

D 275

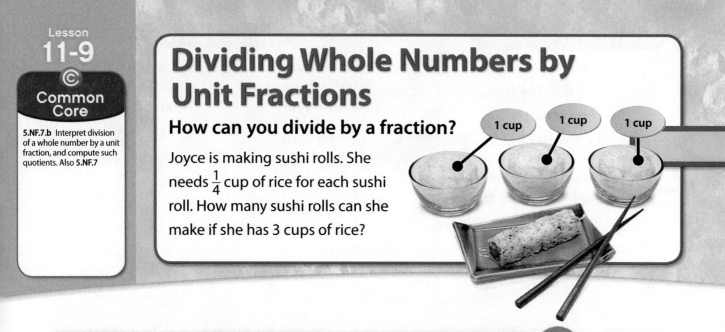

Dividing Whole Numbers by Unit Fractions

© Common Core

5.NF.7.b Interpret division of a whole number by a unit fraction, and compute such quotients. Also 5.NF.7

How can you divide by a fraction?

Joyce is making sushi rolls. She needs $\frac{1}{4}$ cup of rice for each sushi roll. How many sushi rolls can she make if she has 3 cups of rice?

1 cup   1 cup   1 cup

Guided Practice*

© **MATHEMATICAL PRACTICES**

Do you know HOW?

In **1** and **2**, use the picture below to find each quotient. Simplify, if necessary.

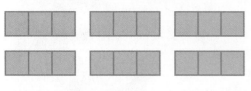

1. How many $\frac{1}{3}$s are in 3? $3 \div \frac{1}{3} = \blacksquare$

2. How many $\frac{2}{3}$s are in 6? $6 \div \frac{2}{3} = \blacksquare$

Do you UNDERSTAND?

© **3. Look for Patterns** In the example at the top, if Joyce had 4 cups of rice, how many rolls could she make?

© **4. Use Structure** In the example at the top, how does the diagram help to show that $3 \div \frac{1}{4}$ is equal to 3×4?

Independent Practice

In **5** and **6**, use the picture to find each quotient.

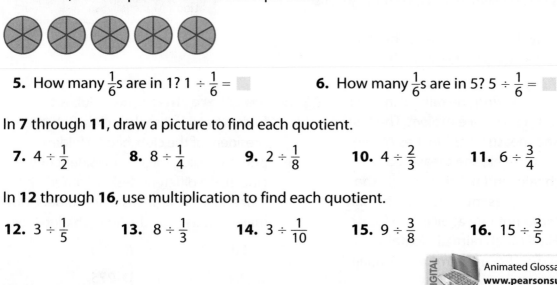

5. How many $\frac{1}{6}$s are in 1? $1 \div \frac{1}{6} = \blacksquare$ **6.** How many $\frac{1}{6}$s are in 5? $5 \div \frac{1}{6} = \blacksquare$

In **7** through **11**, draw a picture to find each quotient.

7. $4 \div \frac{1}{2}$ **8.** $8 \div \frac{1}{4}$ **9.** $2 \div \frac{1}{8}$ **10.** $4 \div \frac{2}{3}$ **11.** $6 \div \frac{3}{4}$

In **12** through **16**, use multiplication to find each quotient.

12. $3 \div \frac{1}{5}$ **13.** $8 \div \frac{1}{3}$ **14.** $3 \div \frac{1}{10}$ **15.** $9 \div \frac{3}{8}$ **16.** $15 \div \frac{3}{5}$

DIGITAL   Animated Glossary
www.pearsonsuccessnet.com

One Way

Draw a diagram.

How many $\frac{1}{4}$s are in 3?

Think $3 \div \frac{1}{4}$.

There are twelve $\frac{1}{4}$s in three whole cups.

So, Joyce can make 12 sushi rolls.

Another Way

The diagram shows $3 \div \frac{1}{4} = 12$. You also know that $3 \times 4 = 12$. This suggests that you can also use multiplication to divide by a fraction.

Two fractions whose product is 1 are reciprocals. For example, $\frac{1}{4} \times \frac{4}{1} = 1$, so $\frac{1}{4}$ and $\frac{4}{1}$ are reciprocals. Dividing by a fraction is the same as multiplying by its reciprocal.

$$3 \div \frac{1}{4} = 3 \times \frac{4}{1} = 12$$

So, Joyce can make 12 sushi rolls.

Problem Solving

MATHEMATICAL
PRACTICES

For **17** and **18**, use the following information.

Bijan is making a banner for his school. Along the bottom edge of the banner is a row of small squares. Each square is 6 inches by 6 inches.

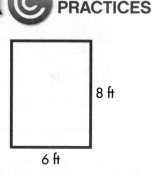

8 ft

6 ft

17. How many small squares can Bijan put along the bottom of the banner?

18. If every fourth square is colored blue, how many blue squares are along the bottom?

Ⓒ **19. Reason** When you divide a whole number by a fraction with a numerator of 1, explain how you can find the quotient.

Ⓒ **20. Communicate** Write a word problem that can be solved by dividing 10 by $\frac{2}{3}$. Include the answer to the problem.

21. As of 2006, the world's largest leather work boot is 16 feet tall. A typical men's work boot is $\frac{1}{2}$ foot tall. How many times as tall is the largest boot as the height of a typical work boot?

Ⓒ **22. Reasonableness** The Nile River is 4,160 miles long. You want to spend three weeks traveling the entire length of the river. Estimate the number of miles you should travel each day.

Ⓒ **23. Model** Maria used one bag of flour. She baked two loaves of bread. Each loaf required $2\frac{1}{4}$ cups of flour. Then she used the remaining $6\frac{1}{2}$ cups of flour to make muffins. How much flour was in the bag to begin with?

Ⓒ **24. Persevere** Rudy has 8 yards of twine. If he cuts the twine into equal pieces of $\frac{3}{4}$ feet each, how many pieces can he cut?

A $10\frac{1}{2}$ **C** 32

B $24\frac{3}{4}$ **D** 96

Lesson
11-10

Common
Core

5.NF.7.c Solve real world
problems involving division
of unit fractions by non-
zero whole numbers and
division of whole numbers
by unit fractions, e.g., by
using visual fraction models
and equations to represent
the problem. Also **5.NF.7**

Dividing Unit Fractions by Non-Zero Whole Numbers

How can you model dividing a unit fraction by a whole number?

Half of a casserole is left over. Ann, Beth, and Chuck
are sharing the leftovers equally. What fraction of the
original casserole does each person get?
Make a drawing to show $\frac{1}{2}$.

Other Examples: Use a number line to find $\frac{1}{3} \div 4$.

Shade $\frac{1}{3}$ on a number line and divide $\frac{1}{3}$ into 4 equal parts.

Each part is $\frac{1}{12}$.

Check with multiplication: $\frac{1}{12} \times 4 = \frac{4}{12} = \frac{1}{3}$

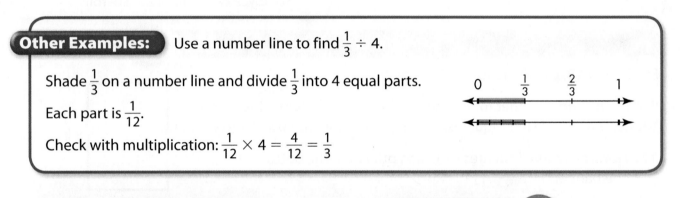

Guided Practice*

MATHEMATICAL PRACTICES

Do you know HOW?

Use the picture below to find each quotient.

1. $\frac{1}{4} \div 2$

2. $\frac{1}{4} \div 4$

Do you UNDERSTAND?

© **3. Construct Arguments** In the example
at the top, how is dividing by 3 the
same as multiplying by $\frac{1}{3}$?

© **4. Reasonableness** When you divide a
unit fraction by a whole number, will
the quotient be greater than or less
than the unit fraction?

Independent Practice

Leveled Practice In **5–10**, find the quotient.

5. $\frac{1}{2} \div 5$

6. $\frac{1}{5} \div 2$

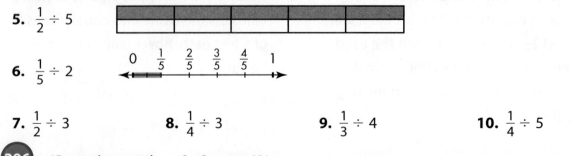

7. $\frac{1}{2} \div 3$ 8. $\frac{1}{4} \div 3$ 9. $\frac{1}{3} \div 4$ 10. $\frac{1}{4} \div 5$

*For another example, see Set G on page 301.

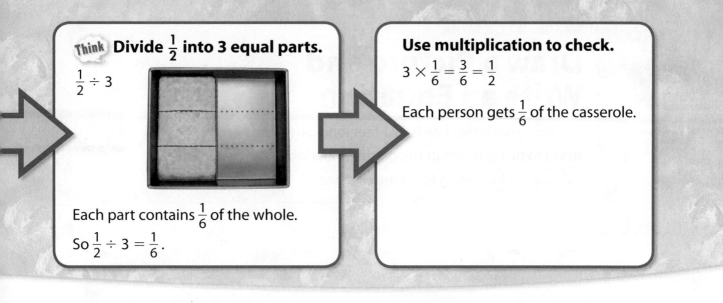

Think Divide $\frac{1}{2}$ into 3 equal parts.

$\frac{1}{2} \div 3$

Each part contains $\frac{1}{6}$ of the whole.

So $\frac{1}{2} \div 3 = \frac{1}{6}$.

Use multiplication to check.

$3 \times \frac{1}{6} = \frac{3}{6} = \frac{1}{2}$

Each person gets $\frac{1}{6}$ of the casserole.

Problem Solving

MATHEMATICAL PRACTICES

11. Sue has $\frac{1}{2}$ gallon of milk. She needs to pour 4 glasses of milk. What fraction of a gallon should she put in each glass?

12. **Use Tools** Who ran the farthest by the end of the week? Use the table below that shows the distances in miles.

Data	Monday	Tuesday	Wednesday	Thursday	Friday
Amir	$2\frac{1}{2}$	$1\frac{1}{2}$	$3\frac{1}{4}$	$1\frac{3}{4}$	$2\frac{1}{2}$
Janie	$2\frac{3}{4}$	$2\frac{1}{2}$	$3\frac{3}{4}$	$2\frac{1}{4}$	$1\frac{1}{2}$

13. **Look for Patterns** Write two decimals whose product is close to 9.8.

14. **Reasonableness** Without multiplying, order the following products from least to greatest.

$2 \times \frac{3}{5}$ $\qquad$ $\frac{1}{4} \times \frac{3}{5}$ $\qquad$ $1\frac{2}{5} \times \frac{3}{5}$ $\qquad$ $\frac{6}{6} \times \frac{3}{5}$

15. Find the area of the rectangle.

$\frac{3}{4}$ m, 16 m

16. What division problem is modeled on the number line below? Find the quotient.

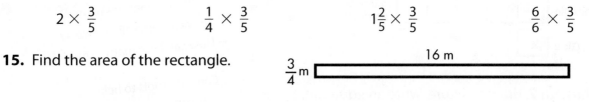

0 $\qquad$ 1

Lesson
11-11

C
Common
Core

5.NF.7.a Interpret division
of a unit fraction by a non-
zero whole number, and
compute such quotients.
Also 5.NF.7

Problem Solving

Draw a Picture and Write an Equation

The string on Josie's kite is $12\frac{1}{2}$ feet long. She wants to use the string to tie up plants in the garden. How long is each garden string if the kite string is cut into 5 pieces?

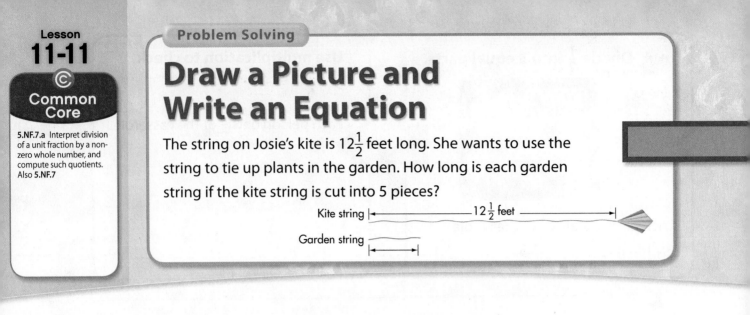

Guided Practice*

MATHEMATICAL PRACTICES

Do you know HOW?

Solve. Draw a picture and write an equation.

1. If a 6 pack of yogurt contains $36\frac{3}{4}$ ounces, how much yogurt is in each container of yogurt?

Do you UNDERSTAND?

C 2. **Reasonableness** How do you know your answer for Exercise 1 is reasonable?

C 3. **Be Precise** Write a real-world problem that you can solve by using division of fractions by a whole number.

Independent Practice

MATHEMATICAL PRACTICES

4. Danielle has a board that is $41\frac{2}{3}$ inches long. It is 5 times as long as the board Gina has. How long is Gina's board? Write an equation, then solve.

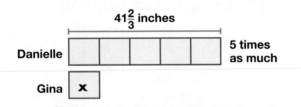

Applying Math Practices

- What am I asked to find?
- What else can I try?
- How are quantities related?
- How can I explain my work?
- How can I use math to model the problem?
- Can I use tools to help?
- Is my work precise?
- Why does this work?
- How can I generalize?

For **5** through **7**, draw a picture, write an equation, then solve.

5. Phil has $\frac{1}{2}$ pound of berries to put equally in to 4 tarts. How many pounds of berries will there be in each tart?

What do I know?

Josie's kite string is $12\frac{1}{2}$ feet long. She needs 5 equal pieces of string.

What am I asked to find?

The length of the strings for each of the garden plants.

Draw a Picture

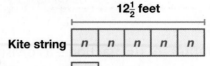

$12\frac{1}{2}$ feet

Kite string | n | n | n | n | n | Cut in to 5 pieces

Garden string | n

Write an Equation

Let n = length of the garden string

$$12\frac{1}{2} \div 5 = n$$

$$12\frac{1}{2} \times \frac{1}{5} = n$$

Each garden string is $2\frac{1}{2}$ feet long.

---

6. Use Structure Josh volunteered at the zoo for $14\frac{2}{5}$ hours over 6 days. About how many hours did Josh volunteer each day?

7. Tina is making a sign to advertise the school play. The width of the sign is $2\frac{2}{3}$ feet. If the length is $4\frac{1}{2}$ times as much, then what is the length of the sign?

8. Brown bats sleep for 20 hours each day. How many hours per week are they awake? How many hours per year are they awake?

9. Construct Arguments Brenda says a good estimate for $50 \times 31\frac{3}{4}$ is 800. Is she correct? Explain.

10. Use Tools Wanda needs to buy at least 50 stickers. Will 1 sheet of stickers be enough? How do you know?

11. Jin's friends collected 149 bottles of water for riders going on a bike trip. If each rider needs 4 bottles, how many riders can they supply with water?

12. Think About the Structure A ticket to Los Angeles costs $390, and a ticket to Hong Kong costs $2\frac{1}{2}$ times as much. Which equation can you solve to show how much the ticket to Hong Kong costs?

A $\$390 + \$390 = c$

B $\$390 \times 2\frac{1}{2} = c$

C $\$390 \div 2\frac{1}{2} = c$

D $(2 \times \$390) + (2 \times \$390) = c$

13. Think About the Structure Each shelf holds 24 books. There are 8 shelves. Which equation could you solve to find how many books there are in all?

A $24 + 8 = b$

B $24 - 8 = b$

C $24 \times 8 = b$

D $24 \div 8 = b$

Set A, pages 276–277

You can represent the fraction $\frac{2}{3}$ as division.

Think $\frac{1}{3}$ of 2 wholes

$$\frac{2}{3} = 2 \div 3$$

Remember that any fraction can be represented as division of the numerator by the denominator.

Write a division expression for each.

1. $\frac{7}{9}$ **2.** $\frac{2}{3}$ **3.** $\frac{11}{17}$

Write each expression as a fraction.

4. $7 \div 12$ **5.** $17 \div 20$

Set B, pages 278–279, 290–291

Find $\frac{2}{3}$ of 6.

One Way

$\frac{1}{3}$ of 6 is 2

$\frac{2}{3}$ is twice as much as $\frac{1}{3}$.

So, $\frac{2}{3}$ of 6 is 4.

Another Way

Multiply first, and then divide.

$$\frac{2}{3} \times 6 = \frac{12}{3} = 4$$

Remember that the fraction bar means to divide.

Find each product. Simplify if possible.

1. $4 \times \frac{1}{2}$ **2.** $\frac{3}{4}$ of 16

3. $24 \times \frac{1}{8}$ **4.** $\frac{4}{7}$ of 28

5. $10 \times \frac{1}{5}$ **6.** $\frac{5}{6}$ of 24

Set C, pages 282–284, 286–287

Find $\frac{5}{6} \times \frac{2}{3}$.

Multiply.

$$\frac{5}{6} \times \frac{2}{3} = \frac{10}{18}.$$

Simplify, if possible.

$$\frac{10 \div 2}{18 \div 2} = \frac{5}{9}.$$

Remember to multiply both the numerator and the denominator.

Find each product. Simplify, if possible.

1. $\frac{3}{5} \times \frac{1}{4}$ **2.** $\frac{6}{7} \times \frac{1}{2}$

3. $\frac{4}{9} \times \frac{2}{3}$ **4.** $\frac{3}{8} \times \frac{1}{3}$

5. $\frac{2}{3} \times \frac{1}{3}$ **6.** $\frac{7}{8} \times \frac{2}{3}$

Set D, pages 280–281, 288–289

Find $3\frac{1}{2} \times 2\frac{7}{8}$.

Estimate. $3\frac{1}{2} \times 2\frac{7}{8}$ is about 4×3 or 12.

Change mixed numbers to improper fractions and multiply.

$$\frac{7}{2} \times \frac{23}{8} = \frac{161}{16} = 10\frac{1}{16}$$

The product $10\frac{1}{16}$ is close to the estimate, 12.

Remember to check your answer against your original estimate to be sure your answer is reasonable.

Find each product.

1. $2\frac{1}{3} \times 4\frac{1}{5}$ **2.** $4\frac{1}{2} \times 6\frac{2}{3}$

3. $7\frac{1}{8} \times 2\frac{3}{4}$ **4.** $3\frac{3}{5} \times 2\frac{5}{7}$

Find and answer hidden questions in multiple-step word problems.

A school sells pizza slices and juice bottles. Pizza slices cost $3 each and juice bottles cost $2 each. On Friday, both items sell for half price. If Remi buys 2 pizza slices and a juice bottle on Friday, how much would he save?

Hidden Question: How much do 2 slices and a juice cost normally?

$(2 \times \$3) + (\$2) = \$6 + \$2 = \$8.$

So, on Friday, 2 slices and a juice would cost $\$8 \times \frac{1}{2} = \$4$. Remi would save $4.

Remember to find and answer the hidden question.

Identify the hidden question. Solve.

1. A bakery sells 20 loaves of bread on Wednesday and 25 loaves on Thursday. It sells as many loaves on Friday as it does on Wednesday and Thursday. How many total loaves does it sell?

A 4-foot board is cut into pieces that are $\frac{1}{2}$ foot in length. How many pieces will there be?

Draw a Picture.

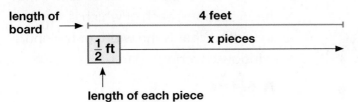

length of board → | 4 feet |
$\frac{1}{2}$ ft — x pieces →
↑
length of each piece

Write an equation: $x = 4 \div \frac{1}{2}$

$$= 4 \times \frac{2}{1} = \frac{8}{1} = 8$$

There will be 8 pieces.

Remember to draw a picture to help write an equation.

Draw a picture and write an equation. Then solve.

1. A total of 60 students are being separated into 5 equal teams. How many students are on each team?

2. A 4-pound package of peanuts is divided into $\frac{1}{4}$-pound packages. How many packages will there be?

Find $\frac{1}{2} \div 4$.

Use multiplication.
Multiply by the recriprocal of the divisor.

$\frac{1}{2} \div 4 = \frac{1}{2} \times \frac{1}{4} = \frac{1}{8}$

Remember that you can multiply by the reciprocal of the divisor when you divide by a fraction.

Find each quotient. Simplify, if possible.

1. $\frac{1}{3} \div 2$ 2. $\frac{1}{7} \div 7$

3. $\frac{1}{2} \div 8$ 4. $\frac{1}{8} \div 2$

1. How many $\frac{3}{4}$s are in 6? (11-9)

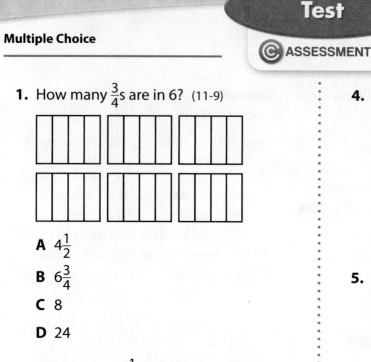

A $4\frac{1}{2}$

B $6\frac{3}{4}$

C 8

D 24

2. Alberto runs $3\frac{1}{4}$ miles each day. Which of the following can be used to find n, the number of miles he will run in a week? (11-11)

n total miles

$3\frac{1}{4}$	$3\frac{1}{4}$	$3\frac{1}{4}$	$3\frac{1}{4}$	$3\frac{1}{4}$	$3\frac{1}{4}$	$3\frac{1}{4}$

A $3\frac{1}{4} \times n = 7$

B $7 \times n = 3\frac{1}{4}$

C $7 \times 3\frac{1}{4} = n$

D $3\frac{1}{4} \div 7 = n$

3. If the diameter of a tree trunk is growing $\frac{1}{4}$ inch each year, how many years will it take for the diameter to grow 8 inches? (11-9)

A 2 years

B 8 years

C 24 years

D 32 years

4. Find the area of a rectangle with sides of lengths $\frac{1}{12}$ foot and $\frac{3}{4}$ foot. (11-5)

A $\frac{1}{12}$ sq. ft

B $\frac{1}{16}$ sq. ft

C $\frac{3}{8}$ sq. ft

D $\frac{1}{9}$ sq. ft

5. Mrs. Webster wants to divide the milk shown into servings that are $\frac{2}{3}$ of a pint in size. How many servings are possible? (11-9)

A 9

B 5

C 4

D 2

6 pints

6. Mary is making a window covering that has 5 sections, each of which is $1\frac{3}{10}$ feet in width. What is the width of the entire window covering? (11-6)

A $6\frac{1}{2}$ feet

B $5\frac{1}{2}$ feet

C $5\frac{3}{10}$ feet

D $3\frac{11}{13}$ feet

7. Which of the following is equal to $\frac{4}{7} \times \frac{14}{3}$? (11-4)

A $\frac{4}{7} \times \frac{3}{14}$

B $4 \times \frac{2}{3}$

C $\frac{7}{4} \times \frac{14}{3}$

D $\frac{2}{7} \times \frac{7}{3}$

8. Tracy took a quiz containing 12 items. If she got $\frac{5}{6}$ of the items correct, how many did she get correct? (11-2)

9. A retaining wall on the playground is shown below. If $\frac{2}{3}$ of the wall is made from brick, what is the height of the brick portion of the wall? (11-6)

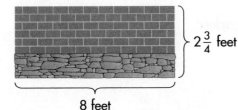

$\left.\begin{array}{c}\end{array}\right\}2\frac{3}{4}$ feet

8 feet

10. What is the area of the retaining wall? (11-5)

11. If the retaining wall in the problems above was a rectangle with dimensions twice as great, what would be the perimeter? (11-6)

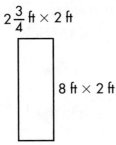

$2\frac{3}{4}$ ft × 2 ft

8 ft × 2 ft

12. Which symbol belongs in the box? (11-7)

$\frac{3}{4} \times \frac{3}{5} \bigcirc \frac{4}{4} \times \frac{3}{5}$

13. Tom and his friends are rolling out clay for an activity in art class. Tom rolled out his clay until it was 2 feet long. Hans rolled his $1\frac{1}{2}$ times as far. Janet rolled hers $\frac{4}{4}$ as far. Noah rolled his $\frac{3}{5}$ as far. Put the students in order of the length of their clay from greatest to least. Explain how you found your answer. (11-7)

14. One-half of a cantaloupe was shared among 3 people. How much cantaloupe did each person get? Explain how you found your answer. (11-10)

15. Lisa has 64 cloth strips to make a rug. There are 8 red strips and 14 blue strips. What fraction of the cloth strips are red? What fraction are blue? (11-1)

16. Gina is buying juice for a class breakfast at school. At the discount store, she can purchase 30 individual juice boxes for $21.99. At the grocery, she can buy $\frac{1}{2}$ gallon cartons of juice. Each carton is $3.99 and contains 5 servings. Which is the better buy? (11-8)

17. Estimate the area of the rectangle below. (11-3)

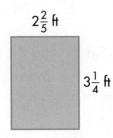

$2\frac{2}{5}$ ft

$3\frac{1}{4}$ ft

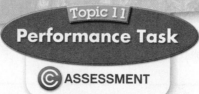

Tammy is planning her training for a 15-mile race. She wants to run in the nearby park on the trails shown in the map.

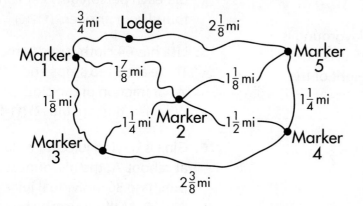

1. For the first few days of her training, Tammy wants to run about $\frac{1}{4}$ the length of the race. Estimate how far she should run.

2. Describe a path in the park that is close to $\frac{1}{4}$ of 15. Explain how to estimate the length of this path.

3. Find $\frac{1}{4}$ of 15 miles and the exact length of the path you chose in exercise 2. With the path you chose, will Tammy run more or less than $\frac{1}{4}$ of 15? How much more or less?

4. Is $\frac{1}{2}$ the distance from Marker 3 to Marker 4 greater than or less than the distance from Marker 2 to Marker 3?

Topic 12 Volume of Solids

▼ Some antique boxes, like this one, were made from special cuts of wood and included intricate carvings. How can you find the volume of this box? You will find out in Lesson 12-5.

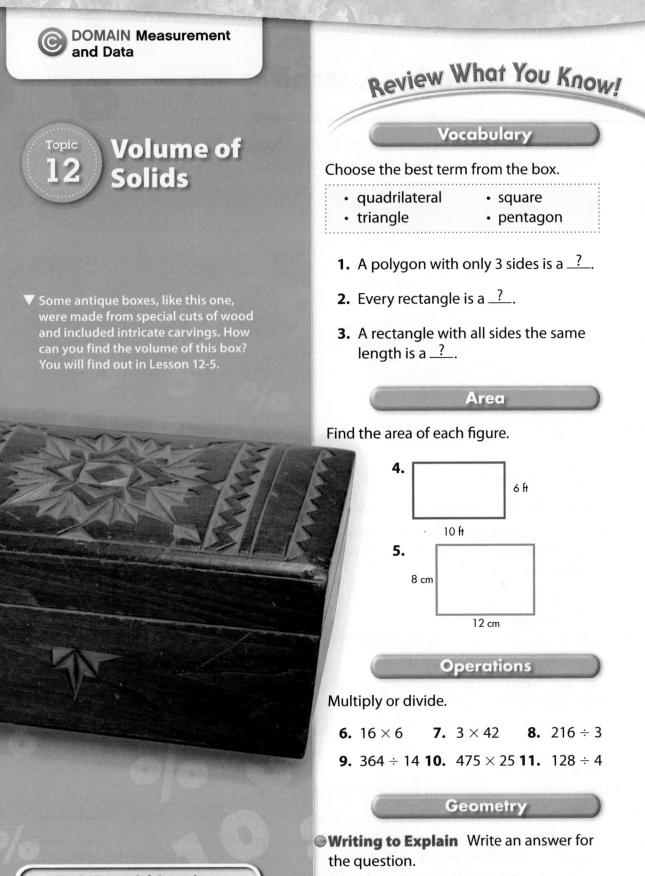

Review What You Know!

Vocabulary

Choose the best term from the box.

- quadrilateral
- square
- triangle
- pentagon

1. A polygon with only 3 sides is a __?__.

2. Every rectangle is a __?__.

3. A rectangle with all sides the same length is a __?__.

Area

Find the area of each figure.

4.
10 ft
6 ft

5.
8 cm
12 cm

Operations

Multiply or divide.

6. 16×6 7. 3×42 8. $216 \div 3$

9. $364 \div 14$ 10. 475×25 11. $128 \div 4$

Geometry

© **Writing to Explain** Write an answer for the question.

12. How are parallel lines different from perpendicular lines?

Topic Essential Questions
- How can three-dimensional shapes be represented and analyzed?
- What does the volume of a rectangular prism mean and how can it be found?

Interactive Learning

Pose the problem. Start each lesson by working together to solve problems. It will help you make sense of math.

Applying Math Practices
- What am I asked to find?
- What else can I try?
- How are quantities related?
- How can I explain my work?
- How can I use math to model the problem?
- Can I use tools to help?
- Is my work precise?
- Why does this work?
- How can I generalize?

Lesson 12-1

© **Communicate** Use objects to help with this task.

How can you describe a cube to someone who can't see it without using the word "cube"? What properties do solids like a cube have?

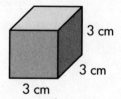
3 cm
3 cm
3 cm

Lesson 12-2

© **Persevere** Solve using the drawing at the right.

Look at these stacked cubes. What would the front view look like – what you see from the front? What would the top view look like? What would the side view look like? Draw pictures to show each view.

Lesson 12-3

© **Use Tools** Solve. Use cubes to help and look for patterns.

The designs at the right follow a pattern. Predict how many cubes in all would be in the design that has 15 cubes on the bottom row. Tell how you decided.

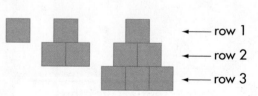
← row 1
← row 2
← row 3

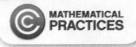
Lesson 12-4

© **Use Tools** Solve. Place a folder in front of your work so your partner cannot see it.

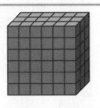

Build a rectangular prism using cubes so your partner cannot see it. Tell your partner how many cubes long, wide, and tall your prism is. Your partner should use this information to build a prism with the same dimensions. What is the total number of cubes that make up the prism? Tell how you decided.

Lesson 12-5

© **Use Tools** Solve. Use cubes to help.

Build a rectangular prism that is 4 cubes long, 2 cubes wide, and 3 cubes high. What is the total number of cubes that make up the prism? How can you decide without counting individual cubes?

Lesson 12-6

© **Use Tools** Solve. Use the solid shown at the right.

Suppose you wanted to find the volume of this three-dimensional shape. How could you do it? Explain.

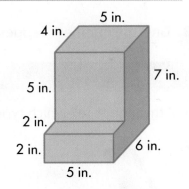

Lesson 12-7

© **Use Tools** Use your cubes to make this solid, then answer the questions below.

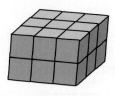

The volume of a single cube in this solid is 1 cubic unit. How many cubic units are needed to make this shape? In other words, what is the volume of this rectangular prism?

Common
Core

5.MD.3 Recognize volume
as an attribute of solid
figures and understand
concepts of volume
measurement.

Solids

What is a solid figure?

A three-dimensional shape, or solid, takes up space. One solid is the cube. It has flat polygon-shaped surfaces called faces. All the faces of a cube are squares. Faces meet along segments called edges, and edges meet at points called vertices. The singular of vertices is vertex.

Hands-On
Power Solids

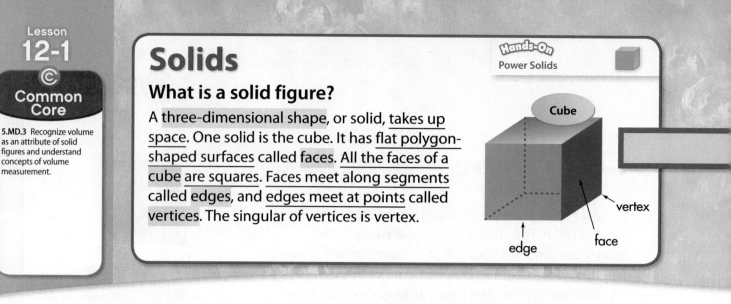
Cube
vertex
face
edge

Guided Practice*

MATHEMATICAL
PRACTICES

Do you know HOW?

For **1** through **3**, use the solid shown.

1. Give the number of vertices.

2. Give the number of faces.

3. Give the number of edges.

Do you UNDERSTAND?

4. Which type of solid figure is shown at the left?

5. Which of the solid figures shown at the top have curved surfaces?

Ⓒ 6. **Construct Arguments** Why is a cube a prism and not a pyramid? Explain.

Independent Practice

For **7** through **9**, tell which type of solid figure each object resembles.

7.

8.

9.

For **10** through **12**, use the solid shown at the right.

10. Give the number of vertices.

11. Give the number of faces.

12. Give the number of edges.

For another example, see Set A on page 324.

Some solid figures have curved surfaces, while others have all flat surfaces.

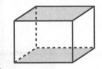

Prism
A solid with two parallel bases that are the same size and shape and faces that are parallelograms.

Cylinder
A solid with two circular bases that are parallel and the same size and shape.

Cone
A solid with one circular base. The points on this circle are joined to one point outside the base.

Pyramid
A solid with one base that is a polygon and whose other faces are triangles with a common vertex.

Problem Solving

MATHEMATICAL
PRACTICES

13. Which of the following decimals is equivalent to 12.45?

   A 12.0045

   B 12.0450

   C 12.4500

   D 124.5000

14. Which of the following solids has a curved surface?

   A Pyramid

   B Cube

   C Prism

   D Cone

15. Which solid has the most vertices?

   A Prism

   B Pyramid

   C Cone

   D Cylinder

16. Which solid has the fewest faces?

   A Prism

   B Pyramid

   C Cone

   D Cylinder

17. Luke's tent weighs $6\frac{1}{2}$ pounds. His fishing tackle weighs $5\frac{1}{4}$ pounds. What is the total weight of both items?

18. Reason Can a prism have an odd number of vertices? Explain.

19. Fillmore Park had 75 spruce trees. Volunteers planted 39 more. Solve $75 + 39 = t$ to find the total number of spruce trees in the park now.

20. Generalize Which of the following is NOT a rectangular prism?

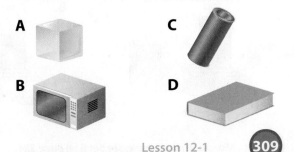

   A

   C

   B

   D

Lesson
12-2
ⓒ
Common Core

5.MD.3.a A cube with side length 1 unit, called a "unit cube," is said to have "one cubic unit" of volume, and can be used to measure volume. Also 5.MD.3.b, 5.MD.4

Views of Solids

How can you get information about a solid by viewing it from different perspectives?

What do the different views of this stack of cubes look like?

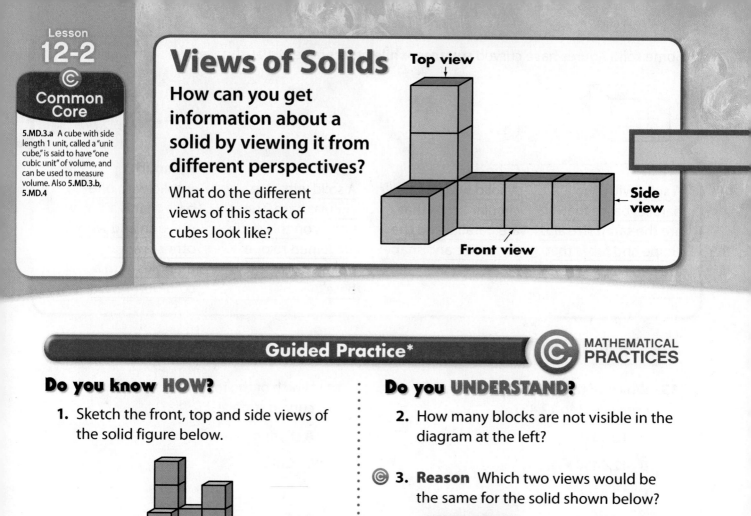

Top view

Side view

Front view

Guided Practice*

ⓒ MATHEMATICAL PRACTICES

Do you know HOW?

1. Sketch the front, top and side views of the solid figure below.

Do you UNDERSTAND?

2. How many blocks are not visible in the diagram at the left?

ⓒ 3. **Reason** Which two views would be the same for the solid shown below?

Independent Practice

In **4** through **9**, draw front, side, and top views of each stack of unit blocks.

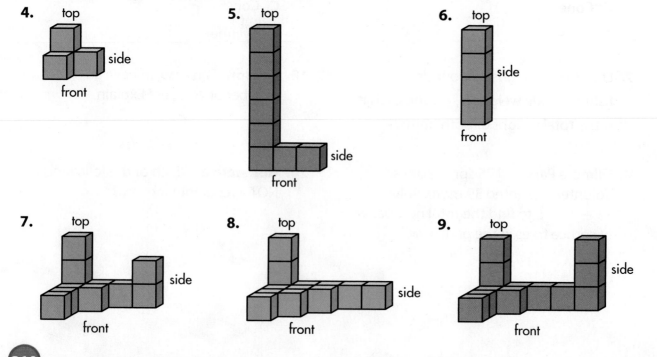

4. top
    side
    front

5. top
    side
    front

6. top
    side
    front

7. top
    side
    front

8. top
    side
    front

9. top
    side
    front

For another example, see Set B on page 324.

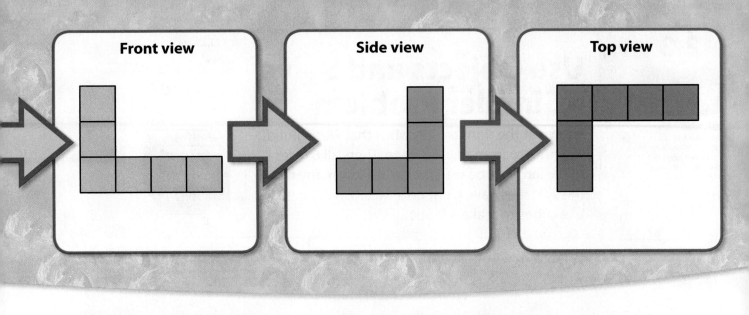

| Front view | Side view | Top view |

Problem Solving

10. Beth, Toby, Juan, and Patricia walked 6 miles to raise money. Beth and Patricia each raised $3.50 for each mile walked. Toby raised $3 for each mile walked, and Juan raised $22 in all. Who raised the most money?

A Beth   **C** Juan

B Toby   **D** Patricia

11. Hina bought 21 stickers and 7 rope bracelets. She wants to make small gift packs for her friends. Each gift pack has 3 stickers and 1 rope bracelet. Stickers cost $1.50 each, and bracelets cost $2 each. How much does it cost Hina to make each gift pack?

A $45.50   **C** $3.50

B $6.50   **D** None of the above

12. Draw the front, side, and top views of this stack of cubes and cylinders.

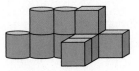

13. If 10 cubes are stacked vertically, how many cubes are not visible from the top view?

14. Look for Patterns How many blocks are not visible from the top view?

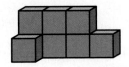

15. Model In the figure below, which face is parallel to face *ABCD*?

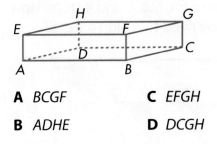

A *BCGF*   **C** *EFGH*

B *ADHE*   **D** *DCGH*

Common Core

5.MD.5 Relate volume to the operations of multiplication and addition and solve real world and mathematical problems involving volume.

Problem Solving

Use Objects and Solve a Simpler Problem

Hands-On
cubes

Shown at the right are 27 cubes that were glued together to form a larger cube. Then, all 6 faces of the larger cube were painted. How many of the 27 cubes have paint on 1 face? On 2 faces? Use cubes to make a model.

Guided Practice*

MATHEMATICAL PRACTICES

Do you know HOW?

1. Use Tools Use cubes and the example of the simpler problem above to build a larger cube with 4 layers. Each layer will have 4 rows of 4 cubes. How many cubes will the larger cube contain?

Do you UNDERSTAND?

2. Think of gluing the cubes together for the $4 \times 4 \times 4$ cube you made. Then, think of painting the outside faces. How many cubes will have paint on 1 face? On 2 faces? On 3 faces?

3. Communicate Write a real-world problem that involves using objects to help solve a simpler problem.

Independent Practice

MATHEMATICAL PRACTICES

In **4** through **9**, use objects to help you solve a simpler problem. Use the solution to help you solve the original problem.

4. Alicia uses wood timbers to build steps. The pattern is shown for 1, 2, 3, and 4 steps. How many timbers will she need to build 10 steps?

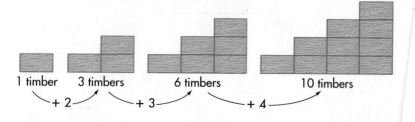

1 timber   3 timbers   6 timbers   10 timbers
+ 2   + 3   + 4

Applying Math Practices

- What am I asked to find?
- What else can I try?
- How are quantities related?
- How can I explain my work?
- How can I use math to model the problem?
- Can I use tools to help?
- Is my work precise?
- Why does this work?
- How can I generalize?

How many cubes have paint on 1 face?

The center cube on each of the 6 faces of the larger cube has paint on 1 face.

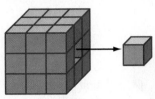

Six of these cubes have paint on 1 face.

How many cubes have paint on 2 faces?

Only 1 cube on each of the 12 edges of the larger cube has paint on 2 faces.

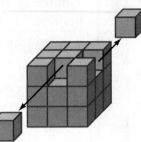

Twelve of these cubes have paint on 2 faces.

5. Look for Patterns Four people can be seated at a table. If two tables are put together, six people can be seated. How many tables are needed to make a long table that will seat 20 people?

6. Jeremiah wants to make a display of CD boxes. He wants a single box on the top layer. Layers that are below the top layer must form a square, with each layer being 1 box wider than the layer above it. The display can only be 4 layers high. How many total boxes will be in the display? Use cubes.

1 layer, 1 cube   2 layers, 5 cubes

7. Katherine is constructing a patio using the design shown at the right.

  a How many total blocks will she need in order to have 5 blocks in the middle row?

  b How many total blocks will she need in order to have 6 blocks in the middle row?

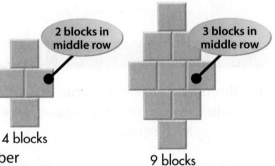

2 blocks in middle row   3 blocks in middle row

4 blocks   9 blocks

  c Generalize What do you notice about the number of blocks in the middle row compared to the total number of blocks?

8. An artist wants to cut 1 square sheet of copper into 16 equal pieces. Before he cuts, he will draw segments on the sheet of copper showing where to make the cuts. How many horizontal and vertical segments will he need to draw?

9. There are 24 balls in a large bin. Two out of every three are basketballs. The rest are footballs. How many basketballs are in the bin?

eTools
www.pearsonsuccessnet.com

©
Common Core

5.MD.3.a A cube with side length 1 unit, called a "unit cube," is said to have "one cubic unit" of volume, and can be used to measure volume. **5.MD.3.b** A solid figure which can be packed without gaps or overlaps using *n* unit cubes is said to have a volume of *n* cubic units. Also **5.MD.4, 5.MD.5.a**

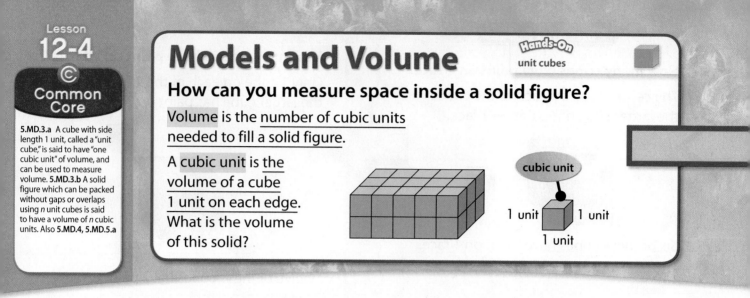

Hands-On
unit cubes

Models and Volume

How can you measure space inside a solid figure?

Volume is the number of cubic units needed to fill a solid figure.

A **cubic unit** is the volume of a cube 1 unit on each edge. What is the volume of this solid?

cubic unit

1 unit   1 unit
1 unit

Guided Practice*

© **MATHEMATICAL PRACTICES**

Do you know HOW?

Use cubes to make a model of each rectangular prism. Find the volume by counting the number of cubes needed to make the model.

1.

2.

Do you UNDERSTAND?

© **3. Model** Make a model of a rectangular prism with a base that is 3 cubes long by 3 cubes wide. The height of the prism is 2 cubes. Then draw a picture of your model.

4. If you add another layer to the top of the prism in Exercise 1, what would the new volume be in cubic units?

Independent Practice

In **5** through **10**, find the number of cubic units needed to make each rectangular prism. You can use unit cubes or you can count the cubes by looking at the drawing.

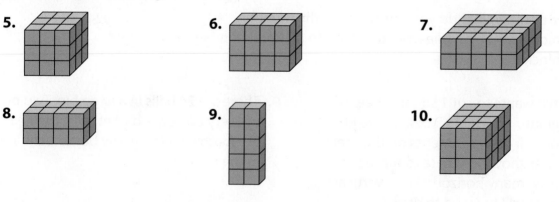

5.

6.

7.

8.

9.

10.

11. How many cubes would it take to make a model of a rectangular prism that is 4 units long × 5 units wide × 3 units high?

DIGITAL
Animated Glossary
www.pearsonsuccessnet.com

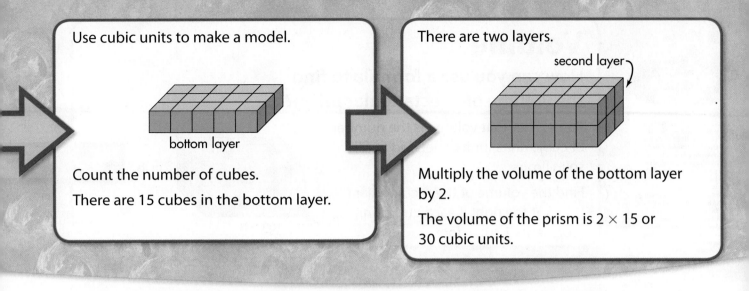

Use cubic units to make a model.

bottom layer

Count the number of cubes.

There are 15 cubes in the bottom layer.

There are two layers.

second layer

Multiply the volume of the bottom layer by 2.

The volume of the prism is 2 × 15 or 30 cubic units.

Problem Solving

For **12** through **16**, use the table at the right.

Compare the volumes of the prisms. Write >, <, or = for each ◯.

12. Prism A ◯ Prism B

13. Prism B ◯ Prism C

14. Prism C ◯ Prism A

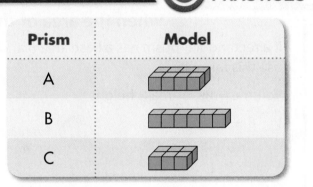

Prism	Model
A	
B	
C	

15. If you added another layer of unit cubes on top of Prism A, what would its volume be in cubic units?

16. If you put Prism C on top of Prism A, what would the volume of the new solid be in cubic units?

© **17. Construct Arguments** A jaguar is 80 inches long. A school's jaguar mascot is 7 feet long. Is the mascot longer or shorter than a real jaguar?

© **18. Reason** Ms. Kellson's storage closet is 3 feet long, 3 feet wide, and 7 feet high. Can she fit 67 boxes that each have a volume of 1 cubic foot in her closet? Explain your answer.

© **19. Think About the Structure** One carton of books had a mass of 8.4 kilograms. Ramon put a book with a mass of 1.2 kilograms into the carton and removed 2 books each with a mass of 1.1 kilograms. Which number sentence could be used to find the final mass of the carton?

A $8.4 + 1.2 + 2.2$

C $(8.4 + 1.2) \times 2 - 1.1$

B $8.4 + 1.2 - (2 \times 1.1)$

D $8.4 + 1.2 + 2(1.1)$

© Common Core

5.MD.5.a Find the volume of a right rectangular prism with whole-number side lengths by packing it with unit cubes, and show that the volume is the same as would be found by multiplying the edge lengths, equivalently by multiplying the height by the area of the base. Represent threefold whole-number products as volumes, e.g., to represent the associative property of multiplication. 5.MD.5.b Apply the formulas V = l × w × h and V = b × h for rectangular prisms to find volumes of right rectangular prisms with whole-number edge lengths in the context of solving real world and mathematical problems. Also 5.MD.5

Volume

How can you use a formula to find the volume of a rectangular prism?

Remember that volume is the number of cubic units (units³) needed to fill a solid figure.

Find the volume of the rectangular prism at the right if each cubic unit represents 1 cubic foot.

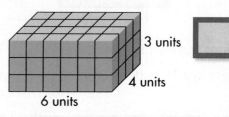

3 units

4 units

6 units

Another Example **How can you find the volume of a rectangular prism when the area of the base is given?**

If a rectangular prism has a base area *B* and a height *h*, use this formula:

Volume = base area × height

$V = B \times h$

Tip *Base area is equal to* $\ell \times w$

height

base

Find the volume of a rectangular prism with a base area of 56 cm² and a height of 6 cm.

$V = B \times h$

$V = 56 \times 6$

$V = 336 \text{ cm}^3$

The volume of the rectangular prism is 336 cm³.

6 cm

Area of base: 56 cm²

Explain It

1. In the example above, what are possible length and width dimensions of the base of the rectangular prism shown? Explain.

2. How is counting cubes related to the formulas for finding volume?

3. How do you know which formula for volume to use?

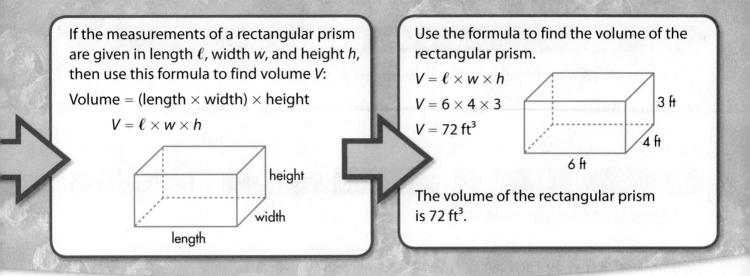

If the measurements of a rectangular prism are given in length ℓ, width w, and height h, then use this formula to find volume V:

Volume = (length × width) × height

$$V = \ell \times w \times h$$

height
width
length

Use the formula to find the volume of the rectangular prism.

$$V = \ell \times w \times h$$
$$V = 6 \times 4 \times 3$$
$$V = 72 \text{ ft}^3$$

3 ft
4 ft
6 ft

The volume of the rectangular prism is 72 ft³.

Guided Practice*

MATHEMATICAL PRACTICES

Do you know HOW?

In **1** through **3**, find the volume of each rectangular prism.

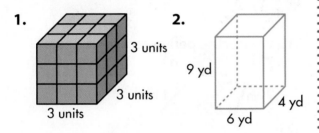

1.
3 units
3 units
3 units

2.
9 yd
4 yd
6 yd

3. Base area: 26 m²
height: 4 m

Do you UNDERSTAND?

4. In the example above, could you first multiply the height by the width?

5. A cereal box measures 6 in. × 2 in. × 10 in. Draw a rectangular prism and label it. What is the volume of the figure you drew?

Ⓒ **6. Model** How can you use different methods to find the volumes of the prisms in Exercises 1–3?

Independent Practice

In **7** through **12**, find the volume of each rectangular prism.

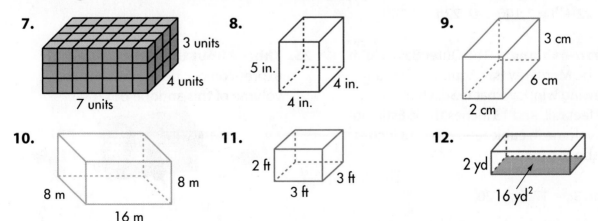

7.
3 units
4 units
7 units

8.
5 in.
4 in.
4 in.

9.
3 cm
6 cm
2 cm

10.
8 m
8 m
16 m

11.
2 ft
3 ft
3 ft

12.
2 yd
16 yd²

For **13** through **15**, find the volume of each rectangular prism.

13. Length: 8 in., width: 7 in., height: 5 in.

14. Base area: 100 ft² height: 17 ft

15. Base area: 72 yd² height: 8 yd

Problem Solving

MATHEMATICAL
PRACTICES

For **16** through **18**, use the information below.

Sixty-four students are planning a field trip to an art museum. Each student will pay $9. Each van can hold 7 students and 1 driver.

16. How much money will be collected if all the students attend?

17. How many vans will be needed if all the students travel to the museum?

18. Persevere The school pays each driver $60 to drive the van. If the round trip takes 4 hours, how much does each driver make per hour?

19. A refrigerator measures 6 feet tall, 4 feet wide, and 3 feet deep. What is the volume of the refrigerator?

20. Only 3 students in each event win medals at the track meet. If 9 students are running the mile, what fraction of them will win a medal?

21. What is the perimeter of this figure?

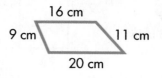

22. Last week 22 people worked a total of 1,100 hours. Each person worked the same number of hours, h. Which equation represents this situation?

A $1,100h = 22$ **C** $h \div 1,100 = 22$

B $22 \div h = 1,100$ **D** $22h = 1,100$

23. Harry is in line at the store. He has 3 items that cost $5.95, $4.25, and $1.05. Explain how Harry can add the cost of the items mentally before he pays for them.

24. Reasonableness The Outer Bay exhibit at the Monterey Bay Aquarium has a viewing window that is 56.5 feet long, 17 feet tall, and 13 inches thick. Estimate its volume in cubic feet. HINT: 13 inches is about 1 foot.

26. Find $3c - 17$ if $c = 20$.

25. Think About the Structure Which expression can be used to find the volume of this antique box?

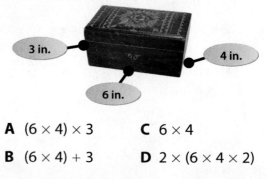

A $(6 \times 4) \times 3$ **C** 6×4

B $(6 \times 4) + 3$ **D** $2 \times (6 \times 4 \times 2)$

Mixed Problem Solving

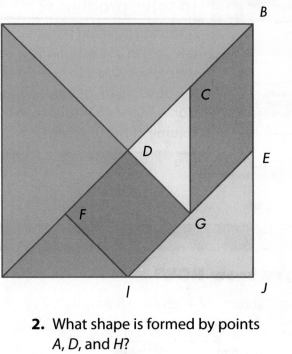

Tangrams are ancient Chinese puzzles made up of geometric shapes. All tangrams have the same seven pieces, which fit together to form a square. The objective is to create a design using all seven pieces, called tans. The tans must all be touching, but they may not overlap.

Use the above tangram for **1** through **7**.

1. What shape do the 7 pieces of the tangram make?

2. What shape is formed by points *A*, *D*, and *H*?

3. Identify three pairs of parallel line segments.

4. Identify a pair of perpendicular line segments.

5. What shape is formed by points *C*, *B*, *E*, and *G*?

6. What shape is formed by points *H*, *B*, and *J*?

7. How many triangles do you see in the tangram?

On a separate sheet of paper, use the above design to create your own tangram. Using the tans from your tangram, try to make the design at the right, using all seven tans. Make sure none of them overlap. Use the puzzle for **8** through **10**.

8. Describe the shape the tangram puzzle forms.

9. Make your own tangram puzzle from the pieces. Name your design and describe what shape your design makes.

 10. Communicate Explain how you created your own shape in Exercise 9.

Common
Core

5.MD.5.c Recognize
volume as additive.
Find volumes of solid
figures composed of two
non-overlapping right
rectangular prisms by
adding the volumes of the
non-overlapping parts,
applying this technique to
solve real world problems.
Also 5.MD.5.b

Combining Volumes

How can you use volume formulas to solve problems?

A storage building has the shape and size shown at the right. The warehouse supervisor wants to find the volume of the building to determine how much storage space is available. What is the volume of the building?

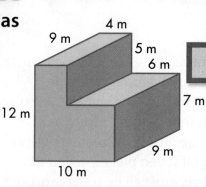

Guided Practice*

MATHEMATICAL
PRACTICES

Do you know HOW?

Find the volume of each solid figure.

1.

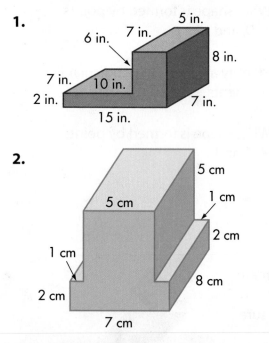

2.

Do you UNDERSTAND?

In **3** and **4**, use the shape below. The dashed line separates it into two rectangular prisms, A and B.

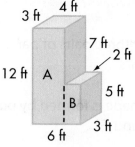

3. What are the length, width, and height of Prism A? What are the length, width, and height of Prism B?

4. Reason How else could you separate the shape into two rectangular prisms?

Independent Practice

In **5** through **7**, find the volume of each solid figure.

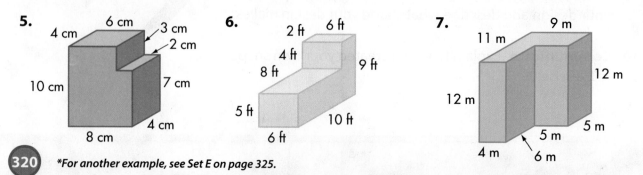

5.

6.

7.

For another example, see Set E on page 325.

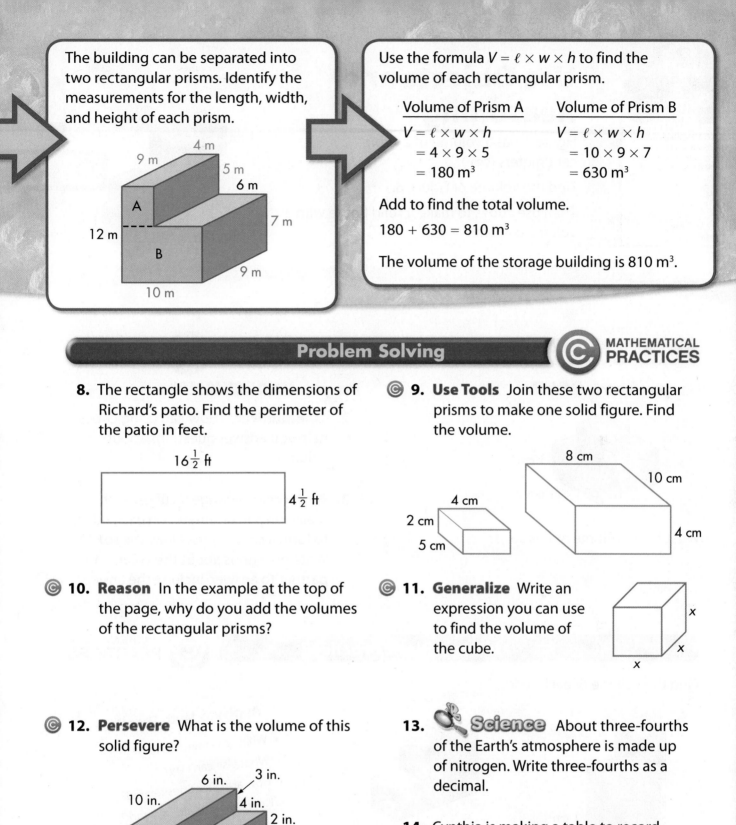

The building can be separated into two rectangular prisms. Identify the measurements for the length, width, and height of each prism.

4 m
9 m
5 m
6 m
A
7 m
12 m
B
9 m
10 m

Use the formula $V = \ell \times w \times h$ to find the volume of each rectangular prism.

Volume of Prism A

$V = \ell \times w \times h$
$= 4 \times 9 \times 5$
$= 180 \text{ m}^3$

Volume of Prism B

$V = \ell \times w \times h$
$= 10 \times 9 \times 7$
$= 630 \text{ m}^3$

Add to find the total volume.

$180 + 630 = 810 \text{ m}^3$

The volume of the storage building is 810 m³.

Problem Solving

MATHEMATICAL
PRACTICES

8. The rectangle shows the dimensions of Richard's patio. Find the perimeter of the patio in feet.

$16\frac{1}{2}$ ft

$4\frac{1}{2}$ ft

© 9. **Use Tools** Join these two rectangular prisms to make one solid figure. Find the volume.

8 cm
10 cm
4 cm
2 cm
4 cm
5 cm

© 10. **Reason** In the example at the top of the page, why do you add the volumes of the rectangular prisms?

© 11. **Generalize** Write an expression you can use to find the volume of the cube.

x
x
x

© 12. **Persevere** What is the volume of this solid figure?

6 in.   3 in.
10 in.   4 in.
2 in.
5 in.   10 in.
10 in.

A 50 in³

C 380 in³

B 260 in³

D 500 in³

13. **Science** About three-fourths of the Earth's atmosphere is made up of nitrogen. Write three-fourths as a decimal.

14. Cynthia is making a table to record the mass of objects for her science fair project. Which power of 10 can she use to convert grams to kilograms?

A 10^1

C 10^3

B 10^2

D 10^4

© **Common Core**

5.MD.4 Measure volumes by counting unit cubes, using cubic cm, cubic in, cubic ft, and improvised units.

Problem Solving

Use Objects and Reasoning

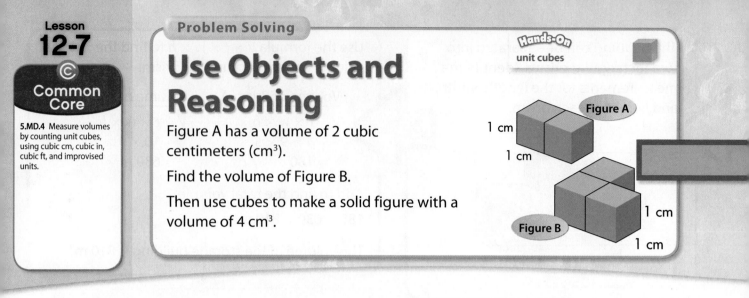

Figure A has a volume of 2 cubic centimeters (cm^3).

Find the volume of Figure B.

Then use cubes to make a solid figure with a volume of 4 cm^3.

Hands-On
unit cubes

Guided Practice*

MATHEMATICAL PRACTICES

Do you know **HOW?**

1.

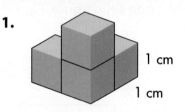

What is the volume of this solid?

Do you **UNDERSTAND?**

© 2. **Communicate** How can using cubes help you answer questions about volume?

© 3. **Be Precise** Arrange 5 cubes, each measuring 1 centimeter on each edge, to form a solid figure. Draw the solid. Write questions about the volume for a partner to answer. Include the answer.

Independent Practice

MATHEMATICAL PRACTICES

Find the volume of each solid.

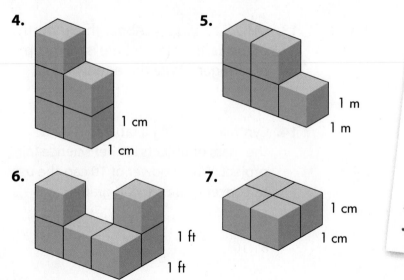

4.

5.

6.

7.

Applying Math Practices

- What am I asked to find?
- What else can I try?
- How are quantities related?
- How can I explain my work?
- How can I use math to model the problem?
- Can I use tools to help?
- Is my work precise?
- Why does this work?
- How can I generalize?

For another example, see Set C on page 325.

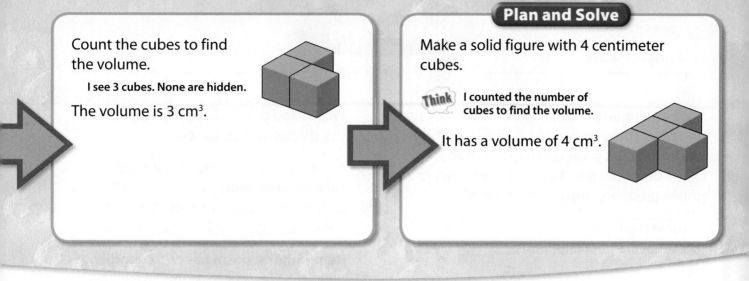

Count the cubes to find the volume.

I see 3 cubes. None are hidden.

The volume is 3 cm³.

Make a solid figure with 4 centimeter cubes.

Think I counted the number of cubes to find the volume.

It has a volume of 4 cm³.

For **8** through **13**, use cubes to make a solid with the given volume. Draw your answers.

8. Draw two other shapes with a volume of 4 cm³ that look different than the shape shown at the top of the page.

9. Look at the 4 cm³ solid shown at the top of the page. How many faces does it have?

10. Reason Matt used inch cubes to make a solid that had a volume of 5 cubic inches. What might his solid have looked like?

11. April and Julie each made differently shaped solids with a volume of 9 cubic inches. What might their 2 solids have looked like?

12. Sebastian made a solid with a volume of 6 cubic inches. What might his solid have looked like?

13. Alberto made a solid with a volume of 8 cubic inches. What might his solid have looked like?

For **14** and **15**, use centimeter cubes to help draw your pictures.

14. Draw a cube that has twice the length, width, and height of the 1 cm cube. What is the volume of the new solid?

15. Use Tools Draw a cube that has triple the length, width, and height of the 1 cm cube. What is the volume of the new solid?

Volume = 1 cubic centimeter

16. At her job, Nancy earns $75 on Saturdays and $50 on Sundays. If she works 4 weekends this month, how much money will she earn in all?

17. Aaron plants vegetables in his backyard. He has 2 separate gardens. Each garden has 4 rows with 12 plants in each row. One of the gardens receives more sunlight than the other. How many total plants does he have in his gardens?

Set A, pages 308–309

A **three-dimensional shape**, or solid, takes up space. Three-dimensional shapes that are made up of flat polygon-shaped surfaces, called **faces**, are **polyhedrons**. Two types of polyhedrons are prisms and pyramids.

A **prism** is a solid with two parallel bases and faces that are parallelograms.

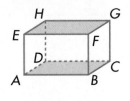

Prism

A **pyramid** is a solid with a base that is a polygon and whose other faces are triangles with a common vertex.

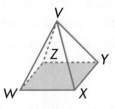

Pyramid

Faces meet along segments called **edges**, and edges meet at points called **vertices**. The singular of vertices is vertex.

Prisms and pyramids can be named by the shapes of their bases.

A pyramid with a rectangular base is called a rectangular pyramid. It has 5 faces, including its base. The faces are ▭*WXYZ*, △*WXV*, △*XYV*, △*YZV*, and △*ZWV*.

Remember A prism has two congruent parallel bases, but a pyramid has only one base.

For **1** through **5** use the solid shown below.

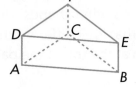

1. Name the figure.

2. Give the number of faces.

3. Give the number of edges.

4. Name the vertices.

5. Do the bases of the prism change if the prism is placed on one of its sides? Explain.

Set B, pages 310–311, 312–313

Draw the front, top, and side views of the solid made from stacked cubes.

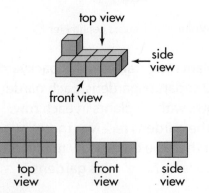

Draw the front, top, and side views of each solid made from stacked cubes.

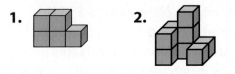

Remember to consider cubes that are hidden from your view.

1.   2.

Find the number of cubes needed to make this rectangular prism.

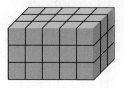

There are 3 rows of 5 cubes in the bottom layer. There are 3 layers.

So the total number of cubes is $3 \times 5 \times 3$ or 45. The volume is 45 cubic units.

Remember that you can find the number of cubes in each layer and then multiply by the number of layers.

Find each volume.

1. 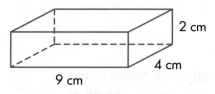 **2.**

Find the volume of this rectangular prism.

2 cm

4 cm

9 cm

Volume = length × width × height.

$V = \ell \times w \times h = 9 \text{ cm} \times 4 \text{ cm} \times 2 \text{ cm}$
$V = 72 \text{ cm}^3$

The volume of the prism is 72 cm^3.

Remember if you know the base area of a rectangular prism, use the formula $V = B \times h$, where B is the base area.

Find each volume.

1. Base area = 42 m^2, height = 3 m

2.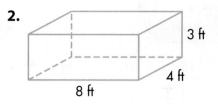

3 ft

4 ft

8 ft

Some solid figures can be separated into two rectangular prisms.

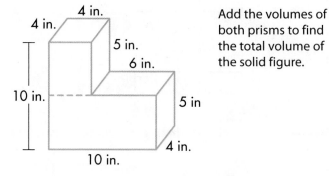

4 in.

4 in.

4 in.

5 in.

6 in.

10 in.

5 in

10 in.

4 in.

Add the volumes of both prisms to find the total volume of the solid figure.

$V = (4 \times 4 \times 5) + (10 \times 4 \times 5) = 280 \text{ in}^3$

Remember to identify the length, width, and height of each prism, so that you can calculate the volume of each part.

1. Find the volume.

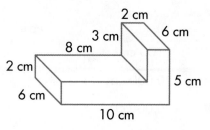

2 cm

3 cm

6 cm

8 cm

2 cm

5 cm

6 cm

10 cm

1. Which solid does the picture below resemble? (12-1)

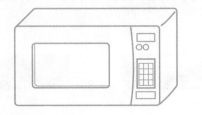

   A Cone

   B Pyramid

   C Cube

   D Prism

2. The rectangular prism below is made up of unit cubes. What is the volume of the prism? (12-4)

   A 18 cubic units

   B 54 cubic units

   C 72 cubic units

   D 108 cubic units

3. What is the volume of the bale of hay? (12-5)

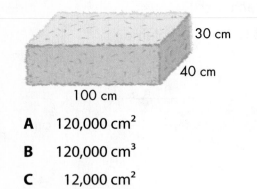

30 cm
40 cm
100 cm

   A 120,000 cm²

   B 120,000 cm³

   C 12,000 cm²

   D 12,000 cm³

4. Todd's mother is setting up a storage unit rental business. She is arranging the units in an L-shape. If she puts 3 units on each side of the L, she has 5 units in all, as shown. How many units does she have if she puts 8 units on each side of the L? (12-3)

   A 13

   B 15

   C 16

   D 17

5. Nita stacked some crates to make a bookshelf as shown. Which of the following is the top view of the crates? (12-2)

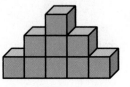

   A

   B

   C

   D

6. Henry made a tower using 9 cubes. How many cubes are NOT visible from the front view? (12-2)

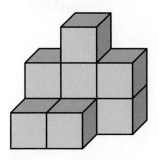

7. Draw the top view of Henry's tower. (12-2)

8. What is the volume of the steps shown? (12-6)

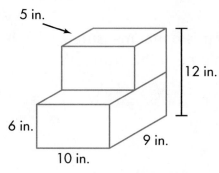

5 in.

12 in.

6 in.

9 in.

10 in.

9. The rectangular prism below is made from cubes that each measure 1 cubic meter. What is the volume of the prism? (12-4)

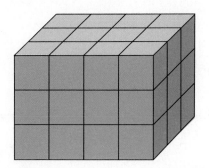

10. What is the volume of the trunk shown? (12-5)

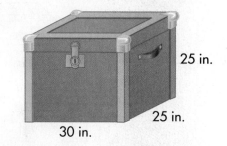

25 in.

25 in.

30 in.

11. How many faces does the trunk shown above have? (12-1)

12. How many edges does a rectangular pyramid have? (12-1)

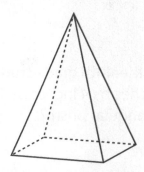

13. Todd's cube has an edge that measures 5 inches. Kara's cube has an edge of 3 inches. If Kara's cube was stacked on top of Todd's cube, what would be the total volume of the combined solid? (12-7)

A fifth-grade student built a rectangular prism shown below. Each cube the student used has a volume of 1 cubic inch.

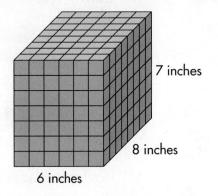

7 inches

8 inches

6 inches

1. What is the volume of the rectangular prism? Explain how you got your answer.

2. Another fifth grade student built a rectangular prism that measured 3 inches by 4 inches by 7 inches. What is the volume of this student's rectangular prism?

3. If the smaller rectangular prism were placed on top of the larger rectangular prism, what would be the combined volume of the new shape? Explain.

4. If the faces of the solid shown above were painted red, how many cubes would still be only green?

5. How many cubes in the red solid would have 3 green faces?

Topic 13 Units of Measure

▼ Diving for lobsters is popular in Key West, Florida. Lobsters typically weigh between 1 and 20 pounds. How many ounces did the heaviest lobster ever recorded weigh? You will find out in Lesson 13-3.

Review What You Know!

Vocabulary

Choose the best term from the box.

- customary
- multiplication
- metric
- subtraction

1. A meter is a unit of length in the ? system of measurement.

2. A foot is a unit of length in the ? system of measurement.

3. Division has an inverse relationship with ? .

Multiplication

Find each product.

4. 60×6 5. 24×3

6. 16×7 7. 12×16

8. 100×34 9. 10×6

Division

Find each quotient.

10. $144 \div 16$ 11. $56 \div 7$

12. $1,000 \div 100$ 13. $176 \div 16$

14. $3,600 \div 60$ 15. $120 \div 24$

Elapsed Time

Find each elapsed time.

16. Start: 4:25 P.M.   17. Start: 10:30 P.M.
    Finish: 5:10 P.M.   Finish: 12:15 A.M.

© 18. **Writing to Explain** Is the elapsed time between 11:40 A.M. and 2:20 P.M. more or less than 3 hours? Explain.

Topic Essential Questions
- What are customary measurement units and how are they related?
- What are metric measurement units and how are they related?

Interactive Learning

Pose the problem. Start each lesson by working together to solve problems. It will help you make sense of math.

Applying Math Practices

- What am I asked to find?
- What else can I try?
- How are quantities related?
- How can I explain my work?
- How can I use math to model the problem?
- Can I use tools to help?
- Is my work precise?
- Why does this work?
- How can I generalize?

Lesson 13-1

ⓒ **Use Tools** Use a ruler and a yardstick to solve.

How long is the strip of paper shown at the right in yards? In feet? In inches? Write equations to show the relationship of yards to feet, yards to inches, and feet to inches.

1 yard

Lesson 13-2

ⓒ **Use Tools** Use containers and water to solve.

A recipe makes 16 cups of soup. How many pints is this? quarts? gallons? Record how you found the measurements on your recording sheet.

Lesson 13-3

ⓒ **Reason** Use drawings, equations, or symbols to solve this problem.

Recall that 1 pound is equal to 16 oz. How many ounces does the box at the right weigh? Tell how you decided.

4 lb

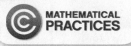

Lesson 13-4

ⓒ **Use Tools** Use your metric ruler to solve.

Choose three objects. Measure the length of each object in centimeters and millimeters. Without using the ruler, how can you convert from centimeters to millimeters and from millimeters to centimeters?

Lesson 13-5

ⓒ **Use Tools** Use containers and water to solve.

Suppose a pitcher holds 4 liters of water. How many milliliters is this? Tell how you decided.

Lesson 13-6

ⓒ **Reason** Use drawings, equations, or symbols to solve this problem.

1 g is equal to 1,000 mg. What is the mass of the marker at the right in grams? Tell how you decided.

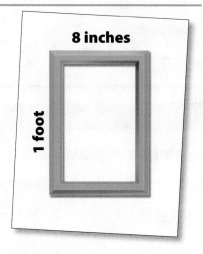

5,000 milligrams

Lesson 13-7

ⓒ **Model** Use the measurement conversions skills you learned in this topic to solve this problem.

What is the perimeter of the picture frame shown at the right? Can you express the answer in more than one way? Explain.

8 inches

1 foot

© Common Core

5.MD.1 Convert among different-sized standard measurement units within a given measurement system (e.g., convert 5 cm to 0.05 m), and use these conversions in solving multi-step, real world problems.

Converting Customary Units of Length

How do you change from one unit of length to another?

| 1 foot (ft) = 12 inches (in.) |
| 1 yard (yd) = 3 ft = 36 in. |
| 1 mile (mi) = 1,760 yd = 5,280 ft |

Some frogs can jump 11 feet. What are some other ways to describe the same distance?

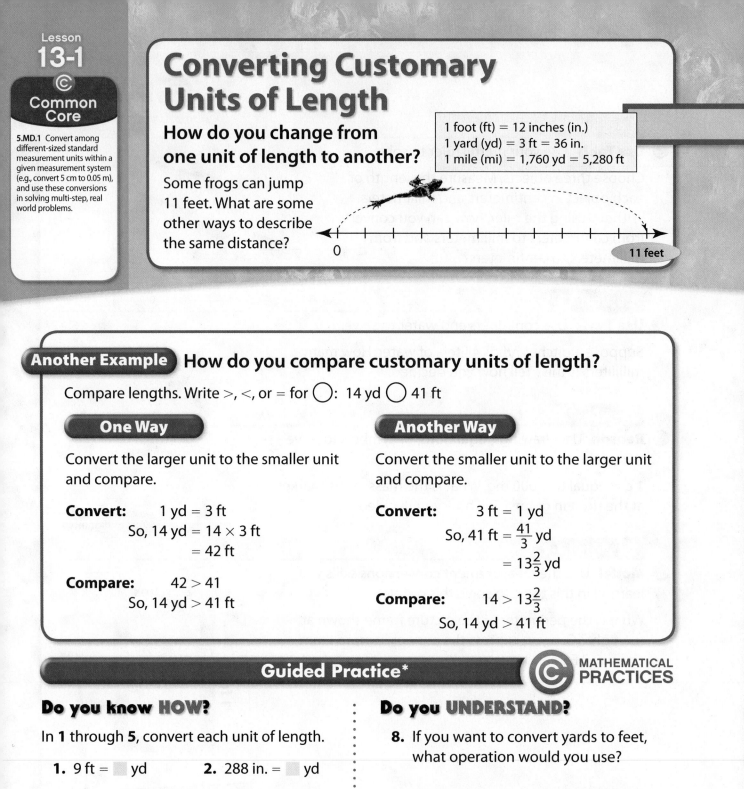

0   11 feet

Another Example How do you compare customary units of length?

Compare lengths. Write >, <, or = for ◯: 14 yd ◯ 41 ft

One Way

Convert the larger unit to the smaller unit and compare.

Convert: 1 yd = 3 ft
        So, 14 yd = 14 × 3 ft
              = 42 ft

Compare: 42 > 41
        So, 14 yd > 41 ft

Another Way

Convert the smaller unit to the larger unit and compare.

Convert: 3 ft = 1 yd
        So, 41 ft = $\frac{41}{3}$ yd
              = $13\frac{2}{3}$ yd

Compare: $14 > 13\frac{2}{3}$
        So, 14 yd > 41 ft

Guided Practice*

© MATHEMATICAL PRACTICES

Do you know HOW?

In **1** through **5**, convert each unit of length.

1. 9 ft = ▉ yd

2. 288 in. = ▉ yd

3. 5 ft = ▉ in.

4. 8 ft 7 in. = ▉ in.

5. 219 in. = ▉ ft ▉ in. or ▉ ft

For **6** and **7**, compare lengths. Write >, <, or = for each ◯.

6. 64 in. ◯ 2 yd

7. 29 yd ◯ 87 ft

Do you UNDERSTAND?

8. If you want to convert yards to feet, what operation would you use?

9. If you want to convert feet to miles, what operation would you use?

© **10. Reason** In the example at the top, explain how you could use a mixed number to write 11 feet as an equivalent measure in yards.

---

*For another example, see Set A on page 346.

To change larger units to smaller units, multiply.

11 ft = ▢ in.

Think 1 foot = 12 inches.

11 ft

| 12 in. | 12 in. | 12 in. | 12 in. | 12 in. | 12 in. | 12 in. | 12 in. | 12 in. | 12 in. | 12 in. |

↑
1 ft

Find 11 × 12.

11 × 12 = 132

11 feet = 132 inches

To change smaller units to larger units, divide.

11 ft = ▢ yd ▢ ft

Think 3 feet = 1 yard.

1 ft
↓

| 1 | 1 | 1 | 1 | 1 | 1 | 1 | 1 | 1 | 1 | 1 |

1 yd　　1 yd　　1 yd　　2 ft left

Find 11 ÷ 3.

11 ÷ 3 = 3 R2

11 feet = 3 yards, 2 feet

Independent Practice

In **11** through **22**, convert each unit of length.

Tip *You may need to make two conversions.*

11. 3 yd = ▢ in.

12. 24 ft = ▢ yd

13. 2 mi = ▢ ft

14. 56 ft = ▢ yd ▢ ft

15. 12 ft 7 in. = ▢ in.

16. 6 in. = ▢ ft

17. 4 yd = ▢ in.

18. 10 yd = ▢ in.

19. 18 ft = ▢ in.

20. 2 mi = ▢ yd

21. 5,280 ft = ▢ mi

22. 15 yd 6 ft = ▢ ft

For **23** through **25**, compare lengths. Write >, <, or = for each ◯.

23. 100 ft ◯ 3 yd

24. 74 in. ◯ 2 yd 2 in.

25. 5,200 ft 145 in. ◯ 1 mi 40 in.

Problem Solving

MATHEMATICAL PRACTICES

26. The lighthouse in Yokohama, Japan, is known as the tallest in the world. It is 348 feet tall. How many yards tall is this lighthouse?

© **27.** **Reason** The dimensions of the nation's smallest post office are 8 ft 4 in. × 7 ft 3 in. Why would you use the measurement 8 ft 4 in. instead of 7 ft 16 in?

28. Ariana had 144 peaches. She has to pack 9 boxes with an equal number of peaches. How many peaches should she pack in each box?

144 peaches

| ? | ? | ? | ? | ? | ? | ? | ? | ? |

↑
Peaches per box

© **29.** **Persevere** The New York City Marathon is 26 miles, 385 yards. How many feet is this?

A 5,306 ft

B 45,760 ft

C 138,435 ft

D 1,647,360 ft

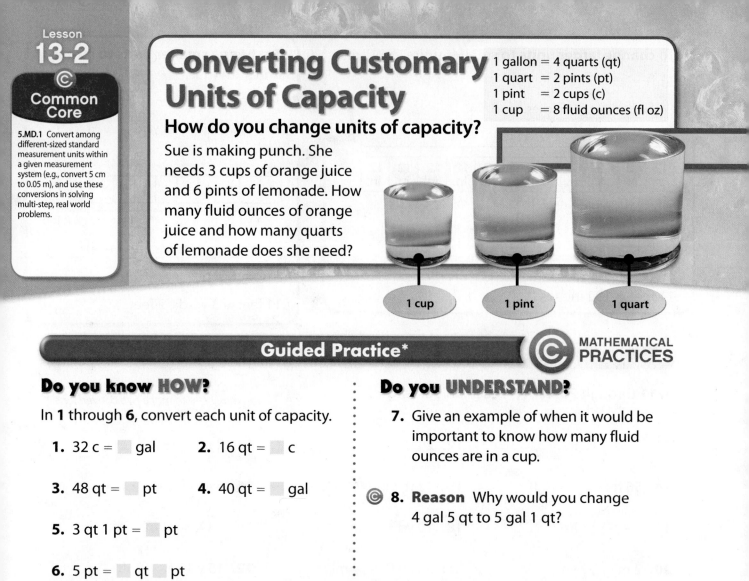

Converting Customary Units of Capacity

1 gallon = 4 quarts (qt)
1 quart = 2 pints (pt)
1 pint = 2 cups (c)
1 cup = 8 fluid ounces (fl oz)

How do you change units of capacity?

Sue is making punch. She needs 3 cups of orange juice and 6 pints of lemonade. How many fluid ounces of orange juice and how many quarts of lemonade does she need?

1 cup   1 pint   1 quart

Guided Practice*

MATHEMATICAL PRACTICES

Do you know HOW?

In **1** through **6**, convert each unit of capacity.

1. 32 c = ☐ gal   **2.** 16 qt = ☐ c

3. 48 qt = ☐ pt   **4.** 40 qt = ☐ gal

5. 3 qt 1 pt = ☐ pt

6. 5 pt = ☐ qt ☐ pt

Do you UNDERSTAND?

7. Give an example of when it would be important to know how many fluid ounces are in a cup.

8. Reason Why would you change 4 gal 5 qt to 5 gal 1 qt?

Independent Practice

In **9** through **26**, convert each unit of capacity. You may need to convert more than once.

9. 10 pt = ☐ qt   **10.** 48 fl oz = ☐ c   **11.** 70 c = ☐ pt

12. 15 pt = ☐ c   **13.** 36 pt = ☐ qt   **14.** 30 qt = ☐ gal ☐ qt

15. 7 c = ☐ fl oz   **16.** 4 qt 1 pt = ☐ pt   **17.** 8 gal = ☐ pt

18. 1 qt = ☐ gal   **19.** 5 gal = ☐ c   **20.** 1 gal 1 c = ☐ fl oz

21. 4 pt 3 c = ☐ c   **22.** 10 gal = ☐ c   **23.** 2 gal = ☐ fl oz

24. 17 pt = ☐ c   **25.** 64 fl oz = ☐ c   **26.** 12 gal = ☐ c

*For another example, see Set B on page 346.

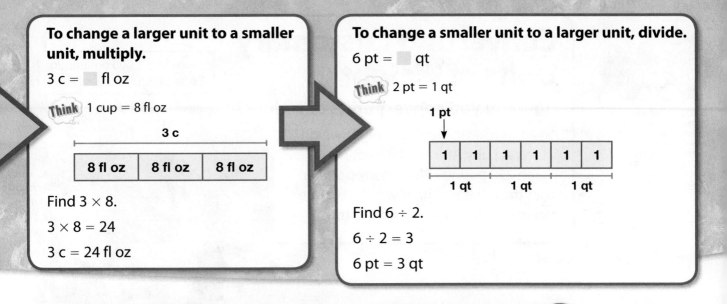

To change a larger unit to a smaller unit, multiply.

3 c = ☐ fl oz

Think 1 cup = 8 fl oz

3 c

8 fl oz	8 fl oz	8 fl oz

Find 3 × 8.

3 × 8 = 24

3 c = 24 fl oz

To change a smaller unit to a larger unit, divide.

6 pt = ☐ qt

Think 2 pt = 1 qt

1 pt

1	1	1	1	1	1

1 qt   1 qt   1 qt

Find 6 ÷ 2.

6 ÷ 2 = 3

6 pt = 3 qt

Problem Solving

MATHEMATICAL PRACTICES

27. The Turtle Bend habitat holds 30,000 gallons of water. How many quarts of water can the exhibit hold?

   A 15,000   **B** 60,000   **C** 120,000   **D** 240,000

28. Model One tablespoon (tbsp) equals 3 teaspoons (tsp) and 1 fluid ounce equals 2 tablespoons. A recipe calls for 3 tablespoons of pineapple juice. A jar of pineapple juice has 12 fluid ounces. How many teaspoons of juice are in the jar?

For **29** through **32**, refer to the aquarium at the right.

29. The class aquarium holds 2 gallons of water. How many cups is this?

30. Use Tools Find the volume of the aquarium in cubic inches.

31. If the class buys two more aquariums that are the same size, how many pints of water will they need to fill all 3 aquariums?

32. What is the perimeter of the base of the aquarium?

33. If all of the dimensions of the aquarium were doubled, what would be the volume of the new aquarium?

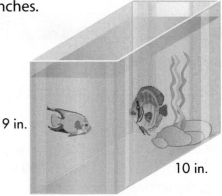

9 in.

10 in.

6 in.

© Common Core

5.MD.1 Convert among different-sized standard measurement units within a given measurement system (e.g., convert 5 cm to 0.05 m), and use these conversions in solving multi-step, real world problems.

Converting Customary Units of Weight

1 ton (T) = 2,000 pounds (lb)
1 pound (lb) = 16 ounces (oz)

How can you convert units of weight?

An adult African elephant might weigh 5 tons. A baby African elephant might weigh 250 pounds. How many pounds does the adult elephant weigh? How can you convert 250 pounds to tons?

about 250 pounds

about 5 tons

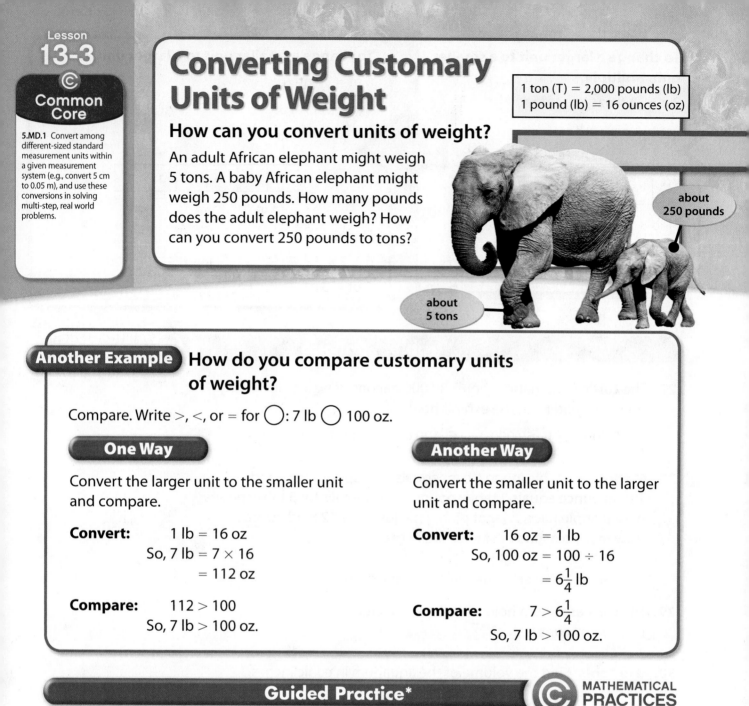

Another Example How do you compare customary units of weight?

Compare. Write >, <, or = for ◯: 7 lb ◯ 100 oz.

One Way

Convert the larger unit to the smaller unit and compare.

Convert: 1 lb = 16 oz
So, 7 lb = 7 × 16
= 112 oz

Compare: 112 > 100
So, 7 lb > 100 oz.

Another Way

Convert the smaller unit to the larger unit and compare.

Convert: 16 oz = 1 lb
So, 100 oz = 100 ÷ 16
= $6\frac{1}{4}$ lb

Compare: $7 > 6\frac{1}{4}$
So, 7 lb > 100 oz.

Guided Practice*

© MATHEMATICAL PRACTICES

Do you know HOW?

In **1** through **4**, convert each unit of weight.

1. 2,000 lb = ▢ T

2. 48 oz = ▢ lb

3. $\frac{1}{2}$ lb = ▢ oz

4. 16,000 lb = ▢ T

For **5** through **8**, compare. Write >, <, or = for each ◯.

5. 33 oz ◯ 2 lb

6. 2 T ◯ 4,500 lb

7. 4 lb ◯ 64 oz

8. 1 T ◯ 1,999 lb

Do you UNDERSTAND?

© **9. Construct Arguments** When you convert 16 pounds to ounces, do you multiply or divide? Explain.

10. Estimate the number of tons in 10,145 pounds.

11. An adult giraffe can weigh up to 3,000 pounds. Does an adult giraffe or an adult elephant weigh more?

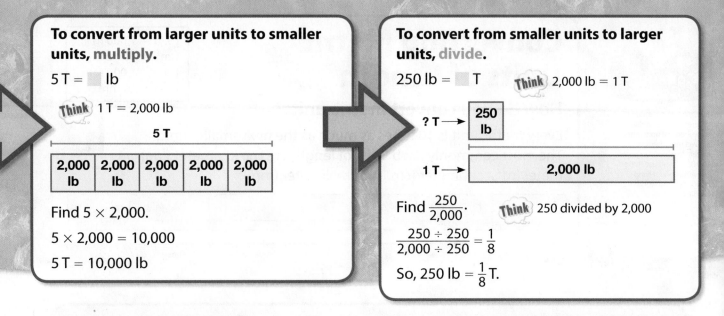

To convert from larger units to smaller units, multiply.

5 T = ▨ lb

Think 1 T = 2,000 lb

5 T

2,000 lb	2,000 lb	2,000 lb	2,000 lb	2,000 lb

Find 5 × 2,000.

5 × 2,000 = 10,000

5 T = 10,000 lb

To convert from smaller units to larger units, divide.

250 lb = ▨ T   **Think** 2,000 lb = 1 T

? T → | 250 lb |

1 T → | 2,000 lb |

Find $\frac{250}{2,000}$.   **Think** 250 divided by 2,000

$\frac{250 \div 250}{2,000 \div 250} = \frac{1}{8}$

So, 250 lb = $\frac{1}{8}$ T.

Independent Practice

In **12** through **20**, convert each unit of weight. Some of your answers will be fractions.

12. 64 oz = ▨ lb

13. 5 T = ▨ lb

14. 6,000 lb = ▨ T

15. 240 oz = ▨ lb

16. 8 T = ▨ lb

17. 8 lb = ▨ oz

18. 8 oz = ▨ lb

19. 1,000 lb = ▨ T

20. 1 T = ▨ oz

For **21** through **23**, compare. Write >, <, or = for each ◯.

21. 5,000 lb ◯ 3 T

22. 24 lb ◯ 124 oz

23. 32,000 oz ◯ 1 T

Problem Solving

Ⓒ MATHEMATICAL PRACTICES

Ⓒ **24. Use Structure** The world's heaviest lobster weighed 44 pounds, 6 ounces. How many ounces did the lobster weigh? Describe the steps you took to find your answer.

Ⓒ **25. Be Precise** How many ounces are equal to $1\frac{1}{2}$ pounds?

In **26** through **28**, use the table at the right to compare the weights of the animals. Write >, <, or = for each ◯.

26. 4 sheep ◯ 6 chimpanzees

27. 1 horse ◯ 4 dolphins

28. 20 chimpanzees ◯ 1 horse

Weights of Animals	
Chimpanzee	100 lb
Sheep	200 lb
Dolphin	400 lb
Horse	1,500 lb

© Common Core

5.MD.1 Convert among different-sized standard measurement units within a given measurement system (e.g., convert 5 cm to 0.05 m), and use these conversions in solving multi-step, real world problems.

Converting Metric Units of Length

1 km = 1,000 m
1 m = 100 cm
1 m = 1,000 mm
1 cm = 10 mm

How do you convert metric units?

Every metric unit is 10 times as much as the next smaller unit. The most commonly used units of length are the kilometer (km), meter (m), centimeter (cm), and millimeter (mm).

1 kilometer 1,000 m	1 hectometer 100 m	1 dekameter 10 m	1 meter 1 m	1 decimeter 0.1 m	1 centimeter 0.01 m	1 millimeter 0.001 m

---

Another Example **How do you compare metric units?**

Compare lengths. Write >, <, or = for ◯ : 12 m ◯ 800 cm

One Way

Convert the larger unit to the smaller unit and compare.

Convert: 1 m = 100 cm
So, 12 m = 12 × 100
= 1,200 cm

Compare: 1,200 > 800
So, 12 m > 800 cm

Another Way

Convert the smaller unit to the larger unit and compare.

Convert: 100 cm = 1 m
So, 800 cm = 800 ÷ 100
= 8 m

Compare: 12 > 8
So, 12 m > 800 cm

Guided Practice*

© **MATHEMATICAL PRACTICES**

Do you know HOW?

In **1** and **2**, convert each unit of length.

1. 1000 cm = ▨ m   **2.** 58 m = ▨ mm

Compare lengths. Write >, <, or = for ◯.

3. 9,000 m ◯ 20 km

Do you UNDERSTAND?

© **4. Construct Arguments** To find the number of meters in one kilometer, why do you multiply 1 × 1,000?

© **5. Use Structure** Convert 12.5 centimeters to millimeters. Explain.

Independent Practice

In **6** through **11**, convert each unit of length.

6. 75 cm = ▨ mm

7. 120,000,000 mm = ▨ km   **8.** 121 km = ▨ cm

9. 17,000 m = ▨ km   **10.** 48,000 mm = ▨ m   **11.** 4 km = ▨ m

*For another example, see Set D on page 347.

The distance between two highway markers is 3 kilometers. How many meters is this?

$$3 \text{ km} = \boxed{} \text{ m}$$

To change from larger units to smaller units, multiply.

(Think) 1 km = 1,000 m

Find 3 × 1,000.

3 km = 3,000 m

The distance between a kitchen and living room is 1,200 centimeters. How many meters is this?

$$1,200 \text{ cm} = \boxed{} \text{ m}$$

To change from smaller units to larger units, divide.

(Think) 100 cm = 1 m

Find 1,200 ÷ 100.

1,200 cm = 12 m

For **12** through **17**, compare lengths. Write >, <, or = for each $\bigcirc$.

12. 25,365 cm $\bigcirc$ 30 m

13. 36 km $\bigcirc$ 36,000 m

14. 1,200 mm $\bigcirc$ 12 m

15. 52,800 cm $\bigcirc$ 1 km

16. 7,500,000 m $\bigcirc$ 750 km

17. 800 m $\bigcirc$ 799,999 mm

Problem Solving

MATHEMATICAL
PRACTICES

For **18**, use the photo at the right.

18. About how many millimeters long is this dinosaur skull bone?

© **19. Use Tools** What is the equivalent length of the bumblebee bat in centimeters?

A 0.03

B 13

C 3

D 300

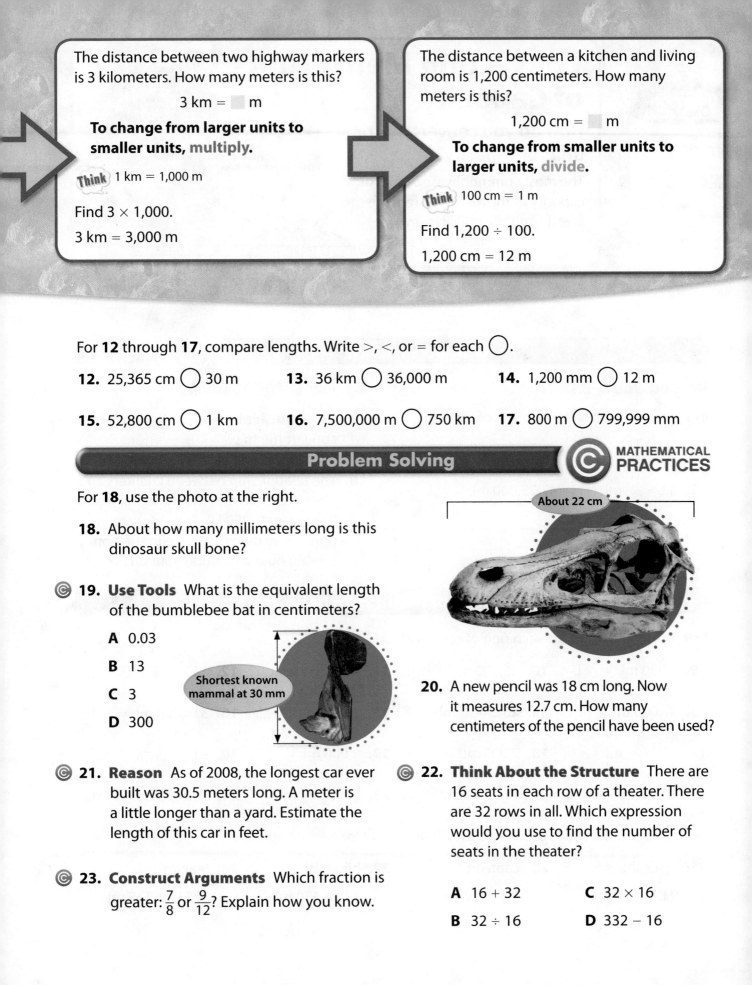

About 22 cm

Shortest known mammal at 30 mm

20. A new pencil was 18 cm long. Now it measures 12.7 cm. How many centimeters of the pencil have been used?

© **21. Reason** As of 2008, the longest car ever built was 30.5 meters long. A meter is a little longer than a yard. Estimate the length of this car in feet.

© **22. Think About the Structure** There are 16 seats in each row of a theater. There are 32 rows in all. Which expression would you use to find the number of seats in the theater?

A 16 + 32

C 32 × 16

B 32 ÷ 16

D 332 − 16

© **23. Construct Arguments** Which fraction is greater: $\frac{7}{8}$ or $\frac{9}{12}$? Explain how you know.

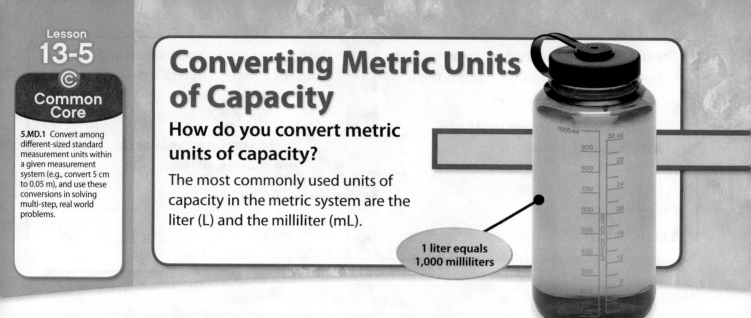

© **Common Core**

5.MD.1 Convert among different-sized standard measurement units within a given measurement system (e.g., convert 5 cm to 0.05 m), and use these conversions in solving multi-step, real world problems.

Converting Metric Units of Capacity

How do you convert metric units of capacity?

The most commonly used units of capacity in the metric system are the liter (L) and the milliliter (mL).

1 liter equals 1,000 milliliters

Guided Practice*

© **MATHEMATICAL PRACTICES**

Do you know HOW?

In **1** through **6**, convert each unit of capacity.

1. 275 L = ▮ mL　　**2.** 34,000 mL = ▮ L

3. 5 L = ▮ mL　　**4.** 25,000 mL = ▮ L

5. 227 L = ▮ mL　　**6.** 40 L = ▮ mL

Do you UNDERSTAND?

© **7. Communicate** Explain how you can convert mL to L.

8. The relationship between kiloliters and liters is the same as liters and milliliters. If there are 2,250 kiloliters of water in a pond, how many liters are in the pond? Explain how you found your answer.

Independent Practice

In **9** through **24**, convert each unit of capacity.

9. 5,000 mL = ▮ L　　**10.** 45,000 mL = ▮ L　　**11.** 427 L = ▮ mL　　**12.** 13 L = ▮ mL

13. 37,000 mL = ▮ L　　**14.** 25 L = ▮ mL　　**15.** 2,000 mL = ▮ L　　**16.** 314,000 mL = ▮ L

17. 6 L = ▮ mL　　**18.** 2,000 mL = ▮ L　　**19.** 8,000 mL = ▮ L　　**20.** 9 L = ▮ mL

21. 10,000 mL = ▮ L　　**22.** 11 L = ▮ mL　　**23.** 27 L = ▮ mL　　**24.** 100,000 mL = ▮ L

In **25** through **28**, which capacity is more reasonable for each container?

25. test tube

9 L or 200 mL

26. canteen

1 L or 100 mL

27. bird bath

4 L or 450 mL

28. teacup

325 L or 325 mL

<table>
<tr><td colspan="2">

From Liters to Milliliters

2 L = ▢ mL

To change a larger unit to a smaller unit, multiply.

Think 1 L = 1,000 mL

Find 2 × 1,000.

2 L = 2,000 mL
</td></tr>
</table>

From Liters to Milliliters

2 L = ▢ mL

To change a larger unit to a smaller unit, multiply.

Think 1 L = 1,000 mL

Find 2 × 1,000.

2 L = 2,000 mL

From Milliliters to Liters

3,000 mL = ▢ L

To change a smaller unit to a larger unit, divide.

Think 1,000 mL = 1 L

Find 3,000 ÷ 1,000.

3,000 mL = 3 L

Problem Solving

MATHEMATICAL PRACTICES

© **29. Be Precise** Café Marissa uses 43 pounds of potatoes every day. How many pounds of potatoes does the café use Monday through Sunday?

30. A drink pitcher holds 5 liters of lemonade. If each person gets 250 mL per serving, how many servings will the pitcher serve?

31. The length of a rectangular garden is 10 yards and its width is 10 feet. What is the perimeter of the garden?

  A 20 ft   **C** 80 ft

  B 20 yd   **D** 100 ft

© **32. Reason** Carla's famous punch calls for 3 liters of mango juice. The only mango juice she can find is sold in 500 mL cartons. How many cartons of mango juice does Carla need to buy?

33. Convert pounds to ounces. Complete the following table.

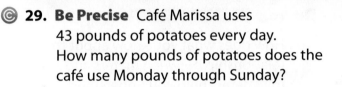

Pounds	3	4	5	6	7
Ounces	48	▢	▢	▢	▢

© **34. Think About the Structure** How can you convert from liters to milliliters?

  A Divide by 100.

  B Multiply by 100.

  C Divide by 1,000.

  D Multiply by 1,000.

35. The CN Tower in Toronto, Canada, is 553 meters tall. How tall is the tower in centimeters?

36. The area of a rectangular garden is 240 sq. ft. If the length is 20 feet, what is the width?

37. The *Canberra* was a cruise ship that had propellers that each weighed 29 tons. How many pounds did each propeller weigh?

38. The width of the *Canberra* was 102 feet. How many yards wide was the ship?

Lesson
13-6

© Common Core

5.MD.1 Convert among different-sized standard measurement units within a given measurement system (e.g., convert 5 cm to 0.05 m), and use these conversions in solving multi-step, real world problems.

Converting Metric Units of Mass

How do you convert metric units of mass?

The three most commonly used units of mass are the milligram (mg), the gram (g), and the kilogram (kg).

about 5 g

1,000 mg = 1 g
1,000 g = 1 kg

100 kg

Guided Practice*

MATHEMATICAL PRACTICES

Do you know HOW?

In **1** through **3**, convert each unit of mass.

1. 925 g = ☐ mg

2. 19,000 g = ☐ kg

3. 1,000,000 mg = ☐ kg

For **4** and **5**, compare. Write >, <, or = for each ◯.

4. 7,000 mg ◯ 7,000 g

5. 100 kg ◯ 10,000 g

Do you UNDERSTAND?

6. How does what you know about the relationship between meters and millimeters help you understand the relationship between grams and milligrams?

© **7.** **Communicate** Which has the greater mass: 1 kg or 137,000 mg? Explain how you made your comparison.

8. If you need to convert kilograms to grams, what operation would you use?

Independent Practice

In **9** through **17**, convert each unit of mass.

9. 17,000 g = ☐ kg

10. 18 kg = ☐ g

11. 420,000 mg = ☐ g

12. 276 g = ☐ mg

13. 438 kg = ☐ g

14. 43,000 mg = ☐ g

15. 238,000 g = ☐ kg

16. 3,000,000 mg = ☐ kg

17. 22 kg = ☐ g

In **18** through **23**, compare. Write >, <, or = for each ◯.

18. 2,000 g ◯ 3 kg

19. 4 kg ◯ 4,000 g

20. 10,000 mg ◯ 13 g

21. 9,000 g ◯ 8 kg

22. 7 kg ◯ 7,000 g

23. 8,000 g ◯ 5 kg

From Grams to Milligrams

$$600 \text{ g} = \boxed{} \text{ mg}$$

To change from a larger unit to a smaller unit, multiply.

Think 1 g = 1,000 mg

Find $600 \times 1{,}000$.

$600 \text{ g} = 600{,}000 \text{ mg}$

From Grams to Kilograms

$$13{,}000 \text{ g} = \boxed{} \text{ kg}$$

To change from a smaller unit to a larger unit, divide.

Think 1,000 g = 1 kg

Find $13{,}000 \div 1{,}000$.

$13{,}000 \text{ g} = 13 \text{ kg}$

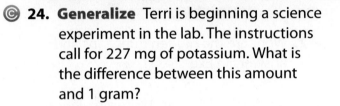

Problem Solving

MATHEMATICAL PRACTICES

ⓒ **24. Generalize** Terri is beginning a science experiment in the lab. The instructions call for 227 mg of potassium. What is the difference between this amount and 1 gram?

25. Sheryl has a recipe for pasta with vegetables. The recipe calls for 130 grams of vegetables and twice as much pasta as vegetables. What is the mass in grams of the pasta needed for the recipe?

ⓒ **26. Look for Patterns** How is converting grams to milligrams similar to converting pounds to ounces? How is it different?

27. If a man weighs 198 pounds on Earth, his mass on Earth is 90 kilograms.

　a What is this man's weight on the Moon?

28. Hummingbirds found in North America weigh about 3 grams. How many milligrams is this?

　b What is his mass on the Moon? Explain.

ⓒ **29. Persevere** Two months out of the 12 months of the year begin with the letter *A*. In simplest form, what fraction of the months begin with the letter *A*?

　A $\frac{2}{12}$

　B $\frac{10}{12}$

　C $\frac{2}{6}$

　D $\frac{1}{6}$

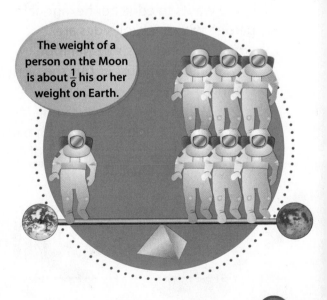

The weight of a person on the Moon is about $\frac{1}{6}$ his or her weight on Earth.

© Common Core

5.MD.1 Convert among different-sized standard measurement units within a given measurement system (e.g., convert 5 cm to 0.05 m), and use these conversions in solving multi-step, real world problems.

Problem Solving

Multiple-Step Problems

A city pool is in the shape of a rectangle with the dimensions shown at the right. What is the perimeter of the pool?

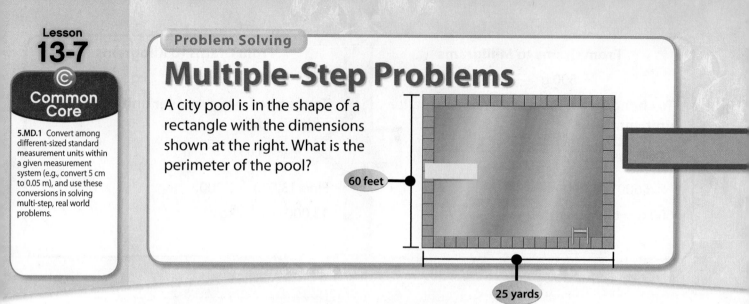

60 feet

25 yards

Guided Practice*

© MATHEMATICAL PRACTICES

Do you know HOW?

1. Stacia needs enough ribbon to wrap around the length (ℓ) and height (h) of a box. If the box length is 2 feet and the height is 4 inches, how much ribbon will she need?

h

Do you UNDERSTAND?

2. What are the hidden questions and answers in Exercise 1?

© 3. **Look for Patterns** Write a real-world multiple-step problem that involves measurement.

Independent Practice

© MATHEMATICAL PRACTICES

In **4** through **10**, write and answer the hidden question or questions. Then solve.

4. Becca wants to edge her hexagonal garden with brick. All sides are equal. The brick costs $2 per foot. How much will it cost to buy the edging she needs?

Becca's Garden

12 feet

5. If Isaac buys 12 tickets, how much money will he save by buying in groups of 4 tickets instead of individually?

$1 per ticket $3 for 4 tickets

Applying Math Practices

* What am I asked to find?
* What else can I try?
* How are quantities related?
* How can I explain my work?
* How can I use math to model the problem?
* Can I use tools to help?
* Is my work precise?
* Why does this work?
* How can I generalize?

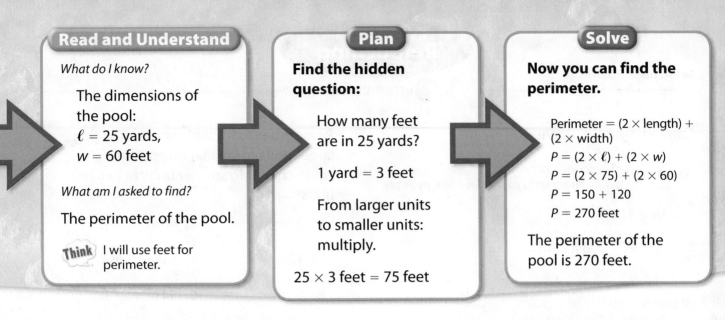

Read and Understand

What do I know?

The dimensions of the pool:
ℓ = 25 yards,
w = 60 feet

What am I asked to find?

The perimeter of the pool.

Think I will use feet for perimeter.

Plan

Find the hidden question:

How many feet are in 25 yards?

1 yard = 3 feet

From larger units to smaller units: multiply.

25 × 3 feet = 75 feet

Solve

Now you can find the perimeter.

Perimeter = (2 × length) + (2 × width)

$P = (2 \times \ell) + (2 \times w)$

$P = (2 \times 75) + (2 \times 60)$

$P = 150 + 120$

$P = 270$ feet

The perimeter of the pool is 270 feet.

6. Matt's family is thinking about buying a family pass to the city pool. The pass is $80 for a family of 4. Individual passes are $25 each. How much money can Matt's family save by purchasing a family pass instead of 4 individual passes?

7. Marcia is attending the annual library book sale. Paperback books are $0.50 and hardcover books are $1.00. Marcia buys 8 paperback books and 7 hardcover books. If she pays with one $10 bill and one $5 bill, how much change does she receive?

8. Raul wants to put wood shavings in his rabbit's cage. The floor of the cage measures 3 ft wide by 5 ft long. One bag of shavings covers 10 square feet.

   How many bags will Raul have to buy to cover the floor of the cage?

9. Cheryl's fish tank is 2 yd long by 24 in. wide by 3 ft high. What is the volume of Cheryl's tank in cubic inches? (Hint: Volume = $\ell \times w \times h$)

© 10. **Model** Joann wants to put a wallpaper border around her room. The border costs $3 per foot. The diagram at the right shows Joann's room. How much money will the border cost?

```
        ⊢ 6 feet ⊣
  ┬     ┌─────────┐
  |     │         │
  |     │         │
8 feet  │         │
  |     │         │
  |     │         │
  ┴ ⊢───────────11 feet───────────┤
```

11. Some statistics about a typical adult Royal antelope are shown at the right.

    a What is a typical Royal antelope's tail length in millimeters?

    b How many centimeters high can a typical Royal antelope jump?

    c What is the mass of a typical Royal antelope in grams?

An Adult Royal Antelope	
Head and body length	43 cm
Tail length	6 cm
Mass	2.4 kg
Vertical leap	2 m

Set A, pages 332–333

Convert 3 yards to inches.

Think 1 yard = 36 inches.
To change larger units to smaller units, multiply.

$3 \times 36 = 108$

So, 3 yards = 108 inches.

1 foot (ft) = 12 inches (in.)
1 yard (yd) = 3 ft = 36 in.
1 mile (mi) = 1,760 yd = 5,280 ft

Remember to multiply when changing larger units to smaller units and to divide when changing smaller units to larger units.

1. 2 ft = ▨ in.   **2.** 48 in. = ▨ ft

3. 12 ft = ▨ yd   **4.** 5 ft = ▨ in.

5. 5 yd = ▨ ft   **6.** 54 in. = ▨ ft

Compare. Write >, <, or = for each ◯.

7. 7 yd ◯ 50 ft   **8.** 212 in. ◯ 2 yd

9. 4 ft 8 in. ◯ 1 yd 2 ft 1 in.

Set B, pages 334–335

Convert 16 cups to pints.

Think 2 cups = 1 pint. To change smaller units to larger units, divide.

$16 \div 2 = 8$

So, 16 cups = 8 pints.

Remember that 1 gal = 4 qt, 1 qt = 2 pt, and 1 pt = 2 cups.

Convert.

1. 32 c = ▨ gal   **2.** 6 pt = ▨ qt

3. 4 qt = ▨ c   **4.** 2 gal = ▨ pt

5. 4 gal = ▨ qt   **6.** 6 pt = ▨ c

7. List 12 pt, 3 gal, and 16 cups in order from least to greatest.

Set C, pages 336–337

Convert 6 pounds to ounces.

Think 1 pound = 16 ounces.
To change larger units to smaller units, multiply.

$6 \times 16 = 96$

So, 6 pounds = 96 ounces.

To compare customary units, convert one of the units first, so that you can compare like units.

Remember that there are 16 ounces in one pound, and there are 2,000 pounds in one ton.

Complete.

1. 2 lb = ▨ oz   **2.** 48 oz = ▨ lb

3. 4,000 lb = ▨ T   **4.** 6 T = ▨ lb

5. 7 lb ◯ 70 oz   **6.** 6,000 oz ◯ 3 T

7. How many ounces are equivalent to one fourth of one ton?

Convert 2 meters to centimeters.

1 km = 1,000 m	1 m = 100 cm
1 m = 1,000 mm	1 cm = 10 mm

Think 1 meter = 100 centimeters.
To change larger units to smaller units, multiply.

$2 \times 100 = 200$

So, 2 meters = 200 centimeters.

Remember to convert to the same unit of measure before comparing two lengths.

Convert.

1. 5 m =   cm   **2.** 2 km =   m

3. 2 km =   cm   **4.** 20 m =   mm

5. 10 cm =   mm   **6.** 2,000 mm =   m

7. 9,000 m =   km

Convert 6,000 milliliters to liters.

Think 1,000 milliliters = 1 liter. To change smaller units to larger units, divide.

$6,000 \div 1,000 = 6$

So, 6,000 milliliters = 6 liters.

Remember that the most commonly used metric units of capacity are the liter and milliliter.

Convert.

1. 6 L =   mL   **2.** 15 L =   mL

3. 2,000 mL =   L   **4.** 9,000 mL =   L

Convert 6 kilograms (kg) to grams (g).

Think 1 kilogram = 1,000 grams.
To change larger units to smaller units, multiply.

$6 \times 1,000 = 6,000$

So, 6 kg = 6,000 g.

Remember that to compare metric units, convert one of the units first, so that you can compare like units.

Complete.

1. 30 kg =   g   **2.** 3,000 mg =   g

3. 5,000 g =   kg   **4.** 17 g =   mg

In a contest, Lina jumped 3 yards and Ed jumped 8 feet. Who jumped farther?

Identify the hidden question or questions.
How many feet are in 3 yards?
1 yd = 3 ft, so 3 yd = 9 ft.

Compare the two distances.
Lina jumped 9 feet, Ed jumped 8 feet. So, Lina jumped farther.

Remember to check if the units in the problem are the same.

1. Max wants to put a fence around his triangular garden. If each side is 6 yards, how many feet of fencing does Max need?

Multiple Choice

1. Which inequality is NOT true? (13-6)

   A   100 mg < 10 g

   B   2,000 kg > 2,000 g

   C   1,000,500 mg > 1 kg

   D   600 g > 6 kg

2. Which of the following is true? (13-4)

   A   100 cm < 500 mm

   B   100 cm > 3 m

   C   100 cm > 1 km

   D   100 cm = 1 m

3. Which inequality is NOT true? (13-1)

   A   3 ft 11 in. < 1 yd 1 ft

   B   75 in. > 2 yd

   C   1 yd 9 ft > 4 yd

   D   3 yd 8 in. < 12 ft 4 in.

4. The nutrition label on a carton of soy milk says that one glass contains 7 grams of protein. How many milligrams of protein does one glass contain? (13-6)

   A   7 milligrams

   B   70 milligrams

   C   700 milligrams

   D   7,000 milligrams

5. Mason made 5 quarts of salsa. Which of the following can be used to find the number of cups of salsa Mason made? (13-2)

   A $5 \times 2 \times 2$

   B $5 \times 4 \times 4$

   C $5 \div 2 \div 2$

   D $5 \times 4 \times 2$

6. Ten bales of cotton weigh about 5,000 pounds. Which comparison is true? (13-3)

   A   5,000 pounds < 10,000 ounces

   B   5,000 pounds = 3 Tons

   C   5,000 pounds < 3 Tons

   D   5,000 pounds > 3 Tons

7. Which of the following can be used to find how many kilograms of sweet potatoes the recipe calls for? (13-6)

Data

Soup Recipe
1 onion
2,000 grams sweet potatoes
3 liters water
15 milliliters chicken stock

   A $1,000 \div 2,000$

   B $2,000 \div 1,000$

   C $2,000 \times 1,000$

   D $2,000 \times 100$

8. A ship is 180 meters in length. How many centimeters are equal to 180 meters? (13-4)

9. The tail of a Boeing 747 is 63 feet 8 inches tall. How many inches tall is the tail? (13-1)

10. Leaving the water running while brushing your teeth can use 11 liters of water. How many milliliters is 11 liters? (13-5)

11. Recently, the largest watermelon on record weighed 269 pounds. How many ounces did it weigh? (13-3)

12. Juanita has a pail with a capacity of 96 fluid ounces. How many pints will the pail hold? (13-2)

13. One event for swim team tryouts is to see how far an athlete can swim. The results of the top athletes are shown in the table. How many meters did Alex swim? (13-4)

Student	Distance
Alex	1 km 200 m
Santo	1,100 m
Jake	1,300 m
Savannah	1 km 500 m

14. A container of orange juice holds 2,000 milliliters. How many liters is that? (13-5)

15. Find the perimeter of the rectangle below in inches. (13-7)

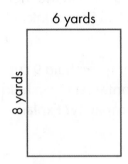

6 yards

8 yards

16. Joann decides to paint one wall in her room with blackboard paint. The wall has the dimensions shown. A can of paint covers 25 square feet. How many cans of blackboard paint does Joann need for the wall? (13-7)

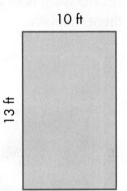

10 ft

13 ft

1. Eric has two rock samples. One has a mass of 600 grams, and the other has a mass of 1 kilogram. He recorded the total mass as 7 kilograms. What did he do wrong? What is the correct answer?

2. Brad read that you should drink at least 2 quarts of water a day. Yesterday he drank 3 cups in the morning, 1 quart in the afternoon, and 1 pint in the evening. Did Brad drink at least 2 quarts of water? Explain.

3. Container A can hold 9 cups of liquid. Container B can hold 5 pints of liquid. Container C can hold 2 quarts of liquid. Which container has the greatest capacity? Explain.

4. Jessica found the number of ounces in 80 pounds. She said it was 5 ounces. What did she do wrong? Give the correct answer.

5. Mihir is building a dog pen and wants to give his dog at least 500 ft² of space. If his side yard is 12 yd by 5 yd, does he have enough space to build the pen there? Explain.

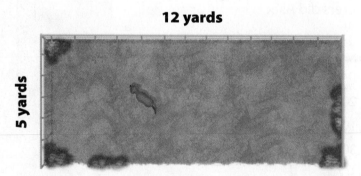

12 yards

5 yards

6. Mihir gets another dog and wants to divide the length of the dog pen in half. What are the new dimensions for each half of the dog yard? What is the area each dog will have to roam in square feet?

Topic
14 **Data**

▼ How many Giant Pandas have been born in United States zoos? You will find out in Lesson 14-3.

Review What You Know!

Vocabulary

Choose the best term from the box.

- minutes   - seconds
- yards   - thermometer

1. A ? is used to measure temperature.

2. There are 60 ? in one hour.

3. There are 60 ? in one minute.

Telling Time

Find the time.

4.   5.

6.   7.

Reading a Thermometer

Find the temperature in Fahrenheit and Celsius.

8.   °F   °C   9.   °F   °C
   90   30   80
   80   70   20
                       60

©10. **Writing to Explain** Yolanda practices piano 2 hours a week. Pete practices piano 120 minutes a week. They both think that they spend more time practicing. Who is correct?

Topic Essential Questions
- How can line plots be used to represent data and answer questions?
- How can numbers be used to describe certain data sets?

Interactive Learning

Pose the problem. Start each lesson by working together to solve problems. It will help you make sense of math.

Applying Math Practices

- What am I asked to find?
- What else can I try?
- How are quantities related?
- How can I explain my work?
- How can I use math to model the problem?
- Can I use tools to help?
- Is my work precise?
- Why does this work?
- How can I generalize?

Lesson 14-1

© **Use Tools** There are 15 students in the class that have pets. Five students have 1 pet, three students have 2 pets, four students have 3 pets, two students have 4 pets, and one student has 8 pets. Work with a partner to display this data.

Number of Pets	Number of Students

Lesson 14-2

© **Be Precise** Take a survey: How many library books has each student in your class read during the last two weeks: 0, 1, 2, 3, 4? Make a tally chart of student responses. Work with your partner to design a different organized way to record the information collected.

Survey Data	
Books?	Students?

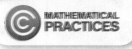

Lesson 14-3

© **Reason** How could you organize the following measurement data?
Heights of Students in Grade 5 (to the nearest $\frac{1}{2}$ inch)

$55, 48, 49\frac{1}{2}, 49\frac{1}{2}, 55, 49\frac{1}{2}, 50, 55, 49\frac{1}{2}, 55, 58\frac{1}{2}, 60, 48, 49\frac{1}{2}, 49\frac{1}{2}, 50, 55, 55, 58\frac{1}{2}, 60$

Lesson 14-4

© **Look for Patterns** Rainfall was measured for 30 days in the Amazon and graphed as a line plot.

Work with a partner to determine how you can find the total rainfall for the month.

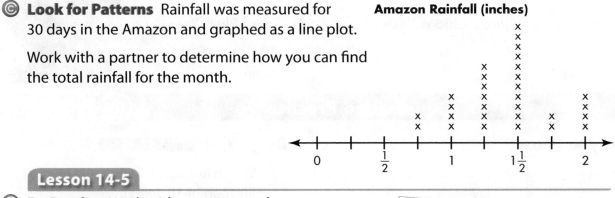

Lesson 14-5

© **Be Precise** Work with a partner and use the information on the graph to write a story about the time Jenna spent reading.

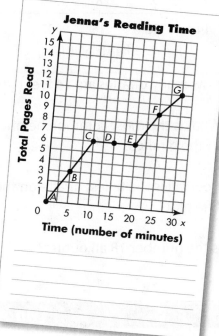

5.MD.2 Make a line plot to display a data set of measurements in fractions of a unit ($\frac{1}{2}, \frac{1}{4}, \frac{1}{8}$). Use operations on fractions for this grade to solve problems involving information presented in line plots.

Line Plots

How can you organize data using a line plot?

A line plot <u>shows data along a number line</u>. Each *X* represents one number in the data set. An outlier <u>is any number that is very different from the rest of the numbers.</u>

The table below shows the average lifespans of certain animals in years. Make a line plot to organize the data.

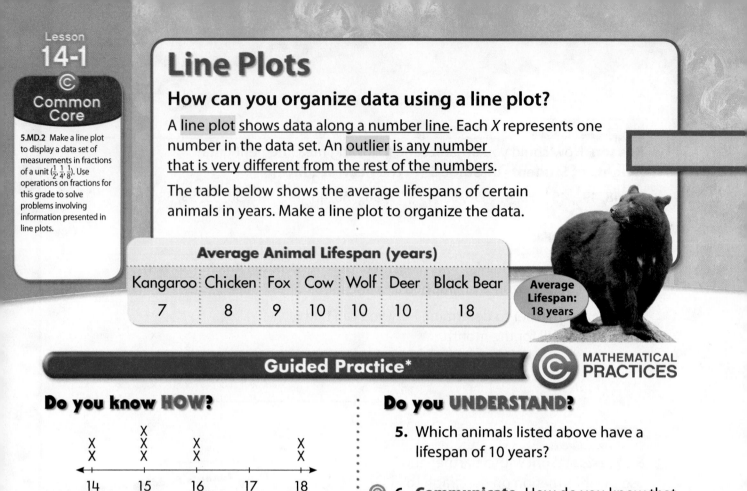

Average Animal Lifespan (years)						
Kangaroo	Chicken	Fox	Cow	Wolf	Deer	Black Bear
7	8	9	10	10	10	18

Average Lifespan: 18 years

Guided Practice*

MATHEMATICAL PRACTICES

Do you know HOW?

```
                X
  X      X      X            X
  X      X      X            X
  +---+---+---+---+---+
  14  15  16  17  18
```
Giraffe Heights (feet)

1. How many giraffes are 14 feet tall?

2. What is the most common height of the giraffes?

3. How tall is the tallest giraffe on the line plot?

4. Is the number 18 an outlier?

Do you UNDERSTAND?

5. Which animals listed above have a lifespan of 10 years?

ⓒ **6. Communicate** How do you know that the lifespan of the bear is an outlier by looking at the line plot?

ⓒ **7. Reason** A mouse has an average lifespan of 2 years. If you included this information on the line plot above, how would it affect the line plot?

Independent Practice

For **8** through **13**, draw a line plot for each data set and identify any outliers.

8. 6, 9, 3, 11, 26

9. 13, 16, 18, 3, 25

10. 18, 17, 11, 15, 29, 14, 16

11. 15, 16, 2, 31, 12

12. 17, 17, 16, 18, 21

13. 25, 28, 22, 24, 27, 28, 21

Animated Glossary
www.pearsonsuccessnet.com

Read the line plot.

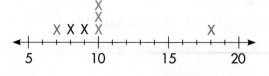

The most *X*s are at 10 so the most common lifespan of the animals in the table is 10 years.

The longest lifespan shown is 18 years and the shortest lifespan shown is 7 years.

Identify any outliers.

The X above the 18 is far from the rest of the Xs on the line plot.

The lifespan of the black bear, which is 18 years, is an outlier.

Problem Solving

For **14** through **16**, use the data to the right.

© **14. Use Tools** Trisha's swimming coach recorded the times it took her to swim one lap each day last week. Make a line plot of Trisha's lap times.

15. Which time is an outlier in the data?

16. If you made a line plot of Trisha's time using 0 and 5 minutes as the boundaries, would the outlier be more or less obvious than if the boundaries of your line plot were 50 and 75 seconds? Explain.

Day	Time
Monday	55 seconds
Tuesday	57 seconds
Wednesday	51 seconds
Thursday	72 seconds
Friday	51 seconds

© **17. Use Tools** A sheet of coupons is in an array with 12 rows. Each row has six coupons. How many coupons are there on 100 sheets?

© **18. Critique Reasoning/Arguments** Bob listed the weights of his friends (in pounds). They were 87, 93, 89, 61, and 93. Bob said there were no outliers. Is Bob correct?

19. Six friends shared some CDs. Each friend received 3 CDs. How many CDs were there in all?

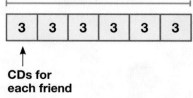

? CDs shared in all

| 3 | 3 | 3 | 3 | 3 | 3 |

CDs for each friend

© **20. Be Precise** Henry and some friends went to play miniature golf. Their scores are shown below. Make a line plot of their scores.

51, 70, 52, 51, 48, 54, 55, 52, 52

Lesson
14-2

Common
Core

5.MD.2 Make a line plot to display a data set of measurements in fractions of a unit ($\frac{1}{4}, \frac{1}{2}, \frac{1}{8}$). Use operations on fractions for this grade to solve problems involving information presented in line plots.

Data from Surveys

How can you display the data collected in a survey?

Your teacher might take a survey to find out how many pets students have at home.

A survey is a question, or questions, used to gather information called data.

When people surveyed represent a larger group, the people are a sample of the larger group. The sample should be selected randomly.

Guided Practice*

MATHEMATICAL PRACTICES

Do you know HOW?

Mr. Willis's students got the following scores on a 20-word spelling test.

16 18 17 19 18 20 18 17
20 19 17 18 19 15 17 16

1. What are the highest and lowest spelling scores?

2. Make a line plot to display the data.

Do you UNDERSTAND?

3. How might the results shown in the above example be different if the survey were taken at a pet club meeting?

4. Generalize A fifth-grade class was surveyed about their favorite type of music. Does this survey represent a sample of the entire population of our country? Why or why not?

Independent Practice

MATHEMATICAL PRACTICES

In **5** through **8**, use the line plot at the right to answer the questions.

5. How many people responded to the survey?

6. How many people have 2 or more brothers and sisters?

7. Make a frequency table that shows the same results as the line plot.

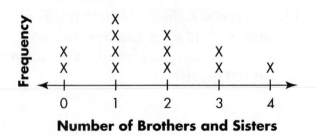

Number of Brothers and Sisters

8. Which is better for displaying a large amount of data, a frequency table or a line plot?

9. Construct Arguments Describe how you might choose a sample of 30 people that represent all the students in your entire school.

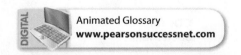
Animated Glossary
www.pearsonsuccessnet.com

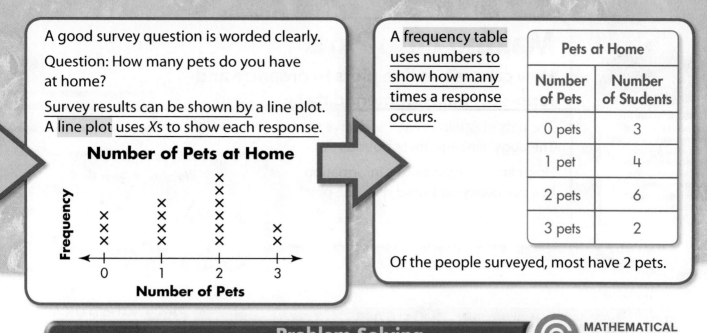

A good survey question is worded clearly.

Question: How many pets do you have at home?

Survey results can be shown by a line plot. A line plot uses *X*s to show each response.

Number of Pets at Home

A frequency table uses numbers to show how many times a response occurs.

Pets at Home

Number of Pets	Number of Students
0 pets	3
1 pet	4
2 pets	6
3 pets	2

Of the people surveyed, most have 2 pets.

Problem Solving

MATHEMATICAL PRACTICES

For **10** through **12**, use the frequency table.

Number of CDs Owned

6 CDs	5
7 CDs	6
9 CDs	12
10 CDs	8

10. How many people responded to the survey?

11. How many people own more than 7 CDs?

12. Make a line plot that shows the same information.

13. Seth has 23 U.S. stamps and 14 foreign stamps. He has 27 U.S. coins and 11 foreign coins. What fraction of Seth's collection is from the U.S.? Write the fraction in simplest form.

© 14. **Use Tools** The base of a rectangular prism has a length of 8 m and a width of 4 m. If the volume is 64 cubic meters, what is the height of the prism?

© 15. **Persevere** If 4 pounds of birdseed cost $6.95, about how much does 1 ounce cost?

    A About $0.01   **C** About $1.00

    B About $0.10   **D** About $1.01

16. Mrs. Dugan plans to serve 100 barbecue sandwiches at the company picnic. How many packages of barbecue buns will she need if buns come in packages of 8? Packages of 12?

© 17. **Model** Janet had $9.25 this morning. She spent $4.50 for lunch and then spent $3.50 on school supplies. Write an expression to show how much money she had at the end of the day.

© 18. **Use Tools** Draw and label a rectangle with an area of 32 square inches.

Common
Core

5.MD.2 Make a line plot to display a data set of measurements in fractions of a unit ($\frac{1}{2}$, $\frac{1}{4}$, $\frac{1}{8}$). Use operations on fractions for this grade to solve problems involving information presented in line plots.

Making Line Plots

How can we use line plots to organize and represent measurement data?

The pets in Paulina's Pet Shop have the following weights. The dogs' weights are in pounds (lb).

How can we organize this information in a frequency table and on a line plot?

Data

Weights of Dogs (in lb)					
$7\frac{1}{4}$	$12\frac{1}{4}$	6	$11\frac{1}{2}$	$2\frac{1}{2}$	$12\frac{1}{4}$
$2\frac{1}{2}$	$12\frac{1}{4}$	$2\frac{1}{2}$	$12\frac{1}{4}$	$12\frac{1}{4}$	6

Guided Practice*

MATHEMATICAL
PRACTICES

Do you know HOW?

1. Draw a line plot to represent the data for weights of pumpkins in a crate.

Weights of Pumpkins (to the nearest $\frac{1}{8}$ pound)	Tally	Frequency
$3\frac{1}{2}$	||	2
$5\frac{1}{4}$	|||	3
7	||||	4
$8\frac{1}{8}$	|	1

Do you UNDERSTAND?

2. How many pumpkins are in the crate?

3. What values do you need to show on the line?

© 4. **Communicate** What observations can you make about the crate of pumpkins?

Independent Practice

In **5–8**, organize the data in a table, then draw a line plot for each data set.

5. $11\frac{1}{4}$, $12\frac{1}{2}$, $11\frac{1}{4}$, $14\frac{1}{8}$, $10\frac{1}{2}$, $11\frac{1}{4}$, 12

6. $1\frac{1}{8}$, 2, $1\frac{1}{2}$, $1\frac{1}{4}$, $1\frac{1}{8}$, 1, 2, $1\frac{1}{2}$, $1\frac{1}{4}$

7. $6\frac{3}{8}$, $6\frac{3}{8}$, $6\frac{1}{8}$, $6\frac{1}{4}$, $6\frac{3}{8}$, $6\frac{3}{8}$, $6\frac{1}{2}$, $6\frac{1}{4}$, $6\frac{1}{8}$, $6\frac{1}{4}$, $6\frac{3}{8}$, $6\frac{3}{8}$

8. List the fractions in order from least to greatest. Use the list to make a frequency table and a line plot. $\frac{1}{8}$, $\frac{1}{2}$, $\frac{1}{4}$, $\frac{3}{4}$, $\frac{1}{4}$, $\frac{3}{4}$, $\frac{5}{8}$, $\frac{1}{4}$, $\frac{1}{8}$

9. How does making a frequency table or line plot help you see which value occurs most often in a data set?

For another example, see Set C on page 365.

Organize the data.

Arrange the weights from least to greatest.

$2\frac{1}{2}, 2\frac{1}{2}, 2\frac{1}{2}, 6, 6, 7\frac{1}{4}, 11\frac{1}{2}, 12\frac{1}{4}, 12\frac{1}{4}, 12\frac{1}{4}, 12\frac{1}{4}, 12\frac{1}{4}$

Make a frequency table to show the data.

Data

Pet Weight (pounds)	Tally	Frequency
$2\frac{1}{2}$	III	3
6	II	2
$7\frac{1}{4}$	I	1
$11\frac{1}{2}$	I	1
$12\frac{1}{4}$	⦀⦀	5

Make a line plot.

First draw the number line. Then make an X for each value in the data set. Then write a title.

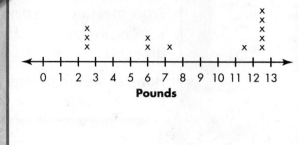

Weights of Paulina's Pets

Pounds

Problem Solving

Use Tools For **10–13,** use the data set at the right.

Marvin's Tree Service purchased several spruce tree saplings. The saplings had the heights listed in the table.

Data

Heights of Saplings (in.)				
$26\frac{1}{2}$	27	$26\frac{3}{4}$	$27\frac{1}{2}$	$26\frac{3}{4}$
$27\frac{1}{2}$	$27\frac{3}{4}$	$27\frac{1}{4}$	$27\frac{1}{2}$	$27\frac{1}{4}$
$27\frac{3}{4}$	$27\frac{1}{2}$	$26\frac{1}{2}$	$26\frac{1}{2}$	$27\frac{1}{2}$
$27\frac{1}{4}$	$27\frac{1}{4}$	$27\frac{1}{2}$	27	$26\frac{3}{4}$

10. Draw a table to organize the data.

11. What is the height of the shortest sapling?

12. How many saplings are $27\frac{1}{4}$ tall?

13. Draw a line plot of the data.

For **14–16,** use the data set. Ten friends have a chili cooking contest. The recipes have the following numbers of cups of beans.

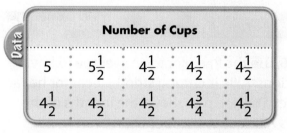

Number of Cups				
5	$5\frac{1}{2}$	$4\frac{1}{2}$	$4\frac{1}{2}$	$4\frac{1}{2}$
$4\frac{1}{2}$	$4\frac{1}{2}$	$4\frac{1}{2}$	$4\frac{3}{4}$	$4\frac{1}{2}$

14. Organize the data in a frequency table.

15. Draw a line plot of the data.

16. Construct Arguments What conclusion does the data suggest?

17. Use Tools Since 2000, a giant panda cub has been born in the following years: 2006, 2008, 2010, 2003, 2005, 2007, 2009, 2005. Draw a frequency table and line plot of the data.

Lesson
14-4

Common
Core

5.MD.2 Make a line plot to display a data set of measurements in fractions of a unit ($\frac{1}{2}$, $\frac{1}{4}$, $\frac{1}{8}$). Use operations on fractions for this grade to solve problems involving information presented in line plots.

Measurement Data

How can we use measurement data represented in a line plot to solve problems?

Bruce measured the daily rainfall while working in Costa Rica. His line plot shows the rainfall for each day in September.

How can we use the line plot to determine the total rainfall for the month?

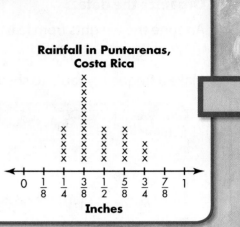

Rainfall in Puntarenas, Costa Rica

Guided Practice*

MATHEMATICAL PRACTICES

Do you know HOW?

Bella's experiment showed how many grams of salt were left after containers of various liquids evaporated. The results are shown in the line plot.

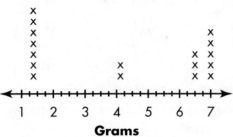

Amount of Salt

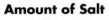

Grams

© **1. Model** Make a frequency table to show the data in the line plot.

Do you UNDERSTAND?

2. How many total grams of salt were left?

© **3. Think About the Structure** Write an equation that shows how to find the total amount of salt.

© **4. Construct Arguments** Rosie says she can find the total rainfall in the example at the top without multiplying. Do you agree? Explain.

Independent Practice

In **5–6**, use the line plot to answer the following questions. Allie is cutting string pieces for her art project. The line plot shows the lengths of the pieces Allie cut to use for her art project.

5. How many total inches of string does Allie have for her art project?

6. Write an equation for the total amount of string.

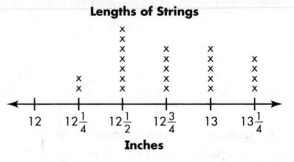

Lengths of Strings

Inches

Think "I can multiply each data value by the frequency to find the amount of rain for that value. Then I can add all of the products to find the total amount of rain for the month."

Use a table to organize the data and multiply. Then add to find the total rainfall.

$$1\frac{1}{4} + 4\frac{1}{2} + 2\frac{1}{2} + 3\frac{1}{8} + 2\frac{1}{4} = 13\frac{5}{8}$$

The total rainfall was $13\frac{5}{8}$ inches.

Rainfall (inches)	Frequency	Multiplication
$\frac{1}{4}$	5	$\frac{1}{4} \times 5 = 1\frac{1}{4}$
$\frac{3}{8}$	12	$\frac{3}{8} \times 12 = 4\frac{1}{2}$
$\frac{1}{2}$	5	$\frac{1}{2} \times 5 = 2\frac{1}{2}$
$\frac{5}{8}$	5	$\frac{5}{8} \times 5 = 3\frac{1}{8}$
$\frac{3}{4}$	3	$\frac{3}{4} \times 3 = 2\frac{1}{4}$

In **7–8** use the line plot to answer the following questions. Susannah made a line plot to show the distances she hiked in the past two weeks.

7. How many miles did Susannah hike in all?

8. Write an equation for the total number of miles she hiked.

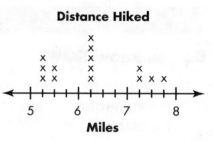

Distance Hiked

Miles

Problem Solving

MATHEMATICAL PRACTICES

In **9–13**, Dominick's class flew toy gliders. He recorded the distances in a line plot.

9. What is the range for the data (difference between the farthest distance and the shortest distance)?

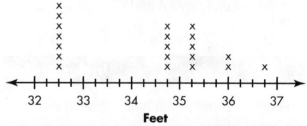

Glider Flight Distances

Feet

10. Write and solve an equation to find d, the total distance for the 20 flights.

Ⓒ **11. Critique Reasoning** Dominick concluded that $32\frac{1}{2}$ is an outlier. Do you agree with him or not? Explain.

Ⓒ **12. Reasonableness** If the X at $36\frac{3}{4}$ were removed, what would the new range be?

   A 37 feet   **C** 5 feet

   B 36 feet   **D** $3\frac{1}{2}$ feet

Ⓒ **13. Communicate** Explain another way to find the total distance of the 20 flights.

14. Molly runs 3 miles on Monday, Wednesday, and Friday. She runs twice as far on Saturday as she does on Monday. How many total miles does she run each week?

15. A square has an area of 81 square feet. How long is each side of the square?

Lesson
14-5

© Common Core

5.G.2 Represent real-world and mathematical problems by graphing points in the first quadrant of the coordinate plane, and interpret coordinate values of points in the context of the situation.

Problem Solving

Writing to Explain

How do you write a good math explanation?

The graph shows a trip that Lynne took to the grocery store. Write a story about Lynne's trip that fits the data on the graph. Explain what happens at each point shown on the graph.

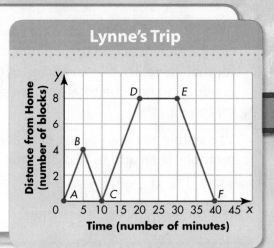

Lynne's Trip

Guided Practice*

MATHEMATICAL PRACTICES

Do you know HOW?

1. How would you infer that Lynne was not at the grocery store at Point *B* on the graph?

2. What does Point *C* tell you about Lynne's location?

3. How can you explain what happened between Points *A* and *C*?

Do you UNDERSTAND?

4. Why does Point *B* represent half the distance to the store?

5. Why can you say Lynne shopped for 10 minutes?

© 6. **Be Precise** Write a problem that uses data from the graph. Your problem should ask for an explanation as part of the solution.

Independent Practice

MATHEMATICAL PRACTICES

The graph shows what happened when Jim went biking.

7. What might have happened between Points *C* and *D*?

8. Between which two points did Jim bike the fastest? the slowest?

9. Write a story to fit the data on the graph. Tell what Jim and his friend might have been doing between each pair of data points.

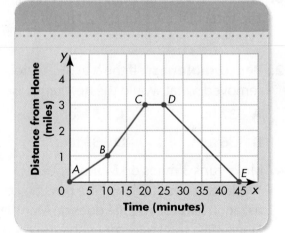

Think I know Points *A*, *C*, and *F* all have a value of 0 on the vertical number line. So Lynne must have returned home once during her trip.

My written explanation should be correct, simple, complete, and easy to understand.

Lynne leaves home at Point *A* to go to the store. At Point *B*, she is halfway to the store but realizes she has forgotten her wallet. So she goes back home at Point *C*. After getting her wallet, Lynne walks to the store at Point *D*. She shops for 10 minutes, to Point *E*. Then Lynne walks home, arriving at Point *F*.

10.  **Science** Scientists believe that the first dinosaurs lived on Earth about 230 million years ago. They believe dinosaurs became extinct about 65 million years ago. Write an equation and solve it to find out about how long (years) dinosaurs roamed the Earth.

11. In July 2008, a wildfire near Yosemite National Park burned about 53 square miles of forest. If one square mile equals 640 acres, about how many acres of forest were burned?

The table at the right shows the amount of time that astronauts have spent in space during several space programs. Use the table for **12** and **13**.

© 12. **Model** Write and solve an equation to find the total number of hours, *h*, astronauts spent in space during the Gemini and Apollo space programs combined.

Program	Years	Total Hours
Mercury	1959–1963	54
Gemini	1965–1966	970
Apollo	1968–1972	2,502
Skylab	1973–1974	4,105
Space Shuttle	1981–1995	12,407

Data

© 13. **Construct Arguments** Explain how estimation can be used to determine if the total number of hours astronauts spent in space during the Space Shuttle program is more or less than the number of hours spent in the other programs combined.

© 14. **Use Tools** Students at Gifford Elementary collected stamps from various countries. The students collected 546 stamps from Africa, 132 from Europe, and 321 from North and South America. If a stamp album can hold 24 stamps on each page, how many pages will the stamps completely fill?

Set A, pages 354–355

The data set below shows the number of goals scored by 20 teams in a soccer tournament. The data is organized as a line plot.

4, 8, 7, 0, 3, 3, 7, 4, 6, 1, 2, 7, 6, 4, 2, 7, 2, 6, 7, 4

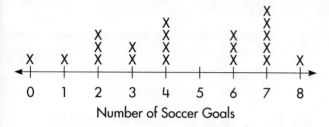

Number of Soccer Goals

Remember that an outlier is a number that is very different from the rest of the numbers in a line plot.

1. How many soccer teams scored 3 goals?

2. How many teams scored more than 5 goals?

3. What was the greatest number of goals scored by a team?

4. How many teams scored only 2 goals?

Set B, pages 356–357

These frequency tables use numbers to show how many times a response to a survey occurs.

Survey A

Favorite Video Games	
Snowboarding	6
Save the Whales	5
Pro Hockey	4

Survey B

Number of Video Games Owned	
2 games	4
3 games	6
4 games	2

Remember that survey results can also be shown on a line plot. Each *X* represents one response.

1. Which survey gathered facts and which gathered opinions?

2. What question do you think was asked in each survey?

3. Show the Survey B data set on a line plot.

Twenty people were interviewed about the amount of time they watch TV on a Saturday. Make a line plot and frequency table to display the data.

2, 3, 1, 4, 3, 5, 1, 0, 1, 1

1, 3, 0, 3, 3, 4, 5, 0, 0, 1

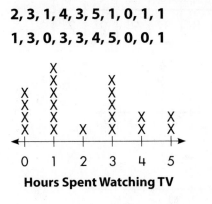

Hours Spent Watching TV

Number of Hours Watching TV	
0 hours	4
1 hour	6
2 hours	1
3 hours	5
4 hours	2
5 hours	2

Remember that you can make a line plot to show the frequency of the data.

1. How many people in the survey watched the most TV?

2. How many hours of TV did the most people watch?

3. What fraction of the 20 people watched 3 hours or more on Saturday? What fraction watched an hour or less?

The graph shows sales of a new video game. Write a story about the first 6 days of the sale.

Sales of a new video game rise during the first 3 days. Sales increase from 4 games on Day 1 to 12 games on Day 3. Sales of the game are flat, or constant, from Days 3 to 5. Sales of the game increase again on Day 6.

Remember that a written explanation should be correct, simple, complete, and easy to understand.

Use the questions to help you complete a story about the graph.

1. What happens to sales on Days 4 and 5?

2. What happens on Day 6?

3. How might you explain what happened on Day 7?

Multiple Choice

ASSESSMENT

1. As part of a class fundraiser, students received money for each lap they ran around the school's parking lot.

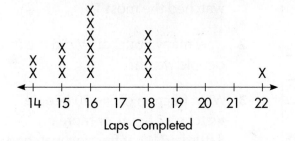

Laps Completed

What is the outlier in this set of data? (14-1)

A 8

B 16

C 22

D There is no outlier in this data set.

2. The line plot shows the results from a survey asking parents how many children they have in the school. How many parents have two children in the school? (14-2)

Children in School

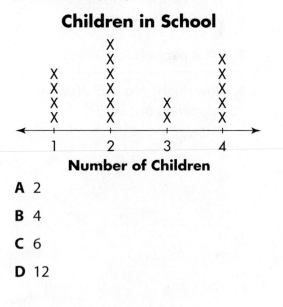

Number of Children

A 2

B 4

C 6

D 12

3. Which line plot shows the data? (14-3)

| 8 | $7\frac{1}{2}$ | $8\frac{3}{4}$ | $7\frac{1}{4}$ | $7\frac{1}{4}$ | $8\frac{3}{4}$ | $8\frac{3}{4}$ |
| $8\frac{3}{4}$ | $8\frac{3}{4}$ | 8 | $8\frac{3}{4}$ | $9\frac{1}{8}$ | $9\frac{1}{8}$ | $7\frac{1}{4}$ |

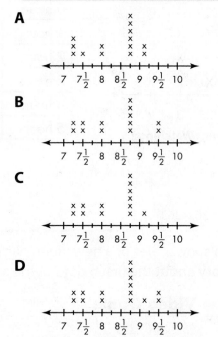

4. Which is the total for the data represented in the line plot? (14-4)

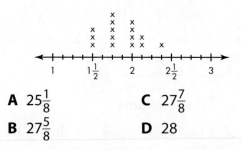

A $25\frac{1}{8}$ **C** $27\frac{7}{8}$

B $27\frac{5}{8}$ **D** 28

5. What is the outlier in the set of data for Exercise 4? (14-1)

A $1\frac{1}{2}$

B 2

C $2\frac{1}{8}$

D There is no outlier in the data set.

6. The graph shows a red-tailed hawk hunting for prey. Explain what could have happened between Point *C* and Point *D*. (14-5)

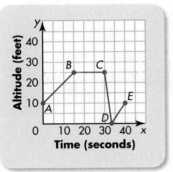

7. Write a story that describes the data in the graph. (14-5)

8. Georgiana made a line plot of her violin practice schedule for the past two weeks.

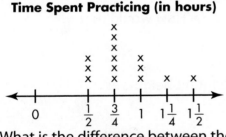

What is the difference between the greatest and least values? (14-3)

9. What is the total amount of time she practiced over the 14 days? Write and solve an equation that represents the total amount of time. (14-4)

For quality control, Sandy weighs every loaf of bread her bakery makes. She recorded how many ounces each loaf weighed one morning.

Bread Loaf Weights (in oz.)					
$23\frac{1}{2}$	24	$24\frac{1}{4}$	$23\frac{1}{2}$	$19\frac{5}{8}$	24
$24\frac{1}{4}$	$23\frac{3}{4}$	24	$23\frac{1}{2}$	$24\frac{1}{2}$	$24\frac{1}{4}$
$23\frac{3}{4}$	$24\frac{1}{2}$	24	$23\frac{3}{4}$	$23\frac{1}{2}$	$24\frac{1}{4}$

10. Copy and complete this frequency table to organize the data. (14-2)

Weight (oz)	Number of Loaves
$19\frac{5}{8}$	
$23\frac{1}{2}$	
$23\frac{3}{4}$	
24	
$24\frac{1}{4}$	
$24\frac{1}{2}$	

11. What is the difference between the heaviest and lightest loaves? Write and solve an equation to show your work. (14-4)

12. Is there an outlier in this set of data? Explain how you decided. (14-1)

13. Construct a line plot for the data. (14-3)

Mr. Aydin's class has 22 students. The table shows the number of absences in Mr. Aydin's class for the last 20 days.

Number of Students Absent

0	1	1	2	3
1	4	2	0	1
0	0	1	2	5
4	3	4	2	0

1. Make a line plot of the data.

2. Copy and complete the table below to find the number of students present each day.

Number of Students Present

3. Suppose 10 students were absent the last day of the data. How would that change the data?

4. If they are not cut, blades of wild grass can grow to different heights as shown in the graph below.

   Look at the illustration that shows how tall 12 blades of grass are. Copy and complete the table to record how many blades are at each height.

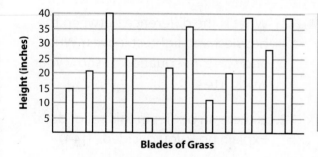

Height	Number of Blades
Less than 10 inches	
11–20 inches	
21–30 inches	
31-40 inches	

Topic 15

Classifying Plane Figures

▼ The Louvre Pyramid serves as the main entrance to the Louvre Museum in Paris, France. How do you classify one of the triangular faces of the pyramid? You will find out in Lesson 15-2.

Review What You Know!

Vocabulary

Choose the best term from the box.

- algebraic expression
- equation
- variable

1. $3x = 15$ is a(n) __?__.

2. $3x$ is a(n) __?__.

3. In the term $3x$, x is the __?__.

Rules and Tables

Write a rule for each table using words, and then write a rule with a variable.

4.
in	out
36	6
42	7
48	8

5.
in	out
5	12
10	17
15	22

Fractions

Write the fraction. Simplify if necessary.

6. If 2 out of 4 bananas are green, what fraction names the green bananas?

7. If $\frac{5}{6}$ of a loaf of bread is eaten, what part of the loaf is NOT eaten?

Multiplying Factors

© 8. **Writing to Explain** Clint bought 3 T-shirts at $9 each and 2 pairs of shorts at $12 each. Explain how to find the total Clint spent.

Topic Essential Questions
- How can angles be measured and classified?
- How can polygons, triangles, and quadrilaterals be described, classified, and named?

Interactive Learning

Pose the problem. Start each lesson by working together to solve problems. It will help you make sense of math.

Applying Math Practices

- What am I asked to find?
- What else can I try?
- How are quantities related?
- How can I explain my work?
- How can I use math to model the problem?
- Can I use tools to help?
- Is my work precise?
- Why does this work?
- How can I generalize?

Lesson 15-1

Use Tools Use eight sticks or straws to work the problem that follows. Suppose the sticks are the sides of a play area for a dog. Make as many different shapes as you can to create a closed play area.

Lesson 15-2

Look for Patterns Work with a partner. Together, draw six different triangles with different properties. Next to each triangle list the properties. Here are some ideas for your drawings: a triangle with 2 equal sides, a triangle with 1 right angle, a triangle with acute angles, and so on.

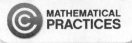

Lesson 15-3

© **Look for Patterns** Work with a partner. Draw as many different quadrilaterals as you can by changing the side lengths and relationships as well as the angles. Make a chart like the one shown and fill it in based on your drawings.

Quadrilateral	Property			
	Only 1 pair of sides parallel	Both pairs of sides parallel	4 right angles	4 equal sides
Parallelogram				
Trapezoid				
Rectangle				
Rhombus				
Square				

Lesson 15-4

© **Look for Patterns** Draw and cut out four different quadrilaterals. Only one may be a square and only one may be a rectangle which is not a square. Work with a partner to describe the properties of each shape. How are your shapes alike and how are they different?

Lesson 15-5

© **Use Structure** Look at the quadrilaterals shown. Which figure is a trapezoid? How do you know?

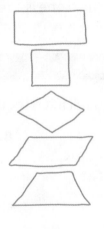

Lesson 15-6

© **Construct Arguments** Work in pairs. Use examples to test whether this statement is correct: *All rectangles are squares.* Record your work. How can you test whether the statement is correct?

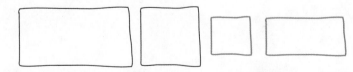

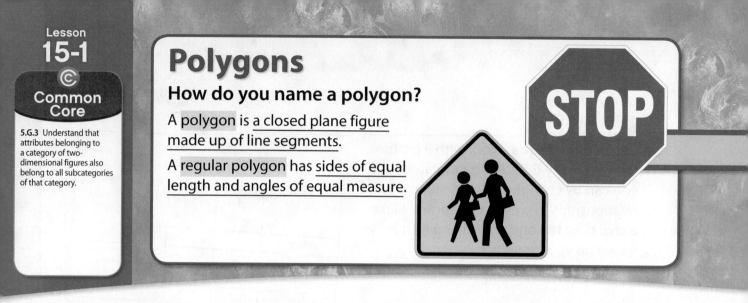

Common Core

5.G.3 Understand that attributes belonging to a category of two-dimensional figures also belong to all subcategories of that category.

Polygons
How do you name a polygon?

A polygon is a closed plane figure made up of line segments.

A regular polygon has sides of equal length and angles of equal measure.

Guided Practice*

MATHEMATICAL PRACTICES

Do you know HOW?

Name the polygon and classify it as regular or irregular.

1.

2.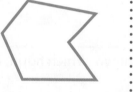

Do you UNDERSTAND?

3. How many sides and how many vertices does a pentagon have? A hexagon?

4. **Look for Patterns** What type of polygon does each road sign in the example at the top appear to be? Which one is a regular polygon?

Independent Practice

In **5** through **8**, name each polygon. Then write *yes* or *no* to tell if it is regular.

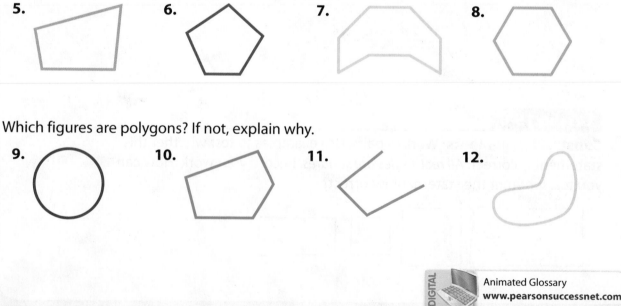

5.   6.   7.   8.

Which figures are polygons? If not, explain why.

9.   10.   11.   12.

Animated Glossary
www.pearsonsuccessnet.com

For another example, see Set A on page 384.

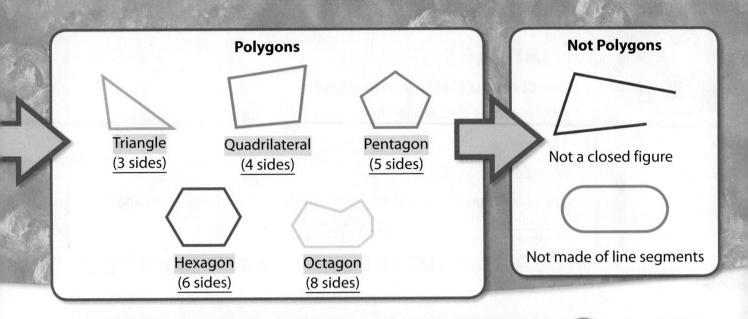

Polygons

Triangle
(3 sides)

Quadrilateral
(4 sides)

Pentagon
(5 sides)

Hexagon
(6 sides)

Octagon
(8 sides)

Not Polygons

Not a closed figure

Not made of line segments

Problem Solving

© MATHEMATICAL PRACTICES

© **13. Reason** A regular hexagon has six angles that are all equal. If the total measure of the angles is 720°, how many degrees is each angle of the hexagon?

   A 40°   **C** 60°

   B 90°   **D** 120°

© **14. Use Structure** What is the value of k in the equation $k \div 12 = 4$?

   A $k = 3$ **C** $k = 60$

   B $k = 48$ **D** $k = 72$

15. If each side of a regular pentagon equals 4 feet, what is its perimeter?

© **16. Use Tools** Divide a square in half by connecting two vertices. What types of polygons are formed? Are they regular or irregular?

© **17. Think About the Structure** Juanita's car gets 28 miles per gallon. Which expression shows how many gallons it will take to drive 720 miles?

   A 720×28 **C** $720 + 28$

   B $720 \div 28$ **D** $720 - 28$

© **18. Reason** Eight pieces of a leftover pizza are shared equally among four friends. Which shows how many pieces each friend got?

   A 8   **C** 4

   B 6   **D** 2

19. While driving, Shania saw a No Passing Zone sign and an Interstate Highway sign. Are these polygons? If so, are they regular?

20. Each cell from a wasps' hive has 6 sides. What is the name of this polygon?

Lesson
15-2

ⓒ
**Common
Core**

5.G.3 Understand that
attributes belonging to
a category of two-
dimensional figures also
belong to all subcategories
of that category.

Triangles

How can you classify triangles?

Triangles can be classifed by the length of their sides.

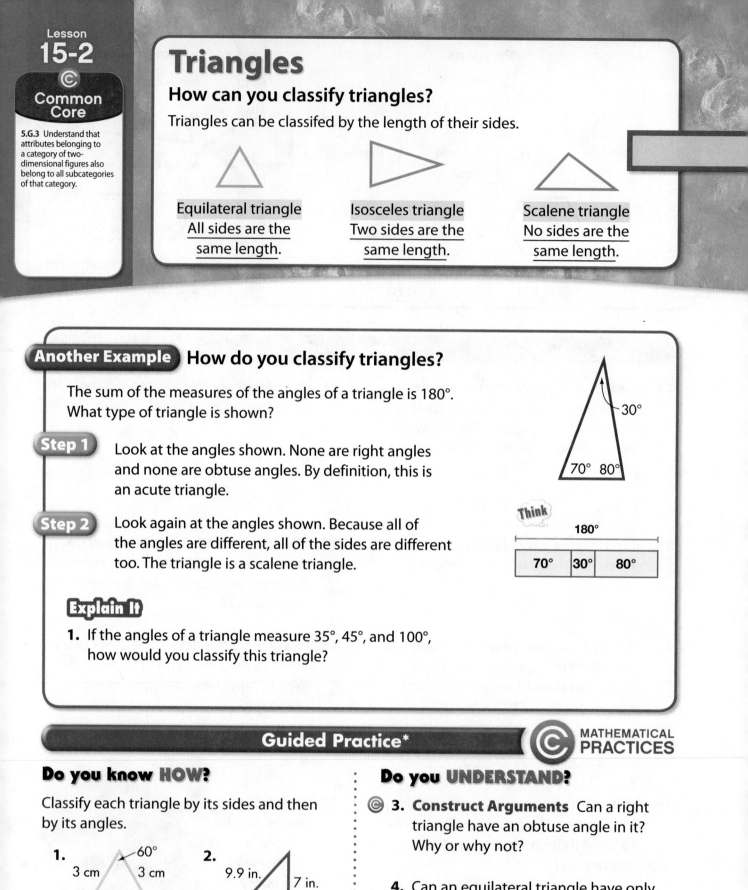

Equilateral triangle
All sides are the
same length.

Isosceles triangle
Two sides are the
same length.

Scalene triangle
No sides are the
same length.

Another Example **How do you classify triangles?**

The sum of the measures of the angles of a triangle is 180°.
What type of triangle is shown?

Step 1 Look at the angles shown. None are right angles
and none are obtuse angles. By definition, this is
an acute triangle.

Step 2 Look again at the angles shown. Because all of
the angles are different, all of the sides are different
too. The triangle is a scalene triangle.

30°

70° 80°

Think
180°

70°	30°	80°

Explain It

1. If the angles of a triangle measure 35°, 45°, and 100°,
how would you classify this triangle?

Guided Practice*

ⓒ **MATHEMATICAL
PRACTICES**

Do you know HOW?

Classify each triangle by its sides and then
by its angles.

1.
60°
3 cm   3 cm
60° 3 cm 60°

2.
9.9 in.   7 in.
7 in.

Do you UNDERSTAND?

ⓒ 3. **Construct Arguments** Can a right
triangle have an obtuse angle in it?
Why or why not?

4. Can an equilateral triangle have only
two sides of equal length? Why or why
not?

Animated Glossary
www.pearsonsuccessnet.com

For another example, see Set B on page 384.

Triangles can also be classified by the measures of their angles.

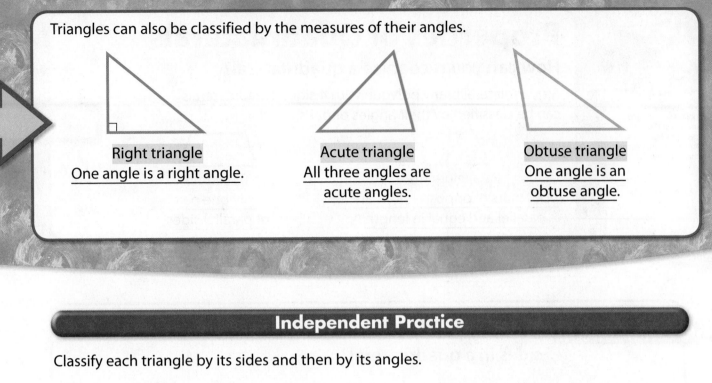

Right triangle
One angle is a right angle.

Acute triangle
All three angles are acute angles.

Obtuse triangle
One angle is an obtuse angle.

Independent Practice

Classify each triangle by its sides and then by its angles.

5.
30°
6 in. 6 in.
75° 75°
3.1 in.

6.
9 yd 12 yd
15 yd

7.
11 cm 60° 11 cm
60° 60°
11 cm

8.
15.1 m
9.2 m 110°
9.2 m

Problem Solving

MATHEMATICAL PRACTICES

For **9**, use the picture at the right.

9. The Louvre Pyramid serves as an entrance to the Louvre Museum in Paris. The base of the pyramid is 35 m long and the sides are 32 m long. Classify the triangle on the front of the Louvre Pyramid by the lengths of its sides and the measures of its angles.

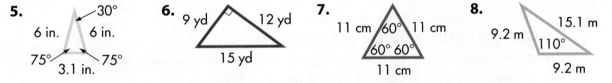

© 10. Construct Arguments The measures of two angles of a triangle are 23° and 67°. Is the triangle acute, right, or obtuse? Use geometric terms in your explanation.

© 11. Be Precise During a sale at the bookstore, books sold for $3 and magazines sold for $2.50. Jan spent $16 and bought a total of 6 books and magazines. How many of each did she buy? Use Try, Check, and Revise.

Lesson
15-3

© Common Core

5.G.3 Understand that attributes belonging to a category of two-dimensional figures also belong to all subcategories of that category. Also 5.G.4

Properties of Quadrilaterals

How can you recognize a quadrilateral?

A quadrilateral is any polygon with 4 sides. Quadrilaterals can be classified by their angles or pairs of sides.

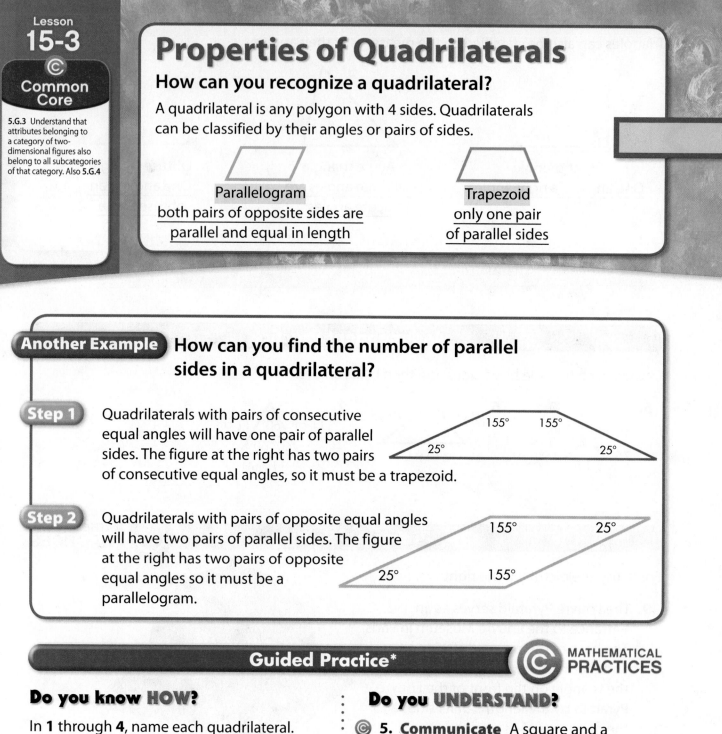

Parallelogram
both pairs of opposite sides are parallel and equal in length

Trapezoid
only one pair of parallel sides

Another Example How can you find the number of parallel sides in a quadrilateral?

Step 1 Quadrilaterals with pairs of consecutive equal angles will have one pair of parallel sides. The figure at the right has two pairs of consecutive equal angles, so it must be a trapezoid.

155° 155°
25°   25°

Step 2 Quadrilaterals with pairs of opposite equal angles will have two pairs of parallel sides. The figure at the right has two pairs of opposite equal angles so it must be a parallelogram.

155°   25°
25°   155°

Guided Practice*

MATHEMATICAL PRACTICES

Do you know HOW?

In **1** through **4**, name each quadrilateral.

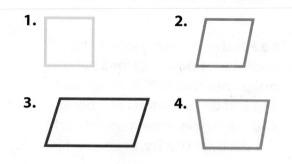

1.

2.

3.

4.

Do you UNDERSTAND?

© 5. **Communicate** A square and a rhombus both have four sides that are equal in length. How can you tell the difference between the two quadrilaterals?

© 6. **Construct Arguments** Why can a rectangle also be called a parallelogram?

Animated Glossary
www.pearsonsuccessnet.com

*For another example, see Set C on page 384.

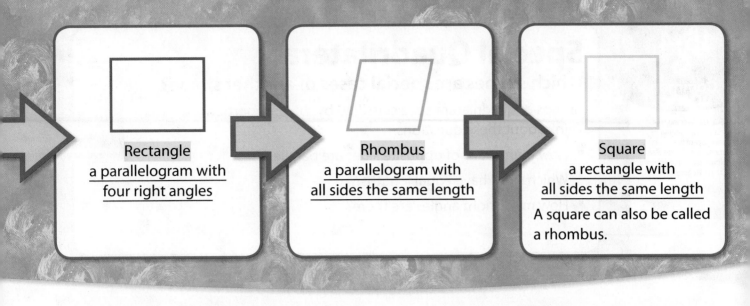

Rectangle	Rhombus	Square
a parallelogram with four right angles	a parallelogram with all sides the same length	a rectangle with all sides the same length

A square can also be called a rhombus.

Independent Practice

Classify each quadrilateral.

7.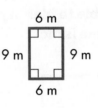

8.
9 ft
9 ft 9 ft
9 ft

9.
6 m
9 m 9 m
6 m

10.
3 ft
3 ft 3 ft
3 ft

The angle measures of a quadrilateral are given in order.
Draw the quadrilateral and name the figure.

11. 54°, 126°, 126°, 54°   **12.** 150°, 30°, 30°, 150°   **13.** 54°, 126°, 54°, 126°

Problem Solving

MATHEMATICAL
PRACTICES

Ⓒ **14. Construct Arguments** Which quadrilateral never has 4 equal sides?

   A Square   **C** Rectangle

   B Trapezoid   **D** Rhombus

15. Draw a quadrilateral that is not a parallelogram.

Ⓒ **16. Use Structure** Draw rectangle *ABCD*. Then draw a diagonal line connecting points *B* and *D*. If triangle *BCD* is a right isosceles triangle, what do you know about rectangle *ABCD*?

Ⓒ **17. Think About the Structure** Hot dog buns come in packages of 12. Which of the following is NOT needed to find out how much you will spend on hot dog buns?

   A The cost of one pack of buns   **C** The number of buns you need

   B The cost of the hot dogs   **D** All of the information is necessary.

Special Quadrilaterals
Which shapes are special cases of another shape?

Groups of quadrilaterals are classified by their properties.
Think about these questions.

- How many pairs of opposite sides are parallel?
- Which sides have equal lengths?
- How many right angles are there?

Lesson 15-4

Common Core

5.G.3 Understand that attributes belonging to a category of two-dimensional figures also belong to all subcategories of that category. Also **5.G.4.**

Guided Practice*

MATHEMATICAL PRACTICES

Do you know HOW?

Use as many names as possible to identify each polygon. Tell which name is most specific.

1.

2.

3.

4.

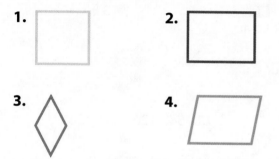

Do you UNDERSTAND?

5. **Look for Patterns** How are a square and a rhombus alike?

6. **Be Precise** How is a parallelogram different from a rhombus? How are they similar?

7. How is a trapezoid different from a parallelogram?

Independent Practice

MATHEMATICAL PRACTICES

8. Identify the polygon using as many names as possible.

9. Identify the polygon using as many names as possible.

10. Why is a square also a rectangle?

11. **Look for Patterns** Which special quadrilateral is both a rectangle and a rhombus? Explain how you know.

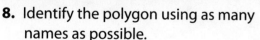

*For another example, see Set D on page 385.

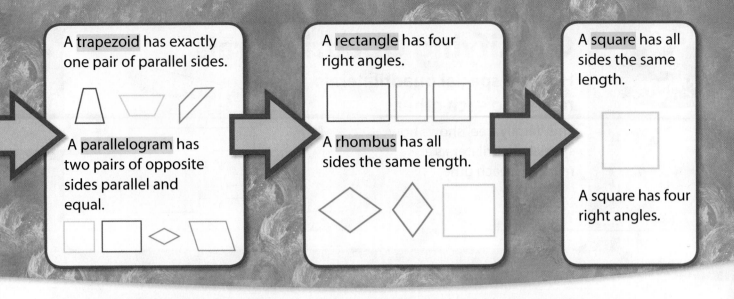

A trapezoid has exactly one pair of parallel sides.

A parallelogram has two pairs of opposite sides parallel and equal.

A rectangle has four right angles.

A rhombus has all sides the same length.

A square has all sides the same length.

A square has four right angles.

Problem Solving

12. Each time she makes a cut to a polygon, Sophie can make a new type of polygon. What kind of polygon appears to be formed by cutting off the top of the isosceles triangle shown?

© 13. Communicate A parallelogram has one side that is 4 cm and one side that is 6 cm. What is the perimeter? Explain how you found your answer.

14. Donald's car gets about 30 miles per gallon. About how many miles can Donald drive on 9.2 gallons of gas? At $3.15 a gallon, about how much would that cost?

15. Is it possible to draw a quadrilateral that is not a rectangle but has at least one right angle? Explain.

16. What properties help you classify a quadrilateral as a parallelogram, but not a rhombus?

© 17. Reasonableness Which shows one way of listing the side lengths of a parallelogram?

A 5, 5, 5, 1   **B** 1, 5, 1, 5

C 4, 1, 1, 1   **D** 1, 1, 1, 5

© 18. Persevere Find two decimals that give a product close to 8.4.

19. Cut a square into two identical triangles. What type of triangles have you made?

20. Howard is doing a science experiment in which he needs several rocks each with a mass of 0.5 kg and a total mass of 34.5 kg. Does he need 6.9 rocks, 69 rocks, or 690 rocks for the experiment? Explain how you found your answer.

© 21. Construct Arguments A parallelogram has four sides that are the same length. Is it a square? Explain how you know.

Lesson
15-5

Common
Core

5.G.4 Classify two-dimensional figures in a hierarchy based on properties.

Classifying Quadrilaterals

How are special quadrilaterals related to each other?

This "family tree" shows how special quadrilaterals are related to each other.

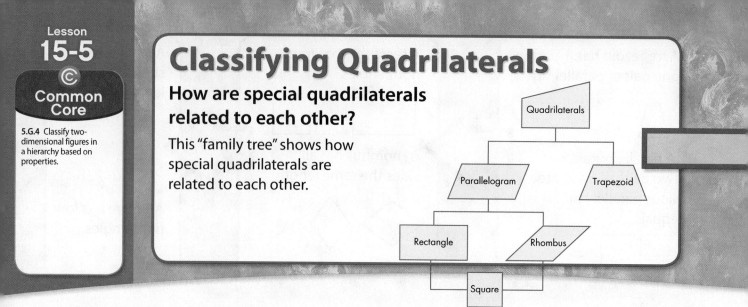

Quadrilaterals

Parallelogram   Trapezoid

Rectangle   Rhombus

Square

Guided Practice*

MATHEMATICAL PRACTICES

Do you know HOW?

Tell whether each statement is true or false.

1. All rectangles are squares.

2. Every rhombus is a parallelogram.

3. Parallelograms are special rectangles.

Do you UNDERSTAND?

4. **Look for Patterns** Explain how the family tree diagram shows that every square is a rectangle.

5. How are a rectangle and a rhombus alike?

Independent Practice

MATHEMATICAL PRACTICES

6. The figure shown below is an isosceles trapezoid. The two sides that are not parallel have the same length. How could you add this shape to the family tree diagram?

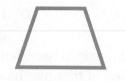

7. What properties does the shape below have? Why is it not a parallelogram?

8. Why is a square also a rhombus?

9. **Look for Patterns** Why is a parallelogram not the same type of quadrilateral as a trapezoid? Explain how you know.

For another example, see Set E on page 385.

Each branch of the tree shows a subgroup of the figure above.

A square is a type of rectangle.

All rectangles are parallelograms.

Each figure shares all of the properties of the figures above it.

A square and a rectangle have four right angles.

All of the figures below the parallelogram have two pairs of parallel opposite sides.

Parallelogram

Rectangle   Rhombus

Square

Problem Solving

MATHEMATICAL PRACTICES

© **10. Construct Arguments** Draw a quadrilateral with one pair of parallel sides and two right angles. Explain why this figure is a trapezoid.

© **11. Use Tools** A rhombus has a side length of 6 m. What is the perimeter? Explain how you found your answer.

12. Classify this polygon using as many names as possible.

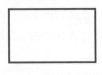

© **13. Critique Reasoning** Ann says the figure below is a square. Pablo says that it is a parallelogram. Felix says that it is a rectangle. Can they all be right? Explain.

© **14. Reasonableness** Which shows the most likely side lengths for a rectangle?

   A 4, 4, 4, 3

   B 3, 4, 3, 4

   C 3, 3, 3, 6

   D 3, 3, 3, 4

15. All parallelograms have opposite sides parallel. Are squares and other rectangles parallelograms?

16. Draw a quadrilateral that is not a trapezoid and not a parallelogram.

© Common Core

5.G.3 Understand that attributes belonging to a category of two-dimensional figures also belong to all subcategories of that category. Also 5.G.4

Problem Solving

Make and Test Generalizations

A generalization or general statement can be made about a rectangle.

Make a generalization.

All rectangles can be cut in half diagonally to make two congruent triangles.

Guided Practice*

© **MATHEMATICAL PRACTICES**

Do you know HOW?

Test the generalization and state whether it appears to be correct or incorrect. If incorrect, give an example to support why.

1. All right triangles are scalene triangles.

2. Two congruent equilateral triangles can be joined to make a rhombus.

Do you UNDERSTAND?

© **3. Critique Reasoning** In the exercise above, how was the conclusion reached?

4. What is another generalization you can make and test about rectangles?

© **5. Generalize** Write a real-world problem that can be solved by making and testing a generalization.

Independent Practice

© **MATHEMATICAL PRACTICES**

In **6** through **10**, test the generalization and state whether it appears to be correct or incorrect. If incorrect, give an example to support why.

6. The sum of the angles of any triangle is 180°.

7. Parallel lines never intersect.

8. All rectangles have four congruent sides.

9. All even numbers are composite.

10. All triangles have at least two acute angles.

Applying Math Practices

- What am I asked to find?
- What else can I try?
- How are quantities related?
- How can I explain my work?
- How can I use math to model the problem?
- Can I use tools to help?
- Is my work precise?
- Why does this work?
- How can I generalize?

Test your generalization.

Draw a rectangle with the length at the base.

I can cut this rectangle diagonally to make two congruent triangles.

Test again if possible.

Draw a different rectangle.

I can also cut this rectangle diagonally to make two congruent triangles.

Conclusion

To prove a generalization incorrect, you need an example of when the test shows the generalization being incorrect.

Based on the results of the tests, this generalization appears to be correct.

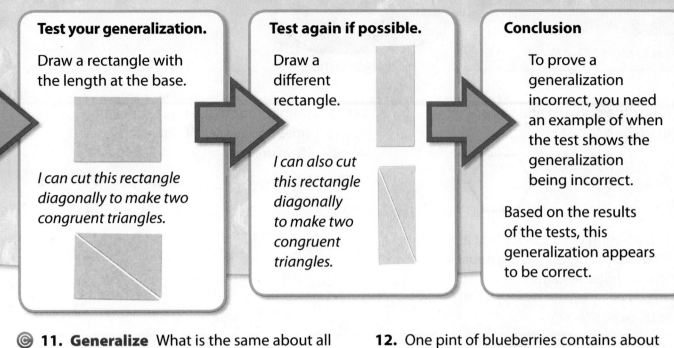

© **11. Generalize** What is the same about all of these polygons?

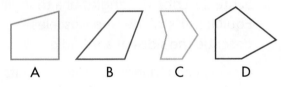

A   B   C   D

12. One pint of blueberries contains about 80 berries. You have a fruit salad recipe that calls for 20 blueberries per serving. You have all of the other fruit necessary for the salad, but only 1 quart of blueberries. How many servings of the fruit salad can you prepare?

13. What is the best estimate of the shaded portion of the picture shown below?

© **14. Look for Patterns** Draw the next figure in the pattern shown below.

15. Mike weighs 24 more pounds than Mark. Together, they weigh 250 pounds. How much do they each weigh?

16. Find the missing numbers in each table. Then, write the rule.

a

Days	1	2	4	7
Dollars	$8	▓	$32	▓

© **17. Model** Marcia and Tim played ping-pong. Marcia won the game with a score of 21. She won by 7 points. Draw a picture and write an equation to find Tim's score.

b

Teams	1	2	4	9
Players	▓	10	20	▓

© **18. Look for Patterns** How many whole numbers have exactly two digits? Hint: 99 is the greatest two-digit whole number.

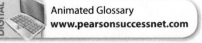
DIGITAL
Animated Glossary
www.pearsonsuccessnet.com

Set A, pages 372–373

Name the polygon and state whether it is regular or irregular.

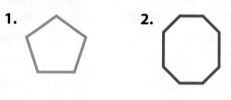

The polygon has six sides that are all equal in length and angles that are equal in measure. It is a regular hexagon.

Remember that a regular polygon has sides and angles of equal length and measure.

1.

2.

Set B, pages 374–375

Classify the triangle by the measure of its angles and the length of its sides.

Since one of the angles is right, this is a right triangle. Since two of the sides are the same length, this is an isosceles triangle.

4 m

4 m

Using both terms, this is a right, isosceles triangle.

Remember that right, obtuse, and acute describe the angles of a triangle. Equilateral, scalene, and isosceles describe the sides of a triangle.

Classify each triangle by the size of its angles and the length of its sides.

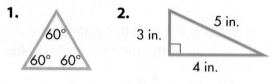

1. 60° 60° 60°

2. 5 in. 3 in. 4 in.

Set C, pages 376–377

Classify the quadrilateral. Then find the missing angle measure.

The quadrilateral has two pairs of parallel sides with all sides the same length. It is a rhombus.

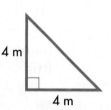

4 cm
? 60°
4 cm 4 cm
60° 120°
4 cm

The sum of the measures of the angles in a quadrilateral is 360°.

$$360° - (60° + 60° + 120°) = 120°$$

So, the missing angle measure is 120°.

Remember that the sum of the angles of a quadrilateral is 360°.

Classify the quadrilateral. Then find the missing angle measure.

1.

3 cm 110° ?
70° 110°
6 cm

2.

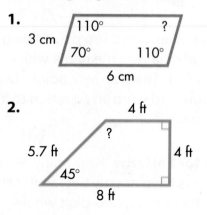

4 ft
?
5.7 ft 4 ft
45°
8 ft

Many special **quadrilaterals** have special **properties**.

A **trapezoid** has exactly one pair of parallel sides.

A **parallelogram** has two pairs of equal parallel sides.

A **rectangle** is a parallelogram with 4 right angles.

A **rhombus** is a parallelogram with 4 equal sides.

A **square** is a parallelogram with 4 right angles and 4 equal sides.

Trapezoid   Parallelogram   Rectangle   Rhombus   Square

Identify each quadrilateral. Describe each quadrilateral by as many names as possible.

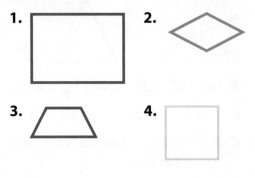

How are special quadrilaterals related to each other?

This "family tree" shows how special quadrilaterals are related to each other.

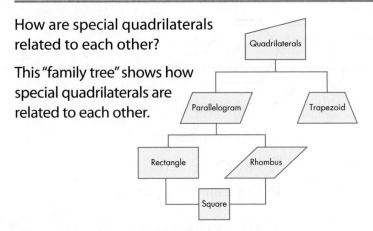

Tell whether each statement is true or false.

1. All squares are rectangles.

2. Every parallelogram is a rectangle.

3. Rhombuses are special parallelograms.

4. All trapezoids are quadrilaterals.

Test the following generalization and state whether it appears to be correct or incorrect. If incorrect, give an example to support why.

Generalization
The sum of the angles in any rectangle is 180°.

Test Your Generalization
Draw a rectangle.
Notice that each of the four angles is 90°.
Add to find the sum of the angles.
90° + 90° + 90° + 90° = 360°

Conclusion
The generalization is incorrect.

Remember to test a generalization more than once before drawing a conclusion that the generalization is true.

Test the generalization. State if it appears to be correct or not. If incorrect, give an example to support why.

1. The sum of two prime numbers equals a prime number.

Multiple Choice

1. Which of the following correctly describes the triangles shown? (15-2)

   A Both triangles have a right angle.

   B Only one triangle has an acute angle.

   C Both triangles have at least two obtuse angles.

   D Both triangles have at least two acute angles.

2. A right triangle has an angle whose measure is 35°. What is the measure of the third angle in the triangle? (15-2)

   A 35°

   B 55°

   C 72.5°

   D 145°

3. Which of the following can be used to describe the square below? (15-3)

   A Opposite sides are perpendicular.

   B All angles are obtuse.

   C Adjacent sides are parallel.

   D All sides are the same length.

4. This quadrilateral has one pair of parallel sides. What is it? (15-4)

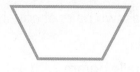

   A Square

   B Trapezoid

   C Rhombus

   D Rectangle

5. Sabra's glasses have lenses that are the shape shown in the picture below. Which of the following could NOT be used to describe the lenses? (15-1)

   A Quadrilateral

   B Regular polygon

   C Hexagon

   D Opposite sides parallel

6. The figures below are rhombuses. Which generalization is incorrect, based on these figures? (15-6)

   A A square can be a rhombus.

   B A rhombus can be a square.

   C All rhombuses are squares.

   D All squares are rhombuses.

7. A sail on a sailboat is a triangle with two sides perpendicular and each side is a different length. What are the two terms that could be used to describe the sail? (15-2)

8. The necklace charm shown has one pair of parallel sides. What type of quadrilateral is the charm? (15-3)

9. Triangle *HJK* is an isosceles triangle. The measures of angles *J* and *K* are equal. The measure of angle *H* is 100°. How do you determine the measure of angle *J*? (15-2)

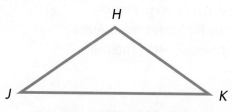

10. Which quadrilaterals must have all four sides of equal length? (15-3)

11. Compare and contrast a rectangle and a parallelogram. Which is the special case of the other? (15-4)

12. Marisol says that a square is a rectangle because it has 4 right angles. Amie says that a square is a rhombus because it has 4 equal sides. Who is correct? Explain. (15-5)

13. Compare the total number of sides in each set of shapes below. Which has more sides, **Set A** or **Set B**? Write an equation to support your answer. (15-1)

Set A

Set B

14. Anwar says that if you cut a regular hexagon in half through two of its vertices, two trapezoids will be created. Do you think Anwar's generalization is true? Explain. (15-6)

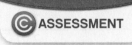

Your Aunt Bea lives in a town you have only visited once. You would like to get an idea of her area of town before visiting, but you only remember the layout of a few streets. The map below shows her area of town as you remember it. Copy the map and use it to complete the following questions.

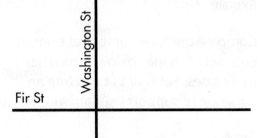

1. Aunt Bea says that Jackson Street is one block east of Washington Street and runs parallel to it. Maple Street is one block north of Fir Street and runs parallel to it. Draw Jackson and Maple Streets on your map.

2. The Crosstown Expressway forms a 30-degree angle with Fir Street between Jackson and Washington Streets. Draw the Crosstown Expressway on your map.

3. Aunt Bea lives at the corner of Jackson and Fir Streets. She lives on the corner that is closest to Maple Street but not closest to the expressway. Place a star where Aunt Bea's house is located. Across Fir Street from Aunt Bea's house is a park shaped like an isosceles right triangle. Add the park to your map.

4. Your Uncle Phil tells you that there is a baseball diamond on the corner of Dupage and Washington Streets that is closest to Jackson Street and the Crosstown Expressway. Dupage Street runs in the east and west direction and is one block south of Fir Street. Draw Dupage Street on your map and label the baseball diamond with a rhombus.

5. Compare your answer with another person who followed the same directions. Notice any differences. What additional instructions could Aunt Bea have included to ensure that only one version of the map is correct?

Topic 16 Coordinate Geometry

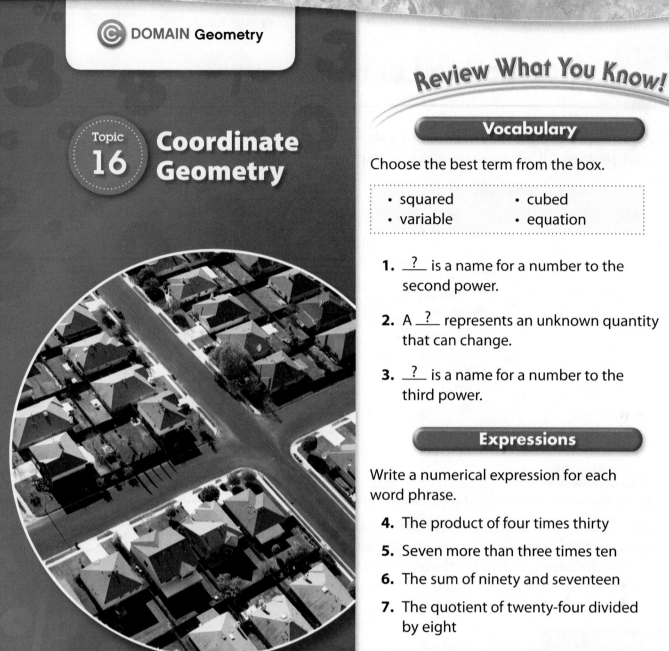

▲ Many cities in the United States are laid out like a coordinate grid. How can this be helpful when finding locations in cities? You will find out in Lesson 16-2.

Review What You Know!

Vocabulary

Choose the best term from the box.

- squared
- cubed
- variable
- equation

1. __?__ is a name for a number to the second power.

2. A __?__ represents an unknown quantity that can change.

3. __?__ is a name for a number to the third power.

Expressions

Write a numerical expression for each word phrase.

4. The product of four times thirty

5. Seven more than three times ten

6. The sum of ninety and seventeen

7. The quotient of twenty-four divided by eight

Solving Equations

Solve each equation.

8. $62 = 39 + n$ 9. $17f = 85$

10. $c - 50 = 27$ 11. $6 = \frac{x}{3}$

© **Writing to Explain** Write an answer to the question.

12. You know that $3 + 5 = 8$. Explain why $3 + 5 + 4 = 8 + 4$.

Topic Essential Questions
- How are points graphed?
- How can we show the relationship between sequences on a graph?

Interactive Learning

Pose the problem. Start each lesson by working together to solve problems. It will help you make sense of math.

Applying Math Practices

- What am I asked to find?
- What else can I try?
- How are quantities related?
- How can I explain my work?
- How can I use math to model the problem?
- Can I use tools to help?
- Is my work precise?
- Why does this work?
- How can I generalize?

Lesson 16-1

© **Communicate** Use the grid paper to complete this task.

Work with a partner. On the first grid, mark a point with a dot where one pair of lines intersects. Do not show your partner. Take turns describing the location of the point and see if your partner can plot that point from your description. Switch roles and repeat with other points.

Lesson 16-2

© **Use Tools** Solve using the diagram at the right.

In planning a miniature village, Glen plotted the post office, the hospital, the school, the library, and the bank at the points shown at the right. Which building is the farthest away from the hospital? Explain how you decided.

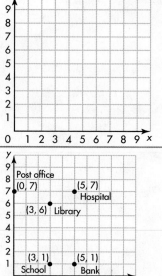

Lesson 16-3

© **Model** Solve. Draw a picture to help.

Hans walked from his home 3 blocks west and 2 blocks north to the hardware store. He then walked 5 blocks west, and 3 blocks north to the supermarket. How far away is Hans' home from the supermarket? Explain how you decided.

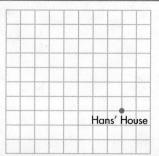

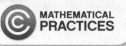

Lesson 16-4

© **Look for Patterns** Make a graph to show the data shown at the right. Let x be the day number and y the height in centimeters. Use the graph to solve this problem.

Day	1	2	5	7
Height (cm)	2 cm	4 cm	10 cm	14 cm

Sally measured the height of her bean plant and got the results shown in the table at the right. If plant growth was consistent each day, how tall was her plant on Day 4? Explain how you decided.

Lesson 16-5

© **Look for Patterns** Make a graph to show the data below. Let x be the length in inches and y the width in inches. Use the graph to solve this problem.

Four rectangles were made following number patterns. What is the width when the length is 10? Extend the table and plot the points on a coordinate grid to decide.

	Rectangle 1	Rectangle 2	Rectangle 3	Rectangle 4
Length (in.)	1	2	3	4
Width (in.)	11	10	9	8

Lesson 16-6

© **Model** Solve any way you choose.

Ben agrees to meet his friends at the ballpark for a 7:30 P.M. game. Trains leave the station near his home at 6:30, 6:50, 7:10, and 7:30 P.M. The train trip takes 30 minutes. He estimates that walking from his home to the train station takes 10 minutes and walking from the train station to the ballpark takes another 5 minutes. Which is the latest train that Ben can take without being late? Tell how you decided.

Lesson
16-1

Common
Core

5.G.1 Use a pair of perpendicular number lines ... to define a coordinate system ... and a given point in the plane located by using an ordered pair of numbers, called its coordinates. Understand that the first number indicates how far to travel from the origin in the direction of one axis, and the second number indicates how far to travel in the direction of the second axis ...

Ordered Pairs

Hands-On
grid paper

How do you name a point on a coordinate grid?

A map shows the location of landmarks and has guides for finding the landmarks. In a similar way, a coordinate grid is used to plot and name the locations of points in a plane.

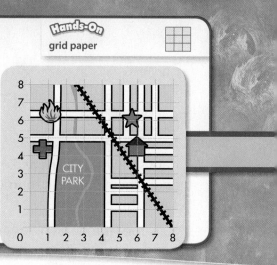

Another Example How do you plot a point on a coordinate grid?

Graph Point *R* at (4, 5).

Step 1

Draw and number the *x*-axis and *y*-axis on grid paper.

Step 2

Move 4 units to the right from 0. Then move 5 units up.

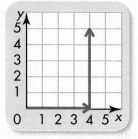

Step 3

Mark a point and label it *R*.

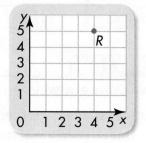

Explain It

1. **Be Precise** Why is the order important when naming and plotting the coordinates of a point?

2. If the location of Point *R* changed to (6, 5), would it be to the right or to the left of its current position?

3. You have labeled the *x*-axis and *y*-axis on grid paper. You want to graph Point *D* at (0, 5). Do you move right zero units or move up zero units? Explain.

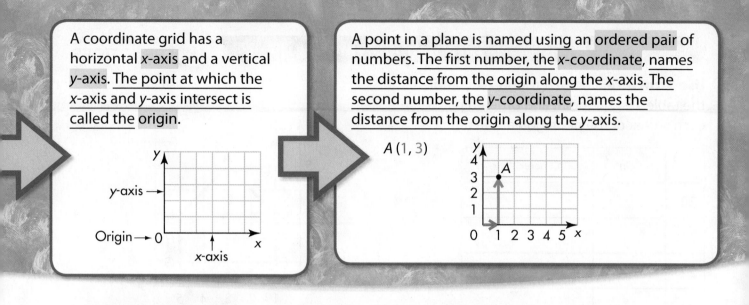

A coordinate grid has a horizontal *x*-axis and a vertical *y*-axis. The point at which the *x*-axis and *y*-axis intersect is called the origin.

A point in a plane is named using an ordered pair of numbers. The first number, the *x*-coordinate, names the distance from the origin along the *x*-axis. The second number, the *y*-coordinate, names the distance from the origin along the *y*-axis.

$A(1, 3)$

Guided Practice*

MATHEMATICAL PRACTICES

Do you know HOW?

In **1** and **2**, write each ordered pair. Use the grid at the right.

1. A

2. B

Graph and label each point on a grid.

3. $C(1, 4)$

4. $D(5, 3)$

Do you UNDERSTAND?

5. Using the example above, name the ordered pair for Point B if it is 3 units to the right of Point A.

6. What ordered pair names the origin of any coordinate grid?

7. Communicate Describe how to locate Point K at $(5, 3)$.

Independent Practice

In **8** through **13**, write each ordered pair. Use the grid at the right.

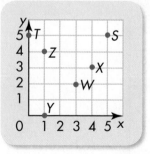

8. T

9. X

10. Y

11. W

12. Z

13. S

In **14** through **19**, plot and label each point on a grid.

14. $L(2, 2)$

15. $M(0, 3)$

16. $N(1, 5)$

17. $O(5, 4)$

18. $P(4, 0)$

19. $Q(0, 0)$

Animated Glossary, eTools
www.pearsonsuccessnet.com

DIGITAL

Ⓒ **Use Structure** For **20** through **24**, complete the table. List the point and ordered pair for each vertex of the pentagon at the right.

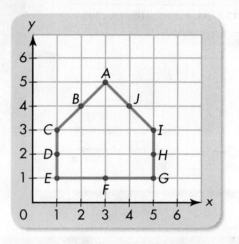

	Point	Ordered Pair
20.		
21.		
22.		
23.		
24.		

Ⓒ **25. Persevere** Use the coordinate grid from Exercises 20–24. Which of the following explains how to move from Point *B* to Point *H*?

   A Move right 3 units and down 2 units

   B Move left 2 units and up 1 unit

   C Move right 1 unit and down 2 units

   D Move right 2 units and down 3 units

Ⓒ **26. Communicate** The streets on maps of many cities in the United States are laid out like a coordinate grid. How is this helpful when finding locations in cities such as Fort Lauderdale, Florida?

Ⓒ **27. Look for Patterns** Write an equation to describe a rule for the table of values. Then complete the table.

x	y
3	1
6	2
12	4
9	■
■	5
24	■

28. A chess board is similar to a coordinate grid. The pieces that look like horses are knights. What letter-number combinations name the locations of the white knights?

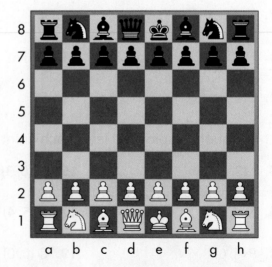

Mixed Problem Solving

© **Use Structure** Objects on Jupiter weigh about two and a half times as much as on Earth.

1. Look for a pattern to complete the table below and then graph the values on the coordinate grid.

Earth weight (lbs)	50	60	70			100
Jupiter weight (approx. lbs)	125		175	200	225	

2. If a dog weighs 40 pounds on Earth, about how much would it weigh on Jupiter?

3. If Tyler weighs 120 pounds on Earth, about how much would he weigh on Jupiter?

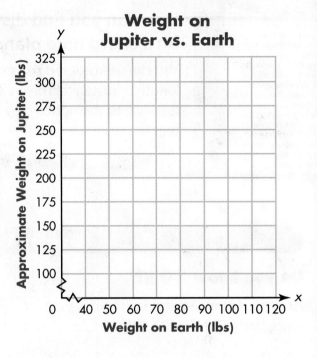

Weight on Jupiter vs. Earth

4. Complete this table using the graph that shows the star positions for the Big Dipper.

Point	Ordered Pair
A	
B	
C	
D	
E	
F	
G	

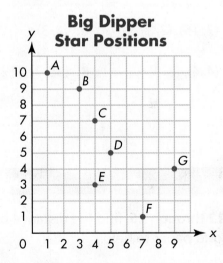

Big Dipper Star Positions

5. If you were to move this drawing of the Big Dipper 3 units to the right on this grid, what would be the ordered pair for Point *D*?

© 6. **Construct Arguments** Examine the ordered pairs for Points *C* and *E*. How do you know that a vertical line can connect those two points? Explain how you decided.

Common
Core

5.G.1 Use a pair of
perpendicular number
lines … to define a coordinate
system … and a given
point in the plane located
by using an ordered pair
of numbers, called its
coordinates. Understand that
the first number indicates
how far to travel from the
origin in the direction of
one axis, and the second
number indicates how far
to travel in the direction of
the second axis …

Distances on a Coordinate Plane

Hands-On
grid paper

How can you find distances on a coordinate plane?

You can use ordered pairs to find length or distance. The *x*-value tells distance to the right. The *y*-value tells the distance up.

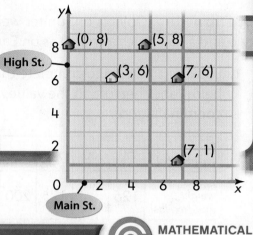

Guided Practice*

MATHEMATICAL PRACTICES

Do you know HOW?

Find the distance between the ordered pairs. Use grid paper to help.

1. (1, 3), (1, 8)

2. (2, 3), (12, 3)

3. (4, 3), (3, 3)

4. (2, 3), (2, 1)

5. (7, 15), (7, 2)

6. (7, 3), (1, 3)

7. (4, 4), (8, 4)

8. (35, 1), (12, 1)

Do you UNDERSTAND?

9. **Construct Arguments** If you are given two ordered pairs, how can you tell if they lie on a vertical line or on a horizontal line?

10. On the grid above, which house did you start at if walking two blocks to the right and two blocks up brings you to another house?

11. On the grid above, what is the distance from the blue house to Main Street? to High Street?

Independent Practice

For **12** through **25**, find the distance between the ordered pairs. Use grid paper to help.

12. (2, 7), (6, 7)

13. (6, 7), (6, 4)

14. (6, 4), (6, 0)

15. (11, 8), (1, 8)

16. (8, 3), (8, 8)

17. (4, 9), (9, 9)

18. (0, 3), (1, 3)

19. (15, 6), (15, 12)

20. (5, 7), (5, 0)

21. (1, 9), (9, 9)

22. (10, 6), (4, 6)

23. (18, 10), (21, 10)

24. (14, 17), (12, 17)

25. (19, 23), (19, 18)

eTools Spreadsheet/Data/
Grapher
www.pearsonsuccessnet.com

*For another example, see Set B on page 406.

How far is the red house from the green house?

Compare the ordered pairs: (7, 1)
(7, 6)

The *x*-values are the same.

Because the points lie on a vertical line, you subtract the *y*-values to find the distance.

6 − 1 = 5

The distance between the red and green houses is 5 units.

How far is the blue house from the purple house?

Compare the ordered pairs: (0, 8)
(5, 8)

The *y*-values are the same.

Because the points lie on a horizontal line, you subtract the *x*-values to find the distance.

5 − 0 = 5

The distance between the purple and blue houses is 5 units.

Problem Solving

MATHEMATICAL PRACTICES

For **26** through **28**, use the coordinate grid at the right.

26. What two points have a vertical distance of 8 units between them?

27. What is the horizontal distance between Point *A* and Point *F*?

Ⓒ **28. Be Precise** Is the horizontal distance between points *A* and *F* greater than or less than the vertical distance between Points *D* and *E*? Explain.

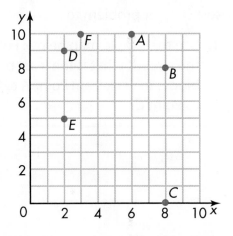

For **29** through **31**, use the map at the right.

29. About how many vertical blocks separate the New York Public Library and the Empire State Building?

Ⓒ **30. Reason** About how many horizontal blocks separate the New York Public Library and Grand Central Terminal?

31. About how many total blocks would you walk from the Empire State Building to arrive at Grand Central Terminal?

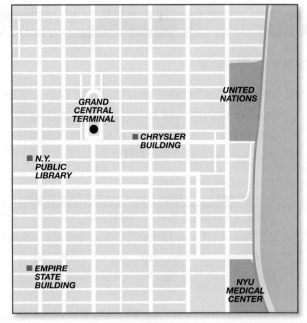

Lesson
16-3

Common Core

5.G.1 Use a pair of perpendicular number lines ... to define a coordinate system ... and a given point in the plane located by using an ordered pair of numbers, called its coordinates. Understand that the first number indicates how far to travel from the origin in the direction of one axis, and the second number indicates how far to travel in the direction of the second axis ...

Problem Solving

Solve a Simpler Problem

If you are riding in a taxi, the shortest distance between two points is usually NOT a straight line.

Find the distance (the number of blocks) from school to the post office and then home. Arrows show one-way streets.

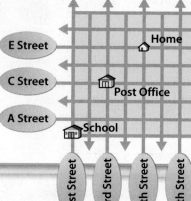

Guided Practice*

MATHEMATICAL PRACTICES

Do you know HOW?

Use a simpler problem to solve.

1. Use the simple map below. Following the streets, what is the least number of blocks to walk from Point *A* to Point *B* to Point *C*?

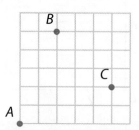

Do you UNDERSTAND?

2. Find another way to travel from school to the post office to home. Is the total distance you found the same as the total distance shown in the example above?

© 3. **Be Precise** Write a problem in which you use a simpler problem to solve. Then answer the problem you wrote.

Independent Practice

MATHEMATICAL PRACTICES

Solve each problem.

4. Rosa walked three blocks west, two blocks north, one block east, and two blocks south. How many blocks was she from where she started?

© 5. **Persevere** Lionel lives 13 blocks south of the library. Randy's house is four times as many blocks south as Lionel's. How many blocks and in what direction does Randy need to travel to get to the library?

Applying Math Practices

- What am I asked to find?
- What else can I try?
- How are quantities related?
- How can I explain my work?
- How can I use math to model the problem?
- Can I use tools to help?
- Is my work precise?
- Why does this work?
- How can I generalize?

I can solve a simpler problem.

First, I'll find the distance from school to the post office.

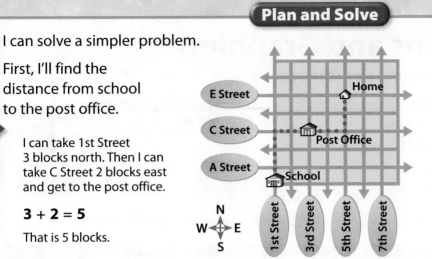

I can take 1st Street 3 blocks north. Then I can take C Street 2 blocks east and get to the post office.

3 + 2 = 5

That is 5 blocks.

Now I can go from the post office to home.

I can go 2 more blocks east on C Street. Then I can go 2 blocks north on 5th Street.

2 + 2 = 4

That is 4 more blocks.

5 + 4 = 9, so it is 9 blocks from school to home.

© **Use Tools** For **6** and **7**, use the map at the right.

6. How far is it from Walter's house to the park if each unit represents 1 block?

7. Nancy rode her bike from her house to Jerry's house, and then to the park. How many blocks did she ride her bike?

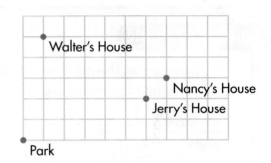

Use the map at the right for **8** through **10**.
In the map, each side of a square equals 5 miles.

8. Estimate how many miles by highway it is from Smithberg to McAllen.

9. Estimate how many miles by highway it is from McAllen to Providence.

10. Estimate how many miles by highway it is from Smithberg to Providence.

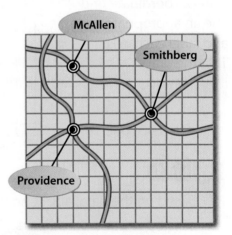

© **11.** **Model** Hayley has set a goal to read all 26 books on the library's Best Books list. She plans to read 2 books each week. How long will it take Hayley to read all the books?

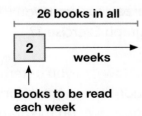

26 books in all

2

weeks

Books to be read each week

© **12.** **Persevere** In a Double Dutch tournament, the winning team jumped 447 times in two minutes. The second place team jumped 375 times in two minutes. How many more jumps did the winning team make?

A 65 jumps   **C** 75 jumps

B 72 jumps   **D** 82 jumps

Lesson
16-4

Common
Core

5.G.2 Represent real
world and mathematical
problems by graphing
points in the first quadrant
of the coordinate plane, and
interpret coordinate values
of points in the context of
the situation. Also 5.G.1

Patterns and Graphing
How do you use coordinate graphs to solve problems?

Amy can hike 2 miles in an hour. At that speed, how far would she walk in 7 hours?

Time (h)	Distance (mi)
1	2
2	4
3	6

Another Example

This table shows the growth of a plant over a period of several days.

Time (days)	1	3	5	7	9
Height (cm)	4	8	10	11	14

Draw a coordinate grid.
Use an appropriate scale
and label each axis.
Title the graph.

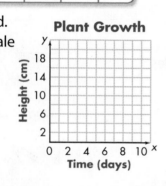

Plot each ordered pair from the table. Use a ruler to connect the points.

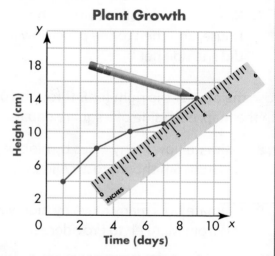

Explain It

1. Based on the data, about how high was the plant on day 4? Day 8?

2. List two other ordered pairs you might plot to show this situation.

Guided Practice*

MATHEMATICAL
PRACTICES

Do you know HOW?

Imagine you have a graph of speed that shows a lion can run four times as fast as a squirrel.

1. What would the point (3, 12) represent?

2. List 2 other ordered pairs that show this relationship.

Do you UNDERSTAND?

3. **Generalize** How you would set up the axes to graph Exercise 1?

4. **Reason** How can you determine information from a graph for a point that is not shown on the graph?

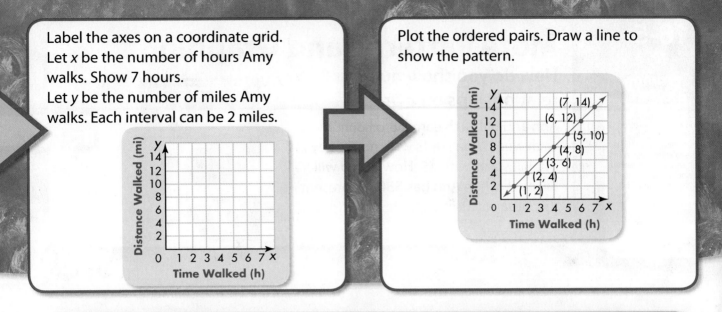

Label the axes on a coordinate grid. Let *x* be the number of hours Amy walks. Show 7 hours.
Let *y* be the number of miles Amy walks. Each interval can be 2 miles.

Plot the ordered pairs. Draw a line to show the pattern.

Independent Practice

For **5** and **6,** find the missing *y*-coordinate for the red point and tell what that coordinate represents.

5. Jet-Car Distance
Distance (m) / Time (sec)
(20, 800), (15, 600), (10, 400), (5, y), (0, 0)

6. Elephant Weight
Weight (lb) / Age (months)
(24, 1,800), (18, y), (12, 900), (6, 300)

For **7** and **8,** use each set of data and the given interval to make a line graph.

7.

A Crawling Ant				
Time (sec)	5	10	15	20
Total Distance (m)	1	2	4	5

Interval: 1 meter

8.

Rainfall at Sunshine Elementary	
Month	**Total Rainfall (in.)**
1	3
2	5
3	10
4	14
5	14

Interval: 2 inches

Problem Solving

MATHEMATICAL PRACTICES

For **9** through **11,** use the table below.

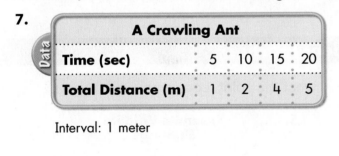

Reading Log						
Time (h)	1	2	3	4	5	
Pages Read	20	40			100	120

9. Fill in the values missing in the table.

10. Use the set of data to make a line graph.

11. Look for Patterns If the trend continues, how many pages will be read after 8 hours? Use your graph to solve.

5.G.2 Represent real world and mathematical problems by graphing points in the first quadrant of the coordinate plane, and interpret coordinate values of points in the context of the situation. Also **5.OA.3**

More Patterns and Graphing

How do you show number relationships on a graph?

Ann and Bill each earn the amount shown each week. Ann starts with no money, but Bill starts with $5. How much will Bill have when Ann has $30? Represent this situation using a table and a graph.

Guided Practice*

MATHEMATICAL
PRACTICES

Do you know HOW?

1. Carl has no money. He saves $2 each week for 10 weeks. Danielle has $20. She spends $2 each week for 10 weeks. Complete the table.

Week	Start	1	2	3	4
Carl	$0	$2			
Danielle	$20	$18			

Do you UNDERSTAND?

2. Let *x* stand for the amount of money Carl has. Let *y* stand for the amount of money Danielle has. What would the point (8, 12) represent?

3. **Reason** What is the relationship between the amount of money Carl has and the amount of money Danielle has?

Independent Practice

For **4** and **5** find the missing coordinates and tell what the point represents.

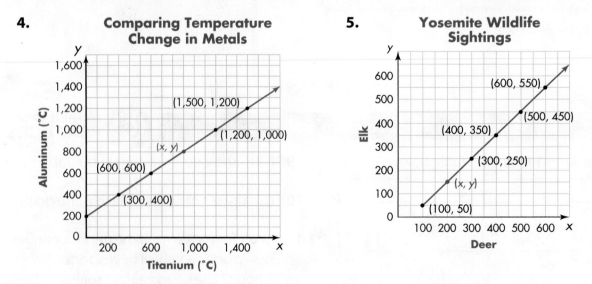

4. **Comparing Temperature Change in Metals**

5. **Yosemite Wildlife Sightings**

For another example, see Set D on page 407.

Make a table showing how much money each person has each week.

Week	Start	1	2	3	4	5
Ann's earnings in $	0	3	6	9	12	15
Bill's earnings in $	5	8	11	14	17	20

Let x = Ann's earnings and y = Bill's earnings.

When Ann has $0, Bill has $5.

Plot the ordered pairs. Draw a line to show the pattern.

Extend your line to the point where the x-coordinate is 30. The corresponding y-coordinate is 35.

Bill has $35 when Ann has $30.

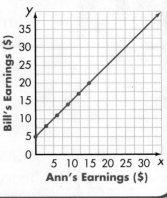

6. Complete the table at the right and graph the data using sunflower for the x-axis and corn for the y-axis.

7. Describe the relationship between sunflower and corn height.

		Plant Height (inches)						
Week	Start	1	2	3	4	5	6	7
Sunflower	10	15	20		30	35	40	
Corn	2		10		18	22	26	

Problem Solving

8. Sue has read 5 books. Joe has read 8 books. If Sue reads 2 more books a day and Joe reads 1 more book a day, how many books will Sue have read when Joe has read 15 books? Complete the table and make a graph to solve.

		Reading Log				
Day	Start	1	2	3	4	5
Sue	5	7		11		
Joe	8	9	10		12	13

9. Mark and Ron are climbing a mountain. They both start at 1,500 ft. If Mark climbs 2,000 ft. a day and Ron climbs 1,500 ft. a day, what elevation will each climber have reached on day 5? Make a table and a graph to solve.

10. A whale swimming 400 m below the ocean surface dives at a rate of 400 m per minute. A submarine is 2,400 m below the surface of the ocean and goes up at a rate of 600 m per minute. How far from the surface will the whale be when the submarine has fully surfaced? Make a table and a graph to solve.

Ⓒ **11. Reason** Anna makes more money than Nancy. Use the graph at the right to make a table and write a rule for the relationship between their earnings.

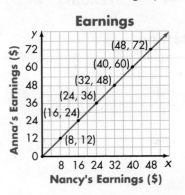

Lesson
16-6

Common
Core

5.G.1 Use a pair of
perpendicular number
lines ... to define a
coordinate system ...
and a given point in the
plane located by using an
ordered pair of numbers,
called its coordinates.
Understand that the first
number indicates how far
to travel from the origin in
the direction of one axis,
and the second number
indicates how far to travel in
the direction of the second
axis ... Also **5.G.2**

Problem Solving

Work Backward

Symbols can show movement
of points on a coordinate plane.

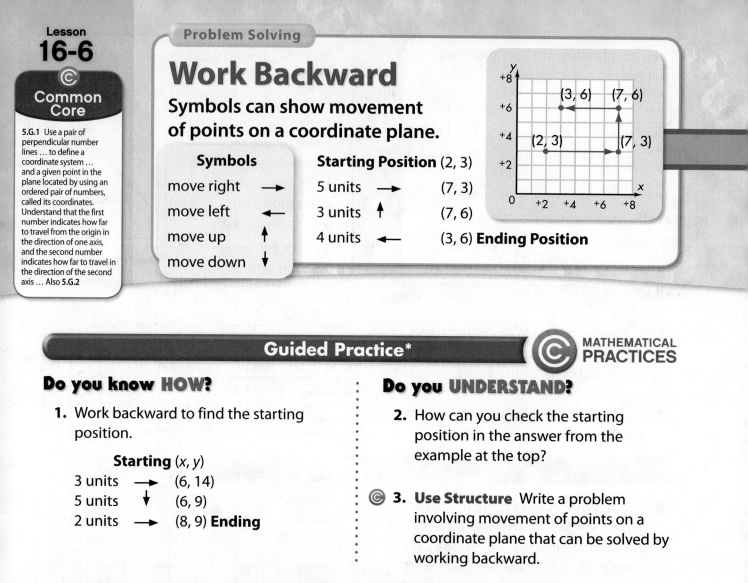

Symbols		Starting Position (2, 3)	
move right	→	5 units →	(7, 3)
move left	←	3 units ↑	(7, 6)
move up	↑	4 units ←	(3, 6) **Ending Position**
move down	↓		

Guided Practice*

MATHEMATICAL
PRACTICES

Do you know HOW?

1. Work backward to find the starting
position.

   Starting (x, y)

   3 units → (6, 14)
   5 units ↓ (6, 9)
   2 units → (8, 9) **Ending**

Do you UNDERSTAND?

2. How can you check the starting
position in the answer from the
example at the top?

3. **Use Structure** Write a problem
involving movement of points on a
coordinate plane that can be solved by
working backward.

Independent Practice

MATHEMATICAL
PRACTICES

Use Tools In **4** and **5**, work backward to find each
starting position.

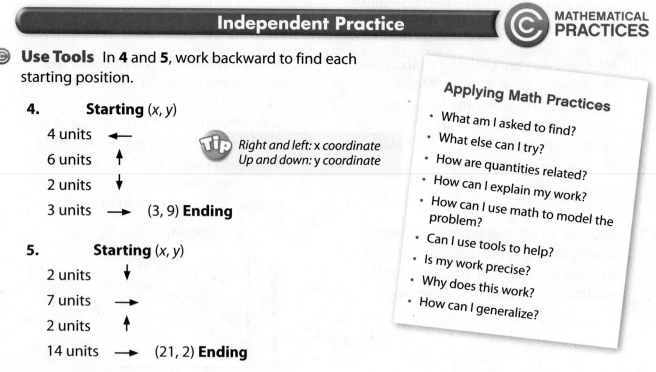

4.   **Starting** (x, y)

   4 units ←

   6 units ↑

   2 units ↓

   3 units → (3, 9) **Ending**

Tip *Right and left: x coordinate*
Up and down: y coordinate

5.   **Starting** (x, y)

   2 units ↓

   7 units →

   2 units ↑

   14 units → (21, 2) **Ending**

Applying Math Practices

- What am I asked to find?
- What else can I try?
- How are quantities related?
- How can I explain my work?
- How can I use math to model the problem?
- Can I use tools to help?
- Is my work precise?
- Why does this work?
- How can I generalize?

What is the starting position?

If you know the ending position and the motions used, you can work backward to find the starting position.

Starting (x, y)

5 units ⟶ (7, 3)

3 units ↑ (7, 6)

4 units ⟵ (3, 6) **Ending**

Plan and Solve

Begin at the ending position. Do the opposite motions and work backward.

Ending (3, 6)

4 units ⟶ (7, 6)

3 units ↓ (7, 3)

5 units ⟵ (2, 3) **Starting**

The starting position is (2, 3).

Solve each problem.

6. Pat decided to bake one evening. First, she used a certain amount of flour to make biscuits. Then, Pat used $3\frac{3}{4}$ cups of flour to make bread and $1\frac{1}{4}$ cups of flour to make pretzels. If Pat used a total of $7\frac{1}{4}$ cups of flour for all of her baking, how much flour did she use to make biscuits?

© 7. **Model** The Tigers scored 20 points during a basketball game. The team scored 6 points during the fourth quarter, 4 points during the third quarter, and the same number of points in both the second and first quarters. How many points did the Tigers score in the first quarter of the game? The second quarter?

8. Heather is thinking of a solid that is made up of a couple of shapes. The solid has 5 faces. One of the faces is a shape that has sides of equal length. The other 4 faces are shapes that have three sides. What is the name of the solid Heather is thinking of?

© 9. **Persevere** Steve, Derrin, Sid, Spencer, and Naji are waiting in line to buy tickets to a movie. Derrin is in front of Spencer and behind Sid. Steve is between Sid and Derrin. Naji is behind Spencer. Who is first in line?

10. Julie kept track of the number of miles she drove over a three-day period. On the first day, she drove 17.25 miles. On the second day, she drove 5.25 miles. On the third day, she drove 24 miles. At the end of the third day, the odometer on Julie's car read 52,607.5 miles. What was the mileage number on Julie's odometer when she began keeping track of her mileage?

11. Philip wants to take the quickest trip to Chicago. Some trains make more stops than others. Which train should he take?

Train Schedule		
Train	**Leave from Elgin**	**Arrive in Chicago**
A	8:45 A.M.	9:55 A.M.
B	2:35 P.M.	3:50 P.M.
C	3:55 P.M.	5:00 P.M.

Set A, pages 392–394

What ordered pair names Point *A*?

Start at the origin. The *x*-coordinate is the horizontal distance along the *x*-axis. The *y*-coordinate is the vertical distance along the *y*-axis.

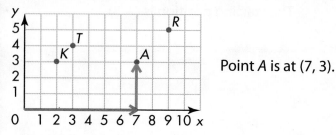

Point *A* is at (7, 3).

Remember to first find the *x*-coordinate. Then find the *y*-coordinate. Write the coordinates in (*x*, *y*) order.

1. Which point is located at (9, 5)?

2. Which point is located at (2, 3)?

3. What ordered pair names Point *T*?

Set B, pages 396–397

What is the length of line segment *AB*?

Because the points lie on a vertical line, you can subtract the *y*-values to find the distance.

Line segment *AB* is 6 − 4 = 2 units.

Remember that if the *y*-values are the same, the line is horizontal.

Find the distance between the ordered pairs.

1. (5, 8), (1, 8)   2. (4, 3), (10, 3)

3. (5, 4), (4, 4)   4. (2, 5), (2, 2)

Set C, pages 398–399

Find the shortest driving distance from school to the park and then home.

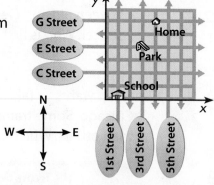

School to park: Go 4 blocks north on 1st Street and 2 blocks east on E Street: 6 blocks.

Park to home: Go 2 blocks north on 3rd Street and 1 block east on G Street: 3 blocks.

The shortest distance is 6 + 3 = 9 blocks.

Remember that arrows show one-way streets.

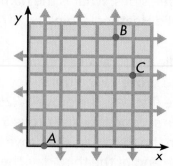

1. Suppose you walk from Point *A* to Point *B*. Then you walk from Point *B* to Point *C*. What is the least number of blocks you could walk?

Use the table to plot the ordered pairs. Then draw a line to connect the points.

x	y
1	1
2	4
3	7

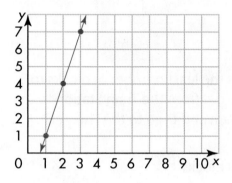

Remember to draw a line connecting the points after graphing them.

1. Copy the grid below. Use the table to plot the ordered pairs and complete the graph. What pattern do you notice?

x	y
2	1
4	2
6	3
8	4

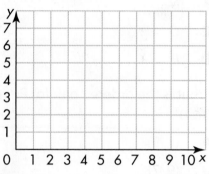

Set E, pages 404–405

Rocio worked on her science fair project for 35 minutes. Then she spent 20 minutes working on math homework. After that, Rocio spent 45 minutes on the computer. If she logged off the computer at 8:10 P.M., what time did Rocio begin working on her science fair project?

You can draw a picture to help you work backward. Use inverse operations for each change.

Rocio began her science project at 6:30 P.M.

Remember that addition and subtraction are inverse operations.

Solve.

1. Barb has $3\frac{1}{4}$ ft of ribbon left over. She used $2\frac{1}{4}$ ft to wrap a gift and $\frac{3}{4}$ ft to decorate a picture frame. She then used $1\frac{3}{4}$ ft for hair ribbons. How many feet of ribbon did Barb start with?

Multiple Choice

Use the grid below for **1** through **4**.

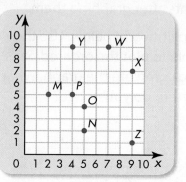

1. Which point is located at (5, 2)? (16-1)

   A M

   B N

   C O

   D P

2. What is the ordered pair for Point Y?
   (16-1)

   A (7, 9)

   B (9, 7)

   C (9, 1)

   D (4, 9)

3. What is the vertical distance between
   Point X and Point Z? (16-2)

   A 9 units

   B 7 units

   C 6 units

   D 1 unit

4. Which tells how to find the horizontal
   distance between Point M and Point P?
   (16-2)

   A Subtract 5 − 2

   B Subtract 4 − 2

   C Subtract 5 − 4

   D Subtract 2 − 0

Use the map below for **5**. Each square
represents 1 city block.

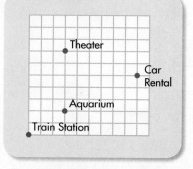

5. What is the least number of blocks to
   walk to get from the Train Station to the
   Aquarium and then to the Theater?
   (16-3)

   A 10 blocks

   B 11 blocks

   C 12 blocks

   D 13 blocks

6. Which ordered pair is located on the line
   shown on the graph? (16-4)

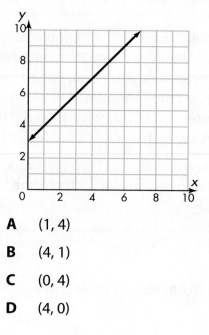

   A (1, 4)

   B (4, 1)

   C (0, 4)

   D (4, 0)

7. After a fundraising dinner, a charity has a balance of $2,530. They spent $700 to host the dinner. If they made $1,400 on the event and another $300 afterwards from a private donation, how much money did the charity have before hosting the dinner? (16-6)

8. Martina drew the graph shown. Copy and fill in the chart with four coordinates on the line. (16-4)

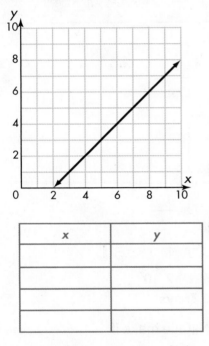

x	y

9. What ordered pair describes point K on the coordinate grid? (16-1)

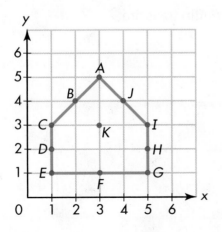

10. If Daneesha walked five blocks north, then three blocks east, then five blocks south, how far was she, in blocks, from where she started? (16-3)

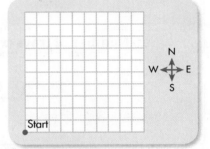

11. Maria and April collected flowers. They both started with zero flowers. Maria collected 2 flowers each day for 5 days. April collected 4 flowers each day during that time. Copy and complete the table to show how many flowers each collected. Then, graph the points that compare the number of flowers Maria and April each has. What patterns do you notice? (16-5)

Day	1	2	3	4	5
Maria	2				
April	4				

12. What is the vertical distance between Points B and E? (16-2)

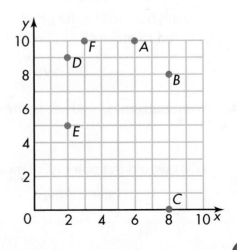

1. Natalie is making muffins. She can make 6 muffins using one tray. Write the *x* and *y* data points as ordered pairs. Use the number of trays as the *x* coordinate. Then plot all points on a grid.

Muffin Trays	
Number of trays (*x*)	**Total number of muffins (*y*)**
1	6
2	12
3	18
4	24

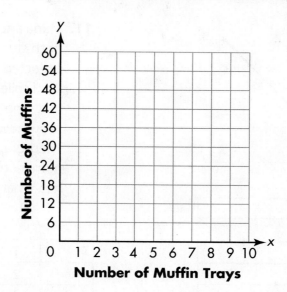

Number of Muffin Trays

2. Extend the line on the grid. How many muffins can Natalie make if she uses 8 muffin trays?

3. Explain how to use the grid to find how many muffin trays are needed to make 42 muffins.

4. What pattern do you see in the ordered pairs?

5. What would the point (0, 0) mean in this context?

Step Up to Grade 6

The following lessons provide a preview of Grade 6 Common Core State Standards.

Lessons

Scott Foresman·Addison Wesley
enVisionMATH®
Common Core

Step-UP
Lesson

1

Common
Core

6.RP.1 Understand the
concept of a ratio and use
ratio language to describe a
ratio relationship between
two quantities.

Understanding Ratios

What is a mathematical way to compare quantities?

Tom's Pet Service takes care of cats and dogs.
Currently, there are more dogs than cats.
Compare the number of cats to the
number of dogs. Then compare
the number of cats to the
total number of pets at
Tom's Pet Service.

17 dogs

14 cats

Guided Practice

MATHEMATICAL
PRACTICES

Do you know HOW?

A fifth-grade hockey team has 4 centers, 7
wingers, and 6 goalies. Write a ratio for each
comparison in three different ways.

1. Wingers to goalies

2. Centers to total

3. Centers to goalies

Do you UNDERSTAND?

4. Communicate What are two different
types of comparisons a ratio can be
used to make? How is this different
from a fraction?

5. In the example at the top of the page,
compare the number of dogs to the
total number of pets.

Independent Practice

MATHEMATICAL
PRACTICES

A person's blood type is denoted with the letters A, B, and
O and the symbols + and −. The blood type A+ is read as
A positive. The blood type B− is read as *B negative*.

In **6** through **14**, use the data file to write a ratio for
each comparison in three different ways.

6. O+ donors to A+ donors

7. AB− donors to AB+ donors

8. B+ donors to total donors

9. O− donors to A− donors

10. B− donors to B+ donors

11. O− donors to total donors

12. A+ and B+ donors to
AB+ donors

13. A− and B− donors to AB−
donors

14. Reason Which comparison does the ratio $\frac{90}{9}$ represent?

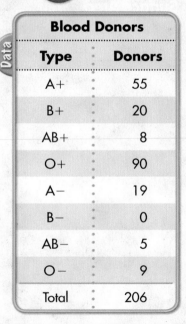

Blood Donors	
Type	**Donors**
A+	55
B+	20
AB+	8
O+	90
A−	19
B−	0
AB−	5
O−	9
Total	206

Data

Animated Glossary
www.pearsonsuccessnet.com

DIGITAL

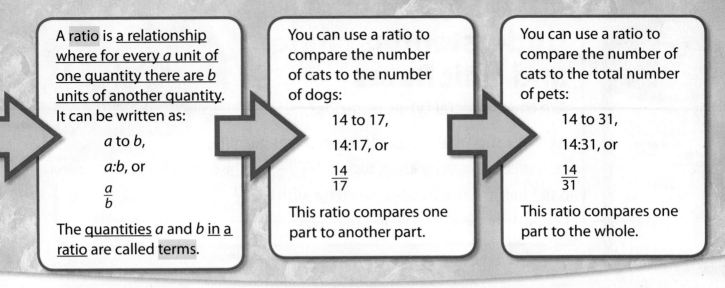

A ratio is <u>a relationship where for every *a* unit of one quantity there are *b* units of another quantity</u>. It can be written as:

a to *b*,

a:*b*, or

$\frac{a}{b}$

The <u>quantities</u> *a* and *b* <u>in a ratio</u> are called <u>terms</u>.

You can use a ratio to compare the number of cats to the number of dogs:

14 to 17,

14:17, or

$\frac{14}{17}$

This ratio compares one part to another part.

You can use a ratio to compare the number of cats to the total number of pets:

14 to 31,

14:31, or

$\frac{14}{31}$

This ratio compares one part to the whole.

Problem Solving

15. Look for patterns in the table. Copy and complete the table.

Number of students with pets	1	3	9		81
Total number of students	3	9		81	

16. A total of 2,021,078 people voted in an election that resulted in a tie. Twice as many people voted in the runoff election. How many people voted in the runoff election? Round your answer to the nearest ten thousand.

17. Think About the Structure Sue's quilt is made of 18 yellow squares and 6 blue squares. Which ratio compares the number of blue squares to the total number of squares?

A 6:18

B 18:6

C 6:24

D 18:24

18. Be Precise Li's class has 13 girls and 17 boys. How do the ratios 13:17 and 13:30 describe Li's class?

19. Look for Patterns Gil has $128 in his savings account. He saves *n* dollars each week. Write an expression for the amount of money in his account in 10 weeks.

20. Pablo surveyed the musical preferences of 42 students. Use the data to write each ratio in three different ways for **a**, **b**, and **c** below.

a Students who prefer punk to students who prefer hip-hop

b Students who prefer classic rock to the total number of students surveyed

c Students who prefer jazz and classic rock to students who prefer all other types of music

Favorite Music Type	Number of Students
Jazz	9
Classic rock	4
Hip-hop	18
Punk	5
Heavy metal	11

Step-UP
Lesson

2

Common
Core

6.RP.2 Understand the
concept of a unit rate *a/b*
associated with a ratio *a:b*
with *b* ≠ 0, and use rate
language in the context of a
ratio relationship.

Understanding Rates and Unit Rates

Are there special types of ratios?

A rate is a special type of ratio that compares quantities with unlike units of measure, such as $\frac{150 \text{ miles}}{3 \text{ hours}}$. If the comparison is to 1 unit, the rate is called a unit rate, such as $\frac{50 \text{ miles}}{1 \text{ hour}}$.
Find how far the car travels in 1 minute.

> 7 kilometers in 4 minutes

Guided Practice

MATHEMATICAL PRACTICES

Do you know HOW?

Write each as a rate and as a unit rate.

1. 60 km in 12 hours

2. 26 cm in 13 seconds

3. 230 miles on 10 gallons

4. $12.50 for 5 pounds

Do you UNDERSTAND?

5. What makes a unit rate different from another rate?

6. **Construct Arguments** Explain the difference in meaning between these two rates: $\frac{3 \text{ trees}}{1 \text{ bird}}$ and $\frac{1 \text{ tree}}{3 \text{ birds}}$.

Independent Practice

MATHEMATICAL PRACTICES

Look for Patterns In **7** through **18**, write each as a rate and a unit rate.

7. 45 minutes to run 5 laps

8. 36 butterflies on 9 flowers

9. 252 days for 9 full moons

10. 18 eggs laid in 3 days

11. 56 points scored in 4 games

12. 216 apples growing on 6 trees

13. 125 giraffes on 20 acres

14. 84 mm in 3 weeks

15. 96 miles driven in 3 hours

16. 210 miles in 7 hours

17. 250 calories in 10 crackers

18. 15 countries visited in 6 weeks

Animated Glossary
www.pearsonsuccessnet.com

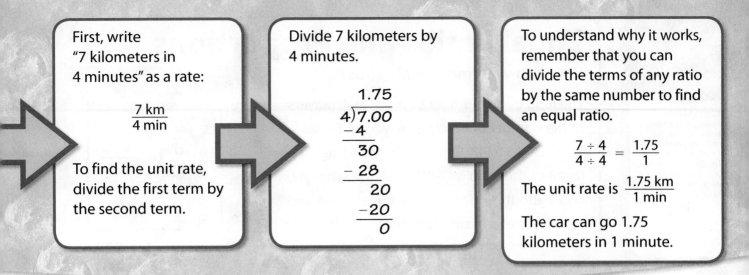

First, write "7 kilometers in 4 minutes" as a rate:

$$\frac{7 \text{ km}}{4 \text{ min}}$$

To find the unit rate, divide the first term by the second term.

Divide 7 kilometers by 4 minutes.

$$
\begin{array}{r}
1.75 \\
4{\overline{\smash{\big)}\,7.00}} \\
\underline{-4} \\
30 \\
\underline{-28} \\
20 \\
\underline{-20} \\
0
\end{array}
$$

To understand why it works, remember that you can divide the terms of any ratio by the same number to find an equal ratio.

$$\frac{7 \div 4}{4 \div 4} = \frac{1.75}{1}$$

The unit rate is $\frac{1.75 \text{ km}}{1 \text{ min}}$

The car can go 1.75 kilometers in 1 minute.

Problem Solving

Use the data table about the speeds of different ocean animals for **19** through **21**.

19. Give three equivalent rates that describe the top speed of a tuna.

20. At top speed how much faster can a swordfish swim than a killer whale?

21. Which animal swims at a top speed of about 0.33 mile per minute? Explain how you found your answer.

Top Speeds of Ocean Animals

(bar graph: Speed (in miles per hour) on vertical axis from 0 to 70; Animal on horizontal axis: Swordfish ≈ 60, Tuna ≈ 45, Shark ≈ 30, Killer Whale ≈ 25, Dolphin ≈ 20)

ⓒ **22. Communicate** Make a list of three rates that describe what you do. For example, you could describe how many classes you attend in a day. For each example, explain why it is a rate.

24. The *SR-71 Blackbird* is the fastest plane in the world. It can reach a maximum speed of 2,512 mph. What is its maximum rate of speed in miles per minute?

ⓒ **23. Think About the Structure** Chen buys 4 tickets to a soccer game. The total cost before taxes is $80. Which equation would you use to determine the price, *p*, of each ticket?

A $4p = 80$ **C** $4 + p = 80$

B $80p = 4$ **D** $p \div 4 = 80$

Step-UP
Lesson

3

Common
Core

6.RP.3a Make tables of
equivalent ratios relating
quantities with whole-
number measurements,
find missing values in the
tables, and plot the pairs of
values on the coordinate
plane. Use tables to
compare ratios.

Equal Ratios and Proportions

How can you find equal ratios?

The ratio of the number of basketball players to the number of baseball players at Grove School is 16 to 48. One way to write the terms of this ratio is $\frac{16}{48}$. You can use what you know about fractions to find equal ratios and to write a ratio in simplest form.

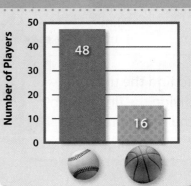

Another Example How can you decide whether two ratios form a proportion?

Use the steps below to decide whether each pair of ratios shown form a proportion.

Ratios to compare	$\frac{7 \text{ laps}}{14 \text{ min}}, \frac{12 \text{ laps}}{24 \text{ min}}$	$\frac{16 \text{ shots}}{12 \text{ baskets}}, \frac{6 \text{ shots}}{4 \text{ baskets}}$
a Compare the units to see if they are the same across the top and bottom.	Top units → laps Bottom units → min The units are the same.	Top units → shots Bottom units → baskets The units are the same.
b Write each ratio in simplest form, dividing by the GCF.	$\frac{7 \div 7}{14 \div 7} = \frac{1}{2}$ $\frac{12 \div 12}{24 \div 12} = \frac{1}{2}$	$\frac{16 \div 4}{12 \div 4} = \frac{4}{3}$ $\frac{6 \div 2}{4 \div 2} = \frac{3}{2}$
c Compare the simplest forms to see if they are the same.	Both equal $\frac{1}{2}$, so the ratios are proportional.	$\frac{4}{3} \neq \frac{3}{2}$, so the ratios are not proportional.

Explain It

© **1. Generalize** What is always true about the simplest forms of two ratios that are proportional?

2. How can you tell the ratios $\frac{24 \text{ pens}}{8 \text{ desks}}$ and $\frac{20 \text{ pencils}}{5 \text{ desks}}$ are not proportional without comparing their simplest forms?

One Way

Use multiplication. Multiply both terms by the same nonzero number. For example:

$$\frac{16 \times 3}{48 \times 3} = \frac{48}{144}$$

So, $\frac{16}{48}$ and $\frac{48}{144}$ are equal ratios.

A mathematical statement that shows two ratios are equal is called a proportion.

So, $\frac{16}{48} = \frac{48}{144}$ is a proportion.

Another Way

Use division. Divide both terms by the same nonzero number. For example:

$$\frac{16 \div 2}{48 \div 2} = \frac{8}{24}$$

You can divide the terms by their GCF (greatest common factor) to write the ratio in simplest form.

$$\frac{16 \div 16}{48 \div 16} = \frac{1}{3}$$

So, $\frac{16}{48}$, $\frac{8}{24}$, and $\frac{1}{3}$ are all equal ratios.

Guided Practice

MATHEMATICAL PRACTICES

Do you know HOW?

In **1** through **3**, write three ratios that are equal to the given ratio.

1. $\frac{12}{21}$ **2.** 1:3   **3.** 6 to 8

Tell if the pair of ratios is proportional.

4. $\frac{3 \text{ hits}}{27 \text{ at bats}}$, $\frac{4 \text{ hits}}{32 \text{ at bats}}$

Do you UNDERSTAND?

5. Communicate How can you write a ratio in simplest form?

6. Use the ratios in the Another Way box at the top of the page to form a proportion.

Independent Practice

MATHEMATICAL PRACTICES

In **7** through **14**, write three ratios that are equal to the given ratio.

7. $\frac{6}{7}$ **8.** $\frac{4}{5}$ **9.** 13:15   **10.** 4 to 9

11. 5 to 5   **12.** 12:60   **13.** $\frac{25}{15}$ **14.** 1 to 7

Look for Patterns In **15** through **18**, tell if each pair of ratios is proportional.

15. $\frac{9 \text{ blue}}{17 \text{ red}}$, $\frac{36 \text{ blue}}{68 \text{ red}}$ **16.** $\frac{20 \text{ balls}}{12 \text{ bats}}$, $\frac{15 \text{ balls}}{9 \text{ bats}}$ **17.** $\frac{14 \text{ dogs}}{20 \text{ cats}}$, $\frac{7 \text{ birds}}{10 \text{ cats}}$ **18.** $\frac{7 \text{ hours}}{56 \text{ times}}$, $\frac{3 \text{ hours}}{24 \text{ times}}$

19. Persevere Look at the rectangle to the right. Write a ratio comparing its length to its width in three different ways.

25 in.

60 in.

Animated Glossary
www.pearsonsuccessnet.com

DIGITAL

Step-UP
Lesson

4

Common Core

6.RP.3a Make tables of equivalent ratios relating quantities with whole-number measurements, find missing values in the tables, and plot the pairs of values on the coordinate plane. Use tables to compare ratios.

Using Ratio Tables

How can you use ratio tables to solve a proportion?

For every 7 cans of tennis balls sold at a sports store, 3 tennis rackets are sold. At this rate, how many cans of tennis balls would be sold if 15 tennis rackets were sold?

Guided Practice

MATHEMATICAL PRACTICES

Do you know HOW?

1. To make plaster, Kevin mixes 3 cups of water with 4 pounds of plaster powder. Complete this ratio table. How much water will he mix with 20 pounds of powder?

Cups of water	3				
Pounds of powder	4	8	12		

2. **Writing to Explain** How would you find the number of cups of water Kevin would mix with 60 pounds of powder?

Do you UNDERSTAND?

3. In the example above, what equivalent ratio can you use to find how many tennis rackets would be sold if a total of 56 cans of tennis balls were sold?

4. **Reason** Suppose 2 out of 3 campers on a trip to the carnival were boys. How many of the 15 campers were boys? Make a ratio table to show how you solved this proportion.

$$\frac{2 \text{ boys}}{3 \text{ campers}} = \frac{n \text{ boys}}{15 \text{ campers}}$$

Independent Practice

MATHEMATICAL PRACTICES

Use Structure The local radio station schedules 2 minutes of news for every 30 minutes of music. Complete the ratio table. Then use the table for **5** through **7**.

5. What is the ratio of minutes of music to minutes of news?

Minutes of music	30	45	60	75	90
Minutes of news	2	3			

6. If there was only one minute of news, how many minutes of music would there be? Write a proportion.

7. How many minutes of news would the disc jockey have to play for every 60 minutes of music?

Write a proportion. Use *x* for the number of cans of tennis balls that would be sold if 15 rackets were sold.

$$\frac{7 \text{ cans}}{3 \text{ rackets}} = \frac{x}{15 \text{ rackets}}$$

Make a ratio table to solve the proportion. Find ratios equivalent to $\frac{7}{3}$. Multiply both terms of the ratio by 2, 3, 4, and so on until you find 15 tennis rackets sold.

Total cans sold	7	14	21	28	
Total rackets sold	3	6	9	12	15

$$\frac{7}{3} = \frac{35}{15}$$

If 15 rackets were sold, then 35 cans of tennis balls would be sold.

In **8** through **13**, answer the question and make a ratio table to show how you solved each proportion.

8. $\dfrac{3 \text{ yellow balls}}{8 \text{ red balls}} = \dfrac{\blacksquare \text{ yellow balls}}{24 \text{ red balls}}$

9. $\dfrac{\$200}{8 \text{ hours}} = \dfrac{\$50}{\blacksquare \text{ hours}}$

10. $\dfrac{120 \text{ mi}}{2 \text{ h}} = \dfrac{\blacksquare \text{ mi}}{6 \text{ h}}$

11. $\dfrac{2 \text{ girls}}{3 \text{ boys}} = \dfrac{\blacksquare \text{ girls}}{24 \text{ boys}}$

12. $\dfrac{6 \text{ ft}}{\blacksquare \text{ sec}} = \dfrac{180 \text{ ft}}{60 \text{ sec}}$

13. $\dfrac{\$5}{2 \text{ oz}} = \dfrac{\blacksquare}{16 \text{ oz}}$

Problem Solving

© 14. Reason Alice found that 6 cars passed her house in 15 minutes. At this rate, how many cars would you expect to pass her house in 2 hours?

© 15. Writing to Explain Explain the difference between a data table and a ratio table.

16. Ryan rode 8 miles on his bicycle in 20 minutes. At this rate, how long will it take him to ride 24 miles?

17. Carol needs $\frac{1}{3}$ yard of ribbon for each bow she makes. If she has $5\frac{1}{2}$ yards of ribbon, how many complete bows can she make?

18. Rosi drove her car 240 miles on 10 gallons of gasoline. At this rate, about how many gallons will she use on a 1,200 mile trip?

A 2,400 gal   **C** 50 gal

B 120 gal   **D** 24 gal

19. Ramon read 12 pages in 10 minutes. At this rate, how many pages can he read in 30 minutes?

Step-UP
Lesson

5

Common
Core

6.RP.3b Solve unit rate
problems including those
involving unit pricing and
constant speed.

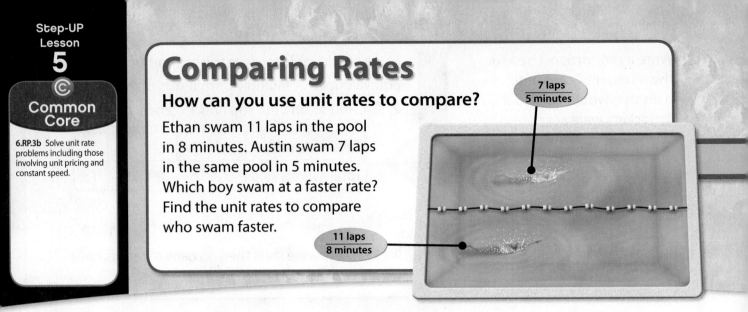

Comparing Rates

How can you use unit rates to compare?

Ethan swam 11 laps in the pool in 8 minutes. Austin swam 7 laps in the same pool in 5 minutes. Which boy swam at a faster rate? Find the unit rates to compare who swam faster.

7 laps
5 minutes

11 laps
8 minutes

Another Example **How can you use unit prices to compare?**

Which is a better buy, 3 tacos for $2.40 or 4 tacos for $3.80?

Find the cost of one taco for each comparison:

- Write each cost as a rate.

$$\frac{\$2.40}{3 \text{ tacos}} \qquad \frac{\$3.80}{4 \text{ tacos}}$$

- Find the quotients of the terms.

$$3\overline{)\$2.40}^{\,\$0.80} \qquad 4\overline{)\$3.80}^{\,\$0.95}$$

- Compare the unit prices $0.80 < \$0.95$, so 3 tacos for $2.40 is a better buy.

Guided Practice

MATHEMATICAL
PRACTICES

Do you know HOW?

Find the unit rates to answer each question.

1. Which has a faster average speed: a car that travels 600 feet in 20 seconds or a motorcycle that travels 300 feet in 12 seconds?

   a Find the unit rate of the car.

   b Find the unit rate of the motorcycle.

   c Compare the unit rates.

2. Which is a better buy: a 16-pack of pens on sale for $0.99 or a 20-pack of pens at the regular price of $1.09?

Do you UNDERSTAND?

3. How does finding the equivalent unit rates allow you to compare two rates?

4. Explain how to decide which is a better buy in Exercise 2.

© 5. **Construct Arguments** Why is a unit price a kind of unit rate?

Find Ethan's unit rate.

- Write his rate. $\dfrac{11 \text{ laps}}{8 \text{ minutes}}$

- Divide the first term by the second term.

$$\dfrac{11}{8} = 1\dfrac{3}{8} = 1.375$$

- Ethan swam 1.375 laps per minute.

Find Austin's unit rate.

- Write his rate. $\dfrac{7 \text{ laps}}{5 \text{ minutes}}$

- Find the quotient of the terms.

$$\dfrac{7}{5} = 1\dfrac{2}{5} = 1.4$$

- Austin swam 1.4 laps per minute.

1.4 > 1.375, so Austin swam at a faster rate.

Independent Practice

MATHEMATICAL PRACTICES

For **6** through **8**, find each unit rate and determine which rate is greater.

6. 280 km in 7 hours or 492 km in 12 hours

7. 24 laps in 16 minutes or 15 laps in 9 minutes

8. 45 strikeouts in 36 innings or 96 strikeouts in 80 innings

© **Be Precise** Find each unit price and determine which is a better buy.

9. 6 days for $45 or 18 days for $135

10. 2 gallons for $5.98 or $\dfrac{1}{2}$ gallon for $1.69

11. 3 crates for $3.90 or 12 crates for $16.80

Problem Solving

© **12. Reason** How can you find which container is the better value?

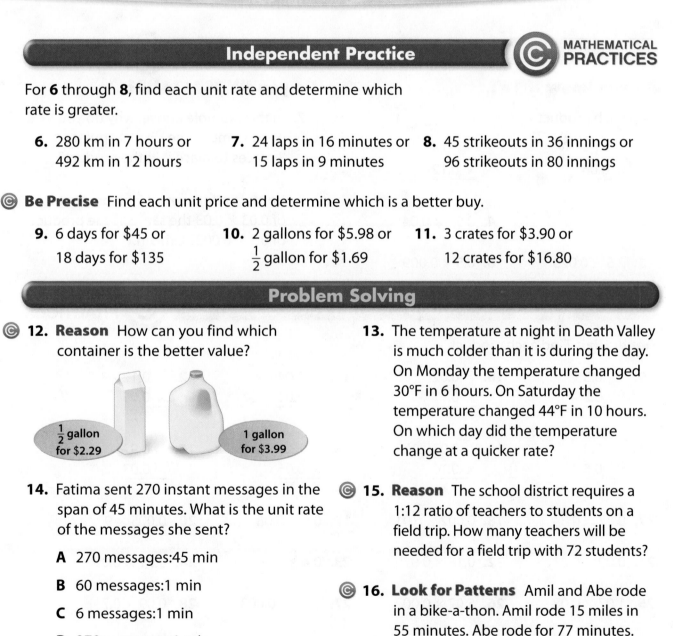

$\frac{1}{2}$ gallon for $2.29

1 gallon for $3.99

13. The temperature at night in Death Valley is much colder than it is during the day. On Monday the temperature changed 30°F in 6 hours. On Saturday the temperature changed 44°F in 10 hours. On which day did the temperature change at a quicker rate?

14. Fatima sent 270 instant messages in the span of 45 minutes. What is the unit rate of the messages she sent?

   A 270 messages:45 min

   B 60 messages:1 min

   C 6 messages:1 min

   D 270 messages:1 min

© **15. Reason** The school district requires a 1:12 ratio of teachers to students on a field trip. How many teachers will be needed for a field trip with 72 students?

© **16. Look for Patterns** Amil and Abe rode in a bike-a-thon. Amil rode 15 miles in 55 minutes. Abe rode for 77 minutes. Their rates were proportional. How many miles did Abe ride?

Common Core

6.NS.3 Fluently add, subtract, multiply, and divide multi-digit decimals using the standard algorithm for each operation.

Multiplying with Zeros in the Product

When do you insert zeros in the product?

The smallest mammal in the world is the bumblebee bat.

The weight of the bumblebee bat is equal to 0.05 times the weight of a mouse. How much does the bumblebee bat weigh?

Choose an Operation Multiply to find 1.5×0.05.

? oz

1.5 oz

Guided Practice

MATHEMATICAL PRACTICES

Do you know HOW?

Find each product.

1.   1.4
    $\times$ 0.06

2.   0.4
    $\times$ 0.12

3. 0.002×9

4. 0.97×0.04

5. 2.5×0.023

6. 0.5×0.009

Do you UNDERSTAND?

7. In the example above, why do you need to move the decimal point 3 places to place it in the product?

8. Look for Patterns Is the product of 0.03×0.03 the same as the product of 0.3×0.003? Explain.

Independent Practice

MATHEMATICAL PRACTICES

Generalize Find each product.

9.   0.3
    $\times$ 0.2

10.   0.02
    $\times$ 0.17

11.   6.04
    $\times$ 0.01

12.   0.12
    $\times$ 0.05

13.   0.4
    $\times$ 0.5

14.   0.03
    $\times$ 0.16

15.   3.1
    $\times$ 0.06

16.   0.92
    $\times$ 0.03

17. 0.87×0.04

18. 0.002×6.01

19. 0.6×0.08

20. 0.005×9

21. 0.09×0.01

22. 0.18×0.07

23. 0.4×0.06

24. 0.71×0.09

25. 1.07×0.08

26. 5.02×0.002

27. 3.74×0.003

28. 0.09×0.7

29. 3.04×0.009

30. 6.03×0.04

31. 8.68×0.5

32. 0.08×0.3

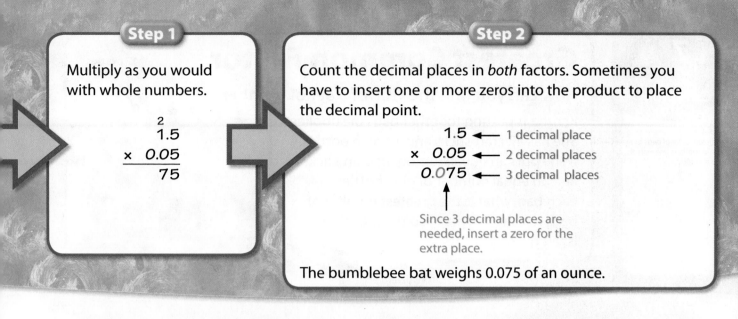

Step 1

Multiply as you would with whole numbers.

$$\begin{array}{r} \overset{2}{1.5} \\ \times\ \ 0.05 \\ \hline 75 \end{array}$$

Step 2

Count the decimal places in *both* factors. Sometimes you have to insert one or more zeros into the product to place the decimal point.

$$\begin{array}{r} 1.5 \leftarrow \text{1 decimal place} \\ \times\ \ 0.05 \leftarrow \text{2 decimal places} \\ \hline 0.075 \leftarrow \text{3 decimal places} \end{array}$$

Since 3 decimal places are needed, insert a zero for the extra place.

The bumblebee bat weighs 0.075 of an ounce.

Problem Solving

33. In a phone survey, people were asked to name their favorite type of television show. The results are shown at the right.

   a How many people named comedy as their favorite type of show?

   b How many people were surveyed in all?

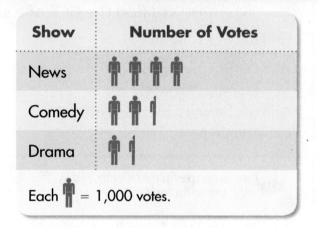

Show	Number of Votes
News	👤 👤 👤 👤
Comedy	👤 👤 👤
Drama	👤 👤

Each 👤 = 1,000 votes.

34. To promote a sale, a local supermarket is mailing postcards. Each postcard costs $0.08 to print and $0.29 to mail. How much will it cost to print and mail the postcards to 10,000 people?

ⓒ 35. Reason The numbers below follow a pattern and are arranged from greatest to least. What number does *x* represent?

678,944   678,942   678,940   *x*

36. Erik spends 2.5 hours each day using his home computer. If the computer uses 0.8 kilowatt of electricity per hour, how many kilowatts of electricity does Erik use each day?

   A 0.02 kilowatt

   B 0.2 kilowatt

   C 2 kilowatts

   D 20 kilowatts

ⓒ 37. Model Find the missing factor represented by the diagram below. Then write and solve the equation.

0.72

?	?	?	?	?	?	?	?

38. A Baltimore oriole weighs about 1.2 ounces. Is the weight of 10 orioles greater than or less than one pound?

Step-UP
Lesson

7

ⓒ

**Common
Core**

6.NS.4 Find the greatest
common factor of two
whole numbers less than or
equal to 100...

Greatest Common Factor

12 bottles
of glue

How can you find the GCF of a set of numbers?

Keesha is putting together bags of supplies.
She has 42 craft sticks and 12 glue bottles.
If she puts an equal number of craft sticks
and an equal number of glue bottles in
each bag, what is the greatest number of
bags Keesha can make so that nothing
is left over?

42 craft
sticks

Another Example How can you use prime factorization
to find the GCF of a set of numbers?

Find the GCF of 40 and 84.

Step 1

Find the prime factorization of
each number.

Tip *You can use factor trees to find
the prime factorizations.*

$40 = 2 \times 2 \times 2 \times 5 = 2^2 \times 2 \times 5$

$84 = 2 \times 2 \times 3 \times 7 = 2^2 \times 3 \times 7$

Step 2

Multiply the common prime factors.

$2^2 = 2 \times 2 = 4$

4 is the GCF of 40 and 84.

Guided Practice

ⓒ **MATHEMATICAL
PRACTICES**

Do you know HOW?

ⓒ Find the GCF for each set of numbers.

1. 18, 90

2. 14, 49

3. 33, 55

4. 25, 100

5. 15, 88

6. 27, 81

7. 39, 69

8. 99, 121

Do you UNDERSTAND?

ⓒ **9. Construct Arguments** Why can the
greatest common factor also be called
the *greatest common divisor*?

10. How are the two ways shown to find
the GCF for a set of numbers alike and
different?

DIGITAL

Animated Glossary
www.pearsonsuccessnet.com

List and compare all the factors of each number in the set.

Factors of 12: 1, 2, 3, 4, 6, 12
Factors of 42: 1, 2, 3, 6, 7, 14,
                     21, 42

1, 2, 3 and 6 are factors of both 12 and 42. These are called common factors.

Identify the greatest common factor (GCF) of the numbers in the set.

You can see that 6 is the GCF of 12 and 42.

This means that 6 is the greatest number that can be divided evenly into 12 and 42. So, Keesha can make 6 bags.

Independent Practice

MATHEMATICAL
PRACTICES

In **11** through **22**, find the GCF for each set of numbers.

11. 21, 70

12. 8, 60

13. 20, 35

14. 21, 36

15. 30, 96

16. 52, 78

17. 29, 99

18. 45, 120

19. 38, 57, 95

20. 56, 63, 81

21. 20, 32, 88

22. 46, 92, 138

Problem Solving

The Venn diagram to the right shows the factors of 12 and 40.

23. What is the meaning of each of the three shaded regions? Which factor is the GCF?

© **24. Use Tools** Draw a Venn diagram to show the common factors of 36 and 54. What is the GCF?

25. About 50 of the 1,500 possibly active volcanoes on Earth erupt every year. What is the GCF of 50 and 1,500?

© **26. Persevere** Mia bought 4 T-shirts and used a $20 coupon to reduce the total. If p equals the price of one T-shirt, write an expression to show the amount Mia paid.

© **27. Writing to Explain** How does finding the prime factorization of a group of numbers help you to find their GCF?

28. What is the GCF of 45 and 75?

    A 5   **B** 10   **C** 15   **D** 20

Step-UP
Lesson
8
Common Core

6.EE.2 Write, read, and evaluate expressions in which letters stand for numbers.

Using Expressions to Describe Patterns

How can you write expressions to describe patterns?

Delvin saves a part of everything he earns. The table at the right shows Delvin's savings pattern.

The INPUT column shows the money he has earned. The OUTPUT column shows the money he has saved.

Write an expression to describe the pattern.

INPUT	OUTPUT
$84	$42
$66	$33
$50	$25
$22	■
$30	■

Guided Practice

MATHEMATICAL PRACTICES

Do you know HOW?

Use the input/output table for **1** and **2**.

INPUT	0	1	2	3	4
OUTPUT	5	6	7	8	9

1. If the input number is 8, what is the output number?

2. Write an algebraic expression that describes the output pattern.

Do you UNDERSTAND?

3. Suppose that Delvin earned $36 mowing lawns. What input and output entries would you add to his table?

4. Critique Reasoning Is it reasonable for an output to be greater than the input in the table above? Explain.

5. What algebraic expression using division also describes the output pattern for the table above?

Independent Practice

MATHEMATICAL PRACTICES

Use this table for **6** and **7**.

Apple Weight	1 lb	2 lb	3 lb	4 lb	5 lb	10 lb
Apple Price	$3	$6	$9	■	■	■

6. What is the cost of 4 lb, 5 lb, and 10 lb of apples?

7. Generalize Write an algebraic expression that describes the output pattern if the input is a variable *a*.

Use this table for **8** and **9**.

Number of Students	12	18	24	30	36	60
Number of Study Groups	■	3	4	■	6	■

8. Copy and complete the table.

9. Generalize Write an algebraic expression that describes the relationship between the input and output values.

Animated Glossary
www.pearsonsuccessnet.com

An input/output table is a <u>table of related values</u>. Identify the pattern.

What is the relationship between the values?

$\frac{1}{2}(84) = 42$ ➝ 42 is half of 84.

$\frac{1}{2}(66) = 33$ ➝ 33 is half of 66.

$\frac{1}{2}(50) = 25$ ➝ 25 is half of 50.

The pattern is: $\frac{1}{2}$ (INPUT) = OUTPUT

Let x = INPUT.

So, the pattern is $\frac{1}{2}x$.

Use the pattern to find the missing values.

$\frac{1}{2}(22) = 11$

$\frac{1}{2}(30) = 15$

INPUT	OUTPUT
$84	$42
$66	$33
$50	$25
$22	$11
$30	$15

Problem Solving

Use the input/output table at the right for **10** and **11**.

10. Myron keeps $\frac{1}{3}$ of the tips he earns. Also, he gets $1 each night to reimburse his parking fee. This information is shown in the input/output table. Write an algebraic expression that describes the output pattern if the input is the variable g.

11. How much money will Myron keep in a night if he takes in $36 in tips?

INPUT	OUTPUT
$12	$5
$27	$10
$36	
$48	$17

Use the input/output table at the right for **12** and **13**.

12. Ms. Bhatia's classroom has a tile floor. The students are making stars to put in the center of 4-tile groups. This input/output chart shows the pattern. Write an algebraic expression that describes the output pattern if the input is the variable t.

ⓒ **13. Writing to Explain** There are 30 rows with 24 tiles in each row on a floor. Explain how to find the number of stars needed to complete the pattern for the floor.

INPUT (tiles)	OUTPUT (stars)
4	1
8	2
12	3

Use the table at the right for **14**.

ⓒ **14. Think About the Structure** Which algebraic expression shows the cost of a chosen number of books b?

A $b + \$3.50$ **C** $b - \$3.50$

B $\$3.50b$ **D** $b \div \$3.50$

Number of Books	Total Cost
1	$3.50
2	$7.00
3	$10.50

Step-UP
Lesson

9

© **Common Core**

6.EE.3 Apply the properties of operations to generate equivalent expressions.

Properties of Operations

How can you use properties of operations to rewrite expressions?

The Commutative Property of Addition states that <u>the order in which numbers are added does not change the sum of the numbers</u>. The Commutative Property of Multiplication states that <u>the order in which numbers are multiplied does not change the product of the numbers.</u>

Commutative Properties

Addition

$a + b = b + a$

$8 + 18 = 18 + 8$

Multiplication

$a \times b = b \times a$

$5 \times 12 = 12 \times 5$

Guided Practice

© MATHEMATICAL PRACTICES

Do you know HOW?

Find each missing number. Tell what property is shown.

1. $19 + (42 + 8) = (\boxed{} + 42) + 8$

2. $12 + 8 = \boxed{} + 12$

3. $42 \times 8 \times 3 = 42 \times 8 \times \boxed{} \times 3$

4. $32 \times 85 = 85 \times \boxed{}$

Do you UNDERSTAND?

© **5. Communicate** For the Identity Property, why does addition involve a 0 and multiplication involve a 1? Why don't they both use 1 or both use 0?

6. Pascal put 3 cartons of markers in the closet. Each carton contains 2 rows of 7 boxes. Use one of the Associative Properties to show two different ways of finding the number of marker boxes.

Independent Practice

© MATHEMATICAL PRACTICES

© **Use Structure** Find each missing number. Tell what property or properties are shown.

7. $\boxed{} \times (29 \times 32) = (5 \times 29) \times 32$

8. $5 + 46 + 4 = 46 + 4 + \boxed{}$

9. $25 + 0 + (3 + 16) = (25 + \boxed{}) + 3$

10. $(7 + 23) + 4 = (7 + \boxed{}) + 23$

11. $(5 \times 7) \times (3 \times 8) = (5 \times 3) \times (8 \times \boxed{})$

12. $(43 \times 1) \times 4 = \boxed{} \times 43$

13. $(27 + 3) + 4 = 27 + (3 + \boxed{})$

14. $(8 \times 9) \times \boxed{} = 8 \times (9 \times 7)$

15. $7 \times \boxed{} = 16 \times 7$

16. $51 + 48 = \boxed{} + 51$

17. $18 + \boxed{} = 4 + 18$

18. $(4 \times 2) \times 3 = \boxed{} \times (2 \times 3)$

DIGITAL Animated Glossary
www.pearsonsuccessnet.com

The Associative Property of Addition states that <u>the way numbers are grouped does not affect the sum</u>.

$$a + (b + c) = (a + b) + c$$
$$2 + (8 + 10) = (2 + 8) + 10$$

The Associative Property of Multiplication states that <u>the way numbers are grouped does not affect the product</u>.

$$a \times (b \times c) = (a \times b) \times c$$
$$2 \times (4 \times 5) = (2 \times 4) \times 5$$

The Identity Property of Addition states that <u>the sum of any number and zero is that number</u>.

$$a + 0 = a$$
$$24 + 0 = 24$$

The Identity Property of Multiplication states that <u>the product of a number and one is that number</u>.

$$a \times 1 = a$$
$$36 \times 1 = 36$$

Find each missing number. Tell what property or properties are shown.

19. $(12 \times 43) \times (3 \times 82) = (12 \times \boxed{}) \times (82 \times 43)$

20. $(6 \times 3) \times \boxed{} = 6 \times (8 \times 3)$

21. $823 \times 1 = \boxed{}$

22. $(34 + 0) \times (1 \times 12) = \boxed{} \times \boxed{}$

Problem Solving

For **23** and **24**, use the table to the right.

23. Zak and Ali live in Bluewater. They rode their bikes to Zink and then to Riverton. Then they rode back home, using the same route. Write a number sentence using the Commutative Property of Addition to show the distances each way.

Where Zak and Ali Rode	Distance
Bluewater to Zink	13 miles
Zink to Riverton	9 miles
Riverton to Red Rock	12 miles
Red Rock to Curry	11 miles

24. Once they rode from Riverton to Red Rock, from Red Rock to Curry, and then back to Riverton. How many miles did they ride that time?

Ⓒ **25. Think About the Structure** Stage 15 of the Tour de France bicycle race includes legs from Gap to Embrun, Embrun to Guillestre, and Guillestre to Arvieux. One way to express the distance of these legs is $33.5 + (20.5 + 21.5)$. Which expression below is another way to express these legs?

A $(23 + 33.5) + (20.5 - 21.5)$

C $33.5 + (20.5 \times 21.5)$

B $(33.5 + 20.5) + 21.5$

D $(33.5 \times 21.5) + 20.5$

26. Write the standard form for 6.45 billion.

Ⓒ **27. Writing to Explain** Can you use the Associative Properties with subtraction and division? Use $(18 - 8) - 2$ and $24 \div (6 \div 2)$ to explain.

Step-UP
Lesson

10

**Common
Core**

6.G.4 Represent three-dimensional figures using nets made up of rectangles and triangles, and use the nets to find the surface area of these figures. Apply these techniques in the context of solving real-world and mathematical problems.

Surface Area

How can you find the surface area of a rectangular prism?

Use what you know about nets and the formula for area of a rectangle to find the surface area of the rectangular prism shown at the right.

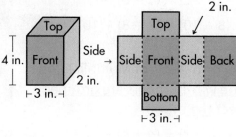

Guided Practice

MATHEMATICAL PRACTICES

Do you know HOW?

For **1** and **2**, use the net of the rectangular prism shown below.

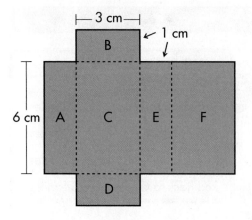

1. What are the dimensions of Face F?

2. What is the surface area of the figure?

Do you UNDERSTAND?

3. List the faces that have the same area.

4. For which type of rectangular prism could you find the surface area by finding the area of 1 face and multiplying that area by 6?

5. What is the surface area of a cube with an edge that measures 7 cm?

© **6. Writing to Explain** A child's shoebox is 6 in. × 3 in. × 7 in. Carla said that the surface area of the box equals 162 inches. Is Carla correct? Why or why not?

Independent Practice

MATHEMATICAL PRACTICES

© **Model** In **7** through **9**, find the surface area of each solid.

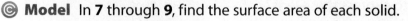

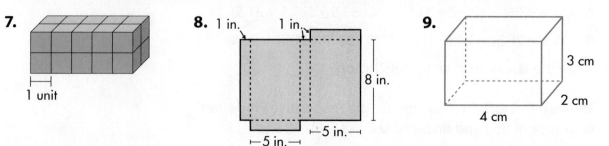

7.

1 unit

8. 1 in. 1 in.

8 in.

5 in. 5 in.

9.

3 cm

2 cm

4 cm

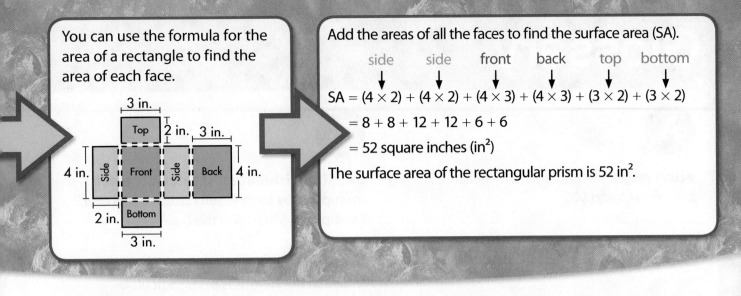

You can use the formula for the area of a rectangle to find the area of each face.

3 in.

Top | 2 in. | 3 in.

4 in. | Side | Front | Side | Back | 4 in.

2 in. | Bottom

3 in.

Add the areas of all the faces to find the surface area (SA).

side   side   front   back   top   bottom

$SA = (4 \times 2) + (4 \times 2) + (4 \times 3) + (4 \times 3) + (3 \times 2) + (3 \times 2)$

$= 8 + 8 + 12 + 12 + 6 + 6$

$= 52$ square inches (in²)

The surface area of the rectangular prism is 52 in².

Problem Solving

For **10** and **11**, use the diagram at the right.

10. Draw a net to represent Jake's cupboard. Find the surface area.

Ⓒ **11. Persevere** If Jake wants to put a wood trim around the base of the cupboard, would he need to find the perimeter or the area of the base?

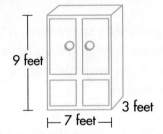

9 feet

3 feet

7 feet

12. What are the coordinates of the triangle below?

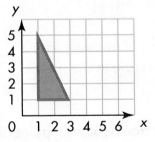

13. Morgan receives a crate that is 5 feet × 3 feet × 4 feet. Kenley receives a crate that is 4 feet × 2 feet × 6 feet. Whose crate has the greater surface area? Explain.

14. The bottom of a vase forms a right triangle with a base of 6 inches and a height of 8 inches. How many square inches of space will the vase occupy on a tabletop?

Ⓒ **15. Reason** Kori's softball team played 19 games. Her team won 5 more games than they lost. How many games did they win?

For **16**, use the diagram at the right.

16. 🌐 **Social Studies** The Pueblo tribe of New Mexico lived in houses that looked like boxes stacked on top of one another. What would the surface area of the outer walls and roof of a pueblo house be if it had the dimensions shown?

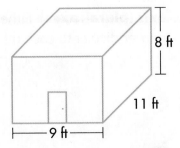

8 ft

11 ft

9 ft

acute angle An angle whose measure is between 0° and 90°.

acute triangle A triangle whose angles are all acute angles.

Addition Property of Equality The same number can be added to both sides of an equation and the sides remain equal.

algebraic expression A mathematical phrase involving a variable or variables, numbers, and operations.
Example: x − 3

angle Two rays that have the same endpoint.

area The number of square units needed to cover a surface or figure.

Associative Property of Addition Addends can be regrouped and the sum remains the same.
Example: 1 + (3 + 5) = (1 + 3) + 5

Associative Property of Multiplication Factors can be regrouped and the product remains the same.
Example: 2 × (4 × 10) = (2 × 4) × 10

axis (plural: axes) Either of two lines drawn perpendicular to each other in a graph.

base (in arithmetic) The number that is multiplied by itself when raised to a power. *Example:* In 5^3, the 5 is the base.

base (of a polygon) The side of a polygon to which the height is perpendicular.

base (of a solid) The face of a solid that is used to name the solid.

benchmark fraction Common fractions used for estimating, such as $\frac{1}{4}, \frac{1}{3}, \frac{1}{2}, \frac{2}{3}$, and $\frac{3}{4}$.

capacity The volume of a container measured in liquid units.

Celsius (°C) A unit of measure for measuring temperature in the metric system.

center The point from which all points in a circle are equally distant.

centimeter (cm) A metric unit of length. 100 centimeters equal 1 meter.

circle A closed plane figure made up of all the points that are the same distance from a given point.

common denominator A number that is the denominator of two or more fractions.

common multiple A number that is a multiple of two or more numbers.

Commutative Property of Addition The order of addends can be changed and the sum remains the same.
Example: $3 + 7 = 7 + 3$

Commutative Property of Multiplication The order of factors can be changed and the product remains the same.
Example: $3 \times 5 = 5 \times 3$

compatible numbers Numbers that are easy to compute with mentally.

compensation Adjusting one number of an operation to make computations easier and balancing the adjustment by changing the other number.

composite number A whole number greater than 1 with more than 2 factors.

cone A solid figure with one circular base; the points on the circle are joined to one point outside the base.

congruent figures Figures that have the same size and shape.

coordinate grid A grid that makes it easy to locate points in a plane using an ordered pair of numbers.

coordinates The two numbers in an ordered pair.

corresponding Matching terms in a pattern.

cube A solid figure with six flat surfaces called faces. All the faces are squares.

cubed A name for a number to the third power.

cubic unit The volume of a cube that measures 1 unit on each edge.

cup (c) A customary unit of capacity. 1 cup equals 8 fluid ounces.

cylinder A solid figure with two circular bases that are congruent and parallel.

data Collected information.

decimal A number with one or more places to the right of a decimal point.

degree (°) A unit of measure for angles.

denominator The number below the fraction bar in a fraction.

difference The number that results from subtracting one number from another.

digits The symbols used to show numbers: 0, 1, 2, 3, 4, 5, 6, 7, 8, 9.

Distributive Property Multiplying a sum (or difference) by a number is the same as multiplying each number in the sum (or difference) by the number and adding (or subtracting) the products. *Example:* $3 \times (10 + 4) = (3 \times 10) + (3 \times 4)$

dividend The number to be divided.

divisible A number is divisible by another number if there is no remainder after dividing.

Division Property of Equality Both sides of an equation can be divided by the same nonzero number and the sides remain equal.

divisor The number used to divide another number.

edge A line segment where two faces meet in a solid figure. ←Edge

elapsed time The difference between two times.

equation A number sentence that uses an equal sign to show that two expressions have the same value. *Example:* $9 + 3 = 12$

equilateral triangle A triangle whose sides all have the same length.

equivalent decimals Decimals that name the same amount. *Example:* $0.7 = 0.70$

equivalent fractions Fractions that name the same part of a whole region, length, or set.

estimate To give an approximate value rather than an exact answer.

evaluate To find the value of an expression.

expanded form A way to write a number that shows the place value of each digit. *Example:* $3{,}000 + 500 + 60 + 2$

expanded form (exponents) A way to write a number involving exponents that shows the base as a factor.

exponent A number that tells how many times the base is used as a factor. *Example:* $10^3 = 10 \times 10 \times 10$; the exponent is 3 and the base is 10.

exponential notation A way to write a number using a base and an exponent.

face A flat surface of a polyhedron. 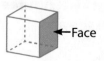 ←Face

factors Numbers that are multiplied to get a product.

Fahrenheit (°F) A unit of measure for measuring temperature in the customary system.

fluid ounce (fl oz) A customary unit of capacity equal to 2 tablespoons.

formula A rule that uses symbols.

fraction A symbol, such as $\frac{2}{3}$, $\frac{5}{1}$, or $\frac{8}{5}$, used to describe one or more parts of a whole that is divided into equal parts. A fraction can name a part of a whole, a part of a set, a location on a number line, or a division of whole numbers.

frequency table A table used to show the number of times something occurs.

gallon (gal) A unit for measuring capacity in the customary system. 1 gallon equals 4 quarts.

generalization A general statement. *Example:* A generalization about rectangles applies to all rectangles.

gram (g) A metric unit of mass. One gram is equal to 1,000 milligrams.

height of a polygon The length of a segment from one vertex of a polygon perpendicular to its base.

height of a solid In a prism or cylinder, the perpendicular distance between the bases of the figure. In a cone or pyramid, the measure of a line segment from the vertex of the figure perpendicular to the base of the figure.

hexagon A polygon with 6 sides.

hundredth One part of 100 equal parts of a whole.

Identity Property of Multiplication The property that states that the product of any number and 1 is that number.

improper fraction A fraction whose numerator is greater than or equal to its denominator.

intersecting lines Lines that pass through the same point.

interval (on a graph) The difference between adjoining numbers on an axis of a graph.

inverse operations Operations that undo each other. *Example:* Adding 6 and subtracting 6 are inverse operations.

isosceles triangle A triangle with two sides of the same length.

kilogram (kg) A metric unit of mass. One kilogram is equal to 1,000 grams.

kilometer (km) A metric unit of length. One kilometer is equal to 1,000 meters.

least common denominator (LCD) The least common multiple of the denominators of two or more fractions.

least common multiple (LCM) The least number that is a common multiple of two or more numbers.

line A straight path of points that goes on forever in two directions.

line graph A graph that connects points to show how data change over time.

line of symmetry The fold line in a symmetric figure.

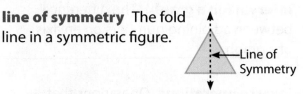

Line of Symmetry

line plot A display of responses along a number line with Xs recorded above the responses to indicate the number of times a response occurred.

line segment Part of a line having two endpoints.

line symmetry A figure has line symmetry when it can be folded along one or more lines that create congruent parts, which can fit on top of each other exactly.

liter (L) A metric unit of capacity. One liter is equal to 1,000 milliliters.

mass The measure of the quantity of matter in an object.

meter (m) A metric unit of length. One meter is equal to 1,000 millimeters.

milligram (mg) A metric unit of mass. 1,000 milligrams equal 1 gram.

milliliter (mL) A metric unit of capacity. 1,000 milliliters equal 1 liter.

millimeter (mm) A metric unit of length. 1,000 millimeters equal 1 meter.

mixed number A number that has a whole-number part and a fractional part.

multiple The product of a given whole number and any other whole number.

multiple of 10 A number that has 10 as a factor.

Multiplication Property of Equality Both sides of an equation can be multiplied by the same nonzero number and the sides remain equal.

multiplicative inverse (reciprocal) Two numbers whose product is one.

net A plane figure which, when folded, gives the original shape of a solid.

numerator The number above the fraction bar in a fraction.

obtuse angle An angle whose measure is between 90° and 180°.

135°

obtuse triangle A triangle in which one angle is an obtuse angle.

octagon A polygon with 8 sides.

order of operations The order in which operations are done in calculations. Work inside parentheses is done first. Next, terms with exponents are evaluated. Then multiplication and division are done in order from left to right, and finally addition and subtraction are done in order from left to right.

ordered pair A pair of numbers used to locate a point on a coordinate grid.

origin The point where the two axes of a coordinate plane intersect. The origin is represented by the ordered pair (0, 0).

ounce (oz) A customary unit of weight. 16 ounces equal 1 pound.

outlier A value that is much greater or much less than the other values in a data set.

overestimate The result of using larger numbers to estimate a sum or product. The estimate is larger than the actual answer.

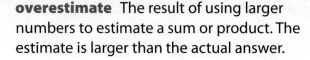

parallel lines In a plane, lines that never cross and stay the same distance apart.

parallelogram A quadrilateral with both pairs of opposite sides parallel.

partial products Products found by breaking one of two factors into ones, tens, hundreds, and so on, and then multiplying each of these by the other factor.

pentagon A polygon with 5 sides.

perimeter The distance around the outside of any polygon.

perpendicular lines Two lines that intersect to form square corners or right angles.

pint (pt) A customary unit of capacity equal to 2 cups.

place value The position of a digit in a number that is used to determine the value of the digit.
Example: In 5,318, the 3 is in the hundreds place. So, the 3 has a value of 300.

plane An endless flat surface.

point An exact location in space.

polygon A closed plane figure made up of line segments.

pound (lb) A customary unit of weight equal to 16 ounces.

power A number that tells how many times the base is used as a factor.
Example: $10^3 = 10 \times 10 \times 10$; 10 is raised to the 3rd power.

prime factorization The process of writing a whole number as a product of its prime factors.

prime number A whole number greater than 1 that has exactly two factors, itself and 1.

prism A solid figure with two congruent parallel bases and faces that are parallelograms.

product The number that is the result of multiplying two or more factors.

proper fraction A fraction less than 1; its numerator is less than its denominator.

protractor An instrument used to measure and draw angles.

pyramid A solid figure with a base that is a polygon and whose faces are triangles with a common vertex.

quadrilateral A polygon with 4 sides.

quart (qt) A customary unit of capacity equal to 2 pints.

quotient The answer to a division problem.

ray Part of a line that has one endpoint and extends forever in one direction.

reciprocal A given number is a reciprocal of another number if the product of the numbers is one.
Example: The numbers $\frac{1}{8}$ and $\frac{8}{1}$ are reciprocals because $\frac{1}{8} \times \frac{8}{1} = 1$.

rectangle A parallelogram with four right angles.

regular polygon A polygon that has sides of equal length and angles of equal measure.

resizing Changing the size of a figure while maintaining the shape of the figure and the measures of its angles.

rhombus A parallelogram with all sides the same length.

right angle An angle whose measure is 90°.

right triangle A triangle in which one angle is a right angle.

rounding A process that determines which multiple of 10, 100, 1,000, etc., a number is closest to.

sample A representative part of a larger group.

scale (in a graph) A series of numbers at equal intervals along an axis on a graph.

scalene triangle A triangle in which no sides have the same length.

scaling Multiplying by a number such that the relation of quantities is maintained.

sequence A set of numbers that follows a pattern.

sides (of an angle) The two rays that form an angle.

simplest form A fraction in which the greatest common factor of the numerator and denominator is one.

solid figure (also: solid) A figure that has three dimensions and takes up space.

square A rectangle with all sides the same length.

squared A name for a number to the second power.

standard form A common way of writing a number with commas separating groups of three digits starting from the right. *Example:* 3,458

straight angle An angle measuring 180°.

Subtraction Property of Equality The same number can be subtracted from both sides of an equation and the sides remain equal.

sum The number that is the result of adding two or more addends.

survey A question or questions used to gather information.

table of *x*- and *y*-values A table used to show how *x* and *y* are related.

tenth One out of ten equal parts of a whole.

terms Numbers in a sequence or variables, such as *x* and *y* in an algebraic expression.

thousandth One out of 1,000 equal parts of a whole.

three-dimensional shape A solid with three dimensions that has volume, such as a rectangular prism.

ton (T) A customary unit of weight equal to 2,000 pounds.

trapezoid A quadrilateral that has exactly one pair of parallel sides.

triangle A polygon with 3 sides.

underestimate The result of using lesser numbers to estimate a sum or product. The estimate is smaller than the actual answer.

value (of a digit) The number a digit represents, which is determined by the position of the digit. See also *place value*.

variable A letter, such as *n*, that represents a number in an expression or an equation.

vertex (plural: vertices) **a.** The common endpoint of the two rays in an angle. **b.** The point at which three or more edges meet in a solid figure. **c.** The point of a cone.

volume The number of cubic units needed to fill a solid figure.

weight A measure of how light or how heavy something is.

whole numbers The numbers 0, 1, 2, 3, 4, and so on.

word form A way to write a number using words.

x-axis A horizontal line that includes both positive and negative numbers.

x-coordinate The first number in an ordered pair, which names the distance to the right or left from the origin along the *x*-axis.

y-axis A vertical line that includes both positive and negative numbers.

y-coordinate The second number in an ordered pair, which names the distance up or down from the origin along the *y*-axis.

Zero Property of Multiplication The product of any number and 0 is 0.

Weight, converting customary units of, 336–337

Whole numbers, 3
   addition, 3
   dividing by decimals, 178–179
   division by, 176–177
   estimating products, 148–149
   multiplication, 61
     by decimals, 152–154, 156–157
     with fractions, 278–279
   non-zero, dividing unit fractions by, 296–297
   rounding, 34–35

Word form of a number, 7

Words, translating into expressions, 210–211

Work Backward strategy, 404–405

Writing to Explain strategy, 226–227, 362–363

x-axis, 393–394

x-coordinate, 393

yard, 332–333

y-axis, 393–394

y-coordinate, 393–394

Zero Property of Multiplication, 65

Zeros
   multiplication by, 65
   in the product, 422–423
   in quotients, 106–108